Courtesy,
Belgian Tourist Bureau

In
the Company
of Ma

*Courtesy, Australian News
Information Bureau*

Edited by

**Joseph B.
Casagrande**

In
the Company
of Man

**Twenty Portraits
of Anthropological
Informants**

HARPER TORCHBOOKS
The University Library
Harper & Row, Publishers
New York, Evanston
and London

IN THE COMPANY OF MAN:
TWENTY PORTRAITS OF ANTHROPOLOGICAL INFORMANTS

Copyright © 1960 by Joseph B. Casagrande
Printed in the United States of America

This book was originally published in 1960 by Harper & Brothers, under
the title *In the Company of Man: Twenty Portraits by Anthropologists.*

All rights reserved. No part of this book may be used or reproduced
in any manner whatsoever without written permission except in the case of
brief quotations embodied in critical articles and reviews.
For information address
Harper & Row, Publishers, Incorporated
49 East 33rd Street, New York 16, N. Y.

First HARPER TORCHBOOK edition published 1964 by
Harper & Row, Publishers, Incorporated
New York, Evanston and London.

Library of Congress catalog card number: 60-5731.

For Mary and the weans

Courtesy, American Museum of Natural History

ontents

vii

Courtesy,
Milwaukee Public Museum

Preface

Most scholars in the several disciplines that deal with man and his works are devoted to the specialized study of but one rather recent variant of human culture, that of Western Man. Unlike his colleagues the anthropologist takes all mankind as his proper subject; and he is concerned with the whole range of socially learned and socially shared behavior patterns that we have come to call *culture*. As the biographer seeks to portray the life of a man, so the anthropologist as ethnographer seeks to describe and understand the *way of life* of a people.

Traditionally, the anthropologist has studied the nonliterate peoples of the world, be they the primitive hunters in the remote corners of the earth or the sophisticates of the florescent civilizations. He is interested alike in the Bushmen of the Kalahari Desert and the sculptors of Benin, in the naked Tierra del Fuegans and the empire-building Inca. In recent years anthropologists have also turned in increasing numbers to the study of peasant communities of the Old World and to the complex societies of modern nations, including their own. But despite the greater compass of his interests the anthropologist's basic methods of research, and perhaps more importantly, his way of looking at human behavior as a whole, remain those that have evolved from his work with the simpler groups.

Where there are no archives and no books other than the memories of men, the anthropologist perforce must take his primary data from life, so to speak—from the actions and words of the people among whom he lives and works. Even if he has recourse to documents, he still relies heavily on his own observations of behavior and on the oral statements of informants. For the anthropologist the field is thus the fountainhead of knowledge, serving him as both laboratory and library. His research is necessarily done in the company of man.

Field work by its very nature is at heart a collaborative enterprise. To come as an inquisitive stranger to live among an alien people is an audacious undertaking. At the very least the anthropologist's presence on the scene must be condoned and his impertinences suffered. But the anthropologist hopes for more than this; he needs the active coöperation of the people if he is to succeed in his work. That such coöperation is so often freely given is eloquent testimony to the universal good will of men. Let it be admitted, too, that the successful outcome of field research depends not only on the anthropologist's own skills, but also on the capabilities and interest of those who teach him their ways.

Like any stranger anywhere the anthropologist on arrival in his community will be an object of curiosity. He will be visited, queried, courted, perhaps resented or suspected. He may be a nuisance and something of a social irritant. He may be a source of some pride. But in either case he will, in the natural course of events, come to terms with the people. The total process of mutual adjustment will not be unlike that, say, of any rather mysterious newcomer who comes to settle in some small provincial town.

With luck and in good time the anthropologist will find an accepted place in the community. His presence will be taken for granted. The people will answer his questions, see that he is fed, invite him to ceremonies, and apprise him of events that they have learned will be of interest. They will laugh at his mistakes and breaches of native etiquette, and they will be amused or perplexed by *his* queer customs. What was strange will in time become familiar. He will become conversant with village gossip, privy to all that is both commonplace and momentous in the daily lives of the people. Individuals, too, will emerge as separate personalities, each as distinct and as predictable as those he knows back home. Indeed, he will recognize beneath the cloak of culture many of the same personality types, and he will come to respond to people as individuals whom he can like or dislike rather than as ethnic prototypes.

In the course of his work, as he sorts out individuals and his reactions to them, the anthropologist will inevitably form closer ties with some persons than with others. Some will serve him as assistant, informant, interpreter, major domo, cook, or house-boy; others may become hangers-on, attaching themselves to his household in the hope of gaining favor for an errand or a scrap of information. One or a few individuals, by virtue of their special knowledge or skills, their authority or qualities of intellect and temperament, may become his particular mentors and close associates.

The relationship between the anthropologist and a key informant has many of the attributes of other kinds of primary relationships: between student and teacher, employee and employer, friends or relatives—as a matter of fact, it is often assimilated to the latter. In some respects it is most closely paralleled by the relationship between the psychiatrist and his patient. There is much of the same depth and intimacy, the same desire to gain insight, in the one case into the personality and in the other into the culture as it is reflected in the personality. There is the same constraint to maintain objectivity, and many of the same psychodynamic currents of transference, countertransference, and identification are at work in the two forms of relationship. But there are marked differences. The relationship between the anthropologist and an informant usually bridges two cultures, it is less episodic, there is greater reciprocity, and it is entered into for quite different reasons. In final analysis it is unique among the various forms of human association. Whatever its emotional tone, whether it be colored by affection and respect or not, such a sustained close relationship cannot but be highly significant for both parties to it.

Immersed in the life around him, the anthropologist may experience an exhilarating sense of coming to understand another people and of being accepted by them. He may also at times undergo a shattering feeling of isolation, of strangeness and disorientation, and yearn for the comfort of accustomed things. Herein lies a dilemma, for he is neither a full participant in the life he studies, nor simply a passive background observer of it. He is something of both, a role nicely summarized in the double term, "participant-observer." Not born to the alien culture or committed to it, the anthropologist must stand at a certain psychological and emotional distance from it. If he is an objective scientist, he cannot "go native." Neither can he hold himself aloof and observe human behavior as a naturalist might watch a colony of ants; with fellow humans there is both the possibility and necessity of communication. Thus one's capacity for imaginatively entering into the life of another people becomes a primary qualification for the ethnographer.

Field research is a challenging scientific undertaking, an adventure of both the mind and the spirit. It is also a memorable *human* experience, yet most anthropological writings tend to obscure the fact. Concerned with cultural patterns and norms, we are accustomed in articles and monographs to treat our data at a highly abstract level several stages removed from the vividness and immediacy of what we have experienced in the field. In our published work remarkably little is vouchsafed about personal reactions to the vicissitudes of field work and to the people among whom we have lived and worked. Most particularly, significant relationships with individuals who have been our close associates for many months are as a rule memorialized in a mere footnote or a few brief prefatory sentences.

In this book we wish to share with the reader the personal experience of field work, and to communicate the essentially humane quality of our discipline in a way that is at once aesthetically, emotionally, and scientifically satisfying. It is first of all a collection of personal memoirs written by anthropologists about individuals they have come to know well during the course of their work. Here are the people who have served us so well in the collaborative enterprise of field work. They are the prismatic lenses, as it were, through which we see refracted the life we would observe.

The subjects of these sketches have been drawn in profile rather than in full biographical detail. The authors' aim has been to reveal the unique personality, to delineate the individual as a credible human being seen against the background of his own locale and culture, and to show him in the context of his social roles rather than simply to chronicle a life. While the native subjects are the central figures, we have written as well about our relationships with those we have sought to portray, about our personal reactions to people and circumstances, and about the way we have gone about our work. I believe my co-authors will agree that these chapters are thus also in some measure autobiographical accounts. They could not but be.

Clyde Kluckhohn in his book *Mirror for Man* has aptly likened anthropology to a great mirror held up to man. To extend that figure, we may think of these several chapters as a virtual gallery, a hall of mirrors in whose shaping glass one may glimpse in full variety the endlessly reflected image of man. We hope that all who enter here will come away with a broader conception of man and the human situation; that the student will gain from this book acquaintance with a side of the discipline seldom touched upon in more technical anthropological writings. We trust, too, that our colleagues will find this book worthy of their professional attention, and that it will awaken in them echoes of their own experiences in the field.

The various chapters are arranged in roughly geographical order, beginning with the Pacific Islands and Australia, and running through India, Africa, South and North America. Within these areas they are further ordered, albeit rather impressionistically, to provide contrasts of style, tone, and subject, and in a few instances, to juxtapose sketches of comparable persons. However, little will be lost if the reader does not choose to read them in the sequence given. Those less familiar with the way anthropologists work in the field may wish to begin with the account by Harold Conklin (page 119) of a "typical" day in his mountain hamlet of Parina in the Philippines.

In planning this book it was hoped that a wide range of geographical areas, of cultures, and of types of individuals might be represented. This has to some extent been achieved, although in a collection of this size one cannot hope to sample all the rich variety of places, peoples, and persons. There are obvious gaps. Except for the sketch of Sulli the Kota from South India, none of the simpler tribal groups of continental Asia is included, nor are Central America, the Middle East, and East Africa represented; there is only one sketch of a South American Indian—and the list could be extended. There are sketches of hunters and gatherers, herdsmen and horticulturists, nomads and villagers, primitives and peasants. But however one might classify the world's cultures, certainly here too there would be omissions. One might, for example, cite the lack of a sketch from one of the more sophisticated groups of Southeast Asia or West Africa.

Perhaps most regrettable is the fact that there are not more sketches in which a woman is the primary subject. To be sure women figure prominently in a number of sketches, but the Hanunóo girl, Maling, and Mrs. Parkinson, Margaret Mead's "informant from the world between," are the only ones of their sex who are themselves the subjects of chapters. I plead no misogynistic bias. Several more such sketches were anticipated, but for various reasons they were not forthcoming. I had hoped also for a piece on an artist—a woodcarver, a potter, a weaver, or a mask-maker—that would give the reader some insight into his techniques, his aesthetic approach to his craft, and his place in the community. There is none. One might easily detail other lacks, but this is tedious and to repair these deficiencies would in any event require another book.

So much for what is not in this volume. What can be said about these twenty sketches, what clusters do we find, what points of comparison and contrast? First, one may note that many in this book have been profoundly affected by contacts with Western culture, and almost all have been touched by it. For Durmugam the Australian aborigine, Bantao the New Guinea "Opening Man," and Ohnainewk the Eskimo hunter, encounters with whites had shattering effects. For them the clash was swift and brutal, leaving them bewildered wanderers in the midst of cultural chaos. These three, all "primitives" living on the world's last frontiers, unlike Marcus the Pueblo G.I., Josie Billie the Seminole, or Bill Begay the Navaho, had neither the personal nor the cultural defenses of those long accustomed to fending off the thrusts of white encroachment. Mrs. Parkinson stands in sharp contrast to all of these. With sustaining pride in her own Polynesian heritage, she skillfully wove the strands of European civilization that reached her islands into the pattern of her own life.

One notes also a recurrent theme of personal tragedy, muted in some sketches and reaching the proportions of a kind of cosmic doom in others. Certainly it appears in the ill-fated lives of Durmugam, Bantao, and Ohnainewk, but even for them the tragic element is not wholly attributable to the traumatic effects of cultural conflict. There is also at work a predisposing temperament and a conspiracy of circumstances, aside from other cultural forces. The latter set of influences combine in purer form to give a tragic stamp to the lives of Shingir the Tiv witch and Muchona the diviner, and in lesser degree, to the life of Surat the village judge. Here, then, is no composite portrait of the "happy savage" as if drawn by a Rousseau. However, the atmosphere of gloom is by no means all-pervasive. The life of the Hanunóo girl, Maling, has a certain idyllic quality that we are pleased to contemplate. Her story is not without its own small tragedy, but it is without despair. Conversely, we meet John Mink the Ojibwa Indian at the end of his long life, but he does not arouse our pity despite the loneliness of his old age. With Maling we have a sense of life's promise, with John Mink of its fulfillment. On the other side of the world, in the Nilgiri Hills of South India, Sulli too has found purpose and satisfaction in a long and vigorous life.

There are in this company a number who occupy positions of authority. One may compare the Muslim Hurgas with the Hindu Surat Singh, the one proud, the other something of a cynic, but both men of power who pull and weave the strings of politics. In these sketches one sees vividly the subtle interplay between personality and the cultural forms within which it must work, each bearing the imprint of the other. One might similarly compare Petrus the Trukese and the Tikopian, Pa Fenuatara, who use their authority in very different ways. The former transcends his culture in embracing his power, while the latter, more of a traditionalist, holds it at arm's length.

Other comparisons on which one might dwell spring to mind—between John Mink the Ojibwa shaman and Josie Billie the Seminole medicine maker, or between the sketches by Cora Du Bois and Ethel Albert of their major domos, Ali the Javanese and Muntu the Mututsi —and the reader will doubtless want to draw other parallels and contrasts. Now, as I review this assembled company, I am most forcibly struck by their individuality and personal worth—not all in this book are admirable men, but most, each in his own way, are exceptional persons. Here perhaps is the crux of the matter and the essential question for anthropology: to explain the simultaneous sense we have of the unique and the universal in our fellow man.

With the exception of Professor Lowie's posthumous article and my own piece on John Mink, published originally in a different version in *The Wisconsin Archeologist,* all of the sketches were written expressly for this volume. Unless otherwise credited, the photographs illustrating the various sketches were taken by the authors. In some instances personal names have been changed and places disguised to shield the privacy of the individuals concerned, but each sketch is firmly grounded in fact.

I owe a first debt to all those who have so graciously contributed to this book. They have forborne both my criticisms and my importunities with remarkably good cheer. I am especially grateful to Thomas Gladwin and Clyde Kluckhohn who have given encouragement and good counsel all the while this book was in the making.

Finally, for all who have contributed to it, let me state here the dedication that is implicit in the conception of this book. It is inscribed to the many persons of other cultures, both those in this book and those who might have been, who have shared their lives with anthropologists. They are our full partners in the study of man.

JOSEPH B. CASAGRANDE

Darien, Connecticut
January, 1960

Courtesy,
Belgian Tourist Bureau

In
the Company
of Man

Note: Place and tribal names are
numerically keyed to the
corresponding chapter

Pa Fenuatara as He Appeared in 1929 (right) and in 1952 (below).

From Raymond Firth, *We, the Tikopia*, George Allen & Unwin Ltd. and The Macmillan Company.

1

A Polynesian Aristocrat

Raymond Firth

Pa Fenuatara was an aristocrat, in a proper sense of the word—one of the ruling class of his community and one of its best representatives. Handsome, intelligent, sensitive, with a proud bearing which had in it some recognition of his high status, he also had that *gravitas,* that unconscious dignity, which marks a man of real character. Born about the turn of the century, he died in an influenza epidemic in 1955. His death was a great loss to his own community of Tikopia, a small remote island in the Western Pacific. But it was an event of little significance to anyone outside it, save a few government officials who had hoped to use his influence to guide and develop Tikopia political life, and two anthropologists, James Spillius and myself, who had come to appreciate the fineness of his character and his worth as a human being.[1]

Pa Fenuatara first became known to me towards the end of 1928, in the early part of my first research expedition on Tikopia. As his title *Pa* (meaning in Tikopia "Mr." or "father" or "Sir," according to circumstances) indicated, he was then married and hence a man of some status. As the eldest son of the premier chief, he was at the very heart of the mysteries of the pagan religion and for some months after my stay was almost inaccessible to me except for superficial social contact. Later, as his courtesy and his hospitality dictated a kindly reception to the intruder, I came to know him well. Viewed first by me as an exceptionally good "informant," he later became my friend.

A friendship of an institutionalized character—"bond" friendship (*tau soa*) as the Tikopia express it—is a recognized feature in their

[1] For some details of this essay, and for discussion of it as a whole, I am much indebted to Mr. James Spillius who was my assistant and colleague on my second expedition to Tikopia in 1952, and who remained on the island for a year after I left. In the preparation of the data for publication I have made use of part of a personal research grant-in-aid from the Behavioral Sciences Division of the Ford Foundation, whose help I gratefully acknowledge. I am greatly indebted also to the Australian National Research Council and to the Australian National University for sponsoring my first and second Tikopia field expeditions respectively.

social life. It can have a wide range of personal relations, from an almost nominal association to deep attachment. In my case, and I am sure also in his, a *tau soa* that began as a matter of policy became one of mutual appreciation. I had many tokens of his friendship in the small thoughtful acts without words that characterized a sincere relationship. For my part the index of our friendship was that, within the technical limitations of his lack of knowledge of the outside world, I could discuss any problem with him frankly and freely, exposing my arguments to him with all the intellectual resources I could muster, and receiving from him question, comment, and elucidation on a similar level. Uninformed, naïve, almost absurd at times in his lack of understanding of science, technology, and Western social behaviour, surprisingly ignorant about some natural processes, he was sensitive and perceptive in his understanding of human relationships and sophisticated to a high degree in his ability to move among his fellows. It was from him above all that I fully appreciated how independent are human relationships of material and educational factors, and how really universal are the basic problems of human beings in relation to one another, with their personal and emotional ties and revulsions, their involvements in status, their irrational reactions to situations to which they themselves are parties. Here his sense of humour and his ability, even in telling a joke about himself, helped to give a predicament its generic or type character.

Scientifically and professionally, in general, I was much indebted to him for a great mass of information about Tikopia culture and many special insights into Tikopia custom. But I was also greatly in his debt personally for two reasons. One was that more than any other person on Tikopia he gave me an easy hospitality—freedom of the house, incorporation into the kin group, food and drink on occasions without number—and all this with very few demands in return. The other reason was that he gave me a kind of intellectual refuge where I could talk, more than in any other Tikopia home, to someone who, while deeply concerned with his own position in Tikopia society, could rise above it and discuss problems in general terms. In the sense that a debt may be a moral and not a material obligation, this essay is in a way an attempt to discharge part of what I owe Pa Fenuatara.

In his young manhood when I first knew him, Pa Fenuatara was a most impressive figure. Tall, well built, with a pleasant light brown skin under which the muscles rippled smoothly, and with an erect carriage, he announced a commanding personality. His chest, back, and upper arms were marked with the blue tattoo patterns of birds, fish, and geometric shapes, commonly worn by Tikopia men. He then was heavily bearded and wore his hair long over his shoulders. His beard was black, contrasting strikingly with his hair that was bleached with lime sometimes to a reddish brown and sometimes to a golden hue. His broad-winged nose was aquiline, his lips fairly thin, his chin well developed. His cheek bones were also prominent, giving his face that faintly hexagonal look which is often characteristic of aristocratic Polynesians. His eyes were dark brown, clear, alert, and expressive. His forehead was high for a Tikopia and scarred by old vertical cuts made with a knife to draw blood as a symbol of sympathy at some of the many funerals he had attended. He was usually clad simply in a rough bark-cloth waist garment such as all Tikopia wear. His appearance was marred only in two respects. His skin in general was of good texture, smooth and velvety, save for an unsightly patch of ringworm on one buttock—a refractory affliction which distressed him greatly and which he was finally able to overcome with European medicine. His other defect was in his walk. Years ago in a fish drive a garfish had pierced his knee with its sharp beak and the injury caused him to walk a little stiffly ever after. But he loved dancing and at times when it was not barred by mourning prohibitions he was frequently to be seen in dance costume—with fringed necklet and hair fillet of sweetly odorous leaf, with trochus shell rings on his arms, beads round his wrists, and other ornaments in his ears, nose septum, and around the neck.

Pa Fenuatara was prominent in the general economic life of Tikopia. Under the aegis of his father, the Ariki Kafika, he acted as senior executive in the affairs of the Kafika lineage, and as a leader in the affairs of his clan. He was not among the hardest workers in the community. However, he was very interested in matters of technique and often devoted himself with quiet, conscientious care to some quite minor employment. As a premier adzeman he took a very active role working with a canoe builder on the repair of a sacred canoe of the Kafika clan. But he also delighted in fashioning for me a noose rat-trap out of bamboo in order to demonstrate traditional Tikopia technology, although for his own use he preferred a European spring trap of the "break-back" variety. He spent much time in carving for me from a solid block of wood a set of sacred emblems, including two fairly lifelike birds.[2] He took pride in all his craftsman's skills. Like many other Tikopia Pa Fenuatara was inclined to vaunt himself as a fisherman and agriculturalist. When the sacred yams of Kafika were poor one season, he commented that if *he* had dug them up they would have been found to have borne heavily. Some people, he said, had "food hands"—the equivalent of our English expression "green fingers"—and others not.

Although heir to a chief, Pa Fenuatara did not claim any privilege of exemption from even the heaviest manual labor. In pursuit of bonito he paddled his canoe as furiously and energetically as any other man and once, with the son of another chief, he joined a score of men in carrying an enormous log half a mile or so across the fields to use in repairing a canoe. He also participated as any other Tikopia in the economic presentations and exchanges which comprised so much of the content of kinship and chieftainship in that society. As a married man, in accordance with custom, he went to the affairs of his wife's family in the capacity of a cook and could be found breaking up firewood, preparing the oven, and sorting over food like any ordinary person. But here too his particular status played a part. Although not averse to manual work, he expected recognition of his social position—not by *relieving* him from jobs, but by giving him the right of *initiating* and *leading* them. On one occasion I missed him from a group of cooks around the oven and asked where he was. The reply was that perhaps he was annoyed because the oven had been kindled before his arrival. This indeed appeared to be the case. He had withdrawn in dudgeon because the other cooks had not waited for him—adopting the common practice of an offended Tikopia, he went off to sleep in a nearby house. But since so much fishing is done at night, sleeping by day may be quite normal, and so he safeguarded his reputation by having an alibi if one were needed.

Pa Fenuatara's knowledge of economic and allied matters more than matched his skills. In some ways he was, if not the best informed, at least the most systematically minded Tikopia in respect to ritual affairs. In addition to his skill as a fisherman he knew many of the ritual formulae used to attract and secure fish. His knowledge of Tikopia belief extended over a wide range. In 1928–1929, apart

---

[2] Illustrated in the *Work of the Gods in Tikopia,* Vol. II, 1940, Frontispiece.

from meeting him in a great number of public contexts, I recorded having about two dozen full-scale discussions with him, each lasting for half a day or over an evening. In these we covered an immense number of topics, ranging from magic formulae to help in handling a canoe at sea, to attitudes towards death and the afterworld of the spirits. On some matters coming under the head of what we would regard as natural science he was vague or inaccurate. He spoke with some authority on the procreation of a species of seabird, saying that the male impregnated the female with saliva when they touched beaks. But he was not simply credulous. He could adopt a critical, experimental attitude. On one occasion he told me that he had heard from elderly men of a peculiar phenomenon occurring at sunset. Parties used to go to the beach on the south side of the island and dig a hole in the sand. Then one would kneel down and put one's ear to the hole. As the sun actually set a thud could be heard. He said he had been told that this was a favourite amusement in olden times. He did not know if the thud could really be heard or not, and suggested that we make an expedition to try it. I have always regretted that I did not take up his offer.

He was particularly lucid in talking about human relationships and found generalisation easy. My book on Tikopia kinship owes much to his explications of the meaning of obligations in the system and of variation in behaviour. Worth quoting again is a brief state-ment he made on family affection. He said, "In this land a man cherishes his daughters and a mother cherishes her sons. Great is the affection of a woman for her male children and of a man for his female children. If a man of this land is about to die and is dividing his property, he will give in small measure to his male children but in great measure to his female children. When a daughter marries he takes secretly his goods from the body of kinsmen and gives them to her. Now he takes his things secretly because her brothers objected to her having gone to marry." This clear-cut recognition of what in modern terms would be regarded as an Oedipal situation was to him an obvious matter. He was himself a family man, having at the time I knew him two sons and four daughters. Gentle and kindly in his treatment of them, he was able to recall in detail their childhood speech and behaviour which he delighted in discussing with me.

Pa Fenuatara's social position was defined by three factors. One was his status as the "seedling chief," the eldest son of the Ariki

Kafika, the premier chief in the Tikopia society. As such he was looked upon by his brothers, the Kafika clan, and the whole community of Tikopia as the natural successor to the ageing chief. This position he bore with dignity and restraint. He was active in promoting the interests of his lineage and clan and, as his father's heir, in assuming responsibility for the welfare of the whole society.

On one occasion when coconuts were in short supply and famine threatened the island, he imposed a taboo on the whole of one mountain area in which the palms grew profusely, in order that the crop might be conserved and used to more advantage later. As he put it to me, "I bound the taboo on the mountain side. I had sympathy for the common people and so I bound it that coconuts might grow until they ripened and fell down in their orchards." He acted without consulting anyone except his father whose support he received. He also set up a similar taboo in one of the major inland areas, and on this occasion he called the people of the two districts of Ravenga and Namo together outside his house and explained to them what he had done. In Tikopia phraseology, "He set up his public assembly."

"Thereupon," he told me, "when the common people heard of it they wished it to be so. They agreed with me; some people objected, but they did not say so to me. They protested silently. Thereupon I asked in this fashion, 'Let whatever man objects announce it to me instantly.' Thereupon all the people called out, 'Oh, there is no man that objects. We give assent completely to you.'" This is a typical instance of his skill in political manoeuvre. Knowing that there was objection he deliberately challenged it, setting the weight of his status against the mute objector and receiving what could only be publicly regarded as the unanimous mandate of the gathering.

Pa Fenuatara said that his imposition of the taboo was conspicuously successful and that a large quantity of coconuts was preserved and accumulated thereby. He contrasted his success on this occasion with that of the eldest son of the Ariki Taumako, who set up a similar taboo on his father's lands but did not make it widely known and therefore people did not respect it. Pa Fenuatara's ability to make his taboo effective depended to a considerable extent upon the severity of circumstances. When the food shortage was only relatively mild the people obeyed, but when the stringency became acute, they broke the prohibition. In 1952, when famine was approaching, his influence was of no avail in restraining people from consuming carefully husbanded food supplies and from stealing those of others. Even in 1929, when there was a distinct scarcity of food—though nothing approaching famine—a taboo that he set up in Nuku was virtually disregarded. He tabooed the area to preserve coconuts, but people went and took them none the less. Pa Fenuatara did not object to their action when he discovered it. Indeed, in full agreement with his father, he removed the taboo earlier than otherwise would have been the case. This incident reveals again Pa Fenuatara's sensitive handling of situations involving him in public discomfort. But it also indicates another trait in his character—the lack of a certain forcefulness in pushing his ideas through to the end. Sensitivity to public criticism or to lack of public support made him, in this case as in many others, withdraw rather than take a firm stand.

Although he took full advantage of the ordinary social privileges of his rank, Pa Fenuatara was not unduly concerned with his purely personal dignity. He told me that as a boy he was once surf-riding with a lad of another clan who was afterwards a great friend of his, each of them riding the breaking waves in a large wooden bowl. They were upon the same wave, the crests of which converged and brought them together so that the bowl of his companion rode up upon his own and struck him upon the forehead, making a large lump. Instead of flying into a passion as the injured son of a chief, Pa Fenuatara only laughed. Again, as one of a party of young men fishing, he lay down on the sand. The young man who later became the Ariki Taumako, much older than he, had a hook on the end of his rod and line, and was sweeping it round from side to side in play. Unexpectedly, the hook caught Pa Fenuatara's cheek and tore a gash in the skin. Greatly concerned, the other young man rushed up and began to wail, "Oh, alas, my friend!" and so on, in this strain, but Pa Fenuatara took no great notice. In fact, he said, he and some of the crowd thought it was rather a joke. Even between members of a chiefly family such an act could have been the occasion of bitter recrimination and a social breach. But it was part of Pa Fenuatara's character to take no offence.

Kinship was the second important factor defining Pa Fenuatara's social position. Socially the children of chiefs formed in many respects a separate category and there was a theoretical or ideal view that they should marry only among themselves. Some chiefs in the last couple of generations have conformed to this view, but it also seems to have been traditional in Tikopia for chiefs' sons to marry women from commoner families. Because of this, the claim that the whole land is one group of kin can be fairly well substantiated. Hence Pa Fenuatara had among his kin persons from a variety of social units, not only from those of chiefly stock. According to the Tikopia kinship system his relationships fell into two broad categories, consanguineal and affinal. On the consanguineal side he had relations of help and coöperation not only from his father's kin but also from his mother's. Thus, he described himself and another man as "linked true brothers, tied through our mothers." The expression "true brother" is given here in Tikopia idiom because their mothers were true sisters and in our terminology they were, therefore, first cousins. With such people Pa Fenuatara had great freedom of relationship in speech and in action. With his kin by marriage, however, it was rather different.

His mother was from the chiefly house of Fangarere. But his wife was from the commoner house of Kamota of Taumako clan. Hence, he had a wide set of affinal kin in the ordinary body of Tikopia and his obligations to them sent him into the heart of the affairs of folk of another clan and lower social status. Moreover, he had also an affinal relationship with the kin of the wives of his brothers and by classificatory extension, of his agnatic cousins as well. According to Tikopia custom, all of them were "in a relationship of constraint," that is, as "in-laws" they had to observe taboos of behaviour—to refrain from calling one another by personal names, from cursing one another, from telling lewd jokes in one another's presence. Between affinal kin, especially brothers-in-law, there might be strong ties of mutual help, supplementing those with a man's blood relatives. Hence, Pa Fenuatara's behaviour was defined in a wide range of social circumstances by his kin ties.

The third factor defining the social position of Pa Fenuatara was his 'bond" friendships. Normally, these traditional friendships are contracted between two young men who use one another as mutual confidants and spend much time in one another's company. They exchange gifts and it is these formal gift exchanges which set the seal upon the friendship as an institutionalized matter. Moreover, friends have a recognized right to call upon one another in time of crisis and they are expected to be especially solicitous about one another. If one has not seen one's friend for some time one may go and "seek him out" to enquire about his health and well-being. On such an occasion, one frequently takes him a small present and receives another in return. Pa Fenuatara had several friendships of the ordinary kind, but one was a little unusual. The initiative had come not from him but from the other party and in an extraordinary way. The other man, much older than he, was clearly subject to some degree of dissociation of personality. In a dissociated state it appeared that he was possessed by the spirit of a dead man, Taurongo, a member of the chiefly family of Kafika who had been lost at sea. As an unmarried man, Pa Fenuatara was himself called Taurongo after the dead man, a half-brother of his paternal grandfather, and the name was still occasionally used by his father and one of his cousins when I first knew him. This spirit announced that he wished the two men to be friends. The link between them was forged in response to the spirit message and was treated by both men with full seriousness and implemented in the usual way.

Pa Fenuatara's friendship with me was also of a somewhat unusual character. Our relationship followed a well-known Tikopia pattern that a man of rank should receive a visitor from abroad and bind him to himself in ties of friendship. The reasons for this were partly to receive the benefit of any gifts the visitor had to offer and partly to have the novelty and attraction of the visitor's news and experiences within his own family circle. I had a similar relationship with Pa Rangifuri, the eldest son of the Ariki Tafua, though we did not develop it as far in mutual understanding. Following the recognized Tikopia pattern, Pa Fentuatara's friendship with me, especially when I was the sole European on the island, did not add to his status, but it did give him access to goods and information not so easily available to others.

In 1928–1929 then, Pa Fenuatara was one of the most influential men in the Tikopia community. There were others who had as much, if not more, influence, but for different reasons. Apart from the four chiefs there was a man who by inheritance had assumed the role of principal officer of the community in charge of maintaining social order. There were also the elders who had public respect because of their wealth, their judgement in social affairs, their ritual privileges, and their control of some of the premier gods of the community.

Pa Fenuatara had neither the formal administrative role of the executive officer, nor the ritual and other religious endowments of the elders. But his status as the eldest son of the chief in conjunction with his personal qualities brought him to the fore on many occasions.

For example, when Pa Rangifuri had been in mourning for many months for his dead son lost at sea, and it was the general wish that he should emerge from seclusion and join in public festivities, it was Pa Fenuatara who had the task of bringing him out of retirement. The Tikopia custom is that the mourner has a festive necklet of flowers or fringed leaf hung upon him. This is the signal for him to rise and dance. The ceremony is preceded by anointing the mourner with turmeric as a formal cleansing of him from his mourning obligations. It is known by the Tikopia as "cleansing his earth." In mid-January, 1929, Pa Fenuatara and his brother went one night in darkness to Faea, taking turmeric with them, and anointed Pa Rangifuri. The next morning Pa Fenuatara returned and hung a necklet of frangipani blossoms upon him. Hearing of this, I asked whether Pa Rangifuri would dance that day. The answer was "No." I arrived at the dance ground to find him sitting down with his face averted from the scene. But later in the morning Pa Fenuatara came to him, put a leaf ornament in his belt at the back, and gave him a length of calico to put around his waist as an ornamental kilt, insisting that he put it on. Then he presented him with a dance bat—a flat, carved stick brandished in rhythmic display—and they both went out to the dance together. Pa Rangifuri took part in the dance quite enthusiastically, although he showed a certain shy reluctance at first. A week or so later, when another dance occurred, he did not take part although requested to do so by his father. He had danced for the earlier festival only at the insistence of the Ariki Kafika and Pa Fenuatara, but for less important occasions he still preserved some remnants of his mourning. I heard then that he had said earlier he would not allow his mourning to be broken, that if any of the people of his own district had come to anoint him with turmeric he would have killed them. But Pa Fenuatara, as a man of equivalent rank and as the representative of another district, was entitled to be treated with utmost courtesy; he could perform the ceremony with impunity.

In public affairs Pa Fenuatara pursued a fairly even course, surrounded by respect and esteem. But what of his private life?

On the whole his earlier years seem to have passed relatively without incident. Apart from the usual small accidents, two of which have been referred to, he seems to have had only one serious illness. In speaking of this he told me that a kind of sea-spell seemed to hang over his family. He had been wounded by a garfish and as a young man he had had a grave illness, apparently a kind of dysentery. Both of these, he said, came from the sea, the latter being attributed to eating some kind of fish. He became very ill. He was carried first to the Ariki Taumako, felt better, and stayed ten days in the chief's house. Then he fell very ill again. He crawled out one night when it was raining heavily and sat at the base of a tree by the oven-house on an old basket. He said that he felt spirits moving all around him, but so grave was his illness he did not feel afraid. For a time he slept, while the rain was falling on him. His wife, who had felt on his sleeping mat beside her with her hand and found it vacant, came out to search for him. She found him and said, "What are you sitting here in the rain for?" "I can't stand it any longer," he replied. Together they made their way very slowly towards the shore for him to empty his bowels, but he was weak and on the way they had to sit down for a time. Finally his wife said she was feeling cold. He told her to go into an adjacent house and sleep and she did so. He stopped outside and again lay down to sleep—still in the rain. After a time, near morning, he dreamed that a spirit came and offered him an orange turmeric-dyed barkcloth. This was a garment for him to wear in the spirit world and was a sign that he would not recover. "I knew then," he said, "that I would die." But he did not die. He crawled into a small house and felt terribly ill. Suddenly his bowels opened and a discharge of blood came in great quantity. As fast as one piece of bark-cloth was placed beneath him it had to be removed and another substituted. At last the discharge ceased. The Ariki Taumako, who had been unable to effect a cure by the intervention of his gods, said that it was better that they should stay no longer with him but seek aid elsewhere. So he was carried to the Ariki Fangarere. This chief, too, applied oil and prayed for health. The patient felt but a brief access of vigour and then collapsed again.

Pa Fenuatara was then carried to Faea on the backs of people of his clan, who set him down at intervals for a rest. When he arrived at the village of the Ariki Tafua he was laid out at the side of the chief's house in a comatose condition or in a faint. He recovered consciousness to find the people of Faea pressing his limbs and head with their hands as is the Tikopia custom to revive a person. The chief was absent at the north of the island but was summoned at once. He arrived just after Pa Fenuatara recovered from his coma. The chief at that time was still unbaptized, a pagan. He proceeded in the customary fashion to pour oil on the palm of his hand and apply it to the patient with the recital of the formula to his gods. "Great was his power," said Pa Fenuatara. He recovered almost immediately. The Ariki Kafika had not come to Faea with his son, but a messenger was now sent to tell him that the sick man was much better. He then came over to Faea and found Pa Fenuatara practically cured.

The cure, said Pa Fenuatara, was due to the gods of the Ariki Tafua. As usual in such cases, they sat or stood around the sick person in a ring, invisible, gazing on him. Some of them drove away the spirits responsible for the illness, others went in search of the soul of the sick man which had been taken away, and restored it to the body. He said that the malevolent spirit who had given him the orange waist-cloth as a token of his reception into the afterworld had been driven away with the rest. Hence, his life was restored to him.

In the explanation of his recovery Pa Fenuatara was talking in effect on two levels. One was the human and personal level of the healing powers of the Ariki Tafua. The other was the extra-human level of the healing powers of the gods of the Ariki Tafua. Yet the explanation was still rather more complex than the narrative Pa Fenuatara gave me, because he knew I was already in possession of certain information. It was this.

The Ariki Tafua was known as a man who exercized black magic. Some time before Pa Fenuatara's illness there had been a dispute in a swamp area, valuable for taro-growing, between Kafika and Tafua. The boundary of their respective interests was marked by a stone. One day Pa Fenuatara found the stone shifted out of position into the middle of the swamp—to the disadvantage of Kafika. He lifted it and put it back in its original place. I was told this by another member of Kafika clan who was standing unseen among the vegetation of the swamp at the time. He said that the

Ariki Tafua was standing in the middle of the swamp when Pa Fenuatara moved the stone and put a spell upon him. My informant heard the chief recite his formula and at the same time the chief saw him and called out loudly, cursing him by his canoe gods. "I left my work in the swamp and came and stood at the side of my house. Then I called on my ancestress Pufine i Tavi and was well," said my informant. But Pa Fenuatara, he said, was unaware of this at the time. Hence, he was struck by the spell and became ill. Thus his cure by the Ariki Tafua was not a matter of chance or due to the superior power of that chief; it was on the principle of "he who kills can also cure." It had been the gods and spirits obeying the Ariki Tafua who had inflicted Pa Fenuatara with sickness and consequently, when Pa Fenuatara came to him for relief, he was able to turn them into protective rather than destructive agents. The double level of explanation is seen again in the parallel statements that the illness of Pa Fenuatara was caused by his eating a certain kind of fish and also by the actions of malevolent spirits. This dualism is resolved by the convention that the spirits were exercizing their power through the fish.

Despite his sophistication in some intellectual respects, Pa Fenuatara operated very largely with concepts derived from his cultural upbringing, as the story of his illness indicates. He accepted without question the full panoply of gods and spirits believed in by all ordinary Tikopia. His analytical powers were displayed in elaboration of the conceptual framework and the provision of reasons for linking concepts together, not in questioning their reality. In fact, towards the end of his life he was very concerned with defining this conceptual framework on the grounds that it was at least as intelligible and moral as that of Christianity.

The intensity with which he felt the existence of these extra-human powers is shown by the story of his experience at his initiation. Initiation, with an incision ceremony—very similar to circumcision —is a major rite for every Tikopia boy, and for a lad of chiefly stock it is an occasion for very great ceremonial feasting and exchanges of property. The emotional high-point of the ceremony is the actual incision performance itself, and for this the boy may be prepared by some ritual act, to fortify his mind.

Pa Fenuatara told me that before the initiation ceremony he was taken to the then Ariki Kafika, predecessor of his father. The chief took a bottle of coconut oil, poured some into his hand, announced it to his gods and then rubbed it on the boy's chest. Pa Fenuatara said, "I felt his hand strike my vitals. I was frightened but I felt as though he had given me food so that I was full. Great is his power. Then my fear quite left me." The old chief himself did not attend the actual ceremony, which was performed by a mother's brother of Pa Fenuatara, a man who afterwards became the Ariki Fangarere. But the incident is an illustration of how, before this ceremony, tension is built up and then released by a social act of reassurance.

Like all other Tikopia, Pa Fenuatara believed firmly in the significance of dreams as indicators of a spiritual world invisible to ordinary human experience. On one occasion he told me about the progress of the soul after death to its heaven and the behaviour of guardian spirits towards it. This led him to say that people in Tikopia saw such spirits only in dreams when they were sleeping at night— in other words, that dreams were evidence of the existence and activities of spirits. He then recounted one of his dreams:

One night as I was sleeping it happened that I found myself standing on the shore and watching a bird swooping down, a great bird. I stood there and looked at it coming. I stood on the shore and I called to the children and to people, "You, there, look at my bird which is coming." Then people called out, "Where?" "Look at it! There it is coming down from above." And so I stood there and gazed at it. It came on and on and there I was standing and I called out, "Look at it there! It is going to come and stand on my hand." People called to me, "No, we don't see it. Where is it?" "Look at it coming down to stand on my hand." The crowd did not see the bird. They simply looked at my hand. Thereupon it kept on flying till it arrived and I stretched out my hand. It flew to me and stood there on my palm. It stood on my hand. As I looked at it it jumped down onto the sand below and as it stood there it was a man. As it stood there, a man, I saw that it was the Ariki Tafua. I said to him, "Well, so it's you. I thought you were a bird." He grasped me by the head, "It is me." Then as he grasped me his right hand held me at my brow. He smoothed back my hair and then put his hand at the top of my head, and I gripped my hand at his left, clasped him and pressed noses with him [in the conventional Tikopia greeting]. And the people stood in crowds on the shore. Thereupon he asked me, "Where is my brother-in-law [the Ariki Kafika]?" I said to him, "He has gone to live in the village over there." Then he said to me, "Are you living in this village here?" "Yes, I myself am living in this village but your brother-in-law has gone to the village over there." Then I asked him, "Where did you come from?" He replied, "I simply went to Namo. I went simply to our place in Namo." Then I said to him, "Let us go up inland farther" [meaning to sit in Pa Fenuatara's house for food and conversation]. He replied, "Oh, you go off inland but I am going. I simply came according to what I told you. I shall go to my brother-in-law in the village over there. Then I shall go off home to Faea." So he went and he was wearing two *kie* [decorated pandanus waist mats]. He did not fly up above, he went on the level ground. Now as I lifted off my hand to go to the village I woke.

I asked Pa Fenuatara what he thought about this dream. He began by saying, "I don't know what kind of talk this was." It was evident that the dream had left a very vivid impression on him. He demonstrated to me just how he spoke to the visitor, extended his hands, and so on. But he was quite clear that this was a dream experience, not a memory of anything that had occurred in ordinary life. He said, "My speech which I made to the chief, it was my dream." The person to whom he spoke in the dream was not in fact the Ariki Tafua: "It was a spirit impersonating him. It was not Pa Tafua. It was a spirit creating a resemblance to him. His body was the semblance of that of the living Ariki Tafua and I thought it was the Ariki Tafua." Pa Fenuatara went on, "When a man sleeps deeply and looks at another man, of course it is a spirit which has taken on the semblance of that other man." This is in fact the Tikopia theory of dreams—that these are ways in which spirits come to men and, by taking on the appearance of human beings, direct men, give them warning, and in general intercede in human affairs.

The anthropologist might offer a different interpretation. As far as I know, there had been no immediate single episode between the Ariki Tafua and Pa Fenuatara which might have given rise to this dream. Nor can I pick out any other figure or circumstance of which the Ariki Tafua may have been the symbol. But two factors relating to the chief himself may have stimulated Pa Fenuatara's dream. Not long before Pa Fenuatara had told me the story of his illness in which the Ariki Tafua had played such a markedly ambivalent role. The other factor was that very recently there had been some speculation that the Ariki Tafua might possibly abandon his Christianity and return to participate in the pagan rites in which he had formerly taken such a prominent part. Pa Fenuatara's dream may then well have been a symbolization of his wish for a resumption in ritual and spiritual matters of the intercourse which now existed only at the social level. The initial identification of the Ariki Tafua as a bird descending from the sky—which is the home of spirits—could support this interpretation.

This is, of course, my speculation. Pa Fenuatara himself had no such interpretation. But I did know at the time that this dream was an illustration of the inadequacy of Durkheim's idea that dreams could be proved false by comparing notes afterwards between the dreamer and the person about whom he dreamed. The Tikopia belief that the figure seen in a dream is not a human being but an impersonation of him by a spirit precludes such an attempt to disprove the actuality of the dream. The Tikopia, although they are very interested in dream interpretation, very reasonably do not try this naïve method of consulting the person about whom they dreamed, because in advance they regard this as useless.

In his beliefs in spirits and in the validity of dreams Pa Fenuatara was not without critical faculty. On one occasion when we were travelling by canoe over the lake he wondered musingly if a certain rite demanding the offering of a large fish would be performed the following day. Then he related a dream of his from the night before. He said that in his dream he went to sea, but as he pushed out his canoe he stepped in some excrement. He asked his companions whether this was a dream portending that they would catch a large fish. One of the crew answered, "A fish dream for certain." "I don't know," said Pa Fenuatara reflectively, and he continued to ponder the matter for some time. On another occasion talk turned to the nets set for salmon trout in the lake. The nets were becoming black, possibly with some organic growth, and tended to rot easily. Pa Fenuatara then told a story to the crowd assembled in the house about how, out on the lake with his nets one time, he felt a spirit going along the net and making it soft. When he held the net up he found it slimy. The spirit had been at work. I asked him then if this was a traditional piece of knowledge that spirits were responsible for the deterioration of the nets. He answered, "No, my own thought." Then he added with a laugh, "My own piece of traditional knowledge."

Such then was the man whom I left in 1929, in the full vigour of his manhood, with a young family growing up around him, heir-apparent to the ageing chief, his father, and a public career ahead of him. We parted with emotion and I wondered whether I should ever see him again.

When I returned to Tikopia in 1952 Pa Fenuatara was one of the first people I met. We greeted each other with the usual Tikopia embrace and pressing of noses. It was obvious from the way he uttered the conventional phrase, *"E aue toku soa,"* literally, "Oh, alas, my friend," that he was much affected. I exchanged personal and family news with him and his aged father who was now somewhat infirm. We were soon immersed in urgent public discussion of the effects of a recent hurricane on the island and the imminent food shortage; but every now and again Pa Fenuatara caught my eye and gave me a warm smile. He was always loyal to his friends, and after more than twenty years it was as if we had only recently parted. From then on, with few intermissions, I saw Pa Fenuatara almost daily or every other day until I left Tikopia again. He had aged markedly in the intervening years. His face was wrinkled, he was much thinner and his cheeks had fallen in through the loss of many of his teeth. His hair was grey and much sparser; and he had shaved his beard. But he had not lost his kindliness or his perceptiveness, and he had acquired a kind of philosophic sweetness which made him even more attractive. His personal dignity was much as it had ever been, but there was now an added authority because of necessity he had taken over a number of the social and political functions formerly exercized by his father.

Relations between Pa Fenuatara and myself were even closer than a generation before. He completely accepted me into his life and we had long discussions about a variety of subjects but in particular about political affairs, which were then giving him great concern. As before I was treated as a member of the Kafika family—a small incident will illustrate this. One day I noticed an elderly woman in a village near the coast and asked who she was. One of the sons of Pa Fenuatara was with me at the time. He replied, "My mother of Tongarutu." Then he asked me, "Do you know what house she is a daughter of?" "No," I replied. He then said, *"Te taina tou taina e nofo i Uta."* This expression can be translated as, "the sibling of your sibling who is living in Uta." Now, my sibling living in Uta might be either a man or a woman, but most generally *taina* means sibling of the same sex, so presumably it was Pa Fenuatara. But since the person referred to was a woman, the first "sibling" is likely to indicate that the second "sibling" referred to would also be a woman. Such a family sibling could not be a sister of Pa Fenuatara because any such kin term would then be *kave*—the relationship must be affinal. My affinal sibling living in Uta who at once came to my mind was Nau Fenuatara, wife of my sibling. Knowing that she belonged to the house of Kamota I said, "Lineage of Kamota?" "Yes," he replied. As shown in this example, the Tikopia always try to include the person spoken to in the mutual kinship group. The lad did not say simply, "my mother's sister," but, "the sister of your sister-in-law who lives in Uta."

I was not only included verbally in the Kafika group; I was treated as a kinsman on many ceremonial occasions. My visit to Anuta was the first I had made and the custom on such occasions is for the novice to have a small ceremony performed for him on his return to celebrate the event. A feast is prepared, a ceremonial bundle of bark-cloth made up and presented to him, and his breast and arms are smeared with turmeric pigment. All this was done for me by my "family." The smearing with turmeric, the culmination of the ceremony, was done as dusk was falling. I went home in the darkness and when I emerged into the lamplight of our house, still bedaubed with turmeric, it was to the consternation of Spillius who thought for the moment that the shining, oily, brilliant red pigment was my blood.

My absorption into the Kafika group was made apparent in another way. After Spillius and I had lived for a couple of months in Tikopia the people began to think of giving us house names in Tikopia style—partly in jest and partly seriously. The suggestion was made that I should be called Pa Te Niu, after the Taumako house in which we were living. The name was derived from the rock Fatutaka on which a single coconut palm once stood, and my name would therefore have meant "Mr. Coconut Palm." When he heard this Pa Fenuatara objected. He said, "No," that I belonged to Kafika and must bear a Kafika name, and he thereupon conferred upon me the title of Pa Munaora. This name was derived from a bachelor house of one of the most famous former chiefs of Kafika. The house used to stand to the east of Pa Fenuatara's old home, but had since been swallowed by the waves. Pa Fenuatara explained to me the meaning of the name, which literally was "speak life." He said, "The Ariki Kafika does not speak in the name of evil, he speaks only for welfare," meaning that his words were words of power, vivifying not destructive. When I inquired further about it he said that the former chief of Kafika gave the name to his house by analogy to his own position; his status laid upon him the obligation not to use witchcraft or attempt other ill, but to speak only for good. "Such are the customs of the Ariki Kafika. He does not speak that a man may be bewitched. He speaks only for good." He was referring here to the ritual speech rather than to the ordinary language of the chief. Pa Fenuatara asked me if I would give this name to my wife. I explained the difference in our naming customs and said that I would give it to my house some time, that I could write it on a sign so that people could see it, but I would not be known by it personally, as in Tikopia.

In his general activities Pa Fenuatara was now somewhat less energetic physically than before, and he was certainly rather more withdrawn from ordinary daily social affairs. This was largely due to his advancing age and change in family position. When I knew him before he lived regularly in a large roomy house near the seashore where he received a continual flow of visitors. As the years had gone by he had in effect vacated that house in favour of his eldest son, now married and with a growing family. Pa Fenuatara alternated his dwellings, inland or by the coast, depending on the season's work and the condition of the orchards. For much of his time he resided in a small house named Karua, hardly more than a hut, in Uta by the lakeshore in the heart of the island. Here he led a simple, semi-isolated life, going down to the coast only when he felt inclined to visit people or to take part in public affairs. This was the house in which he and his father had always spent much time at the turn of the seasons, conducting the great religious cycle of rites termed the "Work of the Gods," but he had now made it virtually his permanent home. The first time I went to see him there he ordered green coconuts to be plucked for the refreshment of myself and my companion. I said to him, "Famine is upon us. Leave them on the tree." He replied in scorn, "What does that matter? Coconuts for my friend," and ordered them to be produced.

In former days I noted that he engaged in a very wide range of occupations. He fished with rod and line and set nets in the lake, he was continually going to the cultivations for coconuts or hibiscus fibre, he helped in house-building and canoe-building, he made himself a wooden bowl, he went out after bonito, he planted taro and other crops. In 1952 I had a much more slender record of his economic pursuits. He rolled cord to make a net, he cleared ground for manioc, he cut hibiscus fibre, he helped his wife to prepare aerial yams, he carved out a dance bat, he dug turmeric, and he took over completely the role of expert in turmeric manufacture. But he moved more leisurely than before and he seemed to spend much more time sitting in his house, talking or sleeping. When the time for turmeric manufacture came, it was difficult to get him to name a day when work should begin. His wife, who was always inclined to rail at him, said he was hard to shift—"He doesn't wake up." There was an element of truth in this. Though not lazy he was leisured in all his economic activities. I saw him most absorbed either when he was engaged with true craftsman's precision in some piece of woodwork and when, on a brief visit to the neighbouring island of Anuta, he immersed himself in exchanges of goods.

He seemed to enjoy dancing as much as ever, and he was always willing to adorn himself and participate. I remember one occasion when a dance had been arranged and he wanted it to be on the grounds at the side of his own house by the sea coast. This would have been appropriate because of the close connection of his clan with the Ariki Fangarere who was the principal sponsor of the dance. But one of his friends said to him, "Brother-in-law, it is better at Asanga," and pointed out to him that there was more space and better facilities there. Pa Fenuatara replied, "Certainly," but in a later talk with his wife he told her he would have preferred to have the dance by his own house. However, he went in sprightly fashion to Asanga, seized a sounding board and its sticks, and joined a band of about six others to beat out a dance. Later, when the dance was fully under way, he was given, in ceremonial fashion, a trailing bark-cloth as acknowledgement of his presence and of his function as beater.

Pa Fenuatara's love of dancing was matched by his interest in dance songs. He knew a large number of these, both sacred and secular, and gave me their texts, very often not when we were talking specifically about dancing or singing, but arising in some quite different context. On one occasion, for instance, we had gone on a trip up a mountain to the Great Cave on the northern shore and were sitting outside a bush house enjoying the cool breeze. As often happens on such a picnic-like occasion, our party plucked fragrant sprigs of leaf and adorned themselves with head fillets, ear and neck ornaments. This stimulated Pa Fenuatara to sing for me songs of the Northern cliffs and the plucking of the fragrant leaflets growing there. His own compositions, while not especially distinguished, seemed to be neat and effective. They were quite popular and were used on many occasions. Here is one, a "dance of the canoe-bow," sung during the sacred rites at Uta when I was there in 1929. The Tikopia text is as follows:

> *Tafito: Ka fakau ki te ikinga vaka*
> *Ku fepeakina ko toko vaka*
> *I te ngoru fokorovo*
> *Kupu: Mataki ki te ainoino*
> *Na ka tetere au i toku motovoko.*

This song was composed in celebration of the narrow channel in the coral reef through which Tikopia canoes on the east side of the island had to paddle. When the weather was bad the heavy surf breaking on the reef could make this quite a dangerous manoeuvre, especially since a beam wave coming from the north side of the channel could strike the canoe hull and throw it over to crash on the coral. Like most Tikopia songs this one is a simple descriptive statement. But its force lies in the neat collocation of its syllables and in the evocative power of the precise terms used. In free translation it is this:

> Lay for the channel mouth,
> My canoe has been thrown off
> By the breaking sea.

> Watch carefully the narrow entrance.
> Now I shall speed along in my canoe prow.

What the song conveys is first the tenseness of beginning the operation, then the anxiety as the wave knocks the canoe sideways, then, as the result of mastery with a strong paddle, the exultation as the canoe races onwards with the breaking wave.

Pa Fenuatara's interest in dancing was not a purely personal one. He had views on its general character and on its functions. He believed, in common with most Tikopia, that dancing was good for the heart of man. But he looked a little further into it than most of his fellows. From him in particular I had observations on dances which involved awareness of sexual attraction and opposition. He pointed out to me that although some dance songs, even at the period of the sacred rites of Uta, had sexual themes, this did not necessarily mean that they were only of bawdy intent. He argued that part of the function of using these songs at dances in the context of the most sacred and awe-inspiring rituals of the community was to help to bring home to the young people the seriousness of sexual matters. They were a form of instruction to the young. This view was by no means shared by all responsible Tikopia, but it was an interesting functional point. Another point to which he drew my attention was that in the dances in which young men and young women tease one another and reply to one another in song (without using overt sexual terms), it was quite legitimate for married men and women to participate. However, he said that in such cases married men should support their daughters and married women support their sons. This was significant. The alignment of a married man with a young woman and a married woman with a young man meant that they were singled out from the younger generation of the same sex—they were marked as it were not for sexual adventure but for sociability and support. If a married man joined the company of the bachelors in opposing young women in song and dance it could be thought that he was seeking personal satisfaction; but if he went to support the young women then it could be regarded as paternal sympathy. This is a direct inference from Tikopia custom and attitude that if the dance was one in which whole districts were engaged, then all the unmarried women of one district are supported by all the married men of the other and vice versa—the support was like that given primarily to one's own son or daughter. Here again is the theme of heterosexual attraction between members of different generations which I have referred to earlier, but this time it is couched more broadly.

Pa Fenuatara's domestic situation did not appear to have changed over the years. His rather shrewish wife had taken on even more termagant qualities as she had aged, but he bore her railings with the same good humour. His children had increased. The youngest, born just as I was leaving the island in 1929 and named Remana after me, was now a grown man and a member of the Solomon Islands Police Force. After I had left, three more children were born to Pa Fenuatara, all boys. The youngest were a pair of twins. He asked me about twins. Did we have them in the West? He said that it was a good thing for both twins to live because in Tikopia if one died his spirit would strike the other dead. To clinch the point he cited a recent example of this from another family, adding, "Twins in this island are bad—damn them!"

The spirit of even a stillborn child can constitute a similar threat to its living siblings. Pa Fenuatara told me, for instance, that after the birth of her second child his wife had had a miscarriage, a male foetal birth. When I asked for details I was told that his name among the spirits was Fakasaka and that he appeared among men in spirit medium. "He comes to look upon his parents and upon his kinfolk. I said to him, though, that he should not come and wreak ill upon the other children. Thereupon he told me he would not. He was right—he has not come. Children like that go turning over in their minds ideas about the children who live among men and they come hither to wreak ill upon them. They turn over in their minds that they have gone and walked in the paths of spirits while the children who are alive walk in the paths of men. They gaze upon these children who eat at the side of their parents. They say, 'Oh, what kind of a thing is that that eats at the side of my parents while I am absent [am dead].'" When I asked Pa Fenuatara specifically if this was *kaimeo,* the Tikopia term for jealousy, he said, "Just that."

After my departure, in the famine of 1952 that followed in the wake of a hurricane and drought, one of Pa Fenuatara's twin sons died. He apparently was the smaller and weaker of the two. (According to Spillius, to whom I owe information on this incident, it is generally reckoned by the Tikopia that one twin is liable to an early death.) The lad himself, his body covered with ringworm, had not been a very prepossessing boy though Pa Fenuatara had seemed reasonably fond of him. His death was a matter of no public regret, and Pa Fenuatara seemed to take his loss stoically. It was a time of severe stringency and curtailment of ceremonies because of lack of food. Pa Fenuatara kept the prescribed mourning for about a month, but the demands of public affairs forced him to foreshorten the customary mourning period. I do not know that he expressed any particular views about the effect of this death upon the surviving twin.

In the years before I came to know him, Pa Fenuatara's personal life had had some dramatic moments. Before 1928, after an early love affair which he abandoned at the wish of his parents, he found a mistress whom in due course he brought home as his wife. On his wedding day an event took place which embarrassed him greatly. An old flame of his rushed up, grasped him round the knees, and refused to release him until she too should become his wife. After some objections and threats, he and his proper wife both accepted her and they set up a polygynous household. But there was too much friction, so finally he left his home and went to live on the other side of the island. He returned at his father's behest, but when it became clear that he did not want her, the second wife went back to her own family. Later she remarried happily. Another incident with his first love had roused his wife's jealousy and Pa Fenuatara's relations with her had degenerated as a result. Here too the woman concerned married elsewhere.

All this had taken place some time before I first met him, and in 1928 he seemed to have settled into relatively placid domesticity. But there had evidently been fires still burning below the surface. I had known that things were not equable between him and his wife. Overtly he was not a man of strong sexual proclivities— unlike his father, who had rather a name for his pursuit of women —but apparently Pa Fenuatara had sought satisfaction elsewhere. I learned that fairly soon after I left Tikopia he had contracted a second marriage and attempted again to have a polygynous household. He married a woman of the lineage of Rangitau and she was known as Nau Karua to distinguish her from his first wife, Nau Fenuatara. The name Karua was an ancient one in Kafika, having been attached to a house belonging to the chiefs of Kafika and formerly standing in Uta near the Kafika temple. When I was there in 1929 the house had long since disappeared, but in accordance with Tikopia custom the name was later revived. But this marriage, like the earlier one, did not last very long. The woman bore Pa Fenuatara a daughter—who was later lost by swimming out to sea with a number of her companions in a mass suicide. Nau Karua was soon "chased away," as the Tikopia put it, by Nau Fenuatara, and went to live in a house of her brother in Namo. Later she became a Christian.

Pa Fenuatara had retained his keen interest in Western goods and ways of doing things. Unlike most Tikopia he was not greedy and very rarely asked me for fishhooks or calico or other desirable items. This was partly because, as his friend, I tried to provide him with a fair share of the wealth which I had to distribute. But it was also his personal fastidiousness and pride which restrained him from appearing grasping. His wife was not so backward and on occasions asked me for beads and berated me for not bringing the family more goods. When this happened Pa Fenuatara was plainly rather embarrassed. However, his eagerness for the novelties of the outside world was revealed in several ways. One was his interest in becoming acquainted with our Western habits of social intercourse. He was not too interested in learning English, although with the fierce desire of the young people to master this new medium he could hardly escape knowledge of a few words. One phrase which he, like nearly all Tikopia, had learned was, "Thank you." In keeping with the Tikopia practice of transforming into their own language any new expression they borrowed, this phrase was treated like a Tikopia word and could be given a causative prefix. On one occasion when I had given Pa Fenuatara's wife a length of calico he said to her, *"Fakathankyou"* (say thank you), whereupon she uttered the polite syllables. On the other hand, Pa Fenuatara was very interested in learning how to use chairs and eating utensils. He was fond of tea and the first time he sat down to a meal with us he acquitted himself admirably with the novel instruments of spoon and fork. His native delicacy enabled him to watch and follow the usages of European table manners without difficulty.

On occasion, however, when his personal status was involved, his interest in European equipment was straightforwardly expressed. This happened with the gun. At the beginning of my second visit Pa Fenuatara complained to me about fruit bats eating food and spoiling coconuts. He had asked the Government for a gun with which to shoot them, but he wanted to know what had happened to the gun which I had had on my previous visit. Had I brought it with me? Did I remember his going shooting with me? The District Commissioner with whom we arrived in Tikopia had in fact brought with him a 12-bore shot gun in response to requests made earlier by the Tikopia. In his public address to the chiefs he mentioned the gun and laid it out in front of the gathering as a present to the four chiefs. It was given to the Ariki Kafika in the first instance but it was left to the chiefs to arrange for its use. The interpreter said, "Now the gun which has been brought here for the Ariki Kafika is the gun for the whole community." But I noted at the time that Pa Fenuatara had his eye on the weapon. He said, "It was I who asked for it and the chiefs have their sprays" (to destroy mosquitoes). The interpreter replied, "Oh it will go round the island, the bats falling before it." To this Pa Fenuatara said, "We will see, we will dispose of it as we will." In fact, he took possession of the gun when the meeting was over and as far as I know it continued to remain his property. His eldest son took it from time to time and after some practice became quite expert at killing bats. I was called upon to produce cartridges for it, but Pa Fenuatara and his son were not backward in putting up money to buy cartridges themselves. In a sense, the gun was the property of the community and the killing of bats with it was of public benefit. But the real point was that a gun in Tikopia was a mark of prestige. In former days a Snider carbine or other gun used to be given by labour recruiters as part payment for men whom they took away to work on the plantations. Such guns, of which a few were left in Tikopia in 1929, gravitated to the men of rank, especially the chiefs. Pa Fenautara was insistent that this new weapon which worked, unlike the ancient guns, was rightfully his to control.

As eldest son and heir-apparent to the chieftainship, Pa Fenuatara's relationship with his father was highly complex. In 1952 as in 1929 he treated his father with a combination of respect and affection, and supported him loyally in social and ritual matters. He was very much in his father's confidence and it was clear from the amount of esoteric information at his command that his father had made known to him all the major secrets of his lineage and of the ritual that devolved upon the leading chieftain in the community. In 1929 the Ariki Kafika told me about the restrictions placed on the land by the ritual cycle of the Work of the Gods. These included a prohibition on the cutting of coconut fronds. If a man should cut fronds in the night to thatch his house, the chief said a storm would strike that man's house, scatter his thatch, and break the ridge pole and drive it into the ground. Thus would the angered god show his wrath, but this destruction could be caused by the chief as well. Seeing coconut fronds freshly cut the Ariki Kafika might address his deity, "You ancestor, look upon the house which has made sport of your things. Set down your sacred foot upon it." Then in the morning news would come that the man's house had been wrecked by a whirlwind.

The Ariki Kafika went on to say that such a formula of destruction is hidden by a chief from all but the son who is to succeed him. He added that this particular formula was still hidden from Taurongo —Pa Fenuatara. He explained that if a chief divulges all his secrets to his son then his gods say among themselves, "Now his things there he has announced completely to his son. He there, will he die?" When a chief imparts his knowledge to his son while still young and vigorous he always leaves a few things unrevealed until the time comes when he can no longer walk about. Then he tells his son to come and he pillows his head on his father's arm. The chief covers them both with one blanket and tells him finally all the formulae of the *kava* and other sacred things. Then he asks his son, "Now you tell me that I may listen and see if it is complete." The son repeats all he knows while the father corrects him and makes additions. When the chief is satisfied he says to his son, "Now all your things are complete." The Ariki Kafika explained to me that he had withheld this particular item from Pa Fenuatara because he himself was still hale and hearty. He did not wish the gods to imagine that he was tired of living. Only much later would he complete his son's knowledge. At this period indeed the Ariki Kafika was very active and there was no reason to think that Pa Fenuatara had any immediate prospects of succeeding him.

On my return to Tikopia, I found the chief an aged man, and his relationship to Pa Fenuatara had undergone a subtle change. When in ordinary health he was still quite active, though he travelled across the lake by canoe and could no longer go by land. With the aid of a staff he used to find his way alone to our house for a cup of tea, and he was so tough that shortly after a severe illness he was to be seen bathing in the cold sea as usual. He was still capable of performing the traditional rituals, but he was infirm, and the regular daily rites of the Work of the Gods were a very great strain upon him. Pa Fenuatara did his best to spare him effort, while at the same time showing respect to his priestly duties and to the chief's right of decision.

One conversation between Pa Fenuatara, his father, and the Ariki Fangarere which I recorded concerned the number of days to be devoted to the rites of one of the sacred temples. Pa Fenuatara said, "You elders go and discuss the matter between yourselves and tell us what you want to do." He himself wanted the rites abbreviated, partly out of concern for his father, but primarily because of the shortage of food. He said, "If we assemble and finish the rites tomorrow, what of it? Where is the harm?" Some of the others supported him, one man saying, "Let each person go home and sleep in his own house." As the discussion went on Pa Fenuatara interjected at intervals, "Will the gods be angry? They know that we have just assembled—without food." Pa Fenuatara put his opinion in very conciliatory terms, "I am simply asking what your intentions may be. It is all right with us whatever opinion you may give to us." His wife echoed his view—she and her husband did not mind what decision the chiefs made, but just wanted it to be clear. (They did in fact mind very much but were being polite about it.) But the Ariki Kafika was resistant to the idea of shortening the rites and the other chief was neutral. Pa Fenuatara returned to the charge. "I am speaking to you, but you listen to your bodies." By that he meant that it depended on how fit and strong the two chiefs felt. Finally, it was decided to have an abbreviated set of rites, although later on the Ariki Kafika did extend them slightly. What was particularly noticeable in all the conversation was that while Pa Fenuatara put his arguments to his father persistently and forcibly, he did so with the greatest politeness and always left the decision to him. Yet all the work in connection with the rites would be done not by the old chief but by Pa Fenuatara and his family.

The reason for this was that only the old chief himself could perform the final esoteric acts to validate the ritual. If he were not present then Pa Fenuatara could operate only at a reduced ritual level. The ultimate role of the chief was illustrated on two other occasions. In one, the manufacture of turmeric, the old chief was present but very ill, lying on a mat in the house where the work was going on with a bark-cloth sheet drawn over him. The turmeric liquid and the wooden oven in which it was to be cooked had been prepared. The next step was to pour the liquid into the cylindrical oven. But this was a ritual as well as a technological act and at this point the chief had to be brought in. Pa Fenuatara, who was the technical expert, went over to his father and said, "Father! The turmeric!" The old chief refused to move and told his son to carry on. So Pa Fenuatara said, "Well, uncover your face then," and he went back to the work. When everything was ready one of the team took coconut oil and poured it into the hand of Pa Fenuatara. He stretched his hand out and called, "Father! Father!" The old chief strained round and stared as Pa Fenuatara tilted his hand and let the drops of sacred oil run as libation on the coconut leaf mat. Pa Fenuatara muttered a formula of invocation to the gods and after a moment the old chief too murmured a few words and then sank back onto his bed, while Pa Fenuatara continued his task. A little later, when the turmeric liquid was about to be poured into its cylinder, Pa Fenuatara again called, "Father! Father!" and held up the bowl to pour. He looked at the chief, who this time was lying still with his eyes closed. Pa Fenuatara himself then recited some phrases, looking at his father as he did so, and then continued the work. Here the contribution of the Ariki Kafika was minimal, but his presence allowed Pa Fenuatara to act in his name and thus validate the proceedings with the gods. The fact that the turmeric pigment turned out very well confirmed the correctness of the proceedings.

On another occasion, the resacralization of a sacred canoe, Pa Fenuatara had to act alone. The old Ariki was absent and ill, and this time the rites were merely a token acknowledgement without the elaboration of an offering and libation which would have been made if the chief had been there. It was difficult to get Pa Fenuatara to act in this matter. Indeed, his wife complained again at his slowness and it seemed to me as if he were almost reluctant to assume some of the functions of the chief.

The question of the succession to the chieftainship lay at the heart of the matter. What were Pa Fenuatara's own feelings and the attitude of the people at large to the situation in which an aged chief continued in office while his heir in turn grew old?

Pa Fenuatara's position was difficult. He acted in many ways as the head of the Kafika clan, making decisions for both his clan and the community as a whole. Yet he was not the chief and his father alone could perform the most sacred rites. In the last resort it was only his word which had final validity. To say that Pa Fenuatara had great influence but no authority is hardly a correct way of putting it, because a legitimacy was accorded to his decisions by virtue of his unchallenged right to be his father's successor. Yet, he had to move carefully. Unlike his father who could give arbitrary decisions because he was the chief and who had all the aura of his ritual powers as sanctions, Pa Fenuatara had no chiefly taboo, no command over gods, no title of *ariki* (chief). His decisions, therefore, had to have some measure of public support to be effective. He was concerned accordingly not to appear in any way to be arrogating to himself privileges that were his father's, and he took at times what seemed to be a line of almost excessive humility. Thus, a meeting of chiefs to discuss with the District Commissioner the approaching famine and measures to counter it took place outside the home of the Ariki Kafika as premier chief. The old Ariki himself was not present because of infirmity and he was represented by Pa Fenuatara. Coconut leaf floor mats were set out for the principal persons and five stools were put upon them, one for each of the three chiefs, one for Pa Fenuatara, and one for the Government official. Other stools were set out at the side for Spillius and myself, the interpreter, and another man of rank. The chiefs took their places, at the specific invitation of a prominent Tikopia, when it developed that they were waiting for the Government officer. Pa Fenuatara sat in the background. When at last one of the leading Tikopia called out to him, "Brother-in-law, go and join the assembly of chiefs," he stood up and very slowly went forward, a stately figure, finely dressed with leaf ornaments in his ears. He moved the stool from the place assigned to him on the mat and gravely set it on the bare ground at the rear where he insisted on sitting despite protests from his neighbour, the Ariki Taumako. On other formal occasions he acted in a similar way, emphasizing that he laid no claim to chiefly status. On the other hand, he regarded himself as fully entitled to consideration as the leader in

Tikopia public affairs and bitterly resented any challenge by the family of the Melanesian Mission priest to assume leadership for the whole community.

The essence of the matter was that to the Tikopia people at large the old chief had held on to life far too long. They saw him decrepit and doddering, barely able to perform his ritual functions, and though still entitled to all the respect and awe which a Tikopia chief inspires, not contributing anything of value to the body politic. Even in ritual matters it was a question whether his survival was of advantage to the community. There was an idea that the ills from which Tikopia suffered in 1952 were in some part due to a correlation between lack of health and prosperity in the land and the waning physical powers of the chief.

This opinion was epitomized and symbolized in a dramatic incident. On the occasion of the illness of his own eldest son, Pa Fenuatara was accused by a spirit medium in the presence of a large gathering of unduly prolonging his father's life so that the gods were moved in anger to destroy the family. Pa Fenuatara rebutted the spirit's accusation and defended himself skilfully. On the one hand he called in filial sentiment and said how could he do anything else but feed and cherish his father. On the other hand he defied the spirit and said that if the gods persisted in afflicting his son with illness he and his son together would go off to sea—in effect, a suicide threat. The spirit—that is the human medium—apologized to Pa Fenuatara and the incident was closed. There was no doubt that the spirit medium was reflecting public opinion—the people wanted Pa Fenuatara as chief. But I had never had any indication from Pa Fenuatara himself that he was in any sense anxious to succeed his father or, indeed, that he was even conscious of the situation. He was always the patient, filial son. However, I had an insight into his attitude as a sequel to this public incident. When I raised it with him privately and asked for explanation on some details—since I myself had not been there—he first told me what had happened, and then, spontaneously, said quietly, "The spirit was right." He explained that according to traditional belief the Ariki Kafika, who is the agent of the supreme god of the Kafika clan, should die young in order that a virile succession be maintained. Otherwise, as the chief grows old and infirm so also infirmities come upon the land as a whole. But even in explaining to me the Tikopia esoteric theory he did not lose his judgement in his ambition. There was no criticism of his father to be detected in what he said, no sense that he himself desired power, but only an expression of belief in a principle which in this case had not been borne out in practice.

The political implications of Pa Fenuatara's relations with his father were kept at a minimum by his own discretion and sentiment. But his political interests were very obvious in other fields. Although he had not the status and rights of a chief, he regarded himself as the *de facto* representative of the Ariki Kafika and therefore trustee for the interests of the community as a whole. In this it was doubtless difficult for him, and indeed for any observer, to separate his actions as leader of a privileged group from his actions on behalf of the whole of Tikopia, if only because even in 1952 the Tikopia community still accepted as part of the natural order the institution of chieftainship and its prerogatives. Granted then that Pa Fenuatara was in many cases defending his class as well as the interests of Tikopia as a whole, he did have a very alert sense of the responsibility as well as the dignity of the chiefly office.

By 1952 Pa Fenuatara was faced by two major political issues, both associated in different ways with social and economic developments. One was the relationship being shaped between the Tikopia community and the Melanesian Mission, the other between the Tikopia and the Solomon Islands Protectorate Government. These issues had existed a generation before but were less critical because of the relative lack of contact between the Tikopia and the outside world. By 1952, as the result of the opening of the external labour market to Tikopia and the increased contact of Tikopia with the outside world, questions of control of policy became more acute. The primary interest of the Mission was conversion of the Tikopia to Christianity. By 1952 about seven-eighths of the Tikopia had become Christian and the remaining hard core of pagans had Pa Fenuatara as one of their major leaders. There was then between Pa Fenuatara and the Mission an unbridgeable ideological gulf. But the local Mission leaders made a bid not only for spiritual but also for temporal control. Pa Fenuatara's opposition to the Mission on religious grounds took only a passive form. He made no counter-movements to secure the allegiance of those who followed the pagan faith. But in the political field it was different.

One of the burning questions in 1952 was whether the Tikopia should be allowed to recruit as labour not only for the Solomons, in whose governmental jurisdiction the island lay, but also for the New Hebrides, foreign territory to them. The attraction of the New Hebrides, as some exploring young Tikopia had found, was the very high wage rate then current there. By 1952 a strong opinion had formed in Tikopia that the New Hebrides was the right place for Tikopia labourers to go. But the Solomon Islands Government, partly as a matter of long-term public interest and partly as an immediate measure of labour conservation, decided otherwise and the Tikopia accepted this with their usual obedience to a decision from above. But the moves prior to this showed that Pa Fenuatara was cleverly appreciative of political strategy and adept in political tactics. A son of the Melanesian Mission priest had announced he was going to hold a public meeting in which he would advocate recruitment to the New Hebrides. On hearing this Pa Fenuatara summoned his own public meeting. He held a meeting in Ravenga and then another in Faea. This shift to the other district was a deliberate challenge to his opponent, whose home it was. Pa Fenuatara himself spoke in Faea. He sent a public messenger to his opponent saying, "You are going to have a public meeting in Motlav style. I recognize only public meetings from the Government. You are going to make a public address to the land—where is your land to address . . ." and so on. This was to be understood in the following way: "I have authority when I speak—as the heir to the chieftainship of Kafika. Who are you to hold a public meeting? What is the basis of your authority? You are a mere nobody. Your father came from Motlav (in the New Hebrides area). You have no rights in Tikopia." This move, which seems to have been undertaken by Pa Fenuatara on his own responsibility, appears to have been effective. Certainly no more was heard of a public meeting by the son of the priest.

More clearly than anyone else in Tikopia, Pa Fenuatara had separated church and state. He saw the Mission as a powerful body, unchallengeable at least in any aggressive way on religious grounds and entitled to respect in its overt sphere. But he recognized, resented, and took measures to counter the ease with which it could assume political control in Tikopia. With increasing governmental interest in Tikopia he saw his opportunity and was able to use the Government as a counterweight to the Mission in the political field.

An instance of his appreciation of the situation was his attitude towards the distribution of relief supplies in the famine. When the question of distribution of food arose he made one significant point. The food was going to be supplied by the Government. He said that any surplus from the initial distribution should be stored in the house of the Ariki Tafua, who could move to another house he had inland. He said that anything which came on the Melanesian Mission vessel should be distributed by the priest, but anything which came from the Government should be distributed by the chiefs. This statement was logical, but it also embodied a political categorization. The Ariki Tafua was the leading Christian chief. By emphasizing his confidence in this chief and suggesting his dwelling as the storehouse for Government food, Pa Fenuatara was in fact stressing the political alignment of chiefs, not their religious alignment.

Pa Fenuatara set out his political position and strengthened it in another way. At the time when the New Hebrides recruitment issue was still very much alive and the view of Government was not yet known, and when Tikopia opinion was almost unanimously in favour of the New Hebrides solution, Pa Fenuatara made his position clear. He came to me one evening to explain that while he agreed with the chiefs at a meeting in which they had expressed their views, it was only for the sake of appearances. He was opposed to the idea of seeking an outlet for work in the New Hebrides. He was in support of the Solomons Government and wanted to defer entirely to their opinion. He was of the view that the pressure to link up with the New Hebrides came from the Mission priest's family, partly because of their connections there, and from their supporter, the Christian Ariki Tafua. He alleged that the priest's family wished to assume leadership in Tikopia and said, "The land here is mine. It is under my control." He stated that earlier the Solomons Government gave agreement to the rule over Tikopia by the chiefs on condition that they agreed to the Government's suzerainty. Since the chiefs assented to this arrangement they were not acting correctly in trying to link up with the New Hebrides. Pa Fenuatara told me he wished this to be brought to the attention of the Government and that he would be content to abide by their views about recruitment.

A month later when the Government officer arrived, Pa Fenuatara had a private interview with him in which, at his request, I acted as his interpreter. He reëmphasized his allegiance to the Government and to their view. He said that the chiefs and the mass of the people had gone astray; they had listened to bad advice. This advice was from the family of the Mission priest who, having relations with the New Hebrides, wished to orient the Tikopia that way. He pointed out that he had opposed this in a public meeting in reply to the views of the son of the Mission priest who had returned from the New Hebrides. But he said that the group of chiefs wished him to be their spokesman and express their views at a meeting with the Government official. He would not do this lest it should seem that he shared the chiefs' views. With the Government's permission, he would sit silent when the public assembly took place.

Thus, the Government official was left in no doubt as to where Pa Fenuatara's loyalties and interests lay. The Tikopia also had no doubt. The following day, while Pa Fenuatara and some other men were in our house, the Ariki Tafua entered. After a little general conversation, Pa Fenuatara opened up. He said, "My eyes were red yesterday. My head was split open . . ." and more to the same effect. This was in reference to the suggestion by a chief that he should head their deputation to Government and request that recruitment to the New Hebrides be allowed. By this expression he signified his embarrassment and anger. He said to the Ariki Tafua, "You and your fellow chiefs can talk. I shall keep silent. But I want you to know the reason why. My mind is different." The Ariki Tafua replied in conciliatory manner, "Oh, don't let it be laid on us only. It is good to be of one speech." But while recognizing Pa Fenuatara's view, the Ariki Tafua, in common with other Tikopia, gave that view perhaps even more importance than it merited. The Ariki Tafua, in particular, attributed the Government's refusal to allow recruiting to the New Hebrides to Pa Fenuatara having spoken first to the Government official when he arrived.

This series of events demonstrated Pa Fenuatara's political influence. No chief himself, he could maintain an opinion contrary to that of the chiefs, and he had been able to demonstrate to the Government and to the Tikopia people at large his right to speak authoritatively in the name of the interests of the community as a whole. He was able to do this not merely because he was in effect exercising the political powers of his father, but also because he had a clear conception of the issues and in particular of the fact that the ultimate political strength lay in the hands of the Government. On the other hand, he was always careful to get sanctions for his attitude whenever he could—to find out, for instance, what the Government view was before he committed himself. Moreover, in practical matters of public order, as against broad policy, he took little initiative himself. By temperament somewhat indolent, as well as being hampered by being only quasi-regent of Kafika, not chief, he tended to leave action in practical affairs to other men of rank.

In one major respect, however, Pa Fenuatara failed, and that was in the religious field. Every anthropologist knows that a pagan can be a religious man—and Pa Fenuatara was markedly so. In a fairly literal sense of the term, he was religious in regarding himself and his family as bound by strong invisible ties to a set of supernatural beings, the gods and ancestors of his family. He believed firmly in the existence of these gods and spirits and in their powers, including those of punishing with illness and death any lack of respect to them. But his support of the pagan religious rites was not simply a response to fear of consequences. He regarded the complex rituals as the fulfillment of legitimate obligations, in one sense a reciprocity by man for the gifts of the gods. More than this, he looked upon these rites as proper and indeed morally good. In the pagan view they were performed not for any evil purpose, not to harm men, but to secure the continued fertility and prosperity of the land. Why then should they be stigmatized by the missionaries as wrong, evil, dark things?

Such was the position in 1929 when the community was almost equally divided between followers of the traditional religion and of Christianity. But a generation later, when only a residuum of pagans remained, his attitude, and his moral position had taken on a note of resignation, almost of despair. In 1929 the pagan religion was still very much alive, not aggressive but with half the island busy in its affairs. When I returned, although the *kava* rites still remained and the cycles of the Work of the Gods were still performed, the flow of participants had shrunk to a trickle. It was a dying religion, especially since the young people, even Pa Fenuatara's own family, were more and more being drawn to the novelty and the sociability of the Church.

It is not fair, perhaps, to say that in this field Pa Fenuatara had completely failed to hold the allegiance of his people. In the first place the primary religious responsibility was not his but that of the chiefs, who were also the major priests. Again, the attitude of leading Tikopia consistently almost from the moment of entry of the Mission had been not to oppose the Mission in any forcible way, but to welcome it socially without conceding its religious claims. Hence, as time went on, the pagans found that in their desire for Western contacts they had conceded a large part of the field before the struggle had really begun. But whatever the element of personal responsibility, Pa Fenuatara was by 1952 confronted with a clear failure of the pagan system. It was apparent that in a short while the system would not be able to maintain itself even at the very low level of ritual participation that then existed. In our discussion of these things Pa Fenuatara's comments were often bitter. This was not surprising since from his point of view the religion which was replacing his own had few obvious advantages. The supreme God it claimed was not very different from his own. He, like most Christian Tikopia, thought of gods and spirits in terms of power politics rather than in terms of existence. The Christian God, they thought, had conquered the others; these other gods did not cease to exist when a person who formerly worshipped them became Christian. Moreover, the ethic of Christianity, whatever its public proclamation, did not seem to have had great effect upon the Tikopia, since Christian Tikopia apparently slandered, lied, and stole food as much as the pagans.

Pa Fenuatara, from his own point of view, had as much ethical justification for his religious position as had any Christian. I personally found him in practice, as well as in precepts, a man of high moral principles. The only occasion on which we really differed was once in 1929 when we were discussing the suicide of a young woman. She had been driven to swim out to sea by a threat of violence of a man of chiefly family. He had wanted her as his mistress but, on learning that she had already had relations with another man, he rejected her angrily and threatened her with death. To me this was a shocking incident, more anomalous because the man concerned had been known for his upright nature. Pa Fenuatara and I differed radically on this. To me it was an inexcusable act; to him it was intelligible, even logical, because of the rank of the man concerned. To him (as to most Tikopia) it was proper that the young woman should have been driven off to sea "because she did not desire the man." The action was justified because "it was a man of chiefly family who took umbrage."

There is no doubt that Pa Fenuatara's ethical and religious views were to a considerable degree bound up with his conception of chiefly status and of his own relation thereto. In our discussions about religion I asked him one day what he thought would be the future of Christianity in Tikopia. He answered in effect, "That's as may be," refusing to commit himself, but it was clear that his thoughts were gloomy. I asked him if he himself had ever thought of becoming a Christian. He said, "No." When I asked him why, he answered in effect that Christianity did not make proper provision for the status of the chief. He drew my attention to one of the Christian chiefs who had to undertake menial tasks such as tending the oven like any common man. In part this offended Pa Fenuatara's notions of the dignity of the office. He was not concerned with his own personal dignity because he himself often undertook such menial tasks, but his conception of a chief was of someone set apart and he did not see why Christianity should alter this status position. But I think that there was more to it than that. In all his discussions about chieftainship, Pa Fenuatara emphasized the responsibility that a chief has to his people, to care for their welfare, not to bewitch people, to act in ways which promote good for all the people and not merely the prosperity of the individual. I think he saw Christianity as an assertion of the rights of the individual to promote his own interest and a reduction of the responsibility of the chief to that of a common man. At no time did I hear him say that Christianity in its religious aspects was untrue. He challenged specific assertions of Christians—for example that the ghosts of Christians did not walk abroad. He reacted sharply against Christian assertions as to the evils of paganism. But he did not deny the possibility that the Christian dogma was true. He merely preferred his own and associated with it notions of communal responsibility which he thought were lacking in Christianity. Here his appreciation of the whole situation was inadequate, due very largely one might think to his lack of education. But in conversation with him one forgot that here was an illiterate pagan. One recognized an aristocrat who could defend his values on a broad human plane in a way that had great point in the context of his own society.

When Pa Fenuatara died in 1955 during a severe epidemic, his own death followed so closely that of his father that I have not been able to find out as yet whether he did in fact ever succeed as chief. Whether he did so or not, the conversion of all the pagan Tikopia shortly afterwards means that he was one of the last of the Tikopia leaders to live and die in the ancient faith.

A man of principle, he had a firm conviction of what was good for his society. Born to high status in it, he was not a careerist. Hampered in the attainment of supreme authority by the accident of his father's longevity, it was not that he had no place in the power structure of his community but that he had had to hold on to his role of heir-apparent too long. Though he was never to achieve the position for which he seemed destined, he did by his personal character succeed in winning a public respect which went far beyond the role his society set out for him. Disposing of his resources skilfully and sparingly, though somewhat indolently, to achieve his ends, he was an example of how acts of personal appreciation and decision can be brought to fulfillment with considerable effect within a given social structure and may, in their turn, help to provide a new framework within which that structure itself must operate.

2

Petrus Mailo,
Chief of Moen

Thomas Gladwin

Petrus Mailo is a man secure, and therefore humble, in the certainty of his own wisdom. He is a statesman who, but for the setting and character of his tasks, could take his place among the historic molders of our common destiny.[1] But he is not a leader of armies and nations, bending the will of multitudes to a great cause. Rather he is the elected chief of a small island boasting perhaps 2000 souls. He stands protectively over his people, who go through their days satisfied that his decisions in a thousand petty matters are unquestionably wise. At the same time he stands, on the organization chart at least, below a group of American administrators, men of good will but often of limited experience. Their understanding of the Trukese can often be clouded by stereotypes they brought with them from America, stereotypes perhaps of the simple savage who knows no morals, of South Sea magic, or of the unique and indispensable virtues of American democracy and free enterprise.

As the pressures and problems, protests and policies flow up and down, Petrus is the eye of the needle through which they all must pass. As each matter goes through his hands it must be scrutinized, and often transformed, so that the cumulative effect of all these transactions will somehow keep his people in harmony with the ever-changing and often dimly seen new patterns of life which constantly emerge. The measure of his statesmanship, then, lies not in conquests or in monuments, but in an endless procession of episodes, most with a fortunate outcome.

Petrus is chief of Moen Island, seat of the American administration and one of half a dozen major islands scattered, along with many smaller ones, throughout the large lagoon of Truk in the western Pacific. Like most tropical islands, these combine the lush beauty of richly wooded slopes, clean white beaches and jewel-clear water

[1] I have shared the pleasure of writing this chapter with several others whose affection and respect for Petrus surely equal my own. In particular, I corresponded at length with Frank J. Mahony during the writing. The passages in this chapter which in my opinion most effectively delineate Petrus in relation to his culture were taken almost verbatim from his letters.

with stagnant inland swamps, areas of drab marsh grass, and occasional inlets which seem somehow to have trapped all the flotsam and refuse of the oceans. Most of the villages are strung along near the water, clusters of unpainted frame houses fashioned of salvaged Japanese lumber and corrugated iron. They are far from beautiful, yet their open porches seem to invite in the trade winds and thus symbolize an appealingly easy relationship with nature. The soil here near the beach is sandy, accenting patterns of light and shadow as the warm sunlight streams through constantly moving coconut fronds. In many villages the South Sea paradise of our dreams becomes a reality—although again our dreams do not usually include the flies and mosquitoes which are necessarily a part of such a tropical scene.

None of the islands is large—Moen is a triangle barely three miles on a side—but together they can support a population far larger than their present 10,000, and in fact apparently did so before smallpox and other diseases invaded the Pacific. More important, the soil of these steep but fertile volcanic islands can grow turmeric, hardwoods, tapioca, and other vital crops impossible to cultivate on low coral islands. Consequently Truk has been since times long forgotten the pivot and focus of all intercourse between islands to the north, to the south, and for hundreds of miles to the west. The cultural influence of Truk extends to the edge of Indonesia, and embraces all of the Caroline Islands except the Palaus, Yap, and Ponape and its outliers—an area which is roughly a mirror image north of the Equator of that covered by New Guinea in the southern hemisphere.

As Western civilization has wrought its varied changes in the patterns of life in these expanses of ocean the high islands have retained their preëminence, now as centers of administration and commerce. Petrus is deeply engaged in both. In addition to being chief of the island on which the administrative center is located, he is president of the Truk Trading Company, an enterprise which totally dominates the economic life of the Truk District. In either role Petrus is uncompromisingly a Trukese. He can understand and often respect the position of an American, or even of those Trukese who, through ancestry or inclination, stand between the cultures. But for himself Petrus knows no middle ground. He is the champion of his people and therefore one of them, with a stubbornness which can sometimes appear quixotic.

Petrus has been chief of Moen for over ten years, and a dominant figure on the political scene of all of Truk for most of this time. This does not appear to be a long time until one realizes that sustained contact with the outer world began for Truk only a scant hundred years ago, and direct foreign rule has been imposed for little over fifty years. Petrus has thus had a share in molding a significant proportion of Truk's recorded history.

This history began with the coming of whalers, followed by missionaries and traders. During this period, in the latter half of the last century, Spain claimed sovereignty over the area, but never implemented its rule. A state of chronic guerrilla warfare, dividing village from village, acquired new menace with the advent of traders' guns which killed too easily for comfort. Chiefs of villages, Petrus' father Mailo among them, raided and conquered and were defeated in turn—although Mailo never suffered the latter fate. At their sides stood men wise in esoteric lore, able through divination to foretell the outcome of battle, who kept their knowledge from the laiety by communicating in a secret chanting jargon called *itang* which they imparted only to their chosen acolytes.

Itang is more than a mode of speech. The summation of the old life and culture of Truk lies in its chants. It is knowledge and wisdom, but it is also terrible in its power. Its words can kill a man. Indeed you need only approach too close to a man who knows *itang* and, although he does not utter a syllable, you can fall mortally ill. *Itang* inspires awe because in it resides the history of the Trukese people, of their origins, migrations, and moments of greatness. It embodies their moral philosophy and is their charter of right and justice. It is also poetry and drama:

> The song of the land bird,
> The cry of the gull from the shore,
> The distant roar of surf on the barrier reef.

This is Truk, attuned equally to land and to sea and protected against the immensity of the surging ocean by the outer reef. Then the scene quickens and is awake:

> The dawn breaks on the horizon.
> The land is peopled
> With men following their nature
> With animals following their nature.

Finally, *itang* is a political philosophy. It tells you how to attain power and how to keep it. (All these things old Mailo knew, and in the peace of his later years he taught them to his favored son, Petrus.)

The mounting chaos of island warfare came to an abrupt end after Germany acquired the Caroline Islands from Spain and in 1904 sent a commercial and administrative party to Truk. An order, impossible to enforce, was issued that all guns be turned in. Almost at once the order was obeyed, resolving an impossible dilemma without loss of face. Thus, the year after Petrus was born on Moen, law and order came to Truk. The Germans developed a network of political control through native chiefs on each island, and established a flourishing trading economy based on the export of copra, the dried meat of the ripe coconut. The Germans made no effort, however, to displace any aspect of the existing Trukese culture which did not come into conflict with their limited policy objectives. Petrus thus had throughout his childhood and early maturity the opportunity— which he grasped diligently—to learn from his father the old ways, to master the chants of *itang,* and to develop a great pride in his culture.

Meanwhile Mailo had learned, even before the advent of the Germans, to read and write in a native alphabet devised by Protestant missionaries. He even served for a time as a native preacher on the island of Fefan, adjacent to Moen. His literacy, combined with the prestige derived from his former war victories as a village chief, made Mailo valuable to the Germans. He was installed as assistant to the man the Germans had selected to be chief of Moen, a distinguished old man who was also Mailo's father-in-law. When the Japanese took over Truk and most of the rest of Micronesia in 1914 Mailo and his superior remained in office on Moen. In 1918 the old chief died and Mailo stepped easily into his shoes. Petrus, then only 15, had also learned to read and write with the missionaries. He became his father's helper in the administrative tasks which steadily grew in complexity.

The Japanese developed Truk, as well as the other island groups under their control, into major sources of economic support for their homeland. This meant many Japanese and Okinawans living on Moen as well as on the other islands of Truk, and many Trukese working for wages and buying increasing varieties of imported goods. It meant powerboats landing at piers instead of canoes being carried up on the beach, roads instead of trails—in short, it brought vast changes to the Trukese scene and complex problems in their wake. The old masters of *itang* went into eclipse and with them much of the old culture, yet the new synthesis which evolved lost nothing in vitality or security for the Trukese, and particularly for Petrus. During these years of bewildering change Petrus was at his father's side, except for a couple of interruptions when he went first to work for a year on Saipan, and later in the phosphate deposits of Angaur over a thousand miles to the east. His perspective broadened and his understanding of the ways of administration and of administrators matured under the tutelage of his father and still further when he was apprenticed for a year as assistant to a chief of one of the villages on Moen.

As enterprises continued to grow on Moen Petrus tried his hand at them: a year operating a powerboat based on the island, three years in the copra trading business on his own, several more years as agricultural supervisor for the Japanese, and finally he was in charge of labor gangs when the Japanese began fortifying the islands in earnest before Pearl Harbor.

With the coming of war and the subsequent blockade of Truk, when the Trukese were competing with four times their number of Japanese for the available food resources, Petrus withdrew from the Japanese to tend the family garden plots and see that his kin did not starve, a responsibility made the greater when his father died at last in 1944 at the age of 90. Petrus remained with his family until, in the closing days of the war, he heeded the urgings of a Japanese administrator of good will. He stepped forward in an attempt to soften the impact on the people of Moen of the undisciplined chaos of despairing soldiers, helpless in the face of the imminent downfall of Imperial Japan.

After the surrender all the Japanese were interned on the neighboring island of Dublon, administrative center for the defeated regime, and Moen shuddered under the impact of Seabees' bulldozers and dynamite as the white quonset huts of a new American regime blossomed on the ridges and valleys of the island.

Guided by the advice of those few half-castes who could speak a little English, the Americans looked to old Mailo's family for a new chief for the island on which they had settled. Petrus, perhaps fortunately, deferred to his older brother, Albert. These were times of confusion and temptation. The United States was pumping in money to get an economy based on worthless Japanese currency back on its feet, and sailors and marines by the hundreds had money and black-market cigarettes to trade for Japanese watches, swords, and souvenirs. Island treasuries and taxes swelled, with little upon which to spend the revenues. When, with American forces greatly reduced, the interim military government changed to a more permanent civil administration under a United Nations trusteeship, Albert was one of the first to come under the scrutiny of the Navy officers who were to be the administrators of Truk for the next four years. Like his fellow chiefs on other islands who were successively removed after him, Albert had only been doing what seemed natural in lining his own coffers and was easily caught in his peccadillos. Petrus was chosen by the administration to succeed his humiliated and embittered brother. Under the popular elections which were instituted shortly thereafter Petrus has invariably been reëlected by overwhelming majorities. Petrus is Moen, and Moen is Petrus; any other combination is unthinkable.

Petrus is also, as I have already mentioned, president of the Truk Trading Company. This is not, however, an office into which he stepped naturally and easily in consequence of his position as chief of Moen. There was perhaps a sense of inevitability about his assuming the presidency, but he attained the office only after several trying and stubborn years of sparring. In this, as in everything he did, he permitted no compromise with his insistence upon being a Trukese free to champion the interests of Truk in the way he felt best. The "T.T.C.," as it is known to Trukese and Americans alike, came into existence shortly after Petrus became chief of Moen, and is the almost single-handed creation of an extraordinary American, Henry Chatroop. Hank came out as an accountant and employee of a temporary agency set up to bring some order into the chaos left by the collapse of the Japanese economy in the islands. He stayed on to build, with native capital and selfless dedication and shrewdness, a fabulously profitable company. The T.T.C. embraces a bewildering array of activities from a fleet of ocean-going vessels to a supermarket and movie theatre, yet its capital stock cannot be held by any outsiders, including Hank himself. Hank's motives in this undertaking, although puzzling to many, were so self-evidently honest and dedicated to the good of the Trukese that several attempts by well-meaning American officials to brand the T.T.C. a dangerous monopoly simply collapsed. It is indeed very nearly a monopoly, but the abuses we expect to flow from a monopoly are just not present in the T.T.C.

However, in building his company Hank leaned heavily on the talents of a small group of men who, although born on Truk of Trukese mothers, had foreign fathers and elected to view themselves as apart from other Trukese. Petrus, loyal to his birthright, could not bring himself to trust a company in the power of men who set themselves at a distance from the culture to which they were born. Although seldom actively opposing the T.T.C., he meticulously withheld any advice and, more important, the support of his prestige. Yet at the same time he tried in various ways to make Hank see that the company needed him. As Petrus grew in stature, so did the T.T.C., yet he would not jeopardize the trust placed in him by his people if the possibility remained that the "half-castes" could compromise the company—and therefore the Trukese customers and stockholders. He was willing to "risk" the island's funds, and his own, by buying T.T.C. stock (which made him all the more a factor for Hank to reckon with) but he would not risk his personal position of trust. After several years of uncomfortable sparring and aloofness —the island office and the T.T.C. office are only a few hundred yards apart—the dilemma was resolved in the only way possible. Petrus was made president of the company and thus able to watch over and control the activities of all the native officials in its employ.

It was shortly after he became chief of Moen that I first met Petrus. His very dark skin, black wavy hair, rotund but compact build, and a mobile face which is also rotund, do not necessarily distinguish him strikingly from other Trukese. But in build, color, features, hair, and indeed every aspect of physical appearance the Trukese are so highly variable—Micronesia seems to be the physical "melting-pot" of the Pacific—that almost any individual one already knows is easily picked out of a crowd, and of course everyone knows Petrus. This logical explanation avoids the necessity of attributing to Petrus a "magnetic" personality—yet I am not sure but that the latter phrase seems to come closer to describing him adequately. He is a man who seldom obtrudes himself into any situation, yet whose presence can somehow never be left out of account. One is invariably surprised in standing next to him to find that he is not actually as tall as he appears to be.

Petrus sitting in thought—withdrawn into himself, almost brooding —is inscrutable but vastly impressive. One waits in respect, although with some slight discomfort, before his dynamic immobility, until he has worked through his thoughts to the point of decision.

I arrived on Moen in early 1948 to be an "anthropological adviser" to the Civil Administrator (a Navy commander), a position whose responsibilities were not very clear to anyone. The real reason, however, for the urgency surrounding my joining the staff lay in my knowledge of the Trukese language. I had learned this during the preceding seven months spent on Romonum, a small island in the western part of the lagoon, where, with four colleagues, I had been doing field work under a U.S. Navy program which embraced all the island cultures of the Trust Territory. The American administrators could communicate with their 15,000 native charges on Truk and its surrounding islands only through a handful of half-castes who knew a little English. These man thereby wielded great power, both formal and informal, and were obviously and rapidly becoming wealthy.

My primary function at the outset, then, was to lend a willing ear to any and all complaints, to monitor translations by the half-castes, and in general, to try to keep them honest. This role was one I fulfilled until, with the passage of a year or two, some of the brighter schoolboys were able to take over routine translation work and the half-castes gradually faded from the scene. To facilitate this communication process I established my office in the house in which my wife and children shortly joined me, rather than in the central administrative office buildings. Petrus was among those who would on occasion come to talk to me there, and it was thus that he and my family came to know each other.

Meanwhile I could not merely sit idle waiting for complainants to come calling. So it was decided I should occupy myself in preparing a map of prewar landholdings in the area of Moen sequestered by the Navy for its civil administration unit, warehouses, airstrip, etc. As chief of the island Petrus was the final arbiter of all questions concerning land ownership or usage, so my very first assignment naturally threw us together in close collaboration. With no funds available for compensation to the former owners and as yet not even a formal legal basis for Navy occupancy of the land, it was fairly clear to Petrus as well as to me that the chances of a practical outcome to our labors were very slim. Yet he never flagged in his determination to see that the work was done properly. (Compensation was finally paid in 1956 on the basis of new maps, the fruition of eight years of unstinting labor by Petrus.)

Many landmarks had been obliterated by time or bulldozers, claims were conflicting, rights of ownership and of usage had to be separately defined, and so on. For hours of every day we walked over the land, surrounded by a vocal group of elders, by interested parties of all sorts, and by curious children. Agreement among the claimants was seldom easily reached and Petrus tried quietly to arbitrate, principally by focusing his attention on those whose opinions he respected. If the bickering went on too long he would turn peremptorily to me, order me to draw it thus and so on the map, and stride off to the next boundary line, the protests dying away as interest turned to new issues. Petrus, I found, knew where his authority lay, but never made a display of its use nor reached a decision until those who might prove wiser than he had spoken their piece.

With me at this time he was friendly but reserved, businesslike in carrying forward our joint task. He did not flatter or defer to an American, nor did he make me uncomfortable in my frequent ignorance of the customs of land tenure. He recognized that anyone who was to do this task would have to be educated. Since the task was an important one even if it might not bear fruit, it must be done properly, and I therefore had to be taught. I recognized this equally with Petrus, so my training proceeded without apology or condescension.

After some months, with interruptions, our map neared completion. Meanwhile the Native Affairs Officer in our Navy administration reached the end of his tour of duty and departed for the United States. To our consternation a change in orders diverted his intended replacement, already en route to Truk, to another post. By default his duties fell to me, and I retained them—later with the official title of Political Affairs and Economics Officer—until I departed three years later when the Navy administration was turned over to the Department of the Interior in 1951.

My new status, and my new power over Petrus as well as the other chiefs, made little difference in our relationship. Perhaps he was a little more reserved, watching me more closely to see whether my judgments and actions were well considered. He was still educating me, replying sometimes to my requests for advice or opinion with questions rather than flat statements. Like a good schoolmaster he led me to my own decisions rather than making them for me. Often he was paternal, gently pointing out solutions alternate to my own when I had already made decisions without consulting him. It was sometimes difficult, especially when the other island chiefs beat a path to my door and paid flattering tribute to my wisdom, not to resent these subtle admonitions from Petrus. Only in time did I come to realize how often he proved to be right. More important to me, I also discovered that his guidance reflected an esteem he would never make explicit: others of equal or greater status than I among the Americans received his opinions directly and unadorned when they asked for them, and otherwise he held his peace. He apparently viewed them as either not worthy or not capable of being educated.

We lived—my wife Flora and our four young children—in a house on the Navy base. Also living with us were a variable number of young Trukese men, some with wives and sometimes children also. These were my "brothers" (by virtue of relationships established during my field work on Romonum) and their relatives. When on Romonum I had lived with them, so naturally when I was established on Moen they stayed with me. Fortunately I had built the house myself (with the help of my brothers) and had allowed plenty of floor space for spreading out sleeping mats. A few of these youths settled in fairly permanently and became the nucleus of the constantly changing work force which, with great good humor and minimal efficiency, operated our household.

The arrival of Petrus on our doorstep invariably precipitated a flurry of activity, rather more activity than took place even when our commanding officer appeared. A chair, centrally located. Coffee, cream, sugar. Someone get a spoon—you fool, you forgot it. Cigarettes, ashtray, the table lighter—no mere matches for Petrus. And get hold of Mr. Tom. I might be anywhere and, with wild turning of the crank of the old wall telephone and a stream of instructions to the Trukese switchboard operator, the base telephone system would be immobilized until I had been located. No other island chief merited this treatment, although all were received with courtesy. I had certainly never given instructions for special deference to Petrus, but both my brothers and he recognized it immediately as his natural due.

By this time Susie would have heard that Petrus was waiting at the house and rushed in breathlessly to greet him. Susie is our younger daughter, not yet 3 years old when she and Petrus became instant friends. She was burned brown by the tropical sun, clad usually only in a pair of shorts, and her hair a rag mop bleached by the same sun to a dazzling blond. She was, and really still is, one of those children who seems to be half wood sprite, loving and being loved by every living being, all the way from stray cats and injured birds to Petrus.

Her standard greeting, whether at our house or, more commonly, in the busy setting of the Moen Island office whither she rode with me in my jeep, was "Hi, Petrus!" The reply from large, black, august Petrus to this blonde mite was equally invariable: "Hi, Susie!" although Petrus did not otherwise essay any words of English in public during these early years. They conversed volubly, she in a child's English and he in equally incomprehensible Trukese, both seemingly quite comfortable in their communication.

The bond between Susie and Petrus was cemented over the island of Mwokomwok. Mwokomwok is a preposterously tiny bit of black rock and red soil which lies in the narrow strait between the big islands of Moen and Dublon. Its handful of coconut trees find themselves so crowded that they stick out at all angles. It is beautiful, yet so tiny that one has difficulty taking it seriously. It has a cave through its center, dug by the Japanese for guns to block the strait, a little marine railway which once berthed a one-man submarine, bushes heavy with bright red berries, and other charms which combined to make it an irresistible magnet for weekend excursions in our outboard motor boat. We all delighted in Mwokomwok, but for Susie it was more than just fun. It was, it had to be, hers.

Plagued by her insistence I finally inquired of Petrus as to the ownership of the island, although, as I had repeatedly and fruitlessly explained to Susie, no foreigners are allowed to acquire any property in the Trust Territory. By a surprising coincidence, it turned out that Mwokomwok was owned by Petrus' family and was therefore his to assign and control. Negotiations began at once. Susie supervised an order from the Sears, Roebuck catalogue for some kitchen knives she felt, with some guidance from her father, represented a fair exchange. The transaction when it finally took place was a solemn affair replete with a formal speech by Petrus, landowner and chief of Moen. It was so solemn in fact that I felt constrained to interrupt, to remind him that a genuine transfer of ownership could not be legal. In return I received one of the few really annoyed glances Petrus ever bestowed upon me, and the proceedings went forward. Ever afterward they met on terms of equality: Susie had her island, and Petrus his.

Petrus with Susie, or gracing our household with a visit, or beaming in good-natured amusement at our annual Trukese Christmas party while my young brothers were convulsed with their own rendition of Japanese love songs—these are the warm bits of recollection which keep alive our fondness for Petrus. But he and I met most commonly over the more serious and complex business of deciding what would be best for the people of Moen, or of Truk as a whole. A new idea or a new development led me almost automatically to try it out with him first, or to seek his advice if no solution was readily apparent. In this I was not alone. We had in succession on the staff two anthropologists, Jack Fischer and Frank Mahony, who were able to devote to a variety of problems the careful study which my administrative role would not permit. Each soon came to respect and to rely upon the wisdom of Petrus' judgment. They also enjoyed the experience so gratifying to an anthropologist but denied to me by the pressure of time, of gathering data on the culture and folklore of the past from an informant who knew his facts and could organize them well, and who could dictate a text with the accuracy and patience necessary for a true transcription.

Another person who respected Petrus and valued his opinion was our Civil Administrator and commanding officer, Commander Robert D. Law, Jr. To him fell the trying responsibility not only of administering wisely the destinies of 10,000 Trukese and their 5000 outer island cousins, but also of maintaining the efficiency, discipline, and morale of a sizeable number of Navy officers and men who were doing jobs they had for the most part definitely not joined the Navy to do. Add to this the special problems of dependents who joined their men in a remote and isolated community, of civilian schoolteachers in a similar situation, of a steady flow of not always appropriate policy directives from higher echelons, of ships which did not arrive on time or arrived without the proper supplies, of the sometimes conflicting interest of missionaries, and of dozens of other situations which he did not join the Navy to meet either—add all these together and Bob

Law had ample excuse to use perfunctorily and arbitrarily the nearly absolute power he wielded over the Trukese. Instead he chose always to seek a balance between higher policy and local culture, perhaps between Navy Regulations and Trukese custom when an enlisted man got into trouble, or between an irate skipper and his native passengers who littered his decks with fermented breadfruit (which is an effective paint-remover).

The fact that during most of the years Petrus and I worked together our "Captain" was such a person, had much to do with the stature Petrus attained. This stature was no greater than his capabilities warranted, but it is all too seldom that a man—especially a man who combines foresight with courage—has the opportunity to be used so fully by his society. This is particularly true in a colonial situation where the distance between governors and governed is so great. Bob Law did not share the bias into which I sometimes fell of believing that Petrus could never be wrong, but he soon perceived that we had in Petrus a man of high prestige and mature judgment, a man who commanded and rewarded our attention as a person, not merely as another island chief. When Petrus and Bob met it was on a basis of genuine respect by each for the status and abilities of the other. Standing between them, I could ask for no more.

The bulk of the time and work Petrus devotes to his job is directed, of course, to the routine of keeping the affairs of his island running smoothly and efficiently. He hears and adjudicates disputes large and small, plans work on roads, sanitation, or construction for the island-wide workday each week, discusses local problems with the village chiefs, and so on. In these tasks he had the help of his two right hand men: quiet, serious Meipung, Assistant Chief, who was often rather puzzled by the humor which so often punctuated my discussions with Petrus, and Efou, the island secretary, a man of intelligence, diplomacy, and dry humor who used to vie with me in solving problems—he with the abacus and I with a slide rule, neither of us ever really understanding or appreciating the other's instrument.

Petrus had been married, but after some years he and his wife had separated. He remarried while I was on Truk, taking a young and attractive bride, but she remained in the background. Trukese wives do not intrude themselves into the affairs of their men, particularly in matters of state, and as a result I saw her only on those rare occasions when I met Petrus at his house instead of the island office.

Petrus works as often as he can in his family garden plots, glistening with sweat as he digs, plants, weeds, or harvests. This is doubtless an example of industry to the men of the island and compels their respect, but I am equally sure that he derives much personal satisfaction from the work. It reassures him that he is a Trukese, able to do and to enjoy the humble tasks which fall to every Trukese. His strong feeling of identity with his people is an important cornerstone of the confidence vested in Petrus not only by his wards on Moen but by all of Truk.

It also establishes for him a consistent basis for judgment of the role he should play when the focus is upon him as intermediary between the American administration and the people of his island. On these occasions he stands alone, in conflict or in acclaim, neither asking nor accepting much help from either Meipung and Efou or, when I was there, from me. He seeks their advice in local problems, and listened to my suggestions when he and his island were shown off to visiting dignitaries. But when he has to represent his people and their interests before the administration and the rest of Truk he trusts only himself. Although his responses are sometimes unexpected they invariably make sense if one recalls that he always sees himself as a Trukese, a Trukese born and raised on his island of Moen.

Yet, in spite of his deep loyalty to his culture, Petrus is anything but a typical Trukese. The ideal Trukese is self-effacing and certain that responsibility, initiative, and public attention can lead only to hard feelings and trouble. As long as each person does his share of the humble tasks which fall within his daily round, kinsman will help kinsman and life will move forward smoothly in peaceful coöperation. Even the Trukese will agree that every society must have some leadership, but equally they hope that this responsibility will fall on someone else's shoulders. In these days of peaceful administration no one will admit to wanting to be a chief. In the majority of cases the reluctance of candidates is so genuine as to suggest that they are truly frightened by the prospect of placing themselves above their fellows, even when forced by public pressure to do so.

In spite of all this Petrus is a chief. Not only is he chief of Moen, but increasingly he speaks for Truk as a whole as the islands move toward larger political unity. He is a born leader in a culture wherein everyone desires and expects to remain completely obscure. He is aggressively intelligent in a culture wherein it is a virtue to be dull and stupid—although protesting the while his own stupidity. Necessary to all this is the final paradox: he is personally ambitious in a culture wherein ambition is a sin. Nevertheless he sees himself and is seen by others as passionately and wholeheartedly a Trukese. Never on any issue was it to my knowledge even whispered that he might be a tool of the American administration.

How can one explain this paradox? And how can Petrus live within it? The key to both questions lies in Petrus' father, in Petrus' relationship with him, and in *itang*. Old Mailo lived in an era when Truk had true leaders, men trained to guide their fellows along paths of wisdom. These were men set apart and obligated to responsibility by the awesome knowledge of *itang*. In the past they had chosen a few young men fit to learn the great secrets and had spent years training them to lead and be wise. But during the Japanese administration they saw the rising generation decked out in imported finery, working for wages instead of their kinsmen, and absorbing the beliefs of foreigners. None was fit, and one by one the old men died with their secrets locked within them.

There was one exception. Mailo saw that *itang* had not lost its meaning, but needed only a man with the vision to understand this meaning in a new context. He apparently felt his eager son Petrus might grow to be such a man. It was hard for him to be sure that his son would not abuse the power he was handing on, particularly when his colleagues in *itang* had decided not to do so, but his pupil was insistent. Petrus recognized that only through *itang* could he justly or wisely assume the power and leadership he wanted. In the end he had learned everything, or almost everything, old Mailo knew. With it he learned that he must be responsible to his people, the more so as only he bore their full heritage.

True power means not merely giving orders, but also making decisions, decisions which will manipulate people so that they will serve the leader's ends. This, above all, is the skill Petrus learned at his father's side—and the skill he must at all costs not abuse. If he is to help and lead his people Petrus must constantly rise in authority and prestige to be able to meet an ever-growing challenge. He can, and certainly does, relish the power which is his, but he must also remind himself that he was given *itang* and its heritage of wisdom for the benefit of his people, not just of himself. This is, everywhere in the world, the dilemma and temptation of power. Petrus masters the dilemma, but it is surely no easy task.

Manipulation of persons and situations is rarely done with certainty, for no man can fully know another man's mind. Nor is it a comfortable process, for it is seldom wise to treat the persons being manipulated with full and open confidence even if they are friends. I discovered how trying this can be one day when Petrus left the island office with the avowed intent of going home to get drunk. Word of this of course spread like wildfire and soon reached me. I felt I knew Petrus well enough to dismiss such a preposterous rumor and went on with my affairs. Yet soon thereafter an emissary from Meipung and Efou arrived to plead for my intervention with such seriousness that I could no longer deny some truth to the story. I hurried down to the village and found that the story, as far as it went, was true. Petrus had indeed gone home, saying he was going to get drunk. No one, however, could offer an explanation for this incongruous act, and it took me some time to make sense out of it even after I had talked to him.

I found Petrus in his house, quite sober but with a bottle or two of beer on the table—contraband under Trust Territory policy—and dressed with conspicuous informality in nothing but a dirty and worn pair of shorts. He greeted me cordially but rather coolly and announced firmly that he had resigned as island chief. I can still recall and feel my sense of confusion and helplessness at this announcement, helplessness coupled with an anger I tried to suppress over what seemed an almost childish display. How could I reason with him when the whole thing made no sense? He said in explanation only that his usefulness as chief was at an end and the people of Moen should elect someone more substantial. Clearly, I was no longer treated as a friend and, with his resignation, we had no official relationship within which to discuss issues. He had closed the door and was not inviting me to try to open it again.

I left, walking through his gardens and over his taro swamp on a narrow bridge, bewildered, angry, and thoroughly frustrated. Suddenly, I recalled that two nights before there had been a disturbance in Mwan, the village closest to the Navy base and the island office. One of the enlisted men had gone to the village after hours, presumably to find a Trukese woman for his entertainment. This happened all too frequently, but such forays were usually negotiated in advance and conducted discreetly on foot. In this case he drove brazenly and drunkenly down the road, past the native policeman at the guard gate, in a loudly roaring jeep loaded with beer. The policeman raised the alarm and set off in pursuit. A fight and tremendous commotion ensued, with the enlisted man finally retreating in his jeep shouting insults as he went.

Local authority had clearly been outraged and justice should have been swift. However, American justice is not precipitate and the greater the offense the more deliberate the legal process. Furthermore, in spite of the hundred or so witnesses the culprit denied everything and produced an alibi. It was a very dubious alibi, but nevertheless had to be examined on its merits.

To Petrus, I realized, all this meant that the man might get away with his misdeed. There seemed to be one law for the Trukese, under which Petrus and the native policeman maintained order, and another for Americans. I hurried back in relief to explain the necessities of legal process and, I believed, to straighten everything out. Instead Petrus professed to have lost his faith in all of us and was adamant in refusing to reconsider his resignation.

Again I walked in despair through garden and taro swamp, perceiving ever more clearly the magnitude of our impasse. The effect of Petrus' resignation under these circumstances would be truly disastrous, yet Navy justice demanded that the accused have an opportunity to demonstrate his innocence. He might even succeed, for there were always available some American sailors who despised their duty assignment and the Trukese with equal fervor, and who would at the same time be delighted to show their loyalty to a fellow enlisted man. This was a chance we could not afford to take, yet could apparently not avoid.

I laid my problem before Bob Law and he promised to look into it. He promised no more than this, but when the weekly airplane came through the offender was quietly transferred to Guam. He may thereby have escaped the justice he deserved, but action had been taken and we were redeemed in the eyes of Petrus. With infinite relief, and some embarrassment, I went down and found him again installed, neat and thoroughly sober, in the island office, and in time our relationship returned to the comfortable informality and trust of old. He had put his personal dignity and the office vested in him by his people on the block. In return he had won an issue which was never again disputed. He might well have lost had our commanding officer been one to react first to the indisputable challenge to Navy authority Petrus had thrown down. Bob's view was never so limited, but I like to believe Petrus would have done the same regardless of who stood above him. But perhaps he would not. With other players on the stage he might have devised an entirely different drama. But whatever the means he might employ, he would never evade the challenge.

This was Petrus in time of travail. It is happier to remember him in times of achievement and acclaim. Perhaps the happiest of these was his dedication of the assembly hall of the Truk Intermediate School.

This building, a dazzling white quonset as large as any built in earlier days by the Seabees on the base, was no mere routinely authorized addition to the base facilities. In fact requests for funds for such a building had repeatedly been struck from the budget. Classroom and dormitory facilities were considered to be all such a school required. Yet on a little ridge across the road stood the consolidated teacher training school for all of the Trust Territory, a showplace for visitors, pride and creation of the High Commissioner's staff—and replete with an admirable assembly hall. The Intermediate School in comparison thus not only lacked any building adequate for student assemblies, but also felt like a neglected poor relative.

This long frustration finally became a challenge to Bob Beck, the Education Officer on the Civil Administration staff. A Naval Academy graduate, he was living refutation of the often cited contention that an officer with primarily military training can never embrace wholeheartedly the tasks of civil administration. He finally obtained little more than a token sum of money with which to start, and permission to salvage any building materials he could find in the supply compound near the dock. He drew up ambitious plans, seemingly totally unrelated to the very limited resources available. Fired by his enthusiasm and a newly found pride in their school, the students worked heroically for months during most of their free time. The whole of the base personnel, American and Trukese alike, and many of the people of Moen, became personally committed to the project as the building took form. As the day of the dedication approached the building swarmed with volunteer labor, from skilled electricians to eager amateurs who covered themselves with white paint.

Somehow on the appointed day the assembly hall was complete. Hundreds of people—everyone from the base and from all the islands of Truk—milled through the building admiring the many facilities, and then assembled in the great central hall. There was singing by the schoolboys: old native chants by the boys from the outer islands, and more modern songs, based mostly on hymns, sung by the whole student body in jubilant but precise harmonies.

Then came the speeches, alternating between Americans and Trukese, each briefly paying tribute not so much to the building as to the manner of its accomplishment. Finally Petrus arose to his turn. His was to be the formal dedicatory oration, and into it he was moved to put every ounce of his personality and a virtuosity of rhetoric I would not have believed possible with the Trukese language.

He wove together a parallel of the growth of the school and its assembly hall with the growth of Truk as recounted in ancient mythology. The school, and indeed the whole base, nestled at the foot of a small rocky peak where the mythological ancestress of all Trukese first touched solid ground after drifting for hundreds of miles on a palm frond. It was in the shadow of this peak that the Germans first established their trading and administrative center, which brought peace, order, and a world view to Truk. Here too the first Trukese were born, and from here they spread out across the lagoon to build their villages on all the other islands. And finally now in this same spot enlightenment was coming to Truk, bringing together knowledge nurtured by centuries of civilization to blend with the culture matured on these islands by generations of Trukese, who were now returned to their original birthplace to receive this new heritage. This vital synthesis of new and of old was reflected in the school, with its goal of making its students better servants of their people rather than aids to the administration as the Japanese had done, and in the assembly hall, whose completion would never have been achieved without the dedicated efforts of Americans and Trukese alike.

As Petrus wove together the themes of present and past he paced his delivery to the styles of America and of the sages of old. At one time he would employ the tension-relieving humorous asides of a skilled Western speaker. When he played on the other theme, of the mythical history of Truk, he became more somber, suggesting reverence. Suddenly, as if to document his authority in citing a bit of history, he several times broke into the chant of *itang*, a thrilling experience for his Trukese audience. Many had never even heard this form of speech, although all knew of it. To hear it, to have it shared with them in this dramatic setting, created an almost awesome impact.

His audience was spellbound—and so was I. In a perfect synthesis the past entered the present. The old did not have to yield its place to the new, but rather entered a hall of vaulting steel to enrich it with a sense of tradition when its paint was scarcely dry.

Only Petrus could have delivered this speech, and perhaps he was least prepared for the overwhelming wave of applause which followed it. To him it was the building and the manner of its creation that were important; he was only striving his best to pay it proper tribute. But in doing so he revealed in himself the embodiment of the very synthesis he had perceived in the hall. Born and schooled to know and respect Truk's often dramatic past, he now guided its present and shaped its future. He neither rejected the old ways nor looked back upon them with wishful sentimentality—as people so often do when the clash of cultures has swept in vast and rapid changes.

Nor did he embalm history for display to the curious. It is rather his greatest gift that he can make history a vital part and servant of the present, not by citing precedent but by bridging the span in his own person. His strong feeling of identity with his culture leads him intuitively but almost unerringly to discriminate those things which would be appropriate and constructive for his people from those which would breed confusion and distress. Thus in his finest speech Petrus revealed also the key to his own greatness.

To every decision he brings the perspective of the history which lies within the span of his years, and indeed within himself. In a sense he is his own anthropologist, yet a far surer one than any outside student of his culture could hope to be. It was doubtless for this reason that I could take almost for granted most major issues and discuss with him only details.

For this same reason Petrus stands foremost in my memory not as chief, politician, or administrator, but as a friend. Trusting each other, we could savor the trivia through which friends express without embarrassment their mutual affection and respect. Such friendship with anyone is the finest privilege of human society. That I, administrator and anthropologist, should have enjoyed it with Petrus, chief and apostle of his culture, was my special and unique privilege.

3

Durmugam,
A Nangiomeri

W. E. H. Stanner

One wintry afternoon, in 1932 on the Daly River in North Australia I saw that some of the men in an aboriginal camp near my own had painted themselves garishly with earth-pigment. I knew this to be a sign of impending trouble but no one would give me any clear idea of what was to come. At about three o'clock the men began to go unobtrusively downriver, and some women and older children drifted off in the same direction. Each man carried a *womerah* or spear-thrower and a handful of mixed spears but this fact, in itself, meant little for in those days every male aborigine went armed on the shortest journey. Curiosity overcame any fear that I might be unwelcome if I followed so I made haste after them as soon as I could. By the time I made my camp and stores as secure as possible the party was lost to sight in the timber. I had to cast about a good deal to find the right direction, but eventually the sound of a distant uproar led me out of the savanna and on to the edge of a clearing where I could see more than one hundred men, my friends among them, locked in noisy battle.

I stood awhile at the edge of the clearing to take the measure of what was happening, for I had not before seen a large-scale fight. The human scene had a savage, vital splendour. The pigments daubed on the men's bodies gleamed harshly in the late afternoon light. The air was filled with flying spears, each making a brief flicker of light as it sped. Some of the overshot missiles slithered with a dry rattle into the timber nearby. One pair of eyes could scarcely take in all that was happening at once. A distracting and continuous din came as much from spectators, of whom there were again over one hundred, as from combatants.

The men were ranged in two groups, one whitened, one yellowed, each in a very rough formation of line, about sixty paces apart. Scarcely for a moment did the lines hold form. Some men, alone or supported, were running forward to throw their spears, others back to retrieve spent weapons or snatch new ones from supporters, others from side to side in challenge to a succession of enemies. Sometimes a solitary man on each side would stand with the others in echelon on both flanks. Old men, capering with excitement on the sidelines, would suddenly run to the battle line to throw spears, and then go back to their former posts. Women, with fistfuls of spears, would come without apparent fear into the danger area to offer the weapons to their menfolk, at the same time shouting in shrill execration of the enemy. On both sides great shows of anger, challenge, and derision were being made. Some men would range up towards the enemy and contort their faces hideously; some, the older, would chew their beards and spit them out; some would bite on the small dilly-bags worn as neck-ornaments or stuff their loincloths into their mouths; here and there one would turn and, with gesticulations of insult, poke his anus towards the other line. Only the light duelling spears were in use but I saw one powerful aborigine, on what seemed the weaker side, run abruptly from the middle of the fight to wrestle fiercely with supporters to gain possession of their heavy, iron-bladed spears. They would not yield them, and sought to pacify him. He returned to continue fighting with the light spears.

The pattern and canons of the fighting eventually showed themselves through the aggregate moil. The struggle could be seen to resolve itself into discontinuous phases of duels between pairs of men with supporters. I could identify various pairs hurling spears at each other and, at the same time, see eddies of movement as others came to support them, so that something like a battle of masses would thus develop. This led to much cross-movement, and a veering of the heat of battle from place to place in the line as principals here became supporters there when an associate or kinsman came under heavy attack. Later, the principals would resume a phase of their own duels.

In trying to sort out the encounters of pairs, my eyes were drawn and held by an aborigine of striking physique and superb carriage who always seemed pinned by an unremitting attack. He seemed, as far as any individual could, to dominate the battlefield. He was so tall that he stood half a head above the tallest there. His muscular power was apparent in his bulk but it was the grace and intensity of his fighting which captured my attention. His favourite posture was to fling arms and legs as wide as possible as though to make himself the maximum target. Having drawn and evaded a spear he would often counter with a dexterity and speed remarkable in so large a man. His fluent movements in avoiding injury—an inclination of the head, a sway of the body, the lifting of an arm or leg, a half turn—always seemed minimal. I saw his spears strike home several times. As they did, the roars of exultation from his own side, and of rage from the other, would bring a rally to both. He himself stayed unwounded through the afternoon after a peerless display of skill and courage.

The battle died, as if by agreement, towards sundown and some of the antagonists began to fraternise, others to drift away. No one had been mortally hurt though many had painful flesh-wounds. There was some talk of continuing the fight another day. As I moved about making my inquiries, the tall aborigine came smilingly across and asked me in the most civil way if I had liked the fight. I asked him who he was and he told me that he was Durmugam, a Nangiomeri, and that Europeans called him Smiler. I then realized that here was the man widely believed by Europeans to be the most murderous black in the region, and whose name I had heard used with respect and fear.[1]

His appearance at this moment was truly formidable. The glaring ochre, the tousled hair above the pipe-clayed forehead band, the spears, and something opaque in his eyes made him seem the savage incarnate. He stood at least 6 feet 3 inches, and must have weighed a sinewy 180 lbs. But his voice was musical, his manner easy, and his smile disarming. I was much taken with him. I noticed particularly how smoothly contoured was his body, how small his feet, how sensitive and finely-boned his hands. Other men present were more heavily muscled but none had so large and so finely moulded a physique. His carriage was perfect, and he walked very erect, with head held high, and with quick, purposeful steps. Yet there was nothing truculent or overbearing about him.

We had a brief but pleasant conversation, at the end of which he said that I should make my camp upriver at The Crossing, near him. I promised that some day I should do so and that we would then talk further.

We did not meet again for several weeks. The next occasion was

[1] Durmugam was named after a locality on the seacoast in the territory of the Murinbata, the western neighbours of the Nangiomeri. In Murinbata, the name is Dirmugam, and has been borne by several men. Possibly Durmugam's mother conceived when she was visiting the Murinbata. This seems likely, for a man of the Nangor or Point Pearce clan captured her sister in marriage, and the place Dirmugam is in Nangor territory.

another intertribal gathering, the initiation of a young boy, a member of the Maringar tribe which was at violent enmity with the Nangiomeri. The bad feeling had been suppressed, after the aboriginal fashion, for a necessarily intertribal affair. On this occasion I was warmly welcomed, not tolerated. The blacks seemed touched that I had walked several times to their distant camps with bags of flour and other gifts, and went to pains to see that I was honoured, even to the point of taking me within the screen which hid the act of circumcision from the throng. Durmugam too was within the screen, seated with three others—all, by rule, classificatory wife's brothers of the initiate—so that their legs made a floor between the boy and the ground.

I saw little of Durmugam during the great events of the ceremony —the vigil of the night, after a warning spear told of the boy's return from isolation; the spectacular, serpentine rush of the boy's abductors from afar soon after dawn; the massed, chanting escort to Mununuk, the camp of the hosts; the rite of sorrow as the boy was passed from kin to kin to be fondled before circumcision; and, later, the healing by fire and the presentation of valuables and insignia. But, as night came on, and the preparations for dancing and festivity were in hand, Durmugam joined me at one of the fires. I soon began to feel that we could become friends. I could not fault his manner and found him quick to see the drift of questions. When he pointed out some of the ceremony's features which I had missed, I began to see him as a new main informant, always one of the most exciting moments of fieldwork.

This particular ceremony had been conducted in the style of Dingiri, which is the name of a mythical ancestor. It is also a term denoting a direction of travel during initiation, a type of dance, a style of decoration, and a set of songs set to a fashion of music. Later, Durmugam told me the myth of Dingiri, the tired hunter who sat singing until he turned to stone. The symbolism is obscure and perhaps the only function of the myth is to give historic credibility to the song and the movements of the dance, which is filled with small intricacy to test the skill of any dancer.

I had already learned that Durmugam was a notable dancer. He flung himself into this dance with zest and gaiety. He must have been at his best but even so was outclassed by Tjimari, a restless wanderer from the distant Murinbata tribe. Where Durmugam had grace and skill, Tjimari had polish and a set of artful tricks which made each dance end in a furore. He would introduce a comical contrast of position and expression, prolong a stance so that it seemed absurd even to my eye, or use some form of caricature too subtle for me to grasp. But the roar of appreciative laughter from the watchers told its own story. I could see no mortification or jealousy in Durmugam or the other dancers. The performances are competitive in a sense but the prestige men gain through them does not seem necessarily to depreciate others.

Durmugam and Tjimari made an interesting comparison. Both were notable men in their own ways. Tjimari was at least Durmugam's equal with fighting weapons, though only half his size. He was so extraordinarily agile that it was almost impossible to hit him with spear, fist, or stick. He claimed to be able to dodge bullets as easily. Since he was deadly accurate with a spear, no one liked to fight him, for it meant being wounded without being able to give wounds in return. Tjimari (or to give him his European name, Wagin, probably a corruption of "wagon") traded on this skill, and took upset with him wherever he went. He was the first aborigine I ever met and, over a quarter of a century, I found him to be a fascinating mixture —a liar, a thief, an inveterate trickster, a tireless intriguer, an artist of high ability, and a man of much if inaccurate knowledge. In the 1930's he was the main *agent provocateur* of the Daly River. The police suspected him, rightly, of using the knowledge gained in court and gaol to instruct other blacks in the limits of police powers. He was adept in playing white against both white and black. Whenever he made a request one had to ask oneself what was Tjimari's "angle," for there was bound to be one. Some aborigines said he was a warlock, and he himself told me how he had cut open a woman at Port Keats and had taken some of her abdominal fat. I established the truth of this independently. Late in life, Tjimari became the friend and confidant of Roland Robinson, the Australian poet, who greatly admired his intelligence, knowledge, and imaginative gifts but took a somewhat sentimental view of other aspects of his character. I thought him an arch-manipulator, with wit and charm but no principles, and ready for any villainy that paid. Durmugam was no manipulator, and had a rocklike steadiness that Tjimari lacked. I feel that he had a deeper and more passionate conviction than Tjimari of the rightness of aboriginal ways. I sometimes felt compassion for Durmugam; for Tjimari, much less frequently, and then mainly because he too typified the vital will of the blacks to make something of the ruined life around them.

In the second half of the dry season I moved upriver to be nearer the Nangiomeri. I had first wanted to learn something of the Mulluk Mulluk and Marithiel-Maringar clusters, which were some distance west by north of The Crossing. Thereafter I saw Durmugam almost daily until my expedition was over. He would come soon after dawn to help Melbyerk, my Mulluk Mulluk follower, fetch wood and water for the day. We would then settle down after breakfast for discussions, usually with other aborigines present, which not uncommonly went on into the night, unless there was business to take us afield—places to visit, ceremonies to see, or game to kill. I was soon compelled to spend part of almost every other day hunting because of the pressure on my food supplies. Each day was something of a battle to keep unwanted natives from settling nearby to live on me. They were peaceable but as persistent as running water. I was importuned at every turn for tobacco, tea, sugar, and flour in about that order of preference. I will say this for Durmugam, that he was never importunate or greedy. He would occasionally ask for tobacco when he was hard up for a smoke, but that was all. He and Belweni, an influential and surly Wagaman who would never work for any European but was the prince of cadgers, or Djarawak, a Madngella whose voice had the whine of the professional beggar, were men from different worlds of personal dignity. There are many aborigines too proud to beg though they will exploit a claim to the full.

The hunting excursions were by no means a waste of time. I learned through them many things much better seen or shown than told. Durmugam was naïvely vain of his skill with spear and gun, and by indulging him I learned not only much about aboriginal ecology but also about motives which powerfully drive the blacks to parasitism. The life of a hunting and foraging nomad is very hard even in a good environment. Time and again the hunters fail, and the search for vegetable food can be just as patchy. A few such failures in sequence and life in the camps can be very miserable. The small, secondary foodstuffs—the roots, honey, grubs, ants, and the like, of which far too much has been made in the literature—are relished tidbits, but not staples. The aborigines rarely starve but they go short more often than might be supposed when the substantial fauna —kangaroos, wallaby, goannas, birds, fish—are too elusive. The blacks have grasped eagerly at any possibility of a regular and dependable food supply for a lesser effort than is involved in nomadic hunting and foraging. There is a sound calculus of cost and gain in preferring a belly regularly if only partly filled for an output of work which can be steadily scaled down. Hence the two most common characteristics of aboriginal adaptation to settlement by Europeans: a persistent and positive effort to make themselves dependent, and a squeeze-play to obtain a constant or increasing supply of food for a dwindling physical effort. I appreciated the good sense of the adaptation only after I had gone hungry from fruitless hunting with rifle, gun, and spears in one of the best environments in Australia.

The blacks vary greatly in their hunting skills. Durmugam was very good with the fish-spear but less skilful than at least one other Nangiomeri, a slightly-built youth with a marvellous ability to judge the depth and speed of fish in spite of the refracted image. Where Durmugam was unsurpassed was in the use of the so-called "shovel" spear. This spear, the main hunting and fighting weapon, may be as much as ten feet long. It is bamboo-shafted and has a lanceolate blade laboriously rubbed down from iron fence-droppers or heavy-gauge roofing. It is not suitable for distances much over sixty paces and, being long and heavy, its efficacy is a function of the strength of the thrower's arm, aided of course by his skill. It was Durmugam's great strength which gave him his superiority by enabling him to give the spear greater force and range. One European who had employed him as a sleeper-cutter told me that he had lifted and carried an ironwood log (which weighs up to 85 lbs. a cubic foot) too heavy for three white men, manual workers in their prime.

I never saw Durmugam use the spear against men or game. After he learned that my scent was too strong, my white skin too visible, and that I made too much noise to let us both get within throwing distance, he gave up any attempt to show me his prowess. Several times he came back with a kill when, rubbed with mud to deaden his scent, he went on alone carrying only his spear and *womerah*. More often we hunted with firearms, I with a Winchester .32, he with my Browning repeater gun, the mechanism of which fascinated him.

He could not use the rifle well, the fine sights evidently being beyond him, but he was an excellent set-piece shot with the gun.

On the hunt, we walked in file, he in the lead. He never went behind me with a weapon of any kind, though I had not asked him to refrain. He was ceaselessly watchful in the bush for the smallest movement, and saw game long before I did. He often grew irritated if I could not pick up targets to which he was looking or pointing. Once, unable to restrain himself, he snatched my rifle from my hands to fire at a wallaby I could not see. Having missed, he was ashamed, and embarrassed by his breach of good manners. Ordinarily, he was courteous in speech and conduct. He addressed me as *maluga,* not a Nangiomeri word, but one from a dialect to the south, and meaning something like "elderly sir" (though I was ten years his junior). He never spared the pace while walking (all aborigines find this difficult and irritating) but if I flagged would turn back and offer to carry things for me. He would break off projecting twigs which might injure me, or hold obstructing branches to one side, or point silently with gun or spear at obscure impediments. When we halted he would often pluck an armful of leaves or grass for me to lie on, and would scuff a place clear with his feet. It was always he who drew the water and fetched the wood. If wildfowl had to be retrieved he would strip and plunge without ado into waters frequented by man-eating crocodiles. True, such services were a convention of black man and white together in the bush, and many other natives performed them for me just as well, but his merit was that he made them seem a courtesy.

Over this period my knowledge of him and confidence in him deepened to the point at which I knew I could safely ask him to tell me about the murders. He did so with what seemed full candour, with no trace of vainglory on the one hand or regret on the other. Wagin, who had himself taken two lives, was no less open, but he also claimed to be "a good man now."

The talk among Europeans was that six, nine, eleven, or some other good round number of murders, were this one man's work. He was supposed to have a monumental cunning in disposing of the bodies, or in otherwise concealing his crimes. Durmugam admitted to taking four lives. The admission was made at a time when he was in real danger of the law, a fact he well knew. I could discover no evidence of other crimes and it seems inherently improbable that, had there been, he would have denied them. If his record of blood is to be considered in an estimate of his personality one should also know something of the social context of which he was in some sense a product and in which the killings took place.

Durmugam's camp, about a quarter of a mile from mine, was on the property of a European farmer for whom he and his wives worked for part of each year. There were two other farms, one owned by a Chinese, over the river and a mile or more away. Down-river were six other farms, the nearest being three miles away. The police station was six miles farther on. This scattered community then constituted the Daly River "settlement" as it was called. It was linked by a rough track with two sidings on the Darwin-Alice Springs railway at Adelaide River and Brock's Creek, respectively sixty and seventy miles away.

The settlers, among whom were two Chinese, were with two exceptions rough, uneducated men with bush backgrounds. They had known little comfort throughout their lives and were inured to hardship and poverty. Each grew a yearly crop of peanuts, sown in the December rains and harvested at the beginning of the dry season. They lived in shanties with earthern floors, and the bare minimum of crude furnishings. Equipment, methods, and life on these farms were so starkly simple that one often felt the year might almost as well have been 1832. The world depression had hit hard. The farmers thought themselves lucky to get sixpence a pound for their crops. They kept going, rarely seeing money, on credit from the distant Darwin stores, and eked out a life on bread, tea, and the simplest condiments which would make tolerable the bush-foods supplied by natives. Wallaby stew was the staple dish. Most of them went hatless, bootless, and shirtless. One or two had decrepit tractors, but the others used horse-drawn ploughs to keep perhaps twenty acres in production. The sandy soil, the opulent weed growth, pests, a parching winter, and a deluge of summer rain were in conspiracy to offer good crops only when there was a glut elsewhere, and bad crops with a frequency guaranteed to keep them in debt.

Each farm had its attached group of aboriginal workers and hangers-on, who were paid nothing but were given a meagre daily ration of the foods which the farmers themselves ate, together with a small allowance of tobacco. Once a year, if the farmers were not destitute, the work-teams were given a handout of the daily commodities and a few articles of clothing. Pitiably small as this real income was, it attracted far more natives than could be employed. Each one at work had others battening on him as adhesively as he on his employer.

All of these men were hard on their natives, some brutally so, but perhaps not much more so than they were on themselves. They supposed that their lives would be insupportable if they lost the physical dominance, and this may very well have been so. They and the aborigines were mutually dependent, desperately so, and no love was lost on either side. The settlers also feuded among themselves, in most cases over the supposed enticement of their more dependable labourers of whom, at this time, there were very few. Unskilled labourers were plentiful enough, within the limits set by the total numbers (the population was about 300) and by the tribal jealousies which I shall mention later, but most of the aborigines were feckless and likely to wander away at whim, usually when most needed for agricultural tasks that could not wait. Dependable men and women able to do unsupervised work were few indeed, and the loss of one from a farm was a serious blow. No agreement about poaching could be depended on, and some of the sophisticated blacks played one employer against another.

The aboriginal women, single or married, were eager for associations with Europeans and Chinese. While ready enough for casual affairs, they tried by any and all means to make semipermanent or permanent attachments. Their menfolk, with few exceptions, not only did not object but often pushed them to such service, which always led to a payment of tobacco, sugar, and tea, and might lead to a steady real income if it could be turned into a squeeze-play against a captured protector. The moment a settler became attached to or dependent on a native woman her close kin and affines put in an appearance, and every artifice and pressure was used to make themselves part of the protector's estate. The same thing tended to happen even with male employees. A single man would have at least classificatory brothers, a married man a set of consanguines and affines, to put him under pressure. Each farm was thus in fact or in aboriginal prospect the locus of a group of natives who made it, or wanted to make it, the centre of their lives. Around them again was a circle of other aborigines using every device of kinship, friendship, and trade to draw on the yield. Since, by aboriginal definition, almost every European and Chinese was concupiscent, any stranger entering the area was likely to be pestered.

Durmugam did not offer his women to me on any occasion, and

prudence made me let his past in this respect go without inquiry. However, I saw no sign in him or in any other aborigine that continence in a European was thought a moral virtue, or that the sexual use of their women led to a loss of repute. The continent man who had much to do with the blacks was like a brother or father, and there was a strong sense that they had a claim on his goods. The concupiscent man was like an affine on whom the claim was even more strong. The murders of two Europeans, one immediately before and one soon after my first visit, had backgrounds of this kind. The male kin of women who had gone with the men felt they had been bilked of due payment.

The river seemed to me a barbarous frontier—more, a rotted frontier, with a smell of old failure, vice, and decadence. I had at first no clear idea of how sombre its history had been since the first effective penetration by Europeans and Chinese after the late 1870's. It was with the utmost surprise that I began to piece together the story of how, over half a century, enterprise after enterprise had failed. A sugar plantation, a Jesuit mission, a copper smelter, a Government experimental farm, and a planned settlement of "blockers" or small farmers, to say nothing of one essay after another by individual fortune hunters, all attracted by absurd optimisms, had failed miserably.

I should have known all this before going, but all my interest had been in the Kimberlies. Radcliffe-Brown, my teacher, had asked me to go to Turkey Creek but when he left Sydney for Chicago late in 1931 a chance meeting with Gerhardt Laves, the linguist, persuaded me to change the plan. Laves told me of half a dozen unstudied tribes, and of scores of *myalls,* i.e., wholly uncivilized natives, who spoke no English, on the Daly River. Turkey Creek faded from sight; I had to see the unspotted savage; I had to be there when the dry season opened; there was not even time to comb the general literature and I knew the anthropological literature; that was enough. It was not enough, when I arrived in Port Darwin, to allow me to assess the innocent misinformation which some of the authorities gave me. Yes, they said, it was truly *myall* country; I would have to look to my skin and possessions; there had been murders and robberies; it was on the fringe of the last unknown part of the North. Nothing I was told was actually incorrect. The trouble was that in capital and province the sense of history was shallow; there was no grasp whatever of the chaos of the past; and there was no understanding of the welter which contemporary life had become for the surviving aborigines.

Each enterprise after the 1870's had drawn more aborigines towards the river and had made them more familiar with Europeans and more dependent on their goods. Each failure had led those now dependent to wander elsewhere to look for the new wealth and excitements—to Pine Creek, Brock's Creek, the Victoria River, even to Darwin itself. In places when no European had ever set foot, or was to do so for many years, a demand had grown up for iron goods, tobacco, tea, sugar, and clothes. There was also a hankering for a sight of such marvels as houses, machines, vehicles, firearms, and bells, one of the most alluring things of all. Unrest and covetousness had drawn in people from tribes on the outer marches, the Moiil and Fitzmaurice Rivers, the Wingate and Macadam Ranges. Whole tribes—like Durmugam's Nangiomeri—had migrated, and large tracts had thus been emptied decades before the authorities or settlers were aware of it. Some of the small tribes of the Daly (Kamor, Yunggor) had ceased to exist. Those members who had not died from new diseases (such as measles, influenza, tuberculosis, and syphilis), or from bullets, or from debauchery by grog and opium, or in the jealous battles for possession of which Durmugam had been a childish witness, had been dispersed by migration or else absorbed into larger tribes on which they had claims by contiguity, kinship, friendship, or affinity. The Marimanindji, Marinunggo, and Madngella were among the tribes which went this way. The dwindling in total numbers, so far as they were visible on the Daly, had been concealed by the inward drift. The Marithiel, Maringar, Mariga, and Maritjavin were already on the river when I arrived, except for a few parties still out in the blue. There were then no more tribes to come, except the Murinbata of Port Keats, and all that held them away was the opening of The Sacred Heart Mission by Father Docherty in 1935. The authorities, in all good faith, could well imagine that the hinterland was still densely populated, for the Daly River seemed to keep on breeding *myalls* continuously.

Durmugam was about 37 years of age when I first met him in 1932. He had been born about 1895 at Kundjawulung, a clan-country of the Nangiomeri, about seventy miles south of The Crossing. About the turn of the century the Nangiomeri had been made restless by tales of the wonders to be seen at the new goldmine at Fletcher's Gully, which lay about half way to The Crossing. In this region of many small tribes, the Nangiomeri were blocked from the Daly River, so they went instead to Fletcher's Gully. Once there, they and the western Wagaman, who accompanied them, never returned to their own country. Durmugam's father died at the mine; how, he does not know. The mine failed and his mother and mother's brother took him on to the Daly; what new circumstances made this possible, so soon after the earlier impasse, he cannot say. He remembers only two things clearly of his earliest days on the Daly, where his mother died at the copper mine—endless, bloody fights between the river and the back-country tribes, and numbers of drink-sodden aborigines lying out in the rain. The few police records which have survived make both memories seem credible enough. Between 1898 and 1911 the police inquired into seventy-three sudden deaths, sixty-two of them Chinese, two aboriginal. Among the genial causes were murder, suicide, accident, alcoholism, lightning, snakebite, fever, and syphilis. But any anthropologist would find indirect genealogical proof that scores, if not hundreds, of aborigines must have died prematurely from unrecorded causes.

Durmugam was a product of this background. He remembers little of his patrikin or matrikin, though he was "grown up" by his mother's brother. One of his bitternesses is that his mother's brother did not tell him anything of the secret male culture of the Nangiomeri. He had to learn this as a man from other tribes which shared it, or had known of it, and he felt there was some element of shame in such a thing. He cannot give a sequential or, indeed, a fully coherent account of how or where he spent his formative years. He seems to have drifted about the region with other Nangiomeri, and with some Wagaman, whose language he understands, sometimes living a truncated aboriginal life in the bush, sometimes a life not unlike that of the Daly River in the 1930's, or working for a succession of Europeans. Some were good men, he says, meaning generous and kindly men. To find a job, when he liked, for as long as he liked, was never difficult: his physique, manner, and general steadiness were in his favour and, unlike many aborigines of his generation, he did not succumb to opium or alcohol, though he has tasted both, and he liked bushwork. He was never in trouble with the police, and he pleased himself where he went. He married a Nangiomeri girl who died, without children. A turning point came in his life when, in the middle of the 1920's, he met an energetic, vital European who gave him work at a variety of jobs—mining, building construction, sleeper-cutting. At the end of the decade this man went to the Daly River to try his fortune as a farmer. Durmugam joined forces with him and, apart from a few interruptions, remained in permanent association with him. It was there that I found him.

Although all this had been, in one sense, central to Durmugam's life, in another sense it had been peripheral. On several occasions, probably during the first world war, of which he knows nothing beyond the fact that it occurred, he had followed up the trade routes which still link the Daly tribes with those of the Victoria. These visits for adventure and trade, in company with other youthful Nangiomeri and Wagaman, were the most decisive and formative events of his life. On the Victoria, he was initiated into the secret rites of the older men. He learned of the religious cult of Kunabibi which Sir Baldwin Spencer had noted in 1914. He was given his first bullroarers. He began to learn too of the lost secret life of the Nangiomeri. He was also "placed" immutably in a fixed locus in the system of eight subsections which, in tribes possessing it, is fundamental to the local organization, the conception of descent, the practices of marriage, residence, and inheritance, and acts reflexively on the sacred culture. In other words, he came for the first time into intimate association with an aboriginal High Culture.

As he told me of these experiences, in the sequence of his life-story, it was as though his mind and heart had suddenly unified. His expression was rapt, his mood earnest, and he seemed filled with passionate conviction. There was no mistaking his gratification when I showed, by a grasp of principles and details, especially of the subsection system, that I really knew what he was talking about. From that time on he treated me as one who understood—the phrase is the aborigines' own. I found myself assigned to the Djangari subsection, that is, as Durmugam's wife's brother.

It was not altogether clear to me at the time, though it is now, that after the failures of the plantation, the mission, and the copper smelter, and over the time when Durmugam was growing up, the weakened tribes had settled down in a protracted tertiary phase of adaptation. I mean by this one of systematic effort to turn to their greater advantage the more or less stable routines imposed on them once the primary phase of contact was over. Many of the preconditions of the traditional culture were gone—a sufficient population, a self-sustaining economy, a discipline by elders, a confident dependency on nature—and, with the preconditions, went much of the culture, including its secret male rites. What was left of the tradition amounted to a Low Culture—some secular ceremonies, magical practices, mundane institutions, and rules-of-thumb for a prosaic life. I found indisputable physical evidences of a regional High Culture—ovoid, circular, and linear piles of man-arranged stones, deep earth-excavations, and some other signs, to say nothing of fragmentary memories of rites evidently last celebrated before the turn of the century. There had been nothing of equivalent force to destroy the High Culture of the Victoria River tribes at this stage and, at the time when Durmugam encountered it, there had been a vivification by the spread of the cult of Kunabibi.

In the 1920's a widespread conviction had grown up on the Daly River that their own culture-hero, Angamunggi, the All-Father, a local variant of the almost universal Rainbow Serpent, had deserted them. Before I had heard a word of Kunabibi I had been told that Angamunggi had "gone away." Many evidences were cited that he no longer "looked after" the people: the infertility of the women (they were in fact riddled by gonorrhea), the spread of sickness, and the dwindling of game were among them. The cult of Kunabibi, the All-Mother, thus came at a beautifully appropriate time. The cult assumed the local form of a cult of Karwadi, by which name the bullroarer, the symbol of the All-Mother, had been known in the days of the All-Father. Karwadi became the provenance of the mixed but connected elements which I term the new High Culture. It was this that the young Nangiomeri brought back from the Victoria—a secret wisdom, a power, and a dream shared by no one else on the Daly River. It is clear that these young men were fired, and also felt under some kind of command. Durmugam was one of a group of three who seem to have set about remodelling their lives and their culture. He was not the leader; it would be more accurate to say that he was the secular force of the movement. And it is here that a connection with his killings is to be sought.

That the cult was at a peak could be seen from the fact that it was spreading intertribally in my early days on the river. Collectively, however, the Marithiel and Maringar remained aloof. The secular plight of the aborigines was also at its worst, for the bottom had fallen out of the white economy on which they were dependent. There was much disenchantment with Europeanism and constant friction with the farmers. I should think that no scrap of European prestige remained. I found an unshaken belief that aboriginal ways were right, even on the level of the Low Culture. But the aborigines were in chains: they could not bear to be without the narcotic tobacco and the stimulating tea; any woman could be bought for a fingernail of one or a spoonful of the other. Their still complex economy also demanded the hardware and softgoods obtainable from Europeans alone. And an increasing difficulty in getting bush food bound them to parasitism on a settlement where the farmers themselves often had barely enough to eat.

In these circumstances the cultivation of a great secret and its expressive rite was, for the aboriginal men at least, a compensatory outlet. What the women thought did not matter. The secret was guarded as closely as possible, and the euphemism "Sunday business" or "big Sunday" came into use to explain to Europeans the nature of the affair which often took men away for a month at a time. I learned of the cult in 1932, not at first from Durmugam, though he confirmed the knowledge and gave me an outline description, but I was required to wait until 1934, on my second visit, before I was invited to attend. I presumed that the delay was deliberate. Durmugam and Belweni, with the knowledge of their leader, used a variety of artifices to make sure of my discretion and goodwill before inviting me to cross the river to Ngurbunmumu, the secret dancing-ring. They told me that I was the only European they had allowed to do so. The farmers of course knew of the existence of the rite but were either uninterested or thought it wiser to look the other way.

It is my hypothesis that the Kunabibi-Karwadi cult belongs to the great family of movements which, for want of better names, have been called "messianic" or "nativistic," although it is probably a distinct species, or at least a very uncommon variety. It is reversionary, mystical, and religious, as well as magical, and is concerned with preserving the continuity of life. At the same time it is in intelligible series with the conventional initiations. The implicit theme of fertility, the sexual symbolisms, and the summoned presence of the All-Mother, are natural images of life and continuity. In all important respects the essential constitution of the cult is comparable, at the level of family likeness, with the Melanesian "cargo" movements. The differences may be explained by the postulates and ontology of aboriginal culture.

I could discover no evidence that the local Europeans were right in attributing all Durmugam's killings to the cult. Only one, I believe, was so connected. My facts were drawn from Durmugam himself, and from other natives, not long after the events. Since that time there has been a tendency in other tribes to believe that offences against Karwadi underlay all the killings. It is an *ex post facto* rationalization: an attempt to adduce a moral justification based on canonized values.

One Lamutji, a Marithiel, had been given a bullroarer by Durmugam as a symbol of admission to membership in the secret circle. Lamutji had promised a substantial payment, a necessary condition of possession, and a condition that the donor had to enforce if, at the very least, his own safety were not to be in danger. When, after five years, Lamutji had paid nothing in spite of many reminders, Durmugam decided to kill him at the first opportunity. He ambushed the bilker in a jungle near the river and transfixed him from behind with a shovel-spear. Lamutji recognized Durmugam before dying and was told why he had been killed. Durmugam then pierced the body with sharp stakes and pinned it in the mud below tide level. On the bank, he left a few traces of Lamutji, obliterated his own tracks, and cleverly simulated the marks of a crocodile to give the impression that this had been Lamutji's fate. The body was never found. Durmugam came under instant suspicion, but he kept silent or denied all knowledge, and the police evidently felt unable to act. On the facts as Durmugam told them, this was the only murder connected with the cult.

He killed Waluk, a Marimanindji who was as powerful and formidable a man as Durmugam himself, in talion for the death of a brother who had sickened and died after a visit by Waluk.

The Marimanindji was alleged to have taken the victim's kidney-fat by physical, not mystical, means. Durmugam's uncle publicly alleged that he had seen an incision in his nephew's side and had seen Waluk with a tin containing human fat and red ochre. Durmugam, with an accessory, followed Waluk to a quiet place, deceived him as to the purpose of the visit, and then killed him with a shovel-spear when a good opportunity came. The body was left where it lay. Again, evidently, no good basis for police action could be found.

His third and fourth victims were also Marimanindji, an old man named Barij and his son Muri. A classificatory brother of Muri had killed an old man in a camp fracas at which Durmugam was present. The murderer, Mutij, fled and was later arrested by a party of natives under the control of police-trackers, then the conventional police method of apprehending criminals. Durmugam was a member of the party. Mutij was sent to gaol for seven years. The Nangiomeri then held a divination to find who had been Mutij's secret prompter. The spirit of the dead man is alleged to have named Barij and Muri as guilty of prime agency. In fact, Barij had done nothing in the fracas and Muri had only run to the aid of his threatened brother, which is a brother's duty. Durmugam and accomplices lured the two men to a quiet place after a kangaroo-hunt, lulled them into a false security, and killed them. Durmugam was arrested but an error of procedure led to his release from custody after five months. He believes he served a gaol sentence expiating the offence. I was told that he wept over this affair, and he once said to me that he had been egged on by others—a standard self-exculpation of the aborigines. This was the nearest I ever heard him come to an expression of regret.

The word "murder" is pejorative and begs a question at issue in these events. Were any of the killings lawful homicide in aboriginal customary law?

All the river tribes believed in mystical agency and in the mystical discovery of it. All practised and acted on the outcome of divinations. Durmugam acted within an established custom and under an acknowledged sanction in killing Barij and Muri. The custom was universal but the sanction had no necessary force in another tribe and, in any case, the Marimanindji were few and decadent. Mutij's real and Durmugam's imagined imprisonment seemed to end the matter. There seemed to be no further consequences. The killing of Waluk worked out differently. All tribes believed in the mystical power of the warlock, and a number of persons were actually cut open for their fat, which was thought to have life-giving and protective properties. A public accusation was, so to speak, a formal indictment, but I never heard of anyone's confessing to his guilt. I could not establish whether Durmugam's uncle made his accusation before or after Waluk's death. But Waluk's kin at once challenged Durmugam. He fought against them three times at just such a fight as I described earlier. Once he was wounded as he stood alone while three men threw spears at him simultane-ously, and there the matter seemed to end. Durmugam had fulfilled the obligation of brotherhood and had met in full the juridical demands of the victim's kin. I would say that he acted within the canons of the ruling Low Culture.

The killing of Lamutji was a duty inherent in Durmugam's mem-bership of the cult. He had to kill or risk his own life. The deep secrecy, the artifices of mystification, and the ominous sanctions of the cult were meant to maintain the value of the main symbol, the bullroarer. The Nangiomeri were very nervous about swinging a bull-roarer by its hair-cord lest the cord break and damage the venerated object. They disliked using them as percussion-sticks in songs, for the same reason. They believed that if the original donors in the Victoria River tribes heard of such accidents, they would seek the deaths of the men responsible. Each member of the cult had an equity in maintaining the valuation of the bullroarer, and each was not only ready, but obliged, to kill a man who damaged the value, or the symbol itself. As I have said, the Marithiel as a whole did not share the High Culture, indeed, had rejected it, but many in-dividuals like Lamutji were flirting with it and were covetous of the new bullroarers. His kin claimed that they wanted Durmugam's life and many threatened to take it, but no one did anything about it. In their eyes the killing was an unjustifiable murder; in Nangiomeri eyes it was a justifiable homicide. If Durmugam's duty coincided too neatly with his personal interest, the same might be said of many honoured men in history.

In 1932, two intertribal coalitions existed which were in acute conflict. The surface of life was, for the most part, peaceable enough but under the surface something like a state of terror existed. All

An Aboriginal Battle·Line. Durmugam is the fourth from the left.

the talk was of warlockry and poison. The death of any man or male child (females did not count) was thought to be evidence of the human use of dark powers, and a divination usually followed, with a plot of talion. No one dared to walk about alone. To do so invited speculation about evil motive, or risked the assassin's spear. An unescorted woman was usually raped. Men, even within eyeshot of their camps, carried a *womerah;* it suggested pacific intention but gave them a means of returning a spear. If they went any distance they carried a spear as well. The camps were fenced in with wire-netting or scraps of roof-iron. No one slept close enough to the fence to be within reach of a warlock's arm.

These fears and tensions were almost exclusively between the two intertribal coalitions. Durmugam had an unconquerable hatred of the Marithiel and Maringar. So too did Melbyerk, the most intelligent and detached aborigine I have known. Neither Nangiomeri nor Mulluk Mulluk would intermarry with the hated tribes, and I am nearly sure they did not trade. They needed each other at initiations and they would then intermingle, but cautiously, and fights were always likely to occur. When I saw Durmugam in 1958, there was no longer much talk of warlocks and poison but his hatred had, if anything, grown. The Nangiomeri epithets could not express his sentiments. He spoke in English about those "bloody f——g bastards of Moiils," even falling into the vulgar European error of lumping both tribes together as "Moiils" whereas a generation before they had been lumped together as "Brinkens."

European law on the river had been feeble, fitful, and sometimes a brutal thing. The police administration sometimes used the station as a penalty-post for men without futures in the force. In general, there was no dependable resort at law for aborigines suffering by felony, misdemeanour, or tort. Many of the police-trackers had served gaol sentences for felonies. The blacks, for the most part, had to look to their own justice.

Thus, in 1932, there was no effective European law interposed between the murk of fear, suspicion, and hatred that lay between the warring coalitions. The white farmers kept a minimum of discipline and in some sense the farms were sanctuaries too. At night, natives would often come out of the darkness and ask to sleep nearby, leaving when daylight came. It was unnecessary to ask for an explanation. Marabut, my main Marithiel informant, was too frightened to leave if kept inadvertently after sundown. Belweni, the Wagaman, was thrown into consternation by a footprint he could not recognize. Melbyerk, when on the southern or "Brinken" bank, would try to defecate at night so as to be within the glow of my campfire. A group of saltwater blacks who came to one initiation sat sleepless, under my own eyes, throughout a whole night. There were, of course, men of greater courage. Durmugam would willingly walk for me the sixty miles to Stapleton or Adelaide River carrying mail in a cleft stick (these were still days of unsophistication) and would do so alone.

I often asked other aborigines what they thought of Durmugam. The most common observation was that he had "a hot belly," was a man of passion. His face suggested rather dignity, strength, and self-possession. While in no sense stony, it was not kindly. There was no trace of brutality or coarseness, but not of great sensibility either—simply a calm, strong face without any excess. He was the authentic Australian in having a rather broad, flat nose and craggy brows, but even these were refined by aboriginal standards. His lips were moderately full, his mouth shapely, his ears small, his jawline clean, and his chin fairly well-formed. Sometimes his eyes left one a little uncertain what to think: they were heavy lidded, perhaps a trifle protuberant, and could wear a hooded and brooding look. This impression may have been only an effect of the aboriginal iris or of the eye diseases from which he was a constant sufferer. I always thought that the smile which had earned him his European name, and was never very far away, was a good index of his most constant temper.

His mind was inclined to be slow and heavy-working. He needed ample time to weigh any question put to him. If pushed he showed perplexity rather than irritation. One felt that his mind worked well only on familiar and unhurried lines, but there was more to it than mental slowness. He had a prudent, judicious quality too. I often waited for minutes in silence while he thought over something. At such times a variety of expressions would show naïvely in his face; he would come several times to the brink of speech only to pause; finally, almost always with a half-smile, he would speak. The quality of his observations usually made up for their slowness. I never proved that he misled me, and found him correct on innumerable occasions. He had a feeling for the truth, whereas Tjimari had none. Durmugam would be very open if he made mistakes and offer the correction candidly. This probity of mind made him invaluable on matters of theoretical significance. Unlike many aborigines he had great mental stamina. He was also gifted, exceptionally so, in making simple visual demonstrations of things. Eventually, I turned one of his demonstrations (in which sticks were used as counters and stick–movements as signs of marriage, parentage, residence, and descent) into a model for teaching the theory of the subsection system, much as the aborigines teach it.

I saw no more of him, after 1935, until the winter of 1952. He was then about 57, white-haired, with failing eyesight, but still erect and still a striking figure of a man. But many things had changed greatly: the farmers were, if not prosperous, no longer poor; the blacks were on wages and very money-conscious; all had European clothes and in their camps, some now reasonably well built, one could find gramophones, torches, kitchenware, even bicycles; some of the younger people, though unable to read, were fond of looking at comic papers and illustrated magazines; the old men had lost authority; and, although I did not have time to make proper inquiry, I had the impression that the traditional culture was on its last legs. There had been no "big Sunday" for some years; the High Culture had not prospered; many of the young men openly derided the secret life; the coalitions now mattered only to those with long memories.

Durmugam was much more difficult to talk to, though still courteous. Many troubles were coming upon him, and he brooded on them so much that I found it hard to keep his mind on other matters. The young men were starting to make overtures to his wives, but he could never catch them. I tried to persuade him, if he did, not to use undue violence, since I had no wish to see him hang or languish in gaol. He promised to be cautious and made himself a bamboo stick loaded with heavy wire. He was filled with angry contempt for the young men of the day. "They can throw a spear," he said, "but can they *make* one? Can they find their own food in the bush?" He told me of a conversation with one youth who was deriding the bullroarer. Durmugam told him that it might cost him his life. The youth said, with a shrug: "If I live, I live; if I die, I die." I asked Durmugam what he said then. Durmugam said: "I said, 'Well, f—— you.'" The use of English for expression in such crises had become common in the area. It was a means of appeal to a wider world, a new code, and a new scale of values.

I met Durmugam again in 1954. His general mood had worsened as his troubles had grown. I noted too, for the first time, an element of desperation and pessimism for the future. At the same time, there were signs of antipathy in him towards Europeanism and a deepening attachment to the old aboriginal ways. He said several times, almost angrily, "the blackfellows have their own laws." Between talks about his own troubles, we went over most of my original notes. They emerged almost unaltered, but I found him able to make more powerful abstractions than twenty years before. He no longer came so freely to me, though I had camped on the same spot; he had to sit, brooding, in his own camp, watching for the next attempt to take his women.

The last time I saw him, in 1958, only a few months before writing this, he told me that great shame had come upon him and that he would be better dead. His favourite wife, the youngest of four, had run away with the son of his first wife, a great humiliation to a man still alive, although in the old law the youth might have inherited her. A married daughter, living for the time being with him, had been abducted by a youth whom Durmugam had befriended all his life. The girl had taken her daughter, the apple of Durmugam's eye, as well. Another wife, the second youngest, had been sexually abused, a traditional penalty, by a number of men, mainly Maringar, on the ground that she had illicitly seen a bullroarer in Durmugam's camp—a pretext, he said vehemently, a lie. Would he, who knew the dangers, be likely to have a bullroarer there? They were all hidden in the bush.

He appealed to me for advice and help. The women, he said, were his, given him by their fathers in the proper way. The blackfellows had their own laws; he had broken none, but the young men had; and the Europeans seemed not to care, to be on their side. Was this right? The young men were "flash" (out of hand, conceited), not listening to anyone, not caring for anything. Much trouble would come from this, trouble for everyone. He grieved over the unfilial conduct of his son. Who ever heard of a son running away with his mother? Who ever heard of a son helping another man to abduct a married sister? Why would no one help him? The police, he said, would do nothing; they had told him no one had broken the Europeans' law; and, if he hurt or killed anyone, they would send him to Fanny Bay (the gaol), or hang him. He said repeatedly: "My belly is like a fire. My brain never stops. It goes round and round."

He had received, or thought he had received, a promise of help from the remote Welfare Department, for he kept speaking of it— a promise to ban the young men from the river and to have the women and child returned. To the aborigines a promise (of which they have a verbalized concept) is a contract. A broken promise is to them iniquitous.

I listened, with all compassion, to the story. I promised, but without much hope, to intercede with the authorities on his behalf. His case had already been pleaded, to no obvious avail, by two other Europeans. One was his employer, the other a Catholic priest who had been until recently the local Protector of Aborigines. Both had seen that Durmugam's natural rights had suffered, that the injustices were compounding, and that an issue had arisen for the administration of the new policy of "assimilation."

The policy of assimilation is meant to offer the aborigines a "positive" future—absorption and eventual integration within the European community. Does it involve a loss of natural justice for the living aborigines? No one answers. Cases like Durmugam's are irritating distractions from loftier things. The policy assumes that the aborigines want, or will want, to be assimilated; that white Australians will accept them on fair terms; that discrimination will die or can be controlled; that, in spite of the revealed nature of the aborigines and their culture, they can be shaped to have a new and "Australian" nature. The chauvinism is quite unconscious. The idea that the aborigines might reject a banausic life occurs to no one. The unconscious, unfocused, but intense racialism of Australians is unnoticed. The risk of producing a depressed class of coloured misfits is thought minimal, although that is the actual basis from which "assimilation" begins.

It would be too far to one side of my purpose here to examine the new policy in detail. The aspirations are high; the sincerity is obvious; everyone is extremely busy; a great deal of money is being spent; and the tasks multiply much faster than the staffs who must do the work. In such a setting a certain courage is needed to ask if people really know what they are doing. I have space only for a single question, which is closely connected to Durmugam's life and problems.

There is such a thing as aboriginal customary law. It is in radical conflict with European law in almost every respect. Our notions of tort and crime, of procedures of arrest and trial, of admissible evidence, and so on do not fit with theirs. Only by extremely high abstraction can the two systems be brought together at all, and then only in a way which is almost useless administratively. The aboriginal system has *in part* widely broken down and cannot be restored. It broke down for a number of reasons. Among them, certainly, was a contempt among Europeans of all classes for all things aboriginal. To the older generations of Australians it seemed an impossible idea that there could be anything in the aborigines or in their tradition to admire. The contempt has perhaps almost gone. In its place one finds, surprisingly widely, both interest and solicitude. But old contempt and new solicitude have a common element: a kind of sightlessness towards the central problems of what it is to be a blackfellow in the here-and-now of Australian life. For this reason hundreds of natives have gone through, and will go through, the torment of powerlessness which Durmugam suffered.

Australia has nothing like the system of local administration which exists in New Guinea, where officials with both executive and judicial powers live in and control given districts. Even if there were, no code of law or regulations exists which is based on aboriginal problems in their own right. It is very doubtful if a European court would recognize an aboriginal marriage as a fact of law. The same is so of most of the other things of life which, to a blackfellow, make life worth the living. For example, the totally inalienable link between a man and his clan-estate, a man's right to hunting tracts, his right to claim material wealth from the husband of his sister or daughter—all these, and a dozen others, are a world away from European minds. The occasional welfare officers whom the aborigines see are not magistrates, and in any case have no code to guide them. The local scene thus tends to be anarchic. If grievance leads to crime then police and magistrates act as might be expected. They may allow a vague sense —it cannot be other than vague—of the aborigines' special problems to mitigate their decisions, but their canons are essentially European. The whole system actually rests on a pretence, rather, on a set of pretences, or fictions about facts. One of them is likely to prove ruinous: the fiction that the aborigines' interest in their rights, as they define them, can safely be ignored while plans are perfected for the greater good which Europeans have in mind. What is produced is a two-sided dissatisfaction among the blacks: a growing rancour among themselves and a projection of the hostility upon Europeans. A strong counterforce against assimilation is thus growing within the anarchy which surrounds the aboriginal pursuit of women, goods, and egoistic satisfaction in the modern period.

The aboriginal tradition permits polygyny. All Durmugam's marriages had had aboriginal sanction. His possession and enjoyment had never been challenged by native or European authority. No statute or common law of the Commonwealth had ever been held explicitly to apply. The Roman Catholic mission (the second, established in 1955) did not seek to interfere, since Durmugam was not Christian and did not wish to be. Tribal institutions acknowledged and upheld his rights but the police would have prevented his defending them, as likely to involve a breach of the peace. No alternative means which an illiterate native could possibly know how to use to advantage were provided. And, between Durmugam and the seat of law, Darwin, were petty officials disinclined to move, since there was no rule or principle, and content to fall back on private judgments: polygamy was wrong, anyway; the game was to the young; he had who could hold; one wife was enough for any man; the blacks had no morals; Durmugam had a criminal record.

The old man's appeals did reach Darwin, but when I passed through the settlement in the middle of the year, nothing had happened. Durmugam then acted on the only matter within reach, the sexual abuse of his wife. He called together all the men concerned, denounced them (in English, so that no one could misunderstand, and Europeans might hear), and soundly thrashed two with his fists. One was Waduwiri, the ring-leader, the other Pundjili. I had seen him striding downriver and, suspecting bad trouble, had vainly tried to intercept him, but he had eluded me. When I told him later that I had searched for him with the idea of holding him back he grinned and said, "I knew what you were going to do." He was feeling very good about the day. "Those bloody Moiils," he said, "they are not men. All they think about is humbugging women." He described where he had hit them, and what poor things they were for not fighting back. He said he would make them pay him £6 each.

After I left the river his wife and daughter were suddenly returned to him, and he was also told that the young men had been banished to Snake Bay. Then, out of the blue, the trouble started again. The youths reappeared in the locality, having tricked the officials in Darwin. They began to send impudent messages to Durmugam, and the young wife was again abducted. The second youth spread the word that he would come for the daughter whenever he felt like it; no one could stop them; the Government was on their side. The perplexed Durmugam asked me on my next visit a few months later if this was so, and I could only say that the Government did not seem to be on his side. I then interceded on his behalf with the authorities.

Among the Mulluk Mulluk, the consanguines of Durmugam's faithless wife, there was a strong feeling of shame. Other Nangiomeri were his defenders too, and the girl's co-wives gave her a thrashing when she returned for (as they told me) bringing shame on an old man. In other tribes, there were mixed feelings, perhaps mainly cynical amusement, but several polygynists were thoughtful and some of the young bloods delighted. They seemed to be drawing the inference that the Government did not mind how they got women.

The emotion of shame is perhaps the most powerful in aboriginal life. But it is not only a restraint; it can be a goad as well. Like most of the emotions of negative valuation, it is stronger than those which are positive. Durmugam may have wept over Barij and Muti, he may have wanted to kill Waluk and Lamutji—he was also ashamed not to. As he himself put it, he was "made" to kill the first two, and "had" to kill the second two. He responded, at least in part, to entirely social pressure. The pressures on him since 1952 have been very great. He wants, he is expected, and, by some, he is dared to do something. The young men ridicule him, behind his back, and out of the reach of his arm. Those "bastards of Moiils" send malicious messages that they will come for his women whenever they feel like doing so. He is not a man to live with expungible shame and, at our last meeting, I had the strong feeling that if his rights were not acknowledged and restored he would either turn his face to the wall and die, or there would be another affair of blood. I do not necessarily mean that Durmugam would himself go out and kill someone, but that several people would die—several, because there is a scale of shame. A single killing will not expunge a great humiliation. The victims could be almost anyone—the youths, the woman, a man like Waduwiri, or even people without apparent connection though, in native eyes, guilty of agency.

A little later, at Port Keats, I picked up a few threads which made me thoughtful. A woman had been abducted from the Victoria River by a Murinbata man, and the secret sponsor of the affair was supposed to be Waduwiri, one of Durmugam's main enemies. Tjimari, the intriguer, was trying by subtle means to frighten the Murinbata into returning the woman on the ground that her abduction had angered the Victoria River aborigines who would otherwise now be bringing bullroarers to Port Keats. He was spreading the story that the woman had slighted Karwadi—in short, was preparing the ground for her mass rape or, possibly, death. Some quiet visits were made to Durmugam by a brother and a classificatory father of the abductor, with a purpose I could not learn. The first outlines were there of the labyrinthine process of gaining support

91

and sanction for two sides. I could not discern Tjimari's deeper intent, nor Durmugam's.

The tension increased when, in spite of the isolation of Port Keats, we heard that Waduwiri had ensnared and killed a certain Split-Lip Mick, a truly villainous man who had completed a gaol sentence for the murder of Tiger Dapan some years ago. Waduwiri had welcomed Split-Lip on his return to the Daly River and had camped with him in apparent amity for some months. A day came when Waduwiri deftly divided a hunting party in two so that he and Split-Lip were left alone. It was then the work of a moment to distract Split-Lip's attention and pierce him through with a shovel-spear. The wounded man showed a ferocious will to live. He shouted for help, ran into the timber, managed somehow to pull the spear through and out of his body, and only then collapsed. Waduwiri stood over him long enough to say, "You forgot about Dapan; well, it is Dapan who is now killing you." Then he too ran, to escape the other party now racing through the timber. He was arrested later but for reasons I am unable to explain was soon out of custody. Split-Lip clung to life for about eight days.

It was now clear that serious trouble was brewing. A number of hatreds were at an intense pitch. How would they align themselves and who would rally to the lines? I spent much time trying to predict what would happen, but there were too many unknowns. Then Alligator Ngundul, Durmugam's mother's sister's son, died at Port Keats for no apparent reason. One of his sons came angrily to me, held out an arm, struck it with his other hand as though to cut the arm in two, and thus showed by how much his father's life had been cut short. He swore then and there to find The Flesh of the Road, the Murinbata name for the warlock. Soon afterwards he set out for the Victoria River with a lock of his father's hair to put the matter to a divination. My guess was that Durmugam's shame, the grief of his new loss, the release of Waduwiri, and the divination going on in secret hundreds of miles away were moving inevitably together. Waduwiri prudently kept away from the Daly River and began to put out feelers as to his reception at Port Keats if he were to come. But I did not see any place as now really safe for him. And there the matter rested when I wrote this article.

The unusual man in unusual circumstances—it is within such a frame that Durmugam's social personality is best seen. His outlook was positive, and his conduct hopeful and constructive, until his great troubles set in, but even then he held on tenaciously, trying to find a solution. Where many aborigines were bewildered or even crushed by the complexity, weight and mysteriousness of Europeanism, or sought sullenly to isolate themselves from it, or became beggars or sycophants, Durmugam tried to come to working terms with it while staying his own man. I never heard him speak harshly of a European, or heard of his being in conflict with one. If spoken to angrily or contemptuously, he would walk away, showing no outward sign of feeling.

He remains for me the most characterful aborigine I have known, but I could not confidently put him in any more specific category. I saw no neurotic or psychotic quality in him. His passions were by nature strong, and he was a man of determined will. He lacked the luminous intelligence of Melbyerk, but had a far stronger sentiment for aboriginal ways. I am sure he was deeply moved to live by the rules of his tradition as he understood it. He wanted to live a blackfellow's life, having the rights of a man, and following up The Dreaming. He venerated his culture; when he grew older, he even found it intellectually interesting. "It comes round again," he would say of the system of sub-sections, "it comes round!" The symmetry and precision of this organizational form fascinated him. His desire to see the aboriginal norms of life realized, and his restraint in the ordinary circumstances of life, were perhaps the two most abiding impressions he left on me. His life-objects, his scale of values, the terms he would accept for their attainment, and the costs he would sustain, all made sense in relation to those qualities.

Aborigines like Durmugam can never be "assimilated." They will retreat from this latterday solicitude as they did from the ignorant neglect of former times. The only thing he liked about Europeanism was its goods. I do not believe he ever formed a deep attachment to any European, myself included. He knew that I was making use of him, and, as a due for good service, he made use of me, always civilly, never unscrupulously or importunately, as with Tjimari. He was told, poor man, that I had great influence; he knew I had commanded a small force during the war, and he developed this fact into the idea that I was the "boss" of all the soldiers he saw; Tjimari told him I was a lawyer who "stood up for the blackfellows." So when he was in trouble he turned to me. He was disappointed that

I could not do much for him but, characteristically, he went away without reproaches to try to find a way to help himself. He was conscious, perhaps for the first time in his life, of a crippling weakness: his eyesight had almost failed. He said to me: "I cannot see where to throw a spear. I cannot see if anyone is sneaking up on me."

Durmugam, in my opinion, represented and embodied all the qualities which the blacks admire in a man, if he is one of their own. A good hunter, a good fighter, and a good brother; a man who kept his promises and paid his debts; a man who left other women alone (he was no philanderer) unless invited to enjoy them; and a man with a "hot belly" for his rights. After his death, his stature will grow in aboriginal eyes. He will be spoken of as "a big man," as, indeed, he always seemed to me.

His fundamental attitude to life was productive. The only negativism appeared in his later years, and even that was, so to speak, positive—a rejection of the mere activism which captivated the young men and women after the trauma of the war (a regiment of troops was stationed at The Crossing, and many aborigines were swept into a labour corps), and the first true impact of a monetary economy in a condition of inflation. The secularization was far-reaching and corrosive, psychically and socially. The young man's remark, "If I live I live, if I die I die," had seemed to Durmugam monstrous. To him, *how* a man lived and what he lived *for* were of first importance. But he himself had in part succumbed. He now spent much time playing poker for money (there were five aces in one of his packs of cards); and, for the first time in his life, he accepted money from me. His material wants were more complex and at a higher level. He still went bootless, but wore a hat and well-kept shirt and trousers.

Aboriginal culture leaves a child virtually untrammeled for five or six years. In infancy, it lies in a smooth, well-rounded *coolamon* which is airy and unconstraining, and rocks if the child moves to any great extent. A cry brings immediate fondling. A child may still cry at three as a sign that it wants something—water, attention, carrying. Its dependence on and command of both parents is maximal, their indulgence extreme. To hit a young child is for them unthinkable. A shake, or a sharp word, both rare, are the most an exasperated parent will do. The behaviour patterns thus formed are rudely broken in males by the initiations (always pubertal, sometimes prepubertal as well) after a gradual softening from the fifth or sixth year, when little boys may be seen throwing stones at their mothers, or abusing them, while the women laugh. At initiation new psychic paths are made by isolation, terror, fatigue, pain, mystery, music, drama, grave instruction—means implicitly prescient and in overt use a memorable spectacle. One inward path is ruptured, another substituted, and life thereafter is one continuous redintegration. There are quite probably neural as well as psychic and social reasons why, after initiation, an aboriginal youth responds but poorly to other possible worlds opened to him. Neural, since there has been a cortical integration of intense quality; psychic, since his responses have been deeply conditioned to limited stimuli; social, since only a limited range of objects of action have positive valence for him.

Durmugam was initiated, as he says, "in the bush," at a time (about 1913) when a relatively large number of aborigines could be assembled and the full panoply of ceremonial forms could be followed. He emerged a blackfellow for life. He did not simply reach manhood: he was *given* it, was *made* a man by men who stood for and taught him to stand for a tradition in part only revealed. Later, as I have narrated, he learned the full tradition, not of his own, but of neighbourly tribes. The conditioning was not only thus completed, but vivified, by the new presence of Kunabibi, and by the repetition and intensification of stimuli consistent with those of the trauma of initiation.

I came to believe, in the end, that the "hot belly" and the calm face of this man were consistent. The initiations teach boys to be men: to know pain and ignore it; to feel fear and master it; to want, but to bear the necessary costs; to grasp that outside society they are nothing (in the isolation of initiation they are called "wild dogs") and, inside it, the masters; that through them The Dreaming is "followed up"; that the tradition is "the road." The vital impulses are not crushed, but steered; the social conscience forecloses these fields only to leave those open; the male ego is beckoned to a defined dominance. The "hot belly" is not only allowable, but premial, in an aboriginal man. The calmness, self-possession, and dignity are the marks of the well-socialized aborigine; and the aborigine following up The Dreaming is a man who has his feet on surety.

The emphasis on rules, forms, norms, and the like, which vexes so many anthropologists who have not encountered aboriginal culture, and seems to be a bias of the analysts, is not an error of scholars. It is objectively there. It is simply a function of a need, or necessary condition, of aboriginal life: an elaboration of means serving ends which have canonized values. The dogma of The Dreaming is the doctrine of those values. The life of the mature, initiated male is the practise of the doctrine.

Durmugam's life, in broad, seems to me to vindicate this thesis. He came to good terms with Europeanism, but found it saltless all his days and, at the end, bitter too. It had some few goods—mundane things which were either substitutes for aboriginal equivalents (axes, knives, houses) or additions in no way competing with anything in "the way"—which he took and used, sensibly. But it never attracted him emotionally, it did not interest him intellectually, and it aroused only his material desires.

He might perhaps be looked on as a study in benign dissociation. At the conscious level he had found a way of living with duality, an oafish Europeanism and an aboriginal idealism. I sometimes thought that his slowness, which was certainly not a retardation, might be the measure of the difficulties of transition, for two scales must always be consulted. His general orientation towards the hard facts of actuality was, however, excellent. He could always tell me the day of the week if I forgot it; his mind held a mass of concrete detail about European things, people and events; he would calculate quite impersonally and rationally about farmer X or Y; and in the same breath, so to speak, pass to the other, an aboriginal, realm of equivalent detail and actuality. It was not that one was conscious and the other paraconscious: they were *co*conscious. Yet, paradoxical and contradictory as it may seem, he could dissociate and not merely separate the two. To be sure, a clinical study by someone competent, and I was not, might transform the picture, but I saw no signs of secondary personality; he was a unified person, who, somehow, could bridge two worlds and, while preferring one, live with two. A clinician might have found evidences of neurotic or psychotic habit because of the fears, hatreds, warlockry, and killing in which he was embroiled. I would argue, however, that these were situational, and not psychogenetic. The postulates of aboriginal culture, and the conditions of aboriginal social transactions in a bizarre context of life, suggest such an explanation. The reality Durmugam saw was defined by a tradition which he believed. If the test of belief is what a man will die for, and if a man is what he loves, I have said enough to enable others to form a judgment of this aborigine. For him, as I understood him, the hills stood, the rivers ran, the sky hung there timelessly, men went on being what they had to be because The All-Father did thus and so in the beginning, and a living man could do that and should do this until he died. Vexing, rather inexplicable things came from outside the tradition. He utilized what he could, endured what he had to, and for the rest did his best to follow up The Dreaming.

All this was written while the old man was still alive. He died in Port Darwin Hospital in August, 1959, of an inoperable cancer of the stomach. Before then he had developed leprosy of one foot and had shown signs of a failing heart. He was cared for through a succession of illnesses at the new Mission of the Sacred Heart on the Daly River and made several trips to Darwin for medical attention.

A European of sensibility who knew him over his last years remarked on his dignity, patience, courtesy to Europeans and readiness to meet any request for help. A nun asked Durmugam if he would like to teach the young aboriginal boys the wood-working in which he excelled, and he responded with delight. He showed the enchanted children how, with no tool but the stub of an old knife, to coax a flawless, complex shape out of wood so tough that it soon dulled axe and saw. The things he best knew how to make were spears, and he carved a great many hooked spears with perfect craftsmanship. All the work showed the love of form, balance, and symmetry which characterized him. In this setting he seemed anything but a man of blood. There was a gentleness about him with children which I had noted even when he was young.

The last illness developed rapidly and though for some time unwilling he consented at last to go to Darwin again. An operation showed that nothing could be done for him. He was not told of his condition and the doctors did what they could to keep him alive and in good spirits. Some of his distant kin told me that when they saw him in hospital he spoke of his sickness as but a little thing. Evidently he did not expect that he would die so soon. At the last he was given Catholic baptism and burial at Rapid Creek not far from where the Jesuits had founded the mission which they transferred to the Daly River a decade before he was born. An unusually large number of aborigines (including Waduwiri) went to the funeral. Many had not known him in life.

It was an unlikely end for such a man. While the old culture still had force Durmugam went long distances to take part in the funerary rites which were once a spectacle of the region. The last time he did so was perhaps twenty years ago. On that occasion he went to Malboiyin, on the border of his tribal country, to stamp into the ancestral earth—after the fashion of the rite—the ashes of a certain Belweni (not the man of the same name mentioned earlier). In other circumstances this would also have been done for Durmugam.

The body of Belweni had been put by affines on a platform of boughs and left there to moulder for years. His chattels, save for one thing, had long since been broken up and burned. One of the two rites of quittance had been held; the last possession had been destroyed in a fire on which close kin had prepared a meal. The preparations for the second rite were complete. The body, dried and shrunken by long exposure, had been broken into pieces, burned to a mixture of ash and charcoal, and then ground to powder. All that was left was a small container of paper-bark and a few handfuls of fine substance. The parcel had been taken from its place under the pillow of Belweni's mother and was now at Malboiyin. It was to help in the due interment of these remains that Durmugam went with many others—kith, kin, friends, and enemies—to Malboiyin, Belweni's ancestral clan-estate.

In the last rite the small parcel of dust was put in a hole within a cleared circle. Valuable things were laid on top as symbolic gifts. The grass around the clearing was then fired. The gift-givers soon withdrew the goods, and two clustered formations of clans ran forward through the smoke and smoulder. Each was daubed with pipeclay and came brandishing spears. The formations alternately encircled the grave, by this time covered with earth, and moved in line by measured and rhythmic steps so as to form an anticlockwise spiral with a point slowly nearing the grave. All the movements were in time to a chant in part melancholy and in part somehow triumphant. Each spiral halted as its leader's feet were on the grave. All the men in the formation then turned and rushed upon the centre. There, crowded together, each man stamped his right foot repeatedly, thrust his spear-point towards the grave, and added his voice to a chorus of chanted cries simulating the calls of wild things, the river currents, and the breaking surf.

Each formation vied with the other to vivify the rite. In the background were wailing women and, at a distance, a solitary singer wandering up and down as he sang in seeming detachment from all else. No one knew the meaning of the song. The singer had learned it by some mystical means he would not or could not disclose. The rite halted at sundown but at intervals throughout the night, while others slept, the singer would rise, go out beyond the glow of the fires, and then wander singing in the darkness.

With the sun the two formations performed the spiral rite once more. Then there was nothing more to do. The spirit of Belweni was now quit of material form and of worldly ties and things of the past. Until now it had had to watch over its own bones and haunt the locality of its bier. The rite had freed it to go somewhere—no one can be sure where—to find a new mode of entry to the visible world. No doubt all this too would have been done for Durmugam had things worked out differently.

According to aboriginal belief at any time now each of his *pule* (friends), of whom I had the honour to be one, will suddenly miss some valuable thing and hunt for it in vain. It will never be found again. This will be the work of Durmugam's spirit making a sign from another plane of life. The belief is tenuous and hard to put into words. The sign is somehow also the mark of a secondary death. The ideas of absolute extinction and of an indestructible soul or spirit may both be found in the belief system. Now one, now the other seems stressed. The same sort of thing is true of the social organization and the associational life generally. It is as though the nature of things were a complementary duality, with human character as the integral.

Every now and then, when one is recording the genealogies of the aborigines, a name is mentioned which brings a great show of animation and admiration. Men hold up their hands as if measuring the size of a huge tree. They say: *kadu pañgoi, kadu ñala, kadu mulak!* ("A tall man, large and fierce"). Quite often such men are known or reputed to have been warlocks, or ghostseers, or wise men, the three classes of spiritists. Durmugam was none of these. Possibly he was thus more free psychologically to come to terms with Europeanism. But by the same token, being no manipulator—and this suspicion always hangs around the three classes—he may have had a simpler and more passionate absorption in his own culture.

How much of the treachery, hatred, and bloodshed in which he was involved was due to the decay of a tradition, and how much was of its very nature, it is not possible to say. A case might be made for either or both. His times were so thoroughly out of joint that ideal and real could only drift farther apart. But the force and integrity he showed could readily be seen by anyone not blinded by the veils of race, culture, and interest.

Maling at Age 7 (right) and as a Young Lady of 11 (below).

4

Maling, A Hanunóo Girl from the Philippines

Harold C. Conklin

Just before dawn, one day in late September, 1953, 7-year-old Maling tiptoed to the edge of my sleeping mat to wake me with a short but sad announcement: *"namatay yi kanmi 'āri' "* (our younger brother is dead). Still an infant, Gawid had succumbed to an unknown ⁻malady during the night. On his death, the Mt. Yagaw Hanunóo family with whom I had been residing in the small hamlet of Parina for almost a year immediately arranged for his burial and began the observance of a five day religious restriction on agricultural work, bathing, and travel. To understand how Maling interpreted this turn of events as she waited for me to get up and help with the preparations, it is necessary to know the part she had played in the activities connected with Gawid's birth eighteen days earlier.

For that occasion, Maling's father, Panday, had rethatched a small, dilapidated annex to the family house and had built a sturdy rail fence around its wooden piles and storm props to keep the foraging pigs away from the space under the bamboo slat floor. Although the period of pregnancy had not been marked by any of the anomalies recognized by the Hanunóo, the customary magical precautions such as refraining from unnecessary binding, tying, or planting activities had been strictly observed for the preceding week by both Panday and his wife, Sukub. On the day before the birth, after a brief final weeding of the maturing rice crop in her steep jungle clearing, Sukub harvested enough bananas for the next two days and returned to Parina to spend most of the afternoon and evening in her rattan hammock-swing.

Maling came to tell me of these things and of how she had helped mend an old buri mat which her father had set up as a screen to shut off the annex from the rest of the house. Her older sister, Hanap, was responsible for most of the family cooking and during this period often relieved Sukub in caring for 2-year-old Iyang. Thus, Maling was relatively free to visit the other four households in our small settlement and occasionally to discuss her views on daily events with me. While I made more systematic attempts to elicit adult interpretations of such events, Maling often volunteered crucial details which her elders deemed either too obvious or too intimate to be mentioned. It was partly for this reason and partly because of her cheerful disposition and youthful enthusiasm that I was immediately drawn to her. Despite her childish exuberance, Maling was an obedient and respectful child, capable of almost infinite patience and concentration if necessary. She was one of those children who felt equally at ease whether sitting for an hour quietly watching her grandfather carve intricate sigmoid curves into a bolo handle or publicly—though jokingly—chiding and poking him for ending a humorous tale with an excessively lewd remark. Her poise with both children and adults in quite varied situations (including even an ethnographer's presence), was a fortunate circumstance for which I became increasingly appreciative.

Early the next morning when I entered the refurbished room that served as the birth chamber, Maling and her two sisters were standing with their backs against the palm-leaf thatch on the side opposite the door, with their eyes glued on the scene directly in front of them. Panday had girth-hitched his loincloth around a low beam at a point only a foot above Maling's head. Sukub, who was facing her daughters in a kneeling position, had wrapped the loose ends of this white cotton fabric securely around her wrists and was pulling—almost hanging—on the taut webbing that stretched from her raised hands to the beam. Sitting on the same floor mat and just behind her, Panday was helping his wife through the first stages of labor by massaging her abdomen and applying arm pressure. No elaborate preparations had been made for the occasion. The usual commonplace objects were left in the room. In the corner beyond the couple were two buri rice sacks, some odd bits of clothing, and a blanket. Winnowing trays, coconut shell dishes, a pitch candle, two bundles of bark and roots used in making incense, and various medicinal herbs filled the remaining corners. Except for a blood-red scarf wrapped tightly around her waist and the broad rattan pocket belt at her side, Sukub was dressed as she had been the day before—in a short homespun sarong with three loose, plaited waist bands and numerous bead necklaces.

The three sisters were dressed like their mother in miniature, except for the addition of loose cotton blouses. Several medicinal charms and an old Spanish silver coin dangled from Maling's beaded necklace. In her tiny sensitive face one could easily read the signs of intense observation. Below a faintly wrinkled brow, her large, somber eyes remained motionless. She had almost succeeded in keeping most of her slightly tousled, shoulder-length hair back from her face with a tight-fitting beaded fillet. One stray lock, however, escaped the encirclement of this headband and fell in a wisp over her smooth brown cheek.

A few minutes after I had sat down next to Iyang, Panday asked Hanap to start heating some rice gruel in the next room. Maling prepared a betel quid for her mother, at the latter's request, and helped Hanap pour some water from a bamboo tube into an earthen cooking pot. By the time Maling returned, her mother had already uttered the first in a series of long, piercing cries, "Udu-u-u-u-y, udu-u-u-u-y, . . . ," which signaled to the settlement at large as well as to those in the room, that the second stage of labor was about to begin.

During the next hour, Maling continued watching every detail intently, often drawing my attention to particular points that differed from the way Iyang had been born in Alyun two years before. "Then," she explained, "Mother's contractions were delayed much longer. And she had to tug on a rough abacá cord instead of a homespun loincloth because Father's was being washed."

A little while later, Maling told me confidently that this looked as if it would be a normal delivery, pointedly adding that her grand-uncle had been a breech baby and still had the name Su'i (legs first) to prove it.

From the beginning, it was obvious that the family wanted a boy. Maling had told me how she envied her girl cousins who had younger brothers to take care of, and how her father would like to have at least one son who, as he grew older, could help with house construction and the felling of larger trees during the annual forest clearance. Even Sukub had once mentioned that she and a mother of three sons (but no daughters) had exchanged waist bands several months earlier to "switch their luck." More recently, Maling had confided to me that she was afraid her Aunt Agum was correct in saying that Sukub's buttocks seemed to be getting flatter—a sure sign that the unborn child was a girl. Consequently, right up to the time the baby was born, considerable anxiety over the sex of the expected offspring was combined with the usual concern about the condition of the mother.

It was a boy, and Maling had the pleasure of announcing the fact to three of her cousins who had gathered outside on the veranda. In a matter of seconds the word reached the rest of the hamlet and attention shifted abruptly from the untouched neonate in front of Sukub to Sukub herself. From previous questioning, I knew that no one would move the baby until the afterbirth was expelled, no matter how long this might take.

During the first hour, Sukub was given all of the comforting treatment customarily provided to induce a rapid expulsion of the afterbirth and to prevent any of the numerous kinds of relapse distinguished by the Hanunóo. Hot, liquid infusions were rubbed over her limbs which were then bathed in sweet pitch incense. She perspired heavily as the room filled with the fragrant smoke. Maling was asked to knot the ends of the loincloth so that Sukub could rest her elbows in the resulting loop.

Never leaving his wife's side, Panday efficiently supervised all of these activities, now in a soft voice asking Hanap or Maling to prepare a betel quid for their mother, now adjusting Sukub's waist band or wiping her forehead with an old shirt, and always checking to see that the requisite magical procedures designed to hasten this last stage of labor were properly carried out. Under his direction, Maling helped Hanap untie everything in the house that either of her parents had lashed, woven, or spliced together in the last few months so that the afterbirth would come "undone" likewise.

Hanap fed her mother some hot rice gruel and kept the fire going while Iyang and two of her cousins spun areca nut tops on a nearby winnowing tray. Periodically, Maling added hot embers to the shell bowl in which fresh scented herbs had been mixed and passed the vessel around her mother several times.

Still, there were no results, even after Sukub's older sister, Ampan, arrived from the settlement across the Silsig valley with additional rice gruel and a new supply of pitch. As the delay extended into the second hour, Sukub became noticeably weaker and even Iyang, who had become extraordinarily quiet—saying she no longer wanted to play outside—began to reflect the urgency of this situation for the entire family.

During the next few minutes, Panday, Hanap, and Ampan conferred hastily on the most effective steps to be taken to help free the afterbirth. Maling had witnessed several such discussions under similar circumstances during the last few years, but this was different. Previously, she had listened to older relatives talk about events which did not concern her directly. Now, however, she found herself involved in almost every activity mentioned.

She had been with her father, for example, when he had planted sweet potato vines three weeks past, and was the only other person present who knew exactly which area in the family clearing he had "seeded." Furthermore, in regard to this particular incident, it was agreed unanimously that Panday should not have planted any new crops so near the end of his wife's pregnancy and that the vines would have to be uprooted. Knowing that Panday could not leave Sukub at this time, Maling offered to take Hanap to the sweet potato patch where both of them could perform this mechanical act of sympathetic magic in hopes of easing the passage of the placenta.

The two girls left almost immediately, stopping on the veranda just long enough to pick up two empty bamboo water tubes to be filled on their way back from the field. I decided to go with them, leaving Panday and his sister-in-law considering other possible sources of Sukub's difficulty. The baby remained untouched, and for the moment, unthought of.

Hanap, followed by her equally slight and even more diminutive younger sister, led the way down the 600 yards of mountain trail connecting Parina with Panday's clearing. As usual for this time of year, the steep, narrow path was muddy and slippery and, at several points where it led around the brim of a 40-foot ravine, even dangerous. Because of their daily trips to fetch water, however, the girls knew every inch of the route intimately. Where recent heavy rains had loosened rocks and made the footing precarious, Maling turned to warn me, adding at one point how only two nights before she had nearly tripped on a wild yam vine that had grown across the trail. Along the way we passed familiar stretches of bamboo forest and second-growth jungle, through two stands of coconut and other fruit trees, and across a small stream where the girls left their heavy containers.

Once in the field, Maling took us straight to the vines Panday had planted, and the girls began pulling them up. As soon as this task was done Hanap hastened back to Parina to inform the others.

Maling and I paused at the stream to talk briefly with one of her young cousins who had stopped there to prepare a betel chew.

Before he went on his way Maling asked him to cut some coconuts for us from a nearby tree which belonged to her family. He appeared happy to do this, and while he was detaching nuts from the crown of the nearest palm she emphasized how useful it is to have a young man in the family who can climb such trees. By the time she had filled her water tube from a stream-side spring, her cousin had opened three of the felled fruits for our immediate consumption, and was husking two other coconuts to make it easier for me to carry them back to Parina. Having had nothing to eat since early morning, we were greatly refreshed by this common midafternoon snack.

After our pause at the stream, Maling and I continued the trip back alone, and although it was a difficult climb most of the way, she kept up a lively conversation about the things she noticed along the trail. On numerous other occasions Parina children had amazed me with their precise knowledge of the plant environment. This was no exception. Before we reached Parina Maling had drawn my attention to five separate clumps of productive perennial crops—ranging from bananas to betel palms—each of which had been planted by her grandfather or by one of his sons, and she had shown me two wild herbs used for making *panrunas,* a medicinal preparation which, when accompanied by appropriate rituals, is believed to be a permanent oral contraceptive.

"They say," noted Maling, "that's the reason why Father doesn't have any younger sisters or brothers. Grandmother took the *panrunas* treatment soon after he was born because his had been such a difficult delivery."

"Do you know," I asked, "what other ingredients are needed to make *panrunas?*"

"I'm not sure," she replied, "but I think *tunawtunaw* weed is one. Hanap says parts of seven different plants are needed; she probably knows what the others are."

In the course of many similar conversations, Maling had demonstrated an astonishing maturity of interests and experience, richly illustrating the way in which a Hanunóo child, without formal instruction, acquires an increasingly detailed acquaintance—direct or vicarious—with all sectors of the local adult world. Geographically, this is a small universe, limited often to an area within ten kilometers of one's birthplace. (Maling had only once been farther than a half-hour's walk from Parina.) But this small orbit comprehends a comparatively vast realm of knowledge in all provinces of which any member of the society is expected to be at home. In this setting, Maling's parents never thought it particularly precocious that on some occasions she should be as interested in contraceptives as in learning to spin cotton or take care of her younger sister. Nevertheless, I was constantly impressed with her independent thinking and utter frankness which seemed to recognize no boundaries, except of degree, between child and adult knowledge. Her status as a child neither prevented her from occasionally accepting some of the responsibilities of her elders nor blocked her intuitive analysis of their adult roles.

As we approached the edge of our settlement, Maling suggested we pick an armload of the soft, leafy heads of the aromatic 'alibun shrub, explaining that not only could we use some of them to wipe the mud from our feet, but that her mother would appreciate having a few in the room because of their fragrance.

After hanging her filled miniature water cylinder on the veranda rack, Maling lifted the screen matting and quietly entered the room where her father, sisters, and aunt were watching Sukub and talking in very low tones. Maling sat quietly looking around the tiny room. Sukub and Panday had both undone their hair knots, and someone, probably Panday, had hung half a dozen untied lashings, unwound arrow bindings, and the like, over a low crossbeam. While we had been gone, many efforts had been made to recall and remedy any recent act by Maling's parents that might be the root of the trouble. Hanap leaned over to tell Maling that at Panday's behest, Aunt Agum had gone to a nearby banana grove to pull up the first and last of thirty banana sets which Sukub had planted in August. This had seemed to please Sukub, but the afterbirth still had not appeared.

Ampan remained attentively at Sukub's side while Panday looked once more through his betel bag, and Maling joined in the search for nooses, slip knots, balls of wound yarn, pegs, and other bound, joined, or fastened objects that might have been overlooked. The muffled voices from the adjoining houses and the occasional gusts of wind up from the Silsig valley only served to underscore the gravity of the quiet but intensive search inside. Maling broke the long silence by inquiring if anyone had undone the leash of the new wooden turtle that Panday had carved for Iyang. No one had, and it was agreed that perhaps this was the knot which was causing the delay.

Maling went into action swiftly, but calmly. By gentle questioning she learned from Iyang that she and her cousins had been playing with the toy turtle earlier in the day. Since their own house had already been thoroughly searched, Maling decided to check in the adjoining house where her cousins were still romping about. Her hunch was right; the toy was returned, and the leash carefully untied, completely unknotted, and thrown over the beam along with the other lines and cords. All eyes again turned to Sukub. After a few more minutes of anxious waiting, and much to everyone's relief, she indicated that the final contractions had begun.

With the expulsion of the afterbirth, the tension relaxed and things moved quickly. Hanap sponged her mother's forehead and adjusted blankets while Maling made her a fresh betel quid. Although Panday could cut the baby's navel cord, it was decided to have Yuktung act as the child's *gupas* (cord cutter) so that the boy would grow up, not only to be like his father, but also to be a good hunter and trapper like his uncle.

Panday cut the tip of an old arrow shaft into a long tapering blade and quickly fashioned one of Maling's empty water-carrying tubes into a small bucket-like vessel to hold the umbilicus and placenta. Maling joined me in the background and, knowing that this was the first time I had observed such a ritual, eagerly explained to me all that she knew about the procedure.

"See," she said, "we can't use an iron blade to cut the cord. Even an arrow shaft is dangerous if the poisoned tip has not first been removed because then the child would grow up to be easily angered. He might even fight his parents, and seriously injure them."

Finally, nine hours after Gawid's birth, and after both the bamboo container and reed knife were prepared, Panday placed the baby on its back and proceeded to tie the umbilicus close to the infant's belly with a piece of homespun yarn. Yuktung, who had been called in from his house, then took Panday's place and with a sawing motion, severed the cord just above the cotton binding with very deliberate short strokes. In rapid succession, he then touched the moist blade tip to the baby's lips, waved the shaft in a zigzag pattern over its head, and uttered a barely audible magical formula to insure rapid healing. As he stuck the shaft in the roof thatch, Maling leaned back to tell me that in a few days her father would shoot it into a tree so that her brother would be a good shot with a bow.

Sukub now handed the afterbirth to Panday who placed it in the bamboo container, filled the tube with earth, and then went off into the forest where, Maling said, he would hang it from a high limb out of reach of large animals. The bamboo floor in front of Sukub was cleared and spread with an unused homespun cloth on which the infant was placed for bathing. While this was Sukub's responsibility, Hanap and Maling helped by heating water and bringing it to their mother's side in large coconut shell bowls. Soon Sukub was holding her young son in a cotton wrap and discussing the events of the past day with her children. Hanap began to winnow rice for the evening meal, Iyang cried for her plaything, and the household gradually settled down to a more normal schedule. When I left, Maling and her mother were still talking about the knot around the turtle's neck.

For the next few weeks Maling was an enthusiastic observer and participant in the care of Parina's youngest resident. Within this settlement of independent nuclear families residing in two lines of veranda-linked dwellings, she served as the chief disseminator of news about the infant's progress. She spent some time in each of these households almost every day, ostensibly to borrow a shellful of salt or a needle, or to check on the identity of an unfamiliar visitor for the folks at home. On these small errands as well as during her casual visits, she could not resist the opportunity to talk about her brother. Her little cousins would sometimes go back with Maling to examine for themselves the various items of behavior and appearance which she had reported. First it was his feeding habits that drew their attention. Then his somewhat flattened head (which Aunt Agum assured Maling would grow "round again" in a few months), then his manual skills, and so on.

One day Maling was sent by her parents to see if the door had been finished on a nearby rice granary which was being built for the family by one of her uncles. She said she wasn't going to be gone long and wondered if I wouldn't walk along with her. On reaching the bamboo and wood storehouse which was hidden from our house-yard clearing by a few yards of low scrub and jungle, we climbed the inclined pole ladder and sat down on the door ledge.

Maling seemed to be in a talkative mood.

"Mother went down to the stream to bathe today," she began,

"and left the baby all alone with Hanap. We were awfully worried that something might happen, but nothing did. He is six days old, and he doesn't have a name yet. Our grandparents are coming up here in a day or two and I suppose we will decide on a name then."

"What do you think would be a good name for your brother?" I queried.

"There are a lot of names that are good for boys, but some we don't like because they sound too much like those used by the lowland Christians. Others we can't use because they belonged to relatives who have been dead only a few years. I think the best name would be the one Father has suggested, Gawid. My great-great-grandfather's name was Gawid. See that peak beyond Alyun? I've never been there, but they say that's where old Gawid once shot two deer with the same arrow. When my brother gets Grandfather Andung to prepare some hunting medicine for him, he should be a good hunter too.

"You know, we used to have a brother, who was several years younger than Hanap, but he died of a sudden illness two rice harvests ago. It was really too bad. He was just learning how to trap and shoot. If he had lived we would now have fish and game to eat with our rice or bananas almost every day. And there are so many things he could have helped Father do. He could have operated the bellows while Father worked at the forge, and he could have built this granary. As it is now, Father will have to forge two bolo blades to repay my uncle for this job. And look there, the cogon thatch seems a bit thin over in that corner, and the lashing here on the floor is poorly knotted. It just isn't the same as having one's own son for a helper.

"With Mother it is different. Hanap already can do most household chores including cooking, and she is pretty good at spinning and weaving baskets. I haven't learned to do all these things yet, but by the time Hanap gets married, I'll be able to take her place."

Our conversation was interrupted at this point by Hanap's call for Maling to go with her to fetch water. As we walked down to the main settlement clearing, Maling asked if girls in America also carry water like the Hanunóo, and whether their brothers ever helped them. Before I had time to answer she had joined Hanap and two other Parina girls on their way to the spring.

The infant's ears were pierced the following day and, not unimpressed by Maling's (and her father's) enthusiasm, the family decided to name him Gawid. Sukub was now able to gather firewood, cook, harvest bananas and beans, and work in the family fields—never, however, without Gawid slung at her side, or in Hanap's care.

During the second week, Maling helped her mother tie small circlets of red and white beads around Gawid's wrists and legs, and a tiny medicinal amulet about his neck. He was now well on his way to becoming accepted as a full-fledged member of the community and Parinans stopped calling him "the infant" as they began to use his proper name.

Parina children were already including Gawid in their play activities, such as the mock feast they held one afternoon behind Panday's house. Sukub whispered to me that they had been dining on twig and turmeric stalk stew and a main dish of ashes for almost half an hour, as I followed her quietly to observe them from a natural blind. Iyang, Maling, their cousin Biru (Yuktung's son), and four other 3-to-8-year-olds had set out a row of banana leaf trays on which these foods had been placed. Mimicking their elders, they were exclaiming loudly about the quality of the meal and shouting for the men to fill up their shell bowls with more "stew." Maling and the gourmandizing tots demanded better service from Gawid and other males not actually present almost as often as they did of Biru and his older brother. This most entertaining make-believe meal ended in a round of laughter on all sides as Gawid himself betrayed our presence by beginning to cry.

Though no one would say so, it was obvious that there would be an abundant rice harvest. Maling evidently knew this should not be stated directly, but at the same time she found it difficult to ignore. Once, for example, she suggested that I visit "her" field in order to gather some cucumbers which were now ripe. "And," she added, "one of the two kinds of rice Father gave me is almost ready to be cut."

Maling was still too young, of course, to do much agricultural work of her own, but she took immense pride in the fact that she possessed some seed of her own which had actually been planted in a full-sized hillside clearing instead of only in a play garden such as the one she had helped Iyang make in their Parina houseyard.

That afternoon I accompanied Sukub and Maling on a brief cucumber-picking visit to their fields, during which I saw for myself that the rats and grubs had not done nearly so much damage as local farmers would have led one to think. In a few months there would be plenty of rice for a large community-wide feast.

Recalling that the last feast her family had sponsored was for the disinterrment of her deceased brother's bones, Maling proposed that this year they should hold a post-harvest rite to celebrate Gawid's birth. On the way back, she composed, in the form of a familiar children's chant, a number of extemporaneous verses addressed to Gawid, informing him of the preparations which would soon be undertaken in his honor, how much rice his different kinsmen would contribute, how many people would participate, and how many pigs would be slaughtered:

'Anung 'ari'ari'an	Oh little brother
kang di waydi sabīhan	I must say again
dūru ti 'gdulud 'aban	That more than fifty
balaw lāmang kalim'an	will attend,
kay pāsung dūru hanggan	And that our feast will
kay bābuy 'imaw diman!	never end!

In a few words set to a very simple melody she expressed the spirit with which the whole family looked forward to the harvest season.

During the third week after his birth, however, Gawid caught a slight head cold which was evidently accompanied by complications other than those observed by his parents. Two days later, on the seventeenth night of his short life, he died quite unexpectedly— while the rest of the family was asleep.

Maling had seen death before. She knew only too well what would happen that morning when she woke me with the sad news. Her father would cut a digging stick and sufficient bamboo poles for the grave mats, while her mother would wash the baby and wrap it in cotton cloth and beads. Hanap would help her mother tie the corpse and carry it out through a hole in the wall on the eastern side of the room in which he died, while Maling herself would assemble some of the usual grave goods, including a small cooking pot, some rice, water, and vegetables in separate shell dishes, and a small betel basket with all essential ingredients—nuts, leaves, lime, and tobacco. Iyang would cry. Many rituals would be performed at the grave and the family would not be able to leave the settlement, even to visit their ripening grain fields for five days, lest all types of misfortune descend upon the already grief-stricken household.

However, there were no tears. While this was a very sad moment for a 7-year-old, Maling was well prepared to accept such events realistically. Her voice reflected sincere disappointment, but, with characteristic optimism, she added that perhaps her mother's next baby would also be a son. As we went to join the other members of her family, she said succinctly, *"mahal māna ti magkabalākih"* (it would be nice to have the same number of both boy and girl children).

This, then, was Maling as I knew her in 1953. Four years later, in the summer of 1957, I returned to the small Yagaw hamlet where she and her family were living. The Maling who greeted me in the houseyard had the same thoughtful eyes and modest smile but she stood at least a head taller than when I had last seen her. Her black hair, still held in place by a beaded band, now fell gracefully down her back to the top folds of her sarong. Her very short blouse was beginning to flare out slightly in front, and she had tightened her corsetlike rattan pocket belt about her otherwise bare midriff in an obvious attempt to accentuate her fast developing wasp-waisted ("ant-waisted" in Hanunóo) figure. And straddled on her now shapely hips was a new member of the family.

This particular pose was to become a familiar one. From early morning until shortly after the evening meal, Maling's time was almost entirely taken up in caring for her younger siblings. She was unassisted by Hanap, who had graduated from this type of surrogate motherhood several years before, and who, in fact after a long series of courtships, was about to leave the immediate family circle to establish one of her own. Iyang of course was still too young to be entrusted with such baby tending duties. And Sukub, except for the feeding and bathing of the youngest child, devoted most of her time to food-getting activities and heavy household chores.

Maling's two young charges were both boys. In 1954, within a year after the death of Gawid, Panday happily took a year-old orphaned baby (and distant cousin) as a foster son. Sukub nursed the infant whose name was Bilug, and Maling soon had the task of caring for him most of the time. When Bilug's mother's bones were ritually exhumed the following dry season, Maling proudly carried him at her side to the grave site several kilometers away. Then, in 1956, Sukub gave birth to a son of her own, Tabul, who immediately became the focus of the whole family's attention. After the first few months, and except for nursing and bathing, Tabul became Maling's main responsibility.

The constant care of two small children in a Hanunóo hamlet is by no means an uneventful or easy task. There are goats, pigs, chickens, cows, dogs, monkeys, and occasionally millipedes, lizards, snakes, and insects for them to watch, play with, or be harmed by. Flat areas being nonexistent on the eastern slopes of Mt. Yagaw, the houseyard itself is usually a steep incline down which a child may slide, tumble, or slip; and the fact that the raised verandas are frequently unrailed does not lessen the danger of falling. When one notes further that favorite playthings, even for a 2-year-old, include such weapons as keen-edged meat knives and fire-hardened bamboo pokers, it is rather remarkable that Maling showed practically no outward signs of fatigue, impatience, or discontent with her lot. On the other hand, she seemed quite indifferent to the fact that her mother was again pregnant. And once I heard her say that when she got married she really wouldn't care if she didn't have any children at all!

Though her former enthusiasm for baby boys had waned, at least temporarily, her interest in older ones was rapidly taking its place. Soon she would become a full-fledged, marriageable young maiden, a status which is the acme of female social existence among the Hanunóo. With this change would come many new privileges and opportunities. Maling, as Hanap before her, would hand over what child care duties remained to her younger sister Iyang, set up living quarters in an adjacent but separate pile dwelling, and, for several—perhaps five or six—years, lead a relatively independent life dominated by the direct but intricate local patterns of courtship ending in pregnancy, or marriage, or both.

Maling was well along in preparing herself for the new role she would be playing. In addition to dressing in a more meticulous manner, she had begun to oil her hair regularly, to trim her eyebrows, and to bind her wrists and ankles with fine red beads. Hanap had given her several decorative tortoise shell combs and a round mirror small enough to be carried in her pocket belt. Whenever her father went to Alyun, she would ask him to dig fresh vetiver roots for her to use as a sachet to keep with her sleeping blanket and extra clothes. Many of these practices she had started years before, but refinements in them had been added more recently by virtue of close observation of Hanap's behavior.

She had also begun to acquire many of the domestic skills that Hanunóo women are expected to learn. During the late morning hours when the children were napping, and by the light of a pitch candle after they had fallen asleep exhausted from a busy day at play, Maling could often be seen weaving a small betel basket, spinning cotton, or repairing a torn blouse. In this way, during the past four years, Maling had found time to learn many of the steps of basket and mat weaving, of producing homespun yarn, and of cooking native dishes. She still was not skilled in tailoring and embroidery, nor could she yet set up a cloth loom by herself.

Maling had learned to conduct herself in a more reserved manner in public, to initiate conversation with male guests only when asking for betel leaf or areca nut, and to communicate simple messages effectively with a minimum of facial gesture. All phases of betel exchange etiquette, which I had first seen her practice with mock chews or red sugar cane four years before, were now perfected. She had become quite versatile with the bamboo jew's-harp and had already learned the rudiments of nose flute playing from her mother and Aunt Agum.

To go with these instrumental skills, however, Maling knew she would need to build up as large a repertoire as possible of chanted verses which form the basis for most serenading and courting activities. While, like all Hanunóo children, she could already sing some 'ambāhan songs, she also knew that to memorize enough appropriate verses to participate successfully in extended repartée, it would be very helpful if she could record new lyrics solicited from her close relatives in some semipermanent form. Hence, about the time I arrived, she was attempting to learn the Hanunóo syllabary.

Inasmuch as Maling's newly acquired reticence in talking openly with men outside the immediate family did not extend to me, I was able to observe and discuss with her at great length the details of these various preparations. The manner in which she learned to read and write, for example, afforded an intimate picture of how she managed to acquire this bit of useful but specialized knowledge without any formalized course or tutor.

From previous visits to the Hanunóo, I knew that their Indic-derived syllabary of forty-eight characters functioned primarily as a vehicle of amorous and often poetic communication, and not as a means of historical, religious, or legal documentation. There are, in fact, no permanent records in this script, the component symbols of which are scratched into the hard but perishable outer surface of bamboo with a sharp steel knife. But what of the actual process of learning how to use this script which is never arranged in an "alphabetic" order or formally taught?

One morning after she had shaped toy animals from a half cylinder of green banana sheathing for Tabul and Bilug, Maling grasped the tip of her small knife blade between her thumb and forefinger and began pushing it across one of the flooring slats. with her other hand so that a series of lightly engraved marks were produced. In reply to my asking her what she was doing, Maling said, "Nothing, just scribbling," and left quickly to stop Tabul from twisting the tail off Bilug's "carabao." She had seemed a bit embarrassed by my question, so I did not press the matter at that time. But later, when I had a chance to examine her "scribbling," I found half a dozen clearly inscribed syllabic characters among what apparently were a good many false starts and scratch-out erasures. That night she admitted that she didn't know what all the characters she had written stood for; she had simply copied them from her mother's tobacco tube. Yet she seemed quite interested in learning and said she would get Hanap to read some of the 'ambāhan their father had written on their lime containers so that she could memorize the words and compare them with characters.

A few weeks later, while her mother was bathing Tabul, Maling came to where I was typing and began to inscribe something along the edge of my large bamboo desk. From the halting way she was singing to herself, it was obvious that she was trying to write down the words:

kang ma-nuk sa bid-la-wan	My dear bidlawan bird,
nu ka-'in-da ma-'u-ran	In a storm like this
pī-san dap ti hu-ru-nan	We are perched together,
nu may . . .	But when . . .

Assuming that she had now learned to use some of the characters adequately, I gave her a simple "dictation test" covering the whole range of syllable types. After every word I paused while Maling inscribed the characters deliberately or told me she didn't yet know them. At the end, she had written eighteen characters correctly.

These represented syllables of high frequency in simple conversation and children's 'ambāhan, and included those symbols necessary to sign her own name.

At six to eight week intervals thereafter I made additional checks to note Maling's progress. Each time she had learned seven or eight new characters, until she had mastered all but those representing the five or six rarest syllable types in the language. By that time she had become quite skilled in rapid transcription, and could and did read almost any verse she could find. Inside of six months, and without giving up any of her family duties she had all but completed the technical training she would need to record and read innumerable songs and letters for the rest of her life. No one person had provided her with more than a fraction of the reading materials she had studied, although Hanap, who at this stage spent a good many leisure hours practicing 'ambāhan, was most frequently consulted.

Although Maling's ability to read and write will probably prove to be very useful, it will not introduce her to any worlds beyond that which she can see from Mt. Yagaw. She has remained close to home all her life and with Hanunóo marriage residence rules as they stand, her future husband will undoubtedly help her set up a new household in Parina or in whatever nearby hamlet her parents are living at the time. He will probably be a distant cousin from one of the other Hanunóo regions near Mt. Yagaw. Several young men of this description have already begun to visit Parina rather frequently. Ostensibly these visits are for medicines or bolo handles, but no one in Parina is deceived.

A Day in Parina

18 JULY 1953

0600   I am awakened by the excited shouting of six Parina children who have found a neighbor's goat giving birth to the last of three offspring right in the middle of the fire pit of my plant-drying shed. I get up, put on my only garment (a pair of shorts), and join the noisy young Parinans. I am impressed with the fact that even two 4-year-old girls seem to understand completely and articulately the physiological event we are witnessing. And I learn much about the process from them.

0630   There is a strong east wind blowing up from the Silsig valley and because we will probably have a few hours of sunlight before the daily monsoon showers commence, I hang out my typewriter, tape recorder, and some clothes on a *siyāpo'* fiber line as a precautionary measure against mold and rust. After rolling up my sleeping mat I am joined by Uming and other members of Badu's household as we eat a breakfast of boiled rice, camote greens, jambo fruits, fresh corn, and rock salt. Food, as always, is served in basket trays and coconut shell dishes set on the bamboo-slat floor.

0700   The dishes cleared away, the floor swept, and most of the kids off jambo gathering, I start to write up detailed notes on last night's curing rite—checking with Badu', who is just outside rekindling the drying fire, on matters of sequence and ritual significance.

0730   Pinungu, the old man of Arasa'as and the best archer on Mt. Yagaw, arrives with a gift of 5 fresh eggs and a handful of medicinal jungle plants which he thought we might have missed (we had). Ayakan and two other Parina elders come into my

This account of a day's activities in Parina, Mindoro, was written by Dr. Conklin in the field as part of a report to the Social Science Research Council from which he then held a fellowship. In an accompanying note, he writes: "No day is really 'typical,' but the . . . sketch gives at least an inkling of what the social framework in which I am living at present is like, of the diversity of activities and field conditions encountered, and of some of my techniques for observation, participation, and documentation."

house to join Pinungu in a chew of betel and a round of gossip. It seems "Nungu" has just come from a nearby settlement where he officiated, as eldest relative, in the trial of his grand-nephew for polygynous marriage sans *pangagduwah* (compensatory payment to first wife). Sitting in a circle on the floor, the others listen intently as the old boy relates the whole affair blow by blow. I appear to be attending to some other business at my bamboo desk, but actually I am recording on $4'' \times 6''$ slips as much of the sociological information uncovered in their conversation as possible.

0800   Three boys come in from Barayung wanting to know what they can do to earn some nylon parachute cord (a now almost universally recognized stronger material for their 3-stringed *gitgit*-violins than the traditionally plucked and twisted strands of their own hair). I am sending them to gather firewood and now hope to get back to the notes on last night's seance.

0830–1200   While writing in my house for three and a half hours and checking on points of detail with two eye-witnesses (at last night's ritual) who are now helping Badu' press and dry the new herbs "Nungu" brought in, the following events transpired—each in its own way an interruption, but each also furnishing me with additional useful documentation of Hanunóo culture patterns:

1. Abala, my sister-in-law by adoption, brings in a staggering load of freshly-picked sweet corn and sets it down on the dance-pavilion and work porch which separates her house from mine. It is the first harvest from her early swidden, and thus she stops to chat and chew betel with me saying that from now on she and her family will be able to eat corn—even from other fields—without fear of losing their own crop by spirit poisoning.

2. Two boys who have been out setting traps bring me a bunch of ripe bananas of a type I have not yet tasted. I give them each a double length of nylon cord and tell them to make replicas of their monkey and civet traps in our "yard" so that I may photograph them.

3. Lin'ay, Ayakan's shy, unmarried daughter, enters my house with a handful of bleached, sweet-scented leaves which constitute a rare but highly valued native form of hair perfume. Lin'ay, who is also quite a singer, tells me several stories about this plant and I copy down two *'ambāhan* chants from her which metaphorically refer to young girls as scented leaves of this sort.

4. Biryu, a wrinkled and slightly bearded old mountaineer from across the Malaw River—and a rare visitor in Parina—jabs his spear into the muddy soil at the back of my house and pays us a surprise call on his way to Randiwan to hunt pigs. I've been meaning to check up on his personal history and certain gaps in his genealogy because he is the oldest member in one of my Yagaw test settlements—so I take off a half hour to check my notes and fill out an individual questionnaire. This he doesn't mind, though he finds it amusing that I should want him to put down in his hand writing all the characters of the Hanunóo syllabary in a completely meaningless (i.e. "alphabetic") sequence.

5. On hearing the first roll of thunder bounce back at us from Mt. Pu'ul, we bring in the sun-dried clothes and equipment just in time to save them from being drenched. These rains are a nuisance even for the Hanunóo, although they often carry effective "umbrellas" in the form of accordion-pleated fronds of the giant fan palm. Biryu has Lin'ay mend one of these with abacá thread so that he may borrow it, inasmuch as there are no signs that it will stop pouring and he wants to return home from Randiwan before nightfall.

6. Giwnay, Ayakan's third wife and one of her daughters fluff cotton on a broad pandanus mat in the next house, using long springy beaters and keeping up a fast duple rhythm which contrasts pleasantly with the patter of the rain.

1200 I join "Nungu" and five Parina men just in from their fields in talking about changes in Hanunóo custom law. I try to work the conversation around to the point where I will get answers to some of the questions which came to mind while listening to "Nungu's" earlier exposition of his grand-nephew's trial. I'm getting what I want.

1230 Visitors and I eat a lunch of fresh corn, dried fish, more jambo fruits, salt, eggs, and limes. Parina folk retire to their own house units for their midday meal or "brunch." Some of them have not eaten since before dawn when they left for their fields. Others ate only a left-over boiled banana or two.

1300 Rain keeps up. Women in next house are spinning thread, old men are carving knife handles and sharpening machetes. Young men are sleeping, two of them in my house. One girl is swinging back and forth in the corner hammock lullabying her younger sister to sleep. I resume writing and for two hours continue almost uninterrupted. I stop once to watch Lig'um's wife dye thread in a pot of indigo.

1500   Some of the adults return to the fields, but Badu' and Ayakan remain in Parina to help catalogue and press a 150-specimen, 30-species collection of medicinal herbs and edible plants which Tigulang just brought in. Tigulang is an old man but in excellent health, and despite the rain had carried this load wrapped in banana leaves from the other side of Mt. Hipi'. It takes four of us two hours to cut, press, label, identify, and discuss briefly the peculiar qualities and medicinal, religious, or sociological significance of each plant type. Tigulang is a great herbalist and although he visits us rarely, he usually comes well laden.

1600   It stops raining and three Parina girls get ready to leave for Badyang Creek to bathe and to fetch water for cooking. I ask them to wash out the newly woven and beautifully embroidered loincloth which I bought yesterday from Yan'ay for a pack of fine red seed beads.

1700   As we finish the last press of Tigulang's collection, Yungit, a young man from Tarubung, arrives with two requests: one, payment in beads for the bamboo jew's-harp he wants to sell me; and two, medication for three swollen bee stings sustained on both eyelids and on his penis. He is in great agony and cannot even stand wearing his G-string. Both Tigulang and I are doing our best to allay the pain with what medicines we have: a mixture of Squibb products and jungle juices.

1730   Discussion centers around Tigulang; the subject: love charms and amulets. In a low voice and probably in full recognition of the intent interest of his audience, he tells us about some of the tricks he has learned from Buhíd mediums on the upper reaches of the Inundungan and Twaga rivers and gives us detailed information with many illustrations of how such charms are best employed.

1745   While the sky remains clear I hurry down the steep and now very muddy trail to the Silsig river for a quick bath. On the way down I visit several traps in the nearby jungle with the boys mentioned above.

1830   Getting dark fast. On returning to Parina I find that the drying fire is burning well and a good supply of firewood has been collected. Three men will help change all the papers, drying blotters, and presses at least once during the evening. Tigulang's collection will be completely dried, packed, and checked for shipment to Manila and Cambridge within three days unless we are interrupted by typhoon winds. Pitch candles have been lit and stuck in three-legged split stick holders in each house at Parina. Pinungu and a few other visitors decide to accept my invitation to stay at my place for the night. Tigulang, however, says he must return and quickly makes a long torch of old split bamboo strips to guide him through the Hipi' forest.

1900 I fill out the daily work, agricultural, sickness, and food charts with the help of representatives of each household at Parina, and take up where I left off with my notes on last night's doings. Several girls from Ayakan's house are now spinning cotton thread on the floor of my house in the reflected light of the drying fire. The older men and those just in from the fields are chewing betel and discussing the prospects of a good rice harvest. The melodic individual calls of four or five Parina women inform us that the water carriers and swidden watchers (for monkeys, birds, and wild pigs) from Badyang are returning. Cooking fires are kindled and women prepare the evening meal while young folks practice chanting and playing musical instruments. Two are strumming bamboo zithers, two are playing a jew's-harp duet, and one boy is practicing on a large but nevertheless all-human-hair-strung guitar.

2000 We eat the evening meal of boiled preripe plantains, rice, several kinds of green vegetables cooked with brown beans in coconut cream, and some roast pork brought over from Tarubong by Bado's sister-in-law. As usual, the evening meal lasts much longer than those taken earlier in the day. Much merrymaking, banter, and jesting among visitors and residents of both sexes is in order. At times the laughter reaches a really high pitch and necessitates a temporary cessation of the normal eating process. Lig'um's boasting of his exploits as a young dandy before he got married and his hilarious mimicking of Bisayan folk trying to speak Hanunóo keep us well entertained.

2100 The meal finished, small work groups of spinners, sewers, and embroiderers assemble wherever there is a source of light. Some of the men help with the ethnobotanical specimens. Several young men take off with blankets, perfumes, and musical instruments for other communities where they will spend the night serenading eligible maidens. I return to my writing which I finish in about an hour. Several youngsters are using my colored pencils to fill up the pages of a blank notebook with geometric designs for garment embroidery and representational sketches of plants, fields, animals, and humans. At one point, Abala asks me for a needle to replace one which just fell through the slat flooring. I mention her name in giving it to her, forgetting to call her by the proper kin designation. Quick as a flash, 7-year-old Maling looks up and asks, *"Ampud, hayga nimu 'iningarnan kanmu bayaw?"* (Ampud [HCC], why did you call your sister-in-law by her name?) I am somewhat embarrassed and most of the spectators are amused to see such a tiny tot take me to task for failing to comply with Hanunóo name taboos.

2200 Giwnay comes into my house, picks up one of the dance gongs, and gets one of her daughters to help her beat out a fast, metallic rhythm. Soon all of the other women and some of the young boys and children stop their various projects and join in the communal gong playing: four players to each set of two gongs. We have three sets in Parina and all are being used at this moment. Older men strum guitars and *gitgit*-violins, others play jew's-harps. Lig'um stops changing presses and leads two younger boys in 15 minutes of vigorous dancing. This spontaneous gong session seems to be going very well, so I take a few 35mm Kodachrome shots using an indoor flash, unpack the Magnemite tape recorder, and proceed to fill two 15-minute tapes with the impelling rhythm of gongs, strings, and the loud clack-clackity-clack of six calloused feet as they crash down, in unison, on the resounding bamboo floor. A new beat called *dinūlut* is presently replacing the older *binalinsay* and several of the unmarried teen-agers here who have learned this rhythm in the southland near Binli are teaching Giwnay and the other leading gong players in Parina. I spend a half hour or so getting notes on the history of these various rhythms and their secular and semi-ritual significance. While doing this I play back the two tapes for the performers to hear.

2300 Gongs are put away and most of the Parina folk retire to their respective homes. The last presses are changed. I give my visitors sleeping mats (they have their own homespun blankets) and they spread them out on the floor amidst mortars, fish-traps, bags of rice, corn, sesame, and salt. Badu' sits in the doorway watching the fire burn down to a bed of embers low enough to be safely left unguarded till morning. My visitors continue to chat while I make plans for tomorrow and write up miscellaneous notes on the evening's activities. If the weather tomorrow turns out to be like it has been today we can expect an evening feast of fried *daldaluh* (a species of fat-bodied white ants the mating forms of which fly about in great swarms during clear, but damp, summer evenings). I can overhear the conversation in the next house. They are making plans for taking a really big catch and they are now debating as to where the most *daldaluh* will be found, at Badyang or Tinapi'.

2345   I spread out my mat, check the fire, say good night to Badu', and retire. But first "Nungu," Balyan, and I discuss indirect manners of speech in Hanunóo and end up having a riddle contest in which, of course, Balyan and I come out losers.

5

A New Guinea "Opening Man"

James B. Watson

The Agarabi discovery of the world beyond their small domain in the Highlands of New Guinea is unbelievably recent. The life of one young man, Bantao, whom I knew in 1954, more than spans it.[1] Bantao was then about 26. He was perhaps 3 years old when his village saw the first white men ever reported in the Eastern Highlands. He was 5 in 1933 when Assistant District Officer Ian Mack was killed in an attack upon Bantao's village and nine village men lost their lives. Two years later the Seventh Day Adventists established their mission at Kainantu, a half day's walk away. In 1943, when bombs were dropped over the district and a Japanese patrol briefly occupied a part of the area of the Agarabi people, Bantao was about 15. In his own account of his life, these intrusions of the outside world are the outstanding time markers. Far more than datable events, however, it has been the penetration of unheard-of ideas and customs into their world that has shaped Bantao and his fellow tribesmen. The sudden events of a mere score of years have thus fundamentally altered the destiny that only a few years before could safely have been predicted for Bantao at birth.

Life then was also eventful for the Agarabi. Violence and treachery

[1] The field work during which the material that forms the basis of this account was collected was made possible by a grant of the Ford Foundation. The debt is gratefully acknowledged. The field trip and residence of a year and a half in the Eastern Highlands of New Guinea were shared by my wife, Virginia, and small daughter, Anne. Both helped me learn much of what I know about the Agarabi. Alan A. Roberts, Director of the Department of District Services and Native Affairs, Port Moresby, and Harry A. West, then A.D.O., Kainantu (now D.C.), and William Brown, A.D.O., together with other people in the Territory, contributed not only to our personal comfort in the field but to any scholarly success we may have had. A special debt for the present paper is of course owed to Bantao himself. He alone could make it possible. We knew him well for some nine months, from the very beginning of our stay with the Agarabi when he helped us build our house. No particular plans were made in the field for a biographical sketch of Bantao but since certain things came up incidentally and I asked about them, he was always concerned to keep track of what was already "in the book." In most things Bantao did the best he could for us and I hope the present sketch will come somewhere near the same measure. Drs. K. E. Read and Melford E. Spiro, my colleagues, have been good enough to read the paper and have made valuable suggestions.

spiced the daily round of gardening, pig-tending, and gossip that occupied the villagers. Adultery, sorcery, vengeance, intrigue, and the most exciting of all human sports, killing in open combat—and the subsequent mutilation of victims and (probably) cannibalism—were the pursuits that gave life its zest. Unnatural death was commonplace and few lived to old age. Like many, the people of Bantao's village knew exile at the hands of enemies; unlike some, they knew the pride and elation of a triumphant return to ancestral lands. Cock-proud boastfulness was the prerogative of the successful man, and the public acclaim his prowess earned was reflected on his kinsmen. Indeed, for the "hot" man equal to the challenge, life held great rewards. But self-realization for some had to be at the cost of failure, or even life itself, for others.

Agarabi life was a complex web of gift and debt, a network of killing and sorcery, of payment for gains and retaliation for losses. Ceremonies to strengthen family and lineage, and actions taken to kill its enemies, or iterative of success, were the most important activities for the men and hence, in their view, for the community. To strengthen the family and lineage required food, friends, and females from outside groups. Food was necessary for ceremonies and for gifts on less formal occasions where friendships and obligations were built or maintained; friends were necessary as allies in fighting and sorcery; and women were necessary to tend pigs and grow food, to enter into exogamous exchanges with other lineages, and to bear the children who as men would carry on and maintain the fighting force. Each important stage in the life of an individual had its place in this cycle of community process, and ceremonies were necessary to sanction and validate every one, including the loss of members of one's own group or the taking of lives in another.

This in brief, then, was the style of life that prevailed until the 1930's. Its violence seemed excessive to even the least scrupulous early white settlers. They opposed the traditional ways of the Agarabi if for no other reason than that they interfered with freedom to move safely about the country and denied them a source of tractable native labor. Others, such as the missionaries and the local government officers, were committed to work toward even more fundamental changes. Inexorably the white man has assumed control in carrying out his various requirements. Native initiative has dwindled away over a period of twenty years replete with both unprecedented possibilities and unprecedented anxieties. Bantao's own life began as the vigor of the old Agarabi life was beginning to wane and his story is that of a man of uncertain expectations and very few solid guides.

In many ways Bantao is like any Agarabi of his village, his generation, his sex. In leaving the village for brief periods to try first this activity and then that in the emergent new scheme of things, his experiences parallel those of other young Agarabi men. He, too, wanted to know the new world and the "station," the tiny European community at Kainantu. The cycle is typical: trying something out, "running away" in the face of a threat or staying to learn, and returning after a while to the village again to "sit down nothing." In other ways Bantao is unique. He seems to have sought more than most of his contemporaries from his relationships with Europeans or with other Agarabi. Because of this search, he has also tried to give more, but it has not brought him any lasting satisfactions. Bantao's self-image corresponds to that of an orphan or unwanted child, though the causes are confused in his account. Perhaps we can see this image mirrored in his questing in an alien world and in his readiness to accept innovation. Such, at any rate, are the gross outlines of a man who is living at an historical moment of dramatic change.

In its Western sense Bantao's name is a poor index to this young man's character. His true name means "thief," but to portray him as a sly, furtive type would be absurd. He has an open countenance and smiles and laughs easily. Probably the tallest man in the village and one of the tallest in the region—a good 5 feet 10 inches—Bantao carries himself well. He is heavily boned and handsomely muscled, although well-contoured muscles are not as uncommon as tall stature in the Central Highlands. His skin is a good deal lighter than most Agarabi, closely approximating the "red-skinned" shade the people recognize. His nose is high, not flat, though not the aquiline type prevalent among the groups farther to the west.

Bantao is generous and certainly more solicitous of approval, if not also more conscientious, than the average of his group. Like most Agarabi men I know, he is distinctly sensitive, even vulnerable, to the opinions of others. On the whole he is gentle, easily disarmed, and ingenuous, a poor hand at dissembling. His readiness to trust the European, his artlessness and sanguine expectations in his relations with whites have led him several times to serious disappointment and disillusion.

Why then "thief" for this rather straightforward person, quick to accept a wrong or a mistake as his own? Bantao says that he was given his name by his foster mother because "I was always taking food as a boy. I was always hungry." By itself such a trait would not be a point of shame, for the Agarabi are ambivalent about stealing. The owner of the pilfered garden may be angry, and perhaps he will set vicious foot-traps of sharpened bamboo by his garden fence. The culprit's relatives, however, while admitting that taking food is "wrong," regard such mischief with covert satisfaction as early evidence of the aggressive nature that will make a hot-tempered man and an outstanding fighter. As would be expected, Bantao's attitude toward his name is not one of wrongfulness but neither is it one of pride; superficially matter-of-fact, his feeling actually amounts to self-pity. Fellow villagers explain the connection a bit patronizingly. Apparently childhood thievery was not regarded in him as the promise of a fighting spirit or else he has singularly failed to live up to that promise. Bantao is generally considered a "cold" man.

Bantao was not a very good informant, though he seemed to want to be. He was quite patient but easily confused. Moreover, his information tended to be either far too abbreviated or else he would by some means work the account around to suggest—rather wistfully —an event which purported to cast him in a favorable light. Since he was better able to talk about himself than to describe other things with much objectivity, I often took the opportunity to ask him about his own life. It was on one of these occasions, sitting in the little thatched "haws story" which he himself had helped to build for the purpose, that he told me how he remembered his early childhood.

Bantao's first mother, Tabike, who bore him, called him Daanoto. His second mother, Ooti, called him Bantao after she took him; quite a few people, Bantao pointed out, have two names. He was born at Koyafa, some miles from where his lineage now lives. In Bantao's words:

My mother was about to kill me in the birth house by the water when Ooti came there and took me. She was Tabike's own elder sister. Tabike wanted to kill me because she had too many children already. Ooti asked her why she wanted to kill me and Tabike told her. [Bantao is himself only the second of an eventual six children. Whatever the real motive of his mother, it could scarcely have been that she had too many children at the time of Bantao's birth.]

Ooti had one child who had recently died. Tabike did not want to give me away and she already had her foot on my neck to shut off my wind. They don't throw children in the water to kill them but shut off their wind with the foot. I don't know why Tabike did not want to give me to Ooti, but Ooti won out. She got me when I was only one day old. Ooti still had milk from her dead child. He was about 8 or 10 when he died. They used to give milk longer in those days. Only when you were a *pumara* [initiated] would you leave your mother's breasts. So Ooti could feed me.

Tabike was not cross when Ooti took me. "That's all right: you can take care of him." Ooti cleaned out my p—s and s—t. [Disposing of the excreta of an infant is considered a symbol of closeness and it is also a form of indebtedness between child and parents.]

Later I grew bigger and Tabike decided she had had a good child and wanted me back. All the time she kept taking me away to Koyafa. Ooti lived at Kokirapa and often when she would come back from the garden to get me, I wouldn't be there—sometimes not for two or three nights. She would go to look at my relatives' and other places, but I wasn't there either. Three times this happened and each time Ooti would fetch me and slap me on the ears all the way home. I cried. She beat me with a stick and kicked me, but I liked Ooti. I didn't like Tabike. I liked Pe?e [2] [Ooti's husband], too, but I didn't help my own father with his garden, his house, or any of his work. Just the same, I did not steal food from my [own] father.

Finally Ooti threatened to fight Tabike if she pulled me away again. She did and Ooti took a fighting stick to her. She bruised and cut her about the head. Tabike did not take a fighting stick but only defended herself with a digging stick. Ooti struck me first of all and I ran into the pitpit [reeds] to hide. Then the two women fought. I didn't see the fight. I thought I was Ooti's child and only when Tabike was dying [much later] I learned from Ooti that Tabike was my own mother. Tabike never mentioned it and I thought she was just a woman who liked me.

The two women finished their fight and settled their dispute. They agreed to cook food on the stones. Tabike gave five pigs to Ooti and Ooti gave four pigs to Tabike. Ooti didn't give as many pigs because raising a child was hard work—cleaning out my s—t and all that. The pigs were ex-

2 "?" is the phonetic symbol representing a glottal stop.

changed all the same day; it was the time for eating pigs. Yes, I ate pig given me by Ooti but I couldn't eat pig from Tabike any more because Ooti tabooed me from going to Tabike's house now that the pigs had been exchanged.

When my number-two mother [Ooti] would kill pigs, I didn't use to hang around. I would go off somewhere and they would all be thinking about me—very sorry I wasn't there. When I came back, they would ask me why I didn't stay around and eat with the rest. They would save me some after the others had all eaten. No, I didn't want to eat together with the rest. Those men were all intent upon eating pig. They might speak harshly to me so I didn't go near them. Time for eating food I could go near—but not eating pig, that's all. I waited until they had all eaten and then I would come and eat a little piece that was left. Yes, I felt sorry for myself. I thought they weren't taking very good care of me.

"Food" usually means garden crops, above all, sweet potatoes. One does not eat the pigs raised by his own family or lineage and given in feast to people of another lineage. It is characteristic of Bantao to phrase this experience in terms of neglect and self-pity. The occasion was certainly not one from which the children of the family were excluded. To be sure, food, security, and love are implicitly equated by the Agarabi, but it is impossible to know the extent to which Bantao's perception of his foster parents' neglect corresponds to the actual facts.

Immediately following this portrayal of neglect and self-pity, Bantao commented: "That is just the way I am. If you go away and ask me to watch your house while you are gone, I will do it. [That is, I think of others first, not my own interest or welfare.] I don't steal things either. If money is found in the road, I go and show it to everyone and try to find the owner. When some men find a thing, it is lost for good. That's the reason that I am always getting into trouble and being put into the calaboose." And in answer to a query, "Yes, I mean I get in trouble because I am like this."

If Bántao's infancy were typical, he would have been indulgently treated, fondled and dandled by parents and relatives, and seldom allowed to cry very long before Ooti attended to him or dispatched some older child to give him attention. There are often second and third mothers about to offer the child the breast if he wants it and normally this period in life seems to be characterized by affection and solicitousness. Bantao said that Ooti had milk when she took

133

him and she appears to have had no more children who would have displaced him. Until able to walk Bantao would have been carried about in his mother's net bag—the same that she used for bringing food from the garden—whenever she had to leave the house or the hamlet. It is not likely that he would have had harsh physical discipline, but as soon as he could understand, he may have been frightened by threats of ghosts to induce compliance with parental instructions.

While we cannot be sure, of course, of Bantao's treatment, children of foster parents are generally loved at least as much as the foster parents' own children. One is tempted to guess that some part of his childhood was atypical in view of his later feeling that he was not well cared for. The squabble between Ooti and Tabike was presumably the culmination of a long-standing dispute which may therefore have had a bearing on his treatment during infancy; but it is not obvious how his rearing may have been affected. It is quite typical at any rate for adoptive parents to conceal from a child his true parentage.

According to his story, Bantao believes that both his own and his foster mother struggled for possession of him but there is no hint of such an interest on the part of either his own father or Pe?e, his foster father. Whether simply because of his early death or not, neither Pe?e nor his own father, who is still alive, seems to have played very strongly the role of father to him. Uwayoro, his own father, lived in different hamlets at various times and appears to have had little interest in his children. When Bantao's own mother died, Bantao says Uwayoro was not sorry for the children nor did he mourn his dead wife. Uwayoro's brother, who ordinarily would have taken over the role of the male parent when needed, did not like either Bantao or Bantao's elder brother. Both Uwayoro and the uncle are rather indifferent to him today, although acknowledging the relationship; and while Bantao would apparently like to be a son and tries to act like one up to a point, their lack of encouragement, together with the enigmatic stain of the past, prevents the relationship from bringing him much strength. It is his elder brother, of whom Bantao speaks as having "looked out for me" after the death of Pe?e, who comes closest to being a father to him.

Unquestionably Bantao's feelings toward his parents and foster parents were largely shaped later in life than during childhood, especially in the case of the father—or not-father—whose relationship should have become increasingly important to him as he grew older. Thus, his confused attitude is an expression of his whole life to the present, and not simply the product or the faithful record of childish experience alone. It is the record as rewritten by the adult, in the light of later experiences as well as of the childhood it purports to recall, even though the revision is the only way now in which we can glimpse the childhood.

Once Bantao had teeth to chew food and legs to run on, he roamed -the village environs in a group with his age-mates. He would spend the day with small bands of youngsters wandering the paths among the gardens, climbing the fences in search of mischief or excitement, spying upon adults, asking for or stealing food to cook by themselves over fires that they built in the kunai grass or in the pitpit. Once in a while these gangs would steal a small pig and eat it, although Bantao said he never did this himself. This was a period in his life that he enjoyed recalling.

Life then as now was full of boyish possibilities, and Bantao smilingly described shooting insects and lizards with tiny arrows of stiff grass shot from small, bamboo bows, or driving and snaring little birds in the heavy cobwebs made in the tops of trees by the *bampoki* spider—which could also be eaten. Sometimes the boys would shoot each other with their grass arrows, painful to the bare skin—even for the youngsters humans were the most important of all targets for this inseparable weapon of manhood. And there were games, essentially contests of shooting skill, luck, or hardiness. Bantao implied that he could hold his own. There was little emphasis here upon an unnatural sportsmanship, and the losers easily give way to invective or physical retaliation. Above all, the rough and ready horse-play stressed the aggressiveness which adults looked for in growing boys as foreshadowing future outstanding men, *ayafabanta*. A running leap and a hard kick in the back of an unsuspecting mate was one of the commonplace pranks as they romped along the village paths. The proper response was grinning repayment in kind at the earliest possible opportunity, although smaller or less aggressive boys sometimes gave way to tears. As likely as not this would provoke rather than lessen further assault; and if some boy were unfortunate enough to be physically or mentally deficient, Bantao admitted, he was likely to be picked on constantly, slapped and kicked, not only by his companions but even by grown men and women when

Preparations for a Feast.

he annoyed them with his staring or got in their way. Because of his size, it would be unlikely that Bantao was always the underdog in such horse-play. If he was nobody's child, as he partly suggested, he may have been the object of adult aggression, but he made no mention of this.

During the daytime, except in cold or rainy weather, a hamlet might be practically deserted, with the adult men and women gone off to their gardens, or to the bush to hunt or fetch betel nut. Except for some ancient, too decrepit ever again to leave the sun in the dooryard, the troop of boys might have the place to themselves. More often than not it was just their noisy games they played, but if someone thought there might be adventure or a piece of pig within one of the boarded-up houses, they quite naturally got themselves involved in an escapade. In some respects this monkey band served as auxiliary eyes and ears to the hamlet for they were fleet and they were everywhere. If a calamity occurred during the day, if a house caught fire or a woman were discovered to have hung herself inside her house, they were likely to discover it and set up a clamor.

When their elders were about, Bantao agreed, the boys did not greatly curtail their boisterous play, but they might receive a kick, a slap, or a smart blow with a stick if they came bumping into the midst of a men's group engaged in smoking and talk—especially if a visitor were present. Sometimes it would be a mere token, with harsh but insincere threats and a symbolic blow delivered in thin air. At this the grinning mob would scamper away, displaying a confidence in their joint defiance that they did not dare individually.

When not running with a gang, the child's lot, between the toddler stage and initiation, was to run errands, fetch food, water, or firewood, and to bring objects such as a lime gourd or some leaf tobacco when suddenly desired. These duties were erratic and obedience was as erratically enforced. Younger boys were more likely than older ones to respond without urging and anyone was more likely to respond to the request of a senior man with prestige. With one's own parents, consistent non-compliance was likely to result in a slap on the ears, as Bantao reported of Ooti, followed by tears and a brief sulk. The ears were a prime target of parental blows because it is the boy's thinking, implicitly associated with his hearing, which was considered at fault. "You slap his ears and then he can hear/ think right," Bantao explained.

The older boy was proud to be taken to the bush with his father to hunt small marsupials. Although not very important economically, game had many ceremonial uses and hunting was the quintessence of masculine activity. Bantao always enjoyed describing his hunting exploits and the dog he trained. In the bush, rather than in the *kunai,* reside nearly all the few supernaturals that threaten the Agarabi. Knowledge of these and especially of hunting ritual and magic became a point of pride with a man, while apprenticeship set off a youth from mere children. It is not clear that Bantao's apprenticeship was very extensive. He was quite defensive when contradicted by other informants after he had declared to me that there was no rule about returning the bones of game to the place where it was taken. "He doesn't have it right," one said within earshot, and Bantao reddened as he floundered fecklessly for excuse. He later tried to make amends by giving me unusually elaborate details of a prehunt ritual.

Another form of hunting had a special interest for bands of late preadolescent boys and girls, although younger ones might also participate. The capturing of rats and small field marsupials by hand and stick took place in the *kunai* in the full of the moon. Although the immediate purpose was sport and meat, stylized sex-play often followed for the older youths. The ultimate symbolism of the rat hunt was connected with the moon and its association with the first menses of a girl and hence her eventual nubility. The occasions were marked by good-natured cries in the clear night air as someone saw a rat dart out of its nest and excitedly called to another to grab it. Gradually the moonlit figures moved farther away and the cries grew fainter as they tired of the sport and the older youths gravitated toward the girls' club house. Bantao recalled such nights with obvious relish.

Until very recently—well after Bantao had left boyhood behind—the range within which the boys' or separate girls' groups could safely roam was quite restricted. It scarcely went beyond the garden fences, but even there the ambushing of men, women, or children with their mothers was all too well known. Women and small children were almost always accompanied, herd-like, by armed men, even to go only as far as the gardens but certainly if they had to go beyond. Heedless indeed was the man who left his bow and arrow beyond arm's reach during the fighting time of year. People rarely went very far on journeys, in marked contrast to the open coming and going on the main roads of the last few years. The little used footpaths were then "like rat trails," according to Bantao.

Even on the paths within the hamlet or district precincts there was danger other than armed ambush. As a small child, too young to know all his kin, Bantao was cautioned against taking gifts of food from strangers. A sorcerer posing as an "uncle" might give him a poisoned banana in feigned affection, he was told. Taking the life of a child or woman was a simple matter, but for a strong man in his prime semen might be the only lethal exuvial substance a sorcerer could employ. For a child faeces is more than sufficient, and so Bantao began a lifelong indoctrination about excretory functions. The prudent man, the one who lives long, is careful where he defecates and where and with whom he copulates. Ultimately his only safety lies in using the streams or in rinsing away the faeces or semen afterwards. Even so, Bantao believes that a sorcerer may lurk in the reeds by a stream and obtain his requirements by means of a long wand held beneath the intended victim. The principal defense of the immature in view of their childish incaution is held to be that their lives are of less interest to sorcerers than those of fighting men.

Within the hamlet itself Bantao and the other Agarabi children learned to fear the dangers that lurk outside at night in human form. Stout slabs are made fast between the doorposts of the houses and the walls are kept tightly thatched. It is not only having to leave the warmth of the black, smoky hut to relieve himself that makes the Agarabi alert and watchful; this is the time when a swift arrow can claim its victim. The death the lurking sorcerer works may be slower but it is hardly more acceptable.

The white man's coming has wrought no perceptible increase in skepticism about sorcery. Bantao not only learned but still accepts his childhood lessons. He was in fact most concerned about the welfare of my wife and daughter during the dry season, as this is the time *par excellence* for sorcerers to practice their black arts. He carefully and soberly pointed out to us the dangers involved—despite his having been baptised in the Adventist faith.

When Bantao was about 3 or 4 years old, what was unquestionably the most remarkable thing in his lifetime occurred. As he recalled it, the first white men were Lutheran missionaries who came with an entourage of coastal or Markham Valley bearers, themselves but for their skin color as awesome as the white men. Bantao's detailed knowledge of their coming is doubtless largely based on hearsay, but the fear and uneasiness that these first disturbing contacts must have created among his elders could scarcely but have impressed him. However, subsequent familiarity with the outsider and reluctance to admit their earlier naïveté, even to themselves, have robbed retrospect of much of the wonder, if not the terror, that the events must have evoked. Some of the Agarabi thought the strangers were ghosts and women would burst out wailing at sight of them, thinking to recognize dead ancestors. They came from the direction—the Finisterre Range across the Markham—where dwelt the ghosts of the departed. Pigs were hastily killed so that the men might smear themselves and their women and children with the blood, the strongest protection they knew against sickness or death from the nameless danger. The pigs were then given over in order to propitiate the strangers with the best that could be offered. In return they received gifts of shell, a few knives, an axe or two, and some cloth. The ornamental shells were practically as new and mysterious to the people as the steel, and all these objects, too, were immediately treated with pig's blood to neutralize the strong and harmful power that must adhere to them. The large cowrie shells, Bantao admitted with smiling embarrassment, were thought by some to be the hardened fruit or nut of an unknown tree; the cloth was at first considered "ghost skin"; the knife blades were explained as the rock-hard leaves of a bush which evidently grew in the distant land whence the ghosts had come. (I did not embarrass him further by asking him what he now considered these objects to be.)

After a brief circuit of the area, their every move anxiously reported, the missionaries went back, leaving behind an incredulous and awe-struck native population to wonder what it all meant. Somewhat later—"a year" as Bantao remembers it—three native evangelists from Finschhafen returned and built a thatched house to serve as a school. However, although nearby, this was in an Agarabi district unfriendly to Bantao's people so they could not go to see the "school." Afterwards, the white missionary came and established the present station at Raipinka in neighboring Kamano territory. In the course of these events the Agarabi were to see their first firearms, which were generally represented to them, and which as fighters they came to accept, as the key to their changing lives. Although the second group of white men to be seen were thought the ghostly fathers of the first, Bantao's people gradually decided these beings were, if not like themselves, at least not actually the ghosts of their ancestors.

Presently other white men came who were said to be looking for "golmoni," prospectors who followed the streams and who seemed mysteriously interested in the sand on the banks or the bottom. Two "golmoni" men built a small hut and stopped briefly on a stream near where Bantao was living with Ooti. He speaks of hanging about their camp and making himself useful by running little errands. He says he remembers being commended by the fossickers for his prepossessing ways—this necessarily in pidgin which presumably no Agarabi then spoke!

Furnishing food and women were the two principal means offered by the *kampan* (company), as the prospecters came to be called, for obtaining the now desired shells, axes, blankets, and other goods.

Another way was shortly discovered for obtaining the new things of which the *kampan* appeared to have an endless supply: theft or open seizure. Bantao relished telling how the men put several *kampan* to flight and took their goods. One of their victims, according to him, told them that soon a *kiap* would come, a man who was a fighter and who would put a stop to all this.

Bantao's life still lay almost wholly before him and if to the elders the strangers had come without warning or explanation, for Bantao's generation the newcomers were but one among a great many other things that had yet to be learned and understood. Of course there was a difference: the young could be oriented authoritatively by parents and elders to some of the experiences which lay ahead; but the other events which punctuated Bantao's youth left the elders as perplexed as if they were children themselves—indeed, more so, for they had no parental authorities other than the white man to explain things to them or by example to help them accept their inherent rightness. Moreover, for the coming generation of Agarabi, parental authority was increasingly shaken in some of the spheres in which it had previously been most developed and most secure, above all in fighting. Nor was there in Agarabi society a central leadership to deal with the exigencies of contact. This was a critical time for a young boy to be starting life, especially a boy who seems, at least in retrospect, to have suffered a keen sense of deprivation, to have been born lost.

When hamlets of the Asupuya district to the north were burned flat, their gardens despoiled, and their pigs shot to teach them a lesson, it was apparent that the *kiap* about whom they had been warned was indeed quite a different sort of man from either the missionary or the *kampan,* whom they had already seen. Many of the Asupuya were taken as captives to Kainantu by the *kiap*. There they were kept by police armed with rifles and bayonets. This punishment was something called "calaboose," they presently learned, and it was to become an important institution in Agarabi life.

Bantao's people could no more understand the *kiap's* "law" at once—if they had yet heard it explained—than the Asupuya could understand that a prisoner did not run away from the calaboose, even if given the opportunity. Like practically everyone else, Bantao knows intimately the details of this hard apprenticeship. His village will not soon forget one day in particular in 1933, when two Asupuya men, Anongke and Afibayo, escaped from their police guards at Kainantu. The route back to Asupuya lay through country into which the two men alone would scarcely have ventured in daylight if there had been any choice, for territory held by the enemy Abiyentu and Kasiyentu lineages and their allies lay athwart the path. Bantao's kinsmen, Abiyentu men, out hunting wild pig, spotted them and immediately gave pursuit. It was several miles before they caught Anongke. Some of them held him while others shot him to death with arrows. Afibayo, who was a stronger runner, lasted long enough to get hold of a bow and arrows, thrust into his trembling hands in full flight by a kinsman of his mother's, who was doubtless as startled to see an unarmed fighter as the poor man was desperate for some means of defense. The gasping Afibayo at last sought refuge in a stand of pitpit. There, after his arrows were spent, the killers found him, knocked him down with their heavy, black wooden shields, and standing over him, shot him again and again. He called the name of his father and his male kinsmen as he lay in agony, and he screamed hoarsely at his tormentors that he was too strong for their arrows to make him die quickly. Then he expired. "He was just like an *ayafabanta,* this man," said Bantao matter-of-factly.

The Abiyentu people could only think that they had been unbelievably lucky in killing two enemies so easily. A few weeks later, however, their hamlet was surrounded one night, the palisade cut and breached with bayonets. The women started screaming and running about. Rifles roared out and men were killed inside the men's house or as they tried to flee through the escape door in the rear. Nearly all who were not immediately killed or seriously wounded ran into the nearby pitpit to escape and presently the police boys began to carry out the dead or wounded that lay inside the house. One man, Ijuke, in his fright had climbed the center pole to hide up next to the roof instead of trying to flee. A police boy heard a rustle in the thatch and looked up, whereupon Ijuke dropped down the pole, grabbed his bow and some arrows, and stood, his young son clinging in panic to his knees. As the police boy came on, he let fly an arrow which took the man in the shoulder. The startled constable dropped his rifle and scrambled back out the passage yelling that there was still a man alive inside. Bantao tells the story in great detail, he has heard it so many times.

For some reason which will never be known, the young Australian

A.D.O. leading the patrol bent down and started inside the door. Firing his revolver blindly several times as he crouched along the posts lining the entryway, he called out some command in pidgin. Ijuke, stepping from behind a post, drew a *kamosa,* one of the most beautiful of all the wicked, barbed arrows of the Agarabi, and discharged it full into the breast of the white man. The *kiap* fell down and Ijuke quickly transfixed him a second time with a *keento.* The police surrounding the men's house on all sides were summoned by the cry of their fallen leader, and all ran and clustered in the doorway to see what had happened. The terror-stricken Ijuke, who had used his last arrow, seized the chance to run out the escape door to the pitpit and safety, tossing his son into the arms of another man in his flight. The young *kiap,* who had just come to this new country, died of his wounds in Salamaua, after being flown from Kainantu in a small plane. The Abiyentu did not even know his name, a rare thing indeed as they knew the names of most of their victims. But Bantao's people lost ten men all told before the affair was over. So many casualties in a single engagement was unheard of in this region and their loss was a stunning blow to the fighting force of so small a community.

Some time later peace ceremonies were conducted with the *kiap* who succeeded Ian Mack. This man made a speech, as they recall it, in which it was said that now the fighting should stop: Australia had lost men and their people had lost men. In view of the disaster which had befallen them, the people were almost pathetically relieved to be able to consider the score even. If they did not yet understand all about the "law," they appreciated fully now that there could be no opposing it. It was a great comfort to them when Bantao's (own) father was subsequently named a *luluai* (government appointed village official), their first and one of the first in the area. He was given the brass badge which identified him—and through him his kinsmen—as being on the side of the *kiap;* but far more important, it signified that the *kiap* was henceforth on their side.

To both the miners and the government officers, these people doubtless still seemed the same "wild pigs," filthy and truculent, as when first seen by the Europeans a few years earlier. On the surface Agarabi life appeared to be the same, but the knowledge that they might no longer undertake their own defense was devastating. "Wild pigs" or not, in their own hearts the people knew that they had now become completely "cold." If dates can be assigned to such matters, 1933 was certainly a turning point in the lives of Bantao and the Agarabi men to follow.

In telling of his initiation, Bantao insisted that he faced the prospect with fears no greater than the rest of his age group. The basic purpose of this painful ceremony, performed jointly for all boys of a certain age, is to assert their masculinity and their manly duties by putting them to a series of cruel tests. The ceremony is also the occasion for severing the boys from their lives as children and from nearly every aspect of the women's sphere. They are admitted into residence in the men's house, a stage that marks the beginning of several years of constant but less formal indoctrination. Formerly *iyampo,* they now become *pumara,* and will be shown the sacred flutes and the bullroarer. They discover closely guarded male secrets such as cane swallowing in which a length of flexible rattan is passed through the mouth to the stomach and then extracted again. The bloody rites of the initiation itself are likewise kept secret from them until now.

Enough is known beforehand of these ordeals to terrify the novices, and the boys will often try to run away at the last moment. Once they have all been herded together, they are escorted toward a stream where the painful part of the business largely takes place. There is a mock battle between the boys and the men, both sides armed with sticks. The battle is real enough so that cuts, bruises, and occasionally more serious injuries are sustained. Some of the initiates cry like children. The death of one boy sometime in the past, from a stone adze wound in his back, was alleged by Bantao, although he insisted that the sham battle was not used by the initiators— fathers among them—as an opportunity to settle scores against the youths. Should a boy slip away from the circle to hide in the pitpit, however, Bantao agreed that the men would use their power mercilessly to discourage further cowardice. It was not the fight that Bantao feared the most, he said—probably because there was still some freedom left to duck and parry. He was much more anxious about the nose-bleeding and the cutting of the glans penis.

After the mock fight the boys are taken directly to the water where each is held by one or more men while another twists sharp blades of grass fastened to sticks up the boy's nostrils. After this has been done with two sets of sticks, the initiate's dripping head is thrust forward and his blood flows into the stream. Then he is held again while one of the men pulls back the foreskin of the boy's penis to reveal the glans, and three or four superficial incisions are made with a bamboo sliver. At this point Bantao said, laughingly, that he cried, "Oh, Mother! Mother! Why didn't you have all girls!" When he heard the command given to hold him for a second time, Bantao said he broke loose and ran and hid in a tree. "Lots of *pumara* do that," he assured me. "Our ancestors used to do it too." (Another man flatly contends that Bantao fled the initiation altogether, taking refuge with his kinsmen in another district, and that he had to be brought back. This he gave as an example of Bantao's cowardice.) There is no blood from the scratches on the glans, Bantao commented, only red marks which are painful for a day or so. An ordeal with a more drastic effect is that of pushing the ribs of stinging nettles up the urethra. Sucking their breath through clenched teeth (which Bantao demonstrated) the boys dance around on tiptoes, every muscle tensed. "It's like fire. After it comes out, you cannot p—s easy for five nights. You begin by p—sing a little bit but it nearly kills you. The big men all stand around and laugh," he said feelingly.

As they are brought back from the water to the men's house the initiates are shielded from the glances of the girls and women by men who walk beside them holding screens of leaves. Once properly inside the men's house for the first time in their lives, the exhausted youths do their best to keep from falling asleep next to the fire while the *akoriye* myth of plant and animal names and origins is sung far into the night. The following morning, when the main pig feast takes place, the women come, and the novices' mothers and sisters and grandmothers will have their first look at the boys of yesterday. The lesson of the ceremony is made clear to the youths in exhortations by an elderly woman and by their mothers' brothers: "In going to live in the men's house, you must forsake the constant company of women, your mother included. You must no longer receive food from the hand of a woman, lest your fathers be angry. Now you are a *pumara*."

It is as a *pumara* that a youth first tries his hand with the opposite sex. Bantao (unseconded by other informants) insisted that younger, uninitiated boys sometimes practice sodomy, usually with a dull boy or half-wit if there is one in the village at the time. In any event the children easily become aware of adult sexual relations, living as they do in small houses with their mothers, and also spying on adults. Like their elders they enjoy the antics of the half-wit who loves to spring from behind on women bending over their garden work. He pulls up their bark skirts and feigns copulation before they turn shrieking upon him with their digging sticks, as he runs away cackling.

After initiation the youths become increasingly involved in courtship and formalized sex play, generally with a series of girls. This continues until marriage and the birth of one's children when manhood really begins. The sex play, now familiarly known in pidgin as "kiss," takes place either at night in the girls' club house or in a secluded spot in the *kunai* during the day. In the traditional recumbent position, which Bantao described with ill-suppressed pleasure, the boy cradles his head on the girl's arm, lying close beside her and the two rub their faces together. Both sexes, once initiated, are quite open about their enjoyment of this form of courtship.

Among the things Bantao as a *pumara* learned from his elders in the men's house was the art of attracting women, for example, by playing the bamboo jew's-harp with seductive skill or wearing a long, waving feather or leaf-plume stuck in his hair. Yet at the same time the admonition to restrict carefully one's contact with females was in Bantao's youth still adhered to and if the older men noticed that a *pumara's* place was too seldom slept in, they would take him out and bleed his nose with the grass sticks. However, Bantao said that this limitation of sexual activity has largely been broken down at present.

The penalties are high for being discovered in adultery, Bantao and all others agreed, but the potential for fornication is obviously higher. Success with women is complexly linked with success in general, which has always meant prowess in all the male activities, such as fighting, oratory, dancing, dreaming, and masculine ostentation. Theoretically a man is irresistible to women, although it is recognized that this is more true for the successful man than for the unsuccessful one. Hence to a young man success with the opposite sex is a measure of his claim to manhood.

Older, married women are likely to introduce a youth to sexual intercourse. Bantao's first invitation was one of this sort although apparently not culminating in copulation: "I was still a new *pumara* and a virgin when a crazy woman from Anabantu chased me and wanted to have intercourse with me. I was afraid. I told myself that she was a bad woman so I did not want to go up her. She is dead now." Either party to adultery typically accuses the other of being the instigator immediately upon any hint or fear that the affair has been discovered. An affair with an older woman may appeal to a youth, therefore, because of the lesser likelihood that she will voluntarily reveal it or that he will be accused of instigating it. Bantao's rejection of the opportunity in this case is probably untypical.

All men have at their command various forms of love sorcery which are compelling to any woman, married or not, and quite beyond her power to resist. The security of a husband, therefore, lies in being an outstandingly successful man, hence attractive to women, but also feared by potential adulterers. Sometimes a man whose wife is unfaithful to him is accordingly accused of not having looked out well for her. This refers ambiguously to a lack of care but often indirectly to a lack of manhood. Bantao was frank to characterize certain husbands this way and a number of men so characterized him. The principal deterrent to adultery is fear of discovery and Bantao assumed that if the probability of discovery were slight enough, nearly any man and perhaps the majority of women would sooner or later seize the chance.

Besides individual magic, Bantao enthusiastically described ceremonial love sorcery for attracting the women of other districts. He claimed to have participated in the last *ampu,* as this is called, although he was at the time an S.D.A. convert. He was criticized for it by a fellow Adventist, but reported being unmoved by the criticism, replying that *ampu* is a "good thing" since it causes no harm and is enjoyable. In learning not only various forms of woman-attracting sorcery but also in learning his role as a man generally, the youth succeeds in being sufficiently attractive to obtain his future wife—or wives if he aspires to a greater measure of success; but in precisely the same measure he also becomes, at least potentially, a challenge to other men, in jeopardizing the fidelity of their wives or fiancées and their ability to keep them.

Bantao was born too late to experience the full apprenticeship in combat undergone by every previous generation. He has of course heard innumerable times each remembered exploit, such as the shooting of the *kiap*. He has once seen fighting—enough to know what it is, at least—and he has seen several enemy men horribly outraged. In one case a man from a nearby district was killed while held at close hand, his belly laid open with the bamboo blade of an arrow while he writhed and screamed. Bantao also remembers with obvious pleasure helping to abuse two enemy men who were accused of sorcery, bludgeoning one of them on the head with a heavy sugar cane. The latter incident occurred only a few years ago, when to kill a man meant serious trouble with the *kiap*.

But Bantao has not worked his way up to the front of the fight in the roughly age-graded system, beginning with carrying bundles of spare arrows as a boy of 10 or 12, handing them forward to older *pumara* who in turn gave them to the shield men. The front line of fighters was followed by youths about ready to carry the fight themselves and these older apprentices could learn the feel of shooting a human being when a fallen enemy was cut off by the retreat of his kinsmen. The *pumara* would immediately run forward with the fighters as they closed in to put arrow after arrow into the dying man. They might then help to disembowel and dismember him, transfixing the severed penis or hand with a shaft into the victim's eye, and perhaps urinating upon the corpse. Bantao can recount such experiences in detail, but he has not had them.

Bantao thus has no final way of knowing how he might measure up to the ideal still flaunted by his elders, and he probably has more than a few self-doubts. Hitting captive sorcerers is not the same as facing flying arrows and a fiercely painted, taunting enemy. Everyone estimates him as a "cold" man. He obviously lacks the self-assurance, the style, and reckless temper, or he would not be so regarded without having been put to a formal test. Bantao's elder brother has shot a man, ambushed with the help of a kinsman while the victim was at work in his garden. The brother is considered a "hot" man and his greater taste for violence, probably more than his few years of seniority, sufficed to prove him the possessor of traditional male virtues. Even if Bantao wants to consider himself a victim of history, being "cold" is not the inevitable consequence. Some of Bantao's own age-mates are among his readiest critics. One says he had the opportunity to fight—presumably during the war years—and deliberately ran away from it.

Though he is among the oldest of the first Agarabi generation to grow up without the bow constantly in hand, Bantao is, of course, not alone in being unproven. Most of his contemporaries have a marked if ambivalent respect for the accomplishments of the older men, as has Bantao despite his recent espousal of mission doctrine. There are certain prestigeful attainments now in the contact world, to be sure, in which the young men, even the unmarried, generally excel their elders, and Bantao often speaks patronizingly of the lack of "savvy" in some of his seniors. But there is at the same time little question that manhood is still largely defined in the qualities, if no longer the exploits, of the aggressive past.

Perhaps the discrepancy between his temperament and his powerful physique has made the issue more poignant for Bantao. There is a clear association between prowess and physical size, even though some of the proven, able men of yesteryear are much smaller than he. Aggressiveness can naturally be recognized, regardless of size, just as the lack of aggressiveness is not concealed by Bantao's stature. Nevertheless, the great fighters (*ayafabanta*) of the past are uniformly described as "big men," both in respect to their physical stature and to their expansive oratory and other aggressive qualities. Indeed, Bantao believes with the others that the great men of "before" were physically larger than anyone living today, as were the pigs, the *kunai,* and nearly everything else that mattered in the landscape. "Now we are diminished," the older men say. Of the generation come of age since fighting was stopped by the *kiap* they sometimes add, "They merely grow up; they do not become big men." Bantao's bigness is only physical although he is proud of a certain ability in village soccer, which he half-consciously equates with fighting prowess.

Although there was but slight military action, the intrusion of the Pacific War into the remote mountain valleys of Kainantu was a period of unbelievable stress—truly at times terror—for the natives. Civilian administration of native affairs was disrupted and the miners and missionaries fled the area. The discovery of the *kiap's* vulnerability was a shock to both sides. This unchallengeable power had constantly been demonstrated to the natives in various ways and they had heretofore witnessed scarcely an exception. For almost ten years no more than two or three government officers at any given time, backed by a mere two score or so of the native constabulary, had been able to dominate the lives of thousands of Agarabi, Kamano, Gadsup, and Tairora. All at once these carefully pacified villagers were "wild pigs" again. They even threatened white men openly. The Agarabi, already confused by the riddles of recent years, suddenly had to cope with another change and a radical reversal of the order of things. The *kiap's* power dwindled and seemed to vanish, whether ever to return, who could say? No one could yet explain why or whence it originally came. Eventually village tempers boiled over at the increase of interdistrict provocations, and the men decided to risk retaliation upon their traditional enemies. To their amazement nothing happened. At the same time, this surprising impunity meant that they could no longer count upon the law in their own favor, so a renewal of fighting was doubly inevitable—and not without pleasure for those with a taste for it. This is the fighting that Bantao remembers.

Police boys deserted their commands and Bantao's people began to sense that the *kiap* himself had some sort of powerful enemy, called "Japan," the cause of his "running away." Moreover, this enemy seemed able to meet him on equal terms, that is, with rifles. The Highland peoples shortly learned, in fact, that there was something even more terrifying than rifles—bombs! The Kainantu station was bombed and strafed and a woman from Anona, another Agarabi district, was killed by bomb fragments in a way these people had never seen. Other bombs fell about the area and swift, snarling planes that spat bullets would sweep suddenly in over the mountain tops without warning. Because of the anxieties of the war years, both more acute and more sustained than any before or since, the period is called in retrospect "the bad time" and Bantao almost inevitably uses it to date occurrences in the recent past—before, during, or since the "bad time."

Eventually the military government regained its balance and was able to stabilize the native situation up to a point until active civilizing work might again be undertaken and scores settled with the "collaborationist" villages. Interdistrict fighting was again suppressed, in the course of which Bantao's village lost two men to police rifles. The police boys also had the villagers dig slit trenches against further bombing and ordered them henceforth to carry any white man's cargo and to supply food to whomever might demand it. When police boys could not be spared, native evangelists of the two local missions were strategically stationed in the villages to keep peace and to insure compliance with the *kiap's* orders. Like the constables for whom they were substituting, the mission boys were for a time issued military rifles and bayonets which earned them nearly as much admiration as the police.

During the later stages of the war a Seventh Day Adventist evangelist came to live in their village and Bantao, along with an agemate, Kurunke, attached themselves to the man as errand boys, cooks, and fetchers of wood and water. Their later affiliation with the Adventist mission doubtless stemmed from influences at this time; and the power of the evangelist and his rifle may have had as much to do with it as some of the Christian teachings. The resident police or mission boy generally exercised a large measure of authority and it was not difficult for a youth like Bantao to regard him as a strong protector, even against the traditional authority of the elder men. One of the mission boys, in fact, intervened to prevent the initiation of Kurunke, who sought his protection.

The war period with its attendant tensions and anxieties brought in its wake a social movement, a form of "Cargo Cult" that rapidly seized many of the Agarabi. It swept over the area so swiftly that people in retrospect have little notion whence it came. In the Kainantu area the physical manifestation was a shivering or shaking seizure as men and women were suddenly possessed by the spirit. The adherents of the movement proclaimed their faith in an impending return of their ancestors with revolutionary consequences. At the same time there was considerable awe about the prospect. It was not necessary to be possessed to become an adherent, although those seized were naturally among the strongest witnesses. Various tentative proofs of the millennium were asserted, including dreams, visitations, ghostly tokens, and promises of supernatural wealth if certain prescribed behavior were carried out.

Bantao was characteristically evasive when asked about his credence in the beliefs that remained in 1954. In fact, he insisted for a time that he had no knowledge of any such thing. He knows that the "whistle" cult, as it is now sometimes called, is opposed by the Seventh Day Adventist mission to which he still nominally adheres, and he shares the general fear that the *kiap* disapproves and might punish the followers of the cult if he found them out. Bantao finally took refuge in his claim that he was too young at the time of the first or wartime phase of the cult to have a firm idea about the ghost prophesy. Nevertheless, it appears that as a youth of 15 or 16 he was involved in at least one of the attempts to achieve the prophesy. He was taken on as a "cook boy" in a group who briefly made such an attempt. A man of his village, Danonke, was persuaded by the promise of Ojabayo, who came from another village, to show them or give them some of the "ancestors' cartridges." Danonke agreed to contribute to the necessary provisions and brought his wife and one or two others along, Bantao among them. Together they built a large house in the style of a men's house, while Ojabayo, who had promised the ghostly ammunition, dressed himself in a facsimile of police boy's clothing and acted as "boss."

All of the group, men, women, and children, lived and slept in the "men's house" they had built, waiting to see their ancestors and the cartridges and other things they would bring. During the day they would "exercise" with their wooden "rifles." Several of them frequently underwent the shivering of possession and listened for ghostly messages. Apparently they did no ordinary work, such as gardening, their needs being supplied by others. To them it seemed possible that the "Japan," who had penetrated the area, might somehow be involved with the prophesy, perhaps in trying to help their ancestors come. Although many "messages" were received during the months they lived there, the cartridges did not materialize. Bantao himself had no seizure, "only the big men and women." Once, however, he saw the surface of the stream nearby splash up and some "messages" written on paper flew into the air and fell at his feet. No one could read them. Ojabayo counseled patience and assured the group of eventual success: the cartridges were imminent. But another event rather than gradual disillusionment caused the house to be abandoned. One day when the "cooks" had gone to get pitpit for the fire, Ojabayo found himself alone with the wife of Danonke. He invited her to have intercourse with him and afterwards ran away. This purely earthly affair seemingly put an end to the immediate quest for the supernatural, although the participants did not all abandon their faith.

Eventually interest in the cult waned, or at least the amount of energy that was devoted to it dwindled. The lack of continued effort did not wholly reflect a lack of conviction, to be sure, for conviction still exists; but unmistakably the failure of the ancestors to come at that time, the dramatic reassertion of authority by the *kiap,* and the cessation of the awful bombings of the Japanese campaign in New Guinea all contributed to a lessening of fervor. Moreover, prewar activities reappeared to claim the cultists' energies, or new ones were introduced.

Apparently it was during the late war years that Bantao had his first experience in regular employment for Europeans. One of his earliest jobs was a brief stint for the "D-D-man" (agricultural agent) at Aiyura. What is now the Highlands Agricultural Experiment Station at Aiyura was established early in the war in order to grow a supply of quinine for the Allies after the Japanese seizure of sources in the East Indies. Indeed, pulling stumps and clearing ground for cinchona seedlings constituted a good part of Bantao's work at Aiyura. The Aiyura station is an easy day's walk from his own district but the work was nonetheless a great adventure for him and the others who went. It was his introduction to the labor line, an important complex of knowledge and social usage of the post-contact caste world. The experience obviously left quite an impression. Bantao worked alongside men with whom such an association would have been suicidal under any conceivable circumstances a few years before; and he saw men from parts of New Guinea, some no more than sixty or eighty miles away, whose very existence was unknown to his grandfathers.

Meeting the sons of hostile Agarabi lineages and districts on neutral, white man's ground, under an alien truce, no doubt made Bantao and his companions "colder" still as heirs of the traditional enmities of their fathers and bearers of the obligation to fight and make sorcery. At the same time, the association with enemies and strangers by no means automatically produced a feeling of brotherhood and charity. In retelling his experiences at Aiyura, Bantao emphasized the physical aggression of the bossboys against Agarabi workers and the fights of Agarabi or men from his village with those from other districts. It is worth noting that Agarabi could, up to a point, still make common cause against men of other areas.

The few coastal natives in the area kept the locals in considerable awe of themselves and one told them that he had a white woman for a wife. He had to leave her in Australia, he alleged, lest every *kanaka* get the idea he would like to marry a white missis. Nothing serious happened to Bantao, he related, although "one of the masters kicked my arse" for ruining a batch of porridge he had been told to cook for the laborers. This mishap was mentioned smilingly with a "we-know-better-now" air.

On the whole Bantao liked the work. He reported with great satisfaction that the master in charge commended him upon their performance: "The men of your village work strong." After having worked "ten moons," they were paid off in knives, tomahawks, calico, and similar goods. Bantao commented that they were now beginning to wear calico as *laplaps* instead of simply as a substitute for the short bark cloak of their fathers. The master in charge asked them if they did not wish to work longer but they said that now they wanted to take it easy. They would go back to their village and after a while try another station. "That is the way with everyone: they don't want to stay a long time at one job. Besides, some of us were thinking about being washed [baptized], some at the Lutheran, some at the Seven Day." An age-mate who enjoyed pointing out weaknesses or inconsistencies in Bantao said that actually he "ran away" from the work at Aiyura without finishing his time. He said the reason was that "the Kainantu men were making sorcery there."

Shortly after the cessation of local hostilities, Bantao and some of the other younger men and youths of his village went as cargo carriers with the police on a patrol to Yawna. That Agarabi district was to be punished for its supposed collaboration with a Japanese detachment during their brief incursion into the area. Two Australian soldiers had been killed in a surprise attack on an outpost near the district and the wartime O.I.C. took it for granted that Yawna people had tipped off the Japanese. Treachery and retaliation are warp and woof of the Agarabi way of doing things, but the extent and ease of this revenge had no native precedent. "The police really broomed that place! But I wasn't sorry for them. They were our enemies," Bantao said. Enemies or not, the demonstration showed that opposition to the *gaman* would continue to be costly despite the recent brief lapse in its power, and those who escaped the fate were as deeply impressed as the Yawna.

During the altercation two police boys to whom Bantao had attached himself raped a captured woman. "You don't belong to the *gaman*," she cried to Bantao. "Why do you help them take me?"

He said that he answered her saying, "Maski! You're no kinsman of mine! If they f——k you, they f——k you! You just lie still!" Bantao did not himself rape her—a foolish thing indeed for an Agarabi, to give semen into enemy hands! But he apparently helped the police boys seize the woman and take her inside a house. "It's all right. It's not the same as shooting people," he commented mildly.

After the war the people of the area had other lessons in the power of the government. Some also had their first real opportunity to see themselves as the European had earlier seen them—this time from the same side of the rifle sights. The chance came when Bantao and some of his age group joined one of the early postwar civilian *kiaps* to "work bush." They went down into newly opened Fore country as cargo boys for the line of police who were to establish the government's authority. Practically never before had they seen people "newer" than themselves, whole districts still dressed in bark with no cloth or *laplaps,* still smeared with pig grease, with long braided hair, and without even a halting use of pidgin. Perhaps they noted the wide stare of fright or bewilderment in the eyes of these people —the "wild look" the Europeans saw. If so, they may have realized that the look mirrored their own expression a scant twelve years or so earlier. Bantao and his kinsmen learned to belittle the Fore as "bush kanaka" and to appreciate the aptness of the name "wild pigs" when these elusive and terrified people deserted their villages and, like game, sought concealment in inaccessible places. In relation to the new *kanakas,* the Agarabi obviously had savvy, just as to a lesser degree Bantao and the younger men had it in comparison with their own elders. They could patronize the Fore and condescend to them as the *kiap* and his police had always done to the Agarabi.

It was on this patrol with the *kiap* that Bantao and a companion were confronted by two Fore bowmen. Challenged, the two Agarabi gave no ground. The Fore made as if to draw arrows whereupon Bantao and his fellow villager shot first. Dropping their bows in fright, the Fore ran up to them and clung tightly to them, begging for their lives. Two police boys appeared at this point and belabored the captives about the head and shoulders with their own bows. Bantao's heroic role in this episode seems at least in part pure fantasy.

Later, or perhaps on another occasion, Bantao found an attractive young Fore woman hiding in the pitpit. "She was surely a good woman." She had an infant which he held when he turned her over to four police boys to be raped. It would be unfair to censure Bantao for acting despicably in this or the instance previously mentioned. Rape or adultery by police boys was a common practice, almost a perquisite of their office; nor do the Agarabi place much emphasis upon chastity or the rights of women, let alone enemy or strange women. Quite possibly Bantao had no way of denying the police. More important is that he was apparently making every effort to ingratiate and affiliate himself with the police, the *kiap,* and the white man at large. So he seized women for police boys, he held Fore fighters at bay, and at Aiyura he worked so well that he drew praise from the master.

Sometime after the war, Bantao was married for the first time. He must have been from 16 to 18 years old, although in indicating his age at the time, he selected for comparison a much younger village lad, a youth who had only just been initiated and was beginning to "kiss" for the first time.

I was still just a new *pumara* like Bese and I decided to work a garden. I was hungry and I did not like to ask my mother and father for food. I wasn't thinking at all of getting married.

I worked quite a piece of ground, dug all the trenches and built the fences myself, near my [own] father's garden. My elder brother came to help me. My father had told me that if I just did nothing, a woman would not come to me—only if I planted a garden. [He had just said that marriage was no part of his motives.] A girl of our village, married into Punano [another district], came to the garden. She asked, "Do you work here?" I said, "Yes, why do you ask?" She said she was just asking. She was already married to the Punano man. She said she would like to stay [i.e., marry Bantao]. I said I planned to marry an unmarried girl. She said that now that she had come, I could not marry an unmarried girl. I laughed. I gave her some sweet potatoes from the garden and sent her away to cook them since the matter had not been straightened. [Although Bantao does not say so, he very likely had intercourse with the woman. The behavior he describes for her is as bold as that he ascribes to himself is passive. When there is possible trouble over adultery, of course, it is conventional to blame the partner, but this incident was already several years in the past, and there was but slight reason on that account, therefore, to ascribe all initiative to the woman.]

She was staying with Pelino [in our village] and Pelino asked her where the sweet potatoes she had came from. She said from Bantao. Pelino said, "Uh! You already have a man!" She said she did not like Punano [district] and wanted to marry me. I had been kissing with her before she was married. Our *tultul* [a village officer] liked her, too, and forced her to kiss with him. He tried to win her from me and we came close to fighting, but I prevailed. [This presumably refers to the time before she married so that Bantao's subsequent adultery and marriage with her probably have no bearing on his claim to having bested the *tultul*. His relationship with this *tultul*, in my observation, was typically anything but the way Bantao describes it here. The two men were on friendly terms, but Bantao was generally subordinate and once backed down without a murmur on an issue where justice was strongly in his own favor.]

The *luluai* from Punano, together with her husband, came and inquired about the woman—why she had not returned. They gave their consent [to the proposed separation and marriage to Bantao] but the husband put sorcery in my doorway and my knees swelled up. He put it there at night. My knees stayed that way a long time and they still swell up if I dig trenches or walk about in damp ground.

Now a [patrol officer] came through, "working bush." The Punano told the [patrol officer] that I had taken his wife. [Bantao, prompted, mentioned her name for the first time at this point; he did not name the husband until later, also when prompted.] He asked him to straighten it out. The [patrol officer] sent word three times for me to come before I could finally go where he was. He looked at my legs and he was sorry for me and agreed to the marriage. So we were married.

In this account Bantao had to make his own garden because he did not have enough to eat and could not ask his mother and father for food. Nor could he ask his elder brother, apparently, whose substitution as "father" would have been at just this stage, before Bantao was married. (Pe²e, his foster father, appears to have died in the outbreak of amoebic dysentery at the end of the war.) The fact is that unmarried youths commonly make gardens but not because they are denied food elsewhere. Indeed, Bantao mentions in his own account that his father recommended the garden as a necessary step toward getting a wife. The contradiction between this motive and hunger is Bantao's own. I do not know whether he was actually begrudged sufficient food. Clearly, however, the account supplies both a culturally "correct" motive and an idiosyncratic motive consistent with Bantao's image of himself as deserted and neglected. Again in this story Bantao had related experiences common to everyone as if they occurred only to him and for reasons peculiar to his misfortune.

For the rest of the story, Bantao said he did nothing to encourage the woman at the outset; she just came to him. Then, despite overtly approving his wife's divorce and prospective remarriage, which certainly should have left Bantao with clean hands, the Punano husband was actually vindictive. He made sorcery against Bantao which partly disabled him, and sought to make him further trouble with the *kiap*. Out of sympathy or pity, as Bantao sees it, for an injury which balanced the advantage of getting another man's woman, the *kiap* approved Bantao's position. This sort of advantage of one Agarabi man over another is *par excellence* symbolic of success in interpersonal rivalry; but Bantao did not willingly seek it, as he relates the case, nor did he achieve it on his own, but rather because of the sympathy of a powerful person for his helpless plight. Both the sorcery of the exhusband and the sentiments of the *kiap,* since they are unverifiable, are pure projection and therefore reveal Bantao's self-image. In this single, brief account, Bantao is trebly victimized: in being driven through neglect and hunger first to make the garden; in becoming involved in a troublesome affair because of the woman's willfulness—although in a way that is naturally a compliment to him; and in being the object of sorcery and a complainant to authority, despite assurances that this would not happen. Bantao can have none of the blame for these things since he did nothing at all.

Bantao continued the story:

My elder brother said that I ought to go Aiyura [village] to get well. I have a half-father there. If I went away from here, the sorcery could not follow me. [My elder brother] could look out for [my wife] while I was gone.

We two went on the road, he carrying me on his back. When we got as far as the Seven Day Mission, he decided to come back. He did not want to be away from his children, his parents, and kinsmen. It was still the time when the Kainantu people were our enemies so we went in the moonlight. We came back about midnight. In the morning, my brother got up and said [to the village], "You people have put something bad on my brother's body. Now take it away!"

Since Bantao had earlier said that the sorcerer was the injured exhusband of his wife, who lived in another district, we might wonder about his brother's haranguing their own village. To be sure, it is commonplace among the Agarabi to make such public declarations in a loud voice, whether or not action is possible or likely as a result. However, it is also fairly common in giving a subsequent account to translate what were actually only one's private thoughts, or even the supposed thoughts of another person, into pseudohistorical occurrences. Thus these suppositions are reported as if they were actual challenges, retorts, or comments. As Bantao recalled it, it was appropriate to say: "You are all (or someone among you is) doing me harm. Let me alone," and it was appropriate to say this to his own village.

Eventually his knees improved a bit and Bantao decided he needed a knife (machete). This implement was rapidly becoming the inseparable equipment of every Agarabi. His elder brother who had briefly been cook boy for a white man at the station had now gone to work for the "doctor" (the European medical officer). Bantao began to live with his brother at the station for periods of a week or two at a time, and finally, at his brother's suggestion, he went to the "doctor" and asked him for some kind of work. The job assigned was as an unskilled "cargo boy." He cleared away sod and planted dracaena and flowers on the grounds for the new infirmary which was about to be built at that time. "I was not yet a 'carpenter' as I had not been taught by the Seven Day." (He is still by no means a carpenter.) He worked "one and a half moons" and got one pound thirteen shillings when the "doctor" said the job was done. With the money he bought his knife and one or two other things.

While I was working for the *haws sick,* I would sometimes stay at Kainantu, sometimes come back to the village at night. This was the custom of many in our village. There was a [barracks] for the cargo boys but I did not want to be given the blanket, cup, and the rest [which legally must be supplied to a resident native laborer by his employer]. If I were given these things and they got lost, they would take it out of my pay.

I did not know much about the way the white man thinks, but I wasn't afraid of him. There was a *tambu* [taboo] on the road to the [old] house sick but I didn't know about it. I was hungry and I was walking on that road one day and was calabooseded for breaking the *tambu.* It was in the daytime and when the police boy took me, my heart was pounding. The number-three *kiap,* who had seen my swollen legs before, called to me. He asked me why I had broken the *tambu.* They told me after that not to go on any road unless there were a lot of men walking there if I didn't want to get into more trouble. They had put up a stick to mark the *tambu* but I didn't know what it meant. [The silhouette of an outstretched hand painted on a piece of packing crate is a sign familiar on the coast but much more recent in the Eastern Highlands.] They kept me in the calaboose just that one day.

There were actually two companions with Bantao on this occasion. This I learned only upon prompting, for he had made no reference to them up to this point, despite his awareness that I knew them both quite well.

In the meantime his first wife bore a son who died shortly after birth. He also acquired a second wife, cast off by an age-mate who almost uniquely appears to have preferred bachelorhood. The second wife did not find the same place in Bantao's affections. He rarely speaks of her or how he came to marry her. She is a strange woman. She killed one of her two children by her first husband, neglected the other; and she had once committed incest with her father. She could scarcely be considered a prize for Bantao. His first wife eventually had another son who lived and whom Bantao recognizes as his own.

Bantao apparently had had no difficulty in finding women to marry. When I knew him he had already had three wives, the third acquired in somewhat more "classical" fashion. She was neither self-invited nor a cast-off, but was given to Bantao by a lineage in another district in exchange for Bantao's sister, Tabike's child. Bantao was the benefactor, in other words, of a reciprocal arrangement, and his acquisition of the girl appears to have been merely incidental to the exchange. This arrangement has been binding upon Teseʔme, at any rate, though for her part she appears to have wanted to marry someone else. Neither his second wife nor Teseʔme have borne him any children.

One of the most important episodes in Bantao's personal life was quite recent: his decision to be "washed" (baptised) by the Seventh Day Adventist mission. Perhaps this was a turning point for him, but if so, an equivocal one as yet. In any case it is a chapter he cannot quite accept as closed. He is so deeply concerned with what has happened to his position in the mission, in fact, that his story about how he decided to join is not very clear.

Three moons after I came back from working at Aiyura I put my name in the book for the Seven Day, to be washed. Some of the leading [Lutheran[3]] spokesmen in the village tried to get me to go to the [Lutherans] but I didn't want to. My [own] father leans toward the [Lutherans] but he was formerly planning to stay in the middle. Lately he has been thinking of his heart [soul]. When he dies he wants his "soul" [breath, shadow] to go to heaven. A [Lutheran's] soul can go to heaven; they don't stay in the ground any length of time. [Hence the father is favoring the Lutherans more strongly.] The Seven Day custom is different. When you die, your soul stays in the ground. Only when the Day of Judgment comes, the ones who are washed can go to heaven. The cutworm is the same: he stays in the ground until his wings come out and then he flies up to heaven. First a Seven Day man rots in the ground and then he goes to heaven.

Two years after I put my name in the book, I was washed. Master G. [the missionary] was very urgent and he persuaded me. I was a kind of "opening man" [i.e., to open up his village and promote further conversions] and I helped the teacher boys. For two years I went all the time on Sundays to the Seven Day mission along with [a number of agemates]. We would hear the [doctrine] and have our names taken. No, they didn't give us any reward for coming, but we went in rain or in sun. [Such fidelity would be a bit exaggerated for most Agarabi, if not for Bantao.]

The people living near the station were familiar with the missions, of course, and with certain aspects of their apocalyptic message. The Seventh Day Adventists' headquarters at Kainantu was one of the very few regular prewar sources of trade goods, and hence attracted the natives. In addition, the S.D.A. carried their millennial gospel into the villages through native evangelists and the white missionary himself. Prior to the government infirmary, the missionary had provided treatment for the dreaded yaws and had had spectacular success. In Bantao's village, however, the Adventist mission had made few conversions, whereas the Lutherans had a number of converts and still other nominal adherents. The "Seven Day" doctrine is a singularly severe one from the point of view of most Melanesian or Papuan cultures, because, among other things, it forbids eating pork, chewing betel, smoking tobacco, dancing, or wearing costumes. In short, it prohibits many of the distinctive enjoyments of native life. Hence, becoming a "Seven Day" convert was not easy and while a few men older than Bantao had briefly attended

---

[3] The native word, from Neo-Melanesian, is "Telatela."

the S.D.A. mission school before the war, it is generally believed, as he himself insists, that his village had no convert until Bantao. Of the group who accompanied him on his weekly visits to the mission, only he and later another man took the final step to baptism without almost at once "losing" the faith.

The motives for Bantao's conversion to the Adventist mission were probably mixed. Personal contact with the mission and the missionary obviously entered into it, quite apart from any conviction about doctrinary matters. During the war Bantao had closely identified himself with the person and prestige of the native Adventist evangelist stationed in their village. Apparently he found the experience somehow satisfying and he noted in his account that the evangelist had authority and the power to back it up. After the war, Bantao felt that Master G. wanted an "opening man" from the village and that he was therefore selected. He was apparently given a strong lead and a good deal of encouragement, as his own account implied, and such support was something he had always wanted from his own parents and from others but which he had not received in very full measure. Now support came from an extremely powerful source indeed, a white man. He characteristically responded in positive terms to the encouragement of the missionary, thereby certainly attracting still further support. For Bantao the Adventists' taboos were perhaps the price to be paid for "finding a father." The fact that the price was not easy is something of a measure of Bantao's need.

There may have been one other thread of motivation in Bantao's affiliation with Adventism. If there is anything that the missions represent in the Agarabi mind it is goodness, love, and trust—insofar as these concepts are translatable. The typical exhortation of the native evangelist, made with all the rhetoric and self-dramatization of the *ayafabanta* of yore, is that people must stop their thievery of pigs, women, and food. If Bantao's trust and his need to be trusted or loved (and surely these traits are fundamental in his character) can be construed as "goodness," then "goodness" may have entered prominently into his conversion. Moreover, just as stealing in the broad sense is a behavioral expression of the Agarabi male ethic of aggression, so is gentleness an expression of the missions' injunction *not* to steal. Bantao says he does not steal and he is a "cold" man when judged by the aggressive male standards of his culture. There is thus a suggestive congruence between Bantao's own character and the ethics prescribed by the mission, a congruence which is precisely lacking between Bantao and the male ideal of the Agarabi. Adventism as such, despite the prohibitions it imposes, could have a strong appeal to a man like Bantao as distinct from many of his fellows; and all the more so when his acceptance of an agreeable morality was rewarded by the encouragement and approval of the powerful white missionary. Thus, Bantao's name, "thief," is doubly ironic. The traits it connotes are highly approved in Agarabi tradition, but Bantao enjoys no such approval. Possessing just the opposite traits, however, he could gravitate toward and be approved by the mission, which in the native mind is practically the antithesis of thieving.

One effect of Bantao's intention to be baptized was that he had to divorce two of his three wives, which he did. Possibly there were impending reasons for the separation, in addition to the forthcoming baptism, but none was clearly indicated. Reasons of this kind, however, must have entered at least *relatively* in determining the two women selected for divorcement. They were his first and second wives. While it is scarcely proof of the reason he kept her, the third wife, Tese?me, was the one who had not previously been married and the one whose marriage with Bantao was arranged by their respective kin groups.

Bantao and the village's other prospective convert, Kurunke, approached the Adventist missionary about building a *haws dotu* or religious meeting house in the village. Master G. was most encouraging and showed them a house on the mission grounds to use for a model. He lent them saws, hammers, and a chisel, and gave them a supply of nails—by now much prized in the region—telling them to come back if they needed more. The missionary left the location of the *haws dotu* to their judgment, but he visited the village to see their progress and spurred them on with his approval. He said that they must *dotu* (teach and preach) all the time and never let up, and they were serious in their intention to do so; and he promised to send out a teacher sometimes on the Sabbath to help them.

The *haws dotu* was located at the entrance to the new, postwar village, situated again on low ground. After it was completed, Bantao and Kurunke would "hit the bell," the broken blade of a shovel, on Saturday afternoons and collaborate in giving talks to the group who came. At the end of the meeting, when Kurunke had spoken, Bantao would *puria* (pray) for all:

I closed my eyes and called the name of Jesus and God. "There is sin and trouble among us. There is evil. When you return to this country, you can fetch us." [4] In the afternoons, after the *dotu,* we would "kick" (play village soccer).

The [Lutherans] think: "The Seven Day master forbids pig, tobacco, betel, and we like these things. Very well. A *dotu* speaks the truth or it lies. You and I cannot know. Later we will see which is strong and which is false. If we are wrong, we will stay here behind [on Earth] when we die and the Seven Days will go to heaven. If the Seven Days are wrong, they can stay behind."

So the people are divided. Some follow one, some the other *dotu.* Even brothers may be different.

No converts emerged from the *haws dotu* meetings but Bantao nevertheless claims that the Lutherans are losing ground to the Adventists. Evidence of such a trend in his village is not obvious.

Certain attitudes were inculcated in Bantao as an "opening man" and informal village evangelist and they are illustrated in an account of his:

One time a Mussau [an island in the Bismarck Archipelago whose population is said to be entirely Adventist] teacher boy was sent to Dabuyantu, in Kamano country [generally strongly Lutheran], by the mission master. The *papatara* [Lutheran village spokesman] said, "This *dotu* cannot come in here." The *papatara* might have struck him then but the Mussau did not answer him back. He just went and reported the words to Master G. Master G. sent the Mussau back to fetch the Dabuyantu *papatara* and he brought him to the Seven Day mission. Master G. then asked the *papatara* why he had made these insults. The *papatara* said he hadn't made any insults but that the Seven Days should go elsewhere and not come into Dabuyantu. Master G. asked the *papatara* if he was taking it upon himself to divide up all the people among the missions. The he took hold of the *papatara's* hair, parted it, and asked him where

---

[4] I have heard Bantao pray and he does not strike me as eloquent. It was my experience once when sick for several days to have his former co-worker, Kurunke, come to my bedside and pray for my recovery and spiritual welfare. My command of Agarabi is limited but the length to which pious sentiments, doctrinal formulae, and the sacred history of the church fathers were woven into the theme of my improvement was impressive. The session lasted a half hour or more and the prayers approached in style the purest Gongorism.

his washwash was. [The rite of baptism is a point of difference between Adventist and Lutheran practice of which the natives have been made very much aware.] The *papatara* pointed to his head and replied doggedly that he had had water turned on him.

Master G. held him by the hair and said, "You Devil-Satan! You are not truly washwashed!" He kicked him and the *papatara* fell down. [Bantao evinced considerable pleasure in relating this part.] The *papatara* got up and Master G. kicked him again, and a third time. The *papatara* was scratched and hurt. Master G. boxed his ears. Later the Mussau [Adventist] went back to that same district and had no more trouble. Master G. asked him about it to be sure. The Seven Days got a man, some women, and boys there at Dabuyantu, but after a while he [the man] gave it up, thinking of pig.

History or fantasy, this account expresses not only the attitude of rivalry of a village spokesman against the other *dotu,* but it shows quite clearly that Bantao regards the white missionary as a powerful figure, one who is not to be trifled with and hence an ally of some consequence. The contrast between the peaceful message of the Adventist *dotu* and the violence he ascribes to the missionary in this instance, if in fact he notices the discrepancy at all, gives Bantao no pause. The figure of the Mussau, like all coastal natives, is also a symbol of strength and relative sophistication in the eyes of a Highland man like Bantao. It is comforting that along with the Europeans these black-skinned coastal men with so much worldly savvy become one's friends and supporters within the mission fold.

One of the consequences of Bantao's having given up his first wife was that she took his only child with her and continued to keep it after she was remarried. Bantao was apparently less concerned about it at first, before his exwife remarried and while he still nursed the hope of having a son by Tese?me. However, as time passed and no child was born to Tese?me, he became increasingly concerned with regaining possession of his son and bitter when he could not. "A girl child I could give up, but a boy is necessary to help me," he said. In addition to the fact that it was a son at stake, it should be emphasized that having children is a mark of status and a point of great concern to both childless men and women.

Because of his concern, Bantao apparently went to the hamlet of his former wife and her husband and in their absence took the boy away with him to his own village, refusing to give him back. At this the former wife or her husband—it is not clear—went to the *kiap* about the matter and "courted" Bantao. Bantao was directed by the *kiap* to return the boy and was put into the calaboose as punishment for the trouble he had caused.

It was while in the calaboose for this offense, so far as I can determine, that he had sexual intercourse with a fellow prisoner, a Tairora woman. This is something which is said to have occurred among the calaboose prisoners from time to time, and much more frequently between the police and the female prisoners. For most of the people of the area such behavior would not so much be "wrong" as simply a violation of the *kiap's* law and hence bad only if it were discovered and led to undesirable consequences. It is hard to tell if Bantao himself considered that the act was wrong or whether it was just his scrupulous acceptance of his Seven Day commitment, as far as he understood it

In any case, shortly after he had finished his "time" in the calaboose, he was attending a ceremony at the mission in which it was customary for the converts to cleanse themselves of their sins. In so doing, Bantao, when it came his turn, stated to the missionary that while in the calaboose he had enjoyed carnal pleasures with a woman not his wife. In all probability he was thinking at the time only of the need to confess the act as a sin in the mission's definition and was not mindful of the *kiap's* law. The missionary, however, sent off a note at once to the *kiap* telling him of the occurrence and the government man had no choice under the circumstances but to send Bantao back to the calaboose for an additional term.

This was a serious blow to Bantao. To be sure there is no strong moral stigma attached to a term in the calaboose. It is not considered a desirable experience, nevertheless, as one is thrown uneasily among enemies and strangers and is denied normal association with his own kin. There is a tinge of failure, too, since with sufficient adeptness and savvy in the white man's world one should not find himself constantly in the calaboose. One term on the heels of the other was certainly an ignominy for a man who had gone so far as to become a Seven Day convert in order to be good. For Bantao himself, naturally, the worst part of it was what he could only regard as a personal betrayal by the missionary for whom he had made such sacrifices. He was undone through his very adherence to the rules of the mission.

Earlier, in recounting how the missionary would despatch a message and quickly obtain the release of any of his people in trouble with the government, Bantao had expressed his belief in the ideal loyalty and support of this powerful man. This was obviously the loyalty one should expect from parents, kinsmen, and their like. The missionary's act in sending him back to the calaboose was a bitter disappointment and a breach of trust.

Of his fall from grace, Bantao's wife, Tese?me, provided more graphic detail than he himself. Bantao had wanted Tese?me to join the Seven Day along with him when he was baptized but she would not although she went to see the baptism and describes the immersion. Her principal reason was that she did not wish to accept the mission's taboos. (She happens also to come from an Agarabi district in which there was not one Adventist convert at the time, but where there were several Lutherans.) One night, after Bantao was out of the calaboose, she was eating a bit of pork that someone had given her. "I cut it up and cooked it and put it on a plate. Bantao's mouth began to water," she related, "and it kept on watering. Then Bakom who was there took a piece of meat, handed it to Bantao, and told him to eat it. Bantao looked at Bakom, took it and ate it, and he thereby gave up the Seven Days. Later on he took to smoking and chewing betel again. So Kurunke is the only one who was baptised that time, the only one from this district who is still left."

Bantao provided little direct comment about "losing" the mission or the effect on him of its loss. When I asked him what had gone wrong, he just muttered, "They were all the time calaboosing me." He did not, however, impute to his withdrawal the probability that he might never return to the mission fold because he has not yet frankly faced that probability himself. To him his estrangement is simply temporary. "When a new man (missionary) comes," he sometimes mused, "I will probably go back." Actually, he is now speaking of a second new man, since the missionary who "betrayed" him has already been succeeded; the immediate successor is apparently strict in his standards for adherence to the rules and he also believes that some of the earlier converts, including Bantao, have proven to be morally unworthy. Unquestionably Bantao has seriously deviated from the rule, and hence he has found little support from Adventists who might have healed his hurt.

By this time Tese'me was becoming quite as concerned over her failure to have a child as Bantao was. For a while her hopes were raised when she managed to obtain a newborn baby from a friend; but, alas, despite her constantly taking the infant back to its mother to be fed, it died. For his own part Bantao still doggedly asserted that his son by his first wife should by rights be his—as presumably he should in keeping with the practice of this patrilineal society. He now says that when a new *kiap* comes he will reopen the matter and the *kiap* will naturally see the right. "I will get my son."

Bantāo has no fuller grasp than other Agarabi of the role of the white man, particularly the *kiap,* in their personal and communal lives. The difference lies, if anything, in his willingness to appeal to alien authority more readily; and even if he understands no better than others, he is willing to defer to its decisions less grudgingly. Bantao scarcely has more cause than others to feel that he has received favorable treatment at the hands of the *kiap,* considering the loss of his son and several periods in the calaboose. Nevertheless, the *kiap,* in Bantao's view, granted him his first wife. Moreover, when he went with several others to the *kiap* to lodge a complaint against the new master of the Seven Day mission (who succeeded Master G.) over pay for their labor in the mission's gardens, he also had occasion to feel gratified. The *kiap* sent a message to the mission master in which, Bantao imagines, he wrote, "You are not a *kanaka.* You have savvy and a good mind. Now you do the right thing for your boys." That they subsequently got their pay confirmed in his opinion that "the *kiap* is the boss of everything, the *kampan,* the [Lutherans], the D-D-man, and the Seven Day, as well as of his *kanakas.*"

Later Bantao was frightened by the threats of a fellow villager to shoot him. "He accused me five times of meddling with his wife, Niriaso, and he 'marked' an arrow for me to my face. I did not meddle with his woman so I reported his threats to the office. Then I told him that his name had gone into the office and now he has stopped threatening me. It was Niriaso who told her husband that I had invited her to have intercourse. I don't know why—she may like me. I told him and told him that I have been tending to my work helping the story master [anthropologist] and that I was being good so that I couldn't have done what he accused me of. I don't know yet what the *kiap* is going to do about it. I will have to ask [the station interpreter]." Bantao was in a state of considerable anxiety during this period and was convinced that Niriaso's husband was actually planning to shoot him. He felt much better after reporting the threat to the *kiap*.

Shortly thereafter Bantao was to have trouble involving his own wife. According to Tese⁹me, she was forced to accept the advances of another man of the village one night after Bantao had left their house to go to a singsing. The next morning she informed Bantao what had happened and he became very angry. He slapped her and then hit her on the head with a stick, making quite a gash on her forehead. In defense she took up a bushknife and threatened him with it whereupon he fled.

Adultery can often nowadays be settled in the village without recourse to court and, wherever possible, such a settlement is preferred because of the enigmas and uncertainties—to the villagers—of the *kiap's* justice. An effort to adjust the matter within the village was made on this occasion. A sum of money was proposed to be paid to Bantao by the adulterer, despite the latter's steadfast insistence that it was Tese⁹me, not himself, who suggested the assignation. But Bantao was adamant. He refused to consider a village settlement and insisted upon taking the case to the *kiap*. As a result, the three of them left the village that same day for Kainantu, each journeying separately, to tell his own story. However, none of the three returned. Tese⁹me and the other man were calaboosed for their affair, and word came back that Bantao was given a term of two months for assault. Unkind jokes were at once passed about the village, especially by kinsmen and friends of the adulterer, that Bantao was truly a "calaboose man." The sarcasm was all the more pointed since it was Bantao's own stubborn faith in the *gaman* that accounted for his plight.

The villagers generally recognized that Bantao and Tese⁹me had their differences. Even before the affair she had made no secret of her dissatisfaction with him and her desire to return to her own district and marry someone there. She criticised him behind his back and sometimes quite openly. (She made a special point of her preference for "black" skin, whereas Bantao's skin is obviously "red.") Their failure to have a child did not help matters between them, and now, in view of her restlessness and her probable part in the recent affair, and in any case her partial responsibility for her husband's being in prison, it was assumed that Bantao would play the man and send her away. Bantao, who was released from the calaboose earlier than the other two, evinced instead an almost desperate concern that Tese?me not leave him when she was eventually freed. For his village critics this was simply one more sign of a basic flaw in his character. Bantao was obviously concerned about their criticism, but he argued that it was hard work for a man to find a wife and that he could count on no help this time from his family. Several times he had hopes of finding another woman, he said, but in each case something fell through. To make matters worse, Tese?me, when she returned, did not immediately come back to live in Bantao's house and it gradually came to light that while at Kainantu she had developed a strong attraction for the police bugler, which the man himself reciprocated.

Now Bantao was indeed in a quandary: how to keep Tese?me and what he conceived as his self-respect if it meant an appeal to the *kiap* against one of his own men. He talked about his problem incessantly but he could think of nothing positive to do. After a period of weeks matters were finally taken out of Bantao's hands for the bugler himself went to the *kiap* to ask permission for the woman to be separated from her husband in order that she might marry him. Calling Bantao and Tese?me to the station, the *kiap* spoke to them separately and ended by denying the bugler and strongly reprimanding Tese?me. Once again Bantao might feel that his faith in the white man had been redeemed.

The *kiap* could not fundamentally change Tese?me, however, nor restore to Bantao the respect of the community. For a while he became quite aimless in his actions and distraught in manner, sometimes going off on long journeys to the Kamano to visit trading partners or on some slight pretext. He had derived considerable satisfaction and support from his association with us variously as companion, guide, cook, factotum, interpreter, and informant and we enjoyed the relationship as well; but at just about this time it became clear to him that we were in the process of pulling up stakes to move to another village fifteen miles away. We would gladly have taken Bantao with us but he was not willing to go because these were enemy people and he feared sorcery. He argued that he should stay behind in order to look out for our house. Of course, it would not have solved anything for him if he had come. It would only have postponed the problem.

The next time I heard of Bantao, he was even more worried about holding on to Tese?me. Her brother and Bantao's sister were apparently on the verge of divorce. This prospect pleased Tese?me considerably and she flaunted the threat of leaving Bantao. News later reached us that Bantao had found another woman to marry, perhaps the clearest break yet with the *dotu* since his initial estrangement from the mission. The last I have heard at the time of writing is a tape-recorded message that Pastor S. A. Stocken of the Adventist Mission was good enough to send me in response to some questions. In it Bantao speaks affectionately and nostalgically of our times together and my daughter Anne, of whom he was very fond. Now he is panning a bit of gold in the streams about the region. He has never done this before though it was almost his first acquaintance with white man's enterprise as a small boy, some twenty-five years ago. Pastor Stocken implies that Bantao lacks any sense of purpose, is ill at ease with himself: "He is a very unhappy man."

There is not much doubt that Bantao is unhappy; perhaps he will always be. There was invariably something wistful and tentative about him while we knew him, even when he was enjoying his best moments, over a joke or some small triumph. He is ill at ease in the world in which he was born, the world that largely made him. The social and psychological cataclysm of 1932 has ultimately brought certain opportunities to the Agarabi, opportunities which have seemed good to Bantao. Government and mission unmistakably have held out some vision of happiness greater than that he knows. He appears to have accepted the vision and the new opportunities and to have gone ahead faithfully to do what he thought was indicated. Yet his sincerest efforts have led him to failure. He not only fails in achieving what he has immediately hoped for, but the failure in the white man's world cruelly underlines, even aggravates, his nonfulfillment in his own—the very reason for his seeking the white man's way. In retrospect, Bantao seems destined to have been an "opening man" but ironically unable to open any of the doors he so hopefully tried for himself.

The quotation to follow is an excerpt from the analysis of a Thematic Apperception Test (Murray, unmodified) given to Bantao by the writer. The analysis is by Dr. Audrey Holliday, Department of Pharmacology, University of Washington, who knew nothing about Bantao except what his T.A.T. responses revealed to her and who had not read this sketch. The sketch, on the other hand, was completed before Dr. Holliday began to work with the T.A.T. material and has not been changed in the light of her results. The writer, who is a tyro in projective interpretation, was quite as impressed with the analysis *per se* as with its general agreement with the life history. Accordingly, Dr. Holliday's general summary of Bantao's character as revealed by the T.A.T. is quoted below. It is of course better rounded than her comments on individual picture responses, while these, for which there is unfortunately not space here, give a better idea of the route by which she has reached her several conclusions. It may be worthwhile to mention that Dr. Holliday worked "blind," knowing next to nothing about New Guinea, and nothing at all about the Agarabi except what I had sketched to her of their clothes, houses, crops, setting, and climate.

Bantao appears to be a passive, dependent, subservient person who is extremely insecure and who has strong feelings of inadequacy and impotency. He seems to be demonstrating a colossal reaction formation against his sex and against his culture. He envies women; he envies white men; nonetheless, he also feels abandoned by women and has apparently been deprived so that he vaguely wants something from women and from white men. He would like to be dependent; he would like to be taken care of and not have to fight and steal as he apparently feels he must as a deprived man in his culture. Therefore, he would like to deny himself both sexually and racially. He would like to be a woman and white.

Bantao's defenses appear to be primarily those of repression, suppression, denial, withdrawal, and rationalization. He does not like to be pushed; he would like to be let alone. He frequently demonstrates a kind of passive-aggressive behavior in his telling of the stories. He retreats into description; he does not tell a story; he is quite concretistic and merely superficially complies.

One might speculate from the foregoing that this man felt that he was abandoned by his mother, that she tore away from him or he was torn away from her. He yearns for his previous passive-dependent relationship in which his oral needs, his needs for closeness and affection and dependence were satisfied. He seems to regard male company as essentially hostile. That is, he envies women who are left to "just live." Men are equated with "beasts." Men kill each other and control each other's thoughts. He does not seem to derive satisfaction from any power which attaches to being a man. He is torn by feelings of inadequacy and impotency; he does not wish to play a male role; he feels that he cannot play such a role; he apparently finds no satisfaction in it. He is too insecure, too anxious, too passive, and too impotent. He apparently feels that he will gain some strength from linking himself with the white man, the white man will take care of him.

Mrs. Parkinson and "Queen Emma" (standing) and Mrs. Parkinson as She appeared about 1929 (below).

6

Weaver of
the Border

Margaret Mead

Many anthropological accounts begin—and go on—as if the anthropologist had arrived in a space ship right in the middle of a completely isolated tribe where, without any help from an interpreter, he learned the culture of people who had preserved it untouched for thousands of years. To study such an "untouched" people becomes the ideal of the anthropological student, and when he goes out to Africa or the South Seas, the dream persists so that the monograph comes out uncontaminated by the days or weeks or even months spent in the world in between where a mysterious process called "culture contact" has a life of its own. The government officials and recruiters, traders and prospectors, missionaries and medical officers, planters, schooner owners, and clerks, who form the population of this world between, who mediate the anthropologist's first contacts in an area, who feed and transport him, find him servants, remit or exact customs duties, give him medical care and medical supplies, pass along to him dozens of stereotypes of the peoples with whom he will presently be working—all these individuals fade out of the picture, appearing at best as a set of unidentified names in the acknowledgements, often to the deep embarrassment of those who have given aid and succor to members of a profession who continually "let white prestige down" and "pick the brains of people who were here before they were born."

This happens when the anthropologist works in remote regions where the only Europeans, Americans, Chinese, or Japanese, or occasionally Africans as in British Guiana, or Indians as in Trinidad, are there as part of the new culture contact conditions, to trade, govern, exploit, or convert the native peoples who are the anthropologist's particular interest and concern. When instead the anthropologist is looking not for an "untouched" people but for the last fragments of a "vanishing culture," again the same process repeats itself. He may actually be living in a hotel in a small town, driving out each day to a reservation to find a few informants. The streets around him are filled with modern Americans of many sorts, farmers and tradesmen, in whose world the Indian is an odd anomaly. The Indians—

as they walk the streets of such towns or sit on a bench outside one of the stores that cater to Indian trade—assume for the benefit of the passers-by their "culture contact faces" of strict unresponsiveness and immobility, learned long before the coming of the white man when war captives were tortured by their Indian enemies and sang as they were burned to death. Again the anthropological report, lovingly and laboriously constructed from the fragmented memories of the old, is written in the setting of the past—great herds of buffalo thunder through the Indians' memories of what their grandparents told them, deer can be sought freely in the forest, buffalo police keep order in the camp. Anthropologist and Indian together inhabit a vanished world, irreplaceable and extraordinarily precious, not to be seen on earth again.

It is because of such omission that I have chosen to write of my most gifted informant from the world between, Mrs. Phebe Clotilda Coe Parkinson, whose mother was a member of a chiefly family in Western Samoa and whose father was the nephew of an American bishop. She was one of eighteen children in a family that first helped to stylize "contact" relationships in Samoa and then, taking their contact style with them, emigrated to New Guinea and built there—in German times before World War I—a second contact culture, in which the Samoans and the part Samoans, no longer the members of the less civilized "aboriginal group," were now in a superordinate position, a people with a style of life already far removed from the aboriginal peoples of New Britain where they first landed. Bigger and stronger and better fed, able to speak German and English, Christian and literate, they were profoundly impressed with the little ceremonies and rituals of civilization in the South Seas—the great clothes presses sent out from Germany; the white table cloths and flowers on the table; the strict codes of behavior which recognized rank among the Europeans, rank among the Samoans and part Samoans, and the rapidly developing functions of "boss boy," "boats' crew," "police boy" and the like among the aboriginal peoples. Into the emergent lingua franca, then called pidgin English, now called Neo-Melanesian, they brought Samoan words, *malolo* (to rest), *tainam* (mosquito net), and words which the early missionaries to Samoa had adapted from the Latin, like *patu,* for duck. The German governing group did not wish the natives of New Britain (then called Neue Pommerania, now part of the Trust Territory of New Guinea) to learn

German; German masters, Samoan mediators, natives who had been black-birded as laborers to Australia, and the many-tongued aboriginal peoples coöperated in the formation of the new language with its Melanesian grammar and its largely adapted English vocabulary.

I was extraordinarily fortunate in finding Mrs. Parkinson at all. In my graduate school days—1923 to 1925—I had worked on Pacific Island literature, and before undertaking a field trip to the Admiralty Islands had read the relevant ethnographic accounts in a German book which was even then a classic, Richard Parkinson's *Dreissig Jahre in der Südsee,* filled with observations on the peoples of the islands, among whom he traveled as a trader, recruiter, and collector of ethnographic information and ethnographic and zoological specimens which he had sent home to Germany. As his widow once remarked to me, "My niece once wrote me when she was traveling in Germany that she saw a cassowary in Stuttgart, which was marked 'Cassowary from Neue Pommerania, sent by Mrs. P. C. Parkinson.' I had forgotten all about it, we sent so many things to so many places."

When my husband and I arrived in Rabaul in the autumn of 1928, we were befriended by the acting Administrator, then Judge, later Chief Justice Sir Beaumont Phillips. In his house, we heard that Richard Parkinson had been dead for many years, that his part Samoan widow was still alive on a remote plantation on the South Coast, and that a young government secretary, named Noel Barry, had undertaken the task of translating the big German book into English. I must have said something about how much I would have liked to meet her. But one did not lightly undertake a journey such as the journey to Sumsum would have been, and we went on to the Admiralties. On our return in the summer of 1929, Judge Phillips suggested that I stay over between boats (six weeks) and "write a book about Mrs. Parkinson." It seemed that an American writer had persuaded Mrs. Parkinson to subsidize him, and put up his wife, his children, and himself while he worked with her. She had given him many papers, photographs, etc., and then nothing had come of this except requests for further subsidy which she didn't feel able to afford. Judge Phillips, always acutely sensitive to any breach in ethics across cultural lines—he himself worked untiringly for nearly forty years to establish British law in the territory—suggested that I could "make it up to Mrs. Parkinson" if I, as an American, now wrote her biography and shared the proceeds with her. I suspect perhaps that Judge Phillips thought I needed a rest, and that in Mrs. Parkinson's capable hands I would be fed and coddled back into a more satisfactory weight than the 98 pounds I weighed after seven months of malaria in Manus. This scheme, hatched at lunch while the steamer was in port, was lent the blessing of fate when it was found that Mrs. Parkinson was in Rabaul and could be invited to the Judge's home that afternoon. I can still see her, a great stately, very heavy woman, her skin browner than it would have been when she was a girl, with the body that had borne twelve living children and cared for many scores of other children, standing serene, proud, friendly, but just a little wary and distant on that verandah, where the spears and clubs and model canoes and carved bowls of the peoples of the islands among whom Judge Phillips had sat in judgment hung on the walls.

Rapport was a matter of seconds, for I still spoke polished Samoan and this was a language she hardly ever heard nowadays. Could I go down with her to Sumsum and stay with her for several weeks while she told me the story of her life, which was also the story of the first attempts to bring New Britain "under control." (We do not speak of colonizing in New Guinea. That word has been reserved for places where the land is good enough to support thousands of Europeans and the natives can be displaced or destroyed.) It was all arranged in a few minutes. I went back to the ship and disentangled my own possessions, my husband went on to a short field trip to Papua to get needed photographs and extra materials, and I stayed in Rabaul. Papers were drawn up by Judge Phillips, and duly sworn and witnessed, giving me the right to use her account and the materials she gave me and promising her half of any proceeds that might come of the publication.[1]

These details may seem tedious and far removed from the romantic autobiographies in which the most minute details of sex and sorcery, vision and ecstasy of identified members of savage tribes are still presented to the eyes of sophisticated readers. As one press photographer said to me on the eve of a field trip, "Why don't you get a soap company to give you some soap and take pictures of those

[1] When it became clear that I would not be able to write a book as quickly as I hoped, I sent her what purported to be half of a publisher's advance so she could use it before she died.

savages using it. I bet *they'd* never sue you for libel." Nor would they, perhaps, although the savages of just a decade ago, now initiate activities which shake the chancelleries of the world. But perhaps because my first field work was among the Samoans who had attained high literacy in their own language and a sophisticated approach to their culture contact problems, I have always felt that the identity of the most savage informant must be given appropriate protection; either he or she must know that I was taking down what they said for publication or making photographs of them and their children to be used, or an absolute cloak of anonymity must be provided for them. When I published the sort of thing which might embarrass them or bring them into jeopardy in any way, I disguised their identity—in Samoa, their names, and among the American Indian group I studied, even the identity of the tribe.

In the in-between world where Mrs. Parkinson was still a reigning power, even though she had never regained the full status she had had under the Germans, these matters were of an infinite touchiness, as considerations of the amount of Samoan or New Guinea "blood," of legal marriage, of Christian identity could all become counters in games of power which were often rough and cruel. (One of her sons had committed suicide soon after a slight he received at a German garden party.) It was very necessary to be extraordinarily clear, both for the reason that one protected an unsophisticated informant and for the reason that one protected a member of one's own society. So the papers were signed and sealed, and we left for Sumsum on a tiny schooner. After a long seasick day we got safely through the reef in a little boat and settled down in a plantation house. Long and high, the house had a wide, windswept corridor in the middle that was used as a dining room. Here everything was as it had been in German times—there were the imported cupboards, the old style mosquito nets, the detached kitchen. There were priceless old pieces of Chinese and Japanese ware, pieces of batik sent from her children who had lived in Java, prim little tidies from Germany, Samoan bark-cloth, and little silver egg cups from Sydney. And the "labor line" of indentured work boys cut the coconuts in the style that had been established forty years before. It was like a window opened suddenly into a past that survived only intermittently on the plantations that fell into the hands of Australian veterans of World War

I when the Australian Expeditionary Forces captured what was then the Bismarck Archipelago and German New Guinea.

Now came the problem of learning to understand what Mrs. Parkinson said—that exploration of which an anthropologist never wearies of the unique perceptions of the informant through whose eyes he will first approach many aspects of the culture. In a native village, one sometimes has a little choice; one can experiment with the three or four who know a little of the lingua franca to start with and select the mind and temperament most congenial for the work, discarding as a major informant someone whose tempo is too different, whose affect seems to introduce an uncomfortable distortion, who is too much at odds with his neighbors, or whose own experience seems too deviant to be used as a guide.

But here I had only one informant, perfectly fitted by circumstance and temperament, for we were completely congenial from the start in those imponderables which make communication possible through any barriers of centuries and hemispheres, and I had the experience of Samoa and of New Guinea to make everything she said intelligible. Samoan culture was there for contrast, as was my intensive Admiralty Island experience and my experience—going and coming —of Rabaul and Lorengau, of the government officials, traders, missionaries, recruiters.

Because of her precise memory and her lively interest in human beings, it was possible to chart from her memories just how the civilizations with which she came in contact reached her, mediated by known personalities, filtered through the receptivities of her own temperament and her experience—an American father; a Samoan mother; a German-reared husband; French nuns; childhood in Apia; adulthood in German New Guinea; old age in the Australian Mandate; one visit to Australia; an Irish brother-in-law; a New Zealand son-in-law; German, Australian, and New Zealand grandchildren; the German Navy; the German Civil Service; the Australian Expeditionary Forces; the Australian civil administration. Her speech was peppered with German scientific words, French cookery phrases, a few American words and idioms, and Neo-Melanesian. She once saw two American Negroes in Samoa, "one of them played the fiddle beautifully"; she had seen a Russian Christmas tree; she learned to play German whist at Finschhafen. She had tasted wines from all over the world on board warships. Each experience had come separately, as if washed up on the shores of her island, to be taken, examined curiously, and either used or rejected, but never forgotten. She never resented a new baby. "I wanted to see their eyes, how they looked." Each significant impression remained sharp and clear:

"There was a *taupou* [ceremonial virgin hostess of a Samoan village] in Upolu [the island of western Samoa on which Apia is located]. She was beautiful. 'A real Grecian profile,' my husband said. I did not know what a Grecian profile was, then. I do now."

A few months later I set down in my notes: "I have been specially fortunate in having fall into my hands the biography of a type of woman who would never have put a line on paper herself—and yet possesses singular gifts as a raconteur. Mrs. Parkinson is 66 and as alive and fascinated by life as she was at 16. She has always seen herself as it were from the outside."

So we set to work.

There was first the task of establishing the main outline of her life, how she had been born in Samoa in 1863, the daughter of a Samoan of high rank and an American father, Jonas Minders Coe, born in Troy, New York, in 1822, who had run away to sea. In the Apia of those days Americans, British, and Germans jockeyed for position. Her father had married four times and had eighteen children. We set their names down—those who had died as children, the one who had been an epileptic, and the one who drowned in the river, her eldest sister Emma, who became such a power in New Britain that she was called "Queen Emma" and ran her little fleet of steamships back and forth from Rabaul, the older brother who had been for a year the governor of Guam, after being banished from New Britain for running the German flag up on an outhouse and who died much later in the Philippines. We followed their children and their children's children; some were in Sumatra, some in Germany, others lived on sheep farms in New Zealand, or were in business in Sydney. Emma had died in Monte Carlo.

Early days in Apia had to be explored; how she, alone of all her brothers and sisters, except for the epileptic sister, had become like her mother a Catholic, entranced by the orderly beauty of the nuns' way of life. She told of the strict upbringing her father tried to give his children, and the contrasts between his standards and the life of the Samoans, in whose ceremonies and gaiety she slipped away from home to participate.

Then at 16 came her marriage to Richard Parkinson, who had been reared in the princely household of Schleswig-Holstein and then aged 36, an ambitious surveyor and amateur ethnologist, had come to Samoa to represent the great trading firm of Gottfried. Two years later, her sister Emma, already established in faraway New Britain was to persuade Richard and Phebe and their first child to join her in the new savage country. It took two months on a sailing vessel, with a baby, a piano, and a parrot, to reach the Bismarck Archipelago. One after another, the half-caste and full-blood Samoan relatives followed them to New Britain, where Queen Emma's fortunes grew. Richard divided his time between managing his sister-in-law's affairs and collecting and writing for museums; Phebe bore twelve children, managed her own plantation and much of her sister's, supervised the twenty-course dinners her sister used to give to the German naval officers, and became to the Germans of the period a kind of ideal of the emerging life in the South Seas. After her husband's lingering death, as the "Widow Parkinson," she became the trusted friend of the German governor, Dr. Hahl. Later, there were troubles between the part-Samoan group and some of the Germans, insults and counter-insults; the second generation proved less sturdy than the first. By the time the Australian Expeditionary Force arrived in New Guinea, Queen Emma was dead, and the hold of the part-Samoan families, who had once owned enormous sections of New Britain and the Duke of York, was slipping.

When the war came, the Germans did not include Mrs. Parkinson among the Germans who were protected, and for the first time she was left deserted, citizen only of an in-between world where there were no principalities and powers to whom to turn for help. The Australians brought in even greater racial self-consciousness and after the war she withdrew almost entirely into plantation life, helping now one child and then another set up plantations, recruit labor, trade in the bush. She was still strong enough to swim ashore if the reef was too rough for a boat to get through. Once on a re-cruiting trip to Buka in the Solomons, she was on a desolate shore with her little cutter rolling out at sea and a dreadful sea running. She was too tired and ill to walk to the nearest village, so she and her companion swam out to sea, diving under the breakers, and reached the cutter. "I could not drown. I can float for miles and never go down. A shark might eat me or I might get cramps now I am old, but I could never drown." She still remembered her husband's collecting activities and occasionally attempted new ones. She was still a good Catholic in spite of many little tiffs with "the fathers" whom she often found on the opposite side from "the sisters."

Throughout it all went her relationships with the natives, whom she had learned to discipline, of whom she was not afraid, whose wives and children she protected, whom she saw as savages in need of protection, as souls who might be brought to God, as people about whom ethnologists wrote and collected—as endlessly interesting: "In the early days I used to take my baby and go up into the bush on Sunday. I had to take Nellie because she was a baby still at the breast. But I had to go because I wanted to see how the natives lived. I took a boy to carry the baby and six boys with Schneider rifles and I took my Winchester and so we went up. The natives—all just as God made them, both men and women—were very glad to see us and I used to come back laden with presents of sugar cane and taros. Later that was very helpful to my husband; when we had trouble with the natives or he wanted to find a special native he would ask, 'Now where does he belong? Where is this village?' and I would tell him."

So, in 1935, she wrote me: "Look, *la'u pele* [my dear] could you find out some museums over there if they are interested in Trepine skulls and what they are willing to pay . . . they have only one in Australia at Canberra, the one I sent Dr. Cilento and it is not so easy to get any nowadays owing the natives left off fighting when the government started here, and no more trepining of skulls and the new generation don't know where the old people are buried . . . but as I am here and knew the old natives who were trepined, I will be able to get one or two if I take the trouble . . . "

Once these broad outlines of her life were established, I could go back and get detailed memories, which I took down in her own words. Her father had arrived in Samoa in a whaling ship, and run away from the ship to stay. "In those days the Samoans still wore only *ti* leaf girdles and there was still a Maliatoa who ate human flesh. The missionaries of course had come but there was still no European settlement. Afterwards there were just a few European families." In Samoa he had built himself a small ship and begun trading with the Samoans; and he had three sets of children, the last of whom remained in Samoa and inherited his lands:

My father was very rich. He had many lands, some of them unplanted but all surveyed in the bush. At the time of the war the Samoans marched into Apia but they did not touch the European property only that of their enemies. We were quite close to the village, I remember them marching into the village and cutting down the posts of the houses and then the roofs would collapse. And then they would cut down the coconut trees. Afterwards we children would go and slide up and down the roofs of the fallen houses. And in the very early days they used to cut off the heads too and hold them up in baskets and the women would dance. I was very little then. My father would shut us up so that we would not see but we would all creep out another way and look. I often think how reckless children are. When my father gave the chiefs ammunition and guns and then when they could not pay they had to give him their lands. My father was a pioneer. He spoke Samoan and all the chiefs used to bring their troubles to him. There were always many chiefs about the house. They wanted to marry us girls and get the *gafa* [genealogy] of our family. Then my father would say, "What! Do you think I take all this trouble to bring up my children and then let them marry Samoans and become Samoans again?"

The Samoans are very proud and they look down on the half castes too. I remember there was a man whose name was Edward S————. He was a very well-educated man and he married a pure Samoan woman, just a bush Samoan, she had not been educated in Apia or anything. And later he came to Apia and built a big house and he brought his wife with him. She used to sit there cross-legged, in the middle of his fine mat. She belonged to the Tui Aana family and they gave the children, there was a boy and girl, they gave them the names of the Tui Aana family. Afterwards he died and also there was no *tamatane* [children of the male line] for the Tui Aana family but only these *tamafafine* [children of the female line]. But the family would have nothing to do with them. They said, "What? Give our high Samoan name to someone who has European blood, and is not a pure Samoan!" Even if someone had high Tongan blood they would look down on them. Oh, yes, I know today some of them marry Fijians and even Solomon Islanders, but these are street girls, fit for nothing but that.

We children used to learn to do our washing in the river. My father's and his wife's clothes were sent out, but we girls did our own. Afterwards at the convent we used to wash with the sisters standing over us and giving us oh, such a little soap, for they were very saving. And we had to rub and rub on the stones.

My father had a lovely house. It was all cut out and planned in San Francisco. The floors were all beautiful narrow boards and all painted white. The walls were all papered in those days. The parlor walls had white paper with a little gold pattern on it. My older brothers used to mix the flour and boiling water and put on the paper. It was very interesting. Every room had different paper on it. And in the parlor the whole of one side was a mirror and two sides were bookcases full of books and with glass doors. But I do not remember my father ever reading any of the books. When the British Consul's children had birthday parties, my father used to go to those shelves and give us each a book to carry as a gift. That is the only use that I remember his making of the books. Our stepmother did nothing but we girls used to keep the house clean and neat. One took one room and one another and we changed around. We were very proud of our home. It burned down in the war when the war ships shelled the town; all that part of Apia burnt.

I was very unhappy as a child. You see, before I was born my father took another wife, that is he did not marry her but he went with her and my mother found out about it and left him, although she was already great with child. She went back to the mission where she had worked as a child and that is why I was born under the Ifififi tree. Then my father married this other woman after he had begged and begged my mother to come back but she would not. She was very proud and so Mr. Pritchard, the first British Consul who had married my father and mother, divorced them. And then later, I remember we were down by the river and my mother was washing in the river, I must have been very small for I remember I was lying on her lap. And my brother came and lifted me up and took me off to the schooner and took me from Falealili to Apia. I remember we got there very early in the morning and they carried me up to my father's house. So I was brought up with that other family and I always think of them as my true sisters. But their mother was very unkind to me. She would not make me any new dresses but when she made them new dresses she put some of their old dresses on me. But I would not have noticed it myself if people outside had not spoken about it. My father would not let me see my mother and I remember she used to come into the little farm back of our house and hide and send one of the girls to get me. Then she used to hug me to her heart and cry and I used to cry for my mother. I do not know where she lived but it must have been close by for once when our house caught fire and was all in flames my mother appeared and carried me out of the fire so she must have been watching over me near by. After that other woman died my father married again. He tried to get my mother to come back but she would not. When my father used to take some of the children to San Francisco to school, she used to come and look after the house while he and his wife and the children went to San Francisco and then when they came back she would go away again. [Phebe had been left home to care for her epileptic half sister, whom she took with her to the convent school, and into her mother's church.]

Then when I was married, I lived three miles away from the sea and my mother came to live with me and she stayed with me until my first baby was born. I heard her in the next room talking with all the old women about girls who had their first babies and how some of them were selfish and thought only of themselves and would say: "Oh, take the thing out, I don't care how, so that this pain stops now." And I made up my mind that I would not be like that. Then after we came up here, my sister, Queen Emma they called her, Mrs. Kolbe was her name, sent for my mother. She built her a real European house and she had her boys and all her Samoan things and she was very happy there. She used to weave fans and sew up strings of the red parrot feathers to send back to Samoa. Every day she had her bottle of beer and then in the night a little brandy. About three o'clock in the night. She could not sleep much at night and so she would have that. Her medicine she called it. Three times she went back to Samoa to visit. After she died we made her house into a rest house for the Naval officers who were our friends to come and rest when they were on leave or feeling a little sick.

The whole theme of Phebe's life can be seen as the acceptance of a set of moving ideals of which she knew very little. Her father's narrow, rigid standards which made the children wear shoes, sent them to bed at eight o'clock until they were married, and forbade them to go to parties if any of the mixed couples were not legally married, would not have been enough for her. She was in continual rebellion against his surveillance, his horsewhipping, his treatment of her mother.

Her shrewd common sense and keen observation would perhaps have made her reject European domesticity if she had had any chance to see it in practice, but she did not. All about were only hard-boiled traders with native wives or more often native housekeepers, fat, spoiled mistresses who sat in their raised doorways, smoking and spitting into the street while servants did the work which they were not skilled enough or interested enough to oversee. The half-caste children were too few and born of too different fathers to form a group in themselves. It was a shifting half-world without standards, without taste. On the one side was the gay, proud Samoan life, the high state kept by the old chiefs, the flowers and the winsome love-making, the festivity of the *malagas* (ceremonial visits). On the other was a world which she dimly glimpsed and chose from rather than grasped at. The brothers and sisters who came back from Sydney and San Francisco brought scattered accounts of this other world. There were her father's proud priestly relatives who had cast him out and who called his children "blacks." There were the young clerks who walked home with them in the evening and went away at eight o'clock. Most of all there was the Convent, where her mother had lived as a girl, where she had been born under the Ififfi tree—so quickly that the nuns had been frightened, for one moment Joana passed them pregnant, and a minute later she had come to the house to get a cake of soap to wash the newborn infant.

When she was a little girl she wanted to be a nun: "The sisters wanted me to learn French, but Father said, 'No. No exceptions. What one child has so must another.' I used to go out and sit in the long avenue of breadfruit trees where the sisters had their playtime, and listen to the French. I used to fall asleep listening to the beautiful language."

But there was still another side to Phebe's world, the life of the Samoans whose "blood" she shared and whose language she spoke. This graceful, happy life appealed to her much more than the strict regimen of her father's house.

My father had very regular habits. Every morning he would go away to the land office and he would not come back again until four o'clock. So I and my sisters had the whole day to ourselves. We used to take off our dresses and just put on *lavalavas* [cloth sarongs] and put *laumaile* [sweet smelling leaves] around our necks and flowers in our hair and we would gather leaves and wood from the bush and make our own little *umus* [ovens] or go swimming in the rivers, or diving under the waves in the sea. Once we got needles and charcoal and tattooed our legs. I tattooed a sea gull and an "M," the first letter of one of my little Samoan sweetheart's names. Afterwards when I was engaged I hurt my foot and it had to be dressed every day. My husband came every day and dressed it and my father saw the tattooing. Oh, he was wild. He said, "If you were not sick with that foot you would have a horsewhipping."

Once I had a real glimpse of Samoan life. My father's third wife was a very young and gay *taupou*. Her brother was a big chief in Manono and on the excuse that her brother was sick she got my father's permission to go home. He sent me with her, for I was always her favorite as she knew the others were cheeky and the Samoans called them *ngutuaitu* [ghost nose]. But when we got there she put me with the *taupou* and she went and stayed with her sweetheart's parents. So for two weeks I slept with the *aualuma* [unmarried girls] and the old women made us *ula* [necklaces] and every night all the boys came. I wore a *lavalava* and flowers in my hair and was very happy.

In the old days when the German officers came we used to go and sit by the river with bare feet and flowers in our hair and talk to them. Father didn't know anything about that.

As a child she delighted in swimming and racing. She fought every full-blood child in the neighborhood until children coming on *malagas* were urged to come and challenge the little half-caste, and standing outside the high fence which surrounded her father's house, they would give the Samoan challenge:

> My left hand is the head of a black fish, Come and fight me.
> My right hand is the head of a red fish, Come and fight me.

In the occasional difficulties with the mixed population, she was always tempted to resort to force, as at the time the wife of a Chinese had a quarrel with her half sister. It was the slender 13-year-old little Phebe who girded a tiny *lavalava* beneath her prim long dress and fought the woman who had insulted her brother and slapped her sister, this within the Chinaman's house because he feared that if the fight were fought outside the others would intervene for the little Phebe whom they all loved. So while the Chinaman danced about holding off the crowd, she beat up the fat wife and knocked her down the steps from the bar into the bedroom, rolled her under the bed for the finish, all the time anxious lest her father or some of her father's gossipy old cronies should pass by and hear of it.

Once, too, she saw the *fa'amase'au* ceremony, the taking of the tokens of virginity of a *taupou*. (This had always worried me, because according to the account which both my Samoan informants and the earlier missionary texts on Samoa had given, if the girl proved not to be a virgin when her husband's talking chief came to take the tokens of virginity with his fingers wrapped in white tapa, she would be beaten to death. This punishment seemed too severe for the Samoan ethos. Mrs. Parkinson had the answer for which I had been seeking.)

"If the girl is not a virgin she will tell her old women, and they will secretly bring the blood of a fowl or a pig and smear it on the *i'e sina* [a fine mat] which was spread on the ground. Then the *i'e sina* is brought out to all the people and all the old women relatives of the woman's side rub the blood on their faces and dance and sing and the husband waves it in the air like a flag, and then goes in, behind a *siapo* [bark-cloth curtain] to his wife."

She also saw the mourning feast of a *taupou*. The woman's side brought many fine mats and the man's side yards and yards of calico. These were all spread about the house while the fine mats were piled up on top of the corpse. Then while the food for the funeral feast was being cooked, all the *polas* (plaited blinds) were lowered, and the young girls and boys and some old people were all shut up naked in there where they cut their hair and painted themselves with *sama* (turmeric) and smeared black *lama* (charcoal) all over themselves as a sign of mourning.

When I was a little girl I used to think what it would be like if I should marry one of the young *manaias* [titled youths of the chief's household] who were my sweethearts. But then I had a dream, a dream which I have always remembered, of a high cliff which had white streaks on it where the ground had been torn away and on the side of the cliff was a beautiful castle and I lived there and walked through those halls. When I would think what it would be like to marry a Samoan then I would remember my dream and think if I married a Samoan I would never live in my castle. Then too I knew how the Samoans left their wives and took new ones and if my husband should stop loving me he would throw me away and I would be no better than a street woman. So I decided to stay on and learn European ways and marry as my father wished. And years later when I came to New Ireland I saw that cliff just as it was in my dream, going up high from the sea, with the white scars there on the side and I pointed it out to my sister and said, "There, I dreamed of that cliff when I was a little girl."

When my sister [Emma, then married to Farrel, a New Zealander of Irish extraction] used to come home I used to sit beside her and watch every little thing she did, the way she held her needle and even the way she would bite off her thread I thought was perfect. I loved her very much and was very jealous of her. When her husband went home to visit his family in New Zealand he brought her and her two children home to my father's house and she brought me up. She used to take the broom to me very often. She took the most pains with me because I tried the hardest; the other girls were lazy and disobedient and they would run and tell their mother, so she gave them all up and only whipped me. When she came up here I was very lonely without her and it was only because I loved her so that my husband and Farrel succeeded in persuading me to come up here. That was the root of their winning.

My husband was born in Augustina in Schleswig-Holstein. His father was an Englishman, a trainer to Prince Christian, and his mother was

German, she was a waiting woman to the empress. My husband was first a teacher of English in Heligoland but he was always wild about anthropology and ethnology and then a man named Kubary, he was in Samoa too, he came back and told my husband and my husband came back there. He was a manager of a plantation and also he surveyed for the firm of Gottfried. I did not want to marry him. He was twenty years older than I was. But there was an American consul there named D——— and he did not mean well by me. I had a little fancy for him and he would always come and see me and if it was my week for cooking my father would set one of my sisters to cook and then he would let me sit and entertain him for it was just me that he came to see. And he would sit and talk to me and say, "Oh, Phebe, I would like you for my little wife. You come and live with me and afterwards we can get married." But I was already a Catholic and I always told the Mother Superior and the sisters everything and they said, "Don't have anything to do with that man, he is no good." So once there was a dance and this wretch was there and my husband also. I did not like my husband particularly but I stayed with him just to get rid of this wretch. Then the next day he went home and wrote to my father and asked to marry me. So my father said, "Well, Phebe, he is a good *parti* for you. He is a good man. He does not drink." I said, "Oh, father, I do not want to get married yet." I was just 15 and just home from the convent. I said, "Let Carrie—that was my older sister—let her get married first." But he said, "It is not Carrie's name here in the letter; it is your name." I was very much afraid of my father, he was always very strict with me. I was the last of the other family and he was too cross with me. The other girls used to love my father, but I did not love him, I feared him. When he was tired and we had to *lomilomi* [massage] him, the other girls used to *lomilomi* with love in their hands but my hands got tired and there was no love in them. But when he said I must marry my husband I knew I must marry him. And all the sisters said, "Yes, this is a good man. True he is not a Catholic, but it is better to marry a good Protestant than a bad Catholic!" We were engaged for six months and all that time I did not look my husband in the face. I did not know whether his eyes were blue or black. He had no teeth, they were all knocked out once when he fell over a fence in Africa.

And all the Samoan *manaias* used to say, "Oh, our little Phebe will soon be chewing food for this old man who has no teeth." And my mother and all the high chiefs of my mother's side came and remonstrated with my father and said, "See, you have had your own way with all the other children. Let us have this one little *tamafafine*. She shall come and live in the chief's house and be an ornament to his rank and do no hard work and marry whom she chooses. Do not make her marry this old man." But my father would not listen. And always when my husband came to see us I would hear his horse coming and I would run away and hide under the bed. I would put on my worst dress and make my hair all untidy so that he would be disgusted with me. Afterwards he told me they were all laughing at me. Once when he took me out driving I said, "Richard, I do not want to marry you. I do not care for you." He said, "Does your father know this?" I said, "Yes." He said, "All right, we will go and talk with him about it." Then I said, "Oh, no, don't. I was just fooling." Then we were married by the British consul and afterwards there was a great party and the ships in the harbor, the *Lackawana* and the *Bismarck* made a great platform, I don't know where they got the wood.

She was just 16 when she was married. After the wedding she jumped into bed with all her wedding clothes on, and turned her back on her husband. Early in the morning, she got up and walked to mass.

After the baby started all her feeling for her husband changed. Where before she had been glad when he flirted with the other girls in an attempt to make her jealous, now she was furious with jealousy. Even after she was pregnant she used to walk about with him on his secret surveying trips in search of guano. Coming home from parties by moonlight he used to lead her horse and teach her to decline *Ich liebe dich* and "give me a kiss." At first she did not know how to cook German food:

My father had a big family and he lived very plain. Just boiled beef and taro, no butter and no bread. Then when I was married my husband said, "I want you to go into the kitchen and superintend the cooking," and I said, "I did not marry you to be a cook!" But he said, "No, but you must learn so that you can train the others to cook." Still I was not interested. Until once we had been out at a party with a group of German officers and it was so late that Mrs. Decker, she was the nearest neighbor we had and she was an Irish orphan who had been trained by the Williams family so that she was a wonderful cook, said, "You had better come home with us." She cooked us all a wonderful dinner and then when we came home my husband said, "Look how she can cook. Now I am ashamed to ask officers here for all that you would give them would be beer and a little bread and radish." Then I was jealous and I started to learn to cook. On Sundays we used to go out to the warships, to morning champagne on one ship and to luncheon on another, and whenever there was a new dish, my husband would taste it and look at me and then I would understand and I would go home and try it. That is the way I learned to cook.

I never learned to cook from a cook book, but later I learned all the medicine and care of the sick which I knew from an old cook book. For five years after we came up here we had no doctor. My husband was very particular about his food, especially about the soup. Everything must come very hot to the table. First I had to see to his food, then to all the children, and then I could get something to eat myself. He was not strong, for about ten years he was all right and then he could no longer work. So I took all the plantation off his hands and he went about recruiting on my sister's ships and went about on the warships and so he could write his books and do the work that he liked. It was not malaria but something internal. But I was sorry for him and I remembered how patient and gentle he had been with me when I first married him and so I tried to make everything as easy for him as possible. My sister used to complain. Her house was very near to ours but sometimes I did not go over there for months. She used to come over and scold and say, "Phebe, Richard keeps you just like an old hen with her eggs. Why do you let him make a slave of you?" But I said, "Emma, he does not make me, I like it. I have enough to do here with my children." My sister said that the reason I was so strong was because I had so many children and with each child all the bad and impure things were drained out of my blood. My sister was a great reader and she read politics and could talk politics with anyone and she read medicine too. And she used to talk to me. Oh, she was very clever, was my sister. She used to give great parties and drink a great deal of champagne but it was only so she could forget her business. Otherwise she could not go to sleep at night but would lie awake figuring and figuring. One thing she was sorry about was that my husband did not teach me bookkeeping. I used to keep a day book for the plantation but that was all. When my husband died she started a ledger for me but I did not keep it up.

From 1881 on, the great sprawling kinship group, of which Queen Emma was the business head, with her two successive male partners, Farrel and Kolbe, and the Parkinsons the intellectual and ethical components, played a major role in establishing the "contact culture." Brothers came from Samoa, with half-caste or Samoan wives; other Samoans were brought up as assistants in the task of surveying and acquiring land and setting up plantations. Germans and Australians and New Zealanders came to the islands and married into the group. The missions came, Protestant and Catholic, and began to establish their domains and procedures. Neo-Melanesian grew into a language.

Every detail of the new way of life had to be transplanted, invented or adapted: the style of house, with great verandahs, the woodwork brought from Germany; the style of cooking; the style of entertaining. Dealings with local natives, methods of recruiting, the style in which the indentured laborers should live, what they ate, what they wore, how their relationships to their employers were regulated—all of these had to be elaborated. In these, memories of Samoan custom, experience of the violence of Jonas Coe, of the formalities of German life, all played a part. In this emerging style of life the Samoans embodied the possibility of intermarriage working well. They also provided a strong population that could withstand the rigors of the territory, and they were a constant reminder of the cultural backwardness of the natives of New Britain and the other islands. Where the Samoans were tall and strong, with a highly developed political system and courtlike etiquette, the natives of New Britain were smaller, darker, thin, and disease ridden, divided into small ineffective political groups, used to head-hunting, slave raiding, and cannibalism; shifty, suspicious, and treacherous in their habits of relating themselves to strangers.

"In Samoa there is sentiment and novelty and romance. Here there is only passion. They are more like animals." (Here Mrs. Parkinson reflected accurately the feeling of the Samoans who treated the indentured Melanesian natives whom the infamous recruiter Bully Hayes brought to Samoa as *meauli,* "black things.") But she had also the mission model of compassion:

"When we first came to the country, Richard and Farrel and I put our heads together and said we would always play fair with the natives, always give them all that they deserved, always keep our words, both our threats and our promises. And they know that that is so, and so we never have any trouble getting laborers. Now [1929] the government regulation is that they must build long houses on the plantation with board or cement floors. The boys don't like that. They steal away on Sundays and build their own little huts where two or three can lie around, have a fire, and enjoy a little bit of fish or some other *kaikai* [food] that they have found. In the big house they are ashamed. I quite understand. If you are to succeed with the natives you must study their comfort a little."

Before the group from Samoa came, "One Father had landed at Rabaul but the natives burnt him out." Then a second group tried to start a mission at Kokopo, and were again burnt out but their lives were spared because they had come to love Miti, as Mrs. Parkinson was called. Later a third mission group came and Queen Emma sold them the land at Vunapope so that her sister might have her religion near her. Every Sunday she went by canoe to mass and brought the altar linen back to wash.

She used to buy the little native children who were captured in war and destined for slavery for life and send them to the sisters to rear. She held markets with the natives from all around and learned to know their names and collect their gossip. Thus she discovered who had slaves and bought them for ten fathoms of *tambu* (shell money) —the price of a large pig—and sent them to the mission.

The first German government station was in the Duke of York Islands, at Kewura. The German flag was hoisted but there was no government for a long time. Richard Parkinson was the station master. Later the "government" moved to New Britain and started a station at Kokopo. The Parkinsons warned them to be careful not to let any of the "station boys" interfere with the *maries* (native women) when they came down to the beach to market. Before in earlier days the Parkinsons had had trouble with their laborers flirting or "pulling" the bush *maries;* the laborers would be killed by the bush natives and a retaliatory expedition would be necessary. But the government was not careful and very soon the trouble began again. The natives came to Mrs. Parkinson and she told them to go to the government, but the government would not listen. The local natives got more and more dissatisfied and stirred up feelings "against all the white men in the country."

Then there was a native named Talavai, who belonged to Pararatawa, who invented a bullet proof paint. You had to come into his enclosure and bring with you a white fowl without any dark or colored feathers on it. Then this fowl was cooked and eaten with Talavai, and you paid so much *tambu*. Only a fathom if you were poor, and then it went up. Then Talavai had a test of the paint. After he has said some words over the paint and talked to the spirits and painted the man—just ordinary red paint, volcanic clay from Matupe such as the natives used to sell in their markets—he would take a gun—in those days the natives had only brass guns and Enfields that had to be rammed with a ramrod—the natives used to make bullets out of bits of lead. I used to make bullets too out of all kinds of lead. You just melt the lead, pour it in a mold, stick it in water and there it is. So Talavai would stand up at one end of the enclosure and have the native stand up at the other. He would hold up his hand and say, "Here is the bullet" and the native couldn't see. Then he would put it in and the powder and the paper and the cap and shoot it off, and the native would find just a little blood-red spot on his chest. But he had not put a bullet in his gun, he had put in a little blood-red fruit like a cherry—we planted some at Kuradui and I used to make a kind of blanc mange of it, lovely and red—into the gun instead, and this would be the red spot. And natives far and near came to be painted and in some faraway districts men who dealt in these things—I call them priests —came and bought the secret for a hundred fathoms of *tambu* and then they painted more people. So it—the *mailan* they called it—spread and spread and the natives attacked Kokopo.

The white men had to watch all the time with arms and they couldn't work their plantations and at night the natives would come down and shoot into the houses. The natives sent word to us that if we stayed at home they wouldn't bother us as we had always been good to them, but that they were going to get those bad white men at Kokopo.

The Germans made one or two expeditions into the bush but they didn't know where to find them, the natives would all hide and they only succeeded in wounding a few. Then the natives would show the wounds to Talavai and he would say, "Ah, yes, you must have broken one of the taboos. You must have slept with a woman or eaten a fowl which was not pure white," and the natives were quite satisfied. Finally the people at Kokopo got tired and they sent for a war vessel. Then the Judge said to Richard, "Now you must come in with us. We are only a handful of white people here in the country and you know well enough that if the natives succeed in killing us and capturing all our ammunition they will come and kill you afterwards." And that was true, they would have done that to rid the country of white people altogether. So Richard said, "Yes, I will help you now and we'll end this."

A plan of attack was formed. Richard went on the warship to direct the shelling, Kolbe led one party and Schmili the other, and Phebe guided a third. The first two parties were to go on top and come down, while the third waited halfway in the center. Phebe planned the march, sent out scouts and spies, and after guiding up the central file, came back and directed operations from the plantations. After a good deal of fighting and killing and burning of houses, the whites came down and told Phebe and Richard to make peace with the natives and make each district pay a peace offering of *tambu.* Phebe pleaded with the natives, offering to put her *tambu* on the pile with theirs, but first they were stubborn and more were shelled. Then finally at night there came little whispers, "Miti?" "Yes, who's that?" "Me with the *tambu.*" "All right, you go and wait until morning." They waited all night long and then she made them tie the *tambu* in rolls and carry it into the district office. Then the station master told her it was all finished and to assure the natives that the affair was over. This she did. But later, at the instigation of the Raluana missionaries, the government wrote asking her to collect further fines. This is her answer:

I have the honour to acknowledge the receipt of your request of the 15th October and in reply would respectfully decline to take any further action in the matter for the following reasons.

At the request of the station master I some time ago assured the natives of Paparatawa that no further steps would be taken against them by the authorities and I fear that to go to them with this demand for additional *diwarra* [shell money] would tend to create a feeling of distrust in the minds of the natives and to impair the friendly relations at present existing between us.

I would add that in the future difficulties of this kind, I would be both obliged and relieved if the authorities could dispense with my assistance and deal with the natives directly.

When the Parkinsons first moved to New Britain word of her fair-haired children spread up into the bush. Once two New Britain natives took ears of Indian corn, which they had also introduced, and made dolls of them with black seeds for eyes, wrapped them in trade cloth and carried them up into the bush, charging a length of shell money for a glimpse of "pickaninny belong missus." One of the dolls accidentally dropped and the deceit was discovered.

Once she started across the island, with only a boy to drive, to help deliver the only white woman on that part of New Britain. She herself was beginning another pregnancy. Suddenly she felt a great pain, dismounted, went behind a bush, put her handkerchief on the ground and miscarried. She wrapped the miscarriage up, put it in her pocket, climbed back into her seat, and told the boy to turn and drive home. When she got home she told her husband to look in her pocket. Then she fainted. "But I always wondered what color that baby's eyes would have been," she said.

When we first started to grow tobacco back of Malapau the natives used to steal it and sell it to a trader away down on the coast. One day one of these traders was at our place and he asked me, "Do these natives have tobacco plantations in the bush?" I said, "No, not that I know of, why?" He said, "Well, they have been selling a lot of tobacco to me." I said, "What natives?" He said, "These natives right up back of your plantation." Then I knew that they had been stealing. I took some tapa and some tin cans and pictures and all kinds of rubbish and I took them out and strung them up on the edge of the plantation and I told the natives, "This is taboo which I have brought from Samoa." There was a road there and they were all so frightened they never even walked on the road any more.

Then when I went down to Kolai all the natives were stealing the fallen coconuts. There were plenty on the trees and none on the ground. So I had two old skulls in my boxes which I had not sent away with some collection that I made. I took painted cloth and put it in their eye sockets and took some hair from an old *tuuiga* [Samoan headdress] and glued it to their heads and tied streamers of tapa on them and I had the boys fasten them up on sticks. Then I told the natives that they were the skulls of my mother's brothers, Talimai and Ma'aona, which I had brought from Samoa to guard my coconuts and that I had told them just to let my own boys gather the nuts and bring them in but that if anyone stole one they would kill them. Oh, they were frightened, especially by the tapa, because there was nothing European about it.

Sometimes the complex traditional life of Samoa intruded even more directly into the new life in New Britain: "My mother was the *tamafafine* and the young people were dying in the *tamatane* side and two of the chiefs made the long journey up here, to get my mother to come down and take off the curse. She would have to get a fine mat and spread it on the graves of those who had died and gather an insect just as in time of war and make a long speech saying she would not curse them any more. My sister was the one whom all my brothers' wives and children had to be very careful not to offend, she was the *matua* [eldest]. My brothers' wives had to wait on her and give her anything that she asked for for fear she would curse their children. And her son could go and ask anything from them."

When she had turned her back on the young Samoan *manaias* and their gaiety and laughter, and prayed God day and night to make her love the tall strange man she had married, she had chosen finally to adhere to the strange beautiful hard path which was the heritage of her white blood. Her sisters turned up their noses at the Samoans. They were educated away from Samoa, and they lost touch with their people. They forgot the tolerance, the high courtesy, the breeding of the finely strung chiefs. They forgot the devices for making life simple and beautiful in the tropics. They put on European clothes and adopted European manners, clinging hard to the trappings of that to which they wished so earnestly to belong. Robbed of pride in their mother's race, they had to seek feverishly for money and place, for some status in the world to which they only half belonged. But Phebe, proud of her Samoan blood, loving devotedly the little disinherited mother who used to come and kiss her secretly in the bushes, had no holes in her pride to patch up with foreign tatters. All that she did in mastering the details of European housekeeping, in learning to keep a garden from which, years later, the harrassed German housewives in Rabaul could borrow to please the palates of their exacting husbands, she did not to be European but "to make Richard happy" for "he was a sick man and I did not like to worry him." She learned German to please him, and so that she could talk to the young officers who came to the house, sitting up at night after the babies were in bed. Queen Emma read omnivorously, that nothing might escape her, that she might be able to meet her guests on their own ground. Phebe read less, but all that she read she remembered and related to the life she knew. Emma remonstrated with her: "If you would urge Richard to make money and to use all his brains and his education to make money for you and the children it would be better than this way. Here you work like a nigger while he runs around making a name for himself. He is just a selfish man." But she said, "Ah, Emma, let him be. He is a sick man and if he can find the things to do which he loves it is enough. We have enough to live on." "But how about the children?" "Well, we are giving them all a good education. They will have to work when they grow up just as we have done, just as Richard has done. I would not spoil his life and keep him from the work he loves just so the children can live without working when they grow up."

Richard Parkinson had been brought to New Britain by Emma, to do the recruiting, the buying of land, the surveying and managing plantations for her, for eight pounds a month. When the New Guinea company came, Richard left and became plantation starter for them, and Phebe had to take over the management of her sister's plantations. She had done much of it before because Richard had never learned to speak pidgin. It was Phebe who talked with the natives, who stuffed the birds to be sent to Germany, who medicated the natives, who labeled the specimens. "Richard did all the brain work."

Richard was a man burning with a desire to establish himself; he wanted to set a good table, he wanted his collars starched more stiffly than those of any dignitary in the little outpost. Phebe had wanted roses in return for the rare plants they sent away. She could never gather enough flowers for her garden. But he refused. They should go as free gifts of science from Richard Parkinson. Everywhere he had debtors, people to whom he had sent beetles, snakes, fish, butterflies, land shells, curios, photographs. When he went abroad in 1893 he wrote her letters filled with names, the names of those at whose tables he had sat, who had received him as a great scientist, a man who had made real contributions. The Sultan of Jahore entertained him in his palace. Even Rome, where he as a Protestant had no part, accepted him. Could he not tell them much of the progress of their missions? Aside from the men he met and the deference he received, his greatest interests were the buildings, the palaces, the evidence of wealth and power. The taste for eminence which he gained in his childhood among the ducal children was rewarded.

He returned to New Britain in 1894, strong and happy and proud. Phebe saw his exultation and was glad that she had laughed down Emma's complaints. What he was doing was good—he was adding to the fine things of the world, things that governments, being wide and informed of Christ, recognized. She was the more confirmed in her faith when Dr. Hahl became the German governor. He recognized the things for which Richard stood; the hospitable roof of the scientist was the roof he found it wise to honor with his friendship. After Richard's death in 1909 the governor did everything he could for the "Widow Parkinson," who also did many things for the government. Among the letters that she had treasured was a letter dated 25 March 1912: "Dr. Hahl wants about twenty police boys for Madang and Eitape (about 20 each). Will you be able to recruit them for us among the *kanakas* here? For every boy the government will pay you thirty M. Wanted strong and big boys all 3 years contract, except those who have served already. These; 2 years contract at least. If possible let us have some boys this week in order that Dr. Hahl may send them to New Guinea in the *Manila*. Yours sincerely, J. A. Steubel."

All her strength which had been channeled for twenty-five years into motherhood and wifehood was now freed. The vigor of the little girl who had fought all comers in Apia, who had swum reefs and advanced unafraid among hostile natives, who had shared the secrets of the Dukduks and crocheted for them emblems of different colors and never betrayed their secrets to their women, now came into its own. But it was the memories of the European half of her life, such as the observances at Christmas, that were her symbols of personal deprivation and grief.

In Samoa we did not have a Christmas tree, we had Santa Claus and my father used to tell us all to hang up our stockings on the side of the chairs. Afterwards, my father went away and my sister filled them, and we peeked and saw them and it was never so nice after that. But in my husband's home we had a Christmas tree. He planted a whole row of avocado trees and he gave one pear to each boy. He was—how do you say, sentimental?—and so he gave each boy a pear and he took the spade and dug the ground and then Otto must plant one and Max one, and then he said, "When you grow up you can say I planted this tree when I was a child." Each Christmas we cut the young top of one of these trees for our Christmas tree. We had a stand which held up the tree and when you "keyed" it, it made music. After it was all trimmed and all the candles there, and the presents piled up, I would stay with the children and Richard would go and light the candles and then throw open the doors. Then we would all join hands and dance around the tree and sing "*Stille Nacht*" and "*Oh Tannenbaum*." Oh, it was lovely. Just our own family. Other people would ask us to go out on Christmas Eve but Richard said no, just our own family. He was always like that, he liked to keep the children at home. In the evening we played games with them, Halma and Uddo, so that they always liked home best. So it was with the cemetery. When he was so ill he had us carry him over in his chair, and he planned out the cemetery where he and I should lie and all the children. He said, "If any of your sisters or your sisters' children want to rest here, put them there on each side but in the center just our own family."

When my mother was very old she knew that she would die soon and she wanted to go back to Samoa to die. My sister and my brother gave their consent but when she asked me, I said, "Oh, Mother, I have taken care of you all these years, and I would like to take care of your grave, too. If you go there you may die and be buried at sea, or in Samoa. Who will look after your grave as I would?" She cried then, and she stayed. When she was dying, for seven months I slept down with her at night, then up to see about my husband's meals, then down again to her. At the New Year they were dancing and having a big party at my sister's and my mother was dying then. I thought of a play I had seen in Sydney where the mother was watching beside a dying child's bed and the father was away carousing, and I was very sad. The next day my sister came and wept and said, "Oh, I should have been here before." Once I had to go up to the house to see about my husband. When I came back my sister said, "Thank God you have come. Twice Mother tried to die but she looked for you and stayed." Then Mother looked at me and then she died.

After my husband died we always had a Christmas tree just for me and my baby boy. Dr. Hahl always urged us to come up to the government house on Christmas Eve and I said, "No, we will stay at home as my husband wished." When my change of life came I went right off my head. I think it was because I had so much trouble then with the death of my husband and of my little son. I used to get up in the night and go out and lie in the graveyard. I would not know what I was doing, but in the morning when it was quite light they would find me there. When they had a Christmas tree here at Sumsum I was too sad and I cried. Silly! So I said, "I will not come any more just to be sad and make you sad," and at Kiep [her last plantation] I said, "Paul, we won't have any Christmas tree."

After Richard's death she still tried to carry on some of his collecting activities. "I remember when I got that great tapa standard from the Baining to send to Chicago. It was one of the things which my husband had promised to send and which he had not sent before he died. I had spies out and I found they were going to have a big feast and dance with this. They cut a man's back specially to receive the end of the standard, and all the men hold it up there just for a minute. All that pain and work just for a little moment. Then they gave it to me and I packed it in with bark and fern, oh, it was a big thing. I could not have sent it if I had not been great friends with the officers of the ship which sent it to Chicago for me."

All through the long years when she had been Richard's wife and the mother of his children, and the assistant in all his collecting schemes, and Emma's assistant manager, she had taken a ceaseless interest in the natives, with whose help they had built the island way of life.

"When my sister sold out she wanted me to sell out too and come to Sydney with her. But I said, 'I have all my children.' She said, 'Never mind, I will educate all your children. You come and live with me in Sydney.' She could not bear to part with me. But I said, 'No, I am ambitious too. I will stay here and run my plantation and bring up my children. This is my life. I have lived here since I was 18. If I went away I would not know what to do.' Once I had to go to Sydney and oh, I was very unhappy. I had to wear gloves and corsets and there was nothing to do. If I went away from here I would miss the natives so. They are my life. I am so interested in everything that happens to them."

She described her first little glimpse of civilization, in Cooktown, Australia, in 1882 when she made a trip south as a young mother.

I had taken with me a native boy who had his hair dyed, to carry the baby. There was a woman there. Oh, she was crazy about that boy and she got out games and sat down on the floor and played games with him. She was quite childish, the old lady. Then there was a railroad about thirty miles it ran out of Cooktown. My sister took me on it so that I could get a little idea of a railroad. At the end of it was a town with whole families living in tents. On the train was a Chinaman with a European wife all loaded down with jewels and she looked so unhappy and turned her face away from him as if she were ashamed to be seen with him. And in Cooktown I saw two half-caste Chinese girls who were language teachers in the schools. They wore simple black dresses with white collars and cuffs and they were very well educated. We saw them when we went to visit the school.

In Sydney I went to a dressmaker and she said, "Oh, are you staying with ————?" "Yes." "Well, a little while ago she had two island ladies staying with her, two princesses." I said, "Well, they aren't from my islands, there are no princesses there." She said, "What island do you come from?" I said, "New Britain." "Yes," she said, "that is where they come from; they are the nieces of Queen Emma." "Oh," I said, very much disgusted, "they are just my niece and my nephew's wife—they are no princesses. My sister is no queen. That is just the name which the people give her in the islands because she is good to them all." I was ashamed.

We were invited to a garden party of the Admiral but I refused to go. The commander of the little war vessel which took us down said, "You are a fool not to go, and if you won't go at least let the children go." But I said, "No, we do not belong there and I haven't the money for the clothes. It is not our place, and if we went and the people at home read about it they would all say, 'Look at those people trying to push themselves in down south where they don't belong.' "

All the tourists on a big steamer that was in were fascinated by that boy's hair and they cut off little pieces. The poor boy came to me frightened and said, "Oh, Missus, I will die now. What do they do this for, I have done them no harm, why do they want to kill me?" So I explained to him that it was just a curiosity.

Her only response to her mixed blood was to look carefully at the ground on which she stood, to be wary of overstepping boundaries. On her own ground she reigned as surely as her sister, but she disliked going beyond it, and refused to climb to any heights to which she could not see the steps clearly. One of the severest blows to her pride came from gossipy criticism when the commander of a German warship had once placed her on his right and Mrs. Hahl, the governor's wife, on his left. Years later, after the Australian regime was established, a district officer had offered to let her go with him on a tax collecting trip, so she could recruit while he taxed. She refused. It was not her place to thrust herself in with government.

She had criticism as well as loyalty for the church.

After all the years that I had supported and been the foundation of the Catholic Mission I had a dreadful fight with the Bishop and I didn't enter the church for six years. Long before when we started the plantation we had Buka boys who would marry local *maries* or New Ireland girls and the mothers would die and leave babies which the fathers could not look after and I kept them and brought them up. I was getting quite a lot of them and so I went to the Bishop and asked about sending them to the mission. We arranged that they should go to the school and if any wished to become catechists or marry catechists or stay in the convent to help the sisters they could do so, but if not they should come back to me. And sometimes the boys ran away but I always sent them back to the fathers because I did not think it was right for the discipline of the school. Then there were two girls who used to come home for the holidays and they wanted to marry two of our boys. I had been sending the boys for a year to the father to receive instruction and they were almost ready to be baptized. So the girls told the sisters and the sisters asked me, and I said, "Let the girls come home for a visit and see if they really like the boys." So they sat on the porch and chewed betel nut and talked and they all liked to marry one another. So I sent them back to the convent and I asked the father to baptize the boys now as they were going to marry the girls. He was very cross and he said, "Does the Bishop know that?" I said, "His Lordship has gone south, but the father in charge knows." He was cross then and would not baptize the boys. When the Bishop came back he got round the girls and made them write me letters saying they did not want to be married. So I went to see him and I told him he had just gotten round the girls and told them what to say. And he said, "We know best. We don't want the girls to marry these boys." But I said, "Father, how about our old agreement?" "Oh," he said, "that is all gone now. The government has come and the government upholds the law that the church is the guardian of all orphans. We made our agreement long ago when the country was young and there was yet no government and it was hard to get children for the school." I argued with him and he said, "Oh, my child, you are not the Mrs. Parkinson of former days. You answer your father in God back. I am your father and you must not talk back to me." I said, "I know, Monsignor, but I am a widow now, I do not have my husband to fight for me and I must speak up, I must fight for my children and for my native children." So he said, "Well, I am very sorry." And I said, "Is that your last word, Monsignor?" He said, "Yes." I said, "Good day, Monsignor," and I walked out. He followed me out and said, "My child, you must not be angry," but I said, "Good day," and drove away—oh, I was wild!

I went to Rabaul and I had them look up all the books, the German laws and the Australian, and there was no such law. Then I could not forgive the fathers. They wanted me to go to court over it and said I would surely win the case, but I would not for the sisters were taking my side and I did not want to drag them in. So for six years I never went near the church and neither did my children. I used to go sometimes to the sisters' chapel, but never where I would see the fathers. The sisters begged me but I said, "When I can forgive them and go to church and think only of our Lord I will go, but now if I went I would only think of how angry I am."

Later she went to Buka, saw a priest there, and went to confession. She was advised to come back and make her peace at Vunapope, and she went back on the day of the new bishop's consecration and was wept over by all the sisters who were supposed to be entertaining the Rabaul ladies. She explained, "It's just crying over the lost sheep that has come back. I do not think there is only one religion, but I do not believe it is right to change. One should stick to one thing, that is my idea of a good woman."

As her precise German husband met her demand for form and orderliness, her religion met her demands for fundamentals, high prices, deep feeling; her life in New Guinea met her need for activity, and her husband's desire for scientific eminence fed her restless curiosity. It was an essential trait of her character never to forget anything, always to seek to relate everything that she saw, and always to want to know how everything was done. "We went to the Admiralty Islands and I saw those spears of obsidian. They told me they did not carve them or cut them out and I was very curious to know how they could make them. So then they took me and showed me how they knocked them off, just as they are on the spears, with one blow of a stone. Very interesting!" Or, "My husband used to buy skeletons and they used to bring them down perfect, even to the little finger bones and toe bones. I was curious to see how they did it and so I made an expedition up into the bush to see. They bind the knees and set them up on a platform and let them rot away in the forest until the skeleton is all whitened. And, oh, the blow flies were terrible." She was the first to give the Bainings an axe, and "Oh, they were happy. Before, it had taken them two years to cut down a tree with their axes of stone." Among the South Coast Arawes she found that the custom of doing the babies' heads up in bark for six weeks led to dreadful sores, that the babies' eyes protruded and their faces were pale and bloated. She took the German doctors down there. Among the Blanche Bay natives the brother and sister taboo was so strict that if a brother passed near a place where a sister was working and a third person saw him pass, they were both killed. Sometimes a powerful chief would delay the killing, if they were relatives of his, and send word secretly to the Parkinsons, and Richard would go up and save them.

July 6, 1929, I tried to sum it all up: "The Germans saw in her a symbol of the peaceful conquest of the strange South Seas, of the gradual combination of island qualities with the Teutonic virtues. They loved her for her ease, her humor, her swift friendliness and tolerance—these recalled to them all that was most appealing about Samoa. They respected and cherished her housewifeliness, her humility, her deference and recognition of authority, of order, of rank. In these things she was a true *Hausfrau*. Her very genuine usefulness to the administration aside from the purely personal contribution made by her home and her hospitality were remembered, doubly remembered. In cherishing and helping her in her widowhood they were serving at once the romance of her origin and the piety of her convictions."

The war undid her cruelly, most cruelly because she could feel no part in it. She did not know which side Richard would have taken had he lived. Since he was half English, half German, and bi-lingual, with friends in both countries, it was impossible for her to imagine what his allegiance would have been. Emma was dead, and her clear decisiveness was denied her. And so it was without emotion, with only curiosity, that she saw the war approaching New Guinea. Her first feeling was symbolic of all that the war was to do to her. The new governor was a comparative stranger. Her relations with the government had been strained since one of her daughters had publicly struck a German officer with a whip for insulting her younger sister. "All the Navy and all the people who had never been in the Army took our part, but all the Army was wild that the Imperial uniform should be so insulted, and by a woman." When the order came for all the German families to prepare to take refuge at Toma in case of attack her name was not among them. The governor explained that he did not think she would be in any danger. She was too experienced to be in danger from the natives; she was after all not a German but a Samoan, the invaders would not harm her. And so the first note of exclusion was struck. Technically she was a German subject, but she shared neither their fears nor was she given their narrow solicitude for their own. Patiently she sought to adjust herself to the situation.

Here was a war at her doors and something of her old curiosity flared up. She made her way into Kokopo to see what a true European war was like. She found a ring of sentries who demanded a pass; this was new and interesting. Within the barriers she encountered a young officer whom she had known as a clerk and who asked her about Louisa (her eldest daughter who was married to a New Zealander). A sense of great familiarity descended upon her. Here was just another set of officers, on another group of warships, to be entertained and fed, given coffee or whiskey, pineapples or guavas, beds or dry shirts. She saw the group of idle casual soldiers chatting, smoking, sitting about on the grass. Her heart misgave her again. This was not discipline. She wasn't sure that this was a real army after all. As she gave tea and whiskey to the young officers who passed her home and danced with her daughters through the years of the military occupation, she came to wonder more and more. There was a casualness here, a lack of form which distressed her. She tried to treat them as she had treated the Germans. She gave them vegetables and fruit, she made them welcome at her table, she gave of her knowledge of the natives.

Through the years of the military occupation she partly succeeded in deluding herself into thinking that the old life would be repeated in new guise; that she would be again the adored hostess, the wise guide, the gentle heroine of a formal governing class. But when the military government departed her slender hopes were shattered. The strange assortment of clerks, engineers, and the like, who came, without tradition or air of authority, without precedent, without form, to govern a country full of *kanakas* and a few half-caste and quasi-Germans who somehow had been allowed to remain, knew her not. Against her they turned the whole weight of their indifference, in some cases their hostility, for was she not a naturalized German? Or they showed her contempt, for did she not have native blood in her veins? And she felt herself shut out from something which she could neither covet nor admire. All her life she had spent in pious conformance to the outer trappings of ideals which she admired. She had accepted the standards of white civilization, its best traditions of loyalty, honor, fidelity. She had believed these standards to be inalienably associated with form, with distinction. That was her Samoan inheritance with its emphasis upon rank. She did not associate civilized standards with Germany alone; actually her father was American, her husband of English descent. All the Europeans she met were either scientists, clothed for her in the robes of great learning whatever their slight deficiencies of manners, or officers of the regular navies or armies of the world. She was unprepared to see the civilization which she had cherished represented so unevenly, so casually, as it was in the first days of the civil government. Expropriation, although she herself was not expropriated, brought her losses, inconveniences. But these did not wound her as did the random discourtesy to which she was subjected. She felt cheated and betrayed of her life's devotion. Richard was dead. His collections were completed and safely in museums. The fabric of the society in which she had once been a happy, active member was gone forever.

Quietly, with hands which were browned from wind and rain, but still slender and beautiful, she put from her all pretense of participation in this new world in which she seemed to have no place. There were still her children and her children's plantations to be looked after. There was still work that she could do, natives who would give her their children gladly; there were little grandchildren with fair hair and German names, little grandchildren with fair hair and English names for whom she could labor. The fundamental things which she had trusted throughout her life were there; the cellar of the house was not burnt in the great flames which had consumed her ideal world. She went back to these simple things; happy to take a swift dip in a river that she must cross, happy to settle some puzzling native dispute, happy to increase the yield of the plantation that worked for her absent children: "I often think of that other grandmother in Germany and how she has no other grandchildren and how she must long to have them now. I have had them so long and I felt selfish." And she said, "My mother used to tell me that she had heard her grandmother and her mother say that when you grow old, your sight gets a little dimmer, your hearing a little poorer. She used to laugh and say, 'I guess it is the second childhood.' So now that I am getting old, I am not surprised or angry. If one did not know, if one's mother had not said what to expect when one began to get old, one might mind. But if one knows what to expect, then it is all right."

The years dealt no more kindly with her. One by one the plantations she had helped to found passed out of the family; she herself eked out a precarious living, sometimes doing a little recruiting, sometimes living with her favorite grandson. In 1934, because of the effects of the depression, a promised job failed to materialize; she and a grandson were left stranded in Buka Passage. Describing her situation, she wrote in a letter, ". . . the mission's financial affairs are very bad, they are cutting down everything to save expenses, no money coming in as copra is very low down, well the long and the short of it. I packed up all the old rubbish left over from my old home besides plants, poultry, and living animals, dogs and so on. . . . for the home now you should see us amongst our goods and chattels without a home or a penny. This hut belongs to an acquaintance of mine—and he kindly told us to put up in it. . . . the sooner we are back to Rabaul the better we will be. There at least I have a little home [this I saw in 1938 when I saw her for the last time, on my way to the Sepik River] and everything convenient. Here I have to go right back to 51 years ago when I first arrived at New Britain, just a little grass roof as a kitchen, cooking on two irons, baking bread between two empty kerosene tins." The letter ended: "Trusting you and your good man are enjoying good health and much luck in this New Year let me hear from you *la'u pele* [my dear] *tele le alofa* [with much love] Yours very sincerely Phebe Parkinson, who *ele galo le uo moni tofa soi fua* [never forgets the true friend, good bye and life to you]."

She died soon after the war ended.

A true child of the South Seas, never denying her inheritance, she took with eager and so skillful hands all that civilization brought to her feet and made a way of life of it. And the World War which wrecked the fabric of European civilization found its echo in Kuradui, when she left it empty-handed. The superstructure of her life, her world of the imagination, crumbled and fell. She remains, the best excuse for European invasion of the graceful Polynesian world, for she showed what a Polynesian can do with European values when they are grafted on to a firm belief and pride in Polynesian blood.

7

The Form and
Substance of Status:
A Javanese-American
Relationship

Cora Du Bois

This is certainly not the life story of Ali ben Usmus, the Javanese "boy" who was, in the course of six months on Alor, to set my domestic standards and to become a friend. It is rather a somewhat halting recapitulation of a relationship for which my egalitarian American background had not prepared me. There had been servants in my home but they were either women who were quasimembers of the family or men who worked primarily on the grounds and were companionable but casual figures in my childhood world. The strangeness for me in my relationship with Ali lay in its closeness and mutual loyalty without intimacy. In a biographical sense, we never knew *about* each other although our relationship was subtle, disciplined, and devoted. To my dishonor, as I review that relationship after twenty years, I gave less than I received and I understood less than Ali about what was happening humanly during a period when we were both experiencing unfamiliar and stressful situations.

I first saw Ali in December, 1937. He was seated cross-legged on the verandah of my room overlooking the court of the old Java Hotel in Djakarta that was still called Batavia in those prewar days. Everyone had strongly advised me to take a trained servant with me from Java to Alor. He would help me travel, handle my innumerable cases of supplies, and settle me in an interior village among the "savages" of that island which lay some 700 miles east of Java at the end of the Lesser Sunda archipelago. No one ever explicitly said that a *djongos,* a "boy," could be one's protector, mentor, and friend. Officially a *djongos* was a personal servant who in this instance was also to be cook and general factotum. But the dependence of the European in the former Netherlands East Indies on his Indonesian servant, on his skill, tact, and competence, although never explicitly stated, came through clearly.

Dr. Pijper a Dutch scholar in the Department of Islamic Affairs, had been kind enough to institute the search for a suitable *djongos* and to screen possible candidates before sending anyone to me for an interview. Hadi had been the first one. He met one of Dr. Pijper's requirements which was experience with the wild "Alfura" of the outer islands. Hadi was brisk and remarkably self-assured in manner for a Javanese. He may indeed have been a Sumatran. He was perhaps a little too self-assured I felt. He left me with the impression that in a very short time he would take charge of me and the field trip and that his convenience, rather than mine, would be served. My command of Malay was minimal, my knowledge of this land nonexistent. It would be too easy for a vigorous and aggressive man like Hadi to have things his own way. And that he had a way, there was no mistaking.

Next a Javanese couple presented themselves. They were outwardly as meek and subservient as Hadi was not. They were also quite obviously intimidated by the thought of the dangers and hardships of life among the savages of Alor—a spot that seemed more frighteningly remote to them than to me who at least had read the little that was written of the island, knew the semimonthly ship schedule through which it kept in touch with the outer world, and cherished that somewhat misleading sense of familiarity provided by the symbols of cartography. The husband of the couple whose name I do not even recall deferred perhaps too patently to his wife who, in turn, was too patently reluctant to go far from their familiar *kampong* on the outskirts of Djakarta.

With Ali, in that first interview on the verandah, it was immediately a different matter. For a Javanese, he was not prepossessing. Although his body was slender, small, and well muscled and his skin an almost golden yellow, his eyes were rather too full, his nose too broad and his jaw too prognathous for beauty by Javanese standards. There was a sturdy peasant aura about his appearance that disguised the sensitivity of perception and feeling he subsequently evinced. In manner he was assured without being aggressive. At first sight I trusted, rather than liked him.

His letters of reference were only moderately numerous but gave the impression of being genuinely appreciative. *Djongos* always acquired such letters from their employers, usually written in Dutch, or even English, French, and German. Their content was often unknown to their bearers. Custom dictated that they be complimentary but one learned to read between the lines a great deal about the writers and even more about the applicants. Ali's letters seemed genuine in their approval. His last letter was from an employer who had found Ali industrious and faithful during a long research trip to the Aru Islands. Of his former employers I never learned more than I could read between those lines for Ali never spoke of them, or for that matter, rarely spoke of anyone. He possessed the impersonal sensitivity that Westerners have sometimes attributed to the Javanese. His world appeared to be one in which human personality in all its variety was recognized and dealt with delicately but was of no importance. So I never learned, or else do not remember, how long that last trip of Ali's had been, or what kind of man he had last served. In any event, the absence had been long enough for Ali to find on his return that his wife had a son he had not fathered. This I learned only later.

All I knew that muggy December afternoon on the verandah was that Ali was not at all sure that he wanted to go off on another *tournée* and that he certainly would not consider staying eighteen months. I also knew that Ali inspired confidence. We talked of little but the most practical affairs; salary—the going *tournée* rate of fifteen dollars a month; food—to be provided by me; his round trip boat fare as a deck passenger was also my responsibility. The length of his service remained unsettled between us. Ali was to return the next afternnon when we both would have had time to think things over. He wanted to talk to his wife and I wanted to talk to Dr. Pijper.

The next afternoon Ali was again squatting on my verandah when I came out from a siesta that the humid heat and early rising hours in Djakarta made so welcome. The tray with its pot of strong, dark tea, the blue milk, coarse sugar, and two dry flat cookies had been left by the hotel room boy. Ali rose and served my tea. I should have sensed from this gesture alone that Ali had decided to accept me as his *nonja* (lady), but, as I said earlier, Ali was always my superior in the delicacy of his gestures and the subtlety of his communications. What I did know that afternoon was that in twenty-four hours I had convinced myself that six months was long enough to have a Javanese servant with me in the field. The conviction was, of course, fully rationalized. In an Alorese village Ali would be as much a stranger and a *tuan* (gentleman) as I would be a stranger and a *nonja*. My image, at that time, was of a village on Alor "uncontaminated" by outside cultural influences. It was to be a primitive community in which somehow I, as the ethnographer, was to be invisible and imponderable, watching, but in no way affecting, community life. I confess this fantasy not because it was accurate, but because I held it. Ali, I reasoned, might be a disturbing outside influence. As I look back, I suppose I reached this conclusion about our respective influences because he was not an ethnographer and I was. In retrospect also, I recall laying much stress in my own mind on the possibility of Ali's becoming involved with the women of the village and entailing me in consequent difficulties. Whether this was a notion of my own or one that my various European advisors suggested I no longer recall. Looking back on these particular concerns, all I can say is that my rationalizations proved unwarranted. What they did reveal, in a deeper sense, was that I unwittingly was ready to assume responsibility for Ali. I was only to learn later, in a hundred subtle ways, that Ali too was ready to assume responsibility for me.

As I recall the conversation of that second afternoon, we reached complete agreement about all external matters despite my extremely limited command of his language. He would sail in two weeks on the *Valentijne* from Djakarta, he would be in charge of my innumerable pieces of luggage; I would join the *Valentijne* in Lombok some ten days after he left Djakarta; half of his salary was to be paid monthly to his wife by the Java Bank. Money for his passage out and an advance on his first month's salary was turned over to him then and there. It all seemed very business-like at the time but again, as I revalue those first two encounters, I am both touched and delighted by the good faith each placed in the other.

Rereading the letters and journals of that period I am astonished how little salience this subsequently crucial relationship had for me at the time. I was absorbed by the facts and events of a new and engaging environment. My journal is filled with details of the Borobudur, the palace of the Mankunegara, the Prambanan, the silversmiths, the batik makers, in central Java; the consulate at Surabaja; the visit on Bali with Gregory Bateson and Margaret Mead; and the drive across Lombok on Christmas Day, 1937, to meet the *Valentijne* at the open roadstead of Labuan Hadji.

I had been on board several hours before I saw Ali. True, I had immediately inquired of the first mate about "my luggage" and "my *djongos*" (I am afraid just in that order). It was only when Ali himself, trim in his long white ducks, his stiff collared mess-jacket, and his neatly folded turban, knocked on the door that separated the first class from deck passengers, that we met and exchanged cordial, if formal, greetings. I am trying to reconstruct an honest, rather than a flattering account of my behavior. If I must make excuses for myself at this late date, I can only plead the formal distance that existed between Ali and me at the time, and that never really disappeared.

I never knew Ali's age. He may not himself have known it. But I was 34 and he must have been somewhat younger. The difference between his formal Mohammedanism and my rearing in a Christian tradition did not occur to me then and rarely obtruded itself later. The significant difference from beginning to end was dictated by our social status. He was a *djongos* and I a *nonja*. The reciprocal attitudes involved in such a status gap demanded distance, formality, and at its best, mutual respect and loyalty. I was unschooled in the role that our status differences required but Ali knew it to perfection. Courteously, step by step, he taught me not only how I must behave toward him but also what symbols of status I must maintain if both of us were to assume the stance proper to our stations in life. To describe social roles and status in one society by comparison to those in another is more often than not misleading. Even though I was a woman, my position in the Indonesia of that day as a European and a mistress (I use this term as more descriptive than employer) not only exceeded but also differed markedly from any I had been accustomed to. Ali's status as *djongos* to a European was lower than had he been serving a member of the Javanese aristocracy; nevertheless, he belonged to what might be roughly equated with the white collar worker of Western society. In Ali's eyes it was clear that his status was linked to mine. He was careful to see that I had an adequate supply of plates, silverware, and table linen, for those seemed to be one of the important symbols of status in colonial society—at least in the eyes of the local servant.

Much later I learned how much they meant. After Ali and I had settled down to what seemed to me a most decorous domestic routine in the mountains of Alor, we were informed that official visitors were expected. I suggested opening several cans of food specially reserved for such state occasions. What I had not considered, but Ali produced, was the full panoply of table linens and wares and in the center of the table a mason jar most inelegantly stuffed full of the argeratum and cannas that were almost the only indigenous flowers of the area. Whatever astonishing apitudes Ali was to evince, flower arrangement was not one of them. I doubt that it was part of either of the two heritages he strove to command—the Javanese and the Dutch.

But these minor questions were still in the future. As we set out for Alor, I feel sure that both of us were to some degree apprehensive. Although Ali had had the experience of at least one trip into "outer savagery," he was after all an urban born-and-bred Djakartan. For me, this was my first trip to the Orient and I was hampered by what was perhaps an excessive seriousness about the task that lay ahead.

During the first days on the *Valentijne* I saw Ali only rarely. Occasionally he was to be seen in his informal dress lounging on the forward deck—barefoot, bare torso, and wearing a pair of knee length blue shorts with a draw string at the waist and the black fezlike cap affected by Indonesian Moslems. But several times Ali asked to see me. Then he always presented himself, eyes downcast, and dressed in impeccable white ducks and his turban. The first time he complained of a headache and wanted *obat* (medicine). After making sure he had no fever, I provided aspirin. The next day he asked for more. The third day, cured, he asked to accompany me and two or three other passengers ashore. Thereafter Ali was always ready and waiting to join us in the rowboat that took us to the beach. He never obtruded himself. In fact he never spoke. But he followed a few yards in the rear wherever I went—making no comment, offering no explanations. I drifted into expecting him to be on hand and found myself turning to him when small purchases were to be made. As the days wore on I tried once or twice to enlist his assistance in studying Malay but it was soon clear that Ali had neither heart nor aptitude for the task. I am sure that he was not unintelligent and that Malay, rather than one of the other languages of Java, was his mother tongue. He was certainly willing to be of service, but perhaps the reversal of roles in which the servant becomes the teacher of his mistress may have disturbed his nice sense of propriety.

Then came the last distraught evening on the *Valentijne* when we reached Alor's only port. The emotions and confusion of the occasion are not relevant to this account of Ali's and my relationship, since Ali had no part of it except possibly, I suspect, as a curious and observant spectator from the bow deck. I know that I worried about his disembarking and, as I moved up the rough, unpaved street from the small concrete landing stage through a velvety black night to the house of the *controleur,* it occurred to me for the first time that I had made no provisions for Ali's housing during the two or three weeks I expected to be the guest of the local administrator. As we stumbled along, blinded by even the dim light of a hurricane lamp, I was aware that Ali was at my heels, and I managed to irritate my host, for the first of many times, by my insistent inquiries about Ali's living arrangements. It all seemed so simple to my host —my *djongos* would find a place in the line of cubicles behind the main bungalow where the servants lived next to the kitchen, bath, and storeroom. In any event Ali disappeared that dark confusing night, out of the arc of light provided by that yellow kerosene flame, carrying under his arm the rolled mat that was his bed and, over his shoulder, the cotton sack that held all his personal belongings. In contrast to Ali's detailed knowledge of all I possessed, I never saw what was in that small sack, but I am sure it contained little more than a pair of sneakers, perhaps two pairs of blue shorts, a couple of singlets, his fez, a large can of carnation scented talcum powder, highly perfumed soap, a mirror, and a largish lump of aromatic resin.

The anticipated week or two in Kalabahi finally stretched out into a month. The radjah and the *controleur* suggested several nearby villages easily accessible by good horse trails to the main settlement with its small Chinese shops (*tokos*), its eight "Europeans," and the semimonthly calls of the Dutch KPM ships. For reasons, good or bad, I finally decided on Atimelang, high in the mountains, a long seven hours on steep trails from the coast, and well out of reach of such Islamic and Christian influences as emanated from the port settlement. Again, these matters are not relevant to the interdependencies that developed between Ali and me during that first month in the still relatively civilized community of Kalabahi.

Ali shared a cubicle with the *controleur's djongos*. He gave every appearance of being quite at ease with the staff—the Makassarese *djongos,* the crotchety old woman cook from Java, the Alorese garden boy. I am sure that he shared their quarters, their meals, and their daily tasks modestly and to everyone's satisfaction. The first morning while I was at breakfast on the rear verandah with my hosts, he moved noiselessly on bare feet and in his white ducks into my bedroom. After breakfast I found the washstand polished, freshly boiled water in the jug, my bed made, the mosquito net tied back. In the evening, the kerosene lamp was lighted, the mosquito net snugly tucked under the mattress, and all mosquitoes carefully brushed out of that high, square cage into which one crawled at night. It must have been during the first day or two that Ali began his morning routine of appropriating all the clothes I had worn the day before, whisking them off to be washed, and returning them ironed in the afternoon. It was perhaps a day or two later that he asked me for my sewing kit to replace a button on one of my blouses. From then on Ali was in charge of the sewing materials although he never removed them from my room. By the end of certainly the first week he had in his charge all the keys to my wooden chests and I have no doubt that he took careful inventory of what were to be our material resources once we settled in Atimelang. I don't quite know how all this happened, so unobtrusive was his gradual assumption of responsibility.

There were other lessons for me to learn during our stay in Kalabahi. Ali and my hosts were teaching me the formalities of social distance. One never visited the kitchen or servants' quarters without advance notice. Master and servant existed in worlds of different concerns, functions, and responsibilities. They could approach each other only by observing the protocol and conventions devised to relate strangers. Close as Ali's and my living quarters were to be in subsequent months, we remained essentially strangers isolated together in a strange society. I entered Ali's room or his kitchen only rarely and after giving him full explanation for the intrusion and explaining the innocence of my intent—an innocence pleaded in terms of either his comfort or my incomprehensible standards of sanitation.

Although I was learning the formalities of distance, I was, of course, depending increasingly on Ali. Did he think my sketches for the house to be built in Atimelang were appropriate? Were his room and the adjacent kitchen large enough? What kind of arrangement would he want for cooking? What final supplies should be acquired in the local Chinese shops? On this last score Ali's ideas were particularly numerous and practical.

I never knew what Ali thought of my financial resources, although I do not doubt that he had carefully counted the contents of a black strong box that I brought with me from the Java Bank—the heavy gray linen sacks of silver rupees and the sausage-like strings of pierced one- and five-cent pieces for small cash. I knew that my financial resources were extremely limited. Perhaps Ali thought so too, for he set about shopping for his own food supplies and the food for the servants we expected to train in Atimelang with both skill and parsimony: canned goods for me, polished rice, onions, and garlic for himself, semihulled local rice for the village staff, but no onions or garlic; bars of crude kitchen soap to be dried and cut into squares for the mountain people, fragrant toilet soaps for himself; bags of coarse, impure local salt for trade purposes in Atimelang, boxes of refined salt for our use; bundles of those Indonesian scented cigarettes for him to smoke, coils of coarse tobacco leaf for the others. (For my use, I had brought from Java sealed tins of those small, strong, and delicious Dieng cigarettes—500 to a tin.) In sum, all the gradations of consumption symbols associated with status were carefully observed.

Morning after morning Ali would suggest what he felt we needed, how much money he wanted, and in his informal clothes would disappear into the intricacies of the daily open market and the street of Chinese shops. Later I would find on the table of my bedroom a meticulous accounting of his purchases. Sometimes there was change from the rupees I had extracted from the strong box that morning. Sometimes it was I who was in Ali's debt. The important change in our relationship was that we had moved into a partnership in these domestic matters—but a partnership in which our difference in status was never forgotten although we were somehow allied against "those others."

That this partnership had undertones more significant than the management of our joint domestic comforts I was to realize during our third week in Kalabahi. I had joined my hosts and the military doctor for tea on the verandah one afternoon. Leaning back in a wicker chair I felt a slight prick on my shoulder that I attributed to nothing more than a sliver of wood until it was repeated. I turned to discover that a wasp had stung me. In not more than ten minutes large welts broke out on my arms and face, I felt feverish, and my heart raced alarmingly. I mentioned my difficulties and went inside to lie on my bed. There set in a frightening series of spasms, a strong and irregular heart action, shortness of breath, all accompanied by a good deal of physical pain. The doctor, somewhat *detraqué* after too many years in the bush without wife or home leave, nodded gloomily, said he was without adrenalin and left. My hosts seemed equally unconcerned. When the symptoms had not abated after two hours, I felt that there were certain letters I would not want to fall under the all too prying eyes of my host in the event matters took a more serious turn. Feeling dizzy and faint I swung my legs over the side of the bed, intending to destroy them, when I realized for the first time that a small kerosene lamp was burning in the room and that Ali was squatting noiselessly and watchfully on the floor near the head of my bed. I gave him the letters to burn in the event that my heart should not start racing again after one of its stifling pauses. At this point severe abdominal cramps set in and I wavered down the central corridor of the house to the toilet in the string of cubicles out back. Ali, without a word and without offering physical support, picked up the kerosene lamp and followed. He waited and returned with me to the bedroom. Soon after this I fell into an exhausted sleep. When I woke in the morning, I found the mosquito net had been carefully tucked in around me. Ali and the lamp were gone. The letters I had entrusted to him were on my table. Neither of us referred to this episode at the time. After all—there was really nothing that could be said.

When the matter came up again it was three weeks later and we had moved up to the mountain community of Atimelang, a day's journey from medical help. I was stung again by a similar wasp. Before any symptoms appeared, I called Ali, told him what had happened, said I was going to lie down and would he look in on me from time to time. If necessary he was to send Thomas (our local interpreter) to the coast for the doctor. After an hour, with not a single one of the anticipated symptoms putting in an appearance, more than a little sheepishly I went back to work on the vocabulary slips that covered my table. Unasked, Ali brought me a glass of juice from the excellent local oranges that he seemed always able to keep in plentiful supply. There was no trace of amusement on his face. But then, Ali practically never smiled and he laughed only on those rare occasions when he broke into a bit of horseplay with Johanis or Nitaniel, two Atimelang youths who soon became attached to our household. If Ali had any sense of humor, it was a small gentle humor, gay rather than sardonic.

As I write, I notice how I have drifted into the use of the phrase "our household." This it indubitably was, but some explanation is in order since it brought out several new facets of Ali's personality

Alorese Men Quarreling over Debts at a Dance.

and our relationship. It had been agreed in Djakarta that Ali would establish me in whatever field quarters were to be built, and would train local people to take over his various tasks when he left at the end of six months. The first part of this agreement Ali executed beyond my fondest hopes. The second part he never achieved.

The Atimelangers finally completed the establishment they were building for us. During an all night dance, it had been named (as all important houses must) in honor of "*my* village," Hamerika. A "two-pig" and "one-goat" feast followed the next day. The goat was out of deference to Ali's real horror, as a Moslem, of eating pork and, I should add, a horror even more intense than mine at the local casualness in killing, butchering, and cooking pigs. That morning, as we saw our first pig slaughtered in Atimelang, was one of the few times I saw Ali's face the bluish-gray that yellow-brown skins turn when their owners pale. The radjah's Kapitan, who was also a Moslem, had come to the mountains for the housewarming. He and Ali were not only friendly, in a rather distant fashion, but they were also the two gentlemen, the two *tuans,* who stood behind me on this occasion. A goat was the minimum tribute I could offer them. Ali had suggested this as soon as he began to grasp the nature of the ceremony to be given in honor of Hamerika. Whereas I was responsible for negotiating the purchase of the two pigs and embroiled myself in noisy, village-wide altercations in the process, Ali's and the Kapitan's goat arrived well in advance, was slaughtered, and turned into succulent *satés* (skewered and broiled with a barbecue sauce) all without fanfare. Finally the village headman smeared chicken blood and rice on the house posts and we were free to move into Hamerika after twenty-four hours of unremitting *brouhaha.*

The window openings in the woven bamboo walls, with swinging shutters to close them, were so out of plumb as to defeat their double purpose of privacy and protection against rain. The storeroom needed a staple and lock. The outhouse had still to be completed. The bamboo aquaduct from the spring on the hillside back of the house was not yet begun. The site of an old pigsty needed fencing if pigs and chickens were to be kept from the vegetable garden we planned. Borers in the green bamboo of the house walls spread an endless film of sawdust over everything. Thatch lice, maddening in the way they crawled over one's flesh, dropped by the thousands, invisible unless swept each morning into dusty piles on the concrete floor. Ali coped with all these matters, evincing skills and ingenuity I had not before suspected. To some he turned his attention before I had really noticed or mentioned them; the others he dealt with promptly if I made a suggestion. At intervals he displayed a passion for rather inept carpentry, cannibalizing the few precious boards of my packing cases until I forbade further inroads.

In those first weeks in Hamerika Ali not only fed me breakfast, lunch, and supper, but a midmorning glass of orange juice and a midafternoon cup of tea. He washed, ironed, and mended my clothes. He brought me warm water in the morning for my washbowl. He tended the smoky kerosene lanterns and the crotchety gasoline pressure lamp. He produced local foods miraculously from heaven knows where. (This was before the children of the village established the custom of a small early morning market on the steps of the verandah.) He concocted a reflector oven out of a five gallon gasoline tin and with yeast from fermented coconut milk baked for me, three times a week, a tiny loaf of bread. All this initiative and energy

I appreciated, but I am afraid I took it for granted. This is what a *djongos* was expected to do in the colonial tradition that had informed me, and how was I to know that Ali was a jewel of a *djongos?* I had no point of comparison and I was much too absorbed in the collecting, typing, and filing of field notes to give domestic details much thought. It was only after Ali left that I realized how carefree those early months had been.

In the midst of all this activity there were only two episodes in the first weeks of settling in to Hamerika that brought back any of the quality of concern that underlay, unspoken, the more human relationship revealed by the wasp episode. On the first Thursday evening in Hamerika, before Ali served supper and as I sat at my desk typing notes, he went systematically through the house with a small flat square tin on which smoldered a fragment of that aromatic resin he carried in his cotton bag of personal belongings. He wore his informal blue shorts, a white singlet, and his more formal turban. He bent low at every house post (there were fifteen) and in the corner of each room. These he asperged with incense. He was so deeply intent on what he was doing that I said nothing. It would have been an intrusion. There was something religious in his gestures, although to my practical mind the only reasonable explanation of his behavior was that he was trying a new material for fumigating bamboo borers and thatch lice. (We had already created bedlam by burning various greens in the house at Thomas' suggestion.)

Later, when Ali served supper, I did venture to ask what he had been doing. He said briefly, and I thought with more than usual reserve, that it was sunset before Friday (the Moslem Sunday in Indonesia). He had driven out the evil spirits from his room and the kitchen in the adjacent building and he felt they should also be exorcized from *nonja's* house. I thanked him. But to pursue the matter further would have been more forthright than even an ethnographer is willing to risk being where human sensitivities and cultural niceties are concerned. Ali never again drove the evil spirits from my house although I was aware that every Thursday night for several successive weeks he was careful to exorcize evil spirits in his own quarters. And again, I can only guess what all this purported. Was Ali worried about that pagan chicken-blood and rice which had been smeared on our house posts during the twenty-four hours of Hamerika's dedication ceremonies? Were my quarters more impregnable than his against the evil geniuses of Atimelang? Was I, as another variety of non-believer, less worthy of protection? Had he sufficiently decontaminated the "big house" to make his own activities there safe? Was the night in his room among these pagans more fearsome for him than he thought it was for me? To fathom one's own mixture of motives is difficult enough; to fathom those of another, particularly one in every respect so distant culturally and psychologically, so reticent in communication, would be sheer impertinence.

The other episode in those first weeks that brought the two of us into a more personal relationship was Ali's acute attack of nausea. Late one evening as I worked, with door and windows closed in what the local people called my *kantoor* (Dutch for office), I heard a violent retching at the edge of the house clearing. Taking a flashlight I went to investigate and saw that Ali was doubled over with spasms of vomiting. Given our relationship, there was no question of going immediately and practically to his aid. All I could do was to waken Thomas and his wife Endirini who slept in a shack across the trail. Neither of them had shown the slightest aptitude for medical care. The only one of the Alorese I ever met that did was Johanis who had volunteered from the beginning to assist me in the "clinic" I conducted each morning. Although Johanis and Ali were playmates (I can find no other word to describe their romping and high spirits on occasion), Johanis slept in the village of Alurkowati, some twenty minutes' walk from Hamerika. I gave Thomas my flashlight and dispatched him, saying that Ali was to come to me when he wished, since I was sure he would not put in his appearance until he regained his composure. In about twenty minutes Thomas and Ali appeared at my door. Ali wore no head covering, a sign of marked disarray. He walked waveringly and supported by Thomas with that officiousness that Thomas seemed to invest in all he did. Ali slumped to the floor and leaned back wanly against the bamboo partition. Even today the whole scene impresses me as having been a bit overdramatic but many foreigners have commented on the dramatic competence of even the simplest Javanese villagers and Ali was by no means a simple villager. Thomas, legs wide spread and barrel chest out, stood as tall as his 4 feet 8 inches permitted. It was Thomas who told me that Ali had eaten from his and Endirini's supper pot, etc., etc. Turning to Ali I went through the "medical" rigmarole that had already become the symbol of my concern in

Atimelang: thermometer in mouth, pulse taken using a radium-dialed watch, examination of throat with the flashlight, a medicine, and a dietary prescription. (Oatmeal was a great favorite.) There was little I could do but reassure Ali, just as, at the time of the wasp sting, there was little he could have done but reassure me in his own way. He was sent off to bed with my hot water bottle and an extra blanket.

Ali's illness had upset me. I remember wondering at the time why Ali had been nauseated by eating Thomas' supper, how often re-assurances would be needed, whether I had been too unappreciative of all Ali had been doing, and whether my attention was too exclusively centered on the Alorese who contributed more directly, if not more importantly, to getting on with the task at hand. Rather belatedly I realized how tryingly isolated Ali must have felt in Atimelang and wondered what inward strengths he marshalled. Whatever made Ali resilient, I suspect it had to do with pride of performance, though this is only a literary and valuational escape clause for my ignorance of his psychological processes.

In any event, I need not have worried. On only two other occasions did Ali's need for reassurance and succor lead him to breach the formality and distance of our relationship. The first was when he was stung by a scorpion. Ali, in the same wan fashion, but this time without Thomas as impressario, appeared at my door late one night and collapsed on the floor. In that area of the world a scorpion sting is no small matter though certainly not fatal as it may be in Mexico. But it is also more serious than most wasp stings. A jigger of my whiskey and cold compresses were all that were required, although some persuasion was involved to convince an unusually pious Moslem, at that point, to down alcohol. The carefully reckoned test and coun-tertest of good faith in an hierarchical, though nevertheless solicitous, relationship had been established.

The other episode was of quite a different order. I had been off on a *tournée* of two weeks seeing other parts of Alor. Ali had been left as master of Hamerika. What he did with his sudden access of leisure I have no idea. I hope he was able to give at least an atten-uated version of a *selamatan,* those cool, formal, neighborhood "feasts" that are symbols of such human solidarity as the Javanese are able to express. There is a hint that one may have been held al-though again I never knew the full story. On my return, early one forenoon, from these two physically gruelling weeks, I found hot water ready, clean clothes laid out, and my small tin of bread (always a treat) cooling on the verandah. My arrival inevitably was announced by the system of vocal telegraph, shouted in an elliptical language from hilltop to hilltop, that kept every stranger's movements well reported two or three hours before arrival. Ali appeared to greet me on the trail and immediately brought the warm water for washing to my bedroom. Instead of leaving quickly and silently, he loitered. He was uneasy; we made conversation. In sum, Ali was not himself. I asked if all had gone well, had he had a good vacation, were there left any of the newly hatched chicks that had a saddening capacity for tragic ends, how was the ferral kitten we were both futilely trying to transform into both pet and rat-catcher but that seemed instead connected with the regular disappearance of the chicks, how was the tomato crop, had Johanis kept him faithfully in wood? In sum, I tried to recall all our familiar domestic problems. Ali's answers were not any more taciturn than usual, but patently he was worried. Finally in that brutish Malay which was our only medium of conversation, and while I pulled off a pair of heavy boots to inspect my blistered feet, I asked Ali the equivalent of "what eats on you." The story poured out, *"Nonja"* would hear. He had been 'naughty' " (that is about as close a translation as I can find for *nakal* in trade Malay). The upshot was that as possessor of Hamerika, its keys and its treasures, he had gone to the bottom of a wooden chest, extracted a .32 Smith and Wesson pistol, and gone hunting doves for a feast. This would seem a simple enough impulse if one were unaware of both the legal and Freudian contexts of guns during the colonial regime in Indonesia. I had been met with every courtesy of Dutch officialdom on my arrival in Java—with the exception of that wretched Smith and Wesson. It had been impounded for two weeks with its ammunition. Every bullet had been counted. I was required to redeclare it on departure and account for the use of each bullet. Officialdom was as vigorously opposed to firearms in "native" possession as it was to the free dissemination of its status language, Dutch. Never have the good offices of a protective American friend who had insisted on providing me with that pistol proved more cumbersome. But in Atimelang I could no more than Ali resist an occasional display of drama. The "gun with six mouths" (as it was locally known) was taken out, shot into the air, and cleaned approximately once a month.

It was always a great dramatic success. During my absence, Ali could scarcely expect to forego that bit of *éclat*.

He had taken the "gun with six mouths" from the chest, set out putatively to hunt doves for a feast, probably duplicating his earlier employment on the Aru Islands where hunting helped to fill the stew pot. He had been ineptly and absent-mindedly peering down the barrel when he pulled the trigger. Fortunately the bullet only grazed his ear. This had happened three days earlier but we still both paled at the telling. Although inwardly I felt only relief at Ali's escape, it seemed clear that censure would alone absolve him. All I could express in the first moment was concern and relief. Then I hardened and engaged in the formal and expected scolding that our role relationship demanded. I could think of no more rigorous punishment than confiscating the key to that wooden chest for two weeks. I believe Ali found this withdrawal of trust a source of genuine expiation. The Alorese told me many versions of the episode, as Ali rightly suspected they would. The ultimate sanction of a primary group relationship is gossip. But of that subtle, interpersonal, status restoring device—the confiscation of a key—no public word was heard. Ali and I reëstablished our hierarchical interdependence privately and in our own way.

It is necessary to include Thomas, his wife Endirini, and Johanis, all three introduced some paragraphs ago, in this account of Ali's and my relationship. Thomas bounced, he scowled, he crossed his arms Napoleonically across his chest. He had once spent several months on Java, and this unparalleled experience for an Alorese gave him his only claim to status among his fellow villagers. Since that trip, one of his favorite "parlor tricks," one that always drew a crowd of guffawing Alorese, was his imitation of Javanese dancing. Even Ali seemed to enjoy it. But after Thomas' first performance in our presence with its subtle implications of ridicule, Ali complained to me, with complete justice, that Thomas was taking no interest in learning the household routine that Ali considered essential to a properly run establishment. Since Ali was not given to unjustified tittle-tattle, I had called Thomas and reminded him that Ali was to leave in June, that he, Thomas, had been engaged to learn how to be a *djongos* and to take over when Ali left. Thomas was all promises and bright agreement. He was also bitter in his complaints against his wife, Endirini, whom he had dressed according to her new status in a sarong and blouse, but who lumpishly refused to acquire any of the other attributes of her higher station in life. Endirini never did show Thomas' yearning for upward social mobility. After all she was so placidly pregnant in very short order! On the other hand, Thomas who had no children was so delighted by her pregnancy that he tried to learn both of their jobs—to cook, wash, iron, mend, and conduct himself with Javanese restraint. It was too much for him. But that had little to do with Ali except to irritate him slightly and to irritate me mightily.

Johanis was a horse of a different color. He was first hired to care for my sandalwood pony that he rather resembled physically but of which he proved to be mortally afraid. He did show real aptitude not only, as I have said, for first aid but also for ingratiation and for never producing enough of the faggots Ali needed for cooking. He and Ali, however, struck it off very well together. When Ali, having failed to either persuade or command from Johanis enough firewood (I never learned which device he preferred), would complain to me, I would offer to find, hopefully, a more reliable wood boy. Ali then invariably interceded for Johanis. Perhaps Johanis, in addition to providing Ali with horseplay and admiration, also served as scapegoat for the stresses Ali must have felt but was never free to discharge. I don't know how close their relationship was but for Ali it seemed to be his only emotional outlet. The bolder and prettier girls who gradually felt free to loiter near Hamerika, and particularly the servants' quarters, found Ali fascinating. He seemed never to have been more than gravely polite to them.

The matter of Johanis came to a head before Ali left. Ali reported that the large, valuable machete that served Johanis as a symbol of office was lost. Johanis blamed the loss on his sister. In the course of the flaming altercation that followed it was clear to me (though I am sure Ali must have know all along) that Johanis had been subcontracting his wood gathering duties to various female "relatives." Nothing, however trivial it might appear on the surface, could occur in Atimelang without embroiling all four neighboring villages and setting off, like the grass fires of the dry season, days of unpredictable recriminations as ominous as the crackling cane that burned on the hillsides and as obfuscating as the attendant pall of smoke. In any event, Johanis was dismissed, the knife was rather improbably found by his sister, and given by me as a gift to her husband. Characteristic of uproars in Atimelang as this one was, it was the only one in which Ali seemed to have been deeply embroiled. How he was involved I never fully knew. But it was clear that he was disturbed and depended on me to support him. This naturally I did. I consulted him on every decision I took. As a result Johanis disappeared to his wife's house in Alurkowati for perhaps ten days. When Ali was making his last preparations for his return to Java, and when it was undoubtedly bruited about that Ali had been paid not only his wages that were accumulating in my strong box, but also a bonus, Johanis reappeared with a large carrying basket of oranges. The last I saw of Ali was his trim figure silhouetted against the ridge in the early morning light, followed by a sandalwood pony and Johanis who carried from a tump line across his forehead the oranges that Ali so prized. Behind them followed other Atimelangers who made up a company of friends bent on two or three days of marketing and fun in Kalabahi, and who hoped to be allowed to set foot on a ship under the guise of seeing off a friend.

But this anticipates the story of Ali's departure. Early in May I asked him whether he would reconsider staying on with me in Atimelang for another year. It was quite clear to both of us that he was the mainstay of a singularly pleasant and smoothly functioning household. It was equally clear that not even a covey of Atimelangers would ever acquire or discharge the many skills and the thoughtfulness that Ali possessed. That May evening Ali and I spoke freely together for the first time. It was then that I learned of Ali's attachment to his wife, his affection for the son he had not fathered, and his real concern, and I think even admiration, for me and the task I was engaged in. Not that he really understood what had brought me to Alor. Neither the intent or content of my long hours of work concerned him. There was in Ali no trace of the ethnographer. It was my Alorese interpreter, Fantan, who showed real aptitude in that respect. Ali lived contained within the boundaries of his role, meticulously discharging its obligations but apparently finding little need beyond them for human relationships or self-expression. It was the Alorese who were curious about Ali, not Ali about them.

We talked for about an hour; it was the longest conversation we ever had. I hope that I communicated to Ali the esteem and appreciation I felt for him. But this I shall never know.

We separated, as we had after that first afternoon's conversation on the hotel verandah in Djakarta, to think things over. In the morning Ali suggested the best compromise he could arrive at. He would return to his family in June and at some indefinite date would come back to Atimelang. This I saw would strain a very meager budget. It was also only temporizing with the inescapable fact that I would have to deal with Atimelangers in their own terms—as kith and kin. Ali had trained me in a singularly congenial mistress-servant relationship. This no Atimelanger would ever understand. It was clear that I must now move from that position to a new one where Alorese staff, whatever their faults or virtues, were to retrain me in their own terms. I must become the rich, old mother to a group of aggressive, if devoted, sons. The complex status relationship of Java had to be exchanged for the equally complex kinship relationships of Atimelang. Within the household a new order seemed inevitable. Ali would leave in June as originally planned. Despite the decision, nothing changed between Ali and me. We continued until the last morning our aloof and formal stances. There was nothing to be done except provide him with a sandalwood pony for his last jaunt down from the hills. Ali had asked for a pony to ride up into the hills five months earlier and I had refused, on the advice of the radjah and *controleur* who assured me it would "spoil" a whole generation of *djongos*. It was the first time Ali had ever requested anything of me that I had refused. He had taken the refusal in good stead. Instead of riding up to Atimelang with the radjah, the kapitan, the doctor, the *controleur,* and me—in other words, instead of arriving in Atimelang as a *tuan,* he had attached to himself the carriers who were charged with my bed-roll and the money chest. He had formed a small cordon at the immediate rear of the riders and arrived in Atimelang in the first wave of outsiders. He left Atimelang leading a pony he was afraid to ride, every inch the gentleman he was, and with the symbol of status no gentleman ever really requires.

I stood below the ridge watching this small procession silhouetted against a sky at dawn and knew that another richly meaningful human tie was severed. I followed the procession in my mind down the slope to the coast and I realized how much I had learned—not about Ali, not about the Alorese, but about myself, about my capacities and incapacities for human relationships and thus also, to a degree, what my areas of competence were as an anthropologist and a human being. I walked back alone to Hamerika seeing again the bamboo, the pineapple, and papayas we had planted on the village boundary, the ostentatious house with its large thatched roof that seemed very much home, and recognized, a little, that age and wisdom combine at best to humble one.

I now understand, twenty years later, as I recapitulate the whole relationship, that I have really nothing to say that is culturally specific. Except superficially, I learned nothing from Ali about even one variety of Javanese. What I have tried to describe, I now realize, is the old, devoted, and increasingly anachronistic relationship of master and servant in its best, almost feudal aspect, an aspect no longer valued in either my world or Ali's, but one that had dignity and depth because it had form and respect. Short of art or philosophy, I know no better avenue to such wisdom than anthropology.

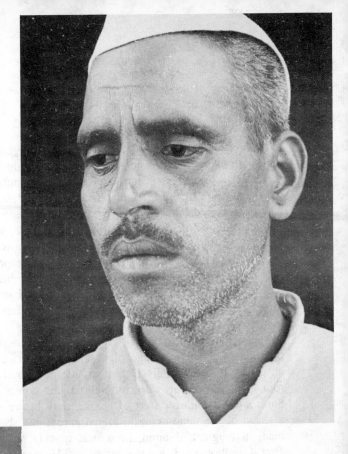

8

Surat Singh, Head Judge

John T. Hitchcock

My first clear memory of Surat had a quality that was typical of many subsequent impressions. One night Narain Singh, my interpreter, co-worker, alter ego, and constant companion during the twenty months I lived in Khalapur, encountered Surat in the village where he was drinking with friends. Narain remarked that he had not seen him at the campsite and invited him to pay us a visit. This brought an announcement from Surat that he was "lord of the village" and would accept the invitation only under specified conditions. 'All formalities' [1] were to be observed and the interview with him was to be conducted 'in private.' Narain agreed to make the necessary arrangements and a few days later, after informing us to expect him, Surat paid his first visit to our camp.

I saw him as he started across the field toward the small outbuilding of the new village high school where we temporarily had an office. It was a chilly December afternoon and in addition to a *topī* (the type of cap worn by Nehru) and homespun cotton *dhotī*, Surat wore a pullover shirt of coarse, dark brown wool. He carried a shawl of the same material folded across one shoulder. A man of medium height and build, he moved quickly and easily, erect and almost motionless from the waist up. He seemed to glide along. Surat slipped off his leather slippers at the door and seated himself crosslegged in the place of honor at the head of the proffered cot. From the start his goodhumored assurance put us at ease. He accepted a cigarette, which he placed in his fist between the third and fourth fingers and smoked through an aperture formed by his curled up index finger and thumb.

"You are here in my village to do 'research,' " he said after we had talked a few minutes. He paused at the English word, looking up with a smile to see if he had pronounced it correctly. At our appreciative assent he went on: "I want to do some 'research' too, some 'research' on this 'project.' " Again the smile and a questioning glance. "Shall I begin now?"

---

[1] Surat knew a little English and his talk was interspersed with English words and phrases. To set these off from the translation of his usual Hindustani, they will be placed in single quotation marks.

We assured him he could and he launched into a series of very searching questions about our purpose in coming to Khalapur. He had a pleasant voice and spoke without hesitation or gesture. The dominant impression was one of ease, purpose, and control.

When he had satisfied himself about the 'project' he began another series of questions ranging from similarities and differences between the Indian and American constitutions to the level of living of laborers in the United States as compared with those in England. It was late afternoon when the interview started and as he continued his questioning the room gradually filled with farmers who stopped off on the way back to the village from their fields. Surat overlooked this inevitable breach in the protocol stipulated for his visit and continued as spokesman for the growing assemblage—a role he was granted rather than seemed to demand. When the questioning became general, as it did in time, he continued to make his presence felt by pithy summarizing quips ("Women quarrel for no reason. They are like the wolf at the brook who killed the goat downstream for muddying the water.") and occasionally by remarking, "Let us go on to another topic." Clearly this self-styled "lord of the village" was a commanding personality, but an engaging one with a very keen mind.

At the time of this first meeting what struck me most forcibly about Surat was a sense of contradiction in his personality. Here was a man who in many ways was like the other village men we were coming to know. Yet in obvious ways he was very different. My awareness of both the similarities and differences between Surat and his fellow villagers deepened as I came to know him better, and along with it, to compound this impression, came the realization that Surat on one day could be quite unlike the person he was on another. On one day he might talk like any number of men in his own high caste: I remember his saying once that "lower caste men were born to obey upper caste men." But it was not long after this that I found him sharing a meal of boiled rice with an Untouchable, even accepting food from the Untouchable's hands. Partaking of food with an Untouchable, and especially food boiled in water, was a reprehensible act to most men of his caste, and two or three decades ago it might have led to his own outcasting.

Surat was the most puzzling, and interesting, of all the men I knew in Khalapur and I often thought of him after I left the village.

I still find him perplexing but my impressions of him have at least become more orderly as I have learned to sort out some of the tangled strands in the immense complexity of the Indian village in which he lives.

Buzzards are always wheeling high above Surat's village. If one could view Khalapur from their vantage point on a spring day after rain has cleared the air of dust, one would see a vast level plain between the two southerly flowing rivers, the Jumna and the Ganges. Some fifty miles to the north lie the foothills of the Himalayas, rising ridge upon ridge until they stand snowclad and almost unbelievably high. The land between the rivers is veined with the broad straight Ganges canal and its angled branches and tributaries. A railroad and hardsurfaced road connect the two large towns to the northeast and southwest of Khalapur, and near each of them is the single tall chimney and patch of white waste that indicate the presence of a sugar mill. The fields around the villages are a vast patchwork quilt of color—brilliant yellow of mustard, variegated green of wheat, sugar cane, pulse, and mango groves.

As one drops lower more details of the villages can be distinguished. Some are very small with only a few mud houses bleached bone-grey by the sun. In the larger villages one can see substantial homes of burnt red brick as well as many smaller ones of mud. In every village there is a pond or tank. There are many villages with the single tapering tower of a Hindu temple, and in a few of the largest, the slender towers of a mosque. All are compact and a web of cart tracks and footpaths spreads out from each through the encircling tillage.

Khalapur itself is spread out along a small brook spanned by a bridge wide enough for bullock carts. With a population of over 5000, comprised of some thirty caste groups, it is one of the largest villages in the district. Beyond the bridge, to the north, lies the new high school. On the opposite side of the village is a large domed shrine, a memorial to a Muslim saint, and beyond it, the buildings of a school devoted to the teaching of Sanskrit. The spire of a Hindu temple rises above the shade trees that obscure much of the village site, a welter of cattle compounds, wide and narrow lanes, and mud and brick houses in a jumble of sizes, shapes, and states of repair. Surat's home and those of his closest relatives lie parallel to the brook at the southern end of the village.

In some respects Surat can be described as one would describe any wealthy landowner of Khalapur. He and his kinsmen belong to the Rajput caste, whose members claim descent from the warrior and ruling class of ancient India. There are some 2000 Rajput men, women, and children in the village. The wives come from other villages but with only a few exceptions the Rajput men have always lived in Khalapur and trace their descent from a man and his sons who founded the village about 400 years ago. The Rajputs in this part of India observe the custom of purdah, or seclusion of married women, and a typical Rajput household consists of both a men's house (*chaupar*) and a women's house (*bagaḍ*). Surat's wife and children share a *bagaḍ* with the families of four other male relatives. These include a brother and three other men who are related to Surat through the same great-grandfather. Although these five families all share the same *bagaḍ*, a large, partially tumbled down brick building with an open compound in the center, they cook and eat separately. In Surat's father's time the land was held in common, but now it has been divided among the five families. Surat and his brother each have farms of about thirty acres, large farms in village terms, and Surat, as well as all the other men who share this *bagaḍ*, are among the wealthiest in the village.

A quarrel led to the partition of the farm which Surat and his brother once owned jointly and since the partition Surat no longer uses the *chaupar* they used to share. He staked out his cattle in a separate compound on one side of the *bagaḍ* and built a separate entrance there. A small brick shelter in this cattle compound serves as a sleeping place for him and his older sons. There is a large shady *nīm* tree growing just beside it and when he is at home he often moves a cot beneath the tree and sits there smoking his water pipe.

Because of purdah restrictions I was not acquainted with the more intimate aspects of Surat's family life. I knew even less about his domestic relations than I did about those of other Rajputs because he was seldom at home except at night. When we met him by prearrangement, in search of a modicum of privacy, it was often at our place on the village outskirts. When we did meet him in the village, it was generally not at his own men's house, as he seldom sat there. Our talk was mostly about the men's world and we seldom asked for details about his life within the *bagaḍ* because we felt such questions would embarrass him as they did other Rajput men. The few references he did make to his wife made it clear he held her and her family in high regard.

The need for help with the farm work establishes the first of many ties that draw Surat's family into the village economy. Some of the land is given to members of other caste groups on a crop sharing basis. Members of families who own little or no land, such as those who belong to the numerous Untouchable caste group of Chamars, are hired for field work from time to time on a daily or monthly basis. There are also a number of caste groups in the village whose members specialize in providing services of various kinds. Surat's family is served by members of a Brahman family, and by members of families who belong to the barber, water-carrier, blacksmith-carpenter, potter, washerman, leather-worker, and sweeper castes. In return, these families are given traditionally determined amounts of grain after each of the two yearly harvests, and some also receive special payments and privileges, such as gifts of food at ceremonies and the right to cut an occasional bundle of fodder for their buffalo or cow. They are regarded to some extent as family retainers. Other needs of Surat's family are met by such village specialists as gold-smiths, weavers, tailors, and shopkeepers. These specialists are not regarded as family retainers and do not receive special privileges. They expect payment when the article or service they sell is obtained. The family depends only to a slight extent, and then mostly for luxuries, on the bazaars of the two neighboring towns, one four miles away, the other twelve. Wheat is Surat's main subsistence crop, but the major cash income from the farm is derived from the sale of sugar cane. With the exception of the large amount of land let out on a share crop basis, the economic pattern exhibited by Surat's farm is much the same as that of other wealthy Rajput families in Khalapur.

In the political sphere Surat and his family also follow the typical pattern in many ways. They are one among a number of Rajput families in Khalapur who possess both power and prestige. Their ascendant position is based upon landed wealth, useful government connections, and strong supporting manpower in the village.

The men of most importance to these petty village principalities are relatives like Surat and his sons who own and work a farm jointly. For political purposes this group is augmented by a greater or lesser segment of the lineage, depending on its solidarity, and by a varying number of close male friends. This is the group the family can count on for support in a court case or for help with quarterstaves if a resort to force is necessary. The family's other political alliances are not as completely dependable. These tend to include families with whom it has close ritual ties and families dependent upon it for economic and political assistance.

The families of highest rank symbolize their power by erecting large brick homes, purchasing spirited imported bullocks, decking their women with expensive clothes and jewelry, and providing guests with ample hospitality. Rank also is symbolized by providing the family head, and perhaps one of the sons, with leisure for looking after family interests in the political and ritual spheres. However, the quintessential symbol of a family's status is an excellent marriage, with a generous dowry for a daughter, an alliance with a high ranking family in another village, and lavish feasting and festivity for friends and relatives.

Surat and his family possessed many of these attributes to an eminent degree. He had a comparatively large landholding and a number of sons to work it. He was well acquainted with the official world outside the village, and also held an important village statutory office. His lineage of eighty members was among the largest in the village, and he could count on the support of many of its male members, a number of them able and educated men. He also had the support of powerful village friends.

There were ways in which Surat did not fit the usual pattern, however, and they were one source of the contradictory quality so characteristic of his life. Most of the twenty-five-odd heads of the highest ranking families were over 50 years of age. Surat was only 42. They wore long moustaches, a mark of their responsible adult status and the martial heritage of their caste. Surat favored the small, close-cropped moustache of the city-educated person. Many of the powerful elders wore turbans. Surat never wore one. When he covered his close-shaved grizzled head at all, he wore a *topī*.

It was a sign of political eminence to be associated with a definite place and coterie. Other high status family heads were often to be found at their *chaupar,* smoking and talking with friends. During the day, and often during much of the night, Surat was absent from his own cattle compound.

Although the heads of ranking families seldom did heavy field work, regarding it as detrimental to their status, they did sometimes go to the fields in a supervisory capacity. Most were interested in farm management and their conversation frequently turned to animal husbandry and agriculture. I never saw Surat in the fields and he almost never mentioned his farm. He had turned the work over to his eldest son, who worked the farm with two rangy local bullocks. Even with the help of the next eldest son, it was a difficult task, and for this reason it was necessary to give out quite a large portion of the farm on a share crop basis each season. Surat also paid but slight attention to the management of his household. The custom in this regard was variable, but few family heads had relinquished control in this sphere so completely. When we were discussing the status of women he once said jokingly, "I have given my wife equality. I have given her complete freedom to manage the household."

Most of the other Rajput prominent men gave the impression of being more completely kin encircled than Surat. They sat with their close kinsmen and consulted them before making decisions, while Surat seldom sat with the men who shared a *bagaḍ* with him. His closest friends belonged to neighboring lineages, and in making decisions he rarely consulted his kinsmen unless they were directly involved. Surat, as one of his friends said, was "a very independent-minded fellow."

I remember being surprised to learn that his brother, Ram, actually was four years older than he. I had come to expect a younger brother to show his elder brother considerable deference, but the relationship between Surat and Ram was not like this. I recall the conversational exchange which first impressed this on me. Narain and I were talking with Surat and his brother at the latter's *chaupaṛ*. Ram was quite proud of his black and luxuriant moustache of the handlebar type, with tips that almost formed a circle, and was claiming he applied clarified butter (*ghī*) to it daily to nourish its growth. Narain noted that Ram and his brother looked much alike, except that Surat wore a different kind of moustache.

"Surat Singh," Narain said, "you should grow a moustache and then you will look like your brother Ram."

Surat retorted, "Why should I look like him? He should shave off his moustache and look like me."

Even though he did not consult them very much about his affairs, and despite his atypical relationship with his elder brother, Surat on the whole was loyal to the members of his lineage. However, there were times when he did not meet their expectations. This was specially conspicuous on the occasion of a dispute over land between two segments of his lineage. As a leading member of the kingroup he was asked to arbitrate. In a "family matter" of this kind he was expected to try to bring about a compromise as rapidly as possible and above all to prevent the matter from assuming large proportions, as would be the case if it were taken to court. But instead of doing this, he became the legal advisor of one of the contending parties and prevented any of the informal councils, or panchayats, called to settle the matter from coming to a decision. At first he hoped to have the dispute decided in court, as he believed his side would be stronger there. In time, however, he changed his mind about this, but still kept the dispute alive, hoping eventually to bluff the other side into thinking that his had stronger legal footing than it did. The bluff was kept up, literally to the court house steps. Only then did Surat and his side back down and agree to a compromise.

In the important matter of hospitality Surat sometimes was careless. He had been known to invite a high police official to come for a meal and then not appear, leaving the task of entertainment to his brother. With the exception of visits to his four sisters' homes, the reciprocities of hospitality among friends and relatives from other villages so important to most villagers did not hold much interest for Surat. He treated us differently than many of the other Rajput family heads. It sometimes was difficult to work in the village because these men "felt it" if we went too long without responding to their hearty and insistent invitations to stop for a talk and a drink of hot milk.

"Come up here! Come up here!" they would call as we passed their *chaupar*. "Come on up here and sit down and have a drink of milk and a smoke."

Even when he was sitting at his own place Surat did not call to us in this way. We always felt genuinely welcome when we were with him, but I can recall only one occasion when he offered us food. The other side of the coin was that he never asked us for anything. It was part of the friendly reciprocity we had established with a number of other landowners that they would ask for transportation to a wedding or to town, or would ask for other kinds of assistance, such as making purchases for them when we visited a city. During

A Traditional Rajput Council or Panchayat.

the whole course of our close acquaintance with Surat there was only one time when he asked for anything—through a very indirect request conveyed by another person, he once asked transportation for his wife who was returning with much luggage from an extended visit to her parents.

The prominent Rajput men of the village are a ruling oligarchy and are expected to act as councilors, or informal leaders. Their basic responsibility is to see that village custom and Rajput caste group sentiment is communicated and prevails. In the role of councilor a prominent man or two is always invited to important Rajput rituals such as marriages. They lend dignity and caste sanction to the occasion, and render decisions on disputed points of procedure. Either singly or in small panchayats they often are called upon to arbitrate disputes. Though tinged with formality these proceedings have a familial tone and the solution arrived at is often a compromise. The major sanction is persuasion, though on occasion there is a threat to act as witnesses against the guilty party in a court case, and the ultimate penalty is outcasting.

The councilors come together as a body to set policy for their own caste group, and in larger panchayats which include representatives from other castes, they make decisions regarded as binding for the whole village. They are expected to mediate between the village and the government, as well as to talk with officials visiting Khalapur and to provide them hospitality. An ideal councilor should be impartial in his interpretation and enforcement of village custom. He should be conciliatory and patient so that discussion may proceed smoothly toward compromise or unanimous agreement.

A few men in the village are regarded as exemplary in their fulfillment of the expectations and ideals associated with the role of informal leader, and in some respects Surat could be called a councilor of the ideal type. He sat on numerous small adjudicatory panchayats which "bore fruit," and he also took a leading role in larger panchayats which secured consensus and brought results. But on the whole it was only a partial fulfillment. He had little interest in ritual, whereas most prominent men were experts in the protocol of ritual and took pleasure in advising others or in performing a function such as counting out the dowry payment note by note before the assembled family and guests. Although Surat enjoyed acting as adjudicator, policymaker, or mediator between the village and the government, his behavior often deviated from that expected of a person who performed these functions of a councilor. In one panchayat, for example, he tossed sand into the machinery of conciliation by twitting an elderly political opponent. In the course of the discussion this high ranking family head remarked that he had never had occassion to use the statutory local village court where Surat presided. Surat murmured audibly that this was because he was not the type of man to be found in such a small court. No one could miss the innuendo —that this man, who actually had had a number of fairly serious brushes with the police, always committed crimes of such magnitude that they fell outside the village court's jurisdiction. No large panchayat was completely free of this kind of sparring, but Surat was so gifted at hitting where it hurt most and could create so many little diversionary skirmishes that panchayats on which he sat would sometimes come to naught.

Soon after Independence the state in which Khalapur is located created new village councils and courts. Both councils and courts, and especially their respective heads, called *Pradhan* and head judge (*Sarpanch*), were given broad powers and their composition was based on village-wide adult suffrage. It was hoped in this way to create a revitalized and more democratic local government. The broadened franchise and the idea of holding elections was repugnant to many Rajputs, for theirs had been the dominant voice in village affairs and from their point of view the proper way of selecting candidates for statutory village office was in a panchayat. The ideal candidate was one who had not sought office openly and who had professed reluctance when selected. Those who sought election and actually campaigned showed a "shameless" egotism. Elections were disliked because they sometimes generated deep-seated animosities and because defeat, like losing a court case, led to serious loss of face. Elections were also feared because in combination the non-Rajput castes held the balance of power and if they maintained a solid front they could secure the important office of *Pradhan*. Such an eventuality was unlikely when decisions about who would hold office were made in large intercaste panchayats. Representatives of the non-Rajput castes were reluctant to express disagreement in front of the more powerful landowners.

Against this background Surat's behavior when elections were announced was clearly different from that expected of a Rajput councilor. He was supporting a Rajput named Prabhu for the office of *Pradhan* and knew his candidate could not win unanimous backing in a panchayat. Surat thought Prabhu's chances would be better in an election—a belief that turned out to be correct. By having Prabhu refuse to withdraw his official ticket of candidacy he was able to hamstring a number of panchayats which were called to secure a compromise candidate. He removed Prabhu from the direct pressures of these panchayats by acting as his representative and seeing that he was absent from the village when they met.

Surat's behavior in the role of councilor, as in this affair, was often parochial and divisive. But taken as a whole it also showed an intermittent adherence to the ideals of informal Rajput leadership. This had to be so or Surat could not have maintained his strong position in village politics. In this as in all phases of his political life, it was a matter of keeping a certain precarious balance.

Rajput martial traditions—a heritage stressing inherent capacity and right to rule, encouraging political ambition and sensitivity to slight, and accenting the use of force—were important factors in Surat's capacity as village lawyer. This calling tended to strengthen the free-booting tradition of his clan as well as propensities to conflict inherent in his caste group. These traditions are important in understanding Surat's activities as a village lawyer.

During the early nineteenth century the clan to which Surat belonged had a reputation for marauding. Such plundering was due partly to the weakening of the central power at the close of the preceding century, partly to straightened circumstances, especially during years when the crops failed or the tax burden was overly heavy, and partly to repeated frustration of clan desire for political hegemony. With the strengthening of British power, pillaging was gradually brought under greater control. But from the British point of view, as well as from the standpoint of surrounding weaker villages, the Rajputs of Surat's clan and village often seemed turbulent and lawless. Surat's great-grandfather, the man who started his lineage on its rise to prominence, was a part of these more boisterous times. During one marauding expedition he had joined, a man from a looted village was killed and to avoid the police Surat's great-grand-father had to spend a number of years "underground." The freebooting tradition, though much weaker than formerly, continues into the present, especially in the guise of a few contemporary cattle theft rings that still operate.

In Khalapur Rajput village politics has long been characterized by the opposition of families. In every generation there emerge a few relatively weak families that aspire to power. This power-seeking takes the form of an attempt to establish a strong and politically effective system of alliances and dependencies—a petty village principality. The creation of such a village domain is phrased in terms of a regal or kingly prototype, a model carried by the Great Tradition of Indian civilization and one to which the Rajputs are especially susceptible. In Khalapur this prototype has been underscored by clan tradition, as well as by local exemplars of regal panoply in the nearby seats of Moghul provincial power and by outstanding petty principalities in the more recent history of the village.

Historically, there has been a marked ebb and flow in the fortunes of individual families in Khalapur, and in family alignments and concentrations of power. Both the law of inheritance, which permits partition of the estate and calls for equal division among all sons, and sheer biological chance are important factors in the rise and fall of these village dynasties. In favorable combination they may work to provide sufficient land, manpower, and leadership to enable an ambitious family to exploit the available avenues to power. To both create and sustain a family's ascendant position requires constant vigilance and aggressive action to ward off the often vengeful challenges of rival families. These ever-present rivals are quick to take advantage of any weakness or defection of purpose and thus a failure of manpower or a lack of self-assertive leadership may leave a family vulnerable to the counterassertions and depredations of its rivals and lead to its decline.

There are, of course, other factors that serve to check competing families and keep them from destroying social cohesion. Among these is the emphasis on familial values associated with the Brotherhood and embodied in the role of the informal leader. There is also a tendency to legitimize leadership in some families even after they have begun to decline. The seclusion of women doubtless helps to remove another possible source of contention, and there is also an inclination to encapsulate quarrels and keep them from spreading. But although such controls are a mitigating and containing force, they do not prevent the continual assertion and counterassertion of families.

The career of Surat's own family, its rapid rise during the late nineteenth century and the subsequent difficulties it encountered, well illustrates this general pattern. The vicissitudes of his family have significantly shaped Surat's own career, and its rather flamboyant history provides insight into the formation of Surat's attitudes toward village politics and his role as a village lawyer.

Surat's grandfather, the latter's two brothers, and their three cousins were members of the same joint family. At that time there were many more Rajputs than now who considered it unseemly for men of their martial heritage to work in the fields, and especially to plow. But the men of Surat's grandfather's generation did not fear the stigma and worked hard on the farm. Surat's great-uncle, Kala, who became head of the family, was a shrewd and ambitious man. He and a cousin hired a teacher to come and live with them and teach them how to read and keep accounts. The surplus grain which resulted from the family's industry was loaned out at 25 percent interest and additional farm land was acquired when debtors defaulted—the family termed these operations "attacks." Loans were much in demand in those days because of the general pattern of Rajput farming. It was the custom to plant only as much as the family could consume. Since more of the land was thus free for grazing, families kept larger herds of cattle than they do today, and milk formed a larger part of the diet. Vagaries of the weather and need for cash to meet such extra expenses as those incurred in marriages, meant that grain was often in short supply. In such circumstances Kala's grain loaning business gradually became so extensive that it was necessary to construct underground granaries in a number of other villages.

Kala and his family also acquired land by taking advantage of those who hadn't made sure their titles were properly recorded. There were a number of landowners who hadn't taken this precaution, as the usual custom was to rely on the help of kinsmen and friends to maintain rights in the land. In these legal machinations Kala and his relatives were assisted by an urban lawyer. The family also started to lend money and eventually hired a member of the village shopkeeper caste to keep their accounts. Kala himself was sometimes spoken of in derision as a "shopkeeper type," but more often he was called "Ranjit Singh," after the feared Sikh who earlier had established a kingdom in the nearby Punjab.

By these methods Kala and his kinsmen succeeded in establishing an exceptionally strong village principality. Grain which was not traded locally or loaned was sold to traders from the Punjab and carried away by long camel caravans. The family owned land in a number of other villages and had created whole subvillages of tenants. Around the turn of the century their total holdings came to about 1000 acres, one of the largest farms in the whole district.[2]

Around 1900, or twelve years before Surat was born, Kala, whose name even today is used as the epitome of wealth, was killed in a fight with a family from whom he had taken much land by legal chicanery.

Surat's father, Rup, had become the head of the family by the time Surat was born, but it was a much weaker family than it had been in Kala's heyday. The men of the previous generation had died

[2] A district is a subdivision within a state and bears some resemblance to a county.

or were very old, and except for Rup, there were no fully adult males in the coming generation to take over. Many Rajputs had been embittered by Kala's methods, but prior to his death and the weakening of his family, they nursed their grievances, not wishing to take steps to regain their land. However, beginning about the time of Surat's birth and for many years thereafter, Rup became involved in a spate of court cases. Surat estimates there were 250 in all. Rup died in 1939, at the age of 72, and Surat recalls that for all but the last ten years of his life he was harassed by one court case after another. "There was not a single Rajput family in the village that wasn't involved directly or indirectly against my father," he said. It is against the rather turbulent background exemplified by the rise and fall of his own family that the need for Surat, the village lawyer, is to be understood.

Surat's ability to meet this need depended upon his education and special kinds of knowledge. He had studied until he was 18, attending schools in both nearby towns, and, for about a month, a European mission school. He was proficient in reading and writing Urdu, knew some Hindi, and could both read and speak a little English. This linguistic proficiency set him apart from most of his fellow villagers and gave him confidence in dealing with documents and town officials. His self-assurance was enhanced by membership in a high status family accustomed to official dealings. Prior to Independence high level district officials, accompanied by large entourages, regularly made the circuit of the area. When they stopped near Khalapur, Surat's father customarily provided them with milk and grain and was one of the elders to whom these officials most often turned for advice and information.

One of Surat's greatest assets was a remarkably precise, detailed, and well-organized knowledge of village landowning families and their histories. Considering the size of this group his knowledge was impressive in scope. Armed with this information he could predict with considerable accuracy the family alignments that would form over any particular issue. Surat attributed much of his knowledge to conversations he had heard as a boy between his father and a man named Bharat.

Bharat knew everything that I know. I would get good marks in history. But Bharat was even better. He could tell the genealogy of every family in the village from memory. And he knew the history of every family.

Bharat and my father were very good friends. Bharat used to come every evening after his meal to sit with my father. They used to eat opium and smoke the water pipe together. Bharat used to do most of the talking. He would talk on and on and my father never had to say "yes, yes" to keep him going. This is a sign of what good friends they were. They would sit and talk until far into the night.

However, Surat's prime qualification for his work as village lawyer was his understanding of legal procedures and the workings of the police department. He had been acquiring such knowledge from boyhood when much of the conversation he heard had to do with the law suits in which his father was engaged. In 1932, when he was 20, his father was made head of the government-sponsored village court. From the beginning Surat helped his father with his judicial responsibilities because Rup was illiterate, and as Rup grew older and became more heavily addicted to opium, he gradually came to leave matters largely in Surat's hands. After Rup's death, Surat assumed headship of the court officially and held it for four years, from 1939 to 1943. However, his involvement in litigation of all kinds did not cease after 1943. His services were as frequently demanded as when he had held formal office. "People turn to Surat," a villager commented, "whether he is head judge or not." In the light of his experience it is small wonder that he seemed to know the Indian Penal Code by heart, and never seemed to be at a loss about how to deal with the police and the courts.

If any of the villagers were asked to name the reward for which Surat pursued his activities as village lawyer, chances are they would say it was for a bottle of the local rum he liked to drink. This was partially true, as rum and food were among his rewards. It would be incorrect, though, to think of the food and rum he received as a form of *quid pro quo* economic exchange. Surat might very well have been describing himself when he made the following observation about the kinds of influence that are most effective:

A friendship maintained on the basis of liquor and meat can do things a friendship maintained on money cannot do. If someone gives money it is believed that he is giving it out of self-interest. But if he supplies liquor and meat four or five times without asking for anything and then does ask for something once, there is much more chance that his work will be done.

If some official accepts money no one knows what he will do. If he is given meat, milk, wine, or fruit, he is likely to be so favorably impressed that he will inscribe his decision right in the man's presence. He will call out, "Sit down! Sit down! See what I'm writing for you here."

Surat was very fond of meat with his rum. During much of the time I knew him he was provided with both by a Rajput whom he had helped in a particularly bitter and protracted lawsuit. Rajput women are more conservative in religious matters than the men. They abstain from eating meat and refuse to cook it or have it cooked over the family fire, so Surat's friend had built a small fireplace against a wall, just beside his *chaupar*. We were invited to eat with him and Surat one evening and reached the *chaupar* just at sundown. The air was full of dust from the hooves of the returning cattle and layered with blue smoke from the cowdung fires. His friend waited until dark to light the fire, then set a brass pot on it, and soon we could smell the highly spiced goat meat. He disappeared inside his *chaupar* for a moment and came back with a bottle. Surat wrapped it carefully in his shawl and pounded it once hard on the ground to loosen the cork. He removed the cork the rest of the way with his teeth and poured some of the rum into a bowl. After we had eaten we talked for a long time. The moon rose and the village became quiet. That night Surat was arguing that the world would never be free of wars until everyone had the same religion and the same language. And Hindi, he held, was the language best suited to be a world language, for it had all the sounds that anyone could wish to make.

It is difficult to say whether meat or speculation and friendly argument were the more important pleasures that accompanied Surat's drinking. The snatch of argument we heard one day was typical of the kind of talk he especially enjoyed. He and a number of other Rajputs were sitting in the shade of an ancient *pīpal* tree just beside the *chaupar* of an elderly Rajput who had been stricken with leprosy. They were arguing about the nature of God. The stricken man, who had once been very prominent in village affairs, was courtly in gesture and his speech was flavored with gracious Urdu turns of phrase. He had been arguing for a pantheistic conception and Surat was objecting that pantheism made it difficult to solve the problem of good and evil. He addressed a question to the elderly man.

"If people who have been bad in a previous life become animals in the next, and if God created everything, why did he create animals?"

"You can't think of God apart from nature," insisted the leper. "God without nature is like a literate man without pen and ink!" He punctuated his statement by vigorously pushing his open palm downward and outward.

At this juncture a slight middle-aged Rajput named Bishambar broke in. A former school teacher, he spoke with great intensity in a thin, high-pitched voice.

"Good and evil are nothing! It is impossible to explain the world in this way. God is not good or evil. He is neither."

Following a few more exchanges in this vein Surat and Bishambar stood up and went off down the lane.

It was not unusual to find these two together when either or both had a bottle. Like Surat, Bishambar was a scion of a wealthy family. He was older and had once been hired to tutor Surat in English. They had since become fast friends and their friendship had healed a breach between their two powerful families, a breach which at one time had divided the whole village into two opposing camps. When Bishambar had been drinking he usually would set out in search of Surat. "He is the engine and I am the rails," he would say.

Surat felt much the same way. "When other men drink," he said, "they want to go to a cinema. I go find Bishambar. He is my entertainment."

It is true that much of what Surat did as a lawyer was in pursuit of a bottle and the various kinds of entertainment that went with it. But his activities also met needs of a different order. Surat was a nascent professional; he pursued something in the nature of a "calling." He keenly followed the law and all the machinery of its administration. He was proud of his knowledge, which was unique in the village, and it was his boast that his "fees" accounted almost entirely for his liquor and meat. In fact, he claimed he took nothing from his household for such sustenance.

In order to keep well informed about village affairs Surat was always moving about. "I must do this," he said. "It's a necessary part of my profession." His understanding of the plight of two elderly prominent men who had gone blind was an indication of how much this occupation meant to him. He often used to go to different ends of the village to sit in turn with both of these men and keep them informed about what was going on in Khalapur. In explanation he said, "Once a man has formed the habit of going about he finds it hard to stop in old age." Surat was not a man who ordinarily showed much sympathy for others.

Although Surat approached being a professional in some respects, such a status was actually impossible in the village. Difficulties a true professional lawyer faces were greatly exaggerated in his case. From Surat's point of view the village was divided into three groups. There were his friends and members of his party, there were his enemies, and there were those who were neither. Among the latter, as a lawyer, he might give assistance in a dispute to whichever side was best able to "please" him. There was some appreciation for such a disinterested "lawyer's" role in the village and Surat more than anyone else was regarded as a man who exemplified it. But his partisan activities on behalf of his friends and against his enemies were too firmly impressed on all minds for him to be able to pursue many cases of this type without the opposite side's thinking he had defined them as "enemies" and in turn regarding him with hostility. So Surat's occupation as a lawyer did involve him, willy-nilly, in party strife. What was characteristic of this phase of his life was that he did not deliberately foment trouble. The trouble existed. He merely profited by it. Creating trouble for personal advantage belonged to a different sphere of his activities.

One of Surat's friends once said that Surat and another village politician were very much alike because they enjoyed getting other people to fight and then standing to one side to watch. It often seemed that manipulating people and dominating them satisfied some compelling need in Surat's make-up. The desire appeared in his earliest schoolboy memories. In the village primary school there was a boy he used to catch hold of and pretend to beat with his palm. "He became so frightened that he used to turn round and round. He wore a dress. When he spun the dress swung out and it was a very pretty sight to see."

Using an image reminiscent of this boy spinning around in fright Surat many years later described the results of his political maneuverings among a group of Rajputs in a portion of the village which had been opposing his candidate for a statutory office. Many of these Rajputs had been former tenants of his family. He regarded them as somewhat stupid and ineffectual and wondered how it was possible that he and they shared the same common ancestor. "The people of this section of the village," he said, "don't have a leader and they go round and round the well like sheep and goats."

It always seemed to me, too, that Surat became involved in intrigue and intricate political maneuvers because he otherwise would have been very bored with village life. His machinations were a way of exercising his mind. They gave tang to his life and were a source of humor.

An example of the kind of maneuver in which Surat delighted had its origins in the years immediately following the founding of the new high school. Much support for the school was derived from contributions solicited from the Rajput landholders. Surat was one of the prominent men responsible for obtaining contributions. The family of the Rajput, Parmal, refused to give any money. In order to bring pressure on them, Surat arranged to have the *Pradhan,* in return for a sum of money, illegally allot some of Parmal's village land which was vacant at the time. The land went to an enemy of Parmal's and this immediately had the desired effect. He agreed to make a payment to the school if Surat would get the allotment cancelled. Surat agreed and the payment to the school was made. However, the *Pradhan* refused to cancel the allotment. This refusal piqued Surat, who then turned against the *Pradhan* and agreed to help Parmal in a court case, as he knew the allotment had been illegal.

During the case Surat took an active part in making contacts with officials and in filling out the necessary petitions and reports. Eventually two other rival village factions became involved, and there was a violent encounter between Parmal and the head of the family who had acquired the land.

As the suspense and anxiety increased, Parmal in a desperate attempt to weaken his opponent, damaged some government property and tried to implicate his rival and entangle him with the police. In discussing this turn of events with a high official Surat, taking the role of staunch village supporter of law and order, expressed righteous indignation and said men like Parmal should be driven from the village.

The case finally was decided in Parmal's favor and he returned from the hearing, obviously elated, with gifts of liquor, sweets, and grapes for Surat and others who had supported him. In this series of maneuvers Surat had not only had the pleasure of exercising his powers as a court case strategist, he had also scored against an old-time political rival who had come to the support of the *Pradhan* as the case developed. Moreover, he had moved back into the good graces of Parmal, who was usually a member of his party, embarrassed the *Pradhan*, with whom he had become annoyed, and obtained the donation for the school.

The nature of Rajput politics and his knowledge of its inner workings had much to do with Surat's success as a wire-puller. He knew what families bore grudges, and toward whom and why. He knew what families had strong political aspirations. All knew it was part of his "profession" to keep a discerning finger on the political pulse and it was relatively easy for him to convince a family head who wished to "get even" that now was the right time. He was assisted at this point by ambiguities inherent in the Rajput system of political alliance.

The mobilized Rajput party consisted of close relatives and friends of the family, plus a crystallization from the web of alliances defined by ritual exchange and dependency. It was difficult to know what kind of support this crystallization would yield. Support varied with the cause of the quarrel. It was a rare conflict which made a neat cleavage between any two total systems of reciprocal obligation. A further complicting factor was a result of the varying degree of obligation people might feel. The possible range spread from simply "not talking against" a person who was involved in a quarrel to wielding a quarterstaff if he was involved in a fight. In between there were all degrees of support, from giving covert advice and loans, or secretly consulting land records and officials, to openly "speaking for" a person and helping to obtain witnesses. In such a system there was always ambiguity and Surat battened on it. He could assure the anxious family head that he had support about which he had been dubious, or he could promise him an unexpected defection from the ranks of an opponent.

This aspect of Surat's life was associated with a philosophy of power politics.

"I drink," he once remarked, "so I am not doing what I should do. But the thing is that when I drink I don't lose track of reality."

Reality meant two things for him: it meant keeping the support of a large 'army' and being cautious not to place himself in a position where he was likely to get his head cracked.

Early in life Surat had learned the utility of manpower in the village. He remembered how his father attributed many of his difficulties to lack of it, saying to his sons: "God should not provide money and property to a family that doesn't have enough men. If there is wealth in a family and not enough men, it is the same as the death of a family."

"Power," Surat remarked one day when we were talking together, "is something you can't see. It doesn't rest in a title like *Pradhan* or head judge. The power a man has," he stated with emphasis, "rests in the support others know he has in the village. The word *Sarpanch* has no meaning unless it is backed by an 'army.' "

This lesson was deeply impressed on him when he was forced to resign from the post of head judge of the village court. The official report, written in 1943, states that his resignation had been called for because he drank, had not been faithfully accounting for court funds, and had been playing politics with his office.

Surat saw it differently. He attributed his deposition to an unnecessary weakness in his village defenses, a weakness which a police official and his enemies had been able to exploit. Because of his activities as village lawyer Surat had become involved in a running feud with a high Muslim police official in the nearby town. This feud reached a climax when he was able to secure the complete legal exoneration of a villager who had killed a petty official, and of a close relative accused of instigating the act. The relative was unpopular and Surat's activities on his behalf lost him some village support. But he never questioned the wisdom or rightness of what he had done in this case. It was his duty as a kinsman.

He did question the wisdom of an act which cost him still more support. He became involved in litigation to help a barber and an oil-presser, both low caste men, whose land had been forcibly taken from them by a powerful Rajput. He recalled that "all the older men who wore big turbans [indicating that they were traditional in outlook] then started saying, 'Oh, this man has gone crazy. Instead of helping his Rajput brothers, he is helping low caste men these days!' " The Rajput with whom Surat had come into direct conflict in this case became "the hand" of the high police official. With the latter's help he provided "all the idlers and thieves with liquor to the tune of about 300 rupees and made them all line up on a platform" against Surat. In the face of this pressure he had resigned.

When Surat pondered the significance of this episode he came to the conclusion that he had foolishly relied on the power of something besides a strong party.

"When I worked for the barber and oil-presser," he said, "I was depending on help from God and Society. But the people of Khalapur made God and Society go sit in a corner."

The incident taught him that "people who believe in justice and humanity" were weak and he resolved from then on not to make the mistake of depending upon these people or upon ideas like "God and Society." "From the year 1943 until the present," he said, "I have been working with the principle that 'might is right.'"

Surat's 'army' consisted of families he spoke of as "families well in hand." They ranged widely over the social scale. A source of support he valued highly came from among the more lawless elements in the village. He attributed his influence over this segment to what he had learned during the interlude he spoke of as his 'rest period.' These were the years from his resignation in 1943 to his reappointment as head judge in 1950. For part of the time he had had a one-third interest in a village liquor shop. He spent much of this time in the company of the customers, a practice he said taught him much "about the business of being a rascal." His easy, friendly relations with many in this group and his ability to speak their language gave him powers other village politicians did not command.

"There are two types of work," Surat commented. "There is work which involves a limited number of people in the village, and there is work which requires the support of everyone. Leaders like the *Pradhan* can do the first type of work without help. But when they want to do the second type, they have to come to me." In this respect Surat was like the big city "boss."

No matter how strong an 'army' Surat was able to maintain, it was of no use to him if he was foolhardy. The game he played aroused sharp enmity and if he exposed himself to it while it was still at white heat, he would have received a beating. One evening when we were talking with him not long after he had reported a number of Rajputs to the police, a young Rajput came running up breathless. He urged Surat to come out to the fields beyond the Sanskrit school, where he said he had just come across some stolen bullocks in a cane field. Surat refused and told the young man to get the bullocks and bring them into the village and then he would come to see them. When the young man had left, Surat explained he was sure the messenger had been sent by relatives of the men he had reported to the police, and they were waiting out there in the fields, hoping to catch him alone dangerously far from the village. Apparently it was only when anger was at its peak that he had to be so careful. At other times a rational calculation of consequences on the part of those who would have liked to have beaten him was a sufficient deterrent. Unlike most villagers he never carried a quarterstaff, and he had never been involved in a violent quarrel.

Surat was walking a political tightrope and he sometimes seemed to sway precariously. Occasionally he would go dangerously far to obtain rum or to satisfy his need to dominate. He would tell a friend that an official who was coming to sit at the friend's house wanted a bottle of liquor. The friend would go to the trouble and expense of securing it and then find the official did not want it after all but Surat did. Or after an election in which his candidate had won, he would go to the section of the village where the defeated candidate lived and taunt him with the title of the office he had just failed to secure.

Both Surat's sometimes excessive thirst and his desire to dominate were strengthened if not orginated by his youthful experiences. A taste for liquor and opium was regarded as characteristic of the Rajputs, and indulgence in both was viewed as part of their warrior's dispensation. Surat was first introduced to intoxicants in his early boyhood by one of his close relatives. It was a habit he took with him when he left his family to go and live in town and attend school there.

The desire to dominate had found expression in the lives of his immediate forbears, men he had been taught to admire. Even more significant perhaps was his boyhood perception of a series of hostile acts against his father and family. This combined with his forced resignation seems to have played a major role in shaping his some-times very aggressive stance.

There is an episode which serves to round out the picture of Surat as a village politican. Surat was clever, so clever that at times he seemed to have all the threads in his fingers and to be able to direct the play of village politics according to his will. He himself at times seemed to accept, and even to foster, the illusion. Yet it was part of his essentially contradictory nature that he would also take pains to destroy the illusion and to insist how impossible it was to foresee all contingencies in the political sphere. We had been discussing benefits that accrued to him through the misdemeanors of others and he told the following tale to illustrate how difficult it was to make predictions in such matters. The incident also revealed the kind of political complication, irony, and humor he savored, and he enjoyed recalling it.

One night he was returning from the village after spending the evening drinking and talking with a friend at the brick kiln located just outside the village. Near the kiln was the mud hut of a member of the vegetable-grower caste named Saudal. Saudal had also been entertaining guests, three young Rajputs. As he approached the hut, Surat encountered a blind man by the name of Budu, who was also a member of the vegetable-grower caste. Surat asked him where he was going and he said he was going to the mud hut to see his caste brother, Saudal. Surat went on his way, but then decided that he, too, would go to the hut and spend some time chatting with the two vegetable-growers. When he arrived he found three young Rajputs and Saudal. But he did not see Budu. This made him wonder what the old blind man could be doing out late at night, and he sent the three young Rajputs to look for him. They didn't return and after talking with Saudal a while, Surat set out again for the village. Just after he left, the three Rajputs returned to the hut. They had found the blind man in the company of four other persons. The young Rajputs thought Budu's companions might have come out of the village to have a drink together and searched them to see if they could find the bottle. Instead they found that all four were carrying sickles used for cutting crops. It was clear that Budu and the others were out to do some thieving.

Saudal, thinking that they intended to steal from his garden, ran out to call Surat back. He called loudly, "Surat! Surat!"

Surat continued the story:

He wanted me to come back. So I went back and asked what the matter was. They said they were searching for liquor and found the sickles. Saudal said they had come to spoil his vegetable garden.

My ears stood up and I began to wonder what it was all about. I abused them and told them to take the chicken position [head down, with arms passed around behind the legs and grasping the ears]. I took a stick and gave each of them a blow on the behind. They were fairly strong men so I thought I ought to do something to make them tell me what they were doing out at night like that. I only gave one blow to the blind man, but I gave two or three good blows to each of the others.

Then I asked them what they were going to do with their sickles. The blind man said that he was going along with these people to steal some onions from Bahadapur, a village on the other side of Rampur.

They said to me, "Oh, *Nambardār* [the title given to leading Rajputs who used to be responsible for collecting revenue and maintaining law and order in the village], we weren't intending to spoil Saudal's garden."

Then I said to the blind man, "*Susrā* [father-in-law, a term of abuse]! Generally people go to their wife's place with a brand new quilt like you are wearing. They don't go with it to steal crops. *Bahenchōd* [lover of your sister, a term of abuse]! *Susrā!* You are a blind man and you are going to commit a theft. Suppose someone saw you, how would you run away? *Bahenchōd!* You would be committing two crimes at the same time. You were going to steal crops, and if you had been caught you would have given the names of the people with you, and they would have been involved too!"

In the morning Attar [a young Rajput who had not been present the night before] heard about this incident. He came to Budu and told him that I was going to go to the police and report him. He began scaring him this way.

Then the blind man asked what he should do about it. Attar assured him he would be able to please me, but he would have to bear the expense of the liquor. Attar said he would ask me to come to his cattle compound and he told the blind man to come along with the liquor at the proper time.

By chance I went to a place outside the village for two or three days. But when I came back Nathu [one of the young Rajputs who had been present that night in the mud hut] met me and said that I should come to Attar's cattle compound. He said he had been looking for me for the past three or four days.

I said to Nathu, "What is the matter?" But he didn't say anything to me. He just said I should come to the cattle compound and he would tell me there. I went to the cattle compound.

There I saw Budu and two of the thieves who were present that night, plus Attar and Nathu. The bottles had been brought to the shelter in the cattle compound. They were there even before I reached the place. We went inside and sat down. They took out one of the bottles and poured some of the liquor. While we were drinking we gossiped and we didn't discuss that previous night at all.

Then Attar took me aside and told me he had taken five or six bottles in my name. He said to me, "You just tell this blind man that no case can be taken into court against him."

Then the next bottle came and it was opened. The blind man and the two other thieves were also given a little to drink. Two or three other people came around. I was there from eight in the morning to one in the afternoon, and all of the six bottles were finished. The six of them cost 27 rupees.

I hadn't thought of Attar as a man who would do this sort of thing. He just happened to come forward on this occasion. There are men like this, and it is very hard to tell beforehand.

In the afternoon Malkhan, the troublemaker and thief, heard that the blind man had given me liquor worth 27 rupees and he went to see Budu.

He said to him, "All right, you provided liquor for the head judge, who lives in another part of the village. But I also have close connections with the police, because I am always going and coming there. I will tell them this secret you are trying to hide."

Then the blind man provided him with a bottle. All this came out of the blind man's pocket.

I had heard the story about what Malkhan had done and when I met the blind man I said, "Sālā [brother-in-law, an abusive term]! You are suffering for whatever you did in your previous life by being blind in both eyes and now you have started stealing. If you had purchased the onion plants with some of the money you have been spending it would have been a lot cheaper!"

In the minds of the villagers Surat was most closely associated with the office of head judge. As head judge he presided over the court that generally was held on Sunday afternoons. The judges sat on the flagstone platform in front of the village temple with the disputants facing them. The clerk of the court, a member of the barber caste and formerly a keeper of government land records, sat cross-legged nearby with the files spread out in his lap. The court messenger, a bearded Muslim and a member of the musician caste, usually squatted on the ground to one side of the platform, sharing a small water pipe with a friend. If the hot dust-laden winds of May and June were blowing or if it were raining, the group would assemble in the nearby council house.

Surat's court existed side by side with the more traditional method of adjudication by means of an informal panchayat—a method still preferred by most people. But panchayats were not always successful. There were persons who rejected a decision because they felt the judges were biased. Others, though clearly at fault, were unafraid to brazen it out. Unless the difficulty subsided or was taken to the town courts, many of these cases eventually were brought before Surat.

The village court was Janus-faced, reflecting both village and town. Village influence was seen in its informality, composition, and place of meeting, but there was much that reflected the town. Unlike the traditional councils, whose only cost was tobacco for the water pipe, the formal court charged a small fee. Petitions had to be filed in writing; meetings were held at regular intervals and summons were delivered to litigants and witnesses by the court messenger. Its decisions could be appealed, but if upheld they were binding and were backed by the police.

Under Surat the village court became largely a personal instrument. There were five judges from Khalapur. Each of the four other villages included in the court's jurisdiction had also elected five judges, making a total of twenty-five. These judges together had elected Surat head judge. By virtue of his office and social status he would in any event have tended to dominate the court, but he further strengthened his hand by means of his authority to select the judges who were to hear any given case.

To avoid serious trouble Surat had to meet certain minimal village and official requirements. He had to hold fairly regular sessions, and he had to prevent too many cases from being appealed to higher courts. His files showed that he was not under heavy pressure to keep careful records or to be meticulous about following correct procedures. The court was a new institution and mistakes of this kind were tolerated, though in appeal cases they were sufficient cause for revision. This was one reason why it was risky to have too many cases appealed to the judiciary outside the village. However, the main reason was that too many appealed cases would have been evidence of serious local dissatisfaction with the way the court operated. The small number of appeals Surat actually had to contend with was largely a result of his reputation as a man who was thoroughly familiar with the ins and outs of the law. Furthermore, appeals were discouraged by the villagers' experience with the vagaries of town justice and their reluctance to spend additional time and money on the petty cases the local court was permitted to consider.

Surat had learned he could ill afford to completely alienate village opinion. He had to be especially chary of the feelings of other high status Rajputs. Unless supported by them, criticism could be quite widespread yet not very dangerous. What he had to fear was their coming together to speak against him openly and unanimously in a panchayat or before outside officials.

"I always watch public opinion very carefully," he said. "I have always been able to keep the important people from going in a body to the officials and telling them I wasn't doing my job properly. My judgments are sometimes revised. But the people of the village don't speak against me openly in a panchayat, though they may privately."

He had more leeway in cases which did not interest the most influential segments of the community. These were the cases which accounted for most of his "fees"—a few rupees, a meal or two, or a bottle. They were also the cases which accounted for the most frequently heard, if not the most effective, criticism. Aside from talk of influence, the charge most often levelled was that he had relied on rigid adherence to the legalism of the town courts in order to tip the beam toward one side or the other. It was said, for example, that instead of making his judgment by taking the character of the witnesses and his knowledge of the total situation into account, he would make it on the basis of recorded evidence alone, as a town judge usually had to do. The result, it was claimed, was a good "paper" case but an unjust decision.

To avoid arousing concerted opposition from the most influential families Surat was cautious about cases in which they were directly or indirectly involved. Such families seldom came to the village court when they were having difficulty with a weaker man. Nor except in rare instances would a weaker man go to court against them. There were many ranking Rajput families who almost never gave anyone cause to file a claim against them, and fear and prudence kept a weaker man from going to court against those who might give cause. Once when a young Rajput, Dharam, stole another's wheat and when the latter, who had only a few close kinsmen and a small farm, approached a prominent Rajput for help in organizing a panchayat, the elder gave him this advice:

"You don't have a shoe in your hand and aren't in a position to do anyone any harm. If I were to organize a panchayat, Dharam might do something else to you. If you take the matter to court, you won't be able to get witnesses. Dharam comes from the largest lineage in the village. You'd better keep quiet and not get him down on you."

When Surat was presented with cases involving two strong Rajput families his usual tactic was delay. If he delayed an embarrassing case it often would solve itself. If this did not happen, Surat would encourage the spirit of compromise by informing each party privately that due to legal technicalities they did not have a chance of winning. Occasionally he was able to avoid embarrassment by declaring such cases out of jurisdiction.

In the face of so much criticism one might well wonder why it was that so many cases (96 in 1952) kept coming to the village court. An explanation is apparent when the different types of dispute are considered. A large number were debt cases; a lack of effective sanctioning authority made it difficult to collect bad debts in the village. Surat's court was backed by the state and since many debts were recorded in writing chicanery was difficult. A biased decision would be appealed and revised. There was one shopkeeper in particular, a man generally held in high repute, who frequently used the village court to collect his debts.

The local court, like the urban courts, provided opponents with a way of contesting with one another, within limits and according to understood rules. The matter at issue generally was minor. One case of this type involved an alleged debt of only a few rupees. The heat of litigation, and the cost, was out of all proportion to this amount. The favor of the judge, helped along by the number and status of the witnesses secured, was what decided the issue. The next round of this quarrel was fought out in the town court. After that it was a contest over a village statutory office, and a number of rounds later there was a fight with quarterstaves. Surat's court was suitable for one round of a contest of this kind.

Some of the cases were inconsequential but interesting "law jobs" to which Surat willingly gave audience. For example, a peaceable man might want to place his opponent in a position where he would have to listen and so he would take his case to Surat. The men of one Rajput lineage kept driving their bullock carts across the field of a neighbor, without bothering to keep to the cart path. Their neighbor, who had objected once or twice but did not want to press the matter in the fields, filed complaint in the court. During the course of the hearing each side brought out a number of things that long had been rankling: the complainant said his neighbor never allowed him to take water from his well. ("The well never goes to the man to ask him to have a drink from it," the owner of the well had replied.) The defendant said the complainant's father had never paid for the land he was accused of damaging. ("People don't give land away," said the complainant, and the two launched into a lengthy reargument of this ancient case.) The appeal eventually was dropped and there was no decision, but as a result of the hearing a fight in the fields had become less likely.

Some cases were a way of getting a man of influence in the community like Surat to listen to domestic troubles. It did not much matter whether the person who was the cause of the complaint were present or not. Who of any stature in the village besides Surat would have listened once more to the old one-eyed Brahman's complaints about his nephew, this time for hitting him with a stalk of sugar cane? Who else but Surat would not only listen to the following story but would order a *bābū* (a clerk, and more generally an educated man) carefully to write it down?

The complainant (a Rajput woman aged 60) alleged that the accused (a Rajput woman aged 30) gave her a beating with a stick. She was injured on the head and on the foot. The reason for the dispute was that both the accused and the complainant went to Allahabad (to attend the great Hindu religious festival, the *Kumbh Mela*). There was a great crowd. The accused asked the complainant to sleep on the other side of her, as there were many males on that side. Now the accused says that the complainant owes her 20 rupees. She also threatens to cut off her nose.

Or what other court of law would have entertained the plea of the father who had given money to a minor government official for getting his son a post, and now wanted his money back, as the son had been fired after working for a few months?

Cases kept coming to Surat's court because it had social utility. A villager who was asked his opinion of the court recognized this when he commented, "It's better to have a broken down bullock than an empty cattle compound."

Surat frequently spoke of how difficult it was to be head judge. It was a difficult post because it was the focus of so many conflicting claims. Justice for one group was not justice for another, and as Surat once put it, his decisions seemed to make him "fifty or sixty enemies every day." There were the traditional claims of the Rajput Brotherhood and village custom, of close kinsmen and friends, and of statutory law. All were not relevent or equally pressing in every instance. But often enough two or more conflicting interests figured in a case.

As the holder of formal office Surat might have been expected to resolve the difficulty by consistently deciding in favor of statutory law, as he frequently did anyway. But there was among the villagers little real understanding of duty to an "office," or of the necessity of adhering to the legal statutes. Surat might have been known as "head judge" but there were always those to whom he was primarily a close friend, a leading man of his lineage, or a Rajput. He had more than the letter of the law to satisfy. There was no source of support from outside the village that could compare even faintly with the psychological and physical protection offered by his loyal village circle of kinsmen and friends. There was no bar association; the police were distant and somewhat capricious in their ministrations; and there was no leaving Khalapur for another place.

With Surat's position in mind, how should he have decided this case? A widow who had been beaten by her husband's kinsmen once came to court insisting on her legal right to manage her husband's property. She did not trust her husband's kinsmen and feared that her only daughter would not be given a dowry large enough to assure her of a good marriage.

The opposing claim of her kinsmen was supported by Brotherhood custom. The land she wished to control was ancestral property and for generations had been handed down from father to son. The holding bore a name and was rich in family associations. According to traditional custom a widow was entitled to the income from her husband's land during her lifetime, but it was to be managed by her husband's kinsmen and remain in their hands at her death. The widow's in-laws attacked her because of their great anxiety. She was letting the land out on shares to a powerful member of one of the strongest lineages in the village and her relatives feared that in time these men, as had happened before in similar cases, would somehow secure title to the land by a legal trick. If this did not happen, they feared that her daughter's husband eventually might come and take possession, as he now had a right to do according to statutory law.

Was he correct in handling the following case as he did? Surat had a lineage cousin named Kartar, a man with a reputation for being very hot-tempered. One day Kartar saw a stranger walking across a cane field he was planting. This made him furious and he chased the stranger into the village and gave him a blow with his quarterstaff. The stranger went to a number of prominent men in search of redress, but each passed him on to someone else, as none of them wished to become involved in a dispute with a member of Surat's lineage, and in particular with Kartar. Finally, the stranger came to Surat and tried to file a petition in the court. Surat refused to accept it, saying that if he took any action he also would get a beating. He then accused the stranger of being nothing but a tramp and ordered him out of the village. In taking this step Surat may well have recalled the judge on his court who had determined to settle all cases without fear or favor, regardless of the claims of kin. To strengthen his resolve this judge often quoted from the *Bhagavad Gītā,* the great Hindu religious classic, in which God, in the form of Kṛṣṇa, advises the hero to do his duty, even to the point of killing his kinsmen. This judge's rigidity in one case had so annoyed his kinsmen and friends that he had lost their support and had been beaten by a strong village party he had decided against.

The incidents could be multiplied but these are sufficient to suggest that the difficulties of his office were real ones. It is clear too that these difficulties were exacerbated in Surat's case because some of his actions were not of the sort that made it easy to maintain the respect and authority due his office. Knowing this I often wondered why Surat seemed so frustrated, and often so truly unhappy about his situation. There was his direct self-criticism, as when he said he was not living up to the requirements of his office because the head judge was supposed to be "like a god, following all the Hindu customs." There was his criticism of the village which sometimes went so far that in actuality it became a form of self-justification. Why wasn't it enough to be the village politician to whom might was right? Or why wasn't it enough to appreciate fully the difficulties inherent in the office and let it go at that?

Surat's sense of frustration and self-criticism, and the murmur of criticism heard throughout the village, implied the existence of standards other than those of expediency. There was a widely held conception of the deportment befitting the office that for both

Surat and the village had been vividly embodied in the person of a lineage uncle of Surat's who had been head judge of an earlier village court.

This man, whose name was Prithivi, had become head judge in 1921 when he was a young man of about 30, and he held the post for nine years. For five years of his term he belonged to the large unpartitioned joint family headed by Surat's father. Since he took office when Surat was 9 and held it until he was 18, Surat had a good opportunity to see how he managed it, though there were periods during these years when Surat was away from the village attending school. His lineage uncle is remembered as the person who led the village in establishing a religious school, building a village temple, and carrying out a number of reforms having a universalist bias, such as changing the nature of a yearly festival which had involved harassment of the shopkeeper caste. He also was remembered as an excellent judge.

A primary feature of Prithivi's leadership was his ability to gain support among most of the Rajput prominent men. There were many reasons for this. He had associated himself closely with the Arya Samaj, a socioreligious reform movement which was very influential during his time. He became its foremost proponent and was able to direct and channel the impulses to change it had stimulated. He himself strove to become an ideal village judge and leader, of the type believed to have existed in ancient India. He used to say he regarded the village as a family of which he was the father.

The Rajput prominent men who supported Prithivi were drawn into the court on important cases as consultants, though officially it consisted of only five members. This fact, plus Prithivi's general attitude toward his office, helped lift it out of partisan village politics. He devoted much of his time and judicial skill to forestalling litigation that might have gone to the town courts and during his term in office the police almost never came to the village. Within the limits of customary law he did much to protect the weaker members of the community against the depradations of the powerful.

The existence of Prithivi helps one understand why Surat again became head judge, even after being forced to resign under circumstances which at best were slightly dubious. There was the close blood tie and the existence of the dynastic principle in village political affairs. Surat's career was similar to Prithivi's. Both had been very young when they took the judgeship, and there was something similar about the times as well. There was a great flush of hope associated with Independence. For a time it seemed easy not only to remake the country but people as well. Surat had shown great promise on his father's court. Despite what had gone before, he might now, with his outstanding talents, mediate as successfully between the village and the ideological currents of the present as his lineage uncle had done twenty years before.

It is against this background that the sharpness of some of the villagers' criticisms and their sense of disappointment must be understood. Something of how many of the older generation felt was apparent in an exchange between Surat and an elderly Rajput named Mungat. We were sitting talking with Surat when Mungat came by on his way to the fields. He carried a small water pipe in one hand and a quarterstaff in the other. A cowdung cake for his hookah was perched on top of a coarse cotton cloth he had folded over his head for protection from the sun. Mungat kept chickens. Surat twitted him for never giving him any eggs, and banteringly threatened to involve him in some cases. Mungat, whose only son had recently died, replied that he was over 50 and didn't care about living any more so it wouldn't matter. After getting Mungat some of the gun oil he insisted was helpful for his stiff joints, we mentioned that we had been talking about Surat's school days.

"All he learned from his books was how to be a rascal," said Mungat.

Surat smiled. "I didn't learn how to be a rascal in school. I learned it when I came back to the village and got to know the people here."

"We had great hopes for this boy," Mungat went on. "We thought he would do something good for the village. But now instead of doing good he does all kinds of bad things. You better have all the talk you want with him now, because we won't allow him to be head judge in the next election."

"I'm not going to fight the election," said Surat, "but my hands will be everywhere."

Mungat said he wasn't greatly worried by such threats. With this he brushed his moustaches with his hand and went off to the fields.

Surat's feelings about Prithivi were tinged with ambivalence. He felt Rup had had to bear the onerous burden of looking after the threatened family interests, a task which Prithivi eschewed, with a touch of irresponsibility, while achieving eminence in politics. Although Prithivi was often compared to a god by the villagers, Surat knew he had been involved in the ordinary human dilemmas and that he too had been obliged to make compromises. He noted that Prithivi had covered up a number of crimes committed by men who were numbered among his strongest supporters, or by their relatives. To have become involved in the lengthy court proceedings and dealings with the police which surely would have ensued if he had reported these men, would have lost him their support and made it impossible to carry out his plans for reform.

But in spite of such reservations Prithivi was an important figure to Surat, an exemplar against whom he measured his own performance. This was apparent when he looked at his own history as judge and divided it into two parts. The dividing line was his forced resignation. He characterized his conduct of the office prior to 1943—a period during which he said he was "a man of principle" —in terms used to describe Prithivi as head judge. And when he criticized himself, saying the head judge should be like a god, what he meant by god, in part at least, seems to have been an amalgam of Prithivi's religious idealism, his universalist bias, and his wisdom in tempering both to village conditions and the conduct of his office.

We might ask finally how Surat regarded the emerging "new order" in Khalapur, and the accompanying realignments of power. The best revelation of Surat's own general attitude was that disclosed one day by a wealthy lineage uncle. This man had been a *Nambardār* (see page 259), and there was a touch of the eccentric about him. He was one of the few villagers who carried a watch—a large silver one regulated by a chart showing the hours of sunrise and sunset and wound with a key worn on a string around his neck. He had a machine for making soda pop, and a sewing machine on which he made most of his own clothes. We were discussing the new order as we sat in the shed of his cattle compound. Without moving from his cross-legged position on the cot, he described his idea of a representative of the new order and vigorously acted out the part. He was a small man, with quick, darting gestures, and was a good mimic.

You can tell who they are! They wear a *topī* which has to be just two fingers in width. [He demonstrated.] When they were of no consequence they wore the cap in the middle of their heads; but as soon as they achieve some power they wear the cap on the side of the head. [He showed how it was pushed to one side, at a rakish angle.] They also wear their *dhotī* in a very special way, draped so it has a tail behind. When they walk they swing their hips and the tail goes, "Lub, jub! Lub, jub!"

When they sit on the new village council they make sweeping gestures, ordering people hither and thither. If a man has a bullock cart, they cry, "Tax that bullock cart!" If a man has a buffalo which is giving milk, they cry, "Tax that buffalo!"

In the old days when I went to Rampur, even though I was wearing the ordinary clothes I work in, people would salute me. When officials noticed the people saluting me, they would ask their assistants who that man was. The assistants would tell the officials and they would offer me a chair and treat me with respect. When judgments were made they were made in favor of men like me, because the officials knew we told the truth. The people who call day night are in the saddle today.

Surat shared these feelings, though not with the same intensity. He was more detached, slightly amused, and patronizing. There was a young Rajput who was actively assisting the new Community Development officials. Surat spoke of him with derogatory humor as "that 'new life' *bābū*." He did not object to these officials who were trying to improve the lot of the villagers, but on the other hand as he put it, he did not "run up and climb on their shoulders." To him most of them were petty officials and on one occasion he threatened to report one to his superior. His attitude was not unlike that of one of his elderly lineage uncles who when angered by a clerk in a high official's office, insultingly told the man he could hire persons like him to work on his farm.

He shared little of the new interest in making farming more productive. Although his high status rested in large part on the efforts of forebears who kept accounts and were devoted to commercial and financial enterprise, Surat spoke with scorn of those of his contemporaries who showed the same propensities. In an ironical echo of the appellation applied to his own great-uncle he spoke of them as "shopkeeper types."

To a degree of course Surat is part of the new order, since he is head judge of the post-Independence court. However, compared to the office of *Pradhan* the present judgeship shows less break in continuity with the past. In the new council the emphasis is upon development schemes and reform. In the court as always it is upon the adjudication of petty disputes.

But Surat is not entirely *ancien régime*. He has many traits which make it impossible to characterize him as backward-looking. During the days of the agitation for Independence he had seen Gandhi and other leaders on the national scene and had become very active in the Indian National Congress. For a number of years he was secretary of a local Congress unit. Though he shares much with his lineage uncle, the old *Nambardār,* there are marked dissimilarities. This uncle would never be seen eating with a Chamar. Nor could he have shared the most vivid intellectual enthusiasm of Surat's life, the teachings of an Indian socialist. As a younger man Surat had been so eager to keep abreast of the movement led by this man that he taught himself to read Hindi script—he had learned to read only Urdu in school.

When thinking of men who in one way or another were breaking with the past Surat sometimes characterized them in mixed Hindustani and English as " 'forward' men." What was most "forward" about Surat was his inquiring, skeptical mind and high degree of intellectual emancipation. This appeared in many ways, among them his detached and critically humorous attitude toward most features of village religion. He viewed ceremonial as "women's work," and he poked fun at a Rajput family whose women became possessed by evil spirits. He delighted in telling the story of one of his own deceased relatives who, on the advice of a shaman, sacrificed a horse, believing it would bring him the son he so much wanted. It was also a source of amusement for him to remember how the same man had refused to believe accounts of airplanes when they were first being flown. For the sake of consistency he had even rejected the tale in the sacred *Rāmāyaṇa* of *Hanumān's* flight to succor *Rāma.*

Rajput landowner and family head, councilor, village lawyer, power politician, trouble-maker, head judge and "forward" man—it is not strange that Surat should seem puzzling and contradictory. But having made this order in my own impressions of the man I keenly realize that somehow the Surat I knew has escaped. This is the final contradiction—the opposition between all these bits and scraps of memory, impression, and thought, and the sense I still have of the whole, living person I knew. His distinct and engaging self has eluded my words, just as he so often delighted me by eluding my expectations. I remember the only occasion he provided us with hot milk. We were sitting on our cot waiting for him to follow the host's almost ritual custom of pouring it back and forth from one brass drinking cup to the other, in order to cool it. Surat noticed our hesitation. He pointed to the brass tray and cups, and said in English, "Self help!"

...ulli, His Wives, and
...is Grandchildren.

9

A Reformer of
His People

David G. Mandelbaum

There is little point in using a pseudonym for Sulli. Anyone who knows the Kotas, knows Sulli. Among them, he stand forth bold and clear.

He is known as Sulli the schoolteacher, although it is many years now since he has taught a class. Even those Kotas who have scant regard for him refer to him respectfully by the honorific title of "Schoolmaster Sulli." His achievement brought honor to all the Kotas; no Kota before him had reached so high as to become a teacher and one who was even able to converse with officials in the official language, English.

The Kotas—some 1200 people living in seven villages—are a tiny group among India's vast millions. They are one of the four indigenous peoples of the Nilgiri plateau in the far south of India. Before the isolation of the plateau was broken over a century ago, the four peoples lived in separate settlements but in close interdependence. The Kotas did some cultivation but were mainly artisans and musicians, providing goods and services for the pastoral Todas, the agricultural Badagas, and the jungle-dwelling Kurumbas.

The Kotas are far less spectacular than are the famed Todas and are outnumbered fifty-fold by the booming Badaga farmers. But though they are overshadowed and outnumbered, the Kotas are far from being abashed. They have a firm sense of their rights as a people. European travelers and officials wrote of them as an undistinguished, even a shabby, lot; the Todas and Badagas looked down upon them as eaters of carrion and practitioners of other base customs. But the Kotas knew well, in earlier years, that without their help the other Nilgiri peoples could carry on neither their economies nor their ceremonies. The Kotas were willing to acknowledge, in formal gesture, the superior status of the Todas and Badagas. They also had clear ideas about the limits of that superiority, and about the obligations which the other peoples owed them. Thus if a Kota family felt that the Badaga families for whom they provided tools and music were not giving them a rightful share of the crop at harvest, a Kota council could be called which might decree that those Badagas were to be boycotted until they paid up properly.

Kota monopolies in crafts and music are now gone. Only vestiges remain of the old interdependence, but they are still an effervescent people, quick to defend their rights, and sure that their neighbors owe them certain obligations. Although so very few in number, they continue to speak their own language and maintain their own culture. It is a society and culture of such vitality and intriguing complexity as to be of absorbing interest to an anthropologist.

Sulli has been one of the more vigorous among them. In his physical appearance he is much like other Kotas, stockier than most, but muscular rather than fat. He is of medium height for a Kota, whose stature is in the medium ranges for South Indian peoples, and he is not especially distinguishable from Kotas, or South Indians generally, in features or complexion.

In other ways he is eminently distinctive. At a time when other Kotas had not yet taken to trousers or shoes, Sulli dared to appear (this was on a suitably important occasion in 1937) in the local Nilgiri version of full English fig, from solar topee down to tweed jacket, fancy shirt, necktie, tropical shorts, woolen hose, and stout brogans.

In his conduct and career he has been unlike any other Kota. His lavish energies have long been directed toward certain social goals. On our first day together, the first of many which were to follow, Sulli told me that he was the one who was working to improve the Kotas, to change their bad habits. Twenty-one years later, toward the end of our most recent series of conversations, Sulli declared in a matter-of-fact tone, but also proudly, "I am now known among the people as the reformer of the Kotas. I am the man who changed the customs of the Kotas. I bring them forward and all the bad customs are left off."

The bad customs are those which tarnish the name and degrade the status of Kotas. The eating of cow and buffalo flesh, even to the eating of carrion, was a prime source of Kota pollution in the view of their neighbors. Another was their association, as players of funeral music, with the inauspicious occasion of death. In the Nilgiris as elsewhere in India, folk whose traditional occupations include service at funerals are considered to be of lowered status. Sulli had also campaigned against the women's seclusion hut, used for childbirth and menstruation, and against the Kota men's custom of wearing long hair.

At age 64, Sulli does not feel that his campaigns are over. He tells of social improvements which he has yet to bring about. He is still full of plans and zeal for bringing his people forward. This zeal has not been unopposed. An ardent reformer of persistent energies does not expect to have smooth sailing and Sulli has fought through many a verbal and legal battle with other Kotas.

One of the greatest of these was the struggle which was precipitated when Sulli cut his hair. Kota men had worn their hair long and tied up in a chignon for as long as myth and memory ran. When a Kota boy reached the threshold of manhood he went through a solemn ceremony in which his hair was ritually tied up. The chignon had religious connotation, it was a sign of manhood, it was a main symbol of being a Kota. So when Sulli had his hair cut, and a few young men followed his example, it seemed to the rest of the Kotas that he was bent on denying the Kota gods and on cutting himself off from all that was well and truly Kota. Men from the seven villages met in solemn conclave, formally cast Sulli out of the community and forbade any Kota to give him food or fire.

But Sulli had no intention of severing himself from Kota life. He showed no desire to be anything other than a Kota, but he was possessed by a burning desire to change those Kota ways which, as he saw them, lowered the Kotas in the eyes of their neighbors. More than other Kotas of his generation, he had been exposed to contacts with other people, had become aware of other values, and knew that his chignon marked him in the Nilgiris as one of a people of polluting custom and lowly status.

So he remained in the village and fought against his expulsion. At first even his wife left his house, whisked back to her father's village. "I have no help and I separately suffer," Sulli recalls. "All the villagers gather to one side and I am alone." Though alone, he was not helpless. Because he had some education, he was able to make his living as a teacher. Further, he used the advantage of his education to obtain land and to launch trading ventures. No other Kota could get along as independently of his fellow Kotas.

Nor was he completely bereft of friends. His wife soon managed to come back to him. His elder brother, dependent on Sulli's support, stood by him. Some of the younger men took his side. And he had powerful means with which to fight back. He alone among Kotas could write his own petition to the government authorities, complaining that the other villagers were violating his civil rights. Only he could plead his own case in English before the officials and consistently secure orders from them which were favorable to him and harmful to his opponents.

In his dealings with officials he did not always get his way. During one of my visits to the Kotas, in 1949, Sulli was absorbed in the problem of getting a license to own and operate a lorry. At that time there was a booming market for Nilgiri-grown potatoes and a great shortage of trucks for their transport. Sulli seized on my coming at once and asked me to tell the Collector, the chief official of the Nilgiri district, to grant him the license. "I want to be the first of my people to own a lorry." There was not only profit to be had from the lorry permit; there was also the undoubted prestige that owning a motor vehicle would bring to both Sulli and Kotas.

I pointed out that as a foreign visitor I could hardly intervene in such matters, but as it happened I did meet the Collector and I mentioned Sulli's request. The Collector remarked that Sulli's qualifications to be a responsible transport operator had been impaired by some alleged irregularities (never proven) in his management of the village ration shop. However, Collectors and their opinions are transferred from time to time and later Sulli did acquire a motor van which, as it turned out, was not one of his more profitable enterprises and had to be sold.

Although some of his business ventures failed, others succeeded, and he was able to build up the resources needed for his long struggle to change Kota customs. As Sulli puts it, "When the people of the seven villages fought against me and tried to make me get down, they taxed each man some rupees. But they cannot make me fall down because if they spend a thousand rupees then I spend a thousand rupees. I have enough money for that."

The money was needed for lawyers and for police protection. Legal charges were filed against him and he filed countercharges. When his opponents sought a court order barring him from the village temples because, as they avowed, he was ritually unfit to worship there, his lawyers charged that the accusers themselves had no rights in the temple. All this long litigation was expensive. So was police protection which Sulli needed when they tried to throw him out of the village. "Every year at the big ceremonies a sub-inspector of police and ten constables would come to the village and I would have to supply them. I had to have them stay with me because I am only one man among the Kotas and all were against me so I needed the police for protection."

He could afford to carry on his fight because he was a successful entrepreneur. Some observers have written that entrepreneurs are rare in village India. But anthropologists who have seen village life at close range have often noticed a good deal of entrepreneurial activity. It is *successful* entrepreneurs who are rare. The institutions and opportunities of village economy are not such as to encourage business success, although they do not extinguish business aspirations. A good many of Sulli's peers have, like him, opened a little shop, or contracted to supply a crew of laborers, or tried to be brokers in potatoes. Most have wound up in debt; Sulli has generally made some profit. He has succeeded not only because of his education and his energy but also because of his powerful motivation to make good in business so that he could realize his regnant ambition to change the ways of the Kotas.

It is not that he is indifferent to personal finances. It is rather that his personal and social goals are the same. He has never held any of the formal positions of religious leadership nor has he ever been the acknowledged headman of his village or of the Kotas. Nor has he ever indicated to me any special desire to hold formal office or to have universal Kota acclaim. The attractions of popularity or of office in themselves hold little appeal for him.

From the time he was outcasted, Sulli has fought through a long succession of village arguments and legal cases. After twenty years of battling, only a few of his bitterest opponents, and those few in his own village, still hold out against him and treat him as outcaste. The younger men do not see Sulli as the heretic he once was thought to be; some of them have now been exposed to the same kind of experiences in the outside world which influenced Sulli.

Several of these younger men have studied English and Sulli's son has had a high school education. But though they know some English they are much too shy to attempt to speak it before those who speak it fluently. Shyness has never been one of Sulli's handicaps. He wields his English freely and forcefully. While he shows little mercy to

English grammar and precise usage, his meaning generally comes through clearly.[1]

His opponents have been many, of many sorts, and not only fellow Kotas. Indeed he has always been ready to drop, temporarily, any quarrel he may be carrying on with Kotas in order to defend the rights and the status of Kotas against any outsiders' threats. With various Badagas, he has long been at odds. He fought for many years against those Badagas who could not bear to have a lowly Kota as teacher for their children. They tried to get him fired, but though he was often transferred, he was never dismissed. More recently he has led the Kota fight for the right to be served wherever others are served in the food shops of the Nilgiri towns. Previously, Kotas could not eat food where customers of higher caste were served. They now can do so in the places they want to patronize. In part, this achievement is the result of the political and social changes of recent Indian history. But, in a more immediate sense, it is the result of Sulli's efforts. His campaigns have been with, rather than against, the tide of history but they have been bitter struggles nonetheless.

Only a man of strong and determined character could have endured so much opposition for so long. He has not been a beloved leader. Some of his early followers changed allegiance; this did not deter Sulli at all. He has pressed his cause with great singleness of purpose (though with considerable tactical footwork) and with substantial success. His aspirations and energies have been concentrated on being the first to change from degrading customs and to convince all other Kotas to change with him.

As we come to know a person of such force and character, whether it be a figure on the grand stage of world history or in the minute microcosm of Kota life, certain questions come to mind. How did he get to be that way? How does he look to others in his

[1] Sulli became accustomed to my typing his responses directly; my notes and the quotations of his words usually preserve the structure of his utterance, but as I typed I would repair, for the sake of future clarity, some of his direct speech. There are more literal notes from my brief visit in 1958 when I was able to use a miniature tape recorder.

When I began my work with Sulli in April, 1937, he had just spent several months as a linguistic informant for Dr. M. B. Emeneau, who introduced us. His English had been improved by that experience. Dr. Emeneau smoothed my understanding of Sulli's diction and facilitated my study of Kota culture. It is a pleasure to express my thanks for his companionship and help.

society? What effect has he really had on his culture? And a reader may be interested in knowing something of the relationship between him and the ethnologist.

How did he get to be so dedicated a personality? What special circumstances induced him to fight for culture change? Until he was 15, there was little in the pattern of his development which was notably different from that of other Kota boys of his generation.

He was born in 1894, the third of five children in a fairly large but not unusual Kota family. He was given a common Kota name, Tu·ǰ; Sulli is a more unusual name which he later adopted. His father's old mother was a dominant presence in the household up to his sixth year. She was generally perched atop the sleeping plank and from that point of vantage she could see into the one other room of the house, the kitchen, and out into the village street. There she sat, sometimes dozing or smoking, often scolding. Her voice ruled the family, as Sulli remembers. "If her wishes were disobeyed, she would curse, 'I have worked all my life for you and now you let [neglect] me.' My father feared her curses and scolding and obeyed her."

His father's widowed and childless sister was also part of the family. Frail and saddened, she devoted herself to taking care of the children and did not go out to gather fuel or work in the fields. "She was a widow and the only sister of my father. He thought that if she had to work hard she would be more mournful than ever. So all she did was nurse the babies."

So it fell to the wife and mother of the household to do the harder chores. It was she who worked in the family's fields, who chopped wood and gathered dung for fuel, who husked the grain and cooked the meals. All this was done under a steady barrage of the grandmother's complaining. No one in the house ever worked hard enough to please grandmother, and especially not her son's wife. But Kota women, even younger women, are not expected to be eternally meek and subservient, as is expected of young wives in the higher castes of Indian village society, and the children's mother often gave as good as she got in the verbal exchange. Such quarreling seems to be taken by Kota children and adults as a kind of unavoidable minor nuisance, like the smoke which comes up from the cooking hearth and gathers in a cloud under the chimneyless roof. It irritates for a while but eventually disappears.

She was not constrained to spare words toward her husband either, but once or twice a week, Sulli recalls, her words were of little avail. His father would come home drunk. "He would kick at the door and come in falling. Then my mother would put rice and broth before him and he would eat. 'Hey fool, this rice is no good.' She answers, 'It is prepared as always.' 'Quiet.' And he would beat her.

"She cries. We children wake. Seeing our mother cry, we cry too. Then my grandmother comes and scolds, 'Who gave you the money for drink? Why do you come like this? Is this what I have suffered long years for?' And with that scolding my father becomes quiet."

The father is thus remembered not as an overwhelming figure, even when he was drunk. Old grandmother can always control him. He is a man, subject to the vagaries of mood expectable in a Kota man and controllable in any mood. He does discipline the children when they deserve it, but he also protects them when they need protection against older children or irate villagers. The children are nourished and tended by the three women of the household. Even grandmother's scolding has a softer edge when she scolds the children. Father's sister provides for their physical needs. Then mother is always the tender recourse for her children.

Sulli's elder brother, some four years his senior, was a docile child (he grew up to be a tractable man) who took care of Sulli as he was told to do. "He would take me by the hand when we went out and he would carry me on his hip. If other boys hit me, he would protect me." Perhaps because his elder brother did so well at tending him, Sulli's next elder sibling, his only sister, did not have as close and affectionate relations with him as are customary between a Kota elder sister and her younger brother.

In the house of their mother's father, the children always had a warm and sure welcome. His village was a day's journey away and they often stayed there for several weeks at a time. He indulged his grandchildren; he was under no social pressure to discipline them, he could enjoy them. "If we didn't come to his house for a while he would send word asking why. Because he was always anxious to see us."

He was not actually their biological grandfather, but their mother's father's brother. Her real father had died when she was young, and her father's brother had taken the widow to wife. He gladly accepted the daughter as his own and, later, her children as his grandchildren.

Kotas like to have children and grandchildren whatever the actual biological facts of relationship may be. Hence a Kota child is usually cradled in a firm network of family relations. When there is a gap in a child's constellation of close family relations, it is generally filled quickly by some adult.

In his earliest years, Sulli thus had a specially secure and nurturing environment. Within the house, the three women looked after him and his siblings. When he would toddle about in the street, his elder brother was always there to care for him. And when he became aware of farther places and peoples, there were the fine visits to the grandfather's house.

When Sulli was about 6 he was sent to the village school. By then his next younger brother, younger by little more than a year, was always trailing him. Sulli recalls that he would go on to school and his little brother walked behind. He was an unwilling scholar. "Always my will is against my father's. So if he sends me to school, I must go and play." When his father found out he would beat him and shut him up in a dark storage bin. As did other Kota parents, he would threaten the truant by pretending to call Kurumbas, the jungle people who were sorcerers.

"Kurumbas, catch this boy!" he would shout as he locked Sulli in the bin. "At that I was in panic. Whenever I went to a dark place I was afraid of the Kurumbas and now I thought that one would surely get me. So I kicked and screamed until my mother came and let me out. At that my father beat my mother.

"When I was let out I would sit with my arms close around mother. And when my father would ask me whether I would go to school I answered, 'Yes, Father, I will. Please don't give me to Kurumbas.' "

The fear of the Kurumbas was inculcated deep into Sulli, as it was with all Kotas of his generation. Somehow, this impress of terror did not devastate Sulli's self-confidence, or that of most other Kota men. Perhaps it was because all active and directed evil could come only through Kurumbas. If one Kota wanted to harm another magically, he had to pay a Kurumba to do so. A Kota who thought that he was being bewitched, hired a Kurumba to parry the evil by countersorcery.

Thus all magical malevolence was assigned outside Kota society. However much one Kota feared or hated another, he knew that a

Kota, by himself, could not work the worst, the really dangerous, harm. If one tried, the intended victim could always hire a countervailing Kurumba. In extreme cases, when a man felt victimized by magic, he or his relatives could thwart the Kurumba agent forever. They would catch him and knock out his two front teeth so that he could no longer enunciate his magical spells properly and could therefore never again harm anyone with magic.

Sulli tells how his father, suitably fortified with drink, did just that to a Kurumba. But this anecdote is perhaps to be understood, not as a literal account of what happened, but as a Kota son's reminiscence of what his father might well have done under the heavy grief of true personal tragedy.

The tragedy was that within the span of a year and a half, when Sulli was about 7, the three women of the family died. First the old grandmother went and the father rallied all his resources and credit to provide her with a suitably grand funeral as a dutiful son should. Then the mother, in the last months of another pregnancy, sickened and suddenly died. Soon after, the children's aunt was gone.

Then a series of women came through the household. A widower with five children needed a woman in the house quickly. Kota marriage is simple and easy. One by one wives came and, divorce being equally simple and easy, soon left. A story Sulli tells about the first of them indicates why they left.

Once she was preparing a meal, wearing only a single cloth tied under the armpits as Kota women do in the heat and smoke of the kitchen. She asked Sulli, then perhaps 9, to get some wood for the cooking fire. He didn't like her ("She always abused and beat us") and so he just refused. She cuffed him and then went out to the woodpile herself. As soon as she was out of the door, he bolted it. She hammered and scolded but he sat still and refused to let her in.

Skimpily dressed as she was, she had to take refuge in a neighbor's house. There she was counselled to go back to her father, because if the boys treated her so now, what could she expect of them when she grew old? She did go back forthwith.

Then the children prevailed on their father to marry their mother's sister. They knew her well from visits to their grandfather's house. Sulli's sister took the proposal to the grandfather and before long a familiar and sympathetic woman was once again in the house. Sulli remembers that she would sit with the children around the hearth and sing with them and play tunes for them. But she was a young woman, only eight years older than Sulli himself, and not entirely happy in her dead sister's place. She went back to her village to nurse her ailing father in what became his last illness. Soon after he died, she died also, and the children were bereft of grandfather and mother's sister.

During the times when there was no woman in the house, father and children frequently ate and slept in the nearby house of the father's closest friend. The two men, clan brothers, worked together, helped each other, and as good Kota friends and brothers should, slept with the woman between them.[2] Sulli's first memory of his father having sex relations is from a time soon after his mother's death when the family was sleeping in the other house. The woman of that house, as well as her husband, was especially fond of Sulli's father. The children slept in one room, the adults in the other. In the dark, Sulli remembers hearing sounds which he understood to be made by the two men taking turns with the woman.

If this memory had any primal significance for Sulli, he is not aware of it. So common were such experiences in Kota domestic life that it might be strange if this memory did carry great emotional freight. Sulli missed his mother, he didn't care much for some of his stepmothers, but his father's sex life was his father's affair. Yet he did remember the sounds in the dark.

How much he missed his mother Sulli tells in this recollection. When he was about 8, he was caught stealing food and sweets which a Muslim had brought to sell in the village. He was hauled over to his father. It was Monday morning just as all the men were coming before the temple to pray.

"So he took me to the temple. 'Stay here and pray!' Afterwards we went to the house. He told my younger brother to get a switch. My brother came back with a small stick. Father spit, 'This is no switch.' He gave my brother a cut with it.

"He locked me in the storage bin and went to get a thorn stick which he wound around a smooth stick. He beat me until blood ran from my behind. I tried to say that the other boys had put me

---

[2] David G. Mandelbaum, "Polyandry in Kota Society," *American Anthropologist,* 1938, *40*:574–583.

up to it, but he replied, 'O, they were weak and you were the brave one. I have fed and fattened you so that you may be strong to be a thief.'

"He beat and beat and I cried and cried. I cried for my mother because if she had been living she would have stopped the blows, but now there was no one to help me."

Though he felt the loss of his mother bitterly, he did not act as though he were helpless. Throughout his boyhood he resolutely took on whatever tasks he had a mind to do, even though some were considerably in advance of his age. It seems as though the special care and security which he received during the first six years of his life had girded him firmly enough so that he had no qualms about his ability. When he wanted to do some difficult chore he would tackle it with confidence, if not with skill.

Meanwhile Sulli was going through the motions of attending school. This was not one of the tasks he was minded to do. His elder brother had been there briefly before him, but when that boy was about 8 he was taken off to his grandfather's house. The grandfather had no sons; he needed a lad to herd his cattle. The father protested; he wanted his son to have schooling. But the old man ridiculed him with what was then a standard quip, "Do you want to make a *tahsildar* of him?" The thought that a Kota could climb to such great heights through education as to become an official (of the very lowest grade), a headman of a subdistrict, was then a ridiculous notion on the face of it.

One son had to be delivered over to grandfather and convention. But the father was firmly determined that the second, at least, should go to school. And when Sulli's father so fixed on something, mere convention was no deterrent. He once decided that he had to keep a horse. Other Kotas objected strenuously. They argued through a stormy series of village assemblies, that it was not the proper thing for a Kota to do; ". . . it was against the ways of the gods for a Kota to have a horse." But Sulli's father stood obstinately firm—as Sulli was to do later—and kept a starveling pony until the issue faded.

He was a peppery character. Apparently his father before him had been of the same stamp, a man who was the first to put a tile roof on his house at a time when it was seemly and ordained for a Kota house to wear only thatch. Sulli's father engaged in a series of feuds, with Badagas as well as with Kotas, sometimes on matters of sheer principle rather than of personal profit.

So when his father decided that Sulli should go through the village school, the boy went. That there was a school in the village at all was an unusual thing. It was partly because the summer capital of Madras Presidency was in the district's main town that special schools were established for the Nilgiri indigenes. And liberal-minded education officers may have considered the village a good place in which to plant a school because of the low status of Kotas.

Sulli attended but, as he recalls, without much gain and with less desire. "I was the most stupid in the class because I didn't care for learning. . . . My father always went to the smithy and to cultivate and I wanted to do the same. My father gave the Badaga teacher an acre of land to use so that he would teach me well. He tried, he beat me like a hammer. Still I didn't learn."

When Sulli was 12 he finally took the examination of the fourth standard, the highest grade of the village school. "A Muslim examiner asked me what caste I was. 'Kota, Sir.' He gave me good marks even though I made a poor showing." He was passed; perhaps only, as he now remembers, because the Muslim examiner was lenient with a candidate of such disadvantaged origin.

"We got our school leaving certificates and from then on when my father would get any little bit of printed paper in the bazaar, he would bring it home for me to read. But I didn't know how to read well and often I couldn't make out what was printed. He would slap me, 'Eh stupid, my fourth standard passer.'"

After his release from school, Sulli entered into the full activities of Kota adolescence, activities in which reading played no part at all and one's schooling could be quickly forgotten. He frequently was part of a Kota band at Badaga funerals. He could not play the main instrument, which resembles a clarinet and carries the melody; that took some skill and a knowledge of the musical repertoire, in neither of which was Sulli then, or later, particularly accomplished. But any Kota boy could beat a drum and a Kota who was assembling a band for a Badaga funeral was usually glad to have a boy substitute for some able-bodied man whose time was better spent in the smithy or the fields. As player, the boy got several good meals, perhaps a few coins, and an opportunity to see something of other villages and people.

There was also work for a boy in his own village. At plowing and at harvest there would be a cluster of Badagas around every smithy, waiting for tools to be sharpened, repaired, or made. Then any likely Kota lad was recruited to work the bellows or hold the hot iron with pincers while a skilled smith worked the metal. As Sulli became able to do a man's work in the fields, his father gave him a plot of land to work by himself. His elder brother was assigned another, and the two youngest boys together worked a third field. "If we worked together, we would laugh and talk and not get much work done. Separately, my elder brother thinks that because he is older he will show that he can get more work done. I want to beat my brothers, so when my father comes to look at the fields he will favor me. So I work hard."

The young brothers, tilling their separate fields, may or may not have entertained the thoughts in 1908 which Sulli mentioned decades later. But this incidental mention does reflect a common situation among Kota brothers. Brothers are supposed to share, to support and protect each other.[3] In a few contexts they can be rivals. Sometimes there is tension when these contexts become confused, yet there usually remains a strong sense of what relation is appropriate to what context. Thus in their later years, Sulli and his next younger brother disagreed about many things. They belong to different factions because this brother is a conservative person and they do not enter each other's homes. But when either is in dire straits, the other comes immediately to his help.

Mutual help was necessary among the brothers in their later adolescence. For weeks and months there was no woman in the house; the boys had to do the cooking and the other women's tasks. Their sister was married off into another village soon after her puberty. There were long periods when their father either had no wife or when the current wife was away in her own parents' house. As Sulli remembers, his elder brother ". . . was foolish. Father would beat him and send him out of the house." The two other brothers were too young to be able to do the household chores. So Sulli would prepare the grain, spread it to dry in the sun, set a younger brother to watch it, go to work in his field, and come back to cook the meal. It is not at all unlikely, gauging from the facts of later years, that Sulli really

[3] David G. Mandelbaum, "The World and the World View of the Kota," in M. Marriott, ed., *Village India,* Chicago, University of Chicago Press, 1955, pp. 234–235.

did manage the family's household economy responsibly as he remembers he did.

Yet he was a boy and he played with the other youths of the village at boys' games. On the two days of the week, Saturday and Monday, when Kotas do not work in the fields or smithy, he joined in their play. Favorite then, as now, was imitating the great occasions of village life. Grand mock funerals are conducted with play processions and pyres. Sacred ceremonies are pretended and some boys (presaging later, non-pretended behavior) throw themselves about as do the diviners when a god enters them.

In those earlier years, the great moments of the grand ceremonies came when several half-wild buffaloes, destined to be sacrificed, were released. Men leapt forth, gave chase, wrestled the beasts by their horns until each animal lay flat (sometimes a pursuer or two also lay flat, his life blood pouring out fast and fatally through a wound from a horn). The best and bravest man in this chase was singled out for special ceremonial acknowledgment. Young men aspired to show their prowess and gain public recognition. Boys prepared for these great events by practicing in the meadows with calves and old cows, worrying the animals until they made resistance enough to give the boys practice.

Sulli, too, practiced for the real chase. As a young man he took part in many such contests and he recalls with great relish those occasions when he shone as a strong brave conqueror of buffaloes. Like other Kota men, he was hot for the buffalo pursuit well into manhood and well after the time when he was in his prime for buffalo chasing. Settled heads of families commonly took a good deal of rough shaking up during buffalo chases, before they would reluctantly realize that younger men with younger sinews could do better in the wild sport of the pursuit. Sulli later came to condemn the sacrifice of the animals and to abjure the chase with its attendant cruelty to the beasts, but he retells with sparkling animation his brave exploits on fierce great buffaloes.

There is another series of exploits, with women, for which Kota boys practice, in which men take pride, and in which, as Sulli tells, he excelled. Just as the children play at staging the grand occasions of Kota life, so do they play frequently at enacting the domestic scene. Boys and girls pair off, set up a few boughs to make a house, pretend to cook and eat meals, lie down together as married people do. And they experiment at intercourse in imitation of the grown-ups.

Throughout his boyhood Sulli had one constant girl companion. She was a girl of his own age, the niece of his father's close friend. She lived for a while in the house of her mother's brother, next but one to Sulli's, and the two children sought each other out as play-mates even before they were 5 years old. When the two families would sleep in the same house, she and Sulli would sleep together, facing each other side by side as married couples do. Far from objecting, the adults thought the boy lucky to have so stable and cordial a friendship with a fine girl.

The boy, in his later recollection at least, thought himself clever to be able to bind a girl so closely that she was always helpful and looked after him. Sulli has detailed memories of his relations with her, as he has of many experiences of his early years. He once remarked, "The things I did from 5 to 15 do not disappear; it always stands just before me. The things I did from the twentieth age up, I have much forgotten."

The girl and he were together constantly. If he was hungry and there was no one in his house to feed him, she would take him to her house where he could always get something to eat. The two helped each other in youngsters' chores, they played at intercourse until the imitating gradually became authentic. As Sulli became adolescent he entered zestfully into the usual man's game of trying to find as many sexual partners among Kota women as possible. With Sulli's drive and ability, many affairs were possible. He played this game well into his middle age, but he also prided himself on being able to hold affection thoroughly, first that of his girl playmate and later of his wife, so that he could always be sure of one woman who would cleave to him, no matter how difficult that might be.

This was not a common concern of Kota boys and Sulli was not an ordinary boy in other ways as well. Yet the course of his life, while he was child and youth, was not particularly different from that of his age-mates. He played at the same games, did the same kinds of work, had undergone the same kind of inconsequential schooling, had the same aspirations about girls and buffaloes.

Then, when he was 15, he made a sharp turn. Thenceforth his career would never again be so much the same as those of his Kota contemporaries. He decided to go back to school.

The moment of decision came, Sulli graphically remembers, one day when he was playing with other boys at catching the horns of young buffaloes. They saw a Badaga boy approaching who had been in the village school with Sulli but had gone on to the higher grades at a mission school. "When the Kota boys saw him coming from school, carrying some books, wearing shoes, trousers, shirt, cap, they ran forward to meet him." They saluted him with the respectful greeting which Kotas gave to Badagas and they escorted him across the fields up to the bounds of the village. Sulli sat still until the boys returned and began playing again.

He asked them why they had made such a to-do about the fellow. They answered that he was going to school and was therefore a "big man" so it was right to salute and escort him respectfully. "From that time on my mind changed. I thought that if I was companion to these boys I would never come forward. They always follow other people and don't know how to do anything for themselves. If I go with them I too will obey others as long as I live."

He suggested to some of the other boys that they go with him to the German-Swiss mission school, three miles from their village. They were aghast at the notion, as Sulli recalls, telling him, ". . . if we go there and back, the Kurumbas will get us and the Badagas will hate us and our fathers will be without sons when the Kurumbas kill us. Throw that thought out of your head or you will be the most foolish of the whole village." And when he told his girl and her friends that he had made up his mind to go to school, they cried because some Badagas who had gone to that school had become converted. He assured them that he would not "join the Christians" and be forever lost to Kotas. He would only study in the school, he said, and freed from wearying toil in the fields and in the house, he would be better able at night to enjoy them.

It was rugged work, going back to school. Sulli had forgotten much of what little learning he had assimilated and he had to start anew on the multiplication tables with the younger boys. But the German headmaster accepted him readily, waived the school fees for him, provided him with slate and books. After some demur, his father supported him and bought him a mission schoolboy's outfit of jacket and knee-length pants. When the boy had to study late into the night, his father did not begrudge buying him a little clay lamp of his own, nor the expense of oil for the lamp.

There was precious little other support for the newly determined scholar. One of his mother's brothers, on hearing the news, hurried to persuade Sulli to give up this dangerous notion, of recklessly and gratuitously exposing himself to Kurumba sorcery by walking alone every day the six miles to the school and back, past a thicket of bluegum trees in which Kurumbas could easily hide. Sulli brushed off his pleas. "If I die, I will die. So many others have died . . ." And the uncle's fond concern turned sour. He spat, made some uncomplimentary remarks about his benighted nephew, and left.

In time, as Sulli proved his ability to go on with schooling, Kota objections were replaced by some pride in his doggedness and ambition. But objections by Badagas to his being educated and in the same school as their children continued for a very long time. There were many harsh encounters with Badagas. Sulli can recount in detail one of the first, which happened soon after he returned to school and was accosted by the father of one of his Badaga schoolfellows.

"Whore son. Have you sense? Dirty Kota, can the turkey [sic] become a peacock? Go back to your village and beat the drum. Don't try to be great."

This slanging upset him, but did not shake his purpose. "I cried bitterly and I made up my mind that there would be a race between the studies and myself. Either I would win and beat the studies or I would die trying. I never forgot those words . . . I didn't play with my friends any longer and didn't lie with the girls . . ."

Before he had finished the first year at the mission school, he had to do something about his steady girl. She was now of an age when suitors were clustering around her and she could hardly avoid marriage to someone else if Sulli delayed any longer. Not that she would be forced by her parents, but rather that she would very likely become pregnant—given the usual proclivities of a young Kota woman —and then she would have to get a father for the child. Many a man would be only too eager to get an attractive young wife, with a child on the way to boot.

She came to Sulli and clasped his feet, he tells, in the gesture of entreaty. "She was 16 and her breasts were so big and she was very beautiful. But the teacher had told me that the boys who get married leave their studies, they don't care for the lessons . . . So that night I thought hard which was best. If I married, I would have a few days happy and then all the rest of my life I would have to dig the earth and sweat. If I worked hard for about four years, then all the rest of the time I would be a teacher or a government servant."

He put her off temporarily with an excuse and disposed of her entreaties permanently with a stratagem. Among her suitors was a gay youth who sang very well and had a persuasive way with the girls. Sulli arranged with this lad to stay the night in a house where the unmarried young men and women of the village often came to sing and then to sleep. Sulli and his girl were there that night. He acted coldly toward her. When the lamp was put out and she came to sleep at his side, he did not cover her with his cloth as usual but straightway turned his back to her and pretended to fall asleep.

Rebuffed and angered, she made little resistance to the singer when he crept over and induced her to move to the other side of the room to lie intimately with him. Then the singer coughed, a signal prearranged; Sulli struck a match and saw her there in the singer's arms. At once she came over to beg his forgiveness but he was adamant and would have nothing more to do with her. But there was one more thing Sulli thought he had to do to clinch the matter. He sought out one of the girl's suitors who was older and wealthier than the others and would therefore be more inclined and better able to make a lasting marriage with her. He told this man that the girl was now ready to marry and go off with him. So it happened. She later came back, appealed to Sulli again, but she no longer figured importantly in his life.

In his second year at the mission school, 1911–1912, there was a major personal crisis, of his own making. He tried to become a convert. Things had not been going well with him in his father's house. He and his elder brother were of the age at which Kota young men can assert their independence and leave the paternal roof. This is more common in the lower social echelons of village India than in the higher, where the father's economic hold and psychological dominance are generally greater than is the case among the Kotas.

After a quarrel with their father, the two brothers moved into another house where they did their own housekeeping. But that meant that Sulli had to do a good deal of the cooking and collecting of fuel; his brother was not a very dependable housemate. His studies suffered. When Sulli was dunned for the contribution which each separate household had to pay toward the expenses of a major ceremony, he had to give up and reluctantly moved back into his father's house.

Thus balked in the village, Sulli gave thought to leaving it. He often walked home from school with a Badaga boy from the next village; the two would sometimes talk about the Bible lessons to which both were exposed and discuss the possibility of becoming converts. One afternoon their resolution quickened and they agreed to meet at the school that evening to take the great step. Even though his schoolmate failed to appear, Sulli went alone to the headmaster and announced his intention of becoming a Christian.

The headmaster took him in and let him stay the night, but instead of sending him forthwith to some distant mission station, as Sulli had imagined he would, he told him to attend his classes as usual. Perhaps that headmaster did not know enough about the temper of the Kotas. There was little enough opportunity for missionaries to come to know anything about them; when a missionary came into a Kota village in the course of his evangelical rounds he was given a standard treatment. Villagers confronted him with a clamor of jeers, imprecations, and barks so that his voice could not be heard and he had to go off to quieter places.

The Kotas did not remain quiet when they discovered what Sulli meant to do. First his father came to the school, called to him, but Sulli brusquely refused to come. Saying nothing more, his father went back to the village and soon returned to the school with some forty angry Kota men. When the teacher saw them coming he locked the classroom door and shouted for help. But they smashed a window, kicked open the door, poured into the room, ". . . grabbed me by the hair, dragged me back to the village. The teachers could not interfere because if they had there would have been murder, for the young men were bad."

That night, Sulli tells, he was very much ashamed. His father cried through the night, lamenting the hard fate that had deprived him of all of life's joys and crushed his will to live now that his best son wanted to become a convert. "For all the crying of my father, I became pity and said, 'Father, I won't leave you and I won't become converted. I will always stay with you and I will light your funeral pyre.'" Then Sulli took a solemn oath, by stepping over his father and giving his promise to God, to his mother, to his father, that he would not leave the village before his father's death and he would fulfill all the filial funeral duties.

His father was reconciled by this but was not fully satisfied until Sulli agreed to quit school and to take a wife. He did both, but neither for long. Within a few months he had convinced his father that he meant to stay in the village and his father let him go back to school. At that, the girl to whom he was quite cordially married told him that if he insisted on going on with his education, she would go back to her father's house. They separated amicably, he was taken back in the mission school, and all was well with Sulli for a while.

Only this one time did he try to leave the community of Kotas and the experience made a deep impression. He told me about it during my brief visit in December, 1958, as he had done at length in December, 1937. The earlier version was given in much greater detail and some of the details differed in the two versions, but in both Sulli made clear that it had been an important event for him. In his earlier account, he says that he was mainly dissuaded by his father's sorrow, in the later account he mentions his fear of being beaten or killed if he became a convert. Whatever the reasons, thenceforth he felt firmly bound to Kota society.

He completed the three years of the course at the mission school. By then he felt able to go right up to the office of the Collector of the District and to ask that high official for a job. He was appointed as a copying clerk in a township office, writing out copies of official papers. Although he was only six months at this post, it gave him a higher education in the ways of officialdom. He learned how to write an effective petition and how to soothe underlings so that their superior officer might take note of the petition.

Next he was awarded a government stipend to attend a teacher training course at Coimbatore, a large town near the foot of the Nilgiri Hills. There he was for the first time completely out of the Nilgiri enclave, in an urban world where the local hierarchy of the Nilgiri peoples was scarcely known. He observed that there too status gradations of caste were highly important and were based on certain general criteria of rank—criteria which a group might manipulate to its own advantage by abandoning demeaning practices and adopting esteemed customs. He had known this before; it was brought home to him in Coimbatore.

His first post as a teacher was as assistant to the Badaga school-master in the very school he had first attended. Now he was ready to marry and, in usual Kota fashion, he went through a series of marriages and divorces before he settled into an alliance that was lasting. One marriage which had promise of being permanent ended when the young woman died.

At one stage a 15-year-old girl caught his eye; she was married but he engineered a divorce for her and took her home. They soon quarreled, she left, and he promptly remarried. But, as Sulli tells the story, she found that she had her heart set on him. She was a bit of a social manipulator herself and she tried various devices to get Sulli back. She finally succeeded in marrying his good-natured younger brother and so lived in the same house with Sulli who by then was temporarily single again. Soon she convinced everyone in the household that she and Sulli were the proper pair. The shift from one brother to the other was easily made and that alliance lasted for years.

Although Sulli was now qualified as a schoolteacher, he felt in need of one further spell of schooling. An Englishman had tried to talk with Sulli about the Kotas and Sulli found that his English was not up to a protracted conversation. So in 1918, at age 24, he took a leave of absence and enrolled for English at the Municipal High School in the town. Sometimes he did not have train fare and walked the twelve miles to the high school. But he did improve his English.

After a term in the high school, he had to begin earning a living again. He was married, his brothers were not great earners, his father was aging. The small pay of a schoolteacher was inadequate so Sulli stopped teaching and opened a small shop in the village. But he had not yet served out the three years as a schoolteacher which he had committed himself to serve when he accepted the government stipend. The school inspector insisted that he fulfill his contract completely and he was assigned to open a new school in one of the Kota villages.

There he found that he could supplement his income by offering a variety of useful services to the villagers, once making a large profit on a shipment of betel leaves, another time handling opium to lucrative effect, always ready to act as scribe or go-between for a fee. Thus fortified financially, Sulli settled into a long term of school teaching. It ended with his resignation during World War II when the demands of his multiple enterprises and new wartime activities, such as managing a ration shop, made it infeasible for him to continue teaching.

As Sulli talked to me about his career as a schoolteacher, some fifteen years after he had stopped teaching, he made plain that it had been a satisfactory, even a victorious, career. It was not that he had risen high in the educational bureaucracy; throughout he had remained a teacher of elementary grades in small village schools. The success came from his triumphs in maintaining that a Kota could be a teacher at all, and could even be a teacher to pupils of any caste—whether Badaga or higher.

Some of the Badagas had objected strenuously to any kind of educational integration of Kotas and Badagas. In Sulli's own village, the schoolhouse was apart from the main settlement area. Both Badaga and Kota children attended the same school when Sulli was a schoolboy, but the Badaga teacher kept the two groups of children spatially and educationally segregated within the one room. When Sulli was assigned to be assistant teacher in that school, he was given charge of the Kota children only.

But he was still called teacher by all the children and soon most of the Badaga parents were stirred to action. It came when a new Badaga teacher replaced the more tolerant schoolmaster. The new man called together the leading Badagas of the neighboring villages and, as Sulli heard later, told them that Sulli had become a teacher to the Badaga children and so he was like their *guru*. "They give him salaams and respect," he charged. "How can a low caste Kota be a *guru* to Badaga children?" They collected money with which to strengthen their complaint before the school authorities. Before long there came an order for Sulli's dismissal. "Now I thought, if they can get rid of me so easily, what is the use of my living beside the Kotas? So I went to the Collector . . . and he ordered strongly that I be reinstated." In his appeals to higher officials Sulli has usually had the firm advantage of being one of the disadvantaged Kotas. So in telling of his reinstatement Sulli mentioned that English officials were "kind and fair," just as in describing another appeal years later, to Indian officials, he referred approvingly to "our kind Congress government."

This reinstatement was not, however, a full victory. He was assigned to a school in another Kota village, in which there were no

Badaga children. From 1919 to 1925 Sulli taught in three such schools, each located in a Kota village.

Then, in April of 1923, there came another test of strength. Sulli managed to get himself transferred to a school which was conveniently located only a few miles from his home village and, more important, had a completely Badaga enrollment. As before, Badaga villagers promptly raised a row. But now the school inspector in charge was sympathetic to Sulli and he simply abolished that school. He assigned Sulli to a nearby school in which about half the students were Badagas and the others from different Hindu groups. Here the Badaga parents, perhaps subdued by the example of the rescinded school, allowed the children to study under a Kota teacher. Later Sulli taught at two other schools where the children were predominantly Badaga. "So I was teaching Badaga children in the different parts of the Nilgiri District and the Badagas' bad aim was spoiled." With these words, Sulli summed up his career as a teacher.

Yet it was not at all enough for him to establish himself personally as a teacher. He had also to establish the Kotas as a people fit to provide teachers and to have rights which others would deny to them. This involved changing those Kota customs which others cited as the reason for shunning Kotas and that, in turn, involved struggles with those of the Kotas who saw no reason to change their ways.

As Sulli's education had progressed, his opportunities for new experiences had widened. He was exposed to new situations which no other Kota had met, and he became increasingly frustrated by the low, polluting status ascribed to Kotas. For example, he once applied to attend the higher elementary school in town. The Brahman headmaster turned him away, explaining that there were many Brahman boys in the school and so a Kota could not come there as a student. It was common knowledge that Kotas were eaters of flesh, not to say of carrion, that they sacrificed buffaloes and even cows at their indigenous rites, that they were called to play music at funerals. All this imparted a polluting aura to any Kota so that Sulli's presence in that school, the headmaster indicated, would disconcert the whole establishment.

Sulli, as we have seen, was not the kind to be crushed by such encounters. He was rather spurred by them to pursue his course with even greater determination. That determination was compounded of many factors. Among them were the self-confidence and security

297

he had received in his family circle, the zest for argument and the defenses against insult he had acquired from his fellow Kotas, the willingness to take a solitary stand which he may have absorbed from his father.

His special career was made possible because his father had insisted on his going through the village school. He set his course resolutely when, repelled by the traditional roles of subservience, he decided to acquire different social roles. Then he came to a juncture where he had to choose between leaving Kota society through the route of conversion or staying with it. When he committed himself to remaining a Kota, he also committed himself—given his career and his temperament—to changing some of the Kota culture patterns. His efforts for personal and group improvement brought him into conflict on two fronts. He had to contend with those Kotas who were unwilling to change and with those Badagas who were unwilling to allow the Kotas to change. Against both, Sulli finds that he has made progress.

Sulli, in his 60's, has come to a certain peace with his society. Not all his reforms have been accomplished but there has been enough change to give him satisfaction. The time is long past when most Kotas met him with angry faces or with turned backs. The factions he sundered within his village have gradually come closer together; differences remain, but are tolerated. The pervasive bite of factional bitterness has, apart from a few older men, been eased.

His household is a prosperous one, filled with his son's children. He has only one son, who has grown into a sturdy, steady man, educated up to the level of college matriculation but not ambitious to leave the village. The wife who had remained steadfast through the most trying years had borne several children; all but this one son died very young. When it became apparent that she would have no more children, Sulli took a series of younger wives, one after the other, in the hope of fathering other sons.

Only one of these younger wives stayed. She came of an unusual family in another village which had chanced to get a regular income from land rental. They had been able to give some schooling even to the daughters and to clothe them in saris, the usual dress of Indian women, rather than in the traditional plain white shift which almost all Kota women still wear.

This woman's modernity endeared her to Sulli. Moreover, she is a strong-minded, strong-voiced, strong-willed woman. Though she bore no children, she came to rule the household. The old wife left, moved to another house in the village where she is supported by her son. For a time she would not enter Sulli's home when the other woman was there, but this animosity too has softened over the years. The old grandmother in her Kota garb comes in to care for her grandchildren, while the housewife in her sari raps out orders to all in the house, not excluding Sulli.

Of his siblings, all except the brother next younger had died by the time Sulli was 64. That brother has always been very different from Sulli, a quiet, unassuming, conservative man who is respected for his good sense and fair judgment. He has held responsible office as village purse-keeper for decades.

Sulli and he do not go into each other's houses because they belong to opposing factions and the brother is very serious about his loyalty to the old tradition. But during the twenty years and more of factional dispute in the village, the two have never reviled each other as factional opponents often did. Each respected the other's stand even though he could not agree with it. When either was in serious straits the other would rally to his aid. Thus when the brother had a severe bout of illness in the late 1940's, Sulli brought expensive doctors from town, paid for the medicines, saw to it that his brother's fields and family were well cared for as long as the illness lasted.

The factional split which Sulli started in the village still existed in 1958, but there has been a gathering rapprochement, especially among the younger men who had not taken part in the bitter early struggles. When Sulli and a few others cut their long locks, they became known as the "karap" men, from their cropped hair. They made up the reformist faction. Under Sulli's instigation the reformists took to a new set of Hindu-like gods which had been introduced into the village[4] and they followed Sulli's lead in demanding that all Kotas abandon the sacrifice of cows and buffaloes, the providing of music, the eating of carrion, and the use of the menstrual seclusion hut.

The conservatives, called the "old rule" adherents, were outraged by these demands which they understood as a disavowal of all that

[4] David G. Mandelbaum, "Social Trends and Personal Pressures," in Leslie Spier et al., eds., *Language, Culture and Personality*, Menasha, Wis., 1941.

was good and truly Kota. Furious arguments raged in the village. Sulli, as we have seen, was formally outcasted by the assembled Kotas. But against the weight of numbers and general sentiment, Sulli brought to bear his formidable capacity to manipulate the power of the police, of civil officials, of the courts, in his favor.

When Sulli began to score over his opponents, the conservatives came to see that he did not mean to undermine all that was traditional. He remained steadfast in the old worship, fighting vigorously to participate in the traditional rituals for the old gods when some tried to bar him from the temples. The reformists, it turned out, did not want to dispute the continuing primacy of the old tribal gods; they only wanted to add the new set of gods and to follow the traditional rites with supplementary worship in a more Hindu fashion. Perhaps the reformists might have been more sweeping in their program had not the conservative opposition been so strong.

In the late 1940's the reformists—mainly financed by Sulli—hired masons from the plains and had an elegant shrine built for the new gods in a meadow beyond the village streets. Ten years later most of the villagers would worship, on due occasion, at this shrine. But it was not well kept up in 1958. The new shrine looked shabby and unattended, while the temples to the traditional triad of Kota gods, refurbished at an annual ceremony, remain trimly kept in the heart of the village. It is as though the reformists were content to have made their point by building the shrine and having the new gods generally accepted; beyond that their prime allegiance was still to the old ways.

A good part of Sulli's original program of reform has been accomplished. Kotas no longer sacrifice cows at their ceremonies and they sacrifice few buffaloes. Many Kotas will not eat beef and few will accept carrion. Only a handful play at Badaga funerals. While the seclusion hut is still in common use, some families have given up this practice.

From time to time Sulli has added new proposals to his reform program. For example, he came to disapprove of the free and gay indulgence which is an important part of the annual second funeral ceremony, performed for the dead of the preceding year.[5] Some of the more riotous features of the ceremony have been dampened—

[5] David G. Mandelbaum, "Form, Variation, and Meaning of a Ceremony," in Robert F. Spencer, ed., *Method and Perspective in Anthropology*, Minneapolis, University of Minnesota Press, 1954, pp. 60–102.

here the state government's prohibition of strong drink has reinforced Sulli's stand.

In recent years, one of the reformist faction decided that a consecrated flame should be brought into the old temples as is done in the usual Hindu tradition. By Kota tradition, the old temples are entered only once a year, at the God Ceremony, and never with a flame.

Sulli took up this proposal and pushed it with his usual stubborn verve. His chief opponent was now the old priest who had come to tolerate certain of Sulli's reforms, though not Sulli himself. The priest would not yield on this proposed infringement of Kota tradition in the very temples, in the holy of Kota holies.

At the God Ceremony of 1948, the reformists managed to get a light into the temples through a ruse. They had secured the right to perform a God Ceremony of their own immediately after the conservatives had finished, and they arranged to have a police detail in the village when they did so. In the course of their rites they began to take a lamp into the old temples. Forthwith the "old rule" adherents learned of this and charged in to stop them. As a fight started, the police promptly intervened to keep the peace and hauled off the objectors. Then the reformists did take a flame into the old temples.

That ruse would only work once; there followed a long series of heated meetings on this matter. Respected Badagas were brought in to help adjudicate this dispute. Their decision was for Sulli but the old priest refused to accept it. Then in 1951, the priest's faction secured a legal injunction which barred the reformists from using the temples or joining in the ritual during any of the three main days of the God Ceremony. Sulli countered by procuring another injunction—it must have seemed fair enough to the issuing magistrate—which similarly barred his opponents from the temples while the reformists were performing their ceremony. Moreover, the writ also stipulated the period when the reformists could carry on their rites and that period was a week before the traditional time for the great ceremony. What the magistrate did not know was that the whole sacred purpose of the ceremony, of renewal and refurbishment, would be destroyed if an unhallowed, imitative rite were performed in the sacred precincts *before* the proper, traditional ceremony.

So the old priest had to retreat and compromise. He has permitted a flame to be brought into the temple, but he has insisted that all the "old rule" villagers have precedence in the course of the ceremony over those of the other faction, thus symbolizing the general superiority of the traditionalists in matters religious. Sulli, for his part, is quite well content to take a formally subordinate part in the ceremony so long as he has gained this change in Kota ritual idiom.

The priest's compromise has also meant an end to the time when the reformists had to carry on separate ceremonies of their own. All in the village now participate together in the ceremonies of the Kota annual cycle. This, too, is an outcome with which Sulli is content.

There has been a like outcome in the other Kota villages. Each had similar factional divisions, though in none was there the protracted acrimony that there was in Sulli's home village, perhaps because Sulli's ardor brought on countervailing fervor. In other villages there was, at first, a general reaction against Sulli's radical measures, especially when he cut his hair. But in the ensuing years there were a series of episodes in which Sulli showed that he could be a staunch and effective defender of some parts of the old tradition even while he opposed others.

One such case, Sulli relates, made a deep impression on all Kotas. It involved a disputed inheritance in another Kota village. According to Kota custom the dead man's brother should have inherited, but his widow had managed to get documents which legally entitled her to the property. The brother came to Sulli's village to enlist his help. Sulli readily agreed; this Kota custom implied nothing derogatory to Kota status. He evidently made a persuasive witness in court, testifying that the widow had secured the documents fradulently and that, in any event, the brother had the right of inheritance by Kota custom, and therefore, his claim should be upheld by the court. Whatever were the judge's grounds for finding in favor of the brother, the Kotas were convinced that Sulli had successfully maintained the "old rule" in the very halls of government power.

Sulli has, in fact, been the foremost defender of Kotas whenever any were demeaned or threatened by outsiders. Such threats have come mainly from the ardent reformers among Badagas.[6] The

---

[6] There are several differing endogamous groups which are called Badagas; in the Kota view these are classed together.

Badagas too have been riven by disputes between reformers and conservatives. A chief issue between them has been on the use of Kota music at funerals. By the standards of high status Hindus, to which many Badagas became sensitive, it is highly improper to dance about a corpse at funerals to the tune of Kota pipes, as was the ancient custom of the Badagas. In the 1920's and 1930's there were riots, even killings, over the issue. More recently, this reform has spread and relatively few Badagas now use Kota musicians. But many are still very touchy about their caste status; the small community of Kotas presents a strong menace to their social aspirations.

In the first place, the Badaga antimusic party has not entirely prevailed. They view those few Kotas who play at Badaga funerals as enemies no less than the Badagas who employ them. More importantly, the Kotas are a constant reminder of what some Badagas would dearly like to forget—that not so long ago the Badagas were an isolated hill people practicing some unworthy customs and more closely linked with a low folk than is seemly for people of respectable status. These status-sensitive Badagas also feel that if they are to maintain a suitable rank for themselves, they must be particularly rigorous in avoiding polluting people like the Kotas. To the degree that the Kotas come up in the local status order, some Badagas feel that they themselves will in like degree go down.[7]

These Badagas were especially vigilant to keep Kotas out of public eating places used by the higher castes. Even before the year of independence, Kotas had certain civil rights in such matters; after 1947, the civil rights were made even more explicit and officials were encouraged to enforce them.

It was Sulli who filed complaint after complaint against tea shop customers who threw out Kotas and against tea shop owners who refused to serve them. One such owner had his license revoked and had to persuade Sulli to withdraw his complaint before the license could be renewed. (It cost him a good meal for a Kota party and additional expenses as well.) Kotas are now generally served without question; in the view of most Kotas, this achievement is mainly Sulli's doing.

In a wider view, Sulli's achievements can be seen as part of a

[7] David G. Mandelbaum, "The Kotas in Their Social Setting," in *Introduction to the Civilization of India*, Chicago, The College, University of Chicago, 1956, p. 29.

great trend in Indian history, a vast, slow, but steadily ongoing revision of differences of status and of the criteria of status. Sulli has played his self-chosen reformer's role on a tiny stage, but on that little stage are exemplified main processes of social change among India's and, indeed, among many of the world's peoples.

Though Sulli has been unique among Kotas in his personality and personal role, other societies have experienced the influence of men of like personality. Their influence can be great. More highly charged and motivated than are the run of their fellows, they have their minds rigidly set on certain social goals. Unwavering as they are about these purposes, they can still be adaptable and adroit in manipulating various means toward their fixed intent. Some of these personalities take on the aura and the devoted following of a charismatic leader. Sulli did not. For one thing, such leaders from village India have generally been religious figures; Sulli is preëminently secular. He could be eminent only among Kotas and they probably know him too well for devotion. Most importantly, Sulli has been much more concerned with accomplishing his purposes than with becoming an acknowledged leader. For a time, when the two factions would not interdine or hold common ceremonies, it looked as though the Kotas would be split into two separate endogamous groups. But Sulli had no desire to be the founder of a separate community; the gradual coming together of the factions—on some of his terms —is fine with him.

There was a reciprocal reinforcement between his personal bent and the experiences which shaped his career. Because he was inclined to take a course of his own, he gained experience in a wider world than any of his fellows had previously known. And because he had these experiences, he became firmly committed to setting a new course for himself and for all Kotas.

To Kotas that new course seemed heretical; to students of village India, it is seen as quite typical of the process of social mobility. There commonly are some groups in a local caste order which strive for higher rank than others will accord them. They do so by trying to abandon degrading practices and to take on customs more elevating. There was little opportunity for changes in status relations in the old Nilgiri social system. But when the ancient relations were made obsolete by the influx of new peoples, new ideas, new economic conditions, there was greater scope and more pressing need for changed status patterns.

Sulli has hurried the pace of these changes among Kotas, but it is well to note that there are certain values which persist and which even Sulli has no notion of changing. One such value is the high importance of group status in a social hierarchy. Even though the Nilgiri people had been relatively isolated from the mainstream of Hindu civilization, they maintained a kind of caste system.[8] And though the Kotas were low in this hierarchy, they prized the status symbols and prerogatives which they did have. Under modern conditions, group rank and the symbols of rank are still of great moment to them as they are to other Indian villagers.

As we look over the whole of Kota culture, we can see that Sulli wanted to change only a very small, if strategic, part of it. It is remarkable how much of the culture remained relatively unchanged after many decades of exposure to influences from the centers of Indian and Western civilizations.[9] The basic patterns of family relations remain much the same as they were in Sulli's original family, the traditional cycle of Kota ceremonies is carried on, the Kota language is used by the still strongly distinctive Kota community.

By the time a new generation has grown up, additional and more drastic changes may come about. Some may come about almost incidentally. There are now a large number of squatters living around Sulli's village, lowland people who were driven by hunger to the hills and attached themselves to any village which would tolerate them. The Kotas did not object to having these people camp in their fields, dependent on them and subservient to them. Now they number as many as the Kota villagers themselves and are always in and about the village. Kota children pick up the Tamil language and Tamil ways from them and use them more regularly than their elders ever did. If Sulli thought that these hangers-on might influence Kota life, he would probably want to clear them out instantly. But he apparently does not suspect that a set of insignificant folk like these squatters could ever affect Kotas.

Those changes which are coming about because of government

[8] *Ibid.*
[9] David G. Mandelbaum, "Culture Change Among the Nilgiri Tribes," *American Anthropologist*, 1941, *43*:19–26.

help, Sulli approves of entirely. He early took advantage of government benefits offered to disadvantaged castes and tribes. His lead has been followed by other Kotas. Some boys are getting free trade training, others a free secondary education; both seem much superior to the schooling that was once doled out in the village schoolhouse. Several Kotas have become teachers or postmen, jobs for which they were given special preferment as members of a backward group.

There is now a road, which even a taxi can traverse, directly to Sulli's village, replacing the cart tracks of old. Wells and new houses have also been built with special government help. A huge hydroelectric project is going up just a few furlongs from a Kota village, constructed with Canadian assistance under the Colombo Plan.

This stream of change, rising from distant sources to impinge on Kota life, makes some Kotas uneasy. Not Sulli; he likes new elements from these sources and welcomes those who bring them. In the same way he welcomed two strangers who came to him years before. First in 1936 there came a linguist, Dr. M. B. Emeneau, to study the Kota language, and in 1937 he introduced to Sulli an anthropologist, myself, who came to study Kota culture and society. Sulli exhibited none of the doubts which Indian villagers tend to have at first about inquiring sahibs.[10] He took to them, not only as sahibs, but as scholars, and did all he could to facilitate their work.

Their work was influenced by Sulli. In the volume, *Kota Texts,* which Dr. Emeneau published, the texts used are entirely of Sulli's dictation. This work has an illuminating section in which Sulli's contributions as a linguistic informant are assayed. He was fluent and adaptable, the author notes, a fine storyteller who adjusted to the slow pace of dictation without losing the narrative and entertainment qualities which are characteristic of Kota tales.

He was just as fluent and communicative over the many hours he spent with me discussing Kota culture. A good part of my Kota interview notes are from Sulli's accounts and another part is devoted to checking, with other Kotas, what Sulli first brought to my atten-

---

[10] These doubts find an echo in Rudyard Kipling's *Kim,* in which an important part of the story is the "Ethnological Survey." This is a cover for what in modern parlance would be called security intelligence agents. Two of the main figures in it (an English Colonel and a Bengali), however, are ardent in pursuing ethnology as a hobby, each dreaming of election to the Royal Society because of the merit of his ethnological publications.

tion. In the main, he has been accurate and has shown a truly remarkable recollection of detail. Yet allowance must be made for two of his traits as ethnological respondent.

One is that his recollection tends to be neater and more integrated than was the historical actuality. His narrative artistry is apt to gloss over inconsistencies or irregularities and to make one episode follow another in logical, abstracted sequences that may have more aesthetic symmetry than historical exactness. Sulli has the kind of integrating, abstracting mind which one may consider to be more properly the prerogative of the ethnological theorist than of the ethnologist's informant.

Secondly, he is like any gifted narrator of events in which he took part and of which he finds reason to be proud. He tends to figure much larger in his account than he may have in the event. But when he gives an impersonal account of, say, ceremonies, these traits do not prevail.

Sulli, in turn, was influenced by his work with the linguist and the anthropologist. In the first instance, the association with two whom he called "our Europeans" added to his prestige. It is not unlikely that this association gave him the final impetus, in 1937, to take the decisive step of cutting his hair. It also gave him opportunity, as mentioned earlier, to polish up his English. Emeneau writes, "Fortunately, the time I was able to spend on the Kota language was long enough to permit the Kota's English to improve about as rapidly as his knowledge of my needs—though not, even at the end, to an exactness which would have solved for me all the difficulties of his none too easy language." [11]

As this work progressed, Sulli enjoyed doing it. Emeneau comments that ". . . in fact he reveled in the activity of dictating texts for five hours a day for weeks on end, accompanying his words with dramatic gestures and laughing heartily at amusing passages." [12] So was it also in his sessions with me. Even during the visit we had together when he was 64, he was as lively a raconteur, as delightful in his zest, in his accounts of his intricate deals, in his self-confidence, as he had been two decades earlier.

On this visit it remained for Thesingh, a Badaga friend of mine

[11] M. B. Emeneau, *Kota Texts*, Berkeley and Los Angeles, University of California Publications in Linguistics, 1944, vol. 2, no. 1, p. v.

[12] *Ibid.*, p. 3.

and of Sulli (his formal antagonism does not preclude being friendly with individual Badagas) to articulate something of what the three of us felt at meeting again. Asked to record something in the Badaga language on a tape recorder I had with me, Thesingh concluded with these words which he also translated, "Now in 1958 he has come again and with great happiness I came to see him. And it is a very good thing that he has come to my house and will take something [to eat] in my house. Though he is living on one side of the world and I am living on the next side of the world, it is human nature that a man should be a friend to another man. There is nothing else in the world, nothing else but that."

Sulli's welcome was warm though he was properly insistent that I call on him first in his village rather than coming immediately to town to see me when he received word of my arrival. And once we got to talking, he lost no time on sentimental reflections or questions; he concentrated on sketching for me an up-to-date outline of the shape and the purpose of his life. It has been a full life, firmly shaped. He has been a purposeful person, who has found satisfaction and success in his life purpose.

10

The Omda

Ian Cunnison

If there are mosquitoes about, you put up a net and you sleep in peace." I was just coming to see that Hurgas Merida had enemies in numbers like mosquitoes, and as troublesome. During the earlier months of my stay in his camp, moving with his cattle from site to site according to the season, it had seemed to me that this man, who for twenty-seven years had been omda of the Mezaghna lineage, and who was clearly welcomed wherever I went in his company, had been born lucky. He was endowed with popularity, a handsome bearing, and wit and facility in speech. From his father he had inherited great wealth in the form of cattle, and the position of omda. But the honeymoon period of my field work, when everyone I met valued their good manners to a stranger above the immediate expression of their inner feelings, was drawing to a close. Hurgas was a remarkable character, but for reasons other than I had thought.

His camp was no different from the dozens of others of the Mezaghna, or the hundreds of others of the Humr tribe.[1] A circle of some fifteen tents, withy-lined and covered with shredded bark and gaily patterned mats, surrounded the cattle dung and the smouldering fires where the animals slept at night and were milked morning and evening. Blue-clad women went about their domestic tasks, occasionally leaving camp to fetch water or firewood, while the white-smocked men sat discussing the affairs of the day under the tree just outside the camp circle.

In one place today, the camp shifted to some sixty other sites in the course of the year. The herds moved along, guided by the men on horseback with their 12-foot spears, who sought out the route. The women followed in slow procession on laden bulls, the richer wives on beasts decorated with cowry headbands, ostrich-plumed horns, and a row of bells behind. One's neighbours today were off into the forests tomorrow, for the leader of each camp had his own ideas about where the best water and fattening grasses

[1] The Baggara (cattle-keeping) Arabs inhabit the area east of Lake Chad as far as the Nile. The Humr, one of the Baggara tribes, lead a nomadic life within their tribal area in the southwest of Kordofan Province of the Sudan Republic.

were to be found, and chose his campsite by weighing these variables with others such as the presence of flies and the condition of the ground underfoot. Or perhaps he just disliked his neighbours of the moment and decamped. Only in the dead heat of summer, among the dried-up meandering watercourses of the south, did a regular local community form, since the wells dug there anchored the herds to them for a period of some weeks.

As omda of the Mezaghna, Hurgas answered to the Sudanese administration for the behaviour and whereabouts of the 7000 Arabs under him. Much of his time was expended in persuading his sheikhs to collect the poll tax from their followers and to hand it over to the administration. He had no court, but he would try to arbitrate in cases brought to his attention, since the court of the Nazir, the chief of the tribe, might be as much as 150 miles from the camps according to the season. So there were days when Hurgas was confined to his camp by the press of litigants before him; and there were days and nights when he was away, going the rounds of his scattered followers, persuading and exhorting them.

His renown was great. His name was on every woman's lips: the omda said this or said that. In the evenings the ringleted girls sang his praises around the drum, remembering the fire in his talk "like salt and red pepper," or singing of the white-robed figure:

> The Omda Hurgas
> Riding his black horse
> A gun in his hands
> The Omda Hurgas
> His spear a bullet.

For food in his travels, his people fed him as they fed all their guests. In their view it was fitting that he should enjoy clean cloth, have his hands soft with little manual work, and sleep in a white sheet as well as a blanket. It was more fitting for him, perhaps, than for the other ten omdas of the tribe because he, almost alone, had been an omda since the adults were young, and his generosity to guests in his own camp was well known.

Hurgas was the last to tell me of his tribulations. I knew he had inherited hundreds of head of cattle from his father, Merida, and that the Nazir of the tribe had appointed him omda when Merida had become old. His fame as son of Omda Merida was justified by his prowess as an elephant hunter. His daring, in riding on horse-back to decoy the elephant into an ambush of young spears, had brought him a renown among young and old, men and women. He mastered, too, the art of galloping down giraffe: tenaciously to course a giraffe, to gallop over miles of pitted ground, to go into its flying hooves, and there to spear it, was the mark of a man among Arabs.

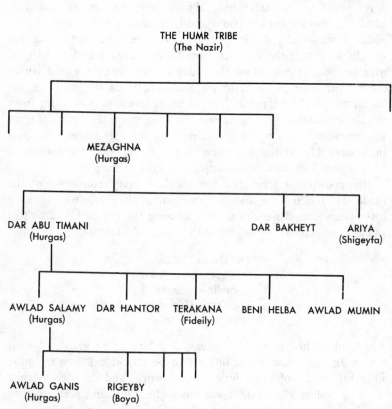

Diagram of the Lineage Segments of the Humr Tribe. The names in parentheses below lineage names denote lineage leaders mentioned in the text. The ancestors of the smallest segments, such as Awlad Ganis, are about five generations removed from present-day adults.

In the 1930's, his cup was full. He had wealth, fame, and position. His name enhanced the prestige of Awlad Ganis, the descendants of his great-great-grandfather; through Awlad Ganis, of Awlad Salamy; and through Awlad Salamy, of Dar Abu Timani, one of the three main lineages of the Mezaghna.[2] During my first months in camp, I was led to believe that the situation was still as it had been then. Awlad Ganis did not always camp together, and I assumed there were cattle elsewhere. But one evening I counted eighty head of cattle in camp, and a youth said, "All the cattle of Ganis are in camp tonight." And so they were; the thirty-seven men of Ganis had eighty head among them.

Hurgas would philosophise without relating his thoughts to his own position:

If a man wants wealth—and every man wants wealth—he has to work hard, and he has to pray five times a day. Wealth is everything; it means you can be generous. With generosity you get a name. With a name you get women, and you get a political seat if you like. What more do you want? But cattle, if you have no sheep, are worthless; with a flock you can give your guests meat as well as milk. These men with great herds of cattle are evil men, for no man could have built a herd of a thousand head and have been generous at the same time. If that man were generous, he would have a smaller herd. A man to be happy must have wives to cook for him, and young sons to herd the cattle. Then he is content, he has milk to drink, and plenty of tea. He may not be a sheikh, but he is a king all the same. He lies under his tree, his sons herd the cattle, his followers do the work of camp, his wives cook and brew tea for him, his cattle low in camp in the evenings as they're milked. When he has guests, he catches a ram and throws it to the ground and slaughters it. These are the sweets of life. You've heard what the minstrel has to say?

> They migrate and they low
> They camp and they low
> They give the liquid butter the old men love
> They carry the maidens with jangling bells
> If their owner's a lizard you'll say he's a crocodile
> If his speech is all curses you'll say it is kind
> You owner of cattle can lie down and rest
> If you have none, go and seek work in the towns.

By God, without cattle a man is nobody.

---

[2] The Humr tribe is a patrilineal lineage, and its political subdivisions follow the lines of lineage segmentation. The diagram on p. 312 names those segments mentioned in the text.

Hurgas had wives to cook and sons to herd. He had cattle, fifty or sixty head. He had a stipend from the government. He had poor relatives in camp with him, who helped with the cattle, fed off him, and became his faithful followers. But Hurgas had no sheep, and his rest beneath the tree was spoiled by the incessant labour of omdaship. He told me that in the old days omdas themselves collected the poll tax and took a tenth of it. Now they had a nominal stipend instead. It wasn't quite the same.

Hurgas ruled his camp with all the hardness of Mahdist tradition; and here, among nomads, the influence of the puritan Mahdi died hard. The omda's autocracy seemed to go unquestioned, but when he snapped out orders that were not only hard but harsh, I was puzzled at the need for this in view of his assured and loved position. His family would do what they could to make his tenure of the omdaship last out. And there were the contradictions between Hurgas' philosophy of the good life and his own practice. There was one thing certainly which had come to my notice early. A part of Awlad Ganis, who usually camped together with the omda, had moved away and pitched a separate circle of tents nearby. This breach in his own family was the outcome of a marriage dispute. Hurgas' sister had been sought in marriage by her second cousin, in the same camp, but the omda had preferred to hand her over to Hammoda, a wealthy and wise man of middle age from the Ariya lineage. The breach was hardly a serious one, and I was assured that the dissatisfied cousin would return to the camp in the course of time.

Sheybun was Hurgas' fey young brother. He had hardly a cow to his name and loved the gay life. I asked him, "I suppose you Arabs know the genealogies of your cattle as well as those of your kinsmen?" We wandered among the cattle and he showed me two cows whose dams were calves from old Merida's herd. But the other cattle in camp, he said, had all come from the market. Disease had on two occasions wiped out the herds. Sheybun led me over to his sister's tent. We sat down near it and as we brewed the dark sweet tea and drank out of little tumblers he remembered his earlier years.

We Arabs are rich one day and poor the next. You see our cattle now? A 10-year-old can herd them by himself. When Hurgas was younger, we had cattle in numbers like the sand. By God, there was no limit to them. I myself had a hundred, and sheep as well. And our sister had sheep, and we all had flocks of sheep. It was in the days before the government stopped us from hunting giraffe, and Hurgas was a famous hunter. Those days we had guests all day long. When they came we gave them calabashes of milk and curds, and they anointed their feet in liquid butter. Never a guest without meat. There was always giraffe meat drying in camp, or if there were no giraffe we vied to be the first to bring a ram for slaughter. And tea? By the Mahdi, we drank tea all day long. The tree was filled with guests; there was brilliant conversation, and the whole lineage of Mezaghna used to come here and talk till they laughed, and they discussed the affairs of the country. And a stranger travelling through the land would know of Hurgas and seek out his camp because he knew he would be hospitably received. And the three lineages of the Mezaghna—Dar Abu Timani, Dar Bakheyt, and the Ariya—they all came and sat at our tree. And as for the women who milled about! "Women are like geese" [he quoted], "they follow the deep waters;" [and he added for good measure], "Women are like flies, they buzz about the calabashes of sour milk." But disease killed off the cattle, and the never-ending guests prevented us from building up a real herd again. He gets money from the government now, yes; but then he has this wife in town—she's high-born, a relative of the Nazir—and she takes half of it every month for her clothes. To keep our cattle it meant that we couldn't replace our sheep as they were slaughtered. We all had flocks. Hurgas finished his off on his guests, then it was the turn of my sheep and my sisters'. Now there are none.

As the dry months proceeded it became even hotter until the first rains broke. At the end of the season in the south of the land, tempers become short and the Arabs wait impatiently for the first thunderstorm; then scouts will go forth to see where the water lies, and the life of moving camp will start again. The Arab welcomes a shift to a new camp site where the ground is clean, and his cattle have untrampled grazing. And at the end of the summer the desire to move is even greater than usual, for it means an end to the tedious watering of cattle from wells in the river beds.

As this summer ended Hurgas had his camp by the side of a dry watercourse. Ahmed, a man of the Ariya, another lineage of the Mezaghna, was camped as he usually was some miles to the east. Among the Ariya we had many good friends and none better than Ahmed, a lively argumentative little man who was a sheikh among them. Hurgas had introduced me months before to this special friend. I was now surprised to find Ahmed with his camp moving in as our neighbours. Ahmed's father, Shigeyfa, had returned from where he had been cultivating cotton. Shigeyfa was a character renowned throughout the tribe for his eternal youth, his loquacity, and his unveiling of embarrassing political situations. He moved about the land like lightning and had a finger in everyone's dish. But among the Mezaghna I knew him only as Hurgas' tried and trusty friend and contemporary.

Hurgas welcomed him in great style. He bought a ram from a neighbouring camp, and they ate and drank tea all day. The talk ran to elephant hunting in the old days, for Shigeyfa too had been an expert. Thereafter Shigeyfa held court at his tree every day; and Hurgas went there also, and was entertained. He saw that the people going to Shigeyfa's tree were more numerous than those who came to his, and also that they came from farther away. Shigeyfa's hospitality was boundless. Every day rams were thrown to the ground and slaughtered, and the guests supped on the delicacies of the land, raw liver and lemon juice, curds and grain, tea and dates from the market, tamarind from the forest. Hurgas was in eclipse.

But fate sent him away from camp on two errands. Trouble had arisen among the Terakana, a brother lineage of Awlad Salamy within Dar Abu Timani. These people had begun their northward trek, and word came back that a Salamy youth and a youth of the Terakana had met and fought in a girl's tent at night. The Salamy youth had accused the other of running away from him, and the Salamy girls sang songs of mockery around the drums in the evenings. Hurgas returned to camp a few days later having achieved some sort of settlement.

A few days later he was summoned to the Nazir of the tribe, who at the time was encamped a day's ride away. When Hurgas returned, he bristled with pomp and importance, and the curt orders to his people at once put the camp on its mettle. Something was up, and it was something big. He had brought back with him Ndalo, a rich merchant who was one of the Awlad Salamy, but who lived in a town and only occasionally put his finger into Mezaghna affairs; but when he did it was to the discomfort of many. In the past he had reported a number of persons for poaching giraffe, among them several from Hurgas' camp. These had served terms in prison and their horses were forfeit.

Now the Nazir had called together some of the omdas to announce a campaign to rid the country of Fellata. The wandering Fellata, from the northern territories of Nigeria, sought pasturage anywhere between their homeland and the Red Sea coast. Many of them were in the land of the Humr, moving quickly with their herds before government authorities could catch up with them. They would stay as long as they could, and then move off somewhere else, as they had moved out of Nigeria and the French Sudan as soon as it seemed to them they would have to pay taxes. The Humr hated the Fellata for using their grass and their scanty water in the dry season. To be put in charge, as Hurgas was, of an operation to rid a part of the land of their enemies, was a grave and important commission. He had to find them, count their herds, and seize sheep to be sold for taxes, for the Fellata had little money. Hurgas persuaded Ahmed Shigeyfa to accompany him and Ndalo.

Hurgas had never looked so stern and purposeful as on the morning he set forth. When the party left in a blaze of importance, Sheybun turned in amusement and said:

"When the mosquitoes are about, you put up a net and you sleep in peace."

I asked him to expound the riddle.

"You saw the look on his face. Well, he smells wealth. Just think of all these Fellata sheep, and no one for miles around. Wealth breeds accusations. He has to involve his enemies to such an extent that they are unable to speak against him. That's why he has taken Ndalo and the son of Shigeyfa. He's putting up a net to sleep in peace."

"These men are his enemies then?"

"Ndalo there, do you know why he informed on these giraffe hunters? It was to try and show the Nazir that Hurgas was shielding them because they were in his camp. Ndalo is wealthy enough to become omda, and more, the people fear him greatly on account of his tongue. And the same with Shigeyfa. That Shigeyfa! It was he who had my father Merida removed from the omdaship over some business about elephant hunting. Shigeyfa even then had a big following—he always appeared with more horsemen than Hurgas himself. But the Nazir loved Hurgas and made him omda to follow Merida. He wouldn't touch Shigeyfa for the omdaship. Shigeyfa's too clever. The Nazir needs men who are not too clever to be omdas otherwise they'd attack the nazirate itself. Hurgas is good to the

Nazir, does whatever he says. But he's an autocrat with his own family. He treats us like slaves. After Hurgas became omda, he made it up with Shigeyfa, but he's still wary of him."

I asked if the Ariya spoke with one voice in this matter.

"Nearly all, but there are one or two who don't like Shigeyfa and stand with us; and there's Isa Ulm, who would also like to be omda, but he has too many cattle and nobody wants him except those in his own camp."

I asked about Dar Bakheyt, the third big lineage of the Mezaghna.

"They are of one voice with the Ariya, because the two houses share descent from one mother."

"I thought Hurgas and Shigeyfa were really friendly. I've seen the way they feast each other, and the camaraderie in their talk."

"That's just a sign of the hostility between them. Hurgas slaughters rams for Shigeyfa because he fears him. Then Shigeyfa whom he hates comes and camps beside him. What do they do? Sit and glour at each other? What else can Hurgas do but laugh with Shigeyfa?"

"So it's only Dar Abu Timani that are faithful to Hurgas?"

"Sometimes even brothers fall out."

Five days after having set off, Hurgas and his band returned to camp, driving before them 300 black and white Fellata sheep. Sheybun said, "Look, the pen is mightier than the spear! In spring they spent three weeks after giraffe and got nothing. Now they spend three days after Fellata with a tax register and bring back 300 sheep to camp!" Hurgas, exhausted after his days of privation in the forest, rested a while and sent his son to deliver the sheep to the Nazir.

It was now time for the northward migration. For three weeks the camp moved slowly towards the region where the cattle graze during the rains. After the searing heat and the black cracked clay of the summer lands, the Arabs breath freshness again, the cattle leave their imprints in sand, and everywhere the greenest of green shoots carpet the forest. It is a season of quickly built camps and blue smoke in an atmosphere at last clear of dust. Politics are forgotten in the long caravan; the Arab revels in abundance of milk and dreams of full granaries a few months ahead. But in the rains, at the end of the migration, he is near the market town which is also the seat of the Nazir's court and the administrative centre of the tribe. The season for politics is the rains, when people camp together in the greatest numbers. It is the season of intrigues, and likewise of peace-making.

On the road north throughout this fragrant spring, Hurgas gave rein to fiery talk. He spoke bitterly, as if he knew that someone would attack him.

This is the age of the government, and that means the age of complaints. If a man has an office, everyone else wants to get it. In the old days they might get it by the spear, but nowadays they get it by lodging complaints with the government. And the big man has many complaints laid against him. You sit and laugh with Arabs, and when your back is turned they speak to the administration with a different tongue. An Arab doesn't fear lions; he hunts elephant with a gay heart. But he fears the tongues of Arabs. They are always ready to betray him.

I mentioned this bitterness to Boya, the head of Rigeyby, the lineage most closely related to Ganis. Boya's father had himself been omda before old Merida, and Boya had on many occasions acted as omda during the absence of Hurgas, expending much wealth on the entertainment of guests, and doing much work for him. Boya said:

Hurgas is a good man, there is none better than he. Only towards me, towards us his close kinsmen, he is hard and ungrateful. He has to spend his life defending his omdaship, and he forgets us; he is even hard to his own children. But he is astute. If he were not politically astute, he would have lost the omdaship long ago. If you see him sitting with the Nazir, he is not the same man. He is humble before him, and his speech is soft and kindly. And the Nazir knows him for his generosity, which is famed throughout the tribe, and hears nothing of the rigour with which he rules his camp and his children. I have my quarrel with Hurgas. I have worked for him, and slaughtered many rams in his name, but he has offered me neither wealth nor kind words. I do not visit him. But I would have none other as omda. Some say a man becomes omda for the renown it brings him. No. A man accepts omdaship for the ascendency it gives his lineage. To have the omdaship in Awlad Salamy is worth much. Awlad Salamy are of one voice. Only that Ndalo makes it hard for us. If Dar Abu Timani were all behind us, it would be well.

I had thought that Dar Abu Timani would be united against the hostility of the Ariya.

"No, between us Awlad Salamy and the Terakana there has been blood for six years now. Dar Hantor stand with the Terakana. Then Awlad Mumin have long quarrelled with us over the matter of garden land, and Beni Helba stand with them. We Awlad Salamy stand alone."

It was Sheybun who later told me the story of the feud. His nature allowed him to look objectively at this tragedy in the lineage, and his first reaction was to say laughingly:

"We Arabs like to keep our family secrets to ourselves, but you are one of us now so you have the right to know. First you thought the Mezaghna spoke with one voice, then you saw the Ariya were against us, and now you see that even we of Dar Abu Timani are divided! One of the Terakana killed one of Boya's men over a woman. The government gave him twelve years in gaol, and we demanded blood money from the Terakana. They gave it to us, sixty head of cattle. To receive blood money is like killing a man in vengeance. But the dead man's brother swore that he now lived only to exact vengeance with the spear. So he killed a man of the Terakana, and then the government killed *him*. But we live in fear of the Terakana because we ate their blood cattle and then avenged ourselves upon them. The Terakana used to be our brothers, and we camped beside their sheikh, Fideily, and shared the same tree. The men don't talk to one another now, but the women pay each other visits and say how sad it is our brotherhood is split. And some of them who married our women pay us short visits."

"Will you never make peace?"

"It's in the hands of the omda. Hurgas is omda of all the Mezaghna—the Terakana among them—but he's also the head of Awlad Salamy. He has heard through his brother-in-law, Daud, that there is great hatred of him among the leaders of the Terakana and he may fear to meet them on that account. But it is we Awlad Salamy who have to make amends, because we are the guilty ones in this matter."

Hurgas, then, was beset on all sides. He had most of what he valued in life. His ambition now was to retain what he held. He saw the attacks upon his position in the past; he looked towards the omdas of other lineages and saw how they came and went. The office of omdaship was essentially insecure, for all lines had equal right to it. To keep his omdaship, he had to fight that poverty which would render him unable to be generous. He realised the truth of the Nazir's words which reached him: that he owed his omdaship to the cattle of old Merida, long dead. In order to be generous to his more distant enemies, he was hard and close towards his own kinsmen, who, he judged, would count blood important above all else. He ordered his personal relationships with the same end in view. He held his camp-mates with tight reins of command. He could do this since the renown of Awlad Ganis was his personal renown, and its wealth, or most of it, was also his. His affability and loquacity he kept for those whom he had to woo politically. It was to further his political ends that he favoured the Ariya, Hammoda, as his sister's bridegroom at the expense of her impecunious cousin. This caused a rift in Awlad Ganis; but it was a satisfaction to Hurgas to know he gained such a good foothold in the enemy's camp.

In daily life, his own personal delights, apart from the sight of his cattle, were his hunting expeditions—nowadays with shotgun after geese and guinea-fowl—and his wives. Of the number of geese he killed and distributed he would boast endlessly. But of his wives he seldom spoke. Perhaps this was because one wife was a favourite, a fact which aggravated and brought into the open the tensions in camp arising from his despotism. Usually he had four wives, and if one should die, or if he should divorce one, he would soon take another. Of the three he had at this time, two were with him in camp. One of these was barren, the daughter of a testy but important sheikh of Awlad Salamy. The other had borne seven children in the course of fifteen years; she was a close cousin, and had two impoverished brothers in the omda's camp. The prolific wife had not the fine mats and the abundance of scents that the barren wife, the favourite, had. The latter used her position to order the children of the other to do errands, and she denied them food, drink, and help. And if the men in camp complained about her behaviour, as they did in this spring migration, it would come to the ears of Hurgas who would lay about him with the acid of his talk: he was the omda, the woman was his wife, his household was his own affair, the camp was his, the lineage was his; others drank his tea, ate from his gun, drank his milk, married with his cattle; he would set up his own camp without them and where would they be then? He silenced the camp and mounted his horse and rode off in a billow of anger and purpose.

The long northward migration was over, and Hammoda was ready to marry. It was to be a quiet affair since he had been married before. There were few guests, and little celebration was expected apart from an evening of tea-drinking and feasting around the campfire. Hurgas was mellowed. A minstrel had heard of the wedding and rode up on a donkey with his one-string fiddle. The men sat around the fire and as the minstrel opened with his songs of love, the women came silently from the tents and sat at a respectful distance out of the firelight. Hurgas half closed his eyes and drank in the surroundings. He was a lover himself.

> Folks call you the daughter of Ahmed
> But to me you're eye of a young gazelle
> Ripple of sand under running water
> Gold of a necklace from Omdurman
> Lotus flower of the southern pool
> Giraffe of the boundless grassy plains. . . .

But then the theme of the minstrel changed, his song became livelier and firmer, as he sang the praises of the men of Ganis dead and gone. Hurgas woke up, and as the wont is, took a piastre and dropped it into the hole in the minstrel's fiddle. Others followed suit as their own relatives were mentioned. The minstrel brought his song up to date and praised famous men of today:

> His mother made the food for the elephant hunts
> And Kibbeyry today leads the best of the horsemen
> A granary of seed for next year's sowing. . . .

The women were stirred, and shrilled at the mention of the brave exploits of their kinsmen. And then the praise was of Hurgas himself. He had led the elephant on and the youths had speared it. His cattle were numbered like the blades of grass. The renown of his generosity was the fireside talk of distant tribes. His horse was black as the night. His women had the grace of horses. Hurgas could contain himself no longer. He seized his gun and shot into the air twice, three, four times. The sound brought people from neighbouring camps who came along and heard the praises of their Omda Hurgas. The half-moon had set by the time the people dispersed, Hammoda went to his bride, and the minstrel lay content with a fiddleful of coins.

That evening was the calm before the storm. The first attack upon

Hurgas took place shortly afterwards. The youth who had been accused of running away from the fight was the son of Fideily, sheikh of the Terakana, and now he brought a suit against his rival who, he claimed, was still slandering him and causing the girls to sing songs of mockery. The court was aware of the circumstance of vengeance between the two families, and gaoled the Salamy youth. But then Fideily addressed the court in castigation of Hurgas, and the words were not lost on the Nazir who presided.

"He is no omda, he is an irresponsible person, he has urged the Salamy youth to rekindle the fire of vengeance. Six years have passed since they broke the bond of blood money and not once has Hurgas tried to come to terms. How can we live like this? We Terakana want him no longer. If he is not removed from the omdaship, we shall go and live with another omda. We will no longer be Mezaghna."

Hurgas was absent from court that day. There was no doubt he was stubborn in his enmities. More than once his people had been set to persuade him that he should approach Fideily in humility, for the Terakana were their kinsmen. But Hurgas would remember this or that event which prevented his doing so with honour. As for Boya, his and Hurgas' men were in constant intercourse, only the two leaders held no converse. Here again it was for Hurgas to make the first steps since the onus of the breach was upon him. And while they were divided, they could not together approach the Terakana. But Fideily had never before threatened to break brotherhood with the Mezaghna completely and move elsewhere. This created a new situation. If they now left, the stigma would be on Hurgas.

Hardly was this case over, than the Ariya launched their offensive. They fought in court, and the battle which raged between Hurgas and Shigeyfa throughout the months of the rains was the talk of campfire and market place. Fellow tribesmen viewed with distress this open split between kinsmen. As court case after court case proceeded, disinterested men approached Shigeyfa to call off his attack, which was bringing shame upon the whole "tribe of Arabs," but to no avail. Insistently, Shigeyfa laid information with the police, who then had to take action. The biggest case, which lasted the whole season, concerned Fellata sheep. But while this was in progress, Shigeyfa gave other information alleging the omda's illicit killing of game, his mounting a poaching expedition against giraffe, and the presence in his camp of unlicensed guns. And by Shigeyfa's side was the merchant Ndalo, while Isa Ulm waited in spotless robes outside the court for the day when Hurgas might be discredited and deposed. Throughout the hearings, well-wishers of Hurgas stayed in the town near him to give him support. And the staunchest of these was Boya, wretchedly treated as he had been.

What prevented the success of Shigeyfa in the minor prosecutions was lack of direct evidence. Certainly portions of giraffe skin were found in the omda's camp but there was none to say they were not from animals killed on a license he held. Certainly there were rumours that a member of the camp was having success with an unlicensed gun but there would have been time to gallop a warning to camp before the police arrived. Certainly the omda had been seen with a dead gazelle slung over the back of my horse, but none could say I had not shot it. The court rightly dismissed all the cases.

The fact that, through my horse, I was indirectly involved in this suit added to the omda's growing friendship with me. It enabled him, as nothing had done hitherto, to speak freely to me about the position in which he found himself. Hurgas had been slow to admit to, and discuss, the difficulties among the Mezaghna and the problems of his omdaship. As events arose, he would dissect them in speech with his followers as a part of his conduct of life, but only as they occurred. If I could understand his analysis of events from his swift, picturesque, but erratic tongue, well and good, but he would not give me specific instruction concerning them. On the contrary, in my position as a quite unusual sort of guest, he felt it proper that I should stay in his camp with enjoyment, unfettered by the worries that daily beset him.

It was only because he was so very much alive, because events occurred and he had to react to them, that he could forget this duty to his guest and speak his mind. Others in camp spoke out as soon as I could converse with them in their language. With Hurgas, I had first of all to know about events and personalities before he would deign to add his own observations. I could never regard him as an informant, for he could hardly be eloquent about events or customs unless there was some pragmatic reason for discussing them. Others knew and gave me the kind of information I as an anthropologist wanted. But Hurgas, after this case which involved us both, did not repay what he supposed was a debt by giving me information;

he repaid it with friendship. As the rains drew their course, and I stayed to watch the progress of the cases and keep his company in the afternoons, he felt his debt increasing. The more I questioned him on Shigeyfa's motives, the more he regarded me as showing a sympathetic interest in his case such as he had had from no one before. He sought out my company, hunted with me, spoke of his father, his earlier wealth, of horses, giraffe, and elephant. Through all this period he continued to administer the affairs of his own people, hearing their disputes, and ordering from a distance the herding of his precious cattle. But he never uttered a word of self-pity.

Allah is my master. A man has got to show manliness whether he be rich or poor. If you are rich or if you are poor, that is in the hands of Allah. But manliness is in the man himself. A man tries his best. If he works hard and gains wealth, that is God. If he works hard and gains not wealth, that too is God. To complain of your life is bad, because God shares things among men. A man goes hunting and kills giraffe. He returns and says, "God has given us." He goes hunting and kills no giraffe. He returns and says, "God has not given us." He is no less of a man. But if he gives up praying, or if he says God has been mean to him, the man who speaks there is no man; he is a woman.

Hurgas was thus prepared to fight the grave accusation which Shigeyfa now brought against him, but at the same time he was resigned to any fate to which he might be directed by the court. Specifically, Shigeyfa said Hurgas had taken Fellata sheep, in addition to the 300 which he had forwarded to the Nazir, and transported them secretly by distant trails to a market. Hurgas at least had the comfort that he was not the only one accused of taking Fellata sheep and selling them discreetly for his pocket. Many had seen their opportunity to down political rivals with such accusations, and if they were all to be believed, then some thousands of the unmistakable Fellata sheep must by this time be flooding the markets of Kordofan.

Here again Shigeyfa lacked direct evidence of seizure and sale. He had various witnesses attest to seeing specified numbers of sheep in Hurgas' possession at various times, but since there was little agreement between their accounts, and no adequate proof that the sheep seen had been illicitly seized, the court sought out witnesses from among the Fellata themselves. A great round-up of Fellata was made, and those whom Hurgas had visited were brought to court. The judges questioned them closely about the number of sheep which they held formerly, and the number now remaining within their thorn fences. Two days of argumentative examination convinced the judges of only one thing: that the Fellata were unable to count their sheep and were therefore unreliable witnesses in the charge under consideration. Thus after many weeks, the judges declared Hurgas not guilty, and he was at last able to return to his cattle.

When Hurgas reached his camp in the sandy scrub of the far north of the country, where the cattle were driven during the latter part of the rains, the welcome those in camp gave him was heartfelt. The women came in a line to meet him; young men came up to him and shook his hand with a relieved, "God be praised"; and Merida's only surviving brother broke into tears as he embraced him. Hurgas was still omda, and Awlad Ganis retained the office it had had since Merida took it.

Hurgas said little about the course of the case itself, but it was clear he regarded it as a great victory. In subsequent days he expended vast amounts of tea to entertain the many guests who came to offer their congratulations. It was of little interest to these visitors whether or not Hurgas had taken sheep. He had defeated the malevolent Shigeyfa and God had favoured him. A victory such as this attracted to his tree men of the Mezaghna who had long remained aloof; and inevitably the question of the unity of Dar Abu Timani was broached. When word finally issued forth from the town that a new court presidency was to be created, and that the Nazir might favour someone from the numerous Dar Abu Timani if they should show a united front, Hurgas reviewed his political fortunes.

His brother-in-law Daud was one of the Terakana, and throughout the feud he had paid short visits, with his wife, to Hurgas' camp and had acted as intermediary between Hurgas and Fideily on those occasions when communication between them had been absolutely necessary. He also kept both of them informed of the attitudes of the opposite camps. Now, in the market, Hurgas met Daud, who assured him that at this time the Terakana might receive his terms with some chance of favour. Hitherto Hurgas' camp-mates had vainly urged him to restore the unity of Dar Abu Timani. Now, interested neutrals, helped by the men of Awlad Ganis and Awlad Salamy generally, seemed to stand a better chance of succeeding. Indeed the relationship of the people of Awlad Ganis and the Terakana was getting beyond endurance, for here were close kinsmen, bound even more closely by intermarriage, who cultivated fields within a few miles of each other and shared the same market, but who were cut off from normal intercourse by the continual threat of vengeance. It was the custom, they knew, for Arabs to compound their feuds after a few years. Hurgas slowly, but finally with conviction, saw the sense in their insistence, and the possibility of success, and realized that other benefits might now follow a rapprochement. Having once resolved to make the attempt, he took immediate action.

His first step was to make peace with Boya. Boya was encamped for the rains only a few hundred yards from Hurgas, and the youths and girls of both camps played together daily. Hurgas sent word in advance that he would come. When the morning arrived, he went, carefully robed, on horseback with a number of well-wishers in his train as well as all the men of Ganis. He bade those who could to go mounted to Boya.

Boya received us in a friendly manner, and over tea, and then a meal, we had casual talk of this and that. Then one of the well-wishers who had come with us opened the proceedings, by saying that Hurgas had come to Boya in order to ask for his brotherhood again, that Hurgas by this act showed that he wanted it, and that he knew it was for him to make the first approach. Others, and finally Hurgas himself, spoke in similar terms. He dwelt on the friendship which was traditional between their closely related lines, and said it was his fault that the estrangement had taken place. Would Boya now hear his words and accept full brotherhood once more? For Boya, whose continued loyalty to Hurgas in spite of personal differences was widely applauded, this was an occasion of deep satisfaction. Wealthier than Hurgas, as clever in speech, as industrious, as brave, and in his personal relations more human, this son of a former omda felt keenly the drama of the situation. He opened his speech and guided it through the ideas of brotherhood, manliness, and generosity to reach the expected conclusion: the omda had shown all of these virtues and he was ready to accept the omda's supplication. He then called on the holy man to declaim the opening chapter of the Koran, while all stood and opened their hands before God. At once the newly cemented alliance resolved upon action to win back the friendship of the Terakana.

And what a triumph for Hurgas! Hurgas, the proud omda, had gone to his younger kinsman, and in the presence of other kinsmen and neutral friends, had laid aside his pride, had said he was guilty and had erred, had come in supplication. He had acted indeed in the traditional manner, and for a purpose which he had achieved; but it must have been difficult indeed for Hurgas to accept even for a moment a role of humility among his kinsmen.

The tribe had moved a short distance south again, to harvest in the gardens surrounding the town. The camps were now pitched more closely together than at any other season. The grass was dry, silvery, and wind-blown. The cattle ate ravenously of the remains of the gardens from which the bulrush millet had been taken.

Hurgas had arranged through Daud to meet the Terakana. On the day set aside for the occasion, the Dar Hantor allies of the Terakana prepared the shade of a large thicket for the meeting. Hurgas, camped on a low sandy ridge, was the focus of men of the Awlad Salamy who came with their white smocks and spears, earnest in demeanour. Hurgas rode his black horse. His elders gathered around him, each voicing his loud opinion. The day's parley would not only concern the Terakana feud; the Mezaghna would be present in numbers and it was likely that all the outstanding issues among them would be raised. About one thing however they were unanimous: there would be no alliance with Shigeyfa's Ariya.

Dar Hantor had worked hard to clear the thicket, and Awlad Salamy found themselves a place to rest. In other parts of the small wood were seated Mezaghna in their various groups: Ariya and Dar Bakheyt together; Awlad Mumin and Beni Helba, Terakana and Dar Hantor. The latter had slaughtered two bulls to provide meat for every man of the multitude present, while their women provided many dishes of grain. It was mid-afternoon before Hurgas suggested to his men that they should approach the Terakana.

This they did, walking with tense solemnity to the tree of their adversaries. All then sat on the ground, the Terakana and Dar Hantor forming one arc of a circle and Awlad Salamy the other. Hurgas and Fideily, the two main antagonists, faced each other in the middle. A close relative of the Nazir had been called to supervise proceedings. The men well knew how to comport themselves on such a grave occasion, the product of two murders and six years of bitterness. Not now that wild undisciplined shouting which usually marked the working out of a political decision. Here was the peace-making with Boya over again but on a much grander scale. The speakers spoke quietly, and the audience made neither move nor sound.

The elders of the Awlad Salamy spoke in turn. One of them said: "When blood was first spilled, you came to us and we made friendship. And now we spilled your blood, and we did not come to you at all; we are wrong and we know how much we have erred. Two of our men are dead; these sons of ours, we shall never see them again. So let us become brothers. We have come here to spread out our smocks before you, to lay our guilt upon them. We know our mistakes; only make it up with us."

Boya arose and addressed the Terakana:

"I am the owner of that blood. You came to us long ago; but I have never gone to you to seek your friendship. I am very wrong indeed. Without you, we do not wish brotherhood with anyone. We want manhood, and there is no manhood without you among us."

And Hurgas with bowed head reiterated the words of those who had spoken before him.

It was now Fideily's turn. In contrast to the contrite bearing of Awlad Salamy, Fideily spoke in a fury.

"I am angry with the omda there. He is the cause of all the trouble. Years ago, when I was trying to meet him he kept deceiving me. We arrange one meeting—he cancels it, says the water is bad. We arrange another—he cancels it, says the birds are eating his millet. Hey, omda, where shall we meet? We arrange another meeting—he cancels it, says he's just moving camp. We met at last; but where was Boya? Where were the dead man's brothers? The omda said he knew their views. Well, we made peace. But then blood was spilled again. What was I to do? Who could I talk to? I could only turn to the Ariya! Your brotherhood? Never!"

After this, it was the turn of the neutrals present to step in. They took over the discussion and exhortation. Since God created the Arabs, they had killed their brothers and come to terms again, they said. The omda had behaved badly, but he had now come to beseech peace; it would be best to grant it, and if the omda should do ill, he would get a bad name in the country. Never-ending hatred between brothers was not to be heard of.

The next of the Terakana who arose to speak began in a fiery manner, but heeding the words of the elders and neutrals, ended by addressing Hurgas in a placatory tone:

"Well, then, after two days, you leave your omdaship and seventy guineas here before us, and we shall be your brothers."

At this Boya and his young brother were on their feet, offering between them cattle whose value covered the required price of peace. As for the omdaship, a neutral pointed out that the Nazir alone could dispose of that. A Terakana then arose, accepting the offer of cattle, and called upon a holy man to put the blessing of God on the pact with the opening verse of the Koran. The men rose to their feet and lifted their hands saying, "In the name of God, the Merciful, the Compassionate."

The feud was over. What had begun as bitter hostility between the kin of the slayer and the slain, soon became a political matter with Hurgas and Fideily as spokesmen of their respective groups. They had not wanted continued acts of vengeance, and they exercised constraint upon the immediate kin of those most closely involved. But if the matter was safely out of the hands of those with blood upon them, the political relationship of Hurgas and Fideily changed more and more to a condition of personal enmity. As Hurgas held back from offering peace, so Fideily heaped ever greater calumnies on his head, and Hurgas in response prevaricated the more. The matter was brought to a head by the girls who sang songs of mockery over Fideily's son; and Fideily was ready to go away for ever. Hurgas was meanwhile constrained by the continuing attacks of the Ariya to come to terms although it meant supplicating before his calumniator. This he had now done in solemn ceremony. And in the eyes of the virtuous Boya, he showed his real manliness, which contains humility, in doing so.

The hot season brought political peace, as the camps dispersed southward in a haze of dust. The rains had dried leaving only stagnating pools here and there. The south called the cattle which, from their regular yearly moves, were aware of the untouched watercourses there with their succulent grasses. The Arab's happiest day is when he comes upon the first splashy green wadi after his weeks of trekking through dusty and burnt bushland. The cattle leap at the sight and plunge like mad beasts belly-deep in the thick juicy grasses.

Hurgas rode with them. He came out of the year's season of political manoeuvre with marked success. But the troubles which beset him would recur year after year. After the settlement of the Terakana feud, Hurgas had approached the Awlad Mumin where they were sitting, and the attempt to settle their lesser argument had broken up in a babble of rage from both sides. Awlad Mumin were set fair to attack the omdaship in the following year; and the Ariya problem was chronic.

But Hurgas could relax a bit. He could say thus: "Where other omdas have fallen, I have repelled attacks for a generation." The Nazir wanted omdas who were not clever. He had plenty of these; they came and they went. But Hurgas held his position for a quarter of a century. He was astute in his own way; in limiting his aims to the retention of his office; and in aiming his humility, his geniality, and his despotism in the proper directions for achieving this limited end. But it was not the clever or the astute omda that his friends extolled. Rather to them, even to the kinsmen he treated so harshly, he was a Mahdist among Mahdists, an Arab among Arabs, a man among men.

Muchona (upper right) with Fellow Ritualists.

11

Muchona the Hornet, Interpreter of Religion

Victor W. Turner

I first became aware of Muchona on a dusty motor road of packed red clay towards the end of a Northern Rhodesian dry season. In one direction the road ran to harsh, colourful Angola, in the other to the distant copperbelt town of Chingola. Along it passed an occasional lorry, mail van, or missionary's car, and many tough black feet, most of them going east to European mines and towns. But on this day the road was almost empty in the hot late afternoon. Kasonda, my African assistant, and I had walked a few miles from our home village to a cluster of villages where we had collected census material. Now we were returning, gay with the millet beer and gossip that usually rounded off our more serious sessions. To make the miles go faster we played a game popular among Ndembu children: each of us tried to be the first to spot the budding *kapembi* shrubs with their frail red presentiment of the rains. Even Ndembu find it hard to distinguish this species from three others. Kasonda, of course, soon had a higher total than myself, for like all Ndembu he prided himself on his knowledge of the mystical and practical properties of the herbs and trees which flourish in this area.

We were so absorbed in our rivalry that we failed to notice a swart elderly gnome who was padding perkily beside us. He was evidently keenly observant, for he joined in our sport and soon took the lead. Kasonda told me he was a *chimbuki*, a "doctor," in several kinds of curative ritual, and "knew many medicines." I pricked up my ears, for ritual symbolism was my major interest. Each plant used in ritual stood for some aspect of Ndembu social life or belief. In my opinion a full interpretation of these symbols would lead me to the heart of Ndembu wisdom. Consequently I seized the opportunity of asking the little man, whose name was Muchona, the meaning of some of the medicines I had seen doctors handle.

Muchona replied readily and at length, with the bright glance of the true enthusiast. He had a high-pitched voice, authoritative as a school-teacher's when conveying information, expressive as a comedian's when telling a tale. Kasonda found his manner and mannerisms both funny and irritating, as he tried to show me by giggling conspiratorially behind his hand whenever Muchona had his back to us. I did not respond, for I liked the doctor's warmth, and thus began Kasonda's bitter jealousy of Muchona. Kasonda was worldly, and a shade spiteful, *au fait* with the seamier side of Ndembu (and indeed human) nature. He took a rancorous zest in the struggles for headmanship, prestige, and money that were the bane of village life. Muchona, for all his battling against witchcraft and the moody, punitive dead, had a curious innocence of character and objectivity of outlook. I was to find that in the balance mankind came off well for Muchona. Between these men lay the gap that has at all times divided the true philosopher from the politician.

Muchona showed me his quality that first day when he pointed to a parasitic growth on a *mukula* tree (a red hardwood). "That plant is called *mutuntamu*," he said. "Do you know why it has that name?" Before I could confess my ignorance he rattled on:

Well, it is from *ku-tuntama,* "to sit on somebody or something." Now, hunters have a drum [a ritual] called *Ntambu,* an old word for "lion." In *Ntambu,* a hunter who has been unlucky and has failed to kill animals for many days, goes into the bush and finds a big *mukula* tree like this one. The *mukula* tree has red gum, which we call "*mukula*'s blood." It is a very important tree for hunters, and also for women. For hunters it means "the blood of animals." They want to see this blood when they go hunting. Now this unlucky hunter puts his bow over his right shoulder and his axe into his right hand—for the right side is for men and the left side for women, who carry their babies on their left arm—and he climbs up the *mukula* bearing bow and axe. When he is high up, he stands with one foot on one branch and one foot on another. Then he shoots an arrow at a *mutuntamu* plant. His arrow goes in strongly. Then he cries, "I have shot at an animal." Then he says, "I have shot you, *Ntambu* spirit. Please bring me quickly to animals." After that he roars, like a lion. Then he puts his strung bow over the *mutuntamu* branches, and breaks them with the strength of the bow-string. He throws the broken twigs on the ground. They will later be mixed with other medicines for washing his body and his hunting gear. Just as the *mutuntamu* "sits on" the tree of blood, so must the spirit come and sit on the animal and blind it, in order that the hunter may kill it easily. He shoots *Ntambu* to show the spirit that he has found him out. He now wants *Ntambu* to help him, and not to trouble him any longer.

Now I had heard many other Ndembu interpret plant symbols before, but never so clearly and cogently as this. I was to become familiar with this mode of exposition, the swift-running commentary on unsolicited details, the parenthetical explanations, the vivid mimicry of ritual speech, and above all, the depth of psychological insight: "What hurts you, when discovered and propitiated, helps you."

But Kasonda was whispering to me, "He is just lying." I could not heed him, for Muchona had already pointed out another tree and had begun to explain its ritual use and significance in a way that also compelled belief. I felt that a new dimension of study was opening up to me. Sympathy was quickly growing between us and when we parted we arranged to meet again in a few days.

But Muchona did not come. Perhaps he hesitated to visit me, for my camp was in Kasonda's village, and it is probable that Kasonda had already hinted that he would be unwelcome there. Perhaps he had been performing curative rituals in distant villages. He was a restless man, seldom at home anywhere for long, like many another Ndembu doctor. Soon afterwards I also had to go away—to Lusaka, for a conference of anthropologists. For one reason or another I did not see him again for two months.

Meanwhile I learned many details of Muchona's life which were common knowledge in his neighbourhood. He did not live in the traditional circular village, but with his two wives occupied a couple of low huts near the motor road. He had seven children, the eldest of whom was a clerk at the Government township, a well-educated youth by Ndembu standards. Kasonda insinuated that this tall son of a meagre father was the by-blow of a youthful affair of Muchona's senior wife. The remark was pure malice. The alert intellect of the father was unmistakably reproduced in his son; and the son's achievement was reflected in his father's pride in him.

Muchona came from Nyamwana chiefdom, just across the Congo border. His mother had been a slave, taken by the Ndembu before British rule was firmly established. His maternal kin were widely scattered over Mwinilunga District and adjacent areas in Angola and the Belgian Congo. The nuclear group of an Ndembu village is a small matrilineage; and no such nucleus had been formed by Muchona's kin. Later he was to complain to me that his two sisters in distant villages had ten children between them, and that if they had come to live with him he could have founded a real village. He ignored the fact that Ndembu women customarily reside with their husbands after marriage, and that indeed his own wives had left their brothers' villages to live with him. But poor Muchona had been doomed to rootless wandering from early boyhood. First of all he had lived in the village of his mother's captors. That village had split, and Muchona and his mother went with the dissident group. His mother was then transferred as a debt slave to yet another group where she was married to one of her owners. It seems that when he was a young man Muchona bought his freedom, and lived in the villages of several successive wives. However, he was never able to achieve a high secular status, nor an established position in a single village. These vicissitudes were both his curse and the source of his great ability to compare and generalize. Living as he had done on the margins of many structured groups and not being a member of any particular group, his loyalties could not be narrowly partisan, and his sympathies were broader than those of the majority of his fellow tribesmen. His experience had been richer and more varied than that of most Ndembu, though all Ndembu, being hunters and semi-nomadic cassava cultivators, travel considerable distances during their lives.

When I returned from Lusaka, I decided to pursue my enquiries into ritual *esoterica* very much further than before. In this quest I was assisted by the senior teacher at the local Mission Out-School, Windson Kashinakaji by name, Ndembu by tribe. Windson was a man of independent mind, obsequious to no European, arrogant to no villager. He was a keen but by no means uncritical student of the Bible. We often discussed religion together, and he became as eager as myself to learn the hidden meanings of Ndembu beliefs and practices. Most of his boyhood had been spent at a Mission Station behind a sort of spiritual *cordon sanitaire* against "paganism."

"I know the very man to talk about these hidden matters with you," he said after my return, "Kapaku. He has very many brains." Next day he brought Kapaku—none other than Muchona! Muchona, fluid and evasive in his movements as wood-smoke, had many names and Kapaku was one of them. It turned out that Muchona and Windson were neighbours, the one inhabiting a big house of sun-dried "Kimberley" brick, the other his pole-and-daub hut. Thus began an association that was to last eight months. Eight months of exhilarating, quickfire talk among the three of us, mainly about Ndembu ritual. Sporadically our colloquy would be interrupted by Muchona's doctoring trips, but most evenings after school Windson would stroll over to my grass hut and Muchona would rustle on its still-green door for admittance. Then we would spend an hour or so running through the gamut of Ndembu rituals and ceremonies. Many I had seen performed, others I had heard about, and still others were now no more than old men's memories. Sometimes, under Windson's prompting, we would turn to the Old Testament and compare Hebrew and Ndembu observances. Muchona especially was fascinated by the fact that the symbolism of blood was a major theme in both systems. My method was to take an Ndembu ritual that I had observed and go through it, detail by detail, asking Muchona for his comments. He would take a symbol, say the *mudyi* tree which is the pivotal symbol of the girl's puberty ritual, and give me a whole spectrum of meanings for it.

Mudyi has white gum [latex]. We say that this is mother's milk. So *mudyi* is the tree of motherhood. Its leaves represent children. So when the women seize *mudyi* leaves and thrust them into the hut where the novice's bridegroom is sleeping, this means that she should bear many live and lovely children in the marriage. But the *mudyi* is also the matrilineage. For our ancestress lay under the *mudyi* tree during her puberty ritual; and women danced round her daughter, our grandmother, when she lay in that place of death or suffering. And our mother who bore us lay there. And the *mudyi* also means learning. It is like going to school today, for it stands for the instruction the girl receives in her seclusion hut.

Later, Muchona would relate the whiteness of the *mudyi* to the white beads which are draped on a miniature bow and placed in the apex of the novice's seclusion hut. "These beads stand for her capacity to reproduce, her *lusemu*—from *ku-sema,* 'to bear children or beget.' When the girl comes out of seclusion and dances publicly her instructress hides these beads in a pack of red clay on her head. No man but her husband may see these beads. She reveals them to him on her nuptial bed." Then he would discuss the meaning of the quality of whiteness which many symbols possess. "It means good luck, health, strength, purity, friendship towards other people, respect for the elders and for the ancestors; it means revealing what is hidden."

At other times, I would ask Muchona to describe a ritual from the beginning, whether I had seen it or not. Sometimes I would mention to him what other Ndembu specialists had said about its symbols

His accounts and glosses were always fuller and internally more consistent than theirs. He had evidently pondered long on the mysteries of his profession, critically comparing the explanations given him by those who had instructed him in the various cults in which he was an adept.

Windson's comments were usually to the point. His father had been a famous councillor in the court of a former sub-chief, and from him as well as from the Mission School, Windson had acquired a flair for elucidating knotty questions. Although he was a product of modern change he had never lost his deep respect for the now passing traditional order, and its "reverend signors." At the time I knew him, he was, like other converts to Christianity, beginning to look askance at the privileged lives of certain of the white missionaries, and to wonder whether the religion of his loved father was really such a farrago of deviltries as he had been led to believe. His major value for me lay in his ability to slow down Muchona's word-spates into digestible sentences and intelligible texts. For, as I have indicated, Muchona was an enthusiast, not only in talk, but, as I have seen him, in professional action as well—brisk, agile, full of prescience and *élan*. Windson spanned the cultural distance between Muchona and myself, transforming the little doctor's technical jargon and salty village argot into a prose I could better grasp. But when taking a text I made him repeat slowly word by word Muchona's staccato speech so as not to water down its vividness. After a while, the three of us settled down into a sort of daily seminar on religion. I had the impression that Muchona had found a home of some kind at last.

I also came to know a few of Muchona's peccadilloes. For example, his knock would now and then be ragged; he would totter into the hut, his greeting an octave higher than usual, and slump on to a stool. He would then boast that his real name was "Chief Hornet" (*Mwanta Iyanvu*). This was his weak pun on the title of the mighty Lunda potentate in the Belgian Congo from whose realm the Ndembu had come some centuries previously. This title, *Mwantiyanvwa,* was the most important name the Ndembu knew. Iyanvu was Muchona's "beer-drinking name" (*ijina dakunwa walwa*), and when he used it he had come from drinking warm honey-beer, a heady brew bobbing with bees. "Like a hornet or a bee," he would say, "I stay near the beer calabashes, talking loudly, and stinging those who annoy me." Hereupon Windson would fix him with a stern look, relieved by a

An *Ihamba* Ritual, Locating the Possible Site of a Dead Hunter's Tooth.

twinkle of amusement, and tell him to go away and stay away until he had become "Mwanta Muchona" again. And the mighty "Chief Hornet," bedraggled with beer, would creep out of the hut.

This was the Muchona at whom men might scoff—at whom some did scoff, although others who had been treated by him for illness took a different view. Along with other motives less altruistic perhaps, Muchona had a genuine desire to cure the ailing and help the unlucky by his magical therapy. For instance, he would often say when describing how he first came to learn some curative technique, "I dearly wanted to cure well by means of *Kaneng'a* [or *Kayong'u* or some other ritual]." *Kaneng'a* doctors are often feared, as well as invoked, for they are the authentic "witch-doctors" who fight off the attacks of those given to the use of black art against their kin and neighbours. There is an implicit threat in the very knowledge the *Kaneng'a* doctors possess about the ways of witches and sorcerers. Muchona himself practised a modified form of *Kaneng'a,* exempt from most of its terrifying elements. Thus, while most *Kaneng'a* practitioners collected medicines from the interior of graves, and some would even brandish human thigh-bones while they danced, Muchona merely took grass from the surface of graves and leaves and bark-scrapings from trees growing in a circle round them. It is difficult to deduce attitudes from the behaviour of members of another culture, but I once attended a *Kaneng'a* of Muchona's in company with a South African artist from Natal who had seen Zulu doctors at work. Muchona was treating an unfortunate woman who was suffering from delusions as the result of puerperal fever. My friend was impressed by what he considered the "compassionateness" of Muchona's demeanour. Gone was the rather uneasy pertness and comicality of his usual manner; in its stead was an almost maternal air—kind, capable hands washing with medicine, a face full of grave concern. My friend commented on the "heroism" with which Muchona, at one phase of the ritual, ventured out alone into the ghost-ridden graveyard, far from the firelight, to exorcise the agencies of evil which were making the poor victim writhe and babble non-sense. He subdued his fear to his curative vocation.

The compassionate side of Muchona's nature also emerged in the form of comments he made from time to time during our sessions on the luckless spirits whom Ndembu call *ayikodjikodji,* "mischief-makers." These are the spirits of persons inimical to society for one reason or other; through their greed and selfishness, because they were sterile, because they loved to stir up trouble, and so on. At many rituals gifts of food and beer are offered to the ancestors and always a small portion is set aside for the *ayikodjikodji,* usually at the margin of the sacred site and far from the person being treated. Instead of emphasizing the outcast position of these entities, Muchona invariably called attention to the fact that despite their delinquencies in life these spirits were still entitled to be fed. "For were they not human beings once, men and women like ourselves? Wicked-ness is in the heart [literally "liver"] and few can change the hearts they are born with. We do not want the *ayikodjikodji* to harm the living, but once they lived in the villages, were our kin." Other Ndembu brought out the propitiatory character of this rite in their interpretations; Muchona had mercy on the disreputable dead. Could it have been because he himself had to wander round the margins of respectable society that he felt fellowship with the despised and the rejected?

In our "seminars" Muchona seldom betrayed the emotional bases of his calling. A new and exhilarating intellectual dimension had opened up to him as well as to myself in our discussions of symbolism. At such times he had the bright hard eye of some raptor, hawk or kite, as he poised over a definitive explanation. Watching him, I sometimes used to fancy that he would have been truly at home scoring debating points on a don's dais, gowned or perhaps in a habit. He delighted in making explicit what he had known sub-liminally about his own religion. A curious quirk of fate had brought him an audience and fellow enthusiasts of a kind he could never have encountered in the villages. In this situation, he was re-spected for his knowledge in its own right. What has become of him since? Can he ever be again the man he was before he experienced the quenchless thirst for objective knowledge?

For Muchona, the homeless, was peculiarly susceptible to nostal-gia. He had a recurrent dream which I translate literally to keep the smack of his speech. "I dream of the country of Nyamwana where I was born and used to live. I am where my mother died. I dream of the village which is surrounded by a palisade, for bad people raided for slaves. Streams which were there I see once more. It is as though I were walking there now. I talk, I chat, I dance. Does my shadow [*mwevulu*—the personal life-principle] go there in sleep?" Here the rational side of Muchona came uppermost, for he went on: "I find that place the same as it was long ago. But if I had really visited it, the trees would have grown big, grass perhaps would have covered it. Would there have been a stockade? No, it is just a memory." He shook his head lugubriously and said, lingering on each syllable, "Ākā" [meaning "Alas" with a flavour of "Eheu fugaces!"].

Muchona appears to have had an exceptionally close relationship with his mother, even for an Ndembu. This emerges in three ways from the history of his inductions into many kinds of ritual. First, it is apparent in the fact that Muchona was initiated into the preliminary grades of certain cults along with his mother, who held the position of senior novice or patient—in Ndembu ritual one must suffer before one is entitled to learn how to cure. Secondly, one finds that after Muchona's mother died she became for him an agent of supernatural affliction in at least one ritual context. The spirits of one's kin in Ndembu society punish one for a number of reasons. But through punishment, bane may become blessing, for the conduct of a ritual to mollify the spirit gives the patient the right of entry into a tribal cult. Affliction may thus well be a blessing in disguise. Thirdly, Muchona's attachment to his mother appears obliquely in that dead male relatives on her side plagued him into the acquirement of expertise in a number of rituals from which women are debarred, such as hunting cults.

My relationship with Muchona was at a professional rather than a personal level; we maintained towards one another a certain reserve about our intimate affairs. I did not ask him direct questions about his past, especially where the delicate question of his slave origin was concerned, but I learned much about it indirectly from his long spoken reveries on rituals in which he had taken part. Now and then, to be sure, he would suddenly take Windson and myself into his confidence about some matter that was currently troubling him. But in the main, the pattern of his personality, like that of a poet in his poems, expressed itself in his accounts and interpretations of ritual, and in the nuances of gesture, expression, and phrase with which he embellished them. In a sense, therefore, Muchona's ritual history is his inner biography, for in ritual he found his deepest satisfactions.

Muchona's mother had been an adept in many kinds of ritual, for among the Ndembu slavery does not debar a person from ritual eminence. She also encouraged her children to acquire ritual skills. Muchona had been initiated into three women's cults concerned with curing reproductive disorders. One of these, *Nkula,* is performed principally to cure menstrual disorders, but also to remove frigidity and barrenness. Its dominant medicine is the red *mukula* tree, which Muchona had mentioned to me at our first encounter. Here the tree symbolizes the blood of birth or motherhood, and the aim of the ritual is to placate an ancestress who is causing the patient's maternal blood to drain away and not to coagulate around the "seed of life" implanted by her husband. At the esoteric phase of *Nkula,* a *mukula* tree is ceremonially cut down and then carved into figurines of infants which are medicated with red substances, and put into small round calabashes, representing wombs. These amulets are then given to the patients to carry on strings adorned with red feathers until they bear "live and lovely children."

Muchona was inducted into the *Nkula* cult when he was about 7 years of age. His mother was principal patient. At her request he was given the role of *Chaka Chankula,* usually taken by the patient's husband or uterine brother, although sometimes a classificatory "brother" or "son" may be chosen. The idea behind these choices is that a male who occupies a social position in which he might be called upon to support the patient jurally and economically should enact a role symbolizing the protective and responsible aspects of the male-female relationship. In practice, however, it is indeed very seldom that a patient's own son becomes *Chaka.*

A *Chaka*'s main task is to squat behind the patient, after she has been washed with medicines by the doctor, and then to lead her backwards, while she rolls her head round and round under the doctor's flat collecting basket, to a small hut built for the afflicting spirit behind her own marital hut. Then the *Chaka* pulls her into the hut, both with their backs to the entrance. Later they emerge in the same fashion and return to the ritual fire. Muchona displayed his interest in "etymological" interpretations—an interest, incidentally, very common among Ndembu—when he told me that *Chaka* was derived from *kwaka,* "to deliver a child," or, more accurately, "to catch it as it drops."

Only a circumcised male can perform the role of *Chaka* since uncircumcised persons are reckoned ritually impure. An uncircumcised boy, like a menstruating woman, is *wunabulakutooka,* "one who lacks whiteness," and hence purity, good luck, and other qualities possessed by "whiteness." Again, an uncircumcised boy represents social immaturity, and a barren woman is also regarded as in some sense immature. As Muchona explained, "*Mukula* and *Nkula* both come from *ku-kula,* 'to grow up or become mature.' When a girl has her first menstruation she has grown up a little. When she has her first child she has grown up still more. Both of these occasions have to do with blood. After a boy is circumcised he sits, with others who have been cut, on a long log of *mukula,* the tree of blood. He has also grown up a little."

Another curious feature of *Nkula* should be noted here, for it may well have influenced Muchona's development as a doctor. In the role of *Chaka* a man is regarded as a midwife, in Muchona's case his own mother's, in contradiction to the strict Ndembu norm that only a woman may deliver another woman in childbirth. Since many *Yaka* (plural of *Chaka*) become *Nkula* specialists, and since such specialists are thought to cure reproductive disorders, the implication is that they are spiritual midwives. In addition, the *Nkula* patient is thought of as being ritually reborn into fruitful maturity, reborn that she too may bear. Muchona's desire to help the unfortunate by the only means known to Ndembu, leechcraft and ritual, may have found its first channel in this early indoctrination in his mother's *Nkula*.

Without being markedly effeminate in his deportment Muchona always seemed more at ease among women than men. In my mind's eye I can still see him pleasantly gossiping with Kasonda's sister, both of them clucking their tongues at the misdeeds of their little world. This gay, full-blown dame had scant time for her scheming brother, whom she often scolded for his meanness to her. Muchona, to his credit, or perhaps through timidity, never to my knowledge said a word out of place about Kasonda, who himself had no hesitation in slandering Muchona behind his back. I fancy that Kasonda's sister more than once, in her imperious way, defended the tiny doctor against Kasonda's insinuations. Certainly, she called him in to perform the *Kayong'u* ritual for her, a ritual I shall shortly describe, for Muchona's first induction into it was a critical point in his development. Muchona might be described as a Tiresias figure, in that he had considerable insight into feminine as well as masculine psychology, especially in the fields of sex and reproduction. It seems certain that he identified himself closely with his mother, even to the extent of speaking in an alto voice. A young man I knew in Kasonda's village used to speak in a similar way, copying his mother, until he went away to work in a European township. When he came back he possessed a rich baritone, but had acquired a stutter in the process of masculinization. Muchona never lost his shrill pitch.

He resembled Tiresias in another important respect, for he was a diviner as well as a doctor. Here again the secret influence of his mother can be seen at work. During her lifetime she had caused Muchona to be initiated into no less than four kinds of ritual. After her death Muchona believed that she came as a spirit to afflict him "in the mode of *Kayong'u*," and thus to make a diviner of him. *Kayong'u* is the name of a specific set of symptoms, of the spirit that inflicts them, and also of the ritual to cure the victim. It has two variant forms, one to cure the illness, and the other to prepare the patient to be a diviner as well as to cure him. Women may suffer from *Kayong'u* and may be treated by the curative ritual, but cannot become diviners. They may, however, carry out minor ritual tasks during subsequent performances of *Kayong'u,* if they have been cured. Muchona's mother had been, in this sense, a *Kayong'u* doctor.

Muchona's initiation into *Kayong'u,* and the events leading up to it, stood out in his memory with harsh clarity. He was in his early 30's at the time, and was living with his recently acquired wife, Masonde, among his step-father's kin on the Angolan border. Apparently it was just about this time that he emancipated himself from slavery. One pictures him then as a minuscule fellow with a needle-sharp and pin-bright mind. He must have already developed a streak of buffoonery to curry the favour of the bigger and better-born. He must already have been something of an intellectual prodigy for his society, half derided and half grudgingly admired—and entirely unable to belong.

He told me that for a long time he had intermittent attacks of "being caught by a very heavy sickness in my body; I found it hard to breathe, it was like being pricked by needles in my chest, and sometimes my chest felt as though it had been blown up by a bicycle pump." A diviner was consulted, and he diagnosed that Muchona was suffering from the sickness of *Kayong'u.* Furthermore, not one but three spirits had come out of the grave to catch him, two full brothers of his mother, and his father. He himself had dreamt of one of his uncles and of his father while he was ill. Both these spirits, he said, were urging him to become a diviner, for they had practised that profession. He had also dreamt of his mother, significantly enough. "She came too," he told me, "but she was so weak that the diviner did not recognize her." It is typical of Muchona that he felt compelled to stress the novelty of his personal lot in religious matters. A whole battery of spirits, not merely a single ancestor, had singled him out for this arduous and dangerous profession.

The values and attitudes expressed and inculcated in Ndembu ritual leave their stamp on its subjects. Personality is shaped at the forge of ritual, especially where the ritual deals with life-crisis, serious illness or, as I believe in Muchona's case, with a severe psychosomatic disorder. Thus, an account of one phase of Muchona's *Kayong'u* and his interpretations of it may reveal something of the man.

Let us go back thirty years or so to the flaring ritual fire of green wood outside Muchona's hut in the dull dawn. All night he has been washed with medicine, shuddering convulsively to the *Kayong'u* drum rhythm, a plaything of the savage spirits within him. At the first faint light, the senior officiant, a hunter-diviner, who was Muchona's father's brother-in-law, brings a red cock to the sacred site and holds it up before the patient by its beak and legs. *Kayong'u* like *Nkula* and the hunting cults is a "red" ritual, full of red symbolism standing for killing, punishment, witchcraft, and in general, for violent breach in the natural and social orders. Muchona, in a sudden spasm, leaps on the cock and bites through its neck, severing the head. Blood spouts out and Muchona "beats the bloody head on his heart to quieten his mind." Then the big doctor orders a goat to be beheaded. Its blood pours on the ground and Muchona laps it up where it puddles. The cock's head is placed on a pole called *muneng'a*, newly cut from the same species of tree from which ancestor shrines of quickset saplings are made, symbolizing ritual death and contact with spirits. The sun now rises and the doctor takes a hoe, a cupful of goat's blood, the hearts of the cock and goat, various "sharp" objects, and leads a procession of the doctors from the village into the bush. They go to a fork in the path and keep straight on instead of following either path. They find the principal medicine tree of the ritual, a *kapwipu* tree, which stands in this context for initial misfortune followed by success—a meaning it also possesses in hunting cults. They pray to the afflicting spirits, then heap up a mound of earth at the foot of the tree roughly in the shape of a crocodile, with legs and a tail. Next they conceal the various small objects, such as a knife, a razor, needles, a bracelet, and a string of beads under the mound, at the head, tail, and sides. Before concealing the razor and needle, the big doctor pricks the cock's and goat's hearts with them. Then they bring the drums and beat out the *Kayong'u* rhythm.

Now Muchona is led out of the village to the crocodile image and seated on its "neck" facing forward. The doctors question him on why he has come to *Kayong'u* and he gives the stereotyped responses regarded as appropriate. Next he has to divine where each of the objects has been concealed. He told me jubilantly that he was completely successful in this, that he seemed to know just where everything was hidden. Each time he answered correctly, he said, the women who had accompanied him to the sacred site trilled their praises aloud, "making me very happy." Suddenly, two doctors dart off to the village to hide something there. Muchona is led home where he begins searching and snuffling about to find what has been concealed. At length he says, "You have kept something here for the name of a dead man." He approaches the *muneng'a* pole, he claws up the earth near it. He shouts aloud, "The name of the dead man is *Nkayi* ["duiker"], for you have hidden a duiker horn here." Someone called *Nkayi,* he said, had recently died in the village. Then he explains to the doctors, showing off a little, one suspects, "A duiker-antelope is an animal of the bush. An animal lives in the bush, but a man lives in the village." He explained this to me by saying that while hunters seek out hidden animals in the bush, diviners hunt out the secret affairs of men in villages. At any rate, according to Muchona, the big doctor is highly impressed and calls out, "This man will make a true diviner." All gather round Muchona and praise him. But he had to pay the doctors many yards of cloth, he added rather ruefully. Nevertheless he had been cured of his malady. It had gone immediately. The spirits that had afflicted him henceforth helped him to divine and protected him from evil. Shortly after the performance he apprenticed himself to a famous diviner and learned the difficult manipulative and interpretative techniques of that profession, many of which he went on to describe in a series of sessions.

Muchona's interpretation of the symbolism of *Kayong'u* was compounded of both traditional beliefs and his own deeper insights: "The cock represents the awakening of people from sleep; at dawn the cock begins to crow and rouses them. The goat too stands for waking up, for at dawn it begins to bleat when it runs after she-goats and it disturbs people with its sound. The *Kayong'u* spirit too awakens people it has caught. It makes them emit a hoarse breathing, like a cock or a goat." I have myself heard Muchona and other diviners make a deep asthmatic wheezing noise in the course of ordinary conversation. This is supposed to be the voice of the *Kayong'u* spirit inside them. The *Kayong'u* then endows its possessor with especial alertness, with the power of the first light that follows the secretive night, full of witches and mysteries.

Muchona continued: "It is the power of the *Kayong'u* spirit that makes a man kill the cock with his teeth. It makes a person a little mad. When he is shuddering he feels as though he were drunk or epileptic. He feels as though he were struck suddenly in his liver, as if by lightning, as if he were being beaten by a hoe-handle, as if his ears were completely closed, as if he could not breathe. He is stopped up. But he is opened when he kills the cock. From the killed animals he gets wakefulness, alertness, for he must be wide awake to become a diviner and seek out hidden things." The orifices of various senses—ears, nostrils, eyes—stopped up during his ritual seizure, the novice experiences a release, an access of heightened sensitivity. Again the curious parallel with Tiresias springs to mind for the Greek soothsayer was smitten with blindness before he attained insight.

Muchona said of the fork in the path:

When people come to a fork, they must then choose exactly where they want to go. It is the place of choice. Usually they have foreknowledge of the way to go. Everyone has such knowledge. But the diviner goes between the paths to a secret place. He knows more than other people. He has secret knowledge.

When the doctor pricks the hearts with needle and razor, he is representing the patient's pain. The patient must not feel it again because it has already been done in the hearts of the cock and goat. But if he becomes a diviner, he will again feel that pricking inside him—while he is divining. It is the thing which tells him to look at the *tuponya* [the symbolic objects shaken up in a basket whose combinations tell the diviner the cause of his client's illness or bad luck or how someone's death was brought about by a witch or sorcerer]. The diviner must be sharp like the needle, cutting like the knife. His teeth must be sharp to bite off the cock's head with one bite. He goes straight to the point in hidden matters. The crocodile in *Kayong'u* stands for divination because it has many sharp teeth, like needles.

A diviner can catch witches by *Kayong'u,* by its sharpness, and also by his divining basket. These help one another. A person who has *Kayong'u* is safe from witchcraft. Thus if someone tries to bewitch me, my three *Tuyong'u* [plural of *Kayong'u*] would kill that witch. For they are terrible spirits.

I have tried to sketch some of the factors that may have been responsible for making Muchona a "marginal man" in Ndembu society. His slave origin, his unimpressive appearance, his frail health, the fact that as a child he trailed after his mother through several villages, even his mental brilliance, combined to make him in some measure abnormal. His special abilities could not overcome the handicaps of his social marginality and psychical maladjustment.

But he found some kind of integration through initiation into curative ritual and especially into divinatory status. For these, his outsider characteristics were positive qualifications. In a ritual context he could set himself apart from the battles for prestige and power that bedevil kinship and village relationships in Ndembu society. Ndembu ritual, like ritual everywhere, tends to assert the higher unifying values of the widest effective congregation. The doctor-diviner heals or judges by reference to commonly held beliefs and values which transcend the laws and customs of everyday secular society. Thus Muchona's very weakness and vulnerability in village life were transmuted into virtues where the maintenance of the total society was concerned.

But the rich symbolism of oral aggression in *Kayong'u* points up a very different aspect of the diviner's role. And since Muchona set so much store by his occupancy of such a role it must have modelled many of his attitudes. In the past, a diviner had to ply a dangerous trade. I have been told of diviners who were shot or speared by the relatives of those they had declared to be witches or sorcerers. Moreover, they had to overcome by aggressive means much fear and guilt in themselves to reach decisions that might result in the death by burning of their fellow men. At its mildest, their profession entailed the probability of declaring in public that someone was a witch. No one but a diviner would do this, for as in all societies, the polite fiction prevails among Ndembu that social intercourse is governed by amity and mutual consideration. Only the diviner, fortified by ritual and protected by ferocious spirits that torment him while they endow him with insight, can publicly expose the hates that simmer beneath the outward semblance of social peace.

One feels, therefore, that there is an aspect of unconscious revenge against the social order in divination. In Muchona's case one may speculate that beneath his jester's mask, and under his apparent timidity, he may have cherished hatred against those more securely placed in the ordered groupings of society. Such hatred may itself have given him a certain clairvoyance into tense relationships in the kinship and political systems. Forever outside the village circle, he could see the villagers' weak spots and foibles more clearly than most. His very objectivity could further his general revenge. But he may himself have felt unconscious fear that those he disliked plotted counter-retribution against him. This fear makes him at once meek and comical in his daily doings. By playing the timorous fool he belittles his own powers and thus defends himself. Moreover, his fear may have something to do with the fact that he invariably rationalized his ritual tasks as being for the good of society. The flower of altruism sometimes has twisted roots.

It was an undoubted fact that Muchona, popular with most elderly women, was disliked by many men. For example, when his junior wife's baby died, a child who he admitted to everyone was none of his, men from a number of villages took pleasure in telling me that they suspected he had bewitched it to death. To discredit these damaging views, communicated to Muchona by innuendo, he took the trouble to make a wearisome journey of several score miles to his parents-in-law to report the details of the baby's illness and the remedial measures he had taken. He told me wryly on his return that they had taken fifteen shillings—a considerable sum for a villager—from him as compensation for the child's loss to their lineage. Muchona, as the husband, was held responsible for the child's welfare. He said that they had taken no account of the money he had already paid a diviner to ascertain the cause of death, nor of the cost of treatment by a herbalist, also borne by Muchona himself. The diviner had declared him innocent of the child's death in the presence of his wife's kin, had indeed nominated as the sorcerer an important headman belonging to her lineage. If Muchona had been a tougher personality in secular affairs he might have refused to pay compensation for an illicit child, and have gotten away with it. As it was he felt constrained to ingratiate established authority whenever he met it—or else to run away and build his hut in a different area.

There is another instance of Muchona's tendency to capitulate without a struggle to public pressure. One day, after he had been working with me for about three months, he strutted in wearing a suit of white ducks, paid for out of my cash gifts. He had informed everyone with some pride, I was told later, that his son Fanuel Muchona had given him the suit. Indeed, poor Muchona often tried to give the impression that Fanuel was more solicitously filial than he really was. It was soon discovered that Fanuel had only put his father in touch with the vendor, not given him the money for the suit. After our session schoolmaster Windson said to me sadly, "That fine suit will make everyone jealous, for people will realize that you have been paying him well, and we Ndembu are a very jealous people."

Sure enough, a few days later Muchona came to us in his usual khaki rags, looking utterly woebegone. "What on earth's the matter?" I asked. He replied, "This is the last time we can speak about customs together. Can't you hear the people talking angrily in the village shelter? When I passed it on my way here, they were saying loudly, so that I could hear, that I was giving away our [tribal] secrets, and that I was teaching you witchcraft matters." I was distressed and a little hurt to hear this, for my relations with the villagers had always seemed extremely friendly. I said as much to Muchona, who went on, "No, it is not the people of this village, at least only a few of them, who are talking like this, but others who come to hear a case discussed in the village shelter. But the people of this village, especially one man—I name no names—say that I am telling you only lies. Before I came, they say, you heard only true things about our ceremonies, but now you just hear nonsense. But one thing I found wonderful. The village people call me a liar, the strangers say I am betraying secrets. Their reasons [for disliking me] don't agree, but they agree with each other!" I knew that it was Kasonda who called Muchona a liar, for he had hinted as much to my wife often enough, but Muchona was too polite or too diplomatic to say so, for everyone knew that Kasonda and I had been friends of long standing.

When Windson heard this sorry tale his expression grew bleak and precipitous, as I suspect it must often have done when he dealt with refractory schoolchildren. "I must have a word with some of these people," he said. "Most of them have children at my school." He turned to Muchona, "Don't take any notice of these troublemakers. They won't say another word." Nor did they. For Windson was not only deeply respected as a man of integrity, but he also had effective sanctions at his command. As village schoolmaster, he could recommend or fail to recommend children for Middle School education at the distant Mission Station. Village Africans in Northern Rhodesia are well aware that a good education is a vital means to such upward social mobility as is available to black people. If the schoolmaster were to become unduly aware of acts of naughtiness on the part of certain borderline cases for promotion he might well send in an adverse report. I don't think Windson would have done this, for he was a gentle, earnest, and not unkindly man, but a hint in the proper quarters that Muchona was not to be bothered again had a wonderfully sobering effect.

Windson had become uncommonly fond of Muchona in the course of our discussions. At first, he had tended to display a certain coolness, bordering on disparagement, towards Muchona's "paganism." But in a very short time he grew to admire the little man's intellect and his appreciation of the complexity of existence. Later still, Windson came to take positive pride in the richness and sonority of the symbolic system Muchona expounded to us. And he would chuckle affectionately at Muchona's occasional flashes of dry wit.

One of those flashes came after we had spent a long session on a painful subject, the *ihamba*. In its material expression, an upper front incisor tooth of a dead hunter imbeds itself in the body of a person who has incurred the hunter's displeasure. The tooth is removed by means of a ritual procedure which includes confession by the patient and by his village relatives of their mutual grudges, and the expression of penitence by the living for having forgotten the hunter-ancestor in their hearts. Only after "the grudge has been found" will the tooth cease "to bite" its victim and allow itself to be caught in one or other of a number of cupping horns affixed to the patient's back by the doctor's principal assistant. After about a couple of hours, Muchona became very restive on his hardwood stool. Full of the zest of enquiry I had become thoughtless and had forgotten to give him his usual cushion. Eventually he burst out, "You have been asking me where an *ihamba* goes. Well, just now I have an *ihamba* in the buttocks." I silently passed him his cushion. But this was not all. We used to punctuate our deliberations pleasantly enough with an occasional cigarette. Today I had forgotten even to pass round the yellow pack of "Belgas." So Muchona said, "I have another *ihamba*." "What's that one?" "The angriest *ihamba* of all, the *ihamba* of drinking [i.e., smoking] tobacco." Like a true professional Muchona could make innocuous quips about his craft.

Muchona normally took *ihamba* beliefs very seriously. He had been treated no less than eight times, he said, to gain relief from an *ihamba* which made his joints sore. But either because the doctors were charlatans—one tried to deceive him with a monkey's tooth—or more often because "the grudge was unknown," the *ihamba* remained to vex him. Several divinations had established to his satisfaction that the *ihamba* came from a mother's brother who had been taken while still a boy by Luba slave-raiders many years ago. Later his mother had learned that her brother had become a famous hunter and a wealthy man in Lubaland, having purchased his freedom there. But she never saw him again. Muchona believed that he held an undying grudge against his maternal kin, perhaps because he had not been captured but had been sold into slavery by them— who could tell so long afterwards? Muchona was being afflicted on account of this grudge. Since no one could now find out what it was, he felt he could never be cured of the biting, creeping *ihamba*. May we not see in this a projection of Muchona's own state? Did he bear an unconscious grudge against his mother—displaced on to her unknown brother—for saddling her son with slavery? Did he not have the fantasy that even a slave could become great, as his uncle was reputed to have done? At any rate, in Muchona's phrasing of *ihamba* beliefs, he seemed to feel that he was in the grip of some irremediable affliction, that indeed his sickness was himself. Although suffering made him a doctor in many curative cults, he never became an *ihamba* specialist. One fancies that this one incurable trouble represented for him the deathless gnawing of his chagrin at being of slave origin and at not really "belonging" in any snug little village community.

No man can do justice to another's human total. I have suggested that in Muchona there was a deep well of unconscious bitterness and a desire for revenge against a society that had no secular place for him compatible with his abilities. But the small man had a big mind. He was only too sensitively aware of the undertone of derision and resentment with which many men regarded him. Yet, although he was paramountly intellectual rather than warm-hearted, he tried on the whole to speak and act civilly and charitably; and he treated his patients with compassion. In our long collaboration he achieved an amazing degree of objectivity about the sacred values of his own society. Whether his outlook was radically altered by our triune discussions I was never to know. All I do know is that shortly before I left his land, probably for ever, he came to see me, and we had an outwardly cheerful drink together. Presently, he grew quiet, then said, "When your motor car sets out in the early morning do not expect to see me nearby. When someone dies we Ndembu do not rejoice, we have a mourning ceremony." Knowing Muchona as I did, I could not help feeling that he was not simply feeling sorry at the loss of a friend. What grieved him was that he could no longer communicate his ideas to anyone who would understand them. The philosophy don would have to return to a world that could only make a "witch-doctor" of him. Had not some kind of death occurred?

12

My "Boy," Muntu

Ethel M. Albert

Find a boy who bakes good bread, and the rest will be easy." This was the most important advice given me as I left Belgium for Africa in February, 1956. I had reason to remember it more than once in the sixteen months I was in Africa. My destination was Ruanda-Urundi, a Belgian trusteeship sandwiched between Belgian Congo and Tanganyika Territory. The first stop was Astrida, in Ruanda. It is an attractive, modern tropical town, the site of the social science center of I.R.S.A.C. (*Institut pour la Recherche Scientifique en Afrique Centrale*), a research institute supported by the Belgian government. From Astrida, I was to proceed to Urundi to carry out the research on African value systems for which I had been granted a Ford Foundation fellowship.[1]

The seasoned researchers of I.R.S.A.C. were ready to help me convert my plans on paper into definite arrangements: a specific research location in Urundi, transportation facilities, provision for funds, mail, and supplies, and a competent African staff of interpreter, chauffeur and "boy." I was warned that all this would require a month or more. Installed in I.R.S.A.C.'s elegant, California-style guest house while waiting to go into the field, I could still enjoy the amenities of electricity, running water, and a kerosene refrigerator and stove.

Within a few days I had learned, among other things, that even in French-speaking Belgian Africa, the English word, "boy," is standard usage for a native male servant of any age. I needed an experienced man who could get along in the bush. When the news of my need spread, a stream of applicants appeared at the guest house. One of the last to arrive was Muntu. Even before the interview was over, I had decided that he would be my "boy." My snap judgment of his worth was well confirmed in his fifteen months as my "boy." We had a lively, intimate relationship that is not easily classified. In a feudal

[1] Grateful acknowledgment is hereby made to the Ford Foundation and to I.R.S.A.C. for the support received for the research. In addition, thanks are due for criticisms and suggestions to Professor Cora Du Bois, Miss May Sarton, and Miss Miriam Gallaher.

environment, he became my privileged personal servant, I his superior and protector.

Muntu's ability to bake good bread was the first item established in our interview. He assured me that he was a good cook and laundry man, and he volunteered the information that he understood white standards of housekeeping cleanliness. Although he was a native of Ruanda, most of his jobs had been in Urundi, several of them in the bush.[2] To my great relief, Muntu spoke passable French. I would not have to learn Swahili, the local master-servant *lingua franca*. He estimated his age at about 38, and I was glad to have a mature hand. He seemed well above average in intelligence and had a very engaging personality. His enthusiastic letters of reference justified in part his demand for twice the going wages. For twenty-four dollars a month and various extras, I would have at my disposal a whole spectrum of skills needed to assure the success of a lone female anthropologist in the central African hinterland.

Very early, Muntu made certain that I knew he was one of the Batutsi, the upper class of Ruanda and Urundi.[3] Six feet tall, he was just average height among these narrow-headed, slender giants. Hamitic herders, the Batutsi had migrated into the area several centuries ago and become the rulers of the Bahutu, the short and broad Bantu farmers who make up more than 85 percent of the population. True to the standards of his aristocratic background, Muntu was dignified, his manners elegant, his speech fluent. Like many of his compatriots, he had adopted Western dress. His white shirt, blue trousers, and tan sweater were spotlessly clean though ragged. Only later did I learn that his good clothes would be left at home until after he had received from me the gift of two tailor-made khaki safari suits, at four dollars apiece.

In my second-hand Ford pick-up truck, driven by Musazi, a chauffeur loaned me by I.R.S.A.C., I travelled about Urundi with Muntu

[2] Ruanda and Urundi are administratively unified under the Belgian trusteeship government. Contiguous but independent kingdoms, they are sufficiently alike in social and political organization, ethnic composition, and language to be indistinguishable to the non-specialist. The peoples themselves, however, with some justification, insist upon keeping their separate identities clear.

[3] In Bantu languages, *mu-* is the singular prefix and *ba-* the plural prefix for terms designating human beings; thus, Mututsi and Batutsi, Muhutu and Bahutu, for the principal ethnic groups of Ruanda and Urundi. Sometimes the alternative form, *W*atutsi, appears in the literature, a reasonable transliteration of the soft "b" sound in the languages of Ruanda and Urundi.

to choose a research site. There were 10,500 square miles and 2,000,-000 people to choose from. Thousands of miles of winding mountain roads led from the few urban centers into the most isolated backwoods. Helpful Belgian administrators directed me to eastern Urundi, where I would find the relatively isolated Bahutu farmers with whom I wanted to begin work. Later, I was to move to Rusaka in the western part of the country to study the Batutsi herders. In both locations, as a non-paying guest of the Belgian administration, I lived in government shelters, well-built brick houses placed in every part of the country for the convenience of travellers.

Muntu knew the roads, the names of the princes and what to do at each stop. When I chose the house at Mutumba, he sent for the local chief—a Mututsi who was about 6 feet 6 inches tall—and instructed him to have ready for my return within a week the repairs needed in the house and three new straw-and-reed houses for my staff. Apparently I had only to tell Muntu what I wanted and leave the rest to him.

With the details of safaris taken care of by Muntu, I was free to look around at the wonderful country and people. Urundi is a land of hills, steeply planted with banana trees, beans, peas, maize, and sorghum. The straw-covered, beehive-shaped houses, encircled by fences, dot the hills at irregular intervals. Each family occupies its own hill. Grazing on the hillsides in small herds of five to ten are the prize possessions of the Barundi, their cows. Their magnificent curved horns spread upwards or outwards to a length of a yard or more.

In the large commercial center of Usumbura and in the capital city of Kitega, I had met the king and some of the princes of Urundi, dressed in well-tailored business suits and driving large American cars. Western influence is in evidence even on the back roads. Many men wear shorts and shirts. Those who can afford them have sweaters or coats. For, although Urundi lies between two and three degrees south of the equator, the altitude is high—6500 to 8500 feet and more—and the average daily temperature 68° F. the year round. In town or country, however, the principal manner of dress is an adaptation of the traditional freely-hanging robe, knotted at one shoulder. Dark cotton cloth and blankets serve for everyday attire. But the wealthy and those on holiday wear two or three long robes, one over the other, of bright colored cotton prints. They are secured at one shoulder with a long, raffia tassel and trail the dust behind. Heavy copper bracelets and other traditional jewelry are now seen only rarely. The long spear or staff persists, as necessary to sartorial elegance in Urundi as the walking stick in England.

Muntu had a roving eye. Following it taught me local standards of feminine beauty: a narrow Hamitic nose, good height, narrow waist, and full hips. It taught me also to distinguish the sexes, not always easy for the newcomer. Barundi women are on the average only slightly shorter than the men, some of the Batutsi women cutting fine figures at over 6 feet in height. Bahutu women, however, like Bahutu men, are usually not much above 5 feet tall. Women also wear robes knotted at the shoulder, sometimes with blouse and long, full skirt barely visible underneath. Most of the women shave their heads, and so do most of the men. Often, especially among Bahutu, the women are as muscular as their husbands. Defined as the stronger sex, the women carry the heavy burdens and do the farm work. Masculine tasks are herding, building, and walking long distances—sometimes fifty miles in two days—on errands or as porters for Batutsi and others in positions of authority.

Settling in at Mutumba was swiftly managed. The brick house was divided into three very large rooms, a kitchen, and a storeroom, all freshly whitewashed. There were some tables and chairs; a bedstead and spring, to which I added a borrowed mattress and pillow; a few cabinets for my linens; and a screened locker for food, ample to hold coffee and tea, flour and oil, jars of jam and cans of fruit, vegetables, fish, and cheese. From I.R.S.A.C., I had borrowed a water filter, some kerosene pressure lamps, pots, pans, and dishes. Curtains went up, hand-hemmed green and yellow cotton that would later be worn as a robe by Muntu's wife. For an anthropological field site, it was indecently luxurious.

On the morning after our arrival, Muntu hired a man to carry up water, another to chop wood for his kitchen stove and my fireplace, and a pair of night watchmen, each at the local rate of fifteen to twenty cents a day. In stormy haggling sessions, he supplemented the canned goods with local produce. He turned out soups of dried peas and peanuts, excellent sauces for chicken, omelettes, sweet potatoes, or cooked bananas as vegetables, and fried bananas or pancakes for dessert. He did not use for my table the chief foods of the neighbors—cassava, beans, and sorghum. About a quart of thin, blue milk each morning, obtained under protest from cow-owning Barundi, was boiled to use with breakfast oatmeal. The bright spot in the menu was each week's batch of fine white bread baked in a makeshift outdoor oven.

Muntu was fanatical about cleanliness. He explained to all its urgency in the dirty and disease-ridden back country. The green cement floors were scrubbed by his assistant every day. His mornings and afternoons were filled with washing and ironing, expertly done. Two pails of water steamed on the stove until I could stop work to have my bath. Sunset was at 6:00 P.M.—plus or minus five minutes according to the season—and the evening began as Muntu lighted the kerosene pressure lamps. The table was laid and dinner served. Quiet descended for a little while on the otherwise noisy and busy household. Some evenings there were interviews after dinner, but sometimes Muntu called me out to watch the dancers he had invited. A small fire against the bitter cold, a 20-liter pot of banana beer from my storeroom for a dozen men dancing and singing, were entertainment enough until bedtime. Muntu had more than made good his claims of competence.

The second day at Mutumba, Muntu asked me for sixty francs ($1.20) to purchase a pot of banana beer. The first in an almost endless series, the pot of beer represented the solution to the problem of how to explain to the Barundi my mission in Mutumba. Muntu had it all figured out, or, clever Mututsi, figured it out on the spot. "For these people," he told me, "you are a *mwamikazi,* like the wife of a king or rich Mututsi. You will have to invite them to visit, and you must offer beer and tobacco, the way any *mwamikazi* in Urundi does." Patiently and intelligently, he explained how princes and aristocrats had in the past placed each of their several wives on separate estates. Each *mwamikazi* governed the household, supervised the workers, kept food and drink in readiness for visitors. She listened to the troubles of her husband's serfs and gave charity to the needy. Above all, she received on her own account formal requests for gifts from those who wished to become her personal followers.

Although I was an *umuzungu*—an outsider, a white—I could prove my good will by being generous with beer and cigarettes, blankets and lengths of cotton cloth, and clothing for the otherwise naked children. Wealthy by local standards and belonging to the same "race" as the powerful administrators of Urundi, I entered the field with the attributes of social superiority as it is defined in the country. I had a great deal to learn about my part as *mwamikazi* in this anthropological play, but it was on the whole wonderfully successful. Nobody was taken in by the fiction, yet it was a legitimate way to give me an acceptable place in the community. People came to visit and to talk. They told others about the new household. I was warned not to offend my guests by suggesting that my beer was purchasing their information. Still, there were rarely objections to my taking notes. The Barundi can play a profitable game as well as any.

The neighbors soon formed the habit of visiting the house at Mutumba in the morning or afternoon or evening, as inclination and leisure permitted. They came singly or in pairs or groups as chance arranged it. Muntu was a versatile impresario for a would-be *mwamikazi*. His air of authority and knowledge of traditional amenities won him immediate approval from the few local Batutsi, who soon came to talk to me. For Bahutu, he used the quite different approach he deemed suitable for peasants. He jokingly proposed marriage to the worn-out widows who stopped to sell a basket of peas or indulge their curiosity. He gave bananas or sweets to the children as he chatted with their mothers about his six youngsters back in Astrida. He gave beer and cigarettes to the men and discussed local affairs with them seriously and wisely.

In the regular course of events, I would look around after breakfast to see who was there and tell Muntu whom I wanted to interview. With appropriate ceremony, he ushered the visitors into the living-room. A camp-bed served as my sofa, and Muntu seated the visitors in the chairs arranged in a circle facing the sofa. To the senior person among them, he gave a gourd of banana beer and a drinking tube, and on the coffee table in front of me he placed my cup of tea or coffee. He called my interpreter and left us to a few hours of conversation. Once the visitors had left, he scrubbed away furiously at the mud or dust their bare feet had tracked in and poured vast quantities of disinfectant around to destroy any chiggers or fleas that might have strayed from the never-washed cotton robes. If a guest became boisterous after too much banana beer, Muntu somehow knew and would come, no matter what the hour, to announce that it was time for me to eat. No Murundi, no matter how drunk, would stay after that, for it is strictly taboo to be present while a superior eats.

Returning visits—and in the process, getting to know something about household affairs in Urundi—presented grave difficulties. It was bad manners to visit anyone at home without advance notice. They would be shamed if there were no beer to offer a distinguished visitor. The yard might not be swept clear of cowdung or banana peels, or it might be cluttered up with mats on which beans or cassava were drying. The mistress of the house would be in work clothes and dirty. Some of the women were rather direct in teaching me my manners. If I arrived uninvited and unannounced, the pounding of cassava in the mortar or the breaking up of firewood would become more vigorous, the noise making conversation impossible. Or, a five-mile hike might end in nothing when a child waiting at the yard entrance offered the socially acceptable lie that nobody was home. Only after several months did I hear the friendly reproach, "You went by our door without stopping to greet us," the signal that I could thereafter drop in unannounced.

By the time my research routine was established, I realized that I much preferred Muntu to Musazi, the chauffeur, or my interpreter, first Charles, then Stanislas. From the first, Musazi was a problem. About 45 years old, half Mututsi and half something else, a Moslem who had first been a Catholic, then a Protestant, a drunkard given to violence, he had little to recommend him other than his skill as a driver. Worst of all, there was almost nothing for him to do. His duties included only a weekly errand to a market-town not ten miles away, an occasional trip to the chief who lived five miles down the road, and the return to Astrida for a week's stay every two months. Charles, in his early 20's and fresh out of the seminary, was competent enough as an interpreter but bored and restless in the bush. Translating the "nonsense" of uneducated Barundi seemed a waste of time to the half-educated Charles. He was replaced by Stanislas. In his 30's and a sober, married man. Stanislas was a quiet, unassuming Mututsi. He worked earnestly, to the limit of his barely adequate linguistic skills, urged on by his interest in learning more about his country's ways. When he was not working with me, he kept to himself in the background.

My preference for Muntu seemed natural enough. He was the first one hired and the only one so competent that I did not have to take time away from field work to supervise him. He was decidedly more intelligent than the others and understood better than they the purpose of my research. We were nearly the same age and early formed the habit of talking about local events, life in general, his youthful experiences or the way things were in my country.

Occasionally, of course, Muntu gave me cause for complaint. His mania for cleanliness did not always reach as far as the kitchen. Worse yet, on his own initiative, he undertook to induct a half-dozen country boys into the arts of housekeeping. As a result, the dishes were not always properly washed, and the fleas of his apprentices sometimes found their way into my bed.

Like virtually every other citizen of Ruanda and Urundi, Muntu drank a great deal. He knew my tolerance for drunkenness was low. Still, he could not prevent himself from coming, in a very dignified stagger, to my living room to describe the wonderful party at which he had got drunk. His one truly puzzling offense was loud quarreling, behavior unbecoming to a Mututsi, usually with Musazi. He was otherwise very decorous in public, even when drunk, no matter whether we were at a wedding near Mutumba or at the great national dance celebrations in Kitega.

There was something about "medicines" in Muntu's quarrels with Musazi. Musazi had smelled out most of the curers and witches in the vicinity. I was glad to know who they were for my own purposes, but surely his interest was of a different order. I interrupted one of the more vociferous quarrels to demand an explanation. Muntu was in a rage and seemed on the point of murdering his kitchen assistant. Stanislas, his head hanging, translated: Musazi had bribed the kitchen boy with a pair of shoes to get him to slip some *inzaratsi* into my soup, and Muntu had caught the lad at it. *Inzaratsi* had been described to me as a potion that would cause the consumer to yearn for the presence of the one who had paid for it. I was certain that Musazi had no amorous designs on me, but what he was up to I could not even imagine.

Brought so close to home, the potions and poisons so constantly discussed by my visitors took on greater importance than material for a file on witchcraft. One day, Musazi himself was found placing a powder of some kind in Muntu's bed. Even without chemical analysis to determine scientifically the properties of the powders and potions, it was obvious that they were active agents in demoralizing my household. I could no longer reasonably assume that I had no right to interfere in the personal affairs of my staff, mature men though they were. I called the three men into my living room for an after-dinner discussion.

The naturalness with which the group assembled seemed most unnatural to me. There was beer, for I wanted to soften a little the blow I intended to deliver. Smiling and relaxed, they were obviously not prepared for me to read them the riot act. Gravely, I announced that this was a serious matter. There was agreement: a meeting of *abashingantahe,* elders sitting in judgment, was always serious, but always a good thing. What was more, it was high time I'd gotten around to it, for the situation was serious.

There is a proverb in Urundi, "You look everywhere for something, and you find it under your arm." I had been trying to learn what the mechanism was in Urundi society for managing discord in family and political affairs. Here it was, the council of elders, assembled in my own living room.

To begin, I announced that the irregularities of behavior of Musazi and Muntu were disrespectful of me, disruptive of my work, and no longer tolerable. Musazi was warned that he would be sent packing back to Astrida the next time he misbehaved. Muntu was warned that no more shouting would be borne. With pained surprise, Stanislas corrected me. There was no sense in a council if the decision were already made. Stanislas could not, as in regular interviews, be merely a translator. He was one of Musazi's peers and owed him support. My place, I was told, was to issue a warning to Musazi in the presence of his friends—not privately as in the past—so that they could try to persuade him to change if he had been doing wrong things. I had also to hear Musazi's complaints against me.

There was always more to be gained from following Barundi rules than from standing on what I viewed as my rights. I restated my complaints against Musazi—his drinking, his quarrels with Muntu, his indiscreet affairs with girls in the vicinity, and so on. I then reasserted my right to fire him, should he disregard a final warning. All three men demurred. I had taken Musazi to work for me, and he was therefore my responsibility. I had to realize that his misbehavior came from the weakness of his character, not from malice. He needed help. Muntu and Stanislas joined together to defend Musazi's rights and their own. Each asked me whether he, too, would be fired if he did something wrong. Mustering my courage, I replied that nobody should expect to be kept on in a job if he did not do it well.

Somehow, the discussion turned to the question of what it was like to be a white, alone in the bush. They wanted to know whether I was afraid. I assured them that I had no reason to be, for I had them to protect me. After a moment of silence, Stanislas, speaking quietly and with eyes lowered, said, "But you know, if we became angry with you, we could do you great harm." Realizing how true this was, I had a bad moment. He continued, "You know, if we were angry, we could all run away." I still do not know whether this was a veiled threat of much worse or Stanislas' idea of real harm to me. I laughed it off, arguing, "That would be very foolish, for then you would have no salary." But from that time forward, my sympathy was somewhat greater for the whites living in Africa, isolated from their own kind, outnumbered, and resented, neither giving nor getting trust and affection, decreasingly certain of the meaningfulness of their "civilizing mission," increasingly certain that they had much to fear.

Musazi at last presented his chief complaint. Every day, I invited people into the house to drink, but never until this night had he been invited. Taken by surprise, I left it to Stanislas and Muntu to explain to Musazi that the beer was not for sociability but for getting information. Nevertheless, to raise morale, I promised to invite him from time to time. The council dispersed, the outcome inconclusive but all of us in good humor.

It was no good. Musazi's brain was soaked in alcohol and his soul in despair. He continued to do the same things, and I sent him back to Astrida in the pick-up truck, telling him I would telegraph when I wanted him to come and get me. About half way there, he wrecked the truck—as he had repeatedly told Stanislas and Muntu he would one day do—killing the two passengers he had picked up on the way.

It was clearly an error—an expensive and dangerous one—to regard my partly Westernized Batutsi staff as my "employees." They were my "children," my dependents. In spite of myself, I was changing in actions and attitudes from democratic, egalitarian liberalism—in which impersonal employer-employee relationships make sense—to the benevolent if burdensome despotism of the *mwamikazi*. What Muntu had told me about the protective role of the head of a household was repeated and elaborated by rich and poor, Mututsi and Muhutu, male and female. The power of the council of elders to decide the fate of inferiors, it was admitted, was relative to the justness of the superior person. Musazi was a bad child, for though I had the duty to be generous, to correct him when he was wrong, to try to make peace between him and my other "children," he owed it to me to be docile and obedient. The wickedness of men like Musazi, it was admitted, was characteristic of Batutsi, who are said never to forgive an injustice and to live only for the opportunity to harm those they hate.

The key to the underlying causes of Musazi's unforgiving hostility came from a detailed discussion of the relationships between superiors and inferiors. In each family household and at each princely court, the superior chooses his *umutoni,* his favorite. To Musazi, to Stanislas, and to my Barundi neighbors, Muntu, technically my "boy," was my *umutoni,* my favorite. People who wanted to visit me or to ask a gift of me had first to offer a gift—a pot of beer or a basket of peas—to Muntu. He, in theory, would then recommend the petitioner to my attention.

Almost nobody sought out Musazi with pots of beer, for he had no influence to open the way for them to obtain a gift from me. Bitter rivalry in the family and at the courts was the common state of affairs. The *umutoni* was hated by the less successful aspirants to the privileged and profitable position. Plotting for his downfall, by calumny or poison, was standard practice. Musazi must have been bitterly resentful of Muntu's advantage, good enough reason for Muntu to be hysterically afraid of him. It cannot have mattered to Musazi, or to Muntu, or to the neighbors, that to me, Muntu's distributing beer and cigarettes was part of his job as my "boy," nor can it have mattered that I had not known I had an *umutoni.*

It is difficult to know how consciously Muntu used my ignorance of his culture to advance his own prestige, how hard he may have jockeyed for position, not so much with me as with the neighbors. Doubtless, he made promises of gifts he nervously hoped I would make. After Musazi's departure, Muntu let his jealousy of Stanislas show. After having spoken against Musazi, he began to speak against Stanislas, though not too harshly. It was enough to make me think he wanted to get rid of everyone on my staff but the laborers. Stanislas must have been most uncomfortable, with Muntu watching his every step to report any slips. One of the duties of the favorite is to be an informer, and Muntu was doing his duty. If I had believed him when he reported Musazi's threats to wreck my truck, I could have prevented the accident, the two deaths, and Musazi's jail sentence. But I was learning. Afterwards, when Muntu said that when he was angry with me, he thought of taking a knife to kill me, I quietly gathered up the sharp knives and locked them up. Nobody had told me how an *umutoni* felt about his *mwamikazi,* so I decided to be cautious.

The psychological discomfort suffered from increased knowledge of the undercurrents of personality and society in this otherwise agreeable feudal kingdom became focused for a time on Muntu. He seemed a fantastic caricature of the brooding, plotting herder, filled with hostilities and anxieties, with jealousy and fear.

I was not beyond the reach of Muntu's jealousy. One morning, he failed to answer my call, and I went to the kitchen to get my coffee for myself. He was there, leaning against his work-table, notebook and pencil in hand. He was talking to one of my informants and appeared to be taking notes. I asked what he was doing. "Anthropological research, like you. But I know the language, so my research will be better than yours." I asked if he meant to turn the notes over to me. He did not. This was his research. Happily, the professional rivalry between us did not last long. The combination of mirth and horror his note-taking produced in me restored my perspective: he was very human and deeply troubled about many things.

Because Muntu spoke French, wore Western clothes, and usually presented a dignified and cheerful face, it was easy to forget how thoroughly he belonged to his culture and how great the conflicts were between the old and new ways. His ambition to fulfill the pattern of the Mututsi aristocrat was intense, perhaps pathological. He was desperately poor and wildly spendthrift when he had money. High social position was expensive. He was a mature man whose judgment was respected in councils, and he was the father of many children in a part of the world where fatherhood defines masculinity. Yet, to earn his living, he did woman's work, a matter about which he occasionally made a bitter joke. Here, then, was Muntu, at dinner time serving a white woman, an hour later drinking on equal and intimate terms with a prince. He must surely have had mixed feelings about himself and about me.

It was not difficult to see Muntu's positive stake in working for me. I was willing to play the generous patroness. My wealth was his wealth: the beer and cigarettes, the blankets and cotton cloth, were given by me, but through his intercession. Property was a sore point with Muntu. He was extremely sensitive about accusations of theft, protesting his reputation for honesty more often than seemed necessary. Since he seemed in fact scrupulously honest in almost everything, I did not split hairs with him over the definition of his generous self-helpings to my tea and sugar. Pilfering was considered virtually a perquisite of household service, and from the outset he had been given permission to use my stores for himself whenever he liked.

The one time in the fifteen months of our association Muntu lost his temper with me was over an imagined accusation of theft. The burst of rage came at a point where my own temper was not under good control. Life in Mutumba was wearing, and I needed a rest. We were both shouting. I stopped making my part of the noise when I found my clenched fist within an inch of Muntu's jaw. The shock of the spectacle of myself at the point of physical violence helped me to recover my control. It gave him a chance to get hold of himself. His parting shot, delivered in a quiet way, was, "After all, mademoiselle, you are *umuzungu* [a white]. If you stay in Urundi a long time, you will become like the other whites." In the earlier, rougher days of European occupation, he had suffered many a whipping, unable to fight back, from white men and women as well. He knew me well enough by then to know that the invidious comparison would hurt, the more so since he was so nearly right.

The *mwamikazi* game had begun to pall. I was feeling foolish, a soft touch for my "boy," my interpreter, for any Murundi who came along. Like anyone else, I am a child of my culture. It took a great many talks with Barundi to grasp the idea that what was good about a gift—whether it was a cigarette or a cow—was not only the material benefit as such but also, and perhaps more important, the meaning of the gift. "You give only to those you like, and everyone wants to be liked." Where I come from, I explained in some humility, we think it is either wealth or affection that is sought, not both at once. Before the lesson was quite driven home, I had burst out to Muntu in anger against a woman who had been rude enough to ask for a gift within an hour after meeting me. "Asking is all the Barundi know how to do! Wealth is all they think about!" Muntu inquired respectfully,

"Do you not also think always of money?" "Of course not!" I countered. "Then, mademoiselle, it is because, unlike us, you have enough." Touché!

The subtleties of a combined materialism and sentimentalism were gradually becoming clear to me. Muntu, not feeling well, started the long walk to the dispensary. He was soon brought back to the house, weak and feverish. Aspirin did not prevent his temperature from rising from 103° to 104° in half an hour. It was a bad moment for me. I had to assume it was malaria and gave him quinine. Fortunately, his temperature dropped rapidly after he took the quinine, and he stopped raving. Despite delirium, he was aware that I had sat by him until he was sleeping soundly. To me, it seemed natural to take care of him when he was ill. To him, it was a kindness about which he spoke to everyone, not only immediately after his recovery but repeatedly and until I left. I had proved that I was his *umuvyeyi*, his benevolent and loving parent.

In our evening talks, Muntu told me a little about his history. His father had not liked him, because he was not brave. He had never claimed his inheritance, though now that his father was old, he was thinking of going to ask for cows and lands. His parents had been divorced, but, like other boys, he was educated by his father. He had to learn how to care for cows, how to speak well, and how to behave toward his betters and his inferiors. His father sometimes sent him with the cows at night to use other men's pastures. This infringement of grazing rights resulted almost inevitably in night fighting with spears, swords, and knives. Muntu lacked spirit for the fights. He showed me the scar on his ankle, a souvenir of the spear his father hurled at him to teach him courage. He ran away to the Catholic mission where he began to learn many things—how to write, to wear Western clothes, to work in the kitchen. One day, he saw one of the fathers slap the face of a boy at the school. "Even at the school, they hit people for nothing." He ran away and found work as a kitchen helper in a private home. There again, he was oppressed by violence and repeatedly ran away from it.

Muntu's father figured in another source of unhappiness, his wife and children. In a country where divorce is frequent, he had been married to Maria for about twenty years. She was terribly jealous, though her own record for fidelity was not very good. She asked me on each return to Astrida whether Muntu had been carrying on with women. I could tell her truthfully that if he had been, I had seen nothing of it.

Muntu had fallen in love with Maria when he was 16 or 17—much below normal marriage age for Batutsi. She had already borne a child to a wandering Arab, but she was beautiful and passionate, and Muntu wanted her. His father objected to the marriage. They had the same clan name, and although there were no direct taboos, the old man was fearful. He consulted a seer, who warned that if Muntu married this woman, she would die, and he would have no children by her. Another woman was suggested, but Muntu refused her. Since his father would not, Muntu himself paid the brideprice for Maria. Several times he repeated the moral of the story: Maria has borne him eight children, of whom six were still alive. The woman his father wanted him to marry had died a few months after her marriage to another man. "That is why I cannot believe in the things that are said by our seers."

It was not a happy marriage. Muntu preferred safari work so that he would not have to be with Maria all the time. She, jealous and always without money, would not leave him but grew thin and unhappy when he was away. Worst of all, she was not bringing up the children properly. Muntu wept when he talked about his oldest daughter. At 15, a stately and beautiful Mututsi girl and fully mature, she was pregnant, but no man had paid for her. He had done so much for her, spending all his money and selling his cows to pay for curing her tuberculosis. He had obtained a scholarship for her to go to school and become educated in European things. Now she had done this. She was in love with a worthless fellow who had begotten children with other women, none of them paid for. He dared not scold her, for she might then run away to Congo or to Uganda and live out her life as a prostitute.

Muntu's oldest son, about 13 years old, was also a keen disappointment. A bright boy, he did not like school and wanted to go to work. It embittered Muntu. "My son is a fool. If I only had had his opportunity, I would not have to be a servant. I could be a clerk or a chief, something worthwhile." He took little comfort from the fact that other fathers the world over faced similar problems with their sons.

Muntu was hardly aware of the three other girls, still children. But the little boy, about 4 years old, really warmed his heart. The child resembled him closely and tagged along with him whenever he was back home in Astrida. Except for this little one, Muntu was a sad old man when he spoke of his children. Yet, usually, he kept a cheerful face and straight posture. As he himself said, one did not always have to think about these things, there were many other things to keep busy with.

The last few weeks of our stay at Mutumba had been difficult. We were all glad to spend December elsewhere. Stanislas went home to his wife and children, with a few texts to work on before the Christmas holiday. Muntu and I returned to Astrida. I left him on enforced vacation, while I spent a few weeks in Kitega studying documents and locating a new research site.

In January, just after the New Year, we went to Rusaka. There, the Batutsi herders far outnumbered the Bahutu farmers. There were many more cows than at Mutumba, and it was chilly and damp. The altitude was about 8500 feet, 2000 feet higher than at Mutumba. It was rainy season, and a fire had to be built in the large fireplace every night. Still, the Mutumba routine for field work and household affairs required very little adjustment to fit Rusaka. We were veterans, we were used to each other, and life was easy and pleasant. In short order, we established relations with the new neighbors and received visits and invitations from them.

The research in Rusaka completed in good order, we returned for the last time to Astrida in May, 1957. The final months there were devoted principally to the translation of texts and to work with I.R.S.A.C. researchers and in the library. There was a definite, conscious process of termination.

Thinking back to the times Muntu had been particularly difficult, I wondered whether I might not have been better off without him. It might have been better to have done without his intelligence and industry for the sake of freedom from his drinking sprees, his jealousies, and his bad temper. But I knew well before I left that I would for a long time be glad that I had known Muntu.

My freedom from all care about household matters was not to be dismissed lightly. The physical care Muntu took of me was not to be underrated. He was unusually scrupulous about the rules of hygiene in the bush. He did the cooking, the laundry, the ironing. When I was careless about my appearance, he would scold. "Mademoiselle, your hair is dirty; go and wash it." If the skirt I was wearing was shabby, he would tell me that it did not look well, that I should put it aside.

He was a very fatherly man in his good moments, and these were many.

Perhaps the most striking part of Muntu's service to me as an anthropologist resulted from his skill in handling people. He reassured the timid, persuaded the recalcitrant, chased away the merely greedy or curious. He was able to procure for me nearly any variety of informant and any kind of object for the museum of Urundi at Kitega. If I wanted to interview an old man who remembered about military organization in the old days, if I wanted to talk to several women about child-rearing, even if I wanted information from a curer or the neighborhood witch, Muntu knew how to get them for me.

For the museum, I wanted the old Arab trade beads I had seen on a shrewd and slightly mad old lady who prized them as amulets against eye disease. Muntu argued with her. "But look at your eyes! They are sick. [They were.] Let me give you good medicine [my boric acid solution] and some money, and you give me the beads." The beads are now in the museum at Kitega. Bracelets, shell ornaments, wooden milk pots, blacksmith's tools, and baskets came the same way. He was not always scrupulous, but he got me what I wanted and needed. His methods and motives perhaps would not stand up under close inspection, nor mine either. But moralizing seems inconsistent with the hard facts we had to deal with in the bush.

In Urundi, as a stranger, I learned what it is like to be pressured by society into appropriate behavior for a social role I did not choose. From Muntu, I learned what an old-fashioned, feudal personal relationship is like. Despite the strains and difficulties of cross-cultural communication, I discovered how important support and forgiveness are between friends living in an unfriendly environment. For a while at least, Muntu had come close to making a *mwamikazi* of me.

The initial sympathy between Muntu and me, lost for a while, returned before my research tour ended. With such different backgrounds and personalities, it is astonishing that we understood each other as well as we did. Muntu's understanding of me was keen. He had surely never read Freud, but he was an uncanny analyst of my actions and accidents, my considered opinions and slips of the tongue. We could not, however, agree about everything. I could not persuade him that my kitchen spices and the flowers in my garden were amenities and not the secret magic by which I, alone among all the whites he had ever known, had avoided becoming ill in the bush. He continued to believe that my curry powder and marigolds had protected me against malaria and dysentery. I could offer no better explanation than his good care and my good luck.

One other matter on which Muntu and I did not agree was the question of my weight. He, following the standards of his country, liked women to be plump. I, typical American, was most unhappy over the ten pounds I had gained on my starchy diet. He was genuinely upset when I spoke of putting off weight. People would think he had not taken good care of me, his wife would reproach him for ingratitude toward me, my brothers back home would be angry. I decided to wait until my departure from Urundi in July, 1957, before going on a diet. It was the least I could do before saying good-by to Muntu.

A Tiv Elder.

13

The Frightened Witch

Laura Bohannan

Most of the Tiv, whom it has been my fortune to know well, I have liked and respected. I could not like Shingir, and the respect that his abilities when sober, forced from me was greatly diminished by his behavior when drunk. Nevertheless, of all the 600-odd people in that particular lineage area, only one man, Anyam, was as able as Shingir and yet more sober in his habits. Anyam, however, was not wholly sane.

Furthermore, neither Shingir, nor the community of which he was the head, is typical, since a general terror of witchcraft is as rare in Tivland [1] as witches are common. The prevalence of witchcraft in Shingir's land was proven to the Tiv by the unusual prevalence there of serious illness. The virulence of the witchcraft, and the absence of any powerful men of good will, was proven to them by the unusually great number of deaths in the community. The insatiability of the witches was proven by the frequency of epidemics, mainly of smallpox, and the hate of the witches for each other by the fact that not even the most powerful escaped unscathed. Everyone was suspicious. Almost everyone was under suspicion. Everyone was afraid. Those who could went away. Those who stayed, drank too much and fell to quarrelling when they tried to joke. Their fear was obvious. All Tiv who saw it and who knew anything of the situation—as neighbors, traders, or visiting relatives—expressed both astonishment and a certain horror in speaking of it. It was also a situation that because of its very rarity attracted my interest.

[1] Tivland lies in the Northern Provinces of Nigeria, on both sides of the Benue River, some 140 miles from its confluence with the Niger, extending approximately from about 6°30′ N. to 8° N. and from 8° E. to 10°. There are about 800,000 Tiv, among whom there are surprisingly slight differences in language, manners, and custom from one to another of the eight lineage segments which compose the tribe. Perhaps the most important variations are the shifts, from south to north, of (1) high to low population density (from as much as 550 per square mile to as little as 25, or less, per square mile), and (2) of what may very loosely be described as the worldly sophistication of the south and the unpolished, unsecular north.

Twenty-eight months' field work among the Tiv between 1949–1953 was financed by the Social Science Research Council, The Wenner-Gren Foundation, the Colonial Social Science Research Council, and the Government of Nigeria, all of whom I wish to thank.

These same circumstances were also responsible for much of my interest in Shingir: the abnormality of the situation almost painfully focused the attention of his people upon him and his deadly rival Anyam. Unquestionably the most powerful two men in the community, and the most feared, everything they did was watched. People who knew Shingir well agreed on one point: he was a man grossly misjudged, whether for good or for ill, by the rest of the world. Therefore, I shall try to show him here as he was seen by four of the people most concerned with him: Ahuma, his crony; Anyam, his greatest enemy; Kusugh, his main heir; and Mfaga, his senior wife. Finally, because all these people were trying to influence me in my opinion of Shingir, I shall begin by sketching my own relationship with him.

Finding a good working site had been a fairly simple matter in the densely populated and relatively sophisticated areas of southern Tivland. In the north, it was rather more difficult.

"If you want to see all the old ceremonies, and find a lot of witches," Tiv from the southern and central lineages advised, "go down there. They still do all the things our grandfathers did, for they sit in the bush, away from everything that's happening." Close friends sometimes added, "They're dirty. They have no respect and no manners. You won't find anyone to talk to; they run away from Europeans—they don't know the mine recruiting stopped years ago. You wouldn't like it there."

Certainly people did disappear at the approach of a European and carriers. After a few days walking, I was immediately prejudiced in Shingir's favor because his was the first homestead that our arrival did not disrupt. Not only were Shingir's people there, they gathered around to look and talk. Shingir himself suggested a longer visit, and when I remarked that I was looking for a spot in which to settle and build some huts, for which I would pay, he made me welcome.

"Look at us," Shingir waved his hand round his homestead. "Some of our wives are even living in the storage huts." Indeed, there were 139 men, women and children crowded into the 41 huts that formed Shingir's homestead circle.

All Tiv homesteads form a series of concentric rings, usually circular but often oval or even irregular, to avoid a muddy depression or some other natural inconvenience. The outermost ring consists of the gardens devoted to tobacco, vegetables, and herbs for spice and medicine. Just within is the ring of storage huts, all round structures of mud with tall thatched roofs, some on stilts for grain, others low and half underground for the storage of yams and other root crops. Every married woman normally has her own granaries, located just behind her sleeping hut. These large round sleeping huts form the next ring, and every married woman with a child is entitled to one. Here she cooks. Here she and her children sleep. The innermost circle is formed by the reception huts, one to each married man, set just in front of the huts of his wives. Here he receives visitors, has ceremonies performed, and here too the whole family gathers on rainy days.

All these rings are concentric about a large open yard, preferably containing one or two large shade trees. In this yard men meet on important occasions, dances are held, story tellers perform on moonlit evenings, children play, and women gossip. It is the heart of the homestead. In this regard, Shingir's homestead was indeed an exception, for it faced in upon an evil-smelling corral occupied by Shingir's fifteen head of cattle. The people of his homestead had little space for themselves.

But no one did anything about it. None of the men was building a hut for his new wife, nor even repairing a tumble-down reception hut. Everyone agreed that the homestead must be moved, but no one could agree where to move it. It lay on the path up from the river, between two slight hills, a site that compressed the homestead into a rather narrow oval. It also lay too near the river. During the rains, the lower part of it, where Shingir's huts lay, was flooded and all of it became intolerably muddy. Shingir thought it would be quite enough if the homestead were gradually shifted uphill. He would start by building at the highest end, the rest would then follow suit until all were back in the same position relative to each other. Everyone else in the homestead wished to move away altogether. Since I wished to build just uphill from the rest of Shingir's homestead, almost precisely on his chosen spot, Shingir found my presence convenient. In the long run, I would have built his huts for him just where he wanted them.

Shingir had other reasons for making me welcome. As Native Authority head (or *taregh*, in Tiv) of a fairly large lineage segment, he felt obliged to entertain visiting Europeans. Some months later, after a beer drink, he confided that he felt himself in the administration's black books and wished me to give a good report of him. More immediately, he wanted medicine for himself and his people: the illness within Shingir's homestead, with its dirt and its cattle, was notorious even locally. The nearest dispensary was a day's walk by the direct route, passable only during the dry season. Even then, few people considered going there until they were too ill to walk. For all practical purposes they were without the benefit of so much as first aid which was all I could offer, but even that proved to be much in itself when babies sat down in fires, neglected sores ate down to the bone, and unwashed cuts became severely infected. Shingir found me useful. I found him a ritual expert, willing to give me a front seat at the many ceremonies he was called upon to perform and able to give me much information about what I had seen and he had done.

Nevertheless, our continued association proved a great strain on both of us. Shingir could never be sure I would be around to witness only his more commendable actions, nor, clearly, was he ever quite sure how to behave towards me. Sober, he vacillated irritatingly between sham servility and spurious bonhomie. Drunk—and during the height of the beer drinking season in the rains, he was customarily drunk five days out of seven—he bullied my servants, and, according to his mood, tried to bully me or to become overly familiar. Several times he tried to get me to drink with him from the same beer calabash, my mouth adjoining his, a Tiv indecency between man and woman.

My servants hated him, feared him, and profoundly respected his ceremonial knowledge, of which they frequently made use when they or their wives were ill. Like myself, they suffered from Shingir's lack of manners and from his inability to understand a hint. We all learned to eye Shingir's approach, to discover whether to welcome or avoid him. If his stocky, corpulent figure came straight towards my hut, if there was a slight stamp in his walk, if the large toga-like cloth which elders wear was decently in place, and if he leaned firmly on his spear, then I went to greet him. On such occasions he had come to tell me the news, to ask for medicine, to invite me to a ceremony, or to discuss with me the ritual of a ceremony he had just taken me to witness and the background of kinship and personalities against which it had taken place. On such occasions, I was grateful both to and for Shingir. I had known several elders who knew more about fetishes and their ritual, but none who could explain them as well.

Shingir did not, however, always come in this manner or for these purposes. As many as four or five days of the seven-day beer-brewing week, he was more than a little drunk by mid-morning. Then, when he stumbled slightly, when his toga swung open, when he held his spear like a yoke across his shoulders, and when the flesh on his face seemed to hang loose, I knew he would be overly familiar with me and extortionate in his demands to my servants. All of us would retreat behind closed doors, hoping that Shingir was merely following the path that led through our cluster of huts either in search of more beer or going home to sleep.

Whenever Shingir, drunk, made for the kitchen, a very few moments brought one of my servants to the door to ask me to rid them of Shingir. Shingir helped himself too freely to my supplies and to their belongings. I would go reluctantly. At the sight of me, Shingir would call out, "Can't you wait for me to come to your door?" and roar delightedly at his own jest. When he laughed, the wen on his neck between ear and chin, shook in its pendulous fold of flesh like a golf ball in jelly. With considerable difficulty—he was, after all, my host—I would pry him from my kitchen and see him home. I did not want Shingir to make my servants' life intolerable, nor did I want him handling my food and my cooking utensils. In addition to some sort of skin trouble, Shingir had gonorrhea, very common in Tivland. From the look of the sores he had showed me, I suspected that he had syphilis as well, rare as that disease is among a people who suffer yaws.

There were awkward moments with Shingir, but we were too useful to each other not to try to forget them as quickly as possible. Eventually, as he began to understand that I did not enjoy a carouse, he again turned to Ahuma in his more jovial moods and these difficulties occurred less frequently.

Shingir and Ahuma were boon companions and particular cronies. Both of them relished their food and their beer, showed the world a bluff and hearty face, and enjoyed the heat of shouted argument. Ahuma was also a knowledgeable elder, with a considerable command of ritual, which he was seldom asked to perform, and a shrewd man, whose shrewdness often just failed of its mark. He was consistently Shingir's ally, and occasionally, one of his greater embarrassments.

It was Shingir who had seen that Ahuma had been named tax collector. Ahuma's first collection coincided with a series of complaints that tax had been twice collected. A few people said that they had two sets of receipts to show for it, and turned them over to Shingir to keep until the District Officer came on tour. These receipts were accidentally eaten by a goat, and Shingir told the complainants that, in the absence of proof, it was no use even mentioning the affair to the District Officer. The victims retired to sulk, while the countryside laughed at their gullibility.

Ahuma's second collection showed no such irregularities. Unfortunately, he did not feel himself able to carry such a weight of pennies and shillings and changed the entire sum into paper money, which Shingir quite providentially had in his possession at that moment. Ahuma and the money fell into the river. Ahuma nearly drowned. The money had wholly disintegrated by the time the box containing it had been recovered. Shingir, who had witnessed this luckless event, supported Ahuma's tearful story to chief and administration. Nevertheless, Ahuma lost his job. In spite of this, however, there still clung to him the not inconsiderable prestige of having been tax collector. Certainly people felt, and Shingir frequently said, that Ahuma had reason to be grateful to him for the whole affair. Consequently, whenever Ahuma was discovered trying to conceal anything from Shingir, Shingir complained loudly over his friend's ingratitude, even while he showed how very much afraid he was that Ahuma might desert him for Anyam. This fear of treachery underlay Shingir's frequent rages at Ahuma, and his quite astounding willingness to swallow insult and trickery once he could surely attribute both to Ahuma's purely personal greed. I first saw this aspect of their relationship in the developments that followed one of the most elaborate series of rituals I had ever watched Shingir perform.

On this occasion the entire lineage in the person of its elders and homestead heads had been summoned to Ahuma's for the performance of curative ceremonies for one of his married daughters. Shingir, as the most influential elder with the command of the necessary fetishes, performed the ceremony. As part of the ritual, the sacrificial chickens are eaten by all the elders of the lineage who have control of those particular fetishes (*akombo,* in Tiv). In this case, there were eight such men, including Shingir. The rest of us were given a purely secular feast: yam porridge provided by the father's household, and meat provided by the girl's husband (who also furnished the chickens and money for the ceremony). Everyone thus has a strong interest in the generosity of the son-in-law; I have known the elders to veto such a ceremony until a larger animal had been provided for the feast. On this particular occasion, the goat paraded before us all could scarcely fail to please for it was large and fat. Nevertheless, the elders were slow to approve it. In Tivland many a man knows his neighbor's livestock and younger children equally well. This goat was Ahuma's, not a new one brought by the son-in-law. Ahuma, leaning across me to Shingir, announced in the stage whisper of politeness, "My son-in-law had no suitable animal. I sold him one. He brought the money." Everyone's face cleared, and the ceremony proceeded.

The next morning, Shingir went off to a beer party and returned within a bare half hour. Ahuma's half-brother had just whispered in his ear that the son-in-law had not merely brought money; he had brought a fat sow, far more valuable than the goat that Ahuma had foisted off on the elders. Shingir, angry at Ahuma for having tried to cheat him and half annoyed because it had been so poor an attempt, went after Ahuma while the men of his homestead searched for the pig.

Only Kusugh, Shingir's heir and his father's brother's son, stayed behind—to explain the event to me: Ahuma tries to do everything that Shingir has done, but "Ahuma bungles. Then Shingir is very angry and forces Ahuma to make reparation. When a fool does a wicked thing everyone can see that it is indeed evil, and then everyone remembers who else has committed such an act, and finds that act evil even when it was done by a clever man who made it seem well done at the time."

Kusugh looked around to make sure no one was listening. He never opposed Shingir publicly, though this was not the first time he had "explained" his actions to me. "You have heard of Ahuma and the tax money that was destroyed. He was a fool, and still has no money. How do you think he paid his witness? And what made Ahuma think of it? Shingir was once keeping some bank notes for someone; they fell into the fire and were burnt. But it was not very much money, and it was the money of a man without influence, not the government's."

Whatever Kusugh might have added was cut off by the noisy approach of the pig, reluctantly dragging at the end of a grass rope tugged by an excited youngster. It was soon followed by Shingir, Ahuma, and most of the elders who had been at the beer drink. Only Anyam was absent.

They paused in my courtyard. "This is the pig," Shingir accused, "that we should have eaten. It was brought to Ahuma for us, and he hid it. And where?" Shingir was angry now, and perturbed. "At Anyam's." It was to Anyam, Shingir's rival and his enemy, that Ahuma had apparently turned.

Ahuma recognized the issue. "Yes, I hid the pig, but I meant to send it across the river where you wouldn't find it. Not to Anyam's." He spoke with a rare sincerity that convinced us all. "Anyam met my son on the path; he took the pig from him, forcibly, and said he'd keep it for me. Where do I stand in this land? With you, Shingir? Or with Anyam? Let the boy tell you himself."

As Ahuma's son told in detail of his meeting with Anyam, Shingir grew slowly less tense. At the end of the story, he was relaxed enough to listen almost sympathetically to Ahuma's claim that the sow was about to farrow and therefore should not be slaughtered.

"Very well," said Shingir, "we will wait and see. Meanwhile, let the sow remain in the care of my senior wife, where we may all watch it. If there is no litter, we will eat the sow. If there is a litter, we will eat them all."

Ahuma shouted his claim to the litter, thereby conceding the sow, and a noisy argument followed it to its new quarters. It was uproar without acrimony. The two men were still allies, united against Anyam. To maintain that alliance, each would forgive the other much.

Anyam was Shingir's opposite in every respect: a small-boned man, tall and nervous, a clairvoyant, and in his youth a diviner. Everyone, my servants included, described his manner and appearance as that of Tiv in the time of their fathers. Anyam wore his hair in a short pigtail; his face was scarred with the old-fashioned raised welts, and he wore earrings that looked like black shoe buttons. He was a soft-spoken man, one who rarely drank or jested. He had command of even more fetishes than Shingir, and was considered his only rival in witchcraft. People who spoke of Shingir as a witch generally used the euphemism, "he knows things." Anyam was bluntly called a "man of *tsav*," when he was not outright dubbed "one of the *mbatsav*."

One cannot long speak about Tiv without speaking of *tsav*. In its most concrete form, *tsav* is a witchcraft substance on the heart, a fatty sac on the pericardium, the presence or absence of which may be established by a post-mortem operation. During a man's life, however, the presence of the substance, and hence the power of witchcraft, can only be assumed. It is so assumed wherever a man's fortunes and behavior reveal the ability, power, talent, and force of personality which both are *tsav* and manifestations of *tsav*.

Is a person in any way outstanding, if only as a singer, dancer, hunter? He has some *tsav*, though perhaps only a little. Is a man healthy, possessed of a large family and prosperous farms? He is a "man of *tsav*," or he could not have warded off the envy of others either in its physical or mystical expression. Is a man solitary? Are his dependents few and ill? Have there been many deaths in his family? Then he is either a victim of the *mbatsav*, who are the men of *tsav* joined together for good or evil, or, quite possibly he is himself one of the *mbatsav* and the cause of these misfortunes. Where fortune as well as misfortune, where the attainment of political and social influence as well as near-ostracism for abnormality of personality or of habit of life, where unusual affluence as well as unusual misery are all manifestations of the working of *tsav*, the only important questions can be whose *tsav*, to what degree, and to what end.

Tsav is effective volition. A man of *tsav* wills death, and the cause of death is his agent, be that cause disease, a falling tree, or a chance arrow. No one in Tivland dies a natural death, for it is considered "natural" for man to go on living. Death then is always due to witchcraft, and the funeral is largely concerned with establishing whose witchcraft and why. Usually the witch is found to be a man of prominence, hence certainly a man of *tsav*, who had a well-known grudge against the deceased. And here, as far as acts of the day are concerned, the matter rests. If any vengeance is taken, it is taken mystically, and appears only when the death of the witch or one of his relatives—of old age, illness, or whatever cause—is found at the funeral to have been willed by a relative of some victim of the witch.

A man of *tsav* may also will and effect the health and welfare of his land and his people. Here the fetishes (*akombo*) of the Tiv and his knowledge of their ritual are his agents. In a very narrow sense, these fetishes are magical forces, the emblems of which may be plants, stones, celts, corn cobs, almost anything. They are non-human forces, established at creation by the Heavens (*Aôndo*), which also gave the Tiv the means—ritual knowledge—and the power—*tsav*—to manipulated these forces. Neither *tsav* nor these forces are good or bad in themselves, though both are dangerous. They are ability and instrument; the moral quality attaches to their use.

Most of these fetishes, the "small fetishes," affect individuals. The great fetishes, on the other hand, affect the fertility, prosperity, and health of entire social groups. While the small fetishes, the minor magical forces, are maintained in full strength by sacrifices of chickens or goats and the concomitant performance of the appropriate ritual performed by a single man, the great fetishes demand the sacrifice of a human life and the performance of ritual by the men of *tsav* of the community concerned. Thus the world cannot prosper without death, and even in their approved role the *mbatsav* cause death. Thus, too, when a pleasant, wholly unimportant adult or a child dies when there are no obvious incidents that might have furnished motive for the death of that individual, then it is assumed that that individual was killed by the witches in concert as the wholly legitimate sacrifice to the great fetishes, the victims of which preferably are persons of minor social importance. But if there are too many such deaths, this explanation no longer serves.

Sometimes, for not all men are good or work together for the common benefit, the *mbatsav* engage in struggles for power. Then they kill not only for necessity and the land, but to weaken each other. Such a situation is "known" to exist when there is much illness in the land, when people die, and when eventually the land itself refuses to bear its crops. Then there is no remedy but to summon all the people of the land to drink sasswood that the evil may die.[2] Today, with this rather drastic social surgery effectively forbidden

---

[2] The bark of sasswood (*Erythrophleum guineense*) is highly poisonous, causing symptoms of depression of the circulation, difficulty of breathing, vomiting, and convulsions, the latter resulting from the direct action on the medulla centre. Drunk as an infusion, Tiv occasionally use it as medicine to cause convulsions, but only when they consider the alternative certain death (as for example to induce the afterbirth when it has not appeared thirty-six or forty-eight hours after birth). Its most common use was in ordeal, either individual or mass. In such ordeals, the innocent drink the infusion, vomit, and live; the guilty are unable to vomit and die.

by the British government, people can only run away or sit out the witches' feud to the end, until only one remains alive and master. This possibility is one of the great cautionary myths of the Tiv, usually told to remind the elders, as the *mbatsav* or witches, of the dangers of a warfare which leaves a land desolate and the conqueror without people. A few men say their grandfathers actually lived through such a battle. The people among whom I lived believed themselves in this situation; they labeled Anyam a witch interested in killing for his own ends, and gave Shingir the bare benefit of the doubt.

Yet, of the two, I found Anyam the more congenial, simply because he was reserved and quiet where Shingir was boisterous and apparently without self-restraint. On the other hand, Shingir could talk well and freely. Anyam would not converse. He would answer questions, and occasionally a direct question would set him off, propounding his views with near fanaticism. He was not a man with whom one could be at ease.

One day when I had found him alone in his reception hut hafting a dagger, nothing I could say drew more than a grunt from him. Nevertheless, since everyone else was drinking beer, I sat on determined to get at least a rest from my walk before I left. Eventually Anyam put aside his work and took up his pipe. I lit a cigarette and had all but finished it, still in silence, before Anyam had finished shredding tobacco and had tamped it into the pipe. As he scrabbled through the ashes for a coal, he spoke, "Once you asked me the names of all my ancestors and of all the children they begot. Where are they all?"

"You have said," I spoke cautiously, not sure to what Anyam was leading, "that your father's eldest brother's children left here, long ago, and are sitting in the bush."

Anyam made no response.

"The rest," I said rather blankly, "are dead."

A glow of hate lit Anyam's eyes and smouldered in his voice. "Dead. All of them. Even my mother's sons. Killed."

"Shingir?" I ventured.

"Shingir." In Anyam's mouth, the name was an expletive. "Shingir! Yes, but it was I, I who killed them, so that I might become great in the land. Like my father. While he lived, we had the greater power, and Shingir was afraid. Now that he is dead, Shingir is trying to kill me. Shingir has already killed those who came between him and what he desired. We have both killed that we may be strong. Now I can protect my own. Now I am as strong as Shingir, but Ahuma still fears. Soon all the land will know my strength."

Tsav is nourished by its exercise, or, in Tiv idiom, by the witch's feeding upon human flesh. Anyam was saying that he had fed his own power of witchcraft upon those under his control that it might quickly wax strong enough for him to turn it upon his enemy. In one sense, he had merely forestalled the death of his dependents at Shingir's hands, an alternative that would have left him just as deprived of followers but without any increment in his own strength as a witch. Nevertheless, Anyam's insistence that he himself killed by witchcraft was abnormal. Normally a Tiv always accuses someone else.

Anyam continued to explain himself. "You ought to know with what sort of man you are dealing. Shingir speaks with a double tongue that deceives many Europeans. I have thrown many times," he laid his hand on his divining apparatus, "and I see, though it is hard to tell about Europeans, that your heart is turned edgewise against Shingir, but that you have no grudge against me. We, the witches of this land, have not met by night since you came, and we shall not meet again until you go. That we decided when you came here. Yet the great owls are heard by night. [Anyam named the species of owl known to be one of the metamorphoses of the witches when they go to warn their victims] and since I have not gone out, it must be Shingir. You have the ability to bear this knowledge, and I want you to know the meaning of what happens in this land while you are here. Then, when you leave, you may tell the District Officer."

"It is useless to speak to the District Officer of witchcraft, Anyam. You know it."

"I know it," said Anyam. "If the Europeans of the government were men with hearts to understand these matters, they might make us all drink sasswood. But that they have forbidden. There is nothing to stop the witches now." The notion amused Anyam. "Tell them that Shingir eats the tax money, that he does not speak truly about the law cases from this land. Tell them of any of the matters to which they do not close their eyes and their ears, then you and I will soon be rid of Shingir. Once he no longer has the government's backing, I can swing the rest of the witches, whom he influences by day, and then I can kill him."

Anyam picked up his dagger and weighed it in his hand somberly. "Shingir plays the fool, drinking beer with the youngsters. He is a man of many quarrels, a noisy man, not one who discusses affairs slowly and quietly and heals the land. He is spoiling the land; he has killed my people, and I shall kill him. Help me in this, and you will do well."

Both Shingir and Anyam were feared as witches. But Anyam was also feared as one fears those who may suddenly become wholly mad. It was, I think, this fear that kept followers from him. Certainly, on the one occasion I saw Anyam publicly open in his enmity to Shingir, it was Shingir that we all followed.

It was at one of the beer drinks Anyam so rarely attended. When the second calabash started around, Shingir, mellow with beer, reminded us all that the well-being of his land and his people was his heart's only desire. He invariably did so, and everyone in earshot invariably made the proper response, chorusing, "You speak well, Shingir."

Before we could turn the conversation, Anyam's voice stopped us all. "Your land is spoiled, Shingir, and your people are dead. Where is Tar? Where is Ndor?"

Shingir was silent. The rest of us sat, not knowing where to look.

Anyam's catalogue of the dead was long, and, though he paused after each name, Shingir found nothing to say. When Anyam finally ceased, Shingir blundered from his seat, down the path out of the homestead, strangely deflated. After some moments we all followed him. Anyam was wrapt in meditation and seemed to want none and nothing of us. It was only later, much later, that Shingir began to roar about "that liar" and to regain firmness of flesh and feature.

Shingir was not widely credited with most of the dead Anyam had named. Yet, even to my knowledge, almost everyone believed that Shingir had killed the three men who had stood between himself and the homestead headship. Certainly those who would discuss such matters with me unanimously attributed the unhealthy state of the people in Shingir's homestead to Shingir's powers of witchcraft, and cited the situation as proof of a reign of fear. Nevertheless, there *were* people in Shingir's homestead, quite a lot of people. Indeed, it was one of the largest I have known in Tivland. Anyam's was nearly empty. The homesteads of "evil" witches are usually empty, and illness in the homestead testifies to their wickedness. Why, then, these people stayed was one of the great riddles of Shingir's position as a witch.

Kusugh, who would almost surely be Shingir's successor to the homestead headship, was during Shingir's lifetime, his right hand man. He was a smooth-skinned, well-spoken man in his late 40's, a man who was never quite in the foreground yet never quite overlooked. Shingir made great use of him, for Kusugh excelled in all practical arrangements, anything from getting a number of men out on the farms at about the same time to extracting further bride-wealth from penniless and goatless sons-in-law.

I had a great deal to do with Kusugh myself. If anything went wrong with my huts, or with supplies of food, water, and firewood, it was to Kusugh that I turned, and Kusugh always solved my difficulties. Many of the elders discussed their farms and their livestock with Kusugh. But no one ever asked his opinion on those matters that lay within the province of the elders, and Kusugh never volunteered any opinion on such matters. If anything of importance came up in Shingir's absence, he always followed the absolutely correct procedure: sooth everyone just enough to keep them from blows until the matter can be decided by the right person, Shingir.

I was never able to discover what Kusugh thought of Anyam. I very soon realized, however, that Kusugh both hated and feared Shingir, though at first I had few "facts" to support this impression: a single remark by Kusugh's wife, that she had once run away from Shingir's only to return when she discovered that Kusugh was "afraid to settle elsewhere," and my own awareness of how much of what I knew to Shingir's discredit was first learned from Kusugh.

It was Kusugh who had brought my full attention to Shingir's refusal to help Ugele, a man widely liked as a pleasant companion and respected as an industrious farmer. Ugele was one of those unfortunates who had been given curative doses of antimalarials while he was in the British army. Consequently, when he returned to his home, he was subject, as few adults among the Tiv are, to acute attacks of malaria. He was often quite seriously ill, and I had given him medicine, enough to break the fever. Shingir had flatly refused to prescribe any herbal remedies, to perform any ritual, or to have the cause of Ugele's illness investigated by a diviner. Such behavior could only mean that it was Shingir who was willing Ugele's illness.

It was Kusugh who had informed me that Agum, another member of the homestead and a great mimic and song-maker, used to hold Shingir up to ridicule in his songs. Traditionally such songs must avoid the libelous: they must be either true or impossible. Shingir had not really minded the song referring to what he did when he changed himself into a boar at night. No one can do such a thing. Moreover, the boar in the song was a most potent and aggressive animal. Shingir did object to the verses about burnt bank notes, sticking to his friends against the prosecution of the British government, and holding his tongue when provoked by Anyam. Worst of all, if common knowledge of the events and the occasion and manner of the singing hadn't plainly shown the satiric intent of the verses, one might have sworn they were meant as praise songs. There is no reason not to repeat praise songs, and since Agum's had good tunes, they were widely sung. After the death of Anyam's father, when Shingir became powerful in the land, Agum came down with smallpox and barely survived. From that time, Shingir was not mentioned in Agum's singing, "for the next time, Shingir will kill him." Smallpox is one of the most blatant manifestations of potent witchcraft. Public opinion concurred with Kusugh's interpretation of Agum's illness.

It was Kusugh who mentioned in the same breath that Shingir commanded the great fetishes which demand life and that too many of the children borne by the wives in the homestead had died. Uvia, Shingir's brother's son, was the only survivor of the ten children his mother had born. Infant mortality in Tivland is high. In Shingir's homestead it was so high that it attracted the attention of the Tiv. They considered it unnatural. Kusugh had even implied that Shingir had taken far more lives than he could possibly need unless he were involved in a flesh debt.

It is believed that witches sometimes share the flesh of their human victims in mystical feasts with other witches, generally of lesser power, who are then under obligation to return the feast. Once such a chain of indebtedness starts in a community, there is, and can be, no end to the deaths needed to continue the feasting, any more than there is ever an end to any of the chains of gift-giving and counterfeasting on any level. Such a situation is believed to exist whenever two features of every day life are prominent: when there are more deaths in a community than the normal rationale of witchcraft can satisfactorily explain, and when an unpopular man is able to impose his will on others and become very influential. Both these conditions certainly existed here. But I still could not see why the people did not adopt the usual Tiv remedy of going away and leaving the witch in isolation. A Tiv can always flee to his mother's people for protection.

I asked Kusugh. He turned, as though he had long been waiting for an opportunity to speak: "Our mother's kin *do not* protect us. Ugele's mother's people sent him back. Agum's mother's people sent him back. Uvia's mother's people sent him back. And mine made me return. All of us who are here have been sent back. That is how we know there is a flesh debt, and that is how we know where Shingir has his flesh debts. Through them he controls not only this land, but all those about us where otherwise we might find refuge. There is no escape for us. There is no escape for the land, for Anyam and Shingir are both killing us. Only if we, the younger men who are not witches, could rise up and force every elder in this land to drink sasswood, then it would end. And then the District Officer would kill us. Why were we here when you came? If you had come to take us to the mines, you would have taken us away from Anyam and Shingir. Why did we want you to stay? The witches would not meet at night while you were here. Why do we still want you to stay? Who of us has died since you came? Not one of us. But the land has been spoiled, and when you go we will die again, those of us who do not please Anyam and Shingir. Both men have killed to obtain power, nor will they cease to kill and kill—Anyam, until he holds this land in the palm of his hand, Shingir until he is able to hold the land undisputed."

Kusugh saw little hope for the land. He himself hoped to survive by doing as little as possible to attract envy while making himself necessary to those whom he feared. Most of the men in Shingir's homestead were pursuing the same course.

Only among the women was I able to find anyone with a real affection for Shingir. Some quality in his personality seemed to arouse in them a peculiar mixture of pity and trust, spiced with a suggestion of sexual attraction. Even Kusugh's wife did not dislike him. Those of Shingir's fifteen wives who had been with him for more than ten years were very fond of him. Although some of the younger ones seemed to prefer his absence to his presence, they all stuck by him.

In his turn, Shingir provided well for them; they had large farms, good clothes, and comparatively many trade utensils. He was indulgent with them, demanding rather less than the normal respect a Tiv wife shows her husband, not noticing if they drank too much, and not suspicious of their trips to visit relatives.

Shingir's senior wife, Mfaga, fussed over his food and worried about his health. Long after I had convinced Shingir that I could not cure his ailments, Mfaga continued to ask me to treat him. "He is ill. It is not because of his age that he can no longer beget children. Give me medicine for him, medicine to heal him, not just medicine for beer headaches." But I had only aspirin to give her.

"You cannot know Shingir," Mfaga once told me. "You have never seen him when he was not ill and afraid at heart. To know him, you should have known him long ago, when I bore him our first child. Then the land was at peace. Anyam's father was alive, and the land prospered. None then could hoe a farm so well as Shingir, nor dance so well. None was so well liked, and none so admired. Then, even then, Anyam, whose heart was black with envy of those who had farms, and livestock, and wives, and children, and friends, even then Anyam hated Shingir. We four who know him, we were married to him then, before Anyam's father died." She stared into the fortunate past.

"And when he died?"

"Then Anyam was free to do evil. He fed the evil within him on the lives that lay in the palm of his hand, his mother's sons and his father's. And so the land began its dying, and we began to know fear. Then, when the water came," she was speaking of the great smallpox epidemic, the marks of which were on children of 10, on adults, and in genealogies, "we, the people of Shingir also died. Kusugh said Shingir was killing us to feed his own power; he lied. I saw Shingir weep when his brothers died, and I know that Anyam was too much for him. I also was afraid, but it was not Shingir that I feared. Anyam! Anyam! Who gave Shingir that wen upon his neck? Who has made him unable to beget children? Do you know how fear can rot the heart of a man? And yet, with fear in his heart, he tries to protect us. There is death in the land, and war at night, but while Shingir yet lives we will remain. Look. Look out that door. In this homestead you can hear the voices of children and the laughter of women, smell the smell of cooking food, and hear the voices of men. But in Anyam's homestead there is nothing to hear; there is only silence."

Not long ago, I had a letter from one of my servants. He wanted some money for a goat for a ceremony for his second wife. At the end of the symptoms and the request came the news: "Taxes are spoiling the land, and there has been no rain for the crops, but everyone you know is alive and well. Except Shingir. Anyam was the stronger, and Shingir is dead."

I sent goat money by the next post, partly in memory of faithful service, partly because his wife's illness had begun during that most unhealthy season at Shingir's, and quite irrationally because Shingir was dead and I had never really liked him. I still don't like him, even in retrospect, though I wonder if I haven't wronged him. Aggressive, loud-mouthed, careless of his person, drunken, bluff in manner, and underhand in dealing—yes. But also a man trusted by his wives, though feared by his relatives. A man without friends, but capable of holding some followers and convives. Above all, a sick and frightened man who believed, as every Tiv there believed, that he was engaged in a deadly duel with a man evil at heart and strong in witchcraft. I find myself sorry for his land, sorry that it was Anyam who conquered.

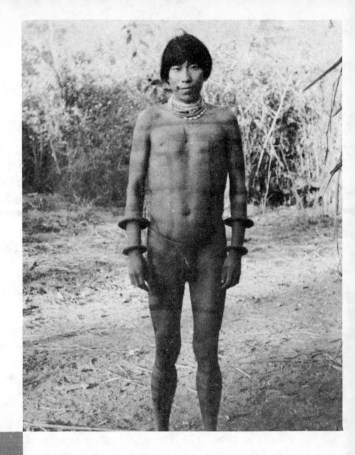

14

Champukwi of the Village of the Tapirs

Charles Wagley

Champuki was not the first person who came to mind when a contribution to this volume was considered. I thought of Gregorio Martin, a dignified and wise old Mayan Indian of Santiago Chimaltenango in Guatemala, who in 1937 had taught me the way of life of his people. I thought of Camirang, the dynamic young chieftain whom I had known in 1941 in a village of Tenetehara Indians along the Pindaré River in northeastern Brazil. I thought also of Nhunduca, a gifted and witty storyteller from a small Amazon community, who in 1948 introduced me to the rich folklore of the Amazon *caboclo* or peasant. But then, among all the people I had known in the various primitive and peasant cultures in which I have done ethnological research, I chose Champukwi, a man of no outstanding talent, yet talented all the same—a man of not the highest prestige in his society, yet admired by all. For the brief span of about a year he was my most intimate friend.

I knew Champukwi some 20 years ago when I lived in his small village of about 175 Tapirapé Indians in central Brazil. I must have seen him at once, for presents were distributed to the whole population on the day of my arrival in late April of 1939. But I did not distinguish Champukwi as an individual, nor did he, at first, stand out in any way from the other men of his village. His name does not appear in the notes taken during my first month among the Tapirapé.

For me, and even more for Valentim Gomes, the Brazilian frontiersman who was my companion and employee, the first weeks in the Village of the Tapirs, as the small settlement was known, were a period of grappling with a strange and often confusing world. The Tapirapé Indians lived between the Araguaia and Xingú Rivers, an area at that time almost entirely isolated from modern Brazil. They had been visited by only a few people from the "outside"— by one or two missionaries; by Herbert Baldus, a German-Brazilian anthropologist; and by a few frontiersmen from the Araguaia River. The nearest Brazilian settlement to the Village of the Tapirs was Furo de Pedra, a town of 400–500 persons that lay some 300 miles away on the Araguaia River. Three Tapirapé youths had spent a few months at mission stations and thus spoke a rudimentary form of Portuguese, using a vocabulary limited to a few basic nouns and verbs. At first our main problem was communication, but these youths were able to help us. Aside from them, the only individuals we knew by name during the first two weeks were the "captains," the older men who were the heads of the six large haypile-like houses arranged in a circular village pattern. These, we later learned, were each occupied by a matrilocal extended family. But even the personal names—such as Oprunxui, Wantanamu, Kamanare, Mariapawungo, Okané, and the like—were then hard to remember, let alone pronounce.

During the first weeks in the Village of Tapirs, I began to study intensively the Tapirapé language, a language belonging to the widespread Tupí-Guaraní stock. Until I could use this language at least passably, I was limited to observing and recording only those forms of Tapirapé culture that the eye could see. Even these usually needed explaining. I visited the extensive Tapirapé gardens in which manioc, beans, peanuts, cotton, and other native American crops were grown. I watched the women fabricate flour from both poisonous and "sweet" varieties of manioc, and make pots out of clay. I watched the men weave baskets out of palm fiber and manufacture their bows and arrows as they sat in hammocks in the large palm-thatched structure in the center of the village circle. This building was obviously the men's club, for no women ever entered. I rapidly became accustomed to nudity. The women wore nothing at all, and the men only a palm fiber band around the prepuce. But even nude women could be modestly seated, and the men were careful never to remove their palm band to expose the glans penis. Obvious also to the uninstructed eye was the fact that the Tapirapé expressed their personal vanity in the elaborate designs carefully painted on their bodies with *rucu* (red) and *genipa* (black). These and many other overt aspects of Tapirapé culture could be recorded in notes and photographs while I studied their language.

The Tapirapé, a friendly and humorous people, seemed rather pleased with the curious strangers in their midst. They found our antics amusing; the gales of laughter that accompanied the conversations that we could hear but not understand seemed evoked by tales of our strange behavior. (It is so easy to presume that oneself is the subject of conversation when listening to a strange language.) Then, of course, our presence was materially valuable—for the salt, knives, needles, beads, mirrors, and other presents we brought were greatly appreciated. However, within a very short time some of these people began to emerge as individuals. Awanchowa, a small boy of about 6, followed me about and literally haunted our little house, staring at our large bag of salt which he ate with the same relish children in other cultures eat sweets. Then there was Tanui, a woman of middle age (whose hair was cropped short indicating that a near relative had recently died) who often brought us presents of food. Gradually most of the villagers emerged as distinctive personalities and among them was Champukwi. I cannot remember when I first came to know him as an individual, but his name begins to appear regularly in my field notebooks about one month after our arrival. Soon, he became my best informant, and after a time, an inseparable companion.

In 1939 Champukwi must have been about 25 years of age. He was tall for a Tapirapé male, measuring perhaps about 5 feet 6 inches, strongly built but lean, and weighing, I should judge, about 150 lbs. Like all Tapirapé men he wore his hair in bangs across his forehead with a braided pigtail tied at the back of his neck. He was somewhat of a dandy, for his feet and the calves of his legs were painted bright red every evening with *rucu*. From time to time he painted an intricate design on his body, and he wore crocheted disc-like wrist ornaments of cotton string dyed red. He was obviously a man of some prestige among men of his age, for youths and younger men treated him with deference, always finding a seat for him on the bench that was built against one wall of our house. I soon learned that he, too, had spent a short period at a mission station several years earlier and that he knew a few words of Portuguese. He was married and had a daughter about 2 years of age. His wife, hardly attractive according to my American tastes, appeared to be somewhat older than he, and was pregnant when we first met.

Champukwi seemed more patient than other Tapirapé with my attempts to use his language and to seek information. He would repeat a word, a phrase, or a sentence several times so that I might write it down phonetically. He resorted to his meager Portuguese and even to mimicry to explain what was meant. His patience was of course requited by gifts of beads, hardware, and salt which I provided judiciously from time to time. After a few days, I began noting questions to be asked of Champukwi in the late afternoon when he now habitually visited our house. But this was the time that others also liked to visit. At this hour of the day our house was often crowded with men, women, children, and even pets—monkeys, parrots, and wild pigs—for which the Tapirapé along with other Brazilian tribes have an especial fondness. Such social gatherings were hardly conducive to the ethnological interview or even to the systematic recording of vocabulary. So I asked Champukwi if I might go with him to his garden. There, alternating between helping him cut brush from his garden site and sitting in the shade, I was able to conduct a kind of haphazard interview. Often, while he worked, I formulated questions in my halting Tapirapé and I was able by repetition to understand his answers. Although the Tapirapé villagers began to joke of Champukwi's new garden site as belonging to the two of us, these days were very valuable for my research.

Walking through the forest to and from Champukwi's garden, we often hunted for *jacu,* a large forest fowl rather like a chicken. I attempted to teach Champukwi how to use my .22 rifle, but he had difficulty understanding the gunsights and missed continually. He attempted to show me how to "see" the *jacu* hidden in the thick branches of the trees, but I seldom caught sight of the birds until they had flown. Thus, our complementary incapacities combined to make our hunting in the tropical forest quite unproductive, and in disgust Champukwi often resorted to his bow and arrow. Only later in the year, after he had practiced a great deal by shooting at tin cans did Champukwi master the use of the rifle, and this new-found skill greatly added to his prestige among the Tapirapé.

My abiding friendship with Champukwi perhaps really began when I came down with malaria about six weeks after our arrival. During the first few days of my illness, I was oblivious to my surroundings. I am told that while one *panché,* or medicine man, predicted my death, another tried to cure me by massage, by blowing tobacco smoke over my body, and by attempting to suck out the "object" that was causing the fever. Evidently his efforts—plus the atabrine tablets administered by Valentim Gomes—were successful, for my fever abated. I realized, however, that convalescence would be slow. Unable to leave the house for almost three weeks, I spent my days and evenings suspended in a large Brazilian hammock. In this state of enervation, I must have been the very picture of the languid white man in the tropics. Each late afternoon our house became a gathering place for the Tapirapé villagers, who came not only to visit with me (communication was still difficult) but also with each other, and to gaze upon the belongings of the *tori* (non-Indian). My illness proved to be a boon for ethnographic research. People were more patient with the sick anthropologist than with the well one. They told stories, not only for my benefit, but also to entertain each other. In attempting to explain to me about a mythological culture hero, a man would find himself telling a myth to the attending audience. Thus, I heard (and saw) Tapirapé stories told as they should be— as dramatic forms spoken with vivacity and replete with mimicry of the animals that are so often characters in these folktales. With my still imperfect knowledge of Tapirapé I inevitably lost the thread of the story and it had to be retold to me more slowly.

Champukwi was a frequent visitor during these days of my convalescence. He came each morning on the way to his garden and he became accustomed to drinking morning coffee with us. And, each late afternoon after he had returned from his garden, he came "to talk"—often slowly retelling the stories and incidents that I had difficulty understanding the evening before. Several days during this period he did not work in his garden but sat for two or three hours talking. He learned when he should pause or repeat a phrase or sentence in order that I might take notes. He came to understand what writing meant, discovering that what I wrote in my notebook I could repeat to him later. In time he appreciated the fact that I was not so much interested in learning the Tapirapé language as I was in comprehending the Tapirapé way of life. As so often is the case when a person understands and speaks a foreign language poorly, one communicates best with but a single person who is accustomed to one's mistakes and one's meager vocabulary. Thus, I could understand and make myself understood to Champukwi better than any other Tapirapé. Moreover, because he spent long hours in our house, he was learning Portuguese from Valentim Gomes, and this was an aid in helping me translate newly learned words and phrases in Tapirapé and even helped me understand his explanations of Tapirapé culture patterns. Champukwi thus consciously became my teacher, and others came to realize that he was teaching me. During the next two months we had daily sessions, some very brief and others lasting two or more hours.

In October of 1939, some six months after my arrival, I found it necessary to leave the Village of the Tapirs to go to Furo de Pedra for supplies and to collect mail that was held there for me. Valentim Gomes and I had come up the Tapirapé River, a tributary of the Araguaia, pulled by an outboard motor belonging to an anthropological colleague who had since returned to the United States. Now we had to paddle ourselves downstream. We could expect little help from the sluggish current and since the river was so low, it might be necessary to haul our canoe through shallows. Malaria had left me weak and I doubted that I was equal to this strenuous task. Several Tapirapé men, including Champukwi, were anxious to accompany us, but having Indians with us in Furo de Pedra was not advisable. First, they were susceptible to the common cold, which among relatively uncontaminated peoples such as these American aborigines often turns into a serious, and even fatal, disease. Second, unaccustomed to clothes, money, many foods, and other Brazilian customs and forms of etiquette, they would be totally dependent upon us during our stay in this frontier community. Nevertheless, the temptation to have my best informant with me during the trip and during our stay in Furo de Pedra was great and so we agreed to take Champukwi.

The trip was made slowly. Two good frontiersmen in a light canoe could have made it in three days, but we took eight. Champukwi was of little help in the canoe; unlike the riverine tribes the Tapirapé are a forest people who know little about the water, and few of them had ever traveled by canoe. Champukwi was unusual in that he could swim. Although he had more endurance than I, his efforts at paddling endangered the equilibrium of our canoe. However, he could shoot fish with his bow and arrow. The dry season had driven game from the open savanna which borders the Tapirapé River so that we were able to kill deer, *mutum* (another species of large forest fowl), and a wild goose to supplement the less palatable fare we had brought with us. Each night we camped on a beach from which we were able to collect the eggs of a small turtle, the *tracaja,* that had been buried in the sand. Only the mosquitoes which swarmed during sundown and early evening marred our trip. The experience remains one of the most memorable

Champukwi on the Trip to Furo de Pedra.

of my life, a feeling that was shared, I believe, by Valentim Gomes and by Champukwi.

Champukwi adjusted to Furo de Pedra with amazing rapidity. His short visit as a youth to the mission station undoubtedly contributed to his quick adaptation although, to be sure, there were minor problems and incidents. The Brazilians of Furo de Pedra were accustomed to Indians, for nearby there was a village of semi-civilized Caraja Indians who frequently visited and traded in the settlement. Yet, Champukwi was a bit of a curiosity—the townspeople had seen only one other Tapirapé. The local Brazilians invited him into their homes and offered him coffee and sweets. Both Valentim Gomes and I watched over his movements with all the anxiety of overprotective parents for fear that he might be exposed to a respiratory infection (he did not contract any) or that the hospitality of the local Brazilians might persuade him to drink *cachaça* (sugar cane *aguardiente*). Alcoholic beverages were unknown to the Tapirapé who are unlike most South American groups in this respect. According to Champukwi's own report, he tried *cachaça* only once in Furo de Pedra and (quite normally) found it distasteful and unpleasant. Yet there were moments that were awkward at the time however humorous they seem in retrospect. One day when I bought several dozen oranges in the street, Champukwi calmly removed the trousers that had been provided for him and made a sack to carry home the oranges by tying up the legs. In Furo de Pedra, he often went nude in the house we had rented for our stay. Even the Brazilian woman who came to prepare our meals became more or less accustomed to his nakedness, but sometimes he forgot to dress before sallying forth into the street. The rural Brazilian diét, derived in large measure from native Indian foods, seemed to please Champukwi, but he could not be comfortable eating at the table. He preferred during meals to sit across the room on a low stool.

Champukwi's reaction to this rural form of Brazilian civilization was not childlike in any way. He in turn became an ethnologist. He wanted to see the gardens that provided the food for so many people (Furo de Pedra had hardly more than 400 people at that time). He was fascinated by the sewing machines with which he saw the women working. He attended the Catholic ceremonies held in the little chapel. He saw pairs of men and women dance face to face in semblance of an intimate embrace. About these and other strange customs he had many questions. But like the inquisitive anthropologist who had come to live in his village, his own curiosity sometimes became obtrusive. He peered into the homes of people and sometimes entered uninvited. And he followed the Brazilian women to their rather isolated bathing spot in the Araguaia River to discover if there were any anatomical differences between these women and those in his village. He even made sexual advances to Brazilian women, actions which, if he had known, were very dangerous in view of the jealous zeal with which Brazilian males protect the honor of their wives and daughters. On the whole, however, Champukwi became quite a favorite of the local Brazilians during his two week visit to Furo de Pedra. His Portuguese improved while he visited in their homes, and he collected simple presents, such as fish hooks, bottles, tin cans, and the like, to take home with him. Even during this short period away from the village, my work with him continued. He told me of antagonisms, gossip, and schisms in the

Tapirapé village which he would have hesitated to relate on home grounds. He told me of adulterous affairs in process and of the growing determination among one group of kinsmen to assassinate Urukumu, the powerful medicine man, because they suspected him of performing death-dealing sorcery.

After two weeks in Furo de Pedra, I found that it would be necessary for Valentim Gomes and me to go to Rio de Janeiro. It was not possible for Champukwi to accompany us and so I arranged for two Brazilian frontiersmen to return him to a point on the Tapirapé River from which he could easily hike to his village in a day. Valentim and I then began our slow trip up the Araguaia River to the motor road and thence to Rio de Janeiro. Two months later, rid of malaria and with a new stock of supplies, we returned to spend the long rainy months from November until the end of May in the Village of the Tapirs. Champukwi was there to welcome us, and he came each day to help repair and enlarge our house. We easily fell into our former friendly relationship, now strengthened by the experience in common of the trip to Furo de Pedra and by the feeling which many anthropologists have shared with the people of their communities—that anyone who returns is an "old friend."

My return to the village that November marked, in a sense, the end of what might be called the first phase of my relationship with Champukwi as friend and as anthropological informant. During the course of at least 200 hours of conversation (many of which may be methodologically dignified as interviews), I had learned much about Champukwi as a person as well as about Tapirapé culture. I knew that as a small boy he had come from Fish Village, where his parents had died, to live in the Village of the Tapirs. He had lived with his father's younger brother, Kamaira, who was the leader of a large household. He even confided to me his boyhood name; Tapirapé change their names several times during their lifetimes and mention of a person's first childhood name, generally that of a fish, an animal, or simply descriptive of some personal characteristic, causes laughter among the audience and considerable embarrassment to the individual. I knew that Champukwi had been married before he took his current wife, and that his first wife had died in childbirth. He revealed that her kinsmen had gossiped that her death was caused by his lack of respect for the food taboos imposed upon an expectant father. This same set of taboos now bothered him again. A series of foods, mainly meats and particularly venison, is prohibited to fathers of infants and to husbands of pregnant women. On two excursions to the savanna (which abounds with deer) Champukwi had eaten venison. Moreover, since the Tapirapé identified cattle with deer, and thus beef with venison, he had broken the taboo several additional times by partaking also of this forbidden meat. The rather scrawny conditon of his 2-year-old daughter, he feared, resulted from his faults. Just after our return to the village in early November, his wife gave birth to a second daughter. She had a difficult delivery, and he remembered his transgressions. Several village gossips, without knowing anything about his misdeeds, had nevertheless accused him of this breach of taboo.

Champukwi's home life was not a happy one. He was frequently in conflict with his second wife, who had, indeed, considerable basis for complaint. She could not claim that he was a poor provider, for Champukwi was a good hunter and a diligent gardener. But he confided to me that he did not find her attractive, or at least not as attractive as other women in the village. Champukwi had a lusty sense of humor and enjoyed joking with Valentim and me. In this mood he told of his many extramarital affairs, which were in truth but slightly concealed. I would in any event have heard of these liaisons; he gave his paramours beads which everyone in the village knew I had given him as presents. This practice caused trouble for the women because their husbands could readily identify the source of the gifts. It also created trouble for Champukwi at home. His wife complained of his affairs and on one occasion, according to Champukwi, she attacked him, grabbing him by his pigtail and squeezing his exposed testicles until he fell helpless into a hammock. On other occasions, she retaliated in a manner more usual for a Tapirapé woman—she simply refused to carry drinking water from the creek, to cook food for him, and to allow him to sleep in the hammock which she and Champukwi shared. For a Tapirapé man to carry drinking water, to cook, or to sleep on a mat is considered ridiculously funny. In other circumstances, Champukwi would have had to seek recourse with a female relative. However, to do so would be tantamount to a public announcement of his marital difficulties; the whole village would have known, to their considerable merriment and jest. But having *tori* friends in the village, Champukwi could come quietly to us at night to drink water, to ask for something to eat, and even to sleep in an extra hammock we had for visitors. His affairs were evidently extensive, for he once divided all of the adult women of the village into two categories—those "I know how to talk with" (i.e., to seduce) and those "I do not know how to talk with." There were many with whom he "could talk."

Unfortunately, by late November of 1939, I knew too much about Champukwi's affairs either for his comfort or for mine. His wife sometimes came to my house to ask if I knew where he had gone (I could generally guess), and once an irate husband even came to inquire of his whereabouts. His Don Juan activities had evidently increased. His friendship with me caused him trouble with other Tapirapé who were envious of the presents he received. The story was circulated that he had stolen a pair of scissors which, in fact, I had given to him. Moreover, several people caught colds, and he was accused of bringing the infection from Furo de Pedra (actually it was probably transmitted by the frontiersman who had helped transport us to the village in November). Champukwi sought revenge by cutting down one of the main supports of the men's house, which promptly caved in. No one died or was seriously injured and the destruction of the men's house was soon forgotten since it is normally rebuilt each year. However, people continued to criticize Champukwi, much of their criticism revolving around his relationship with me. There are no realms of esoteric secrets in Tapirapé culture (as there are in many cultures) that must not be revealed to an outsider; there is only the "secret" of the men from the women that the masked dancers are not supernatural beings but merely masquerading men, but I had been fully and openly brought into this "secret." I was, moreover, exceedingly careful in conversation never to refer to any bit of personal information that some informant, Champukwi or another, had told me. But rumors were rife in the small village—that I was angry and would soon leave (I was by then a valuable asset), that Champukwi told me lies about others, that I refused to give a bushknife to a household leader because Champukwi had urged me not to do so (I refused because I had already given him one bushknife), and the like.

Champukwi reacted moodily, often violently, to this situation. I could no longer count on his visits nor on our research interviews. He now visited us with a glum look on his face, and when he was not at once offered coffee, he left offended. But the very next day he might return, gay and joking, yet without his former patience for teaching or explaining Tapirapé culture. Once he returned tired from a hunting trip, and, irritated by his wife, he beat her with the flat side of his bushknife and marched off in anger, thoughtfully taking the family hammock and a basket of manioc flour, to sleep four nights in the forest near his garden. Soon afterwards, he left his wife to take the wife of a younger man. This did not become a major scandal in the village. After some tense yet calm words between the two men, it seemed clear that the young woman preferred Champukwi and the abandoned husband peacefully moved into the men's house. Champukwi's former wife and their two young daughters continued to live with her relatives as is the Tapirapé rule. But the switch of spouses caused tension between Champukwi and his former wife's kinsmen, and between Champukwi and the abandoned husband's kinsmen; and, to multiply his woes, he now had a new set of in-laws to satisfy. For about a month thereafter I rarely saw Champukwi; he obviously avoided our house. When we met in the village or in the men's house, he simply said that he was busy repairing his house or hunting.

Discussing emotions with someone from a culture as widely different as Tapirapé is from my own was difficult, and the language barrier was still a real one. Although my Tapirapé vocabulary was increasing, it was hardly adequate to probe deeply into emotional responses; nor was Champukwi given to introspection. I shall probably never fully understand Champukwi's temporary rejection of me, but the cause was probably both sociological and psychological. First, his apparent influence with me and our close friendship had created antagonism on the part of other villagers. By rejecting the outsider, he now hoped to reinstate himself in his own society. A second, deeper and more personal reason, contributed to his rejection of me; he had told me too much about himself, and feared that he had lost face in the process. Also, it was obvious that I was growing less dependent upon him for knowledge as my facility with the language improved and my information about the culture grew. Finally, the rejection was not one-sided. Now additional informants were desirable for my research. Also, if I remember correctly (it is not stated in my notebooks), I was annoyed by Champukwi's neglect and disappointed by his lack of loyalty.

When the heavy rains of late December and January set in, we were all more or less confined to the village as the rivers and streams rose to flood the savanna. What had been brooks in the tropical forest became wide streams, difficult, and sometimes dangerous, to ford. It rained many hours each day. The Tapirapé women and children spent most of the time in their dwellings, and the men and older boys lounged in the men's house. Our house again became a meeting place. And as this was of course an opportune time for interviewing, I joined the men in their club or entertained visitors at home. I began to see more of Champukwi—first, in the men's house and then as he again became a regular visitor at our house. Now, he brought his new (and younger) wife with him. He liked to sit up with us late at night after the other Tapirapé visitors had retired to their dwellings or to the men's house for the night-long sings that are customary during the season of heavy rains. Under the light of our gasoline lamp, we again took up our study of Tapirapé culture. Not once did he mention his period of antagonism except to complain that the Tapirapé gossip too much.

Sometime late in January there began what might be considered the second phase of my relationship with Champukwi. Our friendship was no less intimate than before, but our conversations and more formal interviews were not now as frequent. During the next months, Champukwi became almost my assistant, an entrepreneur of Tapirapé culture. He continued to provide invaluable information, but when I became interested in a subject of which he knew little, he would recommend that I talk to someone else. Though he directed me to Urukumu on the subject of medicine men or shamans, Champukwi himself related dreams he had heard other shamans tell. He explained that he did not want to become a shaman himself, for he had seen grieved relatives beat out the brains of Tapirapé shamans whom they suspected of causing a death by sorcery. He was not certain, he said, whether such shamans had actually performed sorcery; but he reasoned that any shaman might come to such an end. Champukwi did have the frequent dreams that are indicative of one's powers to become a shaman and, in some of his dreams, he saw *anchunga,* the ghosts and supernaturals who are the aids of shamans. He had told only one or two of his kinsmen about this, and he did not want it to be known throughout the village lest there be pressure on him to train for shamanism.

Champukwi sketched for me the stories of Petura, the Tapirapé ancestral hero who stole fire from the King Vulture, daylight from the night owl, *genipa* (used for dye) from the monkeys, and other items for the Tapirapé. However, he persuaded Maeumi, an elder famous for his knowledge of mythology, to relate the details although he himself helped considerably to clarify for me the meaning of native phrases and to make the stories told by Maeumi more fully understandable. Champukwi also forewarned me of events that I might want to witness, events that without his warning I might have missed. Such were the wrestling matches which took place upon the return of a hunting party between those men who went on the hunt and those who remained at home. He told me of a particularly handsome basket a man had made, which I might want to add to my collection for the Brazilian National Museum. He came to tell me that a young woman in a neighboring house was in labor, thus enabling me to get a photograph of the newborn infant being washed in the stream, and he urged the men to celebrate for my benefit a ceremony which might easily have been omitted. Champukwi was no longer merely an informant. He became a participant in ethnographic research although, of course, he never thought of it in these terms. He seemed somehow to understand the anthropologist's task in studying his culture, and in the process he gained considerable objectivity about his own way of life.

Yet it must be said that Champukwi did not seem to discredit the norms, institutions, and beliefs of his own people. Although he saw Valentim and me walk safely down the path through the forest late at night, he steadfastly refused to do the same; for the path was a favorite haunt of the lonely ghosts of deceased Tapirapé who might harm the living. He reasoned that the *tori* were probably immune to this danger. When he was ill, he took the pills we urged upon him but he also called in the shaman. His curiosity about airplanes, automobiles, and "gigantic canoes" (passenger boats) which he saw pictured in the magazines we had brought with us, was great; but he boasted that the Tapirapé could walk farther and faster than any *tori* or even the Caraja (who are a canoe people). In fact, his interest in, and enthusiasm for, certain Tapirapé activities seemed to be heightened by our presence. Almost all Tapirapé ceremonials involve choral singing and Champukwi was a singing leader of one of the sections of the men's societies. He was always pleased when we came to listen, particularly if we made the motions of joining in. He was an excellent wrestler in Tapirapé style, in which each opponent takes a firm grip on the pigtail of the other and attempts to throw him to the ground by tripping. Our wrestling match was brief although I was much taller than he; and his match with Valentim Gomes, who outweighed him by more than forty pounds, was a draw. Unlike so many who get a glimpse at a seemingly "superior" cultural world, Champukwi never became dissatisfied with his own way of life.

In June of 1940, my period of residence among the Tapirapé Indians ended. The waters on the savanna which had to be crossed afoot to get to the Tapirapé River where our canoe was moored had not completely receded. Many Tapirapé friends, among them Champukwi, offered to carry our baggage, made lighter after a final distribution of gifts, down to the river. The night before our departure a festival with the usual songfest was held to celebrate the final phase of a ceremony during which a youth, this time the nephew of Kamiraho, became a man. Some Brazilian tribes make this occasion an ordeal by such means as applying a frame of stinging wasps to the body of the novice, but it is characteristic of the Tapirapé that the "ordeal" consists only of decorating the youth with a headdress of magnificent red macaw feathers, painting his body elaborately, and making him the center of dancing and singing—although the youth must himself dance continuously for a day and a night. Champukwi led the singing most of the night, but at dawn he came to our house to supervise the packing of our belongings into the basketlike cases made of palm which are used for carrying loads of any kind. He divided the baggage among the younger men. Even some of the older household leaders decided to accompany us but they, of course, did not carry anything. Our trip was slow because everyone was tired after the all-night festival and because of the water through which we had to wade. At one point, rafts had to be made to transport our baggage across a still-swollen stream. Since the Tapirapé do not swim—or, like Champukwi, they swim but poorly—it was the job of the *tori* to swim and push the rafts. I had the honor of swimming across the stream, pushing the respected chieftain, Kamiraho. (How he got back, I shall never know.) After a day and a half, we reached the landing on the Tapirapé River, and the next morning we embarked downriver. My last memory of Champukwi was of him standing on the bank waving in *tori* style until our boat made the curve of the river.

I did not return to visit the Tapirapé until 1953, but news of them came to me at intervals. Valentim Gomes returned to the region in 1941 as an officer of the Brazilian Indian Service, and his post was charged with the protection of the Tapirapé Indians. In his first year in this capacity, he wrote me: "I report that I was in the village of the Tapirapé on the 26th of July [1941]. They were in good health and there were plenty of garden products such as manioc, yams, peanuts, and the like. There were plenty of bananas. But I am sorry to say that after we left them, twenty-nine adults and a few children have died. Fifteen women and fourteen men died. Among those who died was Champukwi, the best informant in the village, and our best friend." Several slow exchanges of letters brought further details from Valentim. In some manner, perhaps through a visit from a Brazilian frontiersman, several Tapirapé had contracted common colds. Its fatalness to them is indicated by the name they give it—*ó-ó* (*ó* is the augmentative which might be translated as "big, big"). Since they have no knowledge of the process of contagion and have not acquired immunity to the common cold, the disease spread rapidly throughout the village. The Tapirapé realized, I knew, that colds and other diseases such as measles which they had suffered before, were derived from visitors. Yet they also believed that death resulted from evil magic or sorcery. Why do some people who are very sick from colds get well, they asked, while others who are no more ill, soon die? It is only because those who die are the victims of sorcery, they had explained to me. So, following many deaths, including that of a young man like Champukwi, who enjoyed prestige and had many kinsmen, I was not surprised to learn from Valentim Gomes that the powerful shaman, Urukumu, had been assassinated. As Champukwi had told me, suspicion of Urukumu had already been growing even during my residence in the village. After the death of Champukwi, one of his many "brothers" (actually a cousin but called by the same term as brother in Tapirapé) had entered Urukumu's house late at night and clubbed him to death. To the Tapirapé, grief and anger are closely related emotions and there is one word, *iwúterahú,* that describes either or both states of mind. Thus in both word and deed grief can be quickly transformed into vengeful anger.

In 1953, when I returned to the Araguaia River, I found only fifty persons, the remnants of the Tapirapé tribe, settled under the protection of the Brazilian Indian Service in a small village near the mouth of the Tapirapé River. My old companion, Valentim Gomes, was the Indian officer in charge. The history of the intervening years had been a tragic story; the Tapirapé had suffered steady depopulation from imported diseases and they had been attacked by the warlike and hostile Kayapo tribe, who had burned their village and carried off several younger women. They had been forced to leave their own territory to seek the protection of the Indian Service, and then cattle ranchers encroached upon the Tapirapé savannas, once rich with game. Champukwi was but one of the many victims of this disintegration of Tapirapé society. Upon my arrival several of Champukwi's surviving relatives met me with the traditional "welcome of tears"; to the Tapirapé, such a return mixes emotions of joy at seeing an old friend with the sadness of the memory of those who have died during the interim. Both the sadness and the joy are expressed almost ritually by crying. People spoke sympathetically to me of the loss of my friend and they brought a young man, who had been but a small boy in 1940, but who was now known as Champukwi. This boy had visited for many months, and had even studied a little, with the Dominican missionaries on the lower Araguaia River; he therefore spoke Portuguese well. He remembered my friendship with his namesake and perhaps felt, as I did, some strange bond between us. So again for a few days the name of Champukwi was entered into my notebook as my source of information on Tapirapé culture.

In the security of our studies and in the classroom, we claim that anthropology is a social science in which regularities of human behavior and of social systems are studied. But, at its source, in the midst of the people with whom the anthropologist lives and works, field research involves the practice of an art in which emotions, subjective attitudes and reactions, and undoubtedly subconscious motivations participate. Of course, the well-trained anthropologist takes all possible precautions to be objective and to maintain a detached attitude. He gathers information from a "cross section" of the population—from a variety of informants selected for their different status positions in their society. He interviews, as far as is possible, men and women, young and old, rich and poor, individuals of high and low status, so that his picture of the culture may not be distorted. The anthropologist might (he seldom has done so) go so far as to keep a record of his subjective reactions in an attempt to achieve greater objectivity. Yet he is never the entirely detached observer he may fancy himself to be—nor am I sure that this should be so. Anthropological field research is a profoundly human endeavor. Faced over a long period by a number of individuals, some intelligent and some slow, some gay and some dour, some placid and some irritable, the anthropologist almost inevitably is involved in a complex set of human relations among another people just as he is by virtue of his membership in his own society. And each anthropologist is a distinctive personality and each undoubtedly handles in his own way his dual role as a sympathetic friend to key informants and as a scientific observer of a society and culture which is not his own. To me, Champukwi was, above all, a friend whom I shall remember always with warm affection.

15

Ohnainewk,
Eskimo Hunter

Edmund Carpenter

The RCMP constable's wire was brief: "OHNAINEWK DIED JANUARY 29, 1954. TOWTOONGIE HAS THE BOAT." In the end, the boat, not the man, mattered.

Months later, at a trading post, I heard the details of his death. The whites sat around, familiarly discussing a man they had shunned in life. His marriages and their failures, his troubles with the traders, were all described, not from his point of view, but from the point of view of strangers. His association with the evangelist was sneered at. There was not one hint that he was strong and brilliant and complex, and (more exasperating still) not one hint that he was Eskimo.

Yet he was the reincarnation of a mighty Eskimo. At birth his identity was never in doubt: Ohnainewk, deceased hunter whose exploits figured in many tales, was once more among the living.

The first test of his inherited powers came early. Late one spring, while still a child, he was playing just off shore, jumping from ice-cake to ice-cake, when he fell in. Afraid to go to his mother, he stayed out until nearly frozen, and reached home only with the help of an older boy. There he lay, scarcely able to eat, his flesh rubbed raw where bones protruded, until snow once more covered the ground. An old woman shaman, an *angakok,* who had insisted that he eat only from his own vessel, forbidden to others, promised that Ohnainewk himself would be a great *angakok* if he recovered. For months he lay in a semicoma. Often, just before he dropped back into unconsciousness, a recurrent dream possessed him. The tent shook and swelled to astronomical size, billowing out at two corners to reveal the flat, endless tundra. Then one day, after he had recovered sufficiently to get up and about, he entered, by accident, an isolated igloo constructed for a woman recovering from childbirth. The igloo was taboo, for it was believed that such women were full of smoke, blinding to an *angakok's* spiritual eye, and that any male who interrupted their seclusion would die.

That night the familiar trance occurred to Ohnainewk, but instead of flat ground, rushing waves swept the new mother along and finally drowned her. In the morning his parents, hoping to save him from the consequences of the broken taboo, fled with him in their whale-boat. But before they had cleared the harbor, they were overtaken by a hunter in a kayak who told them that the woman had died in her sleep. Then all knew that Ohnainewk enjoyed the protection of a powerful spirit-helper.

A year passed before the dream recurred. His mother had just quarreled with an *angakok* who, in retaliation, tried to kill Ohnainewk by psychic means. Again in his dream the placid sea turned to storm, while above it, swaying over boiling waters, stood the vengeful *angakok*. That night, in real life, the *angakok* publicly confessed and Ohnainewk emerged unharmed.

But the conflict wasn't resolved until several years later when he and another boy encountered this man in caribou country. They traveled with many dogs; he had but three and asked to borrow several. Ohnainewk consented, but arrogantly, at which the older man burst out, as he threateningly advanced: "There is one here without relatives, but he does not fear you! You have no children. So! You lose your power to kill!"

Ohnainewk mocked him, but that year he killed no caribou. One day, seeing two, he took off his parka and ran forward to fire prone from close range, but just as he was about to pull the trigger, the snow squeaked under his elbow, and the caribou jumped. When he fired, only the primer went off and the ejected cartridge exploded in his face. The next cartridge did the same. Then he sprang up, and fired in all directions shouting, "What power prevents me?" From far to the south came the "thunk" of a bullet striking flesh, and a puff of smoke appeared.

Delirious, he staggered home where his parents laid him out and fastening a cord about his head, began the rite of head-raising. He was to answer "No" if his head were raised with ease, "Yes" if it were held by an unseen power. When he answered "Yes," a spirit's voice spoke, saying it was the work of the *angakok,* but that he was now dead.

Ohnainewk rose and killed three caribou and never again had difficulty hunting deer. For that very day, as they all later learned, the *angakok,* who had been traveling far to the south, dropped dead and his family all starved.

Why, Ohnainewk wondered, when he had such powers, had his last two wives betrayed him—worse, betrayed him to the inferior Ookpuktowk, one of them deserting him for Ookpuktowk, the second arranging it so that when he entered his igloo, he would find Ookpuktowk on top of her. Why had they scorned him so? This question troubled him and racked him and would not let him sleep at night.

An outsider, knowing Ookpuktowk, might have guessed. For Ookpuktowk was an ardent progressive, cherishing everything Western with extravagant ardor, revelling in being as un-Eskimo as possible, even getting the trader's daughter with child. By studying white men with care, he managed to make himself into an eager assistant who, if he did not succeed in winning Eskimo friends, succeeded in impressing many with suggestions of power. He lived at the Trading Post, parading his alien attachments, a man driven to torment himself by a desire to succeed in the eyes of others, even though this meant being subservient to the whites.

Ohnainewk could never bring himself to do this. No matter how much he wanted to fit into this new society, to make friends with the whites, he could do so only as Ohnainewk, mighty hunter, and this they would not let him do. He had a better head than any of them, and a better heart than most. He was friendly but never servile and he resented their constant rudeness. In silence he quit a position with the Hudson's Bay Company when he was given only menial, degrading tasks. He hoped the Anglican Church would appoint him a lay catechist, but it found no room for his talents. And when the government nurse—a woman—ignored his offer to take penicillin to a distant camp and closed the door in irritation, leaving him in the dark cold, that was too much: "One will go from this place to a cleaner land."

The land he chose was a barren peninsula, largely comfortless and desolate. The endless tundra, stretching from sea to horizon, had an austere, monotonous charm, a certain cold, clean-edged beauty. Yet throughout it was hard on man.

Here in this wind-swept land, cut off from the surrounding world by ice-filled seas and trackless wastes, Ohnainewk's family and those of his elder sons, forty-two people in all, lived their own lives largely untouched by outside influences. They not only depended upon game for all of life's necessities, but they had the hunter's outlook on the world. Their food was meat, much of it eaten raw, and they dressed in the skins of beasts.

Their camp stood beside a river gorge, overlooking the sea, in a landscape of infernal grandeur. Years later, after Ohnainewk's death, I revisited the spot. The peat-stone igloos were now but stumps, half-strangled with lichens and grass, indistinguishable from ancient ruins. Ice in their centers imprisoned ivory tools made by Ohnainewk and his sons, as well as the stone lamps that had once heated these tiny homes. To the south, hunters robed in fur passed on sleds with silent gliding motion over ice-fields that here and there were stained with blood. It was a scene that had not changed since man first reached this island.

As I stood over the ruins of the igloo where Ohnainewk had lived, it seemed incredible that a family could have wintered in so small a space, yet eight of us had. And there were gay times, especially when bellies were full. He and his sons were true hunters: their greatest delight was the chase. It was a life of constant adventure. They realized this and admitted it, and it was this element of the lottery that attached them to their calling. In the long run they were always hungry, but a tremendous kill made them full for the day, giving them a taste of opulence unsoured by satiety.

It was then that stories were told. With subtle gestures and a dramatist's timing, Ohnainewk took over. He usually began with the crisis, so to speak, and wove backwards and forwards in time, with many omissions and repetitions, his accounts so full of digressions the plots starved while he pursued each passing irrelevant fancy. He once told how he had seen a white bear and a red bear, and chose to pursue the former, which, of course, turned out to be the wrong choice, but we never heard why the other bear was red.

He delighted in recitation, and the genius of the Eskimo language, which is highly expressive, full of onomatopoeic effects, favored him. He used hierarchic expressions: "The man his son," and he could say "bear" in such a way that we were awed as if in the presence of some wondrous ursine power. Statements often began with a *non sequitur,* best translated "So . . . ," used not as a conjunction but as a magic conclusion that had no logical reference to the preceding statement. He spoke only of things we could touch and see, constantly choosing the concrete word, in phrase after phrase, forcing us to touch and see. No speaker so insistently taught the general through the particular. He had mastery over the definite, detailed, particular, visualized image. But the mythic abstract air of the telling blurred the sharp contours of these images, the has-been and the to-be became the now, and particular places, particular people, faded as he recited his litany of the great mysteries—birth, death, famine, water, sky.

He was a brooding, inwardly unquiet man. When bad weather prevented hunting and all went hungry, he and his family sat silently for days, humble in the face of immutable reality. Faced with life which *was,* despite themselves, which they had to accept without question, they hung their heads: *ayongnermut,* "It cannot be helped." Ill, they made little effort to recover, but silently withdrew, resigned to death. When a new-born child was put aside because of insufficient food: *ayongnermut,* "It is our destiny." When asked about the future: *ahmi,* "It cannot be known." When a crack in the ice widened, separating a hunter from his companions, marooning him on an ice-cake where, days later, he must freeze: *ayongnermukput,* "It will not be otherwise," and an old woman began the chant, "Say tell me now, was life so good on earth?"

Death was everywhere. Sealing and walrus hunting might fail; the ice might break up suddenly and go adrift with the sled traveler; a walrus might drag both kayak and hunter down into the depth. Therefore they saw life as a thing of little account, a little thing to give; and if life seemed harder than death, it was a little thing to take.

As I listened to Ohnainewk's tales, where tragedy followed tragedy, grandson replaced grandfather, I wondered in despair: "And is life no more than that?" For despite the brooding beauty of his tales, I did not feel tragic exhilaration so much as the weary sinking of a river into the sea. Nor was I moved by the nobility of his characters so much as by their animal-like persistence in the face of storm until they fell to make room for future generations. Somehow the more aware he made us of how great a part of us was soil and animal, the more stifled we became with our kinship with the All. His resignation, like his fatalism, arrived at a point where the only grandeur consisted not in striving but surviving.

Then suddenly, violence, laughter, ecstasy would erupt, breaking the mood of futility and despair. He had contempt for all outcries, human and animal; a terrible bloodlust came upon him when a bear lay fallen, snapping at his feet. Many days we killed nothing;

one day we killed thirty-two seals and a walrus. Once we captured a live seal, which he then tortured for hours. This was done by a man whose guardian spirit spoke to him in the voice of a seal and who daily offered prayers of great beauty to the animals of the sea. The contrast struck the local Oblate so forcibly that he attributed it to the work of the devil, but what made him think cruelty and love were not compatible, I do not know.

Ohnainewk's successive wives taunted him, annoyed him with their wailing, deceived him, yet loved him and were unhappy after they left him. When he was very young, he lived with a woman, older than his mother, who wanted to get even with her husband for taking a young wife. Ohnainewk fell in love with this older woman and willingly let her husband sleep with his own wife, the young girl to whom he had been betrothed since birth. After six years he moved away, taking his own wife, but shortly afterwards she left him for Ookpuktowk and he in turn acquired Ookpuktowk's wife. There was little happiness in all this and a great deal of mutual anguish.

The strong conventionalized contempt in which women and their opinions and preferences were held did not operate to make them an abashed and inferior sex. When wives were young, they had few privileges and much work, but as they grew older, they gradually took over and ruled. I watched Ohnainewk's wife disdainfully toss him a skin to scraped, women's work—but he silently began. One day his eldest son returned from trapping to find his clothes unmended. His wife defended herself by blaming his mother, who, she said, had forced her to do the mother's work during his absence. She cried and carried on and finally made him confront his mother with this accusation, which happened to be true. But the mother cut him short: "Your wife is lazy." He stood for a moment, confused, then went back and struck his wife.

There was a fight one day in camp, a near-fatal one, between one of Ohnainewk's sons and a hunter from a group that was temporarily camped nearby. The next morning, Ohnainewk, followed by his angry son, and the other men in order of seniority, with the women and children clustered outside their tents, met a similar procession from the adjoining camp. Ohnainewk apologized for his son, but pointed out that he had been right in defending himself. The apology was accepted, the error admitted. However, an older brother of the other fighter was not so easily pacified. Ohnainewk angrily stepped up to him: "Have you forgotten who your wife is? If you do not soon remember, you will have no wife."

That same spring Angotemarek, "the real man," an old *angakok*, killed himself. He'd been wanting to die for years and when a flu epidemic struck, and he was unable to save the children, he became convinced that the only hope for rejuvenating his waning powers lay in death and rebirth. He ordered the younger wife of his eldest son to prepare the cord and help him into position; then, before the assembled group he hung himself, with his daughter-in-law pulling down on his knees to hasten death. Ohnainewk now became the camp's spiritual leader.

An enthusiastic Christian, Ohnainewk was hopeful that we would all be called to the attention of God. But in a crisis it was the old beliefs which held him. Just before he died, he dreamed again of the placid sea turned to storm. Thick darkness gathered around him and it seemed to him as if he were doomed. He was ready to sink into despair and abandon himself to the waves, when a pillar of light, exactly overhead, rested on him, and a being whose brightness and glory defied all description, standing above him in the air, spoke to him, calling him by name, telling him to follow. He was led beneath the sea, to the home of Sumna, Goddess of Sea Mammals, a fingerless cyclopean creature with tangled hair. Just inside her door, beneath a blanket, lay her father, a Cerebus-like dog, who snarled and snapped as Ohnainewk stepped over him.

He was never simple, never ordinary, never deaf to promptings which most of us scarcely hear. His religion was the deepest thing in him. It ought to be studied—neither by the psychologist nor the anthropologist but by the individual who has had similar promptings. He penetrated into rare regions and always hoped that others would follow him there. But the other members of his group were too involved in the immediate machinery of life to bother with such cosmic mysteries. Talk of hunting, sex, personal hatreds, these commanded their attention, but abstract discussions were met with indifference.

Not until I arrived did he have anyone to talk to about such things. During the winter of 1910 he had learned a little English from the wife of a Mounted Policeman, and though there had been little opportunity to use it in later years, he had not forgotten it. In this he was unique, for though a few other Canadian Eskimo had acquired limited English from early whalers, they were never motivated to transmit it to their children, nor even to retain it.

Our association resulted in superb English on his part, limited Eskimo on mine. One oaf at the white settlement, who resented Ohnainewk's "pretensions," gave him a subscription to *Fortune* and *The Wall Street Journal*. If he understood the insult, he ignored it; he was far too grateful for reading matter on this exciting new world of power. Between visits we corresponded, about everything, including the threat to use atomic weapons in Korea: "This is from an eskimo, the entire world seemingly have worked and found a way to distroy people butt are somewhat behind in finding ways to protect their wives and children from the might of thier own distructive weapons. However if you should come up north with your family I would soon find a plase somewere north of here and I tell you, we would not starve even if we should fall back on bows and arrows & harpoons not for a long while anyway."

I offered Ohnainewk immortality, the chance to record the history of his people, but he wasn't interested in the old tales of a dying people; he aspired to leadership. When this was denied him repeatedly, when—after he had sacrificed so much to follow him—even the fanatical evangelist rejected him, he gave up. No man can face life deprived of his false dreams of the past and his baseless hopes for the future. I think he died with relief.

Ohnainewk's death destroyed his family. His wife became a shrew whom children called *aivanigok*, "battleaxe." But in my memory, her mature beauty, her dark eyes, will not go out of sight and be forgotten; I prefer to remember her as she was with him. His eldest son, who had been a fearless hunter and a fine man, became a mission bum. Another son abandoned his children. Two died.

How proud he was of his family! In summer the children ran in and out of the sealskin tent—those going out meeting those coming in, all standing for a moment, then rushing out; the same runny nose here, gone, then back again. When weather was bad and hunters mended gear, Ohnainewk would take his youngest son from its mother's parka (nude except for a little cap), and play with him on the furs while the child squealed.

He never forced himself on people or things. When he started to carve ivory, he would hold the unworked tooth lightly in his hand, turning it this way and that, and whisper, "Who are you? Who hides there?" And then: "Ah, Seal!" He rarely set out, at least consciously, to carve, say, a seal, but picked up the ivory, examined it to find its hidden form, and, if that wasn't immediately apparent, carved aimlessly until he saw it, humming or chanting as he worked. Then he brought it out: Seal, hidden, emerged. It was always there: he didn't create it; he released it. This was his attitude not only toward ivory but toward people, especially children. He was a gentle father, he was a kind husband, he was a loveable friend; he was kind to everyone in his group—such tremendous kindness.

An emergency arose once while we were hunting and we put in at a neighboring camp of poor newcomers whose presence he resented. I entered the cold igloo and in the pinched, chalk faces of five children saw starvation. Their parents were dead, there was no food, and they simply sat there, silently waiting for the oldest boy, who was hunting alone on the sea ice. I looked at Ohnainewk and somehow knew he had known all along.

The children were adopted into various families. Into the igloo where I stayed came a boy of 8, a most unattractive lad with great dark eyes. His foster mother never spoke kindly to him; the other children pointedly ignored him. He couldn't control his bowels and constantly soiled the furs. On this excuse, they forced him to sleep on the damp snow floor, condemning him to pneumonia and inevitable death. Just before the lad died, I saw him standing alone in the center of the igloo, trembling with cold and fright. My heart just went out to him. I took a great knife, a spectacular thing someone had given to me, and offered it to him. He stood confused, then slowly, with the most wonderful light in his eyes (he must have thought he would be spared) reached out for it. But a hand shot out—Ohnainewk's—and the knife was taken from me and given to a favorite son.

It was a hard land. A knife like that went to one who could use it.

16

My Crow
Interpreter

Robert H. Lowie

In 1910 the American Museum of Natural History sent me on my second expedition to the Crow Indians in southern Montana. The young half-breed who had helped me on my previous visit was otherwise engaged, so I cast about for a suitable substitute. In this fashion I came to meet Jim Carpenter, henceforth my chief interpreter on the reservation. Then in his early 30's, he had been a pupil of the Catholic Mission school, and spoke English fluently. Thus he ranked as an "educated" Crow. Yet outwardly he did not noticeably differ from the general run of "blanket" Indians. He wore moccasins and kept coquettish little tin cones dangling from the pigtails on the sides of his temples. For amusement he would get drunk, run footraces, and break in broncos. Spiritually, he then classed himself as a Catholic, though subsequently he was, after a fashion, affiliated with the Baptist Church. Neither of these ties prevented him from zestfully entering into the native dances or from seeking admission to the great religious order of the sacred Tobacco. Nor did his contacts with Christianity and the modern world make him skeptical about the marvelous experiences claimed by the venerable sages of the tribe. "When you listen to the old men telling about their visions," he once said to me, "you've just *got* to believe them."

In 1910 automobiles were still scarce. Of a morning Jim and I would sally forth on horseback or in a buggy to interview the survivors from buffalo-hunting times whose words Jim was to render into English. Most of them had witnessed Sun Dances and had lost at least one finger joint either as a mourning rite or in seeking a vision. All the men had been on the warpath and belonged to one or the other of the military clubs; several were said to have scouted for General Custer. With varying skill the old people of either sex could recite the adventures of mythical heroes.

Indeed, if a person came at the right season and kept his eyes open, there were still plenty of things to observe first-hand. Women were still pounding wild cherries, scraping skins, and painting rawhide bags. Here and there on the reservation loomed burial stages, and everywhere the Indians took the equivalent of Turkish vapor baths in little dome-shaped sweat-lodges. In the spring the members of the Tobacco order planted their sacred weed. Early in the summer they adopted novices with a great display of ceremonial, and a little later they harvested their crop. Although the plant was completely useless in a practical way (they would not smoke the sacred variety), it had great value for them, so that I had to pay five dollars for a plant to be sent East for botanical identification. Because so much of ancient custom was still alive, Jim's duties went far beyond conveying my informants' memories. He had to ferret out the best authorities on ceremonial, the outstanding storytellers, the old folks who knew what clans everybody belonged to and had married into. If someone had recently played the buffoon at a tribal gathering, Jim tracked him down and got him to pose for me in his outlandish clown's costume.

Yet, had I accepted the character given him at the Agency, I should have shunned him as a shiftless, besotted, trouble-making brawler. His unpopularity, in fact, was well grounded. He never minced words when he felt that employees of the Government were betraying the interests of its wards; and being no respecter of persons, he was capable of falling to fisticuffs if a policeman tried to carry out what seemed a nefarious official's orders. No wonder my interpreter's name was anathema at the Agency.

Perhaps there was a compensatory urge at the bottom of Jim Carpenter's intransigence. For this fervid tribune of his people was really not of their stock at all; his father had been white, his mother was a full-blood Piegan Blackfoot and had merely for some reason brought her infant son to be raised among the Crow as a quasi-naturalized member of the tribe.

At first Jim treated me with reserve. However, he later relented, one day going so far as to say that the Indians liked me because I was not "high-toned." Some years later I scored higher still. A part-Indian neighbor was about to drop in for a call on him, but hesitated awe-struck when she heard that the "wise man" from the East was there. But Jim swept away her misgivings: "I told her," he explained to me afterwards, " 'Why, he's as common as you or I!' " Early in the game he made it clear that he would not help me buy specimens for the Museum cheaper than they should be sold.

For a while Jim was prone to chafe me with Indian grievances and white iniquity, always bent on extolling his compatriots' virtues. On one occasion I had persuaded Chief Medicine-Crow to show me his holy shield. In getting it down he could have made a short cut by stepping over my feet, but instead he made a detour. At once Carpenter nudged me. "Did you see that? There's the politeness of an Indian. No white man would have done that!"

Jim was loath to admit that white contact had benefited the Indian. But wasn't any old-time Crow liable to be murdered in cold blood by a marauding Cheyenne or Sioux? Jim spurned the argument. What of it? In the old days a man's ambition was pricked by the chance of glory in battle. What zest does life preserve for an Indian in modern times? What is there in competition with white farmers? Better the old insecurity with the old opportunities to gain renown in fighting.

Gradually Jim developed a spirit of complete loyalty toward me, but it remained without a trace of subservience. It was a foregone conclusion that I was acquiring a deeper insight into Crow mentality than any other white man known to him, but every so often I was given to understand that, after all, I was only the one-eyed among the blind. This attitude came out especially in connection with my spurts at learning the native language. "Lowie," I was informed on one occasion, "you've got a fine pronunciation, but you talk Crow with a foreign accent." Once I was going to surprise him and earn admiration with the translation of a fairy tale from an elementary school reader, but Jim would not allow one of my Crow sentences to stand as it was written.

Our relations were on a plane of *noblesse oblige*. Theoretically, I was paying him four dollars a day for interpreting and transportation, but to insist on the eight hours' daily stint would have proven fatal. If Jim had been on a spree the night before, there was no use expecting him at nine in the morning; he might turn up at noon or he might not turn up at all. I gained stature in his eyes by never reproving him for such irregularities and actually lost nothing at all. For when Carpenter had once overcome his initial suspicions, he worked for me whether I was about or not. If informants disagreed, he spent hours at night interviewing all available authorities. He told me things I had no means of finding out unaided—that so-and-so was willing to sell his sacred rock or that his own father-in-law, for a consideration, might open up and explain the contents of the sacrosanct bundle that had made him a famous warrior.

True enough, it was not altogether devotion to me personally that made Jim add hours to our official working day. He was genuinely interested, intellectually and emotionally. It became a labor of love and a patriotic duty to help record for future generations how the ancient Crow had lived and spoken; and in fulfilling this task Carpenter showed the zeal of a German philologist.

Jim's interest in the Crow language and traditions was not restricted to the times when I was actually present on the reservation. Over the years we corresponded, he in both English and Crow, about a variety of topics, often touching upon recondite points of Crow manners or grammar. The following is excerpted from one of his letters to me:

> Lodge Grass Mont.
> Oct. 30–31

Dear Lowie.

Your question. Birepbakáradec. means. hull. I will illustrat by the following lines The first line we will say is the bearer of the name. <u>Bearer of the name going 2nd</u> This is the Beaver coming. The name conveys a picture both traveling. I was told the beaver was on one of its slides when sliding an otter was going up this slide and passed the beaver It is a vision name. Bapúxta bi réu daꞔkuc. This name to make it clear would be written Bapúxta bíe ūnꞔda kuc The otter water where lives orꞏ stays

The picture I get is (where The Otter Lives or Stays in the water)

I will try to find out the particulars of this name. I know this much. it is a vision name. I will inform you as soon as I can find some one that knows. ūn batsás xiásac. I might be wrong as to the writing this name. but you will know and correct it. This name was given the present bearer, also known as Yellow Brow, by daxpit tsé íc According to y. B's story he was a brave man in former undertakings with his foes. Everybody heard but never seen any of his actions with the enemy. Two battles he had. One about 18 miles below where Hardin now stands Also one above where Billings now is about 4 miles above where the Clarks Fork river enters the Yellow Stone river.

On these two occasions we might say the Mountain Crow Tribe were raided or charged by the Souixs.

This first happened some nine year before Y. B. was born as to the second he told me he would find out and give me the story as he has done in the first battle and which I am enclosing herewith.

He did not tell me all the details but made in breif. Should you like all the details I will try and get it for you in Crow the best I know how. I will say you will find many mistakes but I will ask you to correct those you know. Those you have any doubts about let me know I will then find out or if I see the mistake will correct and send it back.

Yellow Brow tells me his name should be

Baᶜpe kón ūn batsásxiásac   Rock rifs there where my courage was clearest

Rock there where my courage ability was clearest.

I will write you for more tests for the Crows should you need more. I arranged with Jack Stuart to go over to the Cheyenne's for me. Excuse me for my delays. I am doing the best with what money and time I can use. Wishing you in the best of health

> I am
> Your Friend
> Céce

Sometimes I would read him a Crow sentence from some myth recorded in the vernacular, expecting him to translate what I could not make out by myself. Then, when I stopped, Jim, startled, would come out of a trance and apologize: he had not listened because he was still brooding over the rendering of some expletive on the previous page. Was it better to "english" it as "Why" or as "Now, then"? He would drive thirty miles after hours or on a Sunday to allay such scruples by pumping old and young tribesmen; and a fortnight later, possibly, I became the beneficiary of his lucubrations. For the finer points of diction he discriminatingly consulted the acknowledged orators and *raconteurs,* his "dictionaries," as he jocularly called them. Alas! They, too, disagreed at times, so that he came to regard no one of them as infallible. He pitted one authority against another and harried his favorite informant with quotations from his own myths to expose incongruities in the explanations offered by the old narrator.

Jim's attitudes toward religion were those of an experimentalist. He had been Catholic; he had been Baptist. When a new cult made headway with a few of the Crow, who learned to chew part of the peyote cactus or to drink a decoction of it in order to induce exaltation and all sorts of blessings, Jim took up the novel practice and found the experience interesting. But after a while he saw no benefits from indulgence and gave it up. Feeling no further craving for peyote, he concluded that the missionaries talked bosh when they denounced it as a habit-forming drug. As for the peyote religion, well, that all depended on the individual. Some followed it merely to get a substitute for whisky; others—very few—had become reformed characters and were leading exemplary lives since their conversion. Jim respected these few, but he could not follow them. He again called himself a Baptist, but there were many things in Christian doctrine that puzzled him, so that he often lingered after a sermon to challenge the minister's dicta.

Sophistication and naïveté were oddly blended in Jim Carpenter's make-up. When I last saw him in the summer of 1931, he suddenly pounced upon me with, "Say, there's one question I want to ask you: What do you think of these here religions?" He had heard of all sorts of things, even of Darwin and evolution, which he rejected; and he had encountered the name of Shakespeare. Once he pulled up his horses as we were driving along in the earlier days of our acquaintance and asked, "Say, is Shakespeare the greatest white man that ever lived?"

Jim kept an unabridged Webster in his home, but stood rather in awe of it and preferred to have *me* consult it. He read, but did not like fiction, wanting history and facts. But one work of the imagination he stumbled on in his youth intrigued him for years; and thereby hangs a tale. Incarcerated once for assaulting a deputy sheriff, he sent me an S.O.S. to New York for reading matter to beguile his boredom. He wanted extra copies of my papers on Crow custom, for though he had regularly received them on publication they invariably got lost before long. But particularly he craved a wonderful book he had once come across, *Hell up-to-date.* He did not know the author, but he thought it had been published by the International News Company. I eagerly searched in secondhand bookshops, but without avail; and the International News Company had never heard of the volume. This I sadly reported, and Jim had to content himself with an alternative he proposed, a life of Napoleon the Great, which he read twice while in jail.

However, the memory of *Hell up-to-date* lingered, and some years later Jim brought up the subject as we were chatting on the reservation. "Too bad," he said, "you couldn't get that book for me." And he launched into a vivid account of the pictures in it. Suddenly I clicked. Doré's illustrations rose before me. "You don't by any chance mean Dante's *Inferno,* do you?" I asked. "Well," said he, "I *think* Dante was the man's name."

This proved, however, only a provisional *dénouement.* I found the story amusing, and so did a group of editors of the old *Freeman* to whom I told it one day over luncheon. About a week later one of them, Mr. Fuller, rang me up. "Do you remember the story you told us about *Hell up-to-date?*" "Of course," I answered. "Well, it has an epilogue, and I want very much to have you meet a friend of mine." Though I could not conceive any possible connection between my tale and a friend of Mr. Fuller's, I accepted a dinner invitation. My fellow guest turned out to be Art Young, the cartoonist; and now at last the riddle was completely solved. In his student days in Paris, Young had chanced upon a copy of Dante illustrated by Doré. A reader of Ingersoll, he was in an iconoclastic mood, so that the volume roused his risibilities. He dashed off a parody, with Chicago as the modern Inferno, and a mid-Western firm published it under the caption Jim had cited. The book had been long out of print, but Young had with him a copy that explained everything, even Jim's recognition of the poet's name. For the cartoonist had so faithfully travestied Doré that Jim's description naturally recalled his drawings to me; and Dante figured prominently in the opening pages, so that his name called forth an immediate response from Jim when I pronounced it.

In some respects Jim changed with age. He stopped wearing his hair long and when a child of his fell sick he vowed in good old Crow style that if it recovered he would abstain from liquor ever after. As he grew older he naturally also gave up riding broncos; and with typical avidity of new experiences he learned to drive an automobile with expert skill. But at bottom he remained what he had always been—a fervid Crow patriot. He had nothing but disdain for many of his age-mates, whom he considered lacking in reverence for the traditional tribal values; some were even ashamed of their native names if they sounded odd in English translation. One of these social climbers had gone to Washington with a Crow delegation, but tried to be "high-toned" and kept aloof from his fellows. Jim had no patience with such snobbishness or protective mimicry. He thought the younger generation was going from bad to worse; they no longer cared for the claims of kinship, adopting the white man's individualism. Not so Jim. One day in 1931, while I was working with him, a remote female relative came to borrow money to spend at a fair in a Wyoming town. He had no ready cash, but at once asked me to turn over to her some of his hard-earned wages. "I'll never see that money again," he remarked after she had gone—one could not hold a kinswoman responsible for a loan.

That same summer a male cousin and his aged wife came to visit Jim, ostensibly for a fortnight, but stayed for six weeks. What is more, they were not content with eating the vegetables on their host's farm, so without blinking an eyelash he bought beef for them in town as the nearest substitute for the buffalo meat craved by the old crone. One just had to be hospitable. No wonder callers thronged the Carpenter house, no wonder his married daughters and their husbands made it their headquarters or left their offspring there for indefinite periods. But such altruism does not work well without reciprocity, and Jim was hard put to it to make ends meet. "He's the only Indian I've ever known to worry," a white old-timer told me.

Jim continued to revere tradition even when he did not accept its basis. He himself did not worship the sacred rocks of his seniors, yet he hated to see their sons sell them to shopkeepers in nearby towns. It outraged his sense of decency. He was willing to *donate* such objects to a public institution, that was all right. Though not yet ready to part with his father-in-law's bundle of sacred arrows, he intended to bequeath it to some museum; to do otherwise would be disrespectful to the old man's memory. Jim went further. In the old days a menstruating woman had to proclaim her condition when approaching a lodge where holy objects were kept, so that they could be removed and escape contamination. But who can trust women in this unregenerate age? So Jim hung up his prized package—unopened since the deceased owner had allowed me to inspect it in 1914—on the rear porch of his frame house and would lock it up in a special chamber for the winter. That was how one showed respect. Jim showed it in many ways that others considered old-fashioned. Crow etiquette used to demand that a man avoid his wife's mother and conversation between the two was strictly tabooed; even any word forming part of her personal name had to be paraphrased. Jim clung to the rule as it had been transmitted and for that reason never uttered the Crow word for "marking."

As the years rolled by, Jim had plenty to worry about. He had a large family to support, his farm gave constant trouble, he himself was often ill, and in 1934 he lost his eldest son. The following note requires no comment:

Lodge Grass, Mont., Nov. 6, 1934

Dear Friend:

It has been quite a while since I heard from you. Ever since last summer I have had hard luck. I lost my crops on account of shortage of water. I did raise a few spuds. The corn was wormy. What the worms did not get the pheasants destroyed. The worst part was when I lost my oldest boy over a month ago. It has been so hard for us to stand, especially on his mother and grandmother. The only relief we get is by going to his grave and weep. We go every day since the accident happened. The strain is such, all we can do is keep alive. I cannot express what we have stood so far. Wishing you in the best of health, I will close.

Your Friend
James Carpenter

To me, Jim seemed the ideal interpreter. His English, fluent and ample, did not quite equal that of a few others; but none of them matched his feeling for the ancient Crow life, none rivaled his meticulousness in bringing home to me its values, his perfectionism when it came to reproducing shades of meaning in the Crow tongue. Smitten with an incurable heart disease, he wrote me his last letter from his deathbed:

Crow Hospital, Jan. 27, 1937

Dear Lowie,

Many, many thanks for the ten dollars you so kindly sent me some time ago. I should have written before this, but have been so ill and weak that I couldn't write myself and did not wish to ask anyone else to do it for me. About as long as I can read or write consecutively is for a few seconds and then I have to quit and rest.

I do not know whether I shall ever completely recover from this ailment. A young man is writing this letter for me as no one else has offered to write for me. I feel that death is steadily approaching.

If you can spare one of your latest publications, I should be glad to receive one, this also applies to your grammar on the Crow language even though it is not finished.

Tepee burial (a'wanoo) is not a custom, it is only a rich man's burial. Only a chief was accorded this rite.

Another question you have wanted an answer [to] for the last seven or eight years is about [the tale of] Old Man Coyote, the Strawberries and Girls—húric koco cákoce ditdik. This word shown above should read húrikokohōcu'ritdik. This word was taken from the Gros Ventre [Hidatsa tribe] and in the adoption of the story by the Crow the word reached its present usage.

If I survive my last letter to you, I shall clear up the meaning of Absaroka [tribal name of the Crow Indians]. I'm so weak that I must give up any more effort for the time being.

Sincerely
James Carpenter
[signed by himself]

I have had many interpreters among the Crow and elsewhere; but I had only one Jim Carpenter.

Little Schoolboy and
Friends.

17

A Navaho
Politician

Clyde Kluckhohn

He doesn't come to meetings any more. We shouldn't have as our tribal delegate a man who lives so far away. Only once in the last thirty years has he really lived among us. He stays up there at Willow Fence along with his wife's family and most of his own brothers and sisters."

"You are right. He doesn't come down here often enough. That is why our coöperative store is losing money now. Those two young boys, Eddie Mario and John Nez, who run it need advice and direction from an older man like our delegate. But he doesn't watch them closely enough."

"Everyone knows he and his mother-in-law are bootleggers. They work with those Mexicans."

"Yes, and he himself gets drunk. He has had two car wrecks while drunk."

"He takes too much power to himself. He isn't supposed to preside at these meetings—that is the job of our chapter president, Jo Miguel. Little Schoolboy is supposed to represent us at the Council of our tribe. He can tell us about that, but he shouldn't be the head at these meetings."[1]

"No, you are wrong, my fellows. Little Schoolboy is the leader of the people here. He speaks best, and he knows the English language too. He works hard for the people. He respects the old ways, while the young man, Jim Chamiso, whom the missionary wants you to put in is going to destroy them."

"Exactly," whispered the local missionary to an official of the Bureau of Indian Affairs, "Bill Begay is the candidate of those men who still keep two wives."

---

[1] In the 1920's the Indian Service organized Navaho local groups into "chapters" who elected a president, vice-president, and secretary. Later, the Navaho Tribal Council was created, and each group elected a delegate. The existence of both a "president" and a "delegate" is still confusing to the Navaho who were accustomed to a single "chief" or "headman" for each band. In most localities, as at Rimrock, the delegate ordinarily takes over the functions of the headmen of earlier days, but there are occasional attempts to reserve these for the "president."

I am indebted to many collaborators in field work for the materials upon which this sketch is based. I owe a particular obligation to Drs. Alexander and Dorothea Leighton who collected an extended autobiography from the subject. I thank Dr. Bert Kaplan for interpreting the Rorschach protocols of the subject and his wife. This chapter has benefited greatly from the criticisms and suggestions of the Drs. Leighton, and Dr. Kaplan.

"Well," the official replied, "it is true John Mucho has two wives, but you must admit he is smart and progressive. He is a young man and wide awake even if he does hold to some of the old customs."

The talk at this meeting in January, 1948 went on all day. Perhaps 50 adults—mainly men, but a few women—of the 600-odd Navahos in this local group had their say. Most of their speeches were long and involved, and those of the older men were delivered in the florid yet precise style of Navaho oratory. Often there was an hour of history, recollection of ancient days, citation of experience and sayings of fathers or grandfathers before the speaker came to the issues relevant to the decisions to be taken: Should Little Schoolboy be required to vacate his post as delegate? Should he be replaced by Jim Chamiso, a man in his early 30's who was a high school graduate and a devout Christian? Should Eddie Mario and John Nez be forced to turn over the store to Charlie Blackbird who was Christian and generally more "progressive"? The underlying issues, however, centered on a specific personality and then on a complex of more abstract problems. Was Little Schoolboy—known to whites as Bill Begay—of good enough character and sufficiently responsible in the performance of his duties to continue as delegate to the Navaho Tribal Council from the Rimrock band? The more general questions were those which have split tribes and tribelets of American Indians from the periods when they first felt intense pressure from European groups. Should they hold stubbornly to the old ways or should they join wholeheartedly with the whites in stamping them out? Or should they, perhaps, compromise? Should missionaries be welcomed, tolerated, or resisted? How much should they stand up to the Government, passively resist it, or follow its lead—insofar as one could understand this?

It was true that Bill Begay was the favorite of the antimissionary, somewhat conservative faction. His program, however, was basically one of compromise. Respect for custom was to be combined with schooling for children, with support of the Navaho coöperative store, with acceptance of useful techniques and ideas introduced by Government representatives or other whites so long as these did not deny any place whatever to Navaho religion and Navaho methods for curing the sick. Implicitly, Bill's position was: of course, changes must come but not so fast that we repudiate all the values of our ancestors and disrupt the stable fabric of our lives.

In Bill's own passionate defense of his record he made or hinted at all of these points as well as replying to specific accusations (for example: "I've made the long, hard trip down here many times only to find that only a handful of you people showed up at the meeting.") Like other astute politicians, he appealed both to the economic interests of his audience and to their more diffuse sentiments. He spoke of his own situation: of his large family and more remote relatives who were dependent upon him, of the terrible mud on the roads which sometimes prevented his getting to meetings, of the overpowering fatigue he felt when, as now, he had been speaking at length in Navaho and also translating the talks by himself and others into English for the benefit of Government officials. He spoke of the conflict of religions:

There's lots of missionaries who hate the singers [medicine men] and the medicine used among us Navahos, but some of this medicine is pretty old. It carried down from our old people, and we are still taking care of that and the songs and the chants. All this stuff are from the old, way back, and we can't lay off that. We got to go by that and the missionary hasn't anything to do with that. He can't hate that.

He must leave us alone in the meetings, not to butt in or try to say something about the people. All he can do is to preach to our people. Not to baptize them, just to preach to them. If they want to come to church they can. If the children want to come, that's up to their parents.

I have worked hard for the people. I have been a leader of the people for seventeen years. First at Pine Valley, then at Willow Fence, and now here. Most men give out after a little while, but I have stuck to it.

The vote was ninety to twenty against Bill. Some adults present did not vote. Others claimed later that they thought they were voting only to censure Bill for not attending meetings rather than to demand that he vacate his office. Bill left for his home almost immediately after the vote, and an observer noted that he looked "like a drawn and shaking old man." Another observer said Bill looked "like a beaten puppy." It is further recorded that for two weeks thereafter he appeared "sick, tired, depressed." But then he developed a plan to defeat Jim Chamiso decisively and got busy. After the vote had been reported to the Navaho Central Agency at Window Rock, the Agency ruled it illegal to force a delegate to resign in this manner. However, it was suggested to Bill that he might wish to resign voluntarily because of the expression of lack of confidence. Bill did resign but spent several weeks campaigning with quiet vigor for the Rimrock chapter president, Jo Miguel, whom he persuaded to run for delegate against Jim Chamiso. Jo Miguel had two wives and was in every respect entirely satisfactory to the conservative faction. Others who had been mainly aligned with the progressives voted for Jo because they felt guilty about their earlier repudiation of Bill. Jim got only thirty-five votes to Jo's one hundred and nine. Everyone regarded this outcome as a signal victory for Bill, and Jim was so disheartened that he promptly moved away from Rimrock to the land of his wife's family on the reservation. Moreover, Bill obtained more than symbolic success. During the same period he manuevered among Navahos and Government officials in such a fashion that when Jo took over as tribal delegate Bill received a paying job as bus driver for the Navaho school in Rimrock and his wife the position of housekeeper at the school.

I was not a witness of these events of the winter and spring of 1948. I learned about them from letters and from reading the field notes of my associates who were on the ground. When I arrived at Rimrock that summer and went to visit Bill, I did not mention what had happened nor even allude to it obliquely. We carried on small talk for an hour and only after I had said I must leave did Bill give me his account:

They have a new delegate here now. These people got all mixed up this spring. It was those relief checks that got them mixed up. They had quite a lot of money. And every week a whole load of food and clothing. John Mucho got some. So did Margarita Luciano and Mucho. [These three individuals all owned considerable livestock.] My wife and I didn't get any. That's why the store has done better. All those relief checks went to the coöperative store. That's what I told the people in the meeting—that the store would have done better even if John Nez and Eddie Mario had stayed there. But these young boys, Jim Chamiso and Charlie Blackbird, they claimed they were progressive and that's why the store did better. I think they knew this relief was coming—they had some understanding with Albuquerque.

Anyway they had a meeting this spring and elected a new delegate and chapter officers. But that didn't stand. I told them the delegate was Window Rock's business, and Window Rock said a delegate was elected for four years. Just Jim and Charlie and Walter Blackbird and Marcos wanted a change. The rest of the people didn't, but they got mixed up.

At first John Nez and Eddie Mario and some of the other war veterans sided with Jim Chamiso until they found out what he was going to do to pollen [2] and the medicine men and all that. Jim made a speech over at the church. After that the people felt like someone feels when you come and hit them on the back of the head [gesturing excitedly], and they see stars. The people didn't like that at all. Jim Chamiso is a good man in many ways, but he wants to do away with the medicine men. We aren't ready for that yet. We don't understand all of the missionary's religion yet.

So Jim and Charlie Blackbird asked me if I would resign as delegate. I said, yes, I would resign if I could get some kind of steady government job. So they fixed it up with the Government that I get this job I have now.

Then we had another meeting. And I told the people how it was—that they had got mixed up and that Jim and Charlie were only working for some of the people. They just stuck with the missionary. And I had always tried to work for all the people. Sometimes traders and government people had tried to get me to work for them. But I never followed their track. I always stayed right in the middle. So I told the people now they mustn't split. They must stick together, just like we always had been doing. So they asked me to name a good man since I was going to quit and take this government job. So I named Jo Miguel, and almost all of the people voted for him. He used to be with the missionary, but he isn't any more.

It is going to be down here just like it was on the reservation—for a while a lot of people will go with the missionary, and then in a couple of years it will be all over. I spoke with the missionary at that meeting, and I told him how when he was living in Rimrock I helped him get this land down here so he could be right in the center of the people. But I didn't think he was going to try to force the people to take his ways. He shouldn't do that. I told him after all I had done for him I didn't like the way he was acting. When I finished he asked me to interpret. I said: "No, you have your own interpreter." He said: "Well, my interpreter can't always understand what you say. You use hard words." So then he said he didn't have anything against me, and that he wanted to be friends. Now every time I meet him he says that same thing to me.

Bill Begay is one of perhaps 85,000 Navaho Indians whose traditional country was in the present states of Arizona, New Mexico, and Colorado in the area roughly defined by the San Juan River on the

[2] Corn pollen is very important in Navaho religious symbolism and in the carrying out of rites.

Two of Bill's Daughters.

north, the Colorado on the west, the Gila on the south, and the Rio Grande on the east. Today about half the tribe lives on the Navaho Reservation, some fifteen million acres mainly in eastern Arizona and western New Mexico. Additional Navaho, of whom Bill is one, live on individually owned allotments or lands leased by the tribe or the United States Government in areas adjacent to the reservation. Some thousands now work all or most of the year as semi-itinerant railroad, mine, or agricultural laborers far from the Navaho country or have settled more permanently in cities as far away as Los Angeles and Chicago. There are today Navaho living in the remoter parts of the reservation who have grown to maturity wholly within the self-contained orbit of Navaho culture. Others in the cities and on the fringes of the tribal land live largely in the white man's world. Bill's own experience has been overwhelmingly in a Navaho environment. He has seen some of the cities of New Mexico and Arizona and has worked two or three times as a migrant laborer in Utah, but if one excludes the years he spent at school in Albuquerque, all except a few months of his life have been spent within a fifty-mile radius of his birthplace.

He was born in 1892 or 1893 about twenty miles south of Gallup, New Mexico, the eighth and last of his mother's children. His mother died when he was 18 months old. His father shortly remarried, and three more children were born to the second wife. Bill, however, was not brought up by his father and stepmother but by other relatives. He was in school from 1901 until 1906, a time when schooling of even so short duration was a rarity for most Navaho youngsters. The Navaho name by which he is still known is "Little Schoolboy." In his late teens he went to work for the trader at Rimrock, and his time in the trading store appreciably increased the scanty knowledge of English he acquired at boarding school. His knowledge of written English can be judged by this letter he wrote me in 1937:

I will write you a letter today We are getting along alright here at Willow Fence country.
and I have think about the Hunting pipe which me and you talk about the time you left us. I whish you let me know if you still wanting the Two pipe yet. if you do we will send them to you before Christmas.
Wife will send you something to.
I got everything here at home now all I have to do is to go ahead and make Two pipe. these Two pipe wille be Navjo hunting pipe. Whick was made back in old days.
let us know just as soon as you get this letter please
I will go some other place again after Christmas for work.

From yours friend
Bill Begay

In 1914 he married a daughter of a "chief" of the Willow Fence band of Navaho, and a year or two later he married, as a second wife, the younger sister of this woman. To anthropologists Bill has always insisted that he was never married to these sisters at the same time, but his contemporaries—Navaho and white—are unanimous to the contrary. His first wife gave him two sons and a daughter; the second, one daughter. Both of these wives died leaving infant children. About 1925 he married his present wife, Ellen, then a young woman of 18. Her mother was Navaho, but her father was a white trader. She and Bill have had seven daughters and three sons. Only one died in infancy—a rare record among the Navaho. In 1952 Bill had more than thirty living grandchildren, not an exceptionally large number for the prolific Navaho.

At 5 feet 7 inches, and weighing 156 pounds, Bill is slightly taller and heavier than the average Navaho of his age group in this region. Like many Navahos, he had pyorrhea, head lice, and a few minor defects of the head and eyes, but a thorough medical examination in 1948 when he was in his mid-50's showed him in general good health and nutritional status. Today he wears glasses continually, and is as unhappy as a professor when he misplaces them. Except for some excess weight, his body is well proportioned, and his gait and gestures have the smooth and flowing quality that typifies Navaho movement.

In part, Bill's success in the field of power and politics must be attributed to a control of English unusual in a Navaho of his age and to the recognition by other Navahos that Bill understands whites and their ways, both skills deemed important in coping with white deviousness. Yet others who had these qualifications have not entered the political game or have failed at it. Bill likes people, loves to talk with everyone. He also likes to have people feel dependent upon him. And—let it be said candidly—he loves to manipulate people. Finally, his role as "leader of the people" allows him escape from the family scene, ruled firmly by his wife. These dispositions—even more than the prestige and perquisites of office—have kept Bill in the political arena. He is not only adroit in political behavior but is likewise an accomplished orator. When I talked with him last during the summer of 1958, the thing that he said to me with the most feeling was that he had been invited to journey a considerable distance north to make a speech during an Enemy Way rite: "These people way up there said they had heard I could talk better than anyone near there."

As I think of Bill during the many years I have known him intimately, his personality seems to me to embrace at least as many obvious and blatant contradictions as is the case with the rest of us. He is (as he himself says in English) a "leader of the people." Yet he was terrified of his mother-in-law and is under the thumb of his wife. He is the object alike of enormous trust and mistrust from Navahos and others. I have never known a Navaho of his age who was more deeply divided between the Navaho and white worlds. When one comes to his home in 1958, one sees several substantial American-style buildings of mill-processed lumber and cement. There is not even one *hogan,* the traditional mud-domed Navaho dwelling of logs, in which a Navaho rite can properly be carried out. There is no sweat-house. And yet Bill has always refused to become a Christian [3] and has opposed missionaries under circumstances that he knew were politically disadvantageous. He is proud of the fact that he knows certain obsolescent rituals for hunting deer and antelope. He attends and participates in curing chants and other ceremonials with great frequency. He is known to some as a "progressive," as an accepter and introducer of American foods, gadgets, and habits, but he publicly laments the decline of Navaho customs among the younger generations. He insists that his English-speaking children speak some English to their children in the home, but he himself flaunts his classical (sometimes almost archaic) Navaho. His female grandchildren must learn to weave rugs in the old manner, though he comments loudly that this activity has become economically unrewarding. He himself was a silversmith for some years. He and his family own automobiles, farm machinery, and all manner of contemporary machine goods. Nevertheless he treasures an ancient digging stick and a ceremonial fire-drill.

But I believe his most basic attitude is expressed clearly in this quotation:

I can never become a white man. My skin is brown, not white; my eyes are black, not blue; my hair is black instead of some other color. I can never change that. I am an Indian, and I have to go by those things what were given us from way back. Those things are for us Indians. If I can change my skin and become white man, than I take the white man's religion. While I am an Indian, I am not going to throw away all those things which have come down for our people.

My first meeting with Bill Begay in 1936 was hardly friendly. I had dropped into the hogan of the Son of Many Beads to check a few points on the Blessing Way rite of which he was a practitioner. In accord with the custom, he shook hands with the visitor, but he was less than cordial and proceeded immediately to ask the assembled company what business a white man had to pry into matters of Navaho religion. He reminded them that Jake Morgan, a leader from the Farmington area, was urging all Navahos to refuse to talk

---

[3] His third marriage took place in a Catholic church, but he has never attended church services.

with whites except in necessary business transactions. This was a time of strong antiwhite feeling because of the Government's stock reduction program, increased pressure of various sorts from the Bureau of Indian Affairs under John Collier's administration, and the continuing impact of the Depression. Although Jake Morgan was a Christian and indeed an ordained Methodist minister, his movement had strong nativistic overtones, including some disposition to exclude whites from attendance at Navaho ceremonials and to clam up at inquiries about Navaho religion. But I had spent considerable time in the Rimrock country at various periods since 1923, long before I had any acquaintance with anthropology. My relation to the Navaho there had been established as a personal rather than a professional one, and this was the first time that my privilege to ask questions about or indeed to participate in rites had even been questioned. I was hurt and shocked into silence.

The Son of Many Beads replied, however, with some asperity that he didn't know much about Jake Morgan, didn't like some of what he had heard, and in any case Morgan had no right to dictate what was or wasn't done at Rimrock. Moreover, he said, had Bill Begay been much around Rimrock in recent years he would have known that I was a friend of the Navaho, addressed by many in kinship terms, and considered almost as a Navaho. They would continue to discuss with me anything that I wished, just as they had found that I answered at suitable length all queries they put to me. I proceeded with my questions. Bill sat quietly at first. Then he interjected a remark that he was surprised I knew something about Navaho religion. Still later, he joined warmly in an argument among the Navaho men on some technical points. We parted on moderately good terms.

The following summer I found that Bill Begay and his family had moved from their place at Willow Fence, eighteen miles south of Gallup, to some land adjacent to that of his wife's sister and her husband, thirty-odd miles southeast of the village of Rimrock. The late anthropologist, Harry Tschopik, was about to begin his field work on Navaho material culture and needed an interpreter. Bill Begay was at that time the only mature Navaho man in the Rimrock area who had a reasonably fluent, if ungrammatical, command of English. Because of my brush with him the previous year and because the local traders did not speak very well of his character, I hesitated about hiring him to work with Harry, but the two younger men who had adequate English lacked Bill's knowledge of the older Navaho culture. When I did invite him to become Harry's interpreter, he said he must consult his wife. They talked for an hour, and then Bill said he could start the following morning.

Bill worked hard and loyally for Harry that summer and the next. Until 1954 there was not a year in which he did not serve as interpreter for one or more field workers, mainly in the Rimrock and Willow Fence areas, but also in Chaco Canyon for part of a summer. He worked for anthropologists, biologists, psychiatrists, general physicians, psychologists, botanists, philosophers, and sociologists. Some of his employers were young and raw graduate students. Some were experienced and sophisticated men and women who had traveled and done research in many parts of the world. Gradually, he became more a collaborator in the investigations than a hired hand. He himself became committed to the minutiae of ethnography. He took the initiative in writing me letters (without pay, though, as will be seen, money was of constant importance to him) to say that he had observed or heard something new or something contrary to what he knew my associates or I accepted as fact. Increasingly, his role toward me became that of "principal adviser and consultant on the Rimrock Project." He acquired a good deal of the jargon of the profession, and frequently made special trips to tell me that I must admonish so and so "to keep Navaho customs" or to warn me that "the tall young man's rapport is not good." He firmly corrected all newcomers who failed to use the standard English translations of certain Navaho technical terms which had become established in anthropological usage.

Indeed, particularly in more recent years, his behavior toward the young and inexperienced can only be characterized as domineering. He has laid down the law as to what they could and could not do, insisted on setting his own days and hours of work, brutally criticized their field techniques, borrowed money which he has not returned or worked out. From the youngsters since 1946 I have heard more complaints about Bill than praise. A composite of what they have said would go something like this:

Oh, yes, he knows the people and their culture very well. And he can give you a decent translation if he feels like it. But if you don't check him closely he'll give you back three sentences after an informant has talked for half an hour. And he is so undependable. Five times in the last two weeks he stood me up. He told me to come pick him up at his place at a certain hour. When I got there, he was away and his family gave me vague and conflicting stories as to when he would be back. He talks you out of wages in advance or just begs a loan, and you can't trust his promises to make it up one way or another.

This picture is abundantly documented by the facts. There are certainly, however, elements of misunderstanding in the portrayal of Bill's character made by novices to Navaho culture. Many traits attributed to him are characteristic of Navaho in general and not of Bill as a unique personality. "Navaho time" is not equivalent to "American time." The "appointment" does not have the almost sacred character it has with us. As regards money, most Navahos are genuinely convinced that any white has access to an almost unlimited supply. Moreover, the average Navaho considers that one of the most delicate and pleasurable of games is fencing with a white for a gift, advance payment, or loan. With great finesse the Navaho will "test the limits." A too easy or too generous response—taking into account the relationship of the two parties—is an occasion for biting jokes about the gullibility of the whites, a small triumph over the representative of a group which is, rightly enough, believed to have cheated and exploited the Navaho. Finally, the youngsters have underestimated the demands and complications of a Navaho's life which are different from those familiar to us but none the less real. Bill may receive a summons (unexpected when he made the "appointment") to assist in a curing rite for a relative or to attend to some political duty that has suddenly arisen. Or, his wife might simply insist that he take her shopping in Gallup in his pick-up truck or to a ceremonial where she can gossip with relatives and do a bit of trading.

Nevertheless, the uninitiated graduate students are right in inferring that there is something in Bill's make-up that cannot be explained by differences in culture or by situational pressures. There is definitely a psychological dimension which includes a component of hostility toward whites. First, I would say that Bill derives some significant substitute gratifications from his whole role as interpreter or "research assistant." He enjoys directing operations and giving instructions. He has little outlet for these propensities at home, for his wife is not only shrewd and energetic but very strong and, not infrequently, hard. In Navaho politics he can influence and direct as well as cajole. With younger field workers, however, he need no longer mask the iron hand. Moreover, I am certain that he finds a peculiar satisfaction in uttering commands and prohibitions to whites, in extracting unearned money from them, and in keeping their work at the mercy of his caprices.

Bill's attitude toward whites—like that, I believe, of the majority of Navaho—is deeply ambivalent. On the one hand, he respects their power and their skills and wishes to emulate them. All save two of his children have been to school, and the total number of years spent in school by them is considerably in excess of the average for Navaho of their ages and geographical location. He ordinarily responds with sincere warmth to whites whom he judges courteous, understanding, and trustworthy. To their face, he usually behaves with deference, though especially to older persons whom he thinks have authority or position. On the other hand, a great deal of distrust and antagonism comes out. He continually repeats tales (true, partly true, and false) of dishonesty, greediness, arrogance, ignorance, or of ridiculous acts on the part of whites. These stories are told more often, with more fervor, and with more embellishments when Bill's superego has been loosened by alcohol. Then, especially, he will also boast of getting the best of a white, sometimes by means which, according to his own standards, were not altogether ethical. His dreams reveal many incidents of overt aggression toward whites and he repeats such dreams disingenuously as if he were not at all implicated in the attitudes they imply. He talks with gusto and longing of the young days when whites were only beginning to be a real nuisance to the Navaho.

Bill's autobiography, recorded by the Leightons, contains many episodes which describe, in effect, his rediscovery of Navaho culture after his return from school. He tells of attending a ceremonial performed over his sister's husband and of his surprise at learning this was conducted because his brother-in-law had been having frequent bad dreams: "I don't know what bad dreams means. After I came back from school I not trying to believe Navaho way, I believe American way. I don't know any more Navaho way than before I went to school. That man start to telling story about the dream."

A little later he rather reluctantly agreed to have a rite performed over himself:

We started from there early in the morning. This is to my other sister where she is living we going. We got there in the afternoon, late in the afternoon. That's where that little canyon, this side of Rimrock. When we got there, my sister started to talk about the sing. They want to put the sing over there by Many Beads, the singer of Blessing Way. The reason they want to do that I was away in school for. They say they said put that sing, I mean they should have done it for me just after I came back from school. They want the singer, that man, Moustache's father. They ask me, did I want it? Told them I don't want it. [Bill laughs a little.] They keep asking me till I say yeah. But I got no moccasins, they got to make moccasins for me first. First they just start to talk about it. After I say all right, then there's some people around there, what living around there. They come there and they put up new hogan. They sent Joe back over here to this other place. Told the people down there they was going to have a sing down there.

This "sing," Blessing Way, is the ceremonial held by the Divine People when they created mankind and taught them skills and ritual. The Navaho say that Blessing Way is the cornerstone of their whole ceremonial system. Seldom does a family go for six months without having Blessing Way sung at least once in their hogan. Most Navaho rites have the ostensible purpose of curing illness, but Blessing Way, as English-speaking Navahos say, is "for good hope." It places the Navahos in tune with the Divine People and so ensures health, prosperity, and general well-being. It is also considered by the Navaho to be a prophylatic against danger. The rite is far less complicated than most Navaho ceremonials. It has the dignity of great simplicity. There are a few songs one night, a ritual bath in yucca suds with prayers and songs the next day, and singing all that night. Cornmeal and pollen are prominently used throughout, and drypaintings of these materials and pulverized flower blossoms are prepared on buckskin spread upon the ground.

After his own ceremony, Bill learned from his father that the rite had been conducted because Bill had been exposed to the hazards of being among whites. At the same time the father, while disclaiming responsibility for Bill's being sent away to school, showed his own mixture of feelings by affirming that school is a good thing:

When I bring in the sheep that night, I asked my sister why did they had a sing for me. She told me ask my father. My father was still there, and I ask him about it. He says we didn't put you in school; your brother did, he says. And we all was so glad you got back over here without anything wrong with you. And Navaho, all the Navaho, they all do same thing whenever they sent the children to school. They do the same thing.

They put up the Blessing. They all have to put up the Blessing sing for children. He says that's the way we Navaho work it with our children when our children goes to school. He told me that's about all I can tell you. There's some good reason for it, but that's too hard for you to understand. He told me some of the people says that school is very good for the children, and he thinks it's good too himself.

Perhaps his induction into ceremonies made Bill feel at home with his people again. Perhaps he felt something inherently good in the ceremonies. Possibly his father's hint that there was something deeper which Bill did not understand instigated him to apprentice himself to a ceremonial practitioner. At any rate, in his autobiography he relates with evident prides his learning and eventual mastery of the ritual ways of hunting. He is pleased to discover by himself some stones that are used in ceremonies. He exults in describing the minutiae of an unusual rite or in recounting the wisdom and sound moral exhortations of the old men. His satisfactions in finding good things in his own culture are plainly evidenced. Equally clear is his pleasure whenever in his experience a white (or indeed an Indian from another group) expresses interest in Navaho custom. Negatively, if it be true that one can understand people better from what they laugh at than from the gods they worship, Bill's *Schadenfreude* is most particularly directed against whites. Any act or belief that seems to him stupid or ignorant in a way in which a Navaho would hardly be stupid or ignorant brings forth a special laugh and a disdainful expression on his face that is reserved for such occasions. He loves —as do most Navaho—to puzzle and pull the legs of whites. Once he spoke of an idiot as able to talk. When the anthropologist looked amazed, Bill went on with a broad smirk: "Sure she talks. The only thing is—no one can understand her."

His life story suggests that Bill would probably have returned to predominantly Navaho orientations had he not when still a young man gone to work for the trader at Rimrock. This man was intelligent and treated Bill with understanding and affection. Bill's affiliations were split again between the two worlds. This essential ambivalence emerges in the reproach he casts upon his older brother and two of his sisters for having earlier kept him from returning to school so that he could herd for them. Behaviorally, the ambivalence appears also in some events attendant upon his first marriage. Although the arrangements were made, Navaho style, by intermediaries from the two families, Bill took rather more initiative in the matter than was customary. And, on the trader's advice, he refused to agree to work for his prospective in-laws after the marriage. Both Bill's relatives and the girl's wanted a Navaho basket ceremony at the marriage, but Bill held out. He simply took his bride to live with him at the trading store, and announced that henceforth he was going to work for whites. Nevertheless he returned to live among his own people. While Bill, to my knowledge, has always spoken of this particular trader with warmth, he does in his autobiography repeat at length the remarks of other Navahos that when he left the trading store he did not get nearly as much money as he should have received. There are also other indications of his mixed feelings toward this man.

The same vacillation has marked our own relationship—and I think it fair to say that this trader and I have been the whites to whom Bill has been closest and whom he had most nearly accepted without reservation. For the most part Bill has shown himself devoted to me and more than faithful in his obligations. He has given me ritual information in the summer which should be divulged, if at all, only in the winter. He has worked without extra pay for more hours in a day than I was sometimes prepared to work. He has been extremely discreet with my confidences where a single offhand remark in a relaxed or drunken moment could have been exceedingly damaging to my work and the work of my associates. With great effort and skill at manuever, and considerable risk to his political fences, he obtained access for me to the secret rites of Enemy Way—the one aspect of Navaho ceremonialism from which whites are automatically excluded. He insisted, once over protest, that I attend and speak at Navaho political meetings deliberately called at times and places that were designed to prevent the presence of representatives of the Indian Service or other whites. Yet from time to time, in contexts not involving a failure on my part to respond to his requests or meet his expectations, he has turned on me. There have been a few outbursts of open and seemingly unprovoked anger. There have been more instances of moody or sulky withdrawal. There was one flagrant case of his taking advantage of me.

Over the years I had made small loans to Bill. Some other Navahos have never repaid such loans. Most of them have, however, made restitution and on occasion in cash after a long lapse of time during which the debt was never mentioned. Bill never paid back a loan in cash but rather in work or in his wife's rugs, and always during the interval while the debt existed he would frequently make me aware that he had it in mind. Ten years ago he came to me with a plea for an advance that would enable him to buy supplies so that he and his family could sell hot dogs and pop at a "Squaw Dance" of Enemy Way. The sum was sizable enough so that I demurred, but his reminders of our friendship and his need and his categorical assurances that I would be repaid the very morning the three-day rite ended won me over. I presented myself promptly at dawn the final morning because my personal funds happened to be low at the time, and I needed to get most of the money back. He and his family had decamped two hours earlier in spite of the fact that just before their departure customers swarm to such stands. I went immediately to his place and not finding him there then visited the hogans of relatives of both Bill and his wife. It was only a week before I had to return East, and repeated search and inquiry failed to locate Bill. By the time of my next trip to the Navaho country I had decided that Bill deserved a bonus if he felt that way about it, and I was curious as to what tack he would take. But neither he nor any member of his family has ever, however indirectly, alluded to the incident.

In part, I am sure that this behavior must be understood in the light of Bill's inability to resist the exploitation of a white, although a friend.[4] But only in part. There were two other immediate instigations to his deception. There is no doubt in my mind that the money, both my loan and what he got from his sales, was urgently needed to buy clothes and meet other expenses in connection with sending five members of his family off to school within a few days. Second, I am sure (without proof) that Bill's wife who has less conscience but more force than Bill badgered him into this action.

If such an explanation of his deception is correct, his susceptibility to these two immediate instigations must be related to some dominant and recurrent features of Bill's personality. The distinc-

[4] This interpretation is reënforced by a similar occurrence. Bill had a white rancher as a neighbor for many years. The two men were unusually friendly, and the rancher did many favors for Bill. Then a calf was stolen from the rancher who tracked the thieves to Bill's place. Bill denied all knowledge, but it is virtually certain that the calf was taken by Bill's sons with at least his tacit approval and possibly at his prompting.

tive features of that personality, considered against the perspective of other Navahos I have known, suggest the following observations:

1. His feelings toward whites are exceptionally mixed.

2. While he can be generous, he is more often grasping in money matters. (The Leightons have entered into their field notes a characteristic comment by Bill after a discussion of money: "That sounds good.")

3. He is generally skillful in interpersonal relations. Over and above possible material advantages, he takes intrinsic pleasure in having people listen to him, arranging their affairs, in making them dependent upon him. And his skill shades over, in the opinion alike of Navaho and of white observers, into manipulation and calculated cunning. At the same time, one must remember the almost disinterested—as well as prideful—psychological reward he seems to get from reconciling a husband and wife or helping a family to get out of economic straits.

4. His own personality is a curious blend of assurance and almost frightened dependence, of responsibility and irresponsibility, of maturity and immaturity.

It will be instructive to view these tendencies against the background of some crucial facts of the history of his early years and of the conditions he has faced as an adult. But first let us compare them with some Rorschach findings. In 1946 I administered the Rorschach test to Bill and his wife. These protocols were interpreted by a clinical psychologist, Dr. Bert Kaplan, who spent a summer testing subjects from four Southwestern cultures, including the Navaho. Dr. Kaplan met Bill Begay more than once. He has not, however, read Bill's life story or discussed Bill's character with me.

Let us begin with a point with which I am in hearty agreement. Dr. Kaplan sees the total record as "typically Navaho" as ". . . in no sense deviant from the main framework of the Navaho way of life." When it comes to those idiosyncratic features which are—at least in their emphasis—specially characteristic of Bill, my experience likewise fully accords with Dr. Kaplan's interpretations when he writes of ". . . freedom and spontaneity of self expression and a proper appreciation of and sensitivity to the subtleties of the materials with which he is dealing. This ability is generally associated with strong ego forces and emotional maturity."

But the following interpretations are peculiarly congruent with the generalizations I have made above and with the biographical data which are to come:

a. Perhaps the most central theme in the protocol has to do with strength and masculinity. At least a half dozen different responses involve these characteristics in association with bravery, vigorous action, overcoming difficulties through strength and endurance, withstanding challenges from a younger generation, maturity, adequacy as a provider of food, protectiveness toward the young and acquisition of prestige and recognition. These qualities undoubtedly loom large in Bill's self picture and are, I believe, understood as aspects of his idea of strength, and assertion of these qualities in the responses should properly be regarded as a reaction to a basic uncertainty about possessing them. I am inclined to think however that, despite the fact that they are given quite freely and spontaneously, the responses do indicate a need to use energies to maintain this self concept and perhaps therefore a deep lying fear that they may not hold unless effort is made to maintain them.

b. A second theme involves the nurturance-succorance dimension. There is a definite preoccupation with the ideas of taking care of and being taken care of which involves both infantile succorant attitudes and more mature nurturance and protective ones. Bill's identifications, in the balance, seem to be more with the mature protective figures than with the infantile ones. The image of himself as a provider of bounty is an important one and he has apparently adapted a role complementary to the childhood one in which oral dependent attitudes predominated. Food and whatever it might symbolize remains important in Bill's personality economy and one might speculate that he is still working through some residual problem of deprivation from his childhood. A related image involves the juxtaposition of very strong and aggressive figures with weak helpless ones.

c. Another recurring theme has to do with affiliative qualities in his social relationships. In at least two responses such relationships are given a pleasurable, spontaneous, "moving toward" quality. . . .

Because of his mother's early death, the number of his siblings, and his father's remarriage, Bill did not receive even the small inheritance with which many of his fellows of that day started. On his father's death, which occurred when Bill was already married, his sisters received some livestock; Bill and his brothers got nothing. Since the day he came back from school he was on his own economically with only very minor assitance from relatives. His first two wives had expensive ceremonials in connection with their lingering, final illnesses. During a period of more than twenty years there was a new child almost every two years. Before the cycle of children from his third wife was complete his daughter and two sons by his first wife were themselves married but continued to be to a large degree dependent upon Bill. His third wife was always demanding: of luxury items, of traveling about, of aid to her relatives. In addition, Bill himself encouraged his own relatives to expect assistance from him. During most of his life he has been desperately poor, and during a number of periods he has barely been able to provide his family with a minimum diet. He has always been in debt, often to half a dozen trading stores and to even more individuals, Navaho and white, at one time. His creditors pressed him so hard that he found it necessary to work out his debts a little here, then there. His wife's rugs and their few lambs and tiny crop of corn and beans would be zealously watched by traders and others so that they could be seized the very minute they were available. He ordinarily insisted on being paid in cash by anthropologists, for checks meant going to a trading store to cash them. Sometimes Bill had to avoid for years entering a particular settlement lest the trader catch him. A few dollars in cash not infrequently meant the difference between eating and not eating. In the literal sense Bill and his family lived from hand to mouth until the last few years when most of his children had become largely self-supporting or significant contributors to the family income and when he had a meager but assured income as delegate to the Tribal Council. He still works hard at what extra jobs he can get: hauling wood for Zuni Indians or making arduous trips to a sacred lake to get salt he can sell at a profit to other Indians.

It is, I believe, this fierce and unceasing pressure that is primary in understanding certain aspects of his character which both Navahos and whites comment upon unfavorably. Let me sketch two relevant incidents. About twenty years ago Bill married his second daughter to a senile man who who had been a scout for the American Army against Geronimo. The difference in their ages was at least sixty years. Although traditional Navaho culture sanctioned a sizable or in fact a large age gap between spouses,[5] this was a bit too much, especially since it seemed clear that the couple did not live together as man and

[5] Not only did older men take young wives, but it was also not uncommon for a widowed or divorced woman to marry a man ten to twenty years her junior.

wife. In effect, the young girl was a kind of servant and companion to the old man. She prepared and served him his food and kept him clean—or fairly clean, by Navaho standards. Bill candidly rationalized the situation to me as follows: [6] "I know people are talking. But he is a good old man and needs someone to look after him. We need the money—my daughter as much as the rest of us—what he gets from pension and from singing at the Gallup Ceremonial and from telling his stories. He won't live very long and then my daughter can marry somebody else. My wife and I will let her take her own pick next time." As a matter of fact, the daughter accepted the arrangement with good nature most of the time and subsequently did marry another man of about her own age.

Bill had a "cousin" who in the 1930's and early 1940's owned one of the two largest herds of livestock in the Rimrock area. In those days Bill was assiduous in his attentions to this man. The slightest hint that his services would be welcome at lambing or shearing time or advising in some problem with the Government caused Bill to drop all other obligations and rush to his "cousin." The latter, in turn, made liberal gifts to Bill from time to time and guaranteed his accounts, now and then, at more than one trading store. The gossip was that Bill hoped to become his principal heir, for the old man had no son and no sister's sons or sons-in-law whom he liked or trusted. Then the "cousin" fell on evil days. He himself was no longer vigorous, and his shrewdness in Navaho ways no longer enabled him to cope successfully with rapidly changing circumstances. Under these conditions Bill, as everyone noted, ceased to be so readily available as helper and counselor. It would not be accurate to say that he "dropped" the old man completely. He continued to be cordial and, in fact, obsequious when they happened to meet. The malevolent attributed this show of attention to the circumstance that the "cousin" still retained some influence which Bill wanted on his side during political jockeyings. But, a year before he died, the old

[6] To Drs. Alexander and Dorothea Leighton, Bill gave approximately the same account but with some additions and variations. He said the "marriage" was first suggested by the local trader who wanted to continue to handle the ex-scout's pension check. He claimed the decision was made by the girl and her stepmother, both of whom regretted it afterward because the old man drank up most of his income. Bill admitted to the Leightons that he had been criticized for "giving my daughter to that old man" and that the elders were "chewing it over." He added he feared trouble from Indian Service officials.

man commented to me: "I used to think that my cousin was like the old Navahos. Relatives didn't change toward each other when someone became rich or poor. He still talks to me the same way. But I can't depend upon him as I could once. He makes me promises he does not keep. When I send him word, he does not come."

The insecurity of Bill's early life was more than economic. After his mother's death he was shifted from one family of relatives to another. Before his own marriage he called seven different places "home." Orphaned Navahos commonly experience one or two such shifts, but this is an unusual number. His siblings were also scattered about. In his autobiography Bill recalls forgetting all about his sisters for a time, though later his relations with at least two of them were exceptionally close. One sister raised his oldest daughter, and his second daughter lived with the same sister until Bill's third marriage. Bill quotes his father himself as remarking, "After your mother's death I never stayed very long at one place." And there is a matter-of-fact yet still pathetic passage in which Bill describes meeting his father among a group of adults shortly after he had come back from school: "After I shake hands with these people there, one of them was my father, but I didn't remember him. My father used to have a sister there. That sister she is the one that's living there. But my father is living way back over here with my brother."

Bill's relations to his present wife, Ellen, and her mother attest to the validity of the Rorschach interpretation that Bill is not altogether assured in his masculine strength. My hunch is that he was drawn to Ellen because of her intelligence and force, by a sense that she shared his ambitions and would be a helpful economic partner, and possibly, unconsciously or half-consciously, by the very fact that she was half white. She was already obese when I first saw her but must have been beautiful when they were married. She has fine, brown hair with a low wave and her skin is a light color. In her own way she is as complicated and contradictory a person as is her husband. Her Rorschach suggests some pathology, "an unspecified horror." On the other hand, there is evidence of imagination, sophisticated perceptions, and intelligence. Her mind and her control are good enough to repress and intellectualize whatever is profoundly troubling her.

The disturbance could well have had its origins in her infancy. In her autobiography she dwells on whippings and neglect from her mother. She says: "My mother was mean to me. My mother did not want to take care of me." Many Navaho women are shrewish, but there is universal agreement that Ellen's mother was an extreme case. After marrying a succession of Navahos, the mother became for some time the mistress of a white trader, Ellen's father. She called herself, "Mrs. Smith." Then she had still other Navaho husbands. The last one was liked and considered a good man by Ellen and Bill. They merely noted repeatedly his fear of his wife. The mother made a prostitute of one of her younger daughters and forced her to do away with an unwanted baby by exposing it. Ellen and Bill told many stories of her thieving, bootlegging, and conniving. Nor is this all. She was generally regarded as a powerful witch, and for this reason, as well as for her cunning and sharp tongue, she was feared by her own children and other relatives, by her sons-in-law, and by the community at large. "She hates everybody, and everybody hates her."

When Bill married Ellen, he went to live—as the Navaho pattern most often prescribes—where his wife and her mother were established. Navaho custom prohibits, under penalty of supernaturally caused blindness, any direct contact between mother-in-law and son-in-law. Ellen's mother announced her intention of treating Bill as a true son; therefore, she said, they would not observe the taboo. (It is significant for the positive polarity of Bill's feelings toward white behavior that he accepted the proposal.) But the old lady was not satisfied with the fashion in which Bill did her bidding. She determined to "run him off the place," as she had Ellen's first husband. Ellen, however, was loyal to her new husband and claimed the land was really hers rather than her mother's. The mother-in-law complained to the Indian Service authorities. Bill was jailed, and there was a long drawn out quarrel, with Navaho elders, the Gallup sheriff and police, traders, and the Indian Service people all attempting to mediate or adjudicate.

Bill and Ellen at last won out, and Bill escaped—largely—from his mother-in-law. He continued to be terrified of her and on a few occasions to suffer from her machinations. He did not, to be sure, escape from his wife. She is steadier and less vacillating, or torn, as regards her purposes. Bill works hard but more episodically. Ellen loves to buy expensive things, yet she seldom squanders money. Her expenditures bear a far more consistent relation to her central and unchanging values: comfort, opportunity, and prestige for her family.

She has exploited her stepchildren as much as she could. Over a long period she has made a drudge of Bill's second daughter, but to her own children she had been, by Navaho lights, an admirable mother. She demands their respect and can be harsh, but she has slaved and fought for every opportunity and advantage for them, tolerating Bill's political and ceremonial activities only to the extent that she felt they served her primary ends for her family. Bill gratefully recognized this quality and saw that she was a rock of tougher, more abiding and unyielding quality than he. In the families of older Navahos the wife is almost always consulted by the husband on important decisions. In Bill's case, though, he is timid about taking even minor steps without her assent. Up to a point he accepts and, in fact, enjoys his dependence upon Ellen. Theirs has been, as these things go, a happy partnership. It has certainly been a firm one; and Navaho marriage is typically fragile. I have heard Ellen and Bill argue with heat. I have heard angry words. Even one of Ellen's own children once said of her: "She is mad all the time, day and night. I hate her." And Bill added in desperation: "She always gets mad. That's what's the matter all the time." On those rare occasions when Bill got angry enough to express aggression toward his wife, he would actually stand up to her. Once, for example, when he was injured in an accident, she kept nagging him to go to the hospital, but he held out in his refusal.

The surprising thing is that never once, either in my own observation or according to rumor, has there been the slightest intimation of a dissolution of the marriage. Still more amazing—the exceedingly active network of Navaho gossip has never accused Bill of infidelity.[7] And yet there is a wistfulness in some of Bill's utterances about his wife. His unending praise of her intelligence, energy, and dependability does not completely mask a resentment at his surrender of male autonomy. There is an apparent compulsive aspect to his activities in those spheres of behavior where he can, to some degree, assert his autonomy: rituals and politics. His self-assumed role as "provider of bounty" I see also as, among other things, a masculine protest.

It may be meaningful that Bill is a specialist in the hunting rituals. These, along with some of the war rites, are the only ones which exclude women completely and also demand sizable periods of sexual

[7] The single hint in our files of notes came from a Mormon woman who knew little about Bill.

abstinence before the ritual begins and after it has been concluded. Women are, of course, patients in the curing ceremonials, and they attend these exactly as do men. After the menopause, women may even become chanters. But the hunting rituals are defined as exclusively masculine business. Women may not so much as hear most of the songs and prayers, let alone witness the ritual acts.

Navaho women are by no means excluded from political activity. Older women occasionally speak in meetings. In recent years a few women have been elected as chapter officers, and one has been elected to the Tribal Council. But politics remains overwhelmingly a male sphere, and Ellen, who is in many respects conservative, intervenes in Bill's political affairs on one pretext only: that he is neglecting his duties to his family. Politics thus for him is an area of autonomy comparable to his ritual life. It may be added, however, that his political behavior has exhibited more guile than force. He did not, as did Jim Chamiso, condemn or accuse his enemies in public. He lacks the masculine authoritarian quality that characterized Jim as a political leader. Jim was all too ready to make decisions at the top. Bill allowed each person to have his say and then was evasive or reluctant or dilatory in bringing matters to a head.

This relative indecisiveness, this unsureness of himself, is also of a piece with his disposition to flee the field when stress mounts. It would seem that, when his inner tensions become unbearable, Bill's typical response is to escape by leaving the stressful situation or by failing to appear where he was expected. This, I think, is behind his absenteeism from political meetings and sometimes behind his failure to meet his promises to anthropologists and others. To "leave the field" is a frequent Navaho response when the pressures accumulate, but this response is accentuated in Bill.

I have spoken but little of Bill's sly but seldom unkind sense of humor. I have said nothing, directly, of his manifest affection and supportive attitude to his children nor of his warmth and charm in many of his dealings with non-relatives. I leave Bill now with the most recent news I have had of him—making a speech in the Navaho Tribal Council on December 9, 1958 in which he complained of the encroachments of whites on the lands of the Indians he represents and also asked for a clearer definition of the area covered by his constituency. The motives of economic pressure and of mixed feelings toward whites are still prominent. (These he shares with most Navahos, but Bill's case shows characteristic stresses.) The politician and the schemer are also probably behind this speech. And I have no doubt that some of his neighbors are complaining that he irresponsibly failed to attend one or more sessions of the Council or that he neglected to bring up a matter that he had promised to raise. In the account of his speech I also imagine Bill happy in acting as an alert man who can operate successfully without the counsel or intervention of his wife, taking pleasure in his skill with words, in his prestige, in his capacity to move other men to action. Yes, in this final posture I see my old friend, "Little Schoolboy," with great clarity.

Courtesy, Milwaukee Public Museum

18

John Mink,
Ojibwa Informant

Joseph B. Casagrande

John Mink lived out his ninety-odd years in the relative obscurity of Lac Court Oreilles Indian Reservation in northwestern Wisconsin. When he died in 1943, few outside the pale of the reservation lands noticed his passing; and few within it were left to mourn, for the old man had neither progeny nor close kin. No editorials were written to memorialize his death, no epitaph was carved on his gravestone, and he left no monument. Like countless others before him whose lives were outside the mainstream of history, he slipped unobtrusively into eternity.

Yet John Mink's death was more than the end of a man. He was one of the last of a lingering handful who followed a style of life ancient among the primitive hunting peoples of both the Old World and the New. As the spiritual leader of a small company of "pagans," themselves a minority group within the more acculturated Christian majority, he more than any other on the reservation strove to preserve the traditions and customs of Ojibwa life. Thus, his death was not only the end of a life, but marked the passing of a *way of life* as well. Many who were close to him must have sensed this dual loss, but they are unlettered and mute. It is for them, and out of my own respect for his memory that I wish to give John Mink brief respite from oblivion and such small taste of immortality as there may be in print.

Everyone at Court Oreilles seemed to know John Mink. His name was one of the first mentioned to us when we arrived on the reservation in June of 1941. And the more we heard about him the more redoubtable he appeared and the more curious we became. Some called him medicine-man, priest, friend; others called him sorcerer, pagan, scoundrel. But all, Indian and white alike, agreed that his knowledge of the old ways was unsurpassed by any of the 1700 Ojibwa on the reservation. Here might be the paragon among informants that we had hoped to find. He spoke no English, we were told, was somewhat infirm, and lived alone near the Couderay River in a house he had occupied for more than half a century. Bob Ritzenthaler, my companion in the field, and I determined to seek him out as soon as we were settled.

We found his weathered cabin on the southern slope of a small hill overlooking the river and followed the well-worn path that led to the door. A hoarsely shouted "Boju!" [1] came in response to our knock. A moment later another voice greeted us in English and bid us enter. Somewhat apprehensively, we pushed open the door and, blinking away the dazzling summer sun, stepped into the single, barely furnished room. John Mink had another visitor, his good and trusted friend Prosper Guibord, who on this first meeting acted as interpreter. In this capacity he was to become an essential third party to all our future conversations. Prosper had brought the Old Man a meal of venison and wild rice which he had just finished eating. When we arrived the two men were smoking kinnikinnick, a native tobacco made of bark scrapings, whose fragrant smoke hung like cobwebs in the room.

The size of the Old Man's reputation had ill-prepared us for his physical appearance. His large, almost massive head with its mat of unkempt grey hair dwarfed his stocky body and enfeebled legs which he supported with a walking-stick that now lay propped against the cot on which he sat. His gnarled hand clutched a pipe, like a root growing around a stone. Squinting at us out of rheumy eyes, slack mouth held open to reveal a few stumps of teeth, and head cocked sightly to one side as he listened, one had the impression that all sensory avenues to his brain had been dulled by his great age. His clothing—faded outsize overalls, a worn wool shirt, and tennis shoes—lent him a ludicrous yet pathetic air, like that of an orang-utan, "the old man of the forest," dressed up for an appearance at a carnival. The image couldn't be repressed.

Through the good offices of Prosper, we presented the Old Man with a package of tobacco and explained the purpose of our call. Would he, we asked, consent to tell us the story of his own life and something about the old Ojibwa ways? In reply John Mink said that he was old and his life was drawing to a close but that he had lived long and remembered much and would tell us what he could. He added that he would welcome our visits for he was often

[1] The customary Ojibwa greeting, borrowed from the French, *bonjour*.

lonely and said that it would make his heart glad to talk of these things.

Even on brief acquaintance it was apparent that in Prosper Guibord, then in his mid-60's, we had found an ideal interpreter. Born of an Indian mother who had married a French-American lumberjack, he was equally fluent in English and Ojibwa, and he owed allegiance to both ways of life. We arranged to hire Prosper, who had no other regular employment, and left with plans made to meet at the Old Man's house the following morning.

I was born in the time of the ripening strawberries when my people were camped near Rice Lake. My mother's mother helped at my birth and after I was cleaned up my father killed a deer for a feast. I remember being tied up on my cradleboard and watching the bright charms that hung from the hood. My mother put my umbilical cord in a little black bag when it fell off and hung it from the hood. There were strings of colored beads and muskellunge vertebrae hanging there too.

I remember the taste of my mother's milk. It tasted rich and good like bear fat, and I remember crying for the breast. When I was able to eat wild rice and venison and blueberries, I stopped nursing. Later when my parents saw that I was healthy and living good my father gave a feast for my godparents. My mother's father, a speaker of the tribe, gave me the name *shoniagízik* [Sky Money].

When I got off the cradleboard, I got my first moccasins and they had holes cut in the soles to help me walk. I was small and frisky and everyone liked me and laughed at me. My first toys were a little toboggan and a little bow and arrow. I killed squirrels and chipmunks with it and once I killed a partridge that was drumming. The arrow hit him right under the wing and he went straight up in the air and came down with his wings fluttering. My parents gave a big feast when I killed the partridge and the men told about their fasting and their dreams so that I would become strong and a good hunter. There was a big feast too when I killed my first deer with a musket. In those days there was lots of game and I can remember the great flocks of passenger pigeons so thick they darkened the sky.

I fasted all the time when I was young. In the early morning I would paint my face with charcoal and go off into the woods without eating. The spirits came to me in my dreams as I fasted and gave me the power to kill game and to cure people. They taught me songs and charms and how to suck the disease from sick people and make medicines.

Thus begain our colloquy and an almost daily association that lasted until late fall. We quickly became adjusted to Prosper's part in our conversations, even to the point of becoming forgetful of the fact that he was a necessary medium of communication between us. Prosper's habitual deference to the Old Man, for whom he had an almost filial regard, his keen interest in the trend of the discussion, and his patience served him well in the rather anonymous role of interpreter.

After a break for lunch the Old Man continued his story with an account of his marriages:

The government used to make payments to us up at La Pointe. That's where I met my first wife. We saw each other and wanted to be together. We just went to live with her folks for a while and later we made our own wigwam. She was a good worker and our wigwam was always fixed up nice with rush mats on the floor. We were happy together, but she died in childbirth after we had been married five years. I mourned for her and when I ate I put food into a dish for her and I got clothes and other things for her and kept them tied up in a bundle.

After a year I took the bundle and the dish to her folks. They had a feast and gave the bundle of clothes to the guests. Then everyone helped wash and dress me. They combed my hair too and painted my face red and blue. My wife's folks wanted to get another girl for me. She was my wife's first cousin, but I didn't want her and refused. When I was young all the women liked me because I worked hard and was a good hunter, but I loved my first wife most and even now I feel sad when I think of her.

I was single for two years before I married again, and it was then that I began to listen to the old men and to learn from them about our religion and medicine. My second wife was from the whooping crane totem and had been married before and had two girls and a boy. We lived together about ten years.

He had had four wives, he told us, and many children, all of whom had died in infancy or early childhood. "Little Girl," his last wife, died ten years ago, he said, and concluded his story: "That's all the wives I have under the ground. They are all buried down there by the river. That's why I don't want to leave this place." Then he lay back on his bed and closed his eyes.

Like many another of his advanced age, the Old Man's memory had a vagrant quality. In telling his life story and in other narratives, incidents of his middle and later years were blurred in outline and events were telescoped so that it was often difficult to disentangle their chronology. One was never sure, for example, which wife was number three and which was number four. But he had an almost startling ability to recall happenings of his childhood and his youth. He described in vivid evocative detail hunting expeditions and other adventures of his early life, many of which were tinged with a mystical quality. One had the impression that he was recounting reminiscences that had been cast repeatedly into consciousness during his lonely hours and worked upon by his memory as the sea works on a piece of driftwood. He had, moreover, a seemingly endless repertoire of songs and tales, and an encyclopedic knowledge of intricate ceremonial and other lore that, unanchored to time, could be summoned at will from this vast sea of memory. It was his boast that he could remember a song or a story after only a single hearing and his store of knowledge gave easy credence to his claim.

In the days that followed we came also to appreciate other facets of his mind and personality. Other than the tricks his memory played him, his vigorous intellect, so incongruously housed in his old body, showed few signs of senile deterioration. There was no repetitiousness, no idle meandering of talk that ended in blank befuddlement, no groping for words that wouldn't come, and it seems improbable that Prosper could have systematically filtered out such lapses. As we learned our respective parts of anthropologist and informant in the give and take of discussion, he quickly came to understand our interest in the general culture pattern rather than the particular instance and our concern with what must at times have seemed to him to be irrelevant details of behavior. He was quick, too, to grasp the point of any question, and his own sharp observations of Ojibwa customs revealed a subtle analytical habit of thought that made them as precise as those of any anthropologist. Often in giving an account of some custom or a description of a technique he would volunteer information that he thought would be of interest although we had not asked for it, and more than once he corrected or elaborated upon information that he had given us at an earlier session. He had, I am certain, countless answers to questions we had not the wit to frame.

Despite his physical infirmities, of which he rarely complained, the Old Man retained his zest for life. He often greeted us in the morning with a joke or a humorous account of a little incident that had happened since we last saw him. He might, for example, spin to epic proportions the story of how he had engaged in quixotic battle with some small marauding rodent and had routed it triumphantly from his house; or he would tell us of how he had the night before dreamed of love as if he were a young boy. He relished a bawdy joke, and he told them to us, grinning in anticipation of our guffaws as Prosper snickeringly relayed the story. He was always ready to go with us in the car on one or another minor expedition—to the rice fields, to town, to the cool shores of a nearby lake, or to a ceremony. However, on such jaunts he usually sat quietly, hands gripping his knees, as if he didn't quite trust this contraption that jounced rather wildly over the rough roads.

One day not long after our first meeting we discovered that Prosper had arrived at the cabin well before us and had deloused the Old Man and his bedding, cut his hair, shaved him, and attended to his bath. John Mink had submitted to all of these ministrations without protest, but having suffered himself to be bathed, barbered, and deloused, and made thereby presentable to a larger public, he insisted that we take his picture. On another occasion he rummaged through the large trunk that served him as both chest and closet and decked out in all the regalia that could be mustered, he posed happily for us outside his door. Such is vanity.

The news that John Mink had become our mentor in Ojibwa customs spread rapidly throughout the reservation. At first a few were suspicious of our motives and of our relationship with the Old Man, but as his protégés we soon gained acceptance by the pagan group. In his company we were welcomed where before we had been only grudgingly tolerated. Together we made the ceremonial round, attending mourning feasts, dances for the sacred drums, a celebration for a slain bear. On such occasions the Old Man was often called upon to speak. Supported by his staff, he would rise to admonish his hearers to follow the old ways, perhaps telling them to feed the mourners and honor the dead bear as was proper lest the hunter kill no meat or the rice fail to ripen. Prophet-like, he spoke as though for the tribal conscience, exhorting the laggards, reaffirming the faith.

Later that summer the Old Man's sponsorship of us was given formal expression when he gave Bob and me Ojibwa names.

Fifty or so people assembled at the drum-dance grounds for the occasion. After the feast that was a customary part of all such ceremonial affairs, John Mink got up to make his naming speech. He said that we had come to him to learn about the old Ojibwa ways, that we had spent many hours together and had become good friends. The spirits had given him many names to bestow, he said, and now he wished to give us names and make us his god-children. He had neither child nor grandchild to teach these things to, but we had been good to him, the Old Man said, and so he wanted to give us names that were close to him. Then he gave me the name *shoniagízik* after himself, and Bob he called *nibanábe* after the creature, half human, half fish, that symbolized the totem to which he belonged. Thereafter we addressed the Old Man as "god-father" and he called us "god-children."

In a small and simply organized society such as that of the Ojibwa there are few offices that correspond to the professions of civilized societies. Among these are the roles of the shaman, or medicine-man, and the religious leader. In Ojibwa society as in many other loosely structured groups these sometimes merging roles of shaman and priest were the only positions given public recognition. Around them clustered most of the codified native learning, and their occupancy carried both prestige and a certain authority. Thus these primitive professions had a natural attraction for the strong personality of intellectual bent, and John Mink was such a man. Neither afforded a full time occupation, but the Old Man had practiced both specialties for most of his adult life.

As the days passed and his trust in us grew, John Mink's early reluctance to talk about religion, medicine, and other esoteric subjects diminished so that by summer's end our conversations ranged quite freely across the whole of Ojibwa culture. Nevertheless, before broaching sacred themes he always offered tobacco to the supernaturals and when discussing these touchy matters, he was sometimes uneasy lest he be accused of perfidy by revealing to us secrets that we were not qualified to know. Several times his mounting anxiety brought an abrupt end to a discussion of these subjects, although it was often resumed at a later session.

John Mink was a master of most of the healing arts. He was physician, surgeon, obstetrician, pharmacologist, psychiatrist, homeopath, bone-setter, and blood-letter all in one. The treatment he used varied according to the nature and source of the illness, which in the more difficult cases he determined with the aid of his spirit helpers. There were many, both pagan and Christian, who sought his services for which he received modest payment in the form of gifts of food, clothing, money, or tobacco.

His knowledge of blood-letting and authority to practice it had come through a dream in which a giant horse-fly and mosquito had appeared to him. These benevolent insect powers had taught him how the veins course through the body, where they should be tapped for various ailments, and the techniques to use. Before treating a patient he would seek their guidance in both the diagnosis of the complaint and its cure, which he effected either by cupping or by opening a vein with a sharp instrument. In the former method he used a hollow cow horn that was applied to the punctured skin and the blood induced to flow by sucking through a small aperture at the tip of the horn. Others, he said, bled a patient by pricking the skin with the sharp-toothed jaw of a garfish, but he preferred to tap a vein with a steel blade.

As an adjunct to other treatment and to ward off further misfortune, the Old Man often recommended that the patient erect an "offering tree." For this a straight tree ten or more feet in height was felled. Then, stripped of its lower branches but with the topmost boughs left intact, the tree was erected in front of the patient's house and clothes hung from the tuft of branches in propitiation of the supernaturals. There were several such trees hung with tattered remnants to be seen on the reservation.

The Old Man had wide knowledge of an extensive native pharmacopoeia. He had medicines to cure gonorrhea, to staunch bleeding, to reduce fever, and to ease colic. Diuretics, physics, poultices, and tonics were in his repertoire. He had prescriptions to stop menstruation or to start it, and to induce the flow of milk in a new mother. But his favorite medicine was one that he had learned from his paternal grandfather and was used to bring on labor. The expectant mother drank the potion from a birchbark vessel on the inside of which the image of a snake was etched with the head at the place on the rim from which the woman drank. As the liquid was drained, the figure of the snake was revealed and the child thereby frightened from its mother's womb.

Some of his medicines were compounded of numerous ingredients, animal, vegetable, and mineral, including such substances as pulverized beaver testicles, cloves, bear fat, moss from a turtle's back, and Epsom salts. Other recipes called for rare or exotic plants that were traded from hand to hand and tribe to tribe from places as distant as South Dakota and Canada. Bundles of dried medicinal plants were stored in the rafters of the Old Man's house, others he preserved in cans and jars. He used to cultivate around his house a garden of the more common medicinal herbs, but now in his infirmity he was no longer able to tend it and the plantings had given way to weeds.

Scarcely a tree or plant grew for which the Old Man did not know a variety of medicinal uses. Notwithstanding his failing sight he was able to identify all but a few of the specimens we brought to him. When given a plant to identify he would run his hands gently over it, hold it close to his face to examine it, then crush a bit of it, taste it, and after a moment's deliberation, pronounce its name and describe the uses to which it was put and where it usually grew. He carefully admonished me when gathering specimens to place an offering of tobacco beside the tree or bush from which a sprig was taken or in the root-hole of the plant where, he said, a blind toad often crouched.

He prescribed sweat baths in the pungent steam of resinous evergreens as a remedy for such ailments as rheumatism and bronchial infections. Sweat-lodges were built for the purpose and steam made by throwing a brew of evergreens and other medicinal substances over hot rocks. Steam baths, he said, were also taken in a kind of purification ritual by persons who had handled a corpse and by hunters to rid themselves of tell-tale body odors before going out in search of deer or bear. He described one such bath he had made for a large party of hunters who then went out and brought back a record bag of game.

One morning on arriving at the cabin we found the Old Man missing and discovered him in the woods nearby steaming his rheumatic legs. He explained that he had been troubled by his legs ever since he had years ago accidently stepped over a discarded menstrual napkin. A woman's menstrual blood was regarded as a highly dangerous substance. It sickened or killed the tiny spirits that dwelt in one's limbs, he said, and cited instances where inadvertent contact with it had led to paralysis or other crippling affliction. Women are careless these days, John Mink said, and young girls are no longer taught the proper menstrual taboos. He told how his first wife used to eat out of her own special dishes when she was menstruating and wouldn't let him come near her, and how when it was over she would walk up to him and kiss him.

By far the most dramatic and powerful therapy practiced by the Old Man was that performed in a shamanistic seance during which he magically sucked the disease substance out of the patient. This was the treatment he used primarily for those who were the victims of sorcery. Although he had rarely performed such cures in recent years, he assured us that he was willing to have us witness a demonstration of his art. Prosper, who had not been feeling well avowed that he had been wanting the Old Man to treat him. His reluctance to ask for this favor now dispelled by the Old Man's willingness to undertake a cure, he happily volunteered to be his patient. We agreed to act as Prosper's sponsors by providing the necessary payment for the Old Man's services and arrangements were made to hold the curing ceremony on the following evening.

We gathered at the Old Man's cabin shortly after dusk. Besides the principals and us as observers, the company included four others—Andrew Quagan, the drummer, Mary Marten, her daughter, Alice, and her granddaughter, a child of 10. After we had assembled, Andrew, acting as the Old Man's assistant, covered the windows to exclude both prying eyes and the last light of day. He then tightly closed the door, first making a brief tour of the premises to see that there were no dogs about whose barking would frighten away the spirit helpers. A guttering candle burning in the corner provided the only light.

We spectators sat in a semicircle around the supine form of Prosper, our intent faces illumined by the uncertain yellow candlelight. The Old Man, his figure grotesquely silhouetted, stood opposite us. Prosper lay motionless before him on a blanket, eyes closed and arms extended at his sides, his gifts to the Old Man, a pair of tennis shoes and a package of tobacco, displayed for all to see. Andrew put two finger-length tubes from the polished leg bones of a deer into a shallow pie tin half filled with salt water, which he in turn placed on the floor at Prosper's side and covered with a red bandanna. This done, Andrew took his position off to one side, his drum in his lap.

The scene thus set, the Old Man began the ceremony with a recitation of his fasting experience. He told how in a dream on the fifth night of his fast he was led to a conjuror's hut by a flock of wild geese. Inside the swaying hut, which he entered through a hole at the top, were a spikebuck and six spirits. Later, her approach heralded by the sound of singing and laughter, they were joined by a beautifully dressed lady whose home was behind the sun. These were the ones, he said, who taught him how to cure people and told him the songs to sing in summoning their help.

His recitation finished, he took up his rattle (a quart oil can filled with buckshot), and accompanied by Andrew on the tambourine drum, began to sing in his hoarse, rather breathless voice. After singing a cycle of songs to call his spirit helpers, the Old Man dropped to his knees at Prosper's side and shook the rattle over him and also around his own body. As the drumming continued, he put one of the bone tubes into his mouth and after a brief pause, tossed back his head and swallowed it, shuddering and jerking his body as the spirits entered it. Still kneeling, the Old Man then regurgitated the tube and, bending close, sucked through it several times in the region of Prosper's lower abdomen. After each sucking he blew through the tube into the pan of salt water. Finally, obviously winded by his exertions, he spat out the tube. The drumming abruptly stopped and Andrew got up to help the Old Man to his feet.

After a brief interlude the Old Man sang another song and began a second series of suckings. This time he succeeded in extracting a small piece of whitish substance which was passed around in the pie tin for inspection before Andrew disposed of it. The Old Man said that he had gotten out only a part of the disease, but added that he believed he could get the rest of it the following evening, when he would use a stronger spirit.

Prosper, his face flushed, arose somewhat giddily from the floor and made a ribald quip. The hushed, intense atmosphere was immediately dissipated, a lamp was lit, and a bantering conversation began. Old Mary Marten, a giantess among women, suggestively invited the Old Man to go for a walk in the woods—as brother- and sister-in-law an intimate "joking relationship" was customary between them. With elaborate thanks for the compliment, he declined, saying that he had never known a mole to have sexual intercourse successfully with a she-bear. In this light mood the women then served a meal of wild rice and sweet buns which they had brought with them. The food eaten, the Old Man sang four more songs, whooping after each, which he said he did to frighten away the disease. The evening's ceremonies thus concluded, we disbanded at midnight.

We reassembled the following evening at the same hour and with some modifications the ceremony of the previous night was repeated. Prosper, averring that he had slept well for the first night in months, resumed his position on the floor, this time stripped to the waist. His gifts to the Old Man were a pair of gloves and two packages of tobacco.

For the evening's second course of treatments, the Old Man asked Alice to put the bone tube in his mouth and gave Mary the rattle to shake. He did this, he said, because two female spirits were helping him that night. After sucking a couple of times he asked Andrew to get a larger bone which was secreted under the bed. He swallowed the tube, alarming us all by momentarily gagging on it, then he regurgitated it and sucked again near Prosper's navel. On the first attempt he sucked out several pieces of the same white stuff and announced that he had now gotten it all.

The Old Man said that Prosper had been sorcerized by a woman, immediately identified by Prosper as a former mistress with whom he had lived for two years and subsequently deserted. Prosper said that he could feel the bone go right through him and that he could also feel the place in his lower right abdomen from which the disease had been removed. He thanked the Old Man for saving his life, adding that he was sure the disease would shortly have killed him, for the woman had never forgiven him.

In spite of his age, the Old Man's performance had force and high dramatic quality. Here, magically recreated in this cabin was an expression of the human mind and spirit to which we all are heir; a rite that in the same essential form must have been practiced by the forebears of us all before the dawn of history. Watching him as the ceremony unfolded, one could not but be conscious of its impending obsolescence as well as its deep continuity with the past. John Mink was the only one left on the reservation who still undertook such cures and the performance we had witnessed may well have been the last of its kind at Court Oreilles.

For John Mink the line between the natural and the supernatural was thinly drawn. His world was filled with an infinite array of spirits and forces that could influence the affairs of men. Nor was man conceived as a creature apart from the rest of nature. For the Ojibwa, as for many hunting peoples, animals and men are akin and the differences between them lay chiefly in outward form. Animals are motivated as men are motivated, live in societies as men live, act as men act, and their fates are intertwined. Thus, the Old Man told how when a bear was killed its four paws and head were placed in position on a rush mat and a feast was given. He described how the head was decorated with ribbons, beadwork, or a baby's clothes and food and tobacco put nearby; and how people would come and talk to the bear endearingly so that its spirit would return to the village of the bears and persuade other bears to allow themselves to be killed.

Contact with the spirit world was for the most part made by means of formal prayers and ceremonies. However, one might have other more casual encounters with the spirits as well, and the Old Man told us about a number of such confrontations he had had. These often had a sort of mystical quality and it was evident from the manner in which he spoke about them that they had been among the most memorable experiences of his long life. He told how once while hunting he saw a strangely spotted deer step out of the forest and before his eyes walk across the water to disappear into a misty lake. He had glimpsed the monsters that lurked in some lakes, he said, and had seen the water break into boiling whirlpools as they thrust beneath the surface.

The Old Man believed in charms and portents, in sorcery and transformations, and in the power for both good and evil of those who had fasted and dreamed. There were those, he said (and he was one of them), who could make the skins of loons come alive and cry out in order to foretell the future. He told how Old Man Skunk, now long dead, used a downy woodpecker skin that would move its head and make a tapping sound, and how for evil ends he would use the skin of an owl. And John Mink had often seen the "shaking tent" conjurors perform, but although he knew how to construct the conjuror's hut and possessed the power to summon the spirits to the magically swaying structure, he had never practiced the art out of fear of its possible bad consequences.

The Old Man claimed that he had never used his power for evil purposes, but there were many on the reservation who swore that they had been sorcerized by him and laid all their misfortunes at his door. Few doubted his powers and most were prepared to lend some degree of credence to the rumors that circulated about him. Even his staunchest friends, Prosper among them, regarded him with a kind of wary ambivalence compounded of both fear and deep respect. Prosper himself once confided to me that he was careful never to cross the Old Man lest he do him harm.

The second office held by John Mink was that of ceremonial leader in both the Medicine Lodge Society or *midewiwin,* the principal ceremonial complex of the Wisconsin Ojibwa, and in the Drum Dance, a quasisocial society centering about a number of highly decorated sacred drums. As the foremost priest in the *midewiwin,* the Old Man had in his custody a birchbark scroll some six feet long on which pictographs and other mnemonic devices were engraved. Each of the scroll's four panels represented the ceremonial and related lore learned by candidates for one of the four degrees in the *midewiwin,* which in the order taken are symbolized by ornamented pouches made from the skins of the otter, raven, fox, and bear, or animals of related species. Every spring and fall week-long ceremonies were held at the *mide* grounds, culminating in a colorful and elaborate two-day public ceremony in the Medicine Lodge itself, a long, open structure made of arched poles decorated with cedar and pine boughs.

That autumn the ceremonies were held in early October and the Old Man took his usual active part in them. Each morning we drove him to the *mide* grounds where his days were given to the instruction and catechization of the six initiates in one or another of the birchbark wigwams temporarily erected nearby. His evenings and a few afternoons were spent in consultation and celebration with other priests and elder members of the Society. Long into the still autumn nights one could hear the sounds of drumming and singing issuing from the various wigwams where the celebrants were gathered.

Preparations finally completed and the Medicine Lodge freshly repaired and decorated, the public ceremonies began on the morning of the seventh day. The American flag was raised. A black mongrel dog was taken off into the woods by one of the "runners" who

481

assisted the officials. There the dog was killed and its body dragged back to the lodge. The initiates and Society members, several score in all, dressed in their most brightly colored clothes and carrying their medicine pouches in one hand and buckets of food in the other, lined up at the north entrance. After an opening song they began to file clockwise slowly around the Lodge. Too feeble to join in their awkward, halting march, the Old Man was led to his solitary place inside the Lodge. Thus commenced the long and elaborate ceremony. Among its features were the magical "shooting" of the participants with *migis,* the variously colored cowrie shells contained in the pouches, and the cermonial eating of the dog which, cleaned and singed, had been boiled in an iron camp kettle. It required a strong stomach to taste of the coarse meat that was offered to us, permeated as it was with the smell of burnt hair. Dog was eaten, the Old Man told us, so that the human beings who ate it would become as faithful to the supernaturals as a dog is to its master.

The ceremony lasted until sundown of the second day and John Mink was the last to leave the Lodge. He had participated throughout, making numerous speeches and being frequently consulted by other officials about the procedures to be followed. As we drove him home, he complained in a strangely querulous voice that it had gone off too slowly and that too many unnecessary things had been done. He was very tired, he said, and didn't think he would last out the winter—and he told Prosper to make sure that he was buried with his medicine pouch and beadwork bandelier.

As shaman and ceremonial leader, John Mink's services were in demand at every crisis in the life cycle from birth to death, and many were the petitioners who came to his door. He had ushered numerous children into the world, and he had named and been godfather to scores more, one of his boasts being that he had been godfather to child, parent, and grandparent in a single family. He had taken part in many of the mourning feasts that are held on the anniversary of a close relative's death, and he had been summoned many times by a runner bearing a gift of tobacco to officiate at a funeral.

Others came to him as a kind of confessor or to ask his advice on matters both trivial and momentous. Once when we were engrossed in a discussion of some moot point of custom, we were interrupted by a man who brought the paws and some meat of a bear he had just killed. Not knowing the proper ceremony, nor willing to risk its omission, he had come to ask the Old Man to smoke a pipe with him and to say a few words in celebration of the occasion. This he did, and the man left content in the thought that he had done the right thing.

As he was wont to do when queried about a particular observance, the Old Man recounted a personal experience to illustrate Ojibwa mortuary customs, punctuating his account with brief asides when he touched upon points where practice varied. In this instance he had been called to officiate at the funeral of a woman who had died that spring. He told in great detail how he had seen to the proper preparation of the body of the dead woman for burial, taking care that the cheeks were painted and that her medicine pouch was placed on her chest as she lay covered with a sheet on a rude catafalque of planks. He told how he had presented a bowl of food to the corpse during the wake, telling her to eat so that she would be strong for the long journey to the village of the dead; and he repeated the speech he had made for the dead woman when her coffin had been lowered into the grave.

She would have a long trip to the land of the dead, he said, and he told her not to look back, but to go right on, making sure to leave offerings of tobacco and to obey the injunctions of the spirits she would meet along the way. He told her that on the fourth day she would come to a river spanned by what appeared to be a log, but which in reality was a huge snake. Similarly, what appeared to be a clump of red willows growing alongside the river would actually be a wigwam. The bridge, he told her, is guarded by two gaunt dogs and attended by two old women in whose custody the journey would be completed. His oration ended, the grave was filled and marked by a wood stake on which the symbol of the deceased's totem was painted upside down. He added that it made him mad because he always had to make such speeches since no one else would learn them or had the gumption to get up and speak.

The Old Man strongly disapproved of the changes, such as the practice of holding wakes, tossing a handful of earth on the coffin, or burial in distant places, that had been introduced in the mortuary customs. In the old days, John Mink said, the dead were buried close by in graves lined with birchbark and food was regularly placed at the entrance of the grave-houses erected over them. No longer, he said, are poles put up in front of the graves from which passers-by might take the gifts of clothing and necklaces hung there and wear them in honor of the deceased. Nowadays, he said, the dead are neglected and disowned.

The Old Man often expressed a strong craving for the native Ojibwa foods and after long denial would eat ravenously of such delicacies as fresh-killed venison, bear fat, or wild rice. Although frequently in precarious supply, there was variety in the native larder and John Mink described the seasonal round of the food quest with obvious relish. He told in full detail how wild rice, the staple food, was harvested, threshed, and winnowed, how in early spring the hard maples were tapped, the sap boiled down, and cakes of maple sugar made in birchbark or clam shell molds, and how blueberries were gathered, dried, and stored in bark containers.

He described how in early April when the black suckers were running up the cold streams and their flesh was white and firm they were caught by hand or in a variety of simple traps. Gutted and their heads and tails cut off, they were smoked and stored in bales and the Old Man recalled roasting them in hot coals and eating them as a kind of snack when he was a boy. And he told how they used to sit on logs alongside a weir and the men joke and the women giggle as they caught the suckers that swam up onto a rack of poles.

Ice-fishing in the winter, however, was a solitary pursuit. A hole would be cut in the ice over a bar in five to ten feet of water, the Old Man said, and a blanket draped over the fisherman's head and shoulders and tightly secured so that no light would be let in. A weighted decoy in the form of a frog or minnow was bobbed from a short handle and a spear with tines of native copper held ready. When a fish approached the fisherman let the spear slide slowly down into the water until it was about a foot away and then the fish was deftly jabbed. The fish quickly froze solid, the Old Man said, and he would carry them home like a bundle of firewood.

For the hunting peoples of the northern latitudes starvation is a lurking threat that rides the winter blizzards and the biting cold. Stories of cannibalism were related by the Ojibwa and half-believed, for here was a theme, like those of classic drama, fascinating in its horrible possibility. Thus, John Mink told many tales about the *windigo*, legendary cannibalistic monsters that stalked the woods in the lean winter months, in whom these fears were joined and given mythological expression:

One winter morning the people noticed that the kettle hanging over the fire began to swing back and forth, and they were scared because they knew a *windigo* was coming. Everyone trembled with fear and no one was brave or strong enough to challenge the *windigo*. Finally they sent for a wise old woman who lived with her little granddaughter at the edge of the village, but the old woman said she was powerless to do anything. The little girl asked what was the matter and they told her that they were all going to die. Then the little girl asked for two sticks of peeled sumac as long as her arms and took them off home with her while all the others huddled together in one place.

That night it turned so bitter cold that the people's bones came near to cracking open. Early the next morning the little girl told her grandmother to melt a kettle of tallow over the fire. Meanwhile it turned colder and colder until the people looked and there coming over the hill was a *windigo* as tall as a white pine tree. Trees cracked open and the river froze solid when he passed by.

The little girl went out to meet him with a sumac stick gripped in each hand. Her two dogs ran on ahead and quickly killed the *windigo*'s dog, but he kept coming closer. The little girl got bigger and bigger as he approached until when they met she was as big as the *windigo* himself. She knocked him down with one sumac stick and crushed his skull in with the other—they had both turned into copper. After the girl killed the *windigo*, she gulped down the hot tallow and then got smaller and smaller until she was herself again. The people rushed over to the dead *windigo* and began to chop him up. He was made of ice, but in the center was the body of a man with his skull crushed in. The people were all very happy and gave the little girl everything she wanted.

That summer we listened to the Old Man tell many tales, including the epic myths of *Wenabojo*, the mischievous and comic culture hero, whom the Ojibwa affectionately called, "nephew." One long tale of *Wenabojo*, two days in the telling, embodied the Noah-like Ojibwa story of flood and re-creation of the earth wherein after loon, otter, and beaver had failed, muskrat succeeded in diving to the bottom of the deep and all-enveloping sea and coming up with a pawful of mud from which *Wenabojo*, with the help of all the animals and birds, refashioned the earth. The tale was told with a true storyteller's art that not even translation or our meager knowledge of the language could mask. The Old Man gave all the characters their separate voices, enlivened the tale with interjections, songs, and animal cries, and punctuated it with pauses and dramatic gestures.

Although too young to be himself a participant, the Old Man related many stories, too, of the war between the Ojibwa and the Woodland Dakota Sioux. As a boy he had been present at the "Chief Dances" that were held at both the departure and return of a war party. At them he had seen impaled on sticks the bloody trophy heads of the Sioux that had been slain, and he had listened to the returned warriors who, their faces still painted and wearing only a breechclout and an eagle feather in their hair, described their exploits to the last grisly detail.

By mid-autumn I had spent many days and hours with the Old Man and we had discussed virtually all aspects of Ojibwa culture. The intricacies of kinship and social organization, a prime anthropological topic, received particular attention. Using sticks for males and stones for females, we made diagrams in the sand to represent the relationships between various kin. The Old Man supplied the appropriate kinship terms and described the behavior that customarily obtained between persons in specific relationships. In an account spiced with numerous anecdotes, he described the horseplay and broad joking that went on between brothers- and sisters-in-law, and the warm relationships that held between grandparent and grandchild, and between a man and his sister's son. He listed the various *dodems,* the loosely organized patrilineal groups to which the Ojibwa owed allegiance—catfish, wolf, lynx, bear, marten, deer, eagle, sturgeon, bullhead, whooping crane, loon, and the one to which John Mink belonged, *nibanabe,* a mermaid-like creature. If a person's totem or totem animal were insulted, the Old Man said, he would give a feast to which the offender and his totem-mates would be invited and good-naturedly forced to drink huge quantities of whiskey and gorge themselves with food.

He described the old Ojibwa arts and crafts which only a few still practiced, explaining how a birchbark canoe was constructed, how a bow was made, and how the arrows were shaped, pointed, and fletched, how glue was made from the swim-bladder of a sturgeon, and how a lacrosse club was fashioned. In heroic terms he described, too, the bitterly contested day-long lacrosse games that used to be played and on which huge amounts of various personal effects were bet.

The Old Man was familiar as well with the handicrafts that were the women's special province. He told how deer hides were fleshed, soaked in a solution of dried deer brains, then stretched, scraped again, and after they were dried and white as snow, formed into a closed cylinder and smoked over a smudge pot. He described how the women made rush mats, how they would weave beautiful colored patterns out of dyed porcupine quills that had been flattened by pulling them through their clenched teeth, and how they would bite designs into small squares of birchbark.

"That's how things used to be," John Mink said. "The women were proud in the old days. They looked good in their braids and long dresses and they worked hard. Now they are lazy and dress in rags. There was always food in my wigwam then and I had many things. Now I live alone in a cold and empty house. The men no longer believe in anything. It is as though they were lost at a fork in the road and don't know which way to take. There is no one left here to take my place."

I last saw John Mink when we stopped by his cabin on the grey November morning we left the reservation. He came to the door to greet us with the shout, little ponderous jig, and flourish of his stick that had become a joke between us. We sat with him to smoke a pipeful of tobacco and talked for a while in the pidgin of Ojibwa, English, and exaggerated pantomine that we had jointly contrived. But even had Prosper been with us, there would have no words with which to say "good-by." When we got up to go the Old Man came outside with us and watched as we walked away down the path, his stick raised high in a gesture of farewell. Then, as we faded from his dim sight, he turned and went slowly back into his house.

~~~~~~~~~

John Mink was something of an anachronism. Born in the middle of the last century when the old Ojibwa life still flourished, he escaped the dilemma of younger men whose heritage was a moribund culture and who had no pride in the past and little hope for the future. He took what he pleased of things the white man had to offer—a gun, clothes, whiskey—but beyond such furnishings and what he knew of the rowdy company of the lumber camps he had few contacts with white culture. Nor did he want more. His faith in Ojibwa ways held firm, and he lived out a full life secure in a tradition he had mastered and found satisfying. This sense of integrity and a certain dignity of character are the qualities I remember best in John Mink. To me he seemed a truly exceptional man, one who in another time and place might even have achieved greatness. But he was probably no more exceptional than many another unsung tribal elder. Through his eyes I glimpsed another way of life that he saw whole. I am grateful to him for this, and for his friendship.

19

A Pueblo G.I.

John Adair

Soon after arriving at the pueblo, I heard that Marcus Tafoya would make a good informant. He was a veteran of World War II, about 30 years of age, and married into a family prominent in the religious life of his pueblo. His wife belonged to a clan that "owned" many religious offices, including one of the high-priesthoods of the village.

With this tip about Marcus, I approached the house of his wife, Maud Arviso. It was an imposing one near the center of the village, built of morticed stone with the new style gabled roof and front porch. Venetian blinds at the windows gave the place a look of prosperity in contrast to the mud-plastered, flat-roofed houses next door.

A woman about 22 years old, whom I judged to be his wife, greeted me at the door.

"Come in and have a seat," she said in perfect English.

"Is Marcus here?" I asked as I sat down on an elaborate over-stuffed chair.

"No, he has gone to the store, but he will be right back. What do you want?"

Her boldness in meeting strangers set her apart from other Pueblo women I had met; however, her manner was quite in harmony with her house—in both there was a spirit of revolt, yet not so complete that the new fully replaced the old. On one side of the fireplace was a radio; resting on the far side of the mantle was a bowl of sacred corn meal. As my eyes roamed around the room, I spotted other evidences of Pueblo tradition: a cradleboard; a house-blessing fetish, tied to a ceiling beam; and out beyond, in the kitchen alongside the enameled gas range, a metate and mano. The traditional was there all right, but in this house the modern veneer was more blatant than in most.

"I have been talking to veterans here in the village, and I understand he is one," I answered.

She asked me to have some coffee while I waited, and as I drank, she sat down and we continued to talk.

"Where was I from? What was I doing? How long did I intend

to stay? Had I got permission from the Governor to work in the pueblo?" These questions and a dozen others came pouring out. I was as noncommittal as I could be and still satisfy her curiosity. Then quite abruptly she asked, "Are you an anthropologist?"

"Yes, I'm a student from the University," I confessed.

"Do you know ————? He was in the village some years ago."

It was just as well that I answered "No," for she went on: "I never saw what he wrote, but it couldn't be any good. He worked with ————," and she named a bitter rival on the other side of the village who had befriended and worked with anthropologists.

I began to squirm in my chair. Would her husband ever come, I wondered. But with each lull in the conversation, Maud picked it up once more and engaged my attention. She was taking no chances on her husband losing out on informant's fees.

Finally, Marcus arrived, groceries in hand. He was not as short or stocky as most of the young Pueblo men, and a fineness of features gave him a Navaho look. He wore bluejeans, work shoes, and a G.I. shirt—like many of the veterans in the pueblo.

I repeated some of what I had already told his wife and added, "I would like to know how the veterans are getting on in the village, what kinds of jobs they have, and how it seems to be home after those years away in the service."

"I see you are wearing your sun-tans," he said. "At first I thought you were a recruiting sergeant here to sign me up for another hitch."

We both laughed. That led to our obliquely sounding each other out. In contrast to his wife, Marcus was almost bashful. As she was preparing supper, we each found out where the other had been in the service, for how long, and when discharged. Marcus, I learned, got out eighteen months ago. But as members of the family gathered for the evening meal, I decided to wait until another time to continue the interview. It was with some misgivings that I asked if I could see him on the next day. Other veterans had said "Yes," but hadn't shown up.

Marcus was there at the appointed time on the following day. After further exchange of war experiences, I asked him if he would be willing to take a test I was giving the veterans. He was too embarrassed to say "No," and not ready with an excuse, so he lamely said "Yes," and we sat down at a table in the back room.

The test was one of the projective type, the well-known Thematic

Apperception Test. As we looked at the pictures and I asked him to tell me about each, I sensed an uneasiness even before he spoke.

"What am I supposed to say now? I'm not sure I know how to answer this one."

My explanation that there was no correct answer was not reassuring.

"I'm just a dumb Indian. I don't know all that stuff. You should go see Joe Mirabal. He'll give you the right answers. He's studying at the University."

I put the test back in its folder and there followed, much to my surprise, another barrage of questions. "Where was I staying in the pueblo? Did I live right in the house with the family?" And Maud, who had come in from time to time to see how we were doing, joined in.

"How much do they charge you for that room? For your meals? Do they give you enough to eat?" she asked.

"They are real stingy," she added. "At our last fiesta they hardly fed their guests a thing, and look at all the sheep they own."

After a brief pause, she continued, "You should have come here first. We wouldn't have charged you so much. My sister has a house with a couple of spare rooms. I am sure she would have been glad to rent them to you."

I told her I wished I had done so, and then switched back to Marcus and asked him if I could talk to him again another time. Before he answered, he glanced up at Maud and I knew by the set expression on her face that he could not have said "No." When I went out of the house to my car, Marcus followed. I told him I wanted to pay him for his time.

"You don't owe me a thing. I flunked that test," he said.

It didn't go so well in the household where I was staying. The annual *Indian Drums* tourist attraction at one of the towns on the highway had just closed. A few days later I learned that a rumor was going around the village that I had written a piece in the special edition of the local newspaper about the sacred clowns of the pueblo. The article was one from the paper's files based on an ethnologist's account of seventy years back. This they took out every few years and refurbished for a new crop of tourists.

As time passed, I learned that one of the men of the house where I was living had entered my room during my absence and looked through the notes which I had been careful to hide under the mattress. (I was becoming as secretive and suspicious as the Indians themselves.) There he had run across the native name for these clowns in a life history I was taking of one of the veterans.

Needless to say, this discovery didn't help me in my relations with my landlord or his veteran sons. I knew that they were looking for an excuse to be rid of me as they had begun to feel I was bringing shame to their house. Since my family was joining me in the pueblo, I needed larger quarters and this provided the "out" both my landlord and I were looking for.

The house Maud had mentioned would serve our needs if it were fixed up a bit, and when I approached her sister about the matter she was pleased at the prospect. We entered as careful a set of business transactions as any concierge with a promising tenant. These included an agreement that I would purchase all of our firewood from the men in her family.

A good share of the work fixing up the old house fell to Marcus and I assisted him in various ways. But I was of greatest use in driving him to town for supplies. As we drove along, we fell to talking about days in the service. We both had been in the Air Corps.

"I felt free as a bird when I was in the army," he said. "For the first time in my life, I could do just what I pleased. There was no one snooping into my business, no one gossiping about me. It sure felt good."

"Did your buddies from other parts of the country feel the same way?"

"Hell, no," he replied. "They did nothing but bitch all the time. There wasn't anything good about it—the food, the drills, inspection, it was all p—s poor according to them. But for me, it was sure a welcome change.

"Just before I went into the service, I decided the hell with it. I might just as well have some fun before I left. I didn't care what the people in the village would say after I left. I was going to be gone for a long time. Maybe I wouldn't even get home again.

"So I got hold of a case of wine and stayed drunk for two weeks.

493

Me and some of the other fellows sure had fun with the girls. Shacked-up just about every night. We sure left plenty of gossip behind us when we did leave."

Maud and Marcus were not married until after the war. He had courted her some years earlier but she had married another fellow and he turned to another girl. However, Maud was still interested in Marcus, and wrote to him when he was in service camp.

"She got my address from my younger brother," Marcus said. "We wrote back and forth and those letters got hotter and hotter. Then one day her husband went to the Post Office and opened one of those letters. They busted up in 1943."

"Why?" I asked.

"He drank too much and was lazy," Marcus replied.

After several such talks, I asked Marcus if he would tell me the story of his life, saying that I could better tell how he felt about the village and his army life if I knew more about his family, his boyhood, his schooling, and the like.

His first reaction was like the time I gave him the test. I could tell before he replied that he didn't want to do so, yet he didn't want to turn me down. Finally, he agreed but only after I promised that we would work at my house and at night.

"If I were to come over here in the daytime, or if people saw us talking at my house, they would say that you were writing another piece for that paper on the religion of my people," he said with a nervous laugh. "Those old people don't know that there aren't any secrets left. All of that stuff was sold long ago," he added.

I agreed with him but said, "I know, but let's not add to the gossip. There are enough rumors going around about me as it is."

"And what about me," he said. "Already the people call me 'newista.'"

"What's that?" I asked.

"White-lover," he replied.

Marcus was very self-conscious as he started to tell me of his life, and I was never sure he wouldn't find an excuse for breaking off. With each episode he would ask, "Is that the sort of thing you want me to tell you?"

The best reassurance I could give him was to ask that he tell me more. It was not long before he was back to his boyhood, living it over and enjoying the telling of it.

But these early years were recalled in a rather matter-of-fact way—as if that life was so foreign to me that sharing it was futile. It was easier to talk as we had on those trips to town about common experiences in the service. Even his initiation into the tribal dance cult was told stiffly, and in the second person, as if he were summarizing what he had read in some ethnologist's monograph rather than telling me about what had happened to him. The excitement he must have felt, the drama, the brilliantly costumed dancers, these were all omitted from his flat account:

"Now the dancers get in line in the middle of the plaza. They take the clothes off you and put on only two blankets with the canvas covering; this time you are on the back of your guardian again. They all go through, pass the line of dancers, each hits you four times now, this time you could feel the pain. Some boys cry for help. The people laugh."

But as the story of his life progressed, Marcus became more personally involved and that other person he was talking about eventually became him.

He told of his life at school, of fights with the other boys on the playground, and always with special interest he related the summer adventures at the ranch where his family lived, ten miles or more from the pueblo.

Every year when the school ends I went home to the family ranch. The same work each year, nothing new. One day, me and Robert was going through a pine forest, the rain really poured on us, we had to stop. We were riding horseback. Lightning almost struck us, it struck a pine tree about fifteen feet away. The horses kicked and wheeled. We smelled that lightning odor so knowing the Indian superstition we hurried home, on one horse, the other one ran away when I let loose the reins.

My father was out in the corral, and the first thing he asked me was if I was hurt. He thought the horse threw me off. We told him what happened and he didn't let us go in the house. He told us to stay outdoors. It was still raining then. We had to stay outside when he went out to the field to look for them black young beetles, stink-bugs, I think you call them. When he came back, he told us to strip down our clothes, let the rain wash us down. Then he told my mother to make tortillas half-done, also the meat half cooked. He put the black beetles in between the meat and between the tortillas. Before we ate he took us down to the small stream, it was one of those made by the rain. We bathed in there from head to toe and we went up to the house and we ate those stink-bug sandwiches. Boy they tasted bitter. Like chili, they were hot. He picked up some of that stuff, the twigs that come with the flood, made some prayer, and made a motion around in the air and threw the twigs away. After we ate then he let us into the house.

That summer there was an eagle, the same eagle that has his nest about two miles from our place. My dad and I were after that eagle, so one day, we went out to see if its young were ready to fly. There were two of them, she had her nest on top of the highest steep cliff. It was about four times as high as the highest pine tree. I made a strong sling shot, but the pebbles didn't reach. I tried to scare them down. There was a way of going up the west side. But when you get on top of the mesa, you see that tall monument-like cliff is separated from the mesa by a crevasse that is about 50 feet deep. A long time ago a Navaho tried to get across that 50-foot crevasse; he only climbed half way and he fell backwards. So from that time on no one tried to get across.

My father had a .38 revolver so the next day we took it with us. He shot about two feet away from that nest, until one of the young ones got scared and flew down. We watched her till she disappeared among the pine trees. We followed and searched about an hour before we found her. She flew when we got near her, then next time she tried to fly she only jumped ten or fifteen feet at a time. We caught her when she got tired. We tied her around the legs with string and carried her home. We made a cage with a post in the middle for her roost. Whenever it rained hard I used to go out and get prairie dogs by running the water into their holes and I fed them to the eagle. Or else I go out early in the morning and late in the evenings after the rabbits. The people use eagle feathers for their prayer sticks. My father was one of the Snake Society—he was their boss, their chief, he used many feathers on the prayer sticks. So we took care of the eagle well.

School started too soon. When I have a lot to do during the summer when school opens I hate to come to the pueblo. That's when I was always shy when school opens, especially among girls. Everybody seems to be all dressed up. So I had to look my best. Usually I have sunburn 'cause I was always out of doors during the summer. My eighth year in school Teddy, my older brother, went away to the Sante Fe Indian School, so did Dolores, my sister. I and Bill, my younger brother, were the only ones that went to school in the village that year.

I seemed to have chased around quite a bit. I didn't stay home during the evenings mostly. I got a quick bite of supper 'cause there were always some of my friends calling me out. Mrs. Umberto who I stayed with that year didn't like me fooling around late at night so I used to sneak out. Their folks don't want them out late at night so that is why they whistle at each other to come out. When they want to call each other they just whistle, or else they have a special place to meet at a certain time. Nowadays they can visit each other at their homes. That time I went to talk to my girl she has to make a good excuse to go out at night. Sometimes girls have funny excuses, such as if there isn't any washing to do she thinks of things she is going to wash so she can throw the water out. Like handkerchiefs, or bandannas or dishtowels. Just so she could go out to throw the water out and meet her boy friend. Else she tell her folks that she wants to chop some wood. Sometimes if it is all right she will let her boy friend do the chopping.

Those days we had hard times visiting our girl friends at night. During cold days in the winter time the boys always have their blankets on, they are usually dark for the purpose you can't be seen in the night I suppose. That is still the style among the people. They also put a pretty bandanna around their head.

After three or four such sessions at our house, Marcus said he would have to break off his story as he had to take his turn herding at the family sheep camp. I asked him if we could continue his story out there.

"That would be good. I get awfully bored herding those dumb sheep. I follow along just like one of them. I hate it. But I'm sure you wouldn't like it either. You're used to city ways. It's rough out there, just camp style."

I arrived at the sheep camp several days later, threw my bedroll down beside some sagebrush, and set out walking over the rolling range land that stretched to the horizon on all sides. A few piñon trees scattered here and there made the sweep seem more immense. Far to the south I spotted Marcus following the sheep as they headed toward the watering tank marked by a windmill against the sky.

I approached, greeted Marcus, and helped him fix some sandwiches which we ate sitting under a juniper tree close by the ranch house.

"Gee, I'm glad to see you, John. It's sure lonely out here—worse than any guard duty I ever had."

"Well," I said, "it seems good to get away from the village and out to the open country. I guess I'm getting to be like one of your people. I imagine others are gossiping about me all the time."

"That's a sure sign if you really feel that way," Marcus replied.

"But that's not all," I said. "Worse than that—after hearing all those stories about witches that you told us at our house, my wife has been uneasy. She said she heard someone prowling around in that empty room next door. In fact, she didn't like to stay home alone with the children when I came out here." (This I said in complete honesty.)

"My wife is just the same way. She's scared to death of witches. She won't stay in the house alone when I'm gone. She takes the children and goes over to stay with relatives. All of us are the same way. We are constantly watching for those jealous people. Just the other day, my wife was in the trading post and she heard a woman boasting about what a good crop of fat lambs her family had this year. My wife told me it just sent the shivers up her spine to hear her talk like that, because standing right behind her was one of the biggest witches in the whole village."

We talked more about the witches as we got up and moved off, following the sheep.

"That's another thing I liked about being in the army. There were no witches over there. It felt good to be away from all these worries. But they came back again as soon as I returned home."

"Do the people have any way of getting rid of those witches?" I asked.

"No, that's the trouble," Marcus answered. "In the old days they did. They'd string them up from the ceiling beams by their elbows until they confessed or died—at least that's what my folks told me."

"And today?"

"Today the government won't let us do that so these witches just keep multiplying."

"What do you do to try and forget about them?" I asked.

"Well, getting away from the village helps. But even out here you're not completely safe. Those witches go after the sheep, too. Just last month we had a medicine man come out here to suck some stuff out of one of the sheep. It had been placed there by one of those people. We think we know who it was that did it."

The sheep were all bunched up now, browsing in a place where the grass was long and thick.

"I see you brought your paper along. We better start in again on my story, or we'll never finish," Marcus said. "Where were we when we stopped? Oh, I remember now. I had reached England with the troops.

"Another thing I thought was funny, all those English people rode around on those bicycles; and when I first saw that village with all those chimneys in those houses, all just alike in a row. This village was called Little Stockton, and it was about twelve miles to Bedford. Another thing, the sergeant got each of us English bicycles. We used to go out riding on the country roads. It surprised me, all those country roads were paved, no dirt roads. About those English workmen, I got a kick out of them. Every morning at ten o'clock, teatime in those old style jugs. They squatted on the cement and had tea. There is another one at two o'clock in the afternoon. The workmen have those black clothes with narrow pants. That seemed funny. Also those small autos, not streamlined. And they told us that it was only a wealthy person who could own one."

As Marcus continued his story, he became increasingly absorbed in the telling of it. I thought back to the first halting beginning of only a few weeks ago. Now he was the one who urged me on. Each time we were interrupted by sheep straying off from the flock, he brought us back with that same, "Let's get on with the story." These breaks seemed almost painful to him, as if he wanted to remain there in England for a while longer.

"Then I used to go to Winchester to meet this girl, this 15-year-old girl. I met her at a carnival in Bedford, all that way she and her folks came to the fair; they call it a fair, sort of carnival like. I was standing there watching the merry-go-round. She was pretty dizzy. I asked her to go on a ride. She said we could take rides only as long as her mother and grandmother were there. They were about to go home. She gave me her address, and took mine. She wrote me first, the first one I guess you would call an introduction letter—where she lived and so on. The next one told me to meet her at Winchester Station. I had a two-day pass, and when I got there a lot of people were waiting. I didn't recognize her until she came over. We got out of the station and walked through town, a couple of miles. First I thought we would have something to eat, fish and chips, that was their main dish, and brussel sprouts. Those hard leaves—I didn't like that stuff.

"Then we went to a show, a picture about the 8th Air Force.

She knew I was in the Air Force and I guess she felt pretty proud of me. When we got out it was getting dark. I asked her if she could go to a pub. She said she was under age, but we went to the outskirts of town where they let her in one pub. We had ale and light beer, got her dizzy, made me dizzy too. I drank twice as much as she did. Then I said, 'I guess I'd better go home.' She suggested that I take her home on the ten o'clock train to her village five miles away. There were only three cars attached to that locomotive, took about half an hour for that five miles. Had the whole car to ourselves. At first I was very bashful towards her. I didn't get to feel her that time, but I did later at the station. She suggested I stay at Mrs. Hicks' that night. She said she could easily put me up. Mrs. Hicks' place was just like any farm cottage, grass roof, an old time cottage. Walls were green with moss. Those old English style furniture, fireplace. The bed was skreeky. She gave me tea before I went to bed. The next morning early she brought me breakfast in bed. It sure felt funny. I felt funny. I felt rotten that morning with a hangover and here she brings that breakfast on a big tray. But I enjoyed the fresh eggs she gave me. That night before she had said, 'What time are you going to get knocked up?' I said, 'What?' I only knew the other meaning."

"Did that girl or the other ones you dated in England know that you were an American Indian?" I asked.

"I used to tell them I was an Indian, but they wouldn't believe it."

"Why not?"

"They said I was too light to be an Indian. You know those Negroes were over there in England. They got there before we did and they told all those girls that *they* were Indians."

For some while now we had been herding the sheep back toward the corral. As Marcus drove them in and secured them for the night, I sat down and glanced over what I had been writing. This was a curious experience. Marcus, the Indian, was an eager informant on a way of life other than his own. Listening to his experiences in England was like hearing another anthropologist fresh home from the field. The remote was vivid and compelling. The immediate had not yet come back into focus.

Marcus told his story with such relish that I thought he would never end. He piled incident upon incident; he recounted the most minute details of barracks life and gave day by day accounts of each furlough he took.

He told me of a flight in a plane over Europe after hostilities ceased:

"We hit Aachen too, it was on the side of a hill, on the edge of a forest, all cut to pieces, skeletons of buildings, not a soul there, just long tracks passing. Boy, that place was studded with bomb craters, trenches along the hills. I wasn't air sick, but I had a hangover that day and got sleepy; after we passed Aachen I fell asleep. This friend of mine woke me up. He said we were coming to Cologne. We went over the Rhine River, real muddy water. I had seen pictures of that city, this was just like seeing a news reel, all those ruins, on one side that cathedral—not a scratch on it, and railroad tracks with a lot of bomb craters around them. The people were probably burning a lot of that stuff that was crumbled. The bridge, we could see it plainly, broken in half. Then to Coblenz with the bridge in the water. Then from Cologne we went back along the Rhine. There were some other towns, I forget the names. I was feeling bad and dozed off for half an hour.

"Then we went over to Frankfurt; this is a big city—lots of factories. They told us about what the cities manufactured, why they bombed them. From there we headed for Münster where they built planes, and there was a shell industry there. That's where we turned around and came back to the Rhine; oh yes, we were along Hitler's superhighway. We could see the Alps off in the distance—it was a clear day. Somewhere along there we came to three or four German air fields. Saw a lot of crashed planes and B–17's broken up, crashed. All the runways full of bomb craters. We hit, what's the name of that famous concentration camp? We could see long grey buildings with an iron fence around, people milling around in there. Then we went back to Aachen again and flew back; got back around 6:30. That was a long day's trip."

We talked now as close friends and he told of his life in England as he might to a barracks mate, not to an anthropologist with a projective test in hand. He concluded the story of his days in the army with an account of the trip back to the states and across the country to the Southwest.

"Next afternoon I took a bus to ———. It seemed to me like a little village, all those Indians around, it seemed sort of strange. I forget how I felt. I was hiding from those people from my village. I just hid in the shops."

"Why?" I asked.

"Because of gossip," he replied.

"What sort of gossip could it be?"

"I don't know, I didn't want them to know I just got back. There was that Red Cross on First Street where I checked my bag. There were a lot of Mexican G.I.'s around. So I thought I'd walk up the street, and there was Jim S., first one I met. Right away he wanted to take me along. He told me that Robert and Mother were in town.

"When I met Robert, he didn't care about that old superstition, he just came up and greeted me. But when I saw my mother she just said, 'Son, I am glad to see you after all this time away from home, but according to the superstition I am not supposed to touch you until you have had that ceremony for the returned warriors. You didn't have that one when you went away, but you better have this one now. Lots of the veterans have returned home and had that.' I thought that was sort of funny. I never knew about that one before. So we came to the village and that man came out to the bridge and said those prayers. After that she was able to greet me."

Marcus had participated in only a few of the group fertility rituals which play such an important part in the religious life of the pueblo. I had noted this as his story unfolded but did not directly question him until now.

"Do you believe that the dancers bring rain," I asked.

"No, I don't. I think that is just a dance, that there is no power to bring the rain. Weather is weather. It isn't man-made," he replied.

And then later, he added, "I'm not a religious man."

That evening in the ranch house, we had some rum to drink and as time passed the anxieties that bothered me in the pueblo melted away. I had not realized how tense I had become as a result of living constantly under surveillance.

As we talked more, and drank more, my understanding of Marcus increased. I felt I had never before been in such close contact with an Indian. His deeply private beliefs about witchcraft and the powers of the medicine men were clearly revealed to me, as we sat by the campfire and talked.

That night, as I crawled into my sleeping bag, I had an exhilarating sense of having gained a profound new insight into the mind and heart of Marcus and through him into the quality of life in the pueblo. When I woke the next morning, all of it was lost. I could remember very little of what we had talked about. But I did recall that the night before I had said to myself, "Write this down. Keep a record of what Marcus is saying." I got out my paper and began to write as I sat there groggy in the intense early morning light. But there was nothing now to record. All had vanished except the memory of the intense excitement I had experienced. Even this was a hollow thing. My only consolation was the hope that Marcus, too, had forgotten and would not suffer regrets at his lack of reticence.

I left the sheep camp the next day and returned to the pueblo. That wasn't the last time I saw Marcus. We went over his whole life story again and I questioned him in detail about all he had told me. But the easy comradeship of the sheep camp was gone. As we resumed work at my house, the same tensions built up once more in me, and I am sure, in him as well.

We had returned to the atmosphere of anxiety that pervades life in the pueblo and touches all within its reach. Communicated in many ways—by rumors, whisperings, suspicion, envy, secretiveness, and in silent watchful demeanor—this basic Pueblo characteristic is both a strong governing influence on village life and a powerful defense against the outsider. It is by such means that they have preserved their way of life and protected the inner workings of their religion, its medicine and fertility cults, from alien scrutiny.

One day a few weeks later, I went over to the trading post. As I stood there waiting my turn, I saw Marcus with some friends on the other side of the store. I greeted him, but he did not respond in any way—he just looked right through me without a flicker of recognition. Only then did I fully understand what it meant to be a Pueblo veteran. I represented that other world which they had individually enjoyed, but which had to be collectively renounced in order to hold on to that which was theirs.

Courtesy, Tom Dewberry,
December, 1958

20

A Seminole
Medicine Maker

William Sturtevant

The Florida Seminole are among the most isolated and conservative of the Indian groups remaining in the United States. The bitter wars between Indians and whites in Florida, which ended a century ago, remain vivid in traditions that color Seminole attitudes today. When hostilities ceased, the remnants of the tribe had gained refuge at the tip of the Florida peninsula in the Big Cypress Swamp and the Everglades where they and their increasing descendants were, until recently, left pretty much alone. When I began my field work among them they were poorly known to anthropologists. By the time I was convinced that this was because most other Indians are much more approachable, I had passed the most discouraging phase of my first prolonged field research. Josie Billie was the man who made my work possible, and the one to whom I owe most of what I know about the Seminole.

When I first went to Florida in 1950, I had already encountered Josie in the literature on the tribe, and had heard of him from recent visitors to the Seminole. That summer, without an automobile, I was isolated on the Dania Reservation near Miami, and Josie Billie was then living, as he is now, on the Big Cypress Reservation to the northwest, accessible only by an automobile drive of several hours. Nevertheless I heard of him often. Indians and local whites told me repeatedly, "You ought to talk to Josie Billie. He's done that kind of work before." Finally, one Sunday toward the end of summer, Josie came to the Indian church at Dania. I went to see him, and found sitting on the grass near the church, a rather short, well-dressed, and very dignified elder.

He readily agreed to talk into my wire recorder later that day, although he showed scant interest in the reasons for my request. He came, and with little ado sat down before the microphone, and spoke in Mikasuki Seminole for about fifteen minutes. Then he gave me a rough summary in English—he had recorded a brief version of the Seminole origin myth, with more than the usual number of Christian elements. It was a good choice of a text to interest any inquisitive foreigner. After I turned off the machine, he continued in English with a brief story about Christ and the Indians. He then ended the session with a Christian prayer, first in Mikasuki and then in English, an observance that seemed rather odd to me, since the two of us were alone in a little room behind a highway café near the reservation. As he took his leave, I paid him fifty cents. He hadn't asked for pay and was evidently somewhat surprised at being offered it, but he accepted the money politely. Josie had assumed complete control of the interview, and he revealed to me at once his preferred exterior as a dignified, pious, and knowledgeable authority.

The next summer when I returned to Florida I again worked mostly on linguistics at the Dania Reservation. But this time I had an automobile, and at the end of the summer I went to the Big Cypress Reservation to consult Josie Billie and worked with him for some ten or fifteen hours. Again, he did not show much interest in the work, but he was perfectly willing to talk to me. By that time I had gained enough experience with other Seminole to be sure that he was highly unusual and probably the only reasonably good informant in the Mikasuki band of the tribe. When I returned in 1952 for nine months of ethnographic field work, I spent all the time he would give me talking to Josie both informally and in formal interviews. These were by far the most rewarding hours I spent in Florida.

Josie was born about 1887, or possibly somewhat before—he does not know the exact date. Through his mother he derives his affiliation with the "tiger" clan (the eponymous animal is the Florida puma). He belongs to a section of the clan whose name and traditional origin show its derivation from the ancient division of the Creek tribe who lived on the Oconee River in Georgia before moving into north Florida in the early eighteenth century to form the nucleus around which the Seminole grew.

About two days after he was born, probably somewhere near the Big Cypress Swamp, Josie received his boyhood name. As was the custom, an old person (in this case a man whose English name was Old Motlow) gave the child a name which referred to one of his experiences in the Seminole Wars. Josie's name meant "go around," and alluded to an occasion when the Indians avoided a soldiers' camp. When he was about 4 months old, his father took him to visit some white friends in Fort Myers, and one of the women there gave him the name "Josie," which he thinks is a woman's name.

At the age of about 15, like other Seminole boys, Josie was given a new, adult name by which he was to be known in Seminole for the rest of his life. Josie's adult name can be translated "crazy spherical puma." However, the bare translation is misleading, since the components of adult men's names belong to a small stock of possible name elements which are combined without regard for meaning.

Many of Josie's unusual qualities were foreshadowed in his antecedents. He rarely mentions his mother, but his mother's mother, Nancy Osceola, was a prominent figure in his early life. His family lived with her, following the ordinary matrilocal residence rule of the Seminole. She seems to have been a remarkable woman. The Ingraham expedition crossing the Everglades in 1892 met her at the family's home a mile or so northwest of the old site of Fort Shackleford, not far from Josie's present home. Members of the expedition described her as about 75 years old, "bright" and "very talkative for an Indian," "well-preserved and evidently enjoy[ing] good health." Two daughters and some of her grandchildren were with her. Josie evidently was not, but a younger brother was there as a baby in his mother's arms and was given the English name "Ingraham" after the leader of the expedition. If Nancy Osceola was around 75 in 1892, she must have lived through most of the Seminole Wars, and was an adult at the onset of the Second Seminole War in 1835. She died shortly before 1911, when Josie was about 20 years old. Toward the end of her long life she became blind, and Josie used to lead her about. He still talks of her often, and mentions her as the source of much of his knowledge of conditions during "war time," for it was from her reminiscences that he learned of many obsolete customs and bits of tradition, which he remembers after all these years.

Josie's father was also an unusual person and Josie reflects his father's progressive tendencies. This was the man known in English as Little Billie, Little Billie Fewell, Billie Conepatchie, or Billy Koniphadjo, who was born about 1860 and died in 1926. He was a Mikasuki of the Wind clan. Josie says that his father was poor as a boy, because both his parents died when he was young. In fact,

Josie's grandfather was killed by his own Otter clan-mates after he was accused of killing a man by sorcery, although Josie claims that afterwards they discovered the allegation was false. His grandfather was nicknamed "Stutterer," because he had a speech defect; indeed, he must have been called nothing else most of the time, because Josie does not know what his real name was.

In 1879 as a youth of 20 Stutterer's son Little Billie went to Fort Myers to live with Capt. F. A. Hendry and go to school. Hendry wrote that "he learns fast and attends [school] promptly not missing an hour." He attended school for three years, while working for Hendry as a cowboy. In 1881 when Clay MacCauley went to Florida to make the first anthropological study of the Seminole, he met Little Billie—"the one Seminole with whom I could hold even the semblance of an English conversation." He became MacCauley's main informant for both linguistics and ethnography, as well as his guide and interpreter. MacCauley reported that the Seminole were angry with Little Billie and that one man had recently threatened to kill him because "he was the only Seminole who had separated himself from his people and cast in his lot with the whites. He had clothed himself in our dress and taken to the bed and table. . . . 'Me all same white man,' he boastfully told me one day." Soon after MacCauley's departure, threats on his life forced Little Billie to leave school.

The Ingraham expedition in 1892 called Little Billie "chief," and another account of 1896 says, "with his knowledge [he] is an important personage among his tribe." Josie says that his father was a good interpreter, although somewhat slow. It is evident that Little Billie was a sort of unofficial contact man between Indians and whites (the Seminole had and have no "chiefs," and Little Billie held no important ceremonial or political office in the tribe). In 1910 the ethnologist Alanson Skinner met Little Billie in the Everglades, and probably got from him the scraps of information on Seminole religion he put on record. In 1917 the acting Seminole agent visited his camp and described him as "a man 50 years of age, who speaks English very well for an Indian, and is about the most progressive and intelligent member of the Big Cypress bands." He was killed in a drunken fight in October, 1926. According to newspaper reports, his murderer was condemned and executed by the Seminole tribal council which met at the busk (an annual ceremony) the next spring.

Josie's uncle, Little Billie's older brother, was also a deviant. This

Josie and Friend, 1908. *(Courtesy, Mrs. M. K. Carson)*

was Billy Fewell, born about 1846, whom MacCauley called "Key West Billy" and described as "in every way a peculiar character among his people, and . . . objectionably favorable to the white man and the white man's ways." He is said to have gone by canoe to the town of Key West where he lived for a time, an act unheard of for a Seminole in those days. He once built a two-story frame house, perhaps the first one of the few which have been built by Seminole. Josie says he was something of a rake, having had "about seven wives" at various times, "just like a bulldog," and leaving many descendants.

While I obtained relatively full information about his forebears from a variety of sources, I have scant knowledge of Josie's own family affairs. I did not inquire into this aspect of his life, and Josie avoided divulging many intimate details of his marital and family relationships. I do know that about 1916 Josie married a woman named Louise, a member of the Otter clan. They had five daughters, and a son who was born in 1927, and Josie now has several grandchildren. He separated from his first wife,—I wish I knew when and why—and married his present wife, Lucy, of the Bear clan. Divorces are common among the Seminole, although usually not after so many children have been born. Josie and Lucy have no children. They live alone, but Josie's children visit him occasionally, and as far as I could judge he and Lucy enjoy a stable and affectionate relationship.

Josie's interest in medicine, his most absorbing preoccupation, began about the time he received his adult name. He once told me how he entered on his professional training and career. I cannot quote him verbatim or reproduce accurately the flavor of his English, but the following paraphrase includes many of his words and preserves the order of his statements:

When I was very young, I saw doctors come when my brothers and sisters and mother got sick. Sometimes they were able to cure serious sicknesses. Then I thought maybe the doctor's business is all right. When I was about 15 years old I went to a doctor and asked him for instance about coughing—what kind of a song do you use for coughing?—and he told me. It was just a small song. Another time, I asked him about headaches, because at that time I had headaches almost all the time myself. I asked him what kind of medicine is used, and he gave me the medicine and the songs, small things. Another time, I asked him, what do you do when a baby is too young to talk, to tell you what's wrong with him? He told me if the baby cries and is thin, give him this medicine. I came back and asked him again, many times, about different songs.

For about two years I talked to him this way. If somebody cuts his foot with an axe, how are you going to doctor him?—and he gave me a song for that. I asked him a lot of times. The doctor said, he wants to know something, that's all right, and he gave me different songs, different medicines, and told me about different sicknesses. How to cure fever, he told me that too. He just gave them to me, taught me without pay or anything; it didn't cost me anything. There were several doctors I talked to this way: Tommy Doctor, Old Doctor, there were a lot of doctors around at that time, that I talked to. Then, when I was about 17 or 18 years old, Old Motlow knew that I wanted to know things. He said, all right, you fast for a while, maybe by yourself, maybe with two or three boys with you, and you'll learn. I said all right, and got three boys and we went out and camped by ourselves, without any women. We built a little shack and stayed there.

Toward the end of this account Josie refers to the regular old-fashioned Seminole school in which an *ayikcomí* (medicine maker) received his training. During their four-day fast, the instructor, Old Motlow, came each morning to fix two emetics for the novices, which they drank to prepare themselves for the teaching that followed. (Fasting and emesis are thought to increase a person's moral, intellectual, and religious strength.) Each day the old medicine maker lectured on a different subject. The first day he discussed various sicknesses and sang the songs for curing them (not mentioning the plant remedies also used, for these are learned informally and not during the school). The second day he taught them some of the myths and beliefs about the origin and structure of the earth and the heavenly bodies, about the fate of souls and the afterlife, and about the Seminole theory that sickness is due to the wandering of the soul during dreams. The third day he devoted to reviewing and adding to the songs he had introduced the first day. The fourth day he gave them some of the more secret and powerful songs and spells, including magical formulae for personal protection and power and perhaps for magical "poisoning." The school ended with a four-day hunt, during which the students talked over and reviewed among themselves what they had learned.

The next year, Josie returned to Old Motlow for a repetition of the same course of training. The year after, he went again, this time with Tommy Doctor as his teacher. During such schools the teacher inquires about his students' dreams, which he later interprets for them. Josie once dreamed of rain for two successive nights, and his teacher told him this was a sign that he understood well what he was taught. On another occasion, he dreamed of two men walking together, one of whom threatened to kill the other. His teacher explained that this was a bad omen, indicating that a relative, perhaps a brother, might get hurt. Josie believes the prediction was fulfilled many years later, when one of his brothers was killed in an automobile accident, and another brother was lost in the woods and never seen again.

After the last school Josie apprenticed himself to Tommy Doctor. He watched him at his practice, listened to him arrive at diagnoses by questioning the patient or his relatives about his physical and mental symptoms and dreams, learned what kinds of herbs were required for each case, helped collect them, and watched him make medicine from them by adding them to water, singing the proper song, and transferring the power of the song to the decoction or infusion by blowing into it through a tube of cane. He accompanied the *ayikcomí* on professional visits to all the Mikasuki groups and into the territory of the other Florida Seminole band, the Cow Creek, whose language is not Mikasuki but the related Creek, which he learned to speak at this time. "I heard him speak, what kind of sickness, what kind of songs, what kind of herbs, how many herbs; that way I learned for four years."

At the end of his apprenticeship Josie was himself a qualified doctor, and patients began coming to him. However, he was still young; his experience was not yet extensive enough to engender much trust, and Tommy Doctor was still alive. His patients were not numerous. Two or three years later, about 1920, Tommy Doctor died and Josie took over his practice. In 1921, the botanist John K. Small met "Josie Billie, the locally celebrated Medicine-man of the Seminoles," at his home in the Big Cypress Swamp. Small later wrote that "Josie Billie's materia-medica contains thirty-odd native plants" —an indication that Josie was willing to discuss the subject, but also evidence that Small failed to realize the extent of his knowledge of herbal medicine.

His three years of schooling and four years of apprenticeship gave Josie more medical training than any other living Seminole. There were other men in the past who had more training—Billie Motlow, for instance, attended the school for ten years—but among those still living no one except Josie has been as many as three times to a full-fledged school of this sort.

The most important thing that happened during Josie's training was that he was deemed worthy by one of his teachers (probably Old Motlow) of receiving a special medicine that gives him extra curing power and also forms the basis of magical abilities to harm others as well as to help them. This the medicine maker determined by watching Josie's eyes. The doctor sent him to find the principal ingredient, a special plant. (Josie refused to identify it. He smiled when I suggested that it was a strange "stone plant" I had heard about, but he would neither confirm nor deny my guess.) The teacher prepared the plant into a medicine by singing a special song and transferring the power of the song to the medicine by blowing through a cane tube in the usual way. When Josie drank the potion it came alive in his body. It is still living there—perhaps in his heart, he told me—and when he prepares medicine it churns about and gives off a magical "smell" which enters the patient and helps effect a cure. To keep this medicine alive and strong, every month or two Josie must fast for a day and take an emetic concocted with a special "medicine eater's song." Should he fail to cure a patient, he concludes that his "living medicine" has become weak, and he fasts and takes the emetic to restore it. He may not doctor a menstruating woman or one who has just given birth, for fear of damaging this medicine. For the same reason, he must be careful not to violate the taboos which prohibit Seminole men from having close associations with menstruating women or recent widows, and prevent them from having sexual intercourse with their wives until four months after the birth of a child. A breach of these taboos will weaken any man and may make him sick, but it is particularly damaging to the "living medicine" in a powerful doctor.

Skilled and powerful medicine makers are feared as well as valued, for as a corollary to their ability to cure, they are believed to know magical techniques which will cause sickness, or accomplish other nefarious ends not connected with health. When I talked with him, Josie denied having these abilities, although he told me that some people believe he possesses them. However, in 1939 he told an amateur ethnologist that he knew a song to call a person's soul, which he could then mistreat, causing his victim to sicken and die. He also claimed to be able to cause a hunter's gun to go off unexpectedly and kill him. He is said by others to know love magic, which he used for his own ends in his younger days. In 1939, he claimed to be able to make rain, or to cause lightning to strike and kill a person. These are all techniques which Josie discussed with me, although he did not then claim them for himself.

A Seminole who knows medicine is also likely to play important roles on ceremonial occasions, for both require an intellectual bent and some of the techniques and procedures are the same. But the Seminole do not think a doctor is necessarily a priest or medicine man, nor the reverse, and the training as well as the sources of power are different. Josie is still a doctor; he was once a medicine man also, but he is no longer.

A medicine man is a person who serves as custodian of one of the six Seminole medicine bundles. These sacrosanct objects each contain a collection of exceedingly powerful charm "medicines," most of which have traditional uses to give power and to cure wounds during warfare. The existence and proper treatment of the bundles is considered essential for the existence and the continued well-being of the Seminole themselves. Every tribesman is associated with one of the bundles. He is under the care and, in some respects, the political control of the medicine man who holds it, and each spring attends the busk ceremony directed by this medicine man. The busk is the main religious and social affair of the year. There is one other occasion—the Hunting Dance in the fall—when the Seminole gather from their scattered homes, but only at the busk is the medicine bundle opened and its contents examined by the medicine man.

About the same time Josie evinced an interest in medicine, he started his career in the hierarchy of ceremonial positions. When he was small, he and his family had attended busks run by his mother's brother, Old Charley Osceola, usually at a busk grounds about two miles east of the present headquarters of the Big Cypress Reservation. As a youth he worked as a minor official, carrying water and running errands for the medicine man, at a busk directed by Old Motlow in the northwestern Everglades. About 1920 he worked for four successive years as an assistant to the medicine man Jimmy Doctor, who was in charge of another busk. This ceremonial position is second only to that of the medicine man himself, and as a reward for his four years of service Jimmy Doctor gave him a second adult name. This manner of obtaining additional names has replaced the old custom of awarding them for war deeds. Such a name can be compared to an academic degree among ourselves: it indicated Josie's knowledge, application, and intelligence, but did not replace "crazy spherical puma" as his ordinary name.

Some time later he substituted for Jimmy Doctor for four years in running his busk and in looking after his medicine bundle. Charley Doctor, who became the custodian of this bundle after Jimmy Doctor died, gave Josie another war name as a reward for having taken care of the bundle these four years. As it happened, when Charley Doctor died several years later, Josie was the one who assigned this same bundle to its present owner, Frank Charlie.

After his association with Jimmy Doctor Josie began attending a busk connected with another medicine bundle, held by Billie Motlow. In 1930, the outsider then most intimately acquainted with the Seminole reported that the busk council under Billie Motlow consisted of Josie, his younger brother Ingraham Billie, and Cuffney Tiger, all three of whom later became medicine men. Josie was certainly one of the most important men associated with Billie Motlow's medicine bundle, and he may have been the "headman" or chairman of the political and judicial council which meets on the fourth day of the busk, an office Josie has filled several times.

Billie Motlow died about 1937, and his bundle, identified with the Tiger clan, passed to Josie's care. Thereafter for seven years Josie took care of this bundle and conducted the yearly busk associated with it.

At this point in his life, Josie had reached the pinnacle of formal status among his people. As a medicine man, his behavior affected the health and well-being of all those associated with his bundle. If he looked after his people—doctoring is one way of doing so—was generous with aid and advice, and properly performed his ceremonial duties, they would prosper and the medicine in his bundle might even increase in potency. Serious consequences could follow a dereliction of these duties—the medicines in the bundle might turn on his people and cause them to sicken. Josie's performance of his duties did not meet the ideal, and some believed that his shortcomings were in some way responsible for Seminole troubles during the late 1930's and early 1940's.

We first hear of Josie's difficulties with alcohol in 1923. That year he visited Fort Myers where a white man and woman got him drunk and robbed him of $110. Newspapers and Indian Bureau reports tell us that in December, 1928, during a drunken fight over money, he accidentally stabbed and killed a woman who was his first cousin once removed, and, much more importantly, a member of his own clan. At this time and well into the 1930's, white authorities did not interfere with Seminole murder cases—in fact as recently as 1952 the Seminole presented a united front which frustrated the efforts of the police to investigate the death of a well-known Seminole man under suspicious circumstances. But murder is a serious crime in Seminole eyes, too, and mitigating circumstances do not usually carry much weight. Josie's case came up for decision at the council meeting of the next busk, in June, 1929.

Josie himself told me he was once in "bad trouble" (certainly alluding to this case), but managed to exonerate himself because he knew magical techniques to strengthen his abilities in argument. Very likely he was helped by the Seminole belief that a doctor also has abilities in sorcery which he can put into operation very quickly. I have also been told explicitly that the council let him off because they valued and respected his medical and ceremonial knowledge and activities. Perhaps even so he would not have escaped if the dead woman had not belonged to his own clan, for it is the clan of a murdered person that takes the initiative in punishing a killing.

Josie's troubles were by no means unique. Drunkenness has long been a Seminole problem, and the Indian Bureau local agency records are full of reports of accidents and deaths due to drink. However, such behavior is definitely not condoned by other Seminole, particularly in a medicine man. Josie's experience in 1928 did not cause him to stop drinking, for I have been told that he drank heavily until he became a Christian in the early 1940's. He is now a complete abstainer.

As a young man Josie spent much time in the swamps hunting alligators for their hides, as many Seminole were doing. The hides were a rather profitable cash crop—one year he made $200 or $300 in this way. He traversed the Big Cypress Swamp and the Everglades in a dugout canoe, often traveling long distances to trade at the little settlement at Miami and in the small town of Everglades. In the years since his youth the face of the country has changed tremendously, due largely to partial drainage of the Everglades and the explosive population increase in south Florida. Josie has passed by canoe over land now dry, under cultivation, and bearing houses and roads. Many locations near the Tamiami Trail highway are still indelibly oriented in his mind in relation to now obliterated Everglades canoe trails, rather than to the highway and the small Seminole settlements now scattered along it. It is no wonder that Seminole of Josie's generation are acutely aware of the changes in the south Florida scene that have engulfed them, or that they feel threatened by them.

The Tamiami Trail highway, running from Miami across the open Everglades, was opened in 1928. Not long after, Josie moved south and established his home camp beside it. Others made the same move, and today most of the non-reservation Mikasuki Seminole live in family-size settlements called "camps" strung out along some eighty miles of "the Trail." Prior to the opening of the highway nearly all the Mikasuki camps were located on high spots in the Everglades, accessible during the rainy season only by water. Today very few camps remain on these "islands."

About 1943 Josie moved from his camp on the Tamiami Trail to the Big Cypress Reservation. The change was an important one, for it involved shifting from one of the most conservative Seminole groups to one of the most progressive. I have not heard Josie's explanation of the move. Others have said that he was in greater and greater difficulties on the Trail, due to his drunkenness, his frequent associations with whites (including ethnologists in 1932–1933 and 1939), and his difficulties of 1928—all behavior unsuited to a medicine man. One author has said that the Trail Seminole forced him to move, blaming their difficulties during the late depression and early war years on his failure to behave as a medicine man should. I have also heard that he was urged to move by an Indian Bureau employee who was trying to encourage the Seminole to move to the reservations, and thought that Josie's influence would lead others to follow him. The year after he moved he returned to the Trail to supervise his busk again. At that time, however, he was told to give up the medicine bundle and not to return. He turned the bundle over to his brother Ingraham, who already kept another one, and he has not attended a busk since. In 1945 he became a Christian. The chronology of these three events—moving, relinquishing the medicine bundle, and conversion—is important for understanding Josie's motives, and I wish I could be positive that the order I have just given is the correct one.

The early efforts of Christian missionaries among the Florida Seminole met with almost no success, despite many attempts by several sects. Then in 1943 the Muskogee, Wichita, and Seminole Baptist Association, centered in Oklahoma, sent to Florida an active, fairly young former boxer, a member of the Creek town of Arbika, and an eloquent preacher in his native Creek. The Reverend Stanley Smith was successful where so many before him had failed. When he arrived in Florida the Seminole church had a total of eleven members, only three of them active. I had the good fortune to encounter Mr. Smith during a brief trip I made to south Florida in January, 1957. He was no longer a missionary, and he was happy to tell me about his former activities among the Seminole. He said that he made his first convert in 1944, but that during 1947, after transferring his affiliation to the Southern Baptists, he baptized 197 Seminoles—"That was the greatest year of my life!" I then asked him when Josie Billie was baptized. Without hesitation he replied, "1945 —January 2nd." The conversion was a difficult one, he said, because Josie had to give up his "medicine," and in particular the powerful substance called *sapiyá*. (Here Smith was influenced by his knowledge of Oklahoma Creek ways; the *sapiyá* exists among the Seminole, but it plays a lesser role in their belief.)

Smith continued: "Josie had administered to the Indians for thirty-seven years, and he didn't want to give it up. The first time I touched Josie was on the banks of a sugar mill at Clewiston. It was Christmas, and I stuck a branch in the ground for a Christmas tree [at a temporary camp occupied by Seminole workers in the mill]; and I knelt down by it and prayed. Josie was there, but he was drinking and he came up to listen with a bottle of whiskey in his hand. I talked to them some and preached to them." Not long after this he established a mission on the Big Cypress Reservation, under the sponsorship of a church in Immokalee. "I held a revival at Big Cypress that time, and it was then that Josie came up. And when Josie made the break, thirty-seven other Big Cypress Mikasukis followed him. Josie came up and said, 'Brother Smith, I have destroyed many people.' Maybe he'd executed people for the Indian council, killed many people. The white preacher who was there with me asked me what Josie said. [He had spoken to Smith in Creek.] I told him, and the preacher says to me, 'Don't ask him any more about that. Tell him we'll take his word.' So I never did ask him about what he meant. So I told Josie, 'Jesus saves sinners. We'll mark that off.' Then Josie smote his chest, and he cried—tears ran down his face—and he said to me, 'I want to take Jesus into my life!' "

Here was a dramatic situation. It marked the first real break in Seminole resistance to missionizing—no wonder Smith remembers the exact date. For Josie conversion offered an ideal opportunity to escape from a difficult position. He had reached the peak of the formal Seminole organization, and had just been removed from the most important office. He certainly felt guilty about the behavior which had led to his removal, and he tried to tell the preacher about his guilt, only to be told, "We'll mark that off." I would guess that his statement about destroying many people referred not only to the 1928 incident, but to what he believed were the effects on others of his misbehavior while he was in charge of a medicine bundle. In any event, if Smith didn't exaggerate, he showed his relief at Smith's reply in a remarkably open manner for a Seminole, the more so considering that this was a public occasion. That Josie could see conversion as a possible solution for his difficulties is not particularly surprising. We know that he had long been more favorably inclined toward foreign ways than many Seminole; and he was not the very first convert Smith had made, so that he was able to see what conversion meant for a Seminole—principally giving up attendance at the busk and Hunting Dance and instead going to church frequently (and he had already been forbidden to attend the busks). The large number of converts who followed him immediately shows, however, that he had not completely lost his prestige and influence.

Once converted, Josie worked hard to be a good Christian and to advance himself in the church—just as he had striven to get ahead in the old system. Although he was about 60 years old and had never been to school, in 1946 he entered the Florida Baptist Institute for a course of training, along with several other Seminole men who were all much younger and spoke better English. By July of 1948, when a new church was opened on the Big Cypress Reservation, he had become assistant pastor. A church publication of May, 1949, indicates that by that time one Seminole had been ordained by the Southern Baptists and three—including Josie Billie—had been licensed to preach.

In his affiliation with the church Josie has broken with most members of his family. All his children and his one surviving brother are members of the non-Christian group. His brother, Ingraham, is the leading medicine man among the Tamiami Trail Seminole, and one of Ingraham's sons is the most conservative and antiwhite individual among the younger generation of this group. The immediate relatives of Josie's present wife are also Trail people. Only his older sister is a Christian and lives with her husband on the Big Cypress Reservation.

When I came to know him best, in 1952, Josie was distinguished from other Seminole by many characteristics. One can catalogue his deviance in both behavior and belief. He was uncommonly ready to accept innovations in material things: although the buildings in his camp were the universal open-sided Seminole types, several of them were unique in having roofs of tin rather than palm thatch, and one had a cement floor rather than bare earth or a board platform. He washed with scented soap; he bought unusual foods—canned goods that other Seminole did not buy, cookies, cheese, peanut butter, and so on; and he had lately bought a gasoline stove for his wife—nearly all Seminole housewives cook over a wood fire on the ground.

Josie has been an innovator in Seminole men's dress styles, which have changed quite rapidly during the century or so that can be documented by museum specimens and photographs. He claims to have originated the practice, begun soon after 1900, of sewing appliqué strips of brightly colored cloth on men's shirts. The style was resisted at first, but in three or four years it was adopted by most men of the eastern Seminole groups. About 1915 Josie and a friend were the first in their group to break with the traditional men's hair style—close cropped or shaved except for a fringe in front and usually a couple of narrow braids in back. They watched a barber at work in Fort Myers, then bought razors and scissors and gave each other haircuts in the white man's manner, which they displayed at the next busk. There was considerable ridicule and opposition at first, but since that time nearly every Seminole man has changed to this style. In 1921, Josie was photographed in the woods dressed entirely in non-Seminole clothes, including a pair of high laced boots —certainly a most unusual costume in those days. He now wears shoes more regularly than most men his age, and occasionally wears a necktie (I don't think I have seen another Seminole of his generation doing so). He wears a Seminole patchwork shirt only for special occasions, particularly for formal affairs involving outsiders, when such dress becomes a sort of national costume of the Seminole.

Josie has traveled considerably more than most Seminole. During the winter of 1929–1930, he led a group of thirty or forty Seminole who spent the tourist season in an exhibition camp at St. Petersburg. This was one of the first such trips; they are now a common practice, both to Florida cities and occasionally elsewhere. In 1933 Josie spent five months with a group of Seminole at the Chicago World's Fair. In 1938 he visited New York, and in 1940 he went again, staying at the Seminole Indian Village at the World's Fair. In 1945 he made his first visit to Oklahoma. He has returned nearly every fall since, preaching and doctoring among the Creek and Seminole there. These activities pay his expenses for the trips—he will accept cash for doctoring in Oklahoma, as he will not in Florida—and he is apparently in some demand as a doctor there.

In 1952 Josie was one of two Seminole on the Big Cypress Reservation who were members of a white church in a nearby town. He was more favorably inclined toward the Indian Bureau than many Seminole, and had several times been appointed by the Seminole Agency to be a trustee of the reservation. He was active as a foreman and time-keeper of work crews on the reservation and among Seminole working for neighboring farmers. He was wholeheartedly in favor of schooling for Seminole children—a position diametrically opposed to that of the Tamiami Trail conservatives and much less equivocal than that of many reservation Seminole.

Josie has more white friends and acquaintances than any other Seminole his age, and he is much more responsive and unreserved in meeting white people than other Seminole I know. He is the only one, for example, whom I have heard greet a strange clerk in a store (the usual southern custom). Unlike other Seminole, he shakes hands quickly and readily. He is the only Seminole I met who is aware of white people's discomfiture with periods of silence during a conversation, and will try to make small-talk to fill the gaps. He volunteers personal information and gossip on much shorter acquaintance than other Seminole, even among those whose competence in English is much greater than his. He once startled me by rather incongruously acting as he thought an elderly white man would, saying to a white boy he knew, "Come here, boy, here's two pennies for you." He was obviously abashed when the boy treated him as an old Indian by replying, "That's all right, Josie, you keep it."

Josie told me that the conservative leaders say wrong-doers should be executed, following the old custom, but that he tells them that the old ways are gone, that if two men fight now, it is their own affair and no one else's business. The world is changing fast now, he says, and the old ways, the old laws, are no longer valid. He has told the conservatives that he knows these old ways, how the busk should be run and the sacred bundles kept, as well as any of them, but that he thinks they are no longer good. There are too many white people now for that, and there are getting to be more and more every year. The Indians are no longer the only people in the area, and there is no longer any way for them to escape—they can retreat south no farther, because there is "water all around." In effect, the white man's laws and customs, schooling for the children, and eventual assimilation, are the only realistic ways open to the Seminole, in his view.

Josie speaks English fairly well, better than anyone else his age among the Seminole, but not nearly as fluently as many younger men. He can read and write English only with considerable difficulty, but I know no other Seminole of his generation who possesses these skills. He reads and writes Creek with more facility, in the standard orthography developed by missionaries and now in use in Oklahoma. He is probably the only Florida Seminole who can do this. However, it has never occurred to him to try to write his own language in this orthography, although it could be done relatively easily.

Josie learned to read Creek in 1948 in Oklahoma. A Creek or Seminole pastor there presented him with a Creek Bible, and after giving him brief instructions in the spelling system, told him to take the book into the woods at sunrise, where he should fast until midday, not talking to anyone, praying, and keeping his hand on the Bible. He was to do this for four days, fasting and staying out all day beginning the second day. Josie says that he easily learned to read Creek by following this method. Certainly he can read his Creek Bible more easily than his English one, and he often uses it in preaching in Mikasuki, since it is easier for him to translate from Creek into the related Mikasuki than it is from the less familiar and unrelated English. However, he often consults his English Bible, for example to look up a reference in his church literature; he prefers to puzzle out the obscure English, rather than refer to the Creek version, evidently feeling that the English rendition is more authoritative. He told me that he corresponds in Creek with those of his Oklahoma friends who know the writing system; otherwise he writes in English.

Despite his feelings about assimilation and the extent to which he has moved in this direction himself in recent years, Josie is still very much a Seminole, and there are areas of belief and behavior in which he is not ready to change. He believes wholeheartedly in Seminole medicine. He has learned to use two or three Creek medicinal plants, which he discovered during his visits to Oklahoma. However, even though he has a good knowledge of white medical terminology and practice (compared to his general English vocabulary and awareness of other specialized areas of non-Indian knowledge), I noticed no tendency on his part to adopt any white medicines or medical techniques. He knows of, but does not use, enemas and aspirins, for example; he never mentioned any patent medicines; unlike many modern Indian medical practitioners in other tribes, he does not order herbal remedies from commercial drug houses. But Josie does not feel that he is competing with physicians or hospitals. He is more easily available to Indian patients, and his services are less expensive. In addition, his methods are the traditional ones and he has a reputation for a rather high frequency of successful cures. Even the most acculturated Seminole still frequently call for his services, as they do for those of other older people who know some Seminole medicine.

In August and September of 1958 there appeared a spate of Florida newspaper stories and an article in *Time* magazine on Josie's abilities as a medicine maker. The Upjohn Co. pharmaceutical house heard of one of his medicines for mental disorders and dispatched a representative who bought eight gallons of the mixture from Josie. I deduce from the newspaper accounts that the medicine was the principal one drunk by the men at the busks, and which is also used on other occasions to treat certain mental aberrations. The herbal ingredients are numerous, and somewhat variable; Josie is reported to have kept them secret in his dealings with the company. He and the Florida state commissioner for Indian affairs (a former state director of outdoor advertising) were flown by private plane to the Upjohn laboratories in Kalamazoo, Michigan, where they watched pharmacological tests of the brew, referred to by reporters and the commissioner as a "tranquilizer." According to the news stories, the preliminary tests with white rats were encouraging. Josie reputedly signed a contract. Should any of the tranquilizing tea's ingredients yield a marketable product, Josie stands to gain fame and fortune. The publicity immediately resulted in a flood of mail for Josie—apparently there is something irresistible about the combination of a tranquilizer and an old Indian remedy. In the midst of plans for further field work in Florida, I am delighted at Josie's possible good fortune, but perturbed about the effects of his new-found fame on our collaborative studies of Seminole botanical knowledge.

All Seminole today go to physicians in town for treatment of more serious disorders, but they also often come to Josie at the same time. When Josie gets a case he cannot handle, he refers the patient to a hospital, and goes along himself to act as interpreter. As he pointed out to me, this parallels the usage of former times when a doctor sent or accompanied a patient he could not cure to another skilled "medicine maker"—but now, Josie says, there is no one left among the Indians to whom he can refer such cases. Josie has not even succeeded in interesting any young men in attending a doctor's school; nor has he ever taught such a school. He wanted very much to teach his son medicine and to pass on to him the "medicine" that lives in his body, but the boy did not show any particular interest and got married (one cannot attend a doctor's school after marriage). However, the month before I left Florida in 1953, a boy about 17 years old, the son of an arch-conservative among the off-reservation Mikasuki, came to inquire whether Josie would teach him doctoring. Josie told the boy to return in a few months, when he would be glad to teach him—so perhaps he has found a successor by now.

Apparently Josie sees little conflict between the Christian and the older Seminole systems of belief. He told me that whereas Christians go to heaven, good non-Christians go to the pagan afterworld; that before an important meeting or discussion, Christians pray to strengthen their powers of persuasion, whereas non-Christians fast and smoke—each method being effective for the group practicing it. He claims not to believe in the busk, but when I asked him what the non-Christians believe would be the consequences of giving it up, the idea was inconceivable to him and he could give no answer. According to Seminole belief, the living have a double soul. On death the two souls become one, and it is only during dreams that they divide, one wandering and the other staying with the body. Josie shares this belief in a dual soul, but here there is little conflict with Christian belief; Christianity is silent on the relation of the soul to dreams.

Josie once told me that he is strongly opposed to Indian-white marriages, and much upset by the several which have occurred in the last few years. He remarked that such people have "lost their sense," and went on to say that conservative Seminole are particularly antagonistic to such marriages, especially to those between an Indian

woman and a white man (as one might expect from Seminole matri-
lineal descent), on the grounds that the resulting children will have
a double affiliation and are likely to betray the Seminol᷉ to the
whites. Evidently Josie agrees with the conservatives' opposition to
intermarriage, although he no longer believes that the whites are
still attempting to subvert and deport the Seminole (as many conservatives do).

Josie's popularity is not high today among the Indians. The non-
Christians are very suspicious of his pro-assimilation ideas, his close
relations with whites, and his Christianity, and many of them hate
and even fear him. Nevertheless, even the most conservative Indians
regularly come to him for medical treatment, believing him to be
the most skilled and powerful Seminole doctor. The non-Christians
also treat him as the Christian group's equivalent of a medicine
man, a higher status than the Christians themselves accord him.
When occasional political meetings (not those held at the busks)
are called to discuss all-Seminole matters, the non-Christians urge
him to attend as representative of the Christians—just as all medicine men attend such meetings—but he usually refuses to go.

There is considerable opposition to Josie even among the Christians. Many people on the reservations say they do not like him because he meddles too much in the personal affairs of others and
gives unsolicited advice. This behavior is probably a carry-over from
his former role as a medicine man, when he was supposed to "look
after" the people of his group, but he has not reached an equivalently
high position among the Christians, for he is not pastor of a church.
Some Seminole Christians accuse him of "backsliding," but as far as
my observations go this is unjustified. The white church people
among whom he is widely acquainted in general like and admire
him, as a Christian Indian. Like his father before him, he is a
contact-man for the white community.

The strong feelings about him are reflected in the often heard
gossip that Josie killed a man by sorcery about 1942. Josie himself
voluntarily admitted to me that he is suspected of sorcery. He says
the accusation is unjustified, explaining, "That's a little dangerous
for doctor's business—you talk a little too much some people don't
like it. . . . Doctors some of them *hampí·ki,* some of them want to
know *pónłi·ki.* Some only want to know *pónłi·ki.* If I no make
'em well for people I got that kind." This can be translated, "Doctor-

ing is a dangerous occupation, especially if one boasts about it. Some doctors are bad and want to know sorcery, rather than curing. If I don't cure people, I am suspected of sorcery."

Josie impressed me as being very egocentric. He constantly turned conversation to himself, his own activities and their importance. Once, when I was questioning him about the Hunting Dance, in which he held no important position, he kept trying to revert discussion to the busk, reiterating that he had been in charge of the latter for seven years. When I refused to change the subject, he kept repeating the really rather unimportant fact that he had led the Snake Dance at the last Hunting Dance he attended. Several times I heard him explain to other Seminole in a rather pompous manner that I had come especially to talk to him and learn from him. Yet he was not interested in me or in my purpose in working with him, and seemed merely to want a sympathetic ear. I do not remember that he ever asked me a personal question—whereas most of my more casual Seminole acquaintances did so readily.

There can be no doubt that Josie is a person of high intelligence, and dedicated to its exercise. He has a vast amount of knowledge. For example, I recorded the names of more than 225 different plants he recognized, and we collected and identified most of these. Moreover he knows much about their growth habits, their flowers and fruits, preferred habitats, and of course their uses. I am sure I did not exhaust the number of plants he knows, yet he considers this a relatively minor part of his professional equipment. Much more important are the hundreds of curing songs and spells in his repertoire, his acquaintance with the etiology of diseases, and his diagnostic abilities. In addition he has a huge amount of ceremonial knowledge: dance songs, ceremonial procedures, mythological explanations, and so forth. His interest in genealogy is strong and his knowledge of Seminole relationships is extensive. He knows more than most about the details of social organization and kinship and their traditional and mythological origins and justifications. While he is not one of the best Seminole craftsmen, he has a good acquaintance with the techniques involved in silversmithing, wood-working, tanning, and the like, and a superior knowledge of now obsolete items of material culture. He has a strong interest in traditional history. He is a capable farmer and a good woodsman and hunter. At the age of 60, he began learning about Christian belief and practice, and has advanced farther in this study than many others, in spite of his age and lack of any previous formal schooling in English.

He is confident in his knowledge of his own culture and with the exception of religion is not particularly interested in supplementary or conflicting foreign beliefs and facts. He asked me few questions and showed little awareness of Euroamerican specialized knowledge. After all, he has had little or no opportunity to become acquainted with intellectual subjects outside his own culture—younger men, who have attended schools, frequently do show great interest in Euroamerican traditional and scientific learning and belief outside religion. When I introduced Josie to a botanist from the University of Miami, and accompanied the two of them on a collecting trip, he showed no particular interest in the botanist's obviously extensive and detailed acquaintance with the local plants, which plainly complemented and supplemented his own in many ways. He did not for a moment relinquish the role of teacher and informant which had become established by this time in his relations with me. Since that time I have accompanied botanists on collecting trips with other eastern Indian herbalists, and have been disturbed by the effects on the data we were collecting of the informants' interest in and questions about the botanists' specialized knowledge. This problem did not arise with Josie; he simply was not interested in my botanist friend's knowledge of the plants we were discussing and collecting.

There is a tremendous contrast between Josie and every other adult Seminole whom I tried to interview. When I asked him a question, he would often talk unprompted for five or ten minutes in response; others, if they did not merely say, "I don't know" (the most frequent response used to discourage questioners), would answer very briefly and volunteer little information. It was practically impossible to interview them because one could not avoid asking leading questions—hence biasing the responses—in such circumstances. But on the other hand it was very difficult to conduct a formal interview with Josie. Many times I prepared outlines of questions on a topic—to be sure to get the same range of data on all items in a list, for example—but attempts to follow these consistently failed. Josie quickly got bored unless given a rather free hand. The conversation could be guided only to a limited extent, and usually not to the degree desirable in ethnographic work. Josie's untrammeled style made him a poor linguistic informant, for such work requires rather tight control over the interview and constant repetition of questions likely to seem nonsensical to the informant.

Even in the sorts of interviewing which were possible, one had to be constantly on the watch. For one thing, Josie had a tendency to answer before he understood a question. He is slightly deaf, and if he does not hear clearly or if he merely does not understand adequately, he will guess at the question rather than ask for clarification or repetition. He hates to admit that he does not know an answer, and will sometimes avoid a question in such a case by answering another, un-asked question. While these characteristics often provided information I would not have thought of eliciting, they also were likely to introduce confusion into my notes.

Many people who are acquainted with the Seminole, including some amateur ethnologists, do not altogether trust Josie as a source of information. This is partly because he answers before he understands a question, and partly because of the great difference between him and all other Seminole, in that he will talk when they will not. I am certain also that if he thinks one is not serious, or is patronizing, skeptical, or disrespectful, he is not above misleading his questioner or playing a joke on him for his own amusement. Others seriously interested in the Seminole also distrust him because he does not object to commercializing some of the popular interest in the Indians, or at least has not done so in the past. He once played a major role, for example, in a fake and widely-advertised "Indian wedding" at one of the exhibition camps in Miami.

It was very hard to get Josie to keep regular appointments, or to work for more than three or four hours on days when he would work. He would often say he was too busy to work with me, or that something else had come up which demanded his attention. Sometimes this was obviously justified: when someone came for medical care, his primary obligation was certainly to his practice. But sometimes he would make other arrangements patently contrived to avoid working with me. He seemed to derive a certain satisfaction in having me wait around for him, apparently able to do nothing until he could squeeze me into his busy schedule. When I waited for him, and worked on my notes or talked only to my younger friends, he would postpone the chore as long as possible; but when I worked instead with another older person, he almost invariably quickly returned to work with me. One morning he was a bit brusque, and told me that he couldn't work except perhaps for two hours in the evening. Judging from past experience, I did not really expect to see him again at all that day or for some time thereafter. Later the same day I worked for a few hours with his old friend and brother-in-law, Charley Cypress, and that night to my surprise Josie came promptly at the appointed time. I said nothing about what I had been doing, but he prefaced one of the first answers to my questions with the remark, "Maybe Charley Cypress never saw it, but *I* did." On departing he said that he would work again the next evening—and he did—and that he perhaps could give me a few whole days the following week. He did.

In part, this reluctance to work for me seems to have been due to his ambivalence about revealing the more esoteric aspects of Seminole culture. His tendency to hold back became worse the longer we worked together and the deeper we penetrated into Seminole culture. When we were together, his dislike of showing any ignorance prevented him on all but a very few occasions from flatly refusing to answer my questions. Hence the simplest way for Josie to avoid the difficulty was not to see me. Once, after he had sung a few curing songs for me and promised to record some more, he had two dreams which he interpreted as a warning not to tell me all his songs or even all the verses and songs for any one sickness.

About three months later, during my last month in Florida, we talked for several sessions about the medicine bundles and their contents, a subject at the core of the native religion and practically never discussed with outsiders. Josie again became difficult to find and broke several appointments with me. I then went to Miami for a week, thinking perhaps he would relent in my absence. (This was a difficult decision for me to make in view of the amount of last-minute investigation remaining.) When I returned I offered to increase his pay from seventy-five cents to a dollar an hour, in the hope that a raise would provide sufficient inducement. He came to see me later that morning, and finally asked me why I wanted to know all these things. This was the first time he had shown any interest in my motives; I had explained my purposes several times before, but he had paid little attention. I explained again. He then said that he was afraid of going against the Bible, and that it was wrong and "just foolishness" to sing busk dance songs. He had recorded a few such songs early in the summer of 1952, and considerably more the previous summer, but we had not even touched upon the subject for some time. He said that he thought he should not have sung them for me, as he had been reading and studying the Bible all day and had discovered that it was not right. I told him that I'd like to ask him a lot more questions about material culture and social organization (carefully avoiding any mention of the busk or the medicine bundles), which he found unobjectionable, and he agreed to work that evening and the next day. He said that he would give ten cents out of each dollar I paid him to the church, since he was doubtful about the propriety of accepting money for what he was doing. He told me that he considered the church his main and only job, and that (in effect) anything which conflicted with this in ideals or in demands on his time he would not consider doing. I suspect that the trouble was caused not by the songs he had sung so long before, but by my persistent questioning about the medicine bundles that are so important in the non-Christian religion. It seems likely that this is the part of his former beliefs which Josie feels most ambivalent about having given up, and that our talking about them had renewed his doubts.

I had asked him some weeks before to make me full-sized models of two ceremonial wands used in the Hunting Dance. He had the necessary materials and agreed to do it. However, that same day he said that he had decided that he couldn't make them; at first he said it was "too dangerous" because no one had "hired" him to do it. (These wands can be made only by the appointed officials at a Hunting Dance and they may be touched with impunity only by the makers and by the two men whose insignia they are.) This reason surprised me, as I had thought he had discarded this pagan belief. I said nothing, but in the next breath he said it was because he was a Christian, and he thought that God would not want him to do it.

After our conversation, Josie went to the government rancher on the reservation and asked him for a job, saying that he didn't much want to work with me. Though the rancher said that I was paying the same wage that he could give him, and for "easier" work, Josie replied that he knew it was good pay, but he didn't like the work and besides he had lots of other things to do, adding that he might be able to give me a couple of hours in the evenings occasionally.

The rancher gave him a job building houses, and he started in. Fortunately, this was the time the incident mentioned above involving Charley Cypress occurred, so that our relationship quickly returned nearly to normal, although I did not dare renew the discussion of the medicine bundles until the last day I was on the reservation. At that time he answered my questions, as usual, although he was obviously uncomfortable about it.

In many respects I found Josie Billie an admirable person, but not a likeable one. He stands out in my mind from other eastern Indian ritualists and knowledgeable elders not only as the first one I knew, but also because of his imperious personality. My feelings about Josie are doubtless colored by my inexperience at the time I worked with him. At best the relationship between ethnologist and informant is fraught with difficulties, and it was magnified in our case by the gap in our ages. Neither of us was at ease in our complementary roles. Josie relished and even exploited his ascendency over me—undoubtedly a new experience for him with a white person. I have enjoyed more pleasant relationships with younger Seminole, and with old men of other eastern tribes, yet I greatly respect Josie's knowledge and his pride, and I am grateful to him as one of my principal teachers in the rewarding, if sometimes painful, process of field work.

Contributors

JOHN ADAIR, at present a member of the faculty of the Cornell University Medical College, has in recent years been closely associated with its project in public health and preventive medicine at Many Farms, Arizona, on the Navaho Reservation. He received his training in anthropology at the University of Wisconsin, the University of Michigan, Columbia University, and the University of New Mexico, receiving his Ph.D. from the latter institution in 1948. He combines a longstanding interest in primitive art and a later concern with problems of applied anthropology. Dr. Adair is well known as the author of *The Navaho and Pueblo Silversmiths* (1944), and has served as manager of the Navaho Arts and Crafts Guild, a tribal enterprise.

ETHEL M. ALBERT is assistant professor in the Department of Speech at the University of California at Berkeley. After receiving her Ph.D. in philosophy from the University of Wisconsin in 1949, she taught at Syracuse University, becoming in 1953 Research Associate on Harvard University's project on "The Comparative Study of Values in Five Cultures." She is the author of "The Classification of Values: A Method and Illustration," published in the *American Anthropologist* (1956), and of other writings in both anthropology and philosophy. In 1957–1958 she was a Fellow at the Center for Advanced Study in the Behavioral Sciences. Dr. Albert summarizes her interests as "the study of cultural world-views and value systems."

LAURA BOHANNAN received her D.Phil. from Oxford University in 1951. Her extensive researches among the Tiv were undertaken in collaboration with her husband, also an anthropologist now on the faculty of Northwestern University. Under the *nom de plume* of Elenore Smith Bowen, she is the author of *Return to Laughter* (1954), a vivid fictional account of an anthropologist's experiences in the West African bush. She is also the author of a radio script, *Miching Mallecho,* published in *From the Third Programme, A Ten-Years' Anthology,* J. Morris, ed. (1956), and of technical studies including, with Paul Bohannan, *The Tiv of Central Nigeria* (1953).

EDMUND CARPENTER, who teaches anthropology at the University of Toronto, alternates arctic trips with studies in the South Seas and Asia. He met Ohnainewk on Southampton Island in 1950 and lived with him that year and during the winter of 1951–1952. He is co-editior of *Explorations,* an experimental periodical in the field of culture and communication published by the University of Toronto, and the author of numerous studies, the most recent being *Anerca,* a volume of Eskimo poems, and *Eskimo,* co-authored with the documentary film producer, the late Robert Flaherty, and illustrated by the Canadian artist, Robert Varley.

JOSEPH B. CASAGRANDE has since 1950 been a member of the staff of the Social Science Research Council in New York City. He has taught anthropology at Queens College, the University of Rochester, and the American University, and is the author of linguistic and ethnographic studies based on field work among the Comanche, Ojibwa, and Navaho Indians.

HAROLD C. CONKLIN, Assistant Professor of Anthropology at Columbia University, studied at the University of California at Berkeley, and at Yale where he received his doctorate in 1955. He has done extensive field research, begun during his undergraduate days, among a number of Southeast Asian, Indonesian, and Philippine peoples. Dr. Conklin is the author of *Hanunóo-English Vocabulary* (1953) and *Hanunóo Agriculture in the Philippines* (1957), among other studies; in 1955 the Ethnic Folkways Library issued his album of Hanunóo music.

IAN CUNNISON, Lecturer in Social Anthropology at the University of Manchester, studied anthropology and archaeology at Cambridge University and Oxford University from which he received the D. Phil. in 1952. During the years 1948–1951, as a research officer of the Rhodes-Livingstone Institute in Northern Rhodesia, he conducted a study of the Luapula Valley peoples, and from

1952–1955 he did research on the Humr under a Sudan Government Research Grant. Among other writings, he is the author of *History on the Luapula* (1950) and *The Luapula Peoples of Northern Rhodesia* (1959). He is at present preparing a book on the Humr, here represented by Hurgas the *omda*.

CORA DU BOIS has been the Radcliffe College Zemurray Professor at Harvard University since 1954. She has also taught at Hunter and Sarah Lawrence Colleges and at the Universities of California, Hawaii, and Colorado. During and immediately after World War II she served in the Office of Strategic Services, the Department of State, the World Health Organization, and the Institute of International Education. Her research in Southeast Asia was preceded by several years of field work among the Indians of California, Oregon, and Nevada. In 1944 she published *The People of Alor,* based on the field research in which Ali served her so well. Dr. Du Bois is also the author of *Social Forces in Southeast Asia,* first published in 1949 and reprinted in 1958, and *Foreign Students and Higher Education in the United States* (1956), in addition to numerous articles and monographs. In 1958–1959 she was a Fellow of the Center for Advanced Study in the Behavioral Sciences.

RAYMOND FIRTH is Professor of Anthropology in the University of London at the London School of Economics and Political Science with which he has been associated for more than twenty-five years. Among his many publications are *We the Tikopia* (1936), *Art and Life in New Guinea* (1936), *Human Types* (1938), *Primitive Polynesian Economy* (1939), *Work of the Gods in Tikopia* (1940), *Malay Fishermen: Their Peasant Economy* (1946), *Elements of Social Organization* (1951), and *Social Change in Tikopia* (1959). Professor Firth is a Fellow of the British Academy. He has served as president of the Royal Anthropological Institute and has been honored by his academic colleagues on both sides of the Atlantic, receiving among other awards, the Rivers Memorial Medal (1940), the Henry Myers Lectureship (1948), and most recently the Viking Fund Medal in General Anthropology for 1958 and the Thomas H. Huxley Memorial Medal for 1959. In 1959 he was a Fellow of the Center for Advanced Study in the Behavioral Sciences.

THOMAS GLADWIN is at present with the National Institute of Mental Health, Bethesda, Maryland. He went to Truk in 1947 where he devoted seven months to a study of Trukese personality, later becoming Native Affairs Officer in the Navy Civil Administration Unit there. In 1953 he published with Seymour B. Sarason a personality study, *Truk: Man in Paradise,* and in 1958 with the same co-author, *Psychological and Cultural Problems in Mental Subnormality.* Dr. Gladwin has also published a number of articles in various anthropological journals, and has served as president of the Anthropological Society of Washington.

JOHN T. HITCHCOCK, Assistant Professor of Anthropology at the University of California at Los Angeles, received his doctorate from Cornell University in 1956. He has done field work among the Ute Indians of North America and as a Ford Foundation Overseas Training and Research Fellow in North India. While in India from 1953 to 1955 he served as director of a Cornell University India Program station. His publications include "Leadership in a North Indian Village: Two Case Studies," in *Leadership and Political Institutions in India* (1959), and "The Idea of the Martial Rājpūt", which appeared in the *Journal of American Folklore.* With his wife, Patricia J. Hitchcock, he has produced a documentary film, *North Indian Village,* distributed by the International Film Bureau, Inc.

CLYDE KLUCKHOHN is Professor of Anthropology at Harvard University. He was a Rhodes Scholar at Corpus Christi College, Oxford, in 1928, beginning his formal study of anthropology at the University of Vienna in 1930, and receiving his Ph.D. from Harvard in 1936. Among his many works on the Navaho, with whom he has long been associated, are *Navaho Witchcraft* (1944), and with Dorothea Leighton, *The Navaho* (1946) and *Children of the People* (1947). His other writings include *Mirror for Man* (1949), *Personality in Nature, Society and Culture* (co-editor with Henry A. Murray and David M. Schneider, 1953), and two books based on early experiences in Navaho country, *To the Foot of the Rainbow* and *Beyond the Rainbow.* Dr. Kluckhohn has served as consultant to a number of government agencies, and is a former director of Harvard's Russian Research Center. A member of the

National Academy of Sciences, he has received many academic honors, among them election to the presidency of the American Anthropological Association in 1947 and, in 1950, the Viking Fund Medal in General Anthropology.

DAVID G. MANDELBAUM is Professor of Anthropology at the University of California at Berkeley. He began his field work in India in 1937 after earlier work with American Indian tribes. While on a visit to the Nilgiri Hills in South India he was introduced to the Kotas by Dr. M. B. Emeneau who was then studying the Kota language, with Sulli as linguistic informant. Sulli later became Dr. Mandelbaum's first ethnological informant in his Kota studies from April, 1937, to May, 1938. Although in South Asia on military service from 1943 to 1945, he was not able to return to the Kotas until 1949 when he spent several months with them, returning again for a brief visit with Sulli and other Kotas in December, 1958. Dr. Mandelbaum is the author of *The Plains Cree* (1940) and *Soldier Groups and Negro Soldiers* (1952), and has edited *Selected Writings of Edward Sapir in Language, Culture and Personality* (1949), among numerous other publications. He has served as a member of the Executive Board of the American Anthropological Association and in 1957–1958 he was a Fellow of the Center for Advanced Study in the Behavioral Sciences.

MARGARET MEAD is Associate Curator of Ethnology at the American Museum of Natural History, New York City, and Adjunct Professor of Anthropology at Columbia University. At the age of 23, as a Fellow in the Biological Sciences of the National Research Council, she made her first trip to Samoa to study the adolescent girl. On her return she completed her two major publications on Samoa, *Coming of Age in Samoa* (1928) and *The Social Organization of Manu'a* (1930). The results of her second trip to the Pacific were published in *Growing Up in New Guinea* (1930) and *Kinship in the Admiralties* (1934). Later field trips among South Seas peoples are reported in *Sex and Temperament in Three Primitive Societies* (1935) which was republished with earlier works on Samoa and New Guinea in *From the South Seas* (1939), with Gregory Bateson, *Balinese Character: A Photographic Analysis* (1942), with Frances Cooke Macgregor, *Growth and*

Childhood: A Photographic Study of Balinese Childhood (1953), and *New Lives for Old, Cultural Transformation, Manus, 1928– 1953* (1955). Among her other well-known works are *And Keep Your Powder Dry* (1942), *Male and Female* (1949), and her most recent book, *An Anthropologist at Work: The Writings of Ruth Benedict* (1959). In 1958 Dr. Mead was the recipient of the Viking Fund Medal in General Anthropology and was honored by her colleagues as president-elect of the American Anthropological Association.

ROBERT LOWIE at the time of his death in 1957 was Professor of Anthropology Emeritus of the University of California at Berkeley. From 1908 to 1921 he was Assistant and Associate Curator of Anthropology at the American Museum of Natural History in New York City under whose auspices he did his first field research with the Crow Indians. He was a member of the American Philosophical Society and the National Academy of Sciences, and was awarded the Viking Fund Medal in 1947 and the Thomas H. Huxley Memorial Medal a year later. His many publications include *Primitive Society* (1920), *Primitive Religion* (1924), *The Crow Indians* (1935), *The History of Ethnological Theory* (1937), *The German People* (1945), *Social Organization* (1948), and *Indians of the Plains* (1954). Professor Lowie's tribute to Jim Carpenter was written shortly after the latter's death in 1937, but was set aside without publication. It appears here through the courtesy of his wife, Mrs. Luella Cole Lowie.

W. E. H. STANNER, Reader in Comparative Social Institutions at the Australian National University, Canberra, was educated at the University of Sydney and the London School of Economics and Political Science where he received his Ph.D. in 1938. He has done extensive field research in North and Central Australia since 1932, as well as in the South Pacific and Africa where he was the first director of the East African Institute of Social and Economic Research in Kampala, Uganda. From 1953 to 1956, he served as the Australian Commissioner of the South Pacific Commission at Noumea. Among other works he is the author of *The South Seas in Transition* (1953).

WILLIAM C. STURTEVANT, who received his Ph.D. from Yale University in 1955, is Ethnologist on the staff of the Bureau of American Ethnology, Smithsonian Institution, Washington, D.C. In addition to his field work among the Seminole, he has done research among the Seneca of New York, in Burma, and for brief periods among the Catawba, Choctaw, and Cherokee. Since 1953 he has published a number of papers on the Seminole in the *Florida Anthropologist, The Florida Historical Quarterly,* and *Tequesta.*

VICTOR W. TURNER, Lecturer in the Department of Social Anthropology and Sociology of the University of Manchester, began his study of anthropology at University College, London, after war service with a Bomb Disposal Squad. He received his Ph.D. from the University of Manchester in 1955 where from 1956 to 1958 he was Simon Research Fellow. His field work among the Ndembu of Mwinilunga District in Northern Rhodesia was conducted during 1950–1954 while he served as Research Officer of the Rhodes-Livingstone Institute. Among other writings, he has published *Schism and Continuity in an African Society: A Study of Ndembu Village Life* (1958), and another book, *The Forest of Symbols: A Study of Four Ndembu Rituals,* is forthcoming.

CHARLES WAGLEY is Professor of Anthropology at Columbia University where he has been almost continuously since his undergraduate days in Columbia College. Long identified with Latin American studies, his many publications on South and Central American groups include *Economics of a Guatemalan Village* (1941), *The Social and Religious Life of a Guatemalan Village* (1949), *The Tenetehara Indians of Brazil* with Eduardo Galvão (1949), *Race and Class in Rural Brazil* (editor, 1952), *Amazon Town: A Study of Man in the Tropics* (1953). He is also the author, with Marvin Harris, of *Minority Groups in the New World* (1958). Dr. Wagley has served as a member of the staff of the Social Science Research Council and, in Brazil during 1942–1945, as a member of the field staff of the Institute of Inter-American Affairs of the U.S. Government. He is a recipient of Brazil's Order of the Southern Cross. In 1957–1958 he was a Fellow of the Center for Advanced Study in the Behavioral Sciences.

JAMES B. WATSON, now Professor and Executive Officer of the Department of Anthropology at the University of Washington, previously taught in São Paulo, Brazil, and at Beloit College, the University of Oklahoma, and Washington University. He has done field work among the Hopi Indians of Arizona and the Cayúa of the Mato Grosso, Brazil, prior to his later work in New Guinea. In addition to a monograph, *Cayúa Culture Change: A Study in Acculturation and Methodology* (1952), he has published a number of articles in various social science journals. Dr. Watson serves as chairman of an interuniversity Committee on New Guinea Studies established for the development of research on that island.

hARpER ✦ ɕoRchbooɕs

HUMANITIES AND SOCIAL SCIENCES

American Studies: General

American Studies: Colonial

American Studies: From the Revolution to 1860

† The New American Nation Series, edited by Henry Steele Commager and Richard B. Morris.
‡ American Perspectives series, edited by Bernard Wishy and William E. Leuchtenburg.
* The Rise of Modern Europe series, edited by William L. Langer.
** History of Europe series, edited by J. H. Plumb.
¶ Researches in the Social, Cultural and Behavioral Sciences, edited by Benjamin Nelson.
§ The Library of Religion and Culture, edited by Benjamin Nelson.
Σ Harper Modern Science Series, edited by James R. Newman.
° Not for sale in Canada.
△ Not for sale in the U. K.

CLEMENT EATON: The Freedom-of-Thought Struggle in the Old South. *Revised and Enlarged. Illus.* TB/1150

CLEMENT EATON: The Growth of Southern Civilization: 1790-1860. † *Illus.* TB/3040

LOUIS FILLER: The Crusade Against Slavery: 1830-1860. † *Illus.* TB/3029

DIXON RYAN FOX: The Decline of Aristocracy in the Politics of New York: 1801-1840. ‡ *Edited by Robert V. Remini* TB/3064

WILLIAM W. FREEHLING, Ed.: The Nullification Era: A Documentary Record ‡ TB/3079

FELIX GILBERT: The Beginnings of American Foreign Policy: *To the Farewell Address* TB/1200

FRANCIS GRIERSON: The Valley of Shadows: *The Coming of the Civil War in Lincoln's Midwest: A Contemporary Account* TB/1246

FRANCIS J. GRUND: Aristocracy in America: *Social Class in the Formative Years of the New Nation* TB/1001

ALEXANDER HAMILTON: The Reports of Alexander Hamilton. ‡ *Edited by Jacob E. Cooke* TB/3060

THOMAS JEFFERSON: Notes on the State of Virginia. ‡ *Edited by Thomas P. Abernethy* TB/3052

JAMES MADISON: The Forging of, American Federalism: *Selected Writings of James Madison. Edited by Saul K. Padover* TB/1226

BERNARD MAYO: Myths and Men: *Patrick Henry, George Washington, Thomas Jefferson* TB/1108

JOHN C. MILLER: Alexander Hamilton and the Growth of the New Nation TB/3057

RICHARD B. MORRIS, Ed.: The Era of the American Revolution TB/1180

R. B. NYE: The Cultural Life of the New Nation: 1776-1801. † *Illus.* TB/3026

JAMES PARTON: The Presidency of Andrew Jackson. *From Vol. III of the Life of Andrew Jackson.* ‡ *Ed. with an Intro. by Robert V. Remini* TB/3080

FRANCIS S. PHILBRICK: The Rise of the West, 1754-1830. † *Illus.* TB/3067

TIMOTHY L. SMITH: Revivalism and Social Reform: *American Protestantism on the Eve of the Civil War* TB/1229

ALBION W. TOURGÉE: A Fool's Errand. ‡ *Ed. by George Fredrickson* TB/3074

A. F. TYLER: Freedom's Ferment: *Phases of American Social History from the Revolution to the Outbreak of the Civil War. 31 illus.* TB/1074

GLYNDON G. VAN DEUSEN: The Jacksonian Era: 1828-1848. † *Illus.* TB/3028

LOUIS B. WRIGHT: Culture on the Moving Frontier TB/1053

American Studies: The Civil War to 1900

W. R. BROCK: An American Crisis: Congress and Reconstruction, 1865-67 ° △ TB/1283

THOMAS C. COCHRAN & WILLIAM MILLER: The Age of Enterprise: *A Social History of Industrial America* TB/1054

W. A. DUNNING: Essays on the Civil War and Reconstruction. *Introduction by David Donald* TB/1181

W. A. DUNNING: Reconstruction, Political and Economic: 1865-1877 TB/1073

HAROLD U. FAULKNER: Politics, Reform and Expansion: 1890-1900. † *Illus.* TB/3020

HELEN HUNT JACKSON: A Century of Dishonor: *The Early Crusade for Indian Reform.* ‡ *Edited by Andrew F. Rolle* TB/3063

ALBERT D. KIRWAN: Revolt of the Rednecks: *Mississippi Politics, 1876-1925* TB/1199

ROBERT GREEN MC CLOSKEY: American Conservatism in the Age of Enterprise: 1865-1910 TB/1137

ARTHUR MANN: Yankee Reformers in the Urban Age: *Social Reform in Boston, 1880-1900* TB/1247

WHITELAW REID: After the War: *A Tour of the Southern States, 1865-1866.* ‡ *Edited by C. Vann Woodward* TB/3066

CHARLES H. SHINN: Mining Camps: *A Study in American Frontier Government.* ‡ *Edited by Rodman W. Paul* TB/3062

VERNON LANE WHARTON: The Negro in Mississippi: 1865-1890 TB/1178

American Studies: 1900 to the Present

RAY STANNARD BAKER: Following the Color Line: *American Negro Citizenship in Progressive Era.* ‡ *Illus. Edited by Dewey W. Grantham, Jr.* TB/3053

RANDOLPH S. BOURNE: War and the Intellectuals: *Collected Essays, 1915-1919.* ‡ *Edited by Carl Resek* TB/3043

A. RUSSELL BUCHANAN: The United States and World War II. † *Illus.* Vol. I TB/3044; Vol. II TB/3045

ABRAHAM CAHAN: The Rise of David Levinsky: *a documentary novel of social mobility in early twentieth century America. Intro. by John Higham* TB/1028

THOMAS C. COCHRAN: The American Business System: *A Historical Perspective, 1900-1955* TB/1080

FOSTER RHEA DULLES: America's Rise to World Power: 1898-1954. † *Illus.* TB/3021

JOHN D. HICKS: Republican Ascendancy: 1921-1933. † *Illus.* TB/3041

SIDNEY HOOK: Reason, Social Myths, and Democracy TB/1237

ROBERT HUNTER: Poverty: *Social Conscience in the Progressive Era.* ‡ *Edited by Peter d'A. Jones* TB/3065

WILLIAM L. LANGER & S. EVERETT GLEASON: The Challenge to Isolation: *The World Crisis of 1937-1940 and American Foreign Policy*
Vol. I TB/3054; Vol. II TB/3055

WILLIAM E. LEUCHTENBURG: Franklin D. Roosevelt and the New Deal: 1932-1940. † *Illus.* TB/3025

ARTHUR S. LINK: Woodrow Wilson and the Progressive Era: 1910-1917. † *Illus.* TB/3023

GEORGE E. MOWRY: The Era of Theodore Roosevelt and the Birth of Modern America: 1900-1912. † *Illus.* TB/3022

RUSSEL B. NYE: Midwestern Progressive Politics: *A Historical Study of Its Origins and Development, 1870-1958* TB/1202

WILLIAM PRESTON, JR.: Aliens and Dissenters: *Federal Suppression of Radicals, 1903-1933* TB/1287

WALTER RAUSCHENBUSCH: Christianity and the Social Crisis. ‡ *Edited by Robert D. Cross* TB/3059

JACOB RIIS: The Making of an American. ‡ *Edited by Roy Lubove* TB/3070

PHILIP SELZNICK: TVA and the Grass Roots: *A Study in the Sociology of Formal Organization* TB/1230

IDA M. TARBELL: The History of the Standard Oil Company: *Briefer Version.* ‡ *Edited by David M. Chalmers* TB/3071

GEORGE B. TINDALL, Ed.: A Populist Reader ‡ TB/3069

TWELVE SOUTHERNERS: I'll Take My Stand: *The South and the Agrarian Tradition. Intro. by Louis D. Rubin, Jr., Biographical Essays by Virginia Rock* TB/1072

Anthropology

JACQUES BARZUN: Race: *A Study in Superstition. Revised Edition* TB/1172

JOSEPH B. CASAGRANDE, Ed.: In the Company of Man: *Twenty Portraits of Anthropological Informants. Illus.* TB/3047

W. E. LE GROS CLARK: The Antecedents of Man: *Intro. to Evolution of the Primates.* ° △ *Illus.* TB/559

CORA DU BOIS: The People of Alor. *New Preface by the author. Illus.* Vol. I TB/1042; Vol. II TB/1043

RAYMOND FIRTH, Ed.: Man and Culture: *An Evaluation of the Work of Bronislaw Malinowski* ¶ ° △ TB/1133

DAVID LANDY: Tropical Childhood: *Cultural Transmission and Learning in a Puerto Rican Village* ¶ TB/1235

2

L. S. B. LEAKEY: Adam's Ancestors: *The Evolution of Man and His Culture.* △ *Illus.* TB/1019

EDWARD BURNETT TYLOR: Religion in Primitive Culture. Part II of "Primitive Culture." § *Intro. by Paul Radin* TB/34

W. LLOYD WARNER: A Black Civilization: *A Study of an Australian Tribe.* ¶ *Illus.* TB/3056

Art and Art History

WALTER LOWRIE: Art in the Early Church. *Revised Edition. 452 illus.* TB/124

EMILE MÂLE: The Gothic Image: *Religious Art in France of the Thirteenth Century.* § △ *190 illus.* TB/44

MILLARD MEISS: Painting in Florence and Siena after the Black Death: *The Arts, Religion and Society in the Mid-Fourteenth Century. 169 illus.* TB/1148

ERICH NEUMANN: The Archetypal World of Henry Moore. △ *107 illus.* TB/2020

DORA & ERWIN PANOFSKY: Pandora's Box: *The Changing Aspects of a Mythical Symbol. Revised Edition. Illus.* TB/2021

ERWIN PANOFSKY: Studies in Iconology: *Humanistic Themes in the Art of the Renaissance.* △ *180 illustrations* TB/1077

ALEXANDRE PIANKOFF: The Shrines of Tut-Ankh-Amon. *Edited by N. Rambova. 117 illus.* TB/2011

JEAN SEZNEC: The Survival of the Pagan Gods: *The Mythological Tradition and Its Place in Renaissance Humanism and Art. 108 illustrations* TB/2004

OTTO VON SIMSON: The Gothic Cathedral: *Origins of Gothic Architecture and the Medieval Concept of Order.* △ *58 illus.* TB/2018

HEINRICH ZIMMER: Myth and Symbols in Indian Art and Civilization. *70 illustrations* TB/2005

Business, Economics & Economic History

REINHARD BENDIX: Work and Authority in Industry: *Ideologies of Management in the Course of Industrialization* TB/3035

GILBERT BURCK & EDITORS OF FORTUNE: The Computer Age: *And Its Potential for Management* TB/1179

THOMAS C. COCHRAN: The American Business System: *A Historical Perspective, 1900-1955* TB/1080

THOMAS C. COCHRAN: The Inner Revolution: *Essays on the Social Sciences in History* △ TB/1140

THOMAS C. COCHRAN & WILLIAM MILLER: The Age of Enterprise: *A Social History of Industrial America* TB/1054

ROBERT DAHL & CHARLES E. LINDBLOM: Politics, Economics, and Welfare: *Planning and Politico-Economic Systems Resolved into Basic Social Processes* TB/3037

PETER F. DRUCKER: The New Society: *The Anatomy of Industrial Order* △ TB/1082

EDITORS OF FORTUNE: America in the Sixties: *The Economy and the Society* . TB/1015

ROBERT L. HEILBRONER: The Great Ascent: *The Struggle for Economic Development in Our Time* TB/3030

ROBERT L. HEILBRONER: The Limits of American Capitalism TB/1305

FRANK H. KNIGHT: The Economic Organization TB/1214

FRANK H. KNIGHT: Risk, Uncertainty and Profit TB/1215

ABBA P. LERNER: Everybody's Business: *Current Assumptions in Economics and Public Policy* TB/3051

ROBERT GREEN MC CLOSKEY: American Conservatism in the Age of Enterprise, 1865-1910 △ TB/1137

PAUL MANTOUX: The Industrial Revolution in the Eighteenth Century: *The Beginnings of the Modern Factory System in England* o △ TB/1079

WILLIAM MILLER, Ed.: Men in Business: *Essays on the Historical Role of the Entrepreneur* TB/1081

RICHARD B. MORRIS: Government and Labor in Early America △ TB/1244

HERBERT SIMON: The Shape of Automation: *For Men and Management* TB/1245

PERRIN STRYKER: The Character of the Executive: *Eleven Studies in Managerial Qualities* TB/1041

Education

JACQUES BARZUN: The House of Intellect △ TB/1051

RICHARD M. JONES, Ed.: Contemporary Educational Psychology: *Selected Readings* TB/1292

CLARK KERR: The Uses of the University TB/1264

JOHN U. NEF: Cultural Foundations of Industrial Civilization △ TB/1024

Historiography & Philosophy of History

JACOB BURCKHARDT: On History and Historians. △ *Introduction by H. R. Trevor-Roper* TB/1216

WILHELM DILTHEY: Pattern and Meaning in History: *Thoughts on History and Society.* o △ *Edited with an Introduction by H. P. Rickman* TB/1075

J. H. HEXTER: Reappraisals in History: *New Views on History & Society in Early Modern Europe* △ TB/1100

H. STUART HUGHES: History as Art and as Science: *Twin Vistas on the Past* TB/1207

RAYMOND KLIBANSKY & H. J. PATON, Eds.: Philosophy and History: *The Ernst Cassirer Festschrift. Illus.* TB/1115

ARNALDO MOMIGLIANO: Studies in Historiography o △ TB/1283

GEORGE H. NADEL, Ed.: Studies in the Philosophy of History: *Selected Essays from History and Theory* TB/1208

JOSE ORTEGA Y GASSET: The Modern Theme. *Introduction by Jose Ferrater Mora* TB/1038

KARL R. POPPER: The Open Society and Its Enemies △
Vol. I: *The Spell of Plato* TB/1101
Vol. II: *The High Tide of Prophecy: Hegel, Marx and the Aftermath* TB/1102

KARL R. POPPER: The Poverty of Historicism o △ TB/1126

G. J. RENIER: History: Its Purpose and Method △ TB/1209

W. H. WALSH: Philosophy of History: *An Introduction* △ TB/1020

History: General

WOLFGANG FRANKE: China and the West. *Trans by R. A. Wilson* TB/1326

L. CARRINGTON GOODRICH: A Short History of the Chinese People. △ *Illus.* TB/3015

DAN N. JACOBS & HANS H. BAERWALD: Chinese Communism: *Selected Documents* TB/3031

BERNARD LEWIS: The Arabs in History △ TB/1029

BERNARD LEWIS: The Middle East and the West o △ TB/1274

History: Ancient

A. ANDREWES: The Greek Tyrants △ TB/1103

ADOLF ERMAN, Ed. The Ancient Egyptians: *A Sourcebook of Their Writings. New material and Introduction by William Kelly Simpson* TB/1233

MICHAEL GRANT: Ancient History o △ TB/1190

SAMUEL NOAH KRAMER: Sumerian Mythology TB/1055

NAPHTALI LEWIS & MEYER REINHOLD, Eds.: Roman Civilization. *Sourcebook I: The Republic* TB/1231

NAPHTALI LEWIS & MEYER REINHOLD, Eds.: Roman Civilization. *Sourcebook II: The Empire* TB/1232

History: Medieval

P. BOISSONNADE: Life and Work in Medieval Europe: *The Evolution of the Medieval Economy, the 5th to the 15th Century.* o △ *Preface by Lynn White, Jr.* TB/1141

HELEN CAM: England before Elizabeth △ TB/1026

NORMAN COHN: The Pursuit of the Millennium: *Revolutionary Messianism in Medieval and Reformation Europe* △ TB/1037

3

G. G. COULTON: Medieval Village, Manor, and Monastery
TB/1022

CHRISTOPHER DAWSON, Ed.: Mission to Asia: *Narratives and Letters of the Franciscan Missionaries in Mongolia and China in the 13th and 14th Centuries* △
TB/315

HEINRICH FICHTENAU: The Carolingian Empire: *The Age of Charlemagne* △
TB/1142

GALBERT OF BRUGES: The Murder of Charles the Good. *Trans. with Intro. by James Bruce Ross*
TB/1311

F. L. GANSHOF: Feudalism △
TB/1058

DENO GEANAKOPLOS: Byzantine East and Latin West: *Two Worlds of Christendom in the Middle Ages and Renaissance*
TB/1265

EDWARD GIBBON: The Triumph of Christendom in the Roman Empire *(Chaps. XV-XX of "Decline and Fall," J. B. Bury edition)*. § △ *Illus.*
TB/46

W. O. HASSALL, Ed.: Medieval England: *As Viewed by Contemporaries* △
TB/1205

DENYS HAY: Europe: The Emergence of an Idea
TB/1275

DENYS HAY: The Medieval Centuries ° △
TB/1192

J. M. HUSSEY: The Byzantine World △
TB/1057

ROBERT LATOUCHE: The Birth of Western Economy: *Economic Aspects of the Dark Ages.* ° △ *Intro. by Philip Grierson*
TB/1290

FERDINAND LOT: The End of the Ancient World and the Beginnings of the Middle Ages. *Introduction by Glanville Downey*
TB/1044

ACHILLE LUCHAIRE: Social France at the Time of Philip Augustus. *New Intro. by John W. Baldwin*
TB/1314

MARSILIUS OF PADUA: The Defender of the Peace. *Trans. with Intro. by Alan Gewirth*
TB/1310

G. MOLLAT: The Popes at Avignon: 1305-1378 △
TB/308

CHARLES PETIT-DUTAILLIS: The Feudal Monarchy in France and England: *From the Tenth to the Thirteenth Century* ° △
TB/1165

HENRI PIRENNE: Early Democracies in the Low Countries: *Urban Society and Political Conflict in the Middle Ages and the Renaissance. Introduction by John H. Mundy*
TB/1110

STEVEN RUNCIMAN: A History of the Crusades. △
Volume I: *The First Crusade and the Foundation of the Kingdom of Jerusalem. Illus.*
TB/1143
Volume II: *The Kingdom of Jerusalem and the Frankish East, 1100-1187. Illus.*
TB/1243
Volume III: *The Kingdom of Acre and the Later Crusades*
TB/1298

SULPICIUS SEVERUS et al.: The Western Fathers: *Being the Lives of Martin of Tours, Ambrose, Augustine of Hippo, Honoratus of Arles and Germanus of Auxerre.* △ *Edited and trans. by F. O. Hoare*
TB/309

J. M. WALLACE-HADRILL: The Barbarian West: *The Early Middle Ages, A.D. 400-1000* △
TB/1061

History: Renaissance & Reformation

JACOB BURCKHARDT: The Civilization of the Renaissance in Italy. △ *Intro. by Benjamin Nelson & Charles Trinkaus. Illus.* Vol. I TB/40; Vol. II TB/41

JOHN CALVIN & JACOPO SADOLETO: A Reformation Debate. *Edited by John C. Olin*
TB/1239

ERNST CASSIRER: The Individual and the Cosmos in Renaissance Philosophy. △ *Translated with an Introduction by Mario Domandi*
TB/1097

FEDERICO CHABOD: Machiavelli and the Renaissance △
TB/1193

EDWARD P. CHEYNEY: The Dawn of a New Era, 1250-1453. * *Illus.*
TB/3002

G. CONSTANT: The Reformation in England: *The English Schism, Henry VIII, 1509-1547* △
TB/314

R. TREVOR DAVIES: The Golden Century of Spain, 1501-1621 ° △
TB/1194

G. R. ELTON: Reformation Europe, 1517-1559 ** ° △
TB/1270

DESIDERIUS ERASMUS: Christian Humanism and the Reformation: *Selected Writings. Edited and translated by John C. Olin*
TB/1166

WALLACE K. FERGUSON et al.: Facets of the Renaissance
TB/1098

WALLACE K. FERGUSON et al.: The Renaissance: *Six Essays. Illus.*
TB/1084

JOHN NEVILLE FIGGIS: The Divine Right of Kings. *Introduction by G. R. Elton*
TB/1191

JOHN NEVILLE FIGGIS: Political Thought from Gerson to Grotius: 1414-1625: *Seven Studies. Introduction by Garrett Mattingly*
TB/1032

MYRON P. GILMORE: The World of Humanism, 1453-1517. * *Illus.*
TB/3003

FRANCESCO GUICCIARDINI: Maxims and Reflections of a Renaissance Statesman *(Ricordi). Trans. by Mario Domandi. Intro. by Nicolai Rubinstein*
TB/1160

J. H. HEXTER: More's Utopia: *The Biography of an Idea. New Epilogue by the Author*
TB/1195

HAJO HOLBORN: Ulrich von Hutten and the German Reformation
TB/1238

JOHAN HUIZINGA: Erasmus and the Age of Reformation. △ *Illus.*
TB/19

JOEL HURSTFIELD: The Elizabethan Nation △
TB/1312

JOEL HURSTFIELD, Ed.: The Reformation Crisis △
TB/1267

ULRICH VON HUTTEN et al.: On the Eve of the Reformation: "*Letters of Obscure Men." Introduction by Hajo Holborn*
TB/1124

PAUL O. KRISTELLER: Renaissance Thought: *The Classic, Scholastic, and Humanist Strains*
TB/1048

PAUL O. KRISTELLER: Renaissance Thought II: *Papers on Humanism and the Arts*
TB/1163

NICCOLÒ MACHIAVELLI: History of Florence and of the Affairs of Italy: *from the earliest times to the death of Lorenzo the Magnificent.* △ *Introduction by Felix Gilbert*
TB/1027

ALFRED VON MARTIN: Sociology of the Renaissance. *Introduction by Wallace K. Ferguson*
TB/1099

GARRETT MATTINGLY et al.: Renaissance Profiles. △ *Edited by J. H. Plumb*
TB/1162

MILLARD MEISS: Painting in Florence and Siena after the Black Death: *The Arts, Religion and Society in the Mid-Fourteenth Century.* △ *169 illus.*
TB/1148

J. E. NEALE: The Age of Catherine de Medici ° △
TB/1085

ERWIN PANOFSKY: Studies in Iconology: *Humanistic Themes in the Art of the Renaissance.* △ *180 illustrations*
TB/1077

J. H. PARRY: The Establishment of the European Hegemony: 1415-1715: *Trade and Exploration in the Age of the Renaissance* △
TB/1045

BUONACCORSO PITTI & GREGORIO DATI: Two Memoirs of Renaissance Florence: *The Diaries of Buonaccorso Pitti and Gregorio Dati. Ed. with an Intro. by Gene Brucker. Trans. by Julia Martines*
TB/1333

J. H. PLUMB: The Italian Renaissance: *A Concise Survey of Its History and Culture* △
TB/1161

A. F. POLLARD: Henry VIII. ° △ *Introduction by A. G. Dickens*
TB/1249

A. F. POLLARD: Wolsey. ° △ *Introduction by A. G. Dickens*
TB/1248

CECIL ROTH: The Jews in the Renaissance. *Illus.*
TB/834

A. L. ROWSE: The Expansion of Elizabethan England. ° △ *Illus.*
TB/1220

GORDON RUPP: Luther's Progress to the Diet of Worms ° △
TB/120

FERDINAND SCHEVILL: The Medici. *Illus.*
TB/1010

FERDINAND SCHEVILL: Medieval and Renaissance Florence. *Illus.* Volume I: *Medieval Florence* TB/1090
Volume II: *The Coming of Humanism and the Age of the Medici*
TB/1091

R. H. TAWNEY: The Agrarian Problem in the Sixteenth Century. *New Intro. by Lawrence Stone*
TB/1315

G. M. TREVELYAN: England in the Age of Wycliffe, 1368-1520 ° △
TB/1112

VESPASIANO: Renaissance Princes, Popes, and Prelates: *The Vespasiano Memoirs: Lives of Illustrious Men of the XVth Century. Intro. by Myron P. Gilmore*
TB/1111

History: Modern European

FREDERICK B. ARTZ: Reaction and Revolution, 1815-1832. * *Illus.*
TB/3034
MAX BELOFF: The Age of Absolutism, 1660-1815 △
TB/1062
ROBERT C. BINKLEY: Realism and Nationalism, 1852-1871. * *Illus.*
TB/3038
EUGENE C. BLACK, Ed.: European Political History, 1815-1870: *Aspects of Liberalism*
TB/1331
ASA BRIGGS: The Making of Modern England, 1784-1867: *The Age of Improvement* ° △
TB/1203
CRANE BRINTON: A Decade of Revolution, 1789-1799. * *Illus.*
TB/3018
D. W. BROGAN: The Development of Modern France. ° △
Volume I: *From the Fall of the Empire to the Dreyfus Affair*
TB/1184
Volume II: *The Shadow of War, World War I, Between the Two Wars. New Introduction by the Author*
TB/1185
J. BRONOWSKI & BRUCE MAZLISH: The Western Intellectual Tradition: *From Leonardo to Hegel* △
TB/3001
GEOFFREY BRUUN: Europe and the French Imperium, 1799-1814. * *Illus.*
TB/3033
ALAN BULLOCK: Hitler, A Study in Tyranny. ° △ *Illus.*
TB/1123
E. H. CARR: German-Soviet Relations Between the Two World Wars, 1919-1939
TB/1278
E. H. CARR: International Relations Between the Two World Wars, 1919-1939 ° △
TB/1279
E. H. CARR: The Twenty Years' Crisis, 1919-1939: *An Introduction to the Study of International Relations* ° △
TB/1122
GORDON A. CRAIG: From Bismarck to Adenauer: *Aspects of German Statecraft. Revised Edition*
TB/1171
DENIS DIDEROT: The Encyclopedia: *Selections. Ed. and trans. by Stephen Gendzier*
TB/1299
WALTER L. DORN: Competition for Empire, 1740-1763. * *Illus.*
TB/3032
FRANKLIN L. FORD: Robe and Sword: *The Regrouping of the French Aristocracy after Louis XIV*
TB/1217
CARL J. FRIEDRICH: The Age of the Baroque, 1610-1660. * *Illus.*
TB/3004
RENÉ FUELOEP-MILLER: The Mind and Face of Bolshevism: *An Examination of Cultural Life in Soviet Russia. New Epilogue by the Author*
TB/1188
M. DOROTHY GEORGE: London Life in the Eighteenth Century △
TB/1182
LEO GERSHOY: From Despotism to Revolution, 1763-1789. * *Illus.*
TB/3017
C. C. GILLISPIE: Genesis and Geology: *The Decades before Darwin* §
TB/51
ALBERT GOODWIN, Ed.: The European Nobility in the Eighteenth Century △
TB/1313
ALBERT GOODWIN: The French Revolution △
TB/1064
ALBERT GUÉRARD: France in the Classical Age: *The Life and Death of an Ideal* △
TB/1183
CARLTON J. H. HAYES: A Generation of Materialism, 1871-1900. * *Illus.*
TB/3039
J. H. HEXTER: Reappraisals in History: *New Views on History and Society in Early Modern Europe* △
TB/1100
STANLEY HOFFMANN et al.: In Search of France: *The Economy, Society and Political System in the Twentieth Century*
TB/1219
A. R. HUMPHREYS: The Augustan World: *Society, Thought, & Letters in 18th Century England* ° △
TB/1105
DAN N. JACOBS, Ed.: The New Communist Manifesto and Related Documents. *Third edition, revised*
TB/1078

LIONEL KOCHAN: The Struggle for Germany: *1914-45*
TB/1304
HANS KOHN: The Mind of Germany: *The Education of a Nation* △
TB/1204
HANS KOHN, Ed.: The Mind of Modern Russia: *Historical and Political Thought of Russia's Great Age* TB/1065
WALTER LAQUEUR & GEORGE L. MOSSE, Eds.: Education and Social Structure in the 20th Century. ° △ *Vol. 6 of the Journal of Contemporary History*
TB/1339
WALTER LAQUEUR & GEORGE L. MOSSE, Eds.: International Fascism, 1920-1945. ° △ *Volume 1 of Journal of Contemporary History*
TB/1276
WALTER LAQUEUR & GEORGE L. MOSSE, Eds.: The Left-Wing Intellectuals between the Wars 1919-1939. ° △ *Volume 2 of Journal of Contemporary History*
TB/1286
WALTER LAQUEUR & GEORGE L. MOSSE, Eds.: Literature and Politics in the 20th Century. ° △ *Vol. 5 of the Journal of Contemporary History*
TB/1328
WALTER LAQUEUR & GEORGE L. MOSSE, Eds.: The New History: *Trends in Historical Research and Writing since World War II.* ° △ *Vol. 4 of the Journal of Contemporary History*
TB/1327
WALTER LAQUEUR & GEORGE L. MOSSE, Eds.: 1914: *The Coming of the First World War.* ° △ *Volume 3 of Journal of Contemporary History*
TB/1306
FRANK E. MANUEL: The Prophets of Paris: *Turgot, Condorcet, Saint-Simon, Fourier, and Comte*
TB/1218
KINGSLEY MARTIN: French Liberal Thought in the Eighteenth Century: *A Study of Political Ideas from Bayle to Condorcet*
TB/1114
ROBERT K. MERTON: Science, Technology and Society in Seventeenth Century England ¶ *New Intro. by the Author*
TB/1324
L. B. NAMIER: Facing East: *Essays on Germany, the Balkans, and Russia in the 20th Century* △
TB/1280
L. B. NAMIER: Personalities and Powers: *Selected Essays* △
TB/1186
L. B. NAMIER: Vanished Supremacies: *Essays on European History, 1812-1918* °
TB/1088
NAPOLEON III: Napoleonic Ideas: *Des Idées Napoléoniennes, par le Prince Napoléon-Louis Bonaparte. Ed. by Brison D. Gooch*
TB/1336
FRANZ NEUMANN: Behemoth: *The Structure and Practice of National Socialism, 1933-1944*
TB/1289
FREDERICK L. NUSSBAUM: The Triumph of Science and Reason, 1660-1685. * *Illus.*
TB/3009
DAVID OGG: Europe of the Ancien Régime, 1715-1783 ** ° △
TB/1271
JOHN PLAMENATZ: German Marxism and Russian Communism. ° △ *New Preface by the Author*
TB/1189
RAYMOND W. POSTGATE, Ed.: Revolution from 1789 to 1906: *Selected Documents*
TB/1063
PENFIELD ROBERTS: The Quest for Security, 1715-1740. * *Illus.*
TB/3016
PRISCILLA ROBERTSON: Revolutions of 1848: *A Social History*
TB/1025
GEORGE RUDÉ: Revolutionary Europe, 1783-1815 ** ° △
TB/1272
LOUIS, DUC DE SAINT-SIMON: Versailles, The Court, and Louis XIV. ° △ *Introductory Note by Peter Gay*
TB/1250
HUGH SETON-WATSON: Eastern Europe Between the Wars, 1918-1941
TB/1330
ALBERT SOREL: Europe Under the Old Regime. *Translated by Francis H. Herrick*
TB/1121
N. N. SUKHANOV: The Russian Revolution, 1917: *Eyewitness Account.* △ *Edited by Joel Carmichael*
Vol. I TB/1066; Vol. II TB/1067
A. J. P. TAYLOR: From Napoleon to Lenin: *Historical Essays* ° △
TB/1268
A. J. P. TAYLOR: The Habsburg Monarchy, 1809-1918: *A History of the Austrian Empire and Austria-Hungary* ° △
TB/1187
G. M. TREVELYAN: British History in the Nineteenth Century and After: 1782-1919. ° △ *Second Edition* TB/1251

RELIGION

Ancient & Classical

Biblical Thought & Literature

The Judaic Tradition

Christianity: General

Christianity: Origins & Early Development

Christianity: The Middle Ages and The Reformation

Christianity: The Protestant Tradition

Christianity: The Roman and Eastern Traditions